EUROPEAN CULTURE

EUROPEAN CULTURE
A Contemporary Companion

edited by
Jonathan Law
(Market House Books Ltd.)

CASSELL

Cassell
Villiers House, 41/47 Strand
London WC2N 5JE

387 Park Avenue South
New York, NY 10016-8810 USA

First published 1993

British Library Cataloguing-in-Publication Data
A catalogue entry for this book is available
from the British Library.

Library of Congress Cataloging-in-Publication Data
available from the Library of Congress

ISBN 0-304-32718 2 (hardback)
ISBN 0-304-32720 4 (paperback)

Compiled, designed, and typeset by Market House Books Limited, Aylesbury
Printed and bound in Great Britain by Mackays of Chatham Plc

PREFACE

The question of what it means to be European has perhaps never received so much attention. Since the collapse of communism in eastern Europe, the concept of a single European culture, extending from Ireland to the Urals, is once again being discussed. Recent moves towards greater EC cooperation have focused attention both on our common European heritage and on the many ways in which we continue to differ. In the last few years we have seen a redrawing of the political map of Europe unparalleled since 1919, with the creation of seven or eight wholly new states and the re-emergence of others that seemed to have disappeared from history. Basques, Catalans, Croats, Serbs, and Slovakians have all claimed the right to their own distinctive cultures. The new perspectives thus revealed have made many of us in Britain realize how inadequate is our knowledge of European life and culture.

For all these reasons, there could not be a more fitting moment for a general survey of European culture as it has developed over the course of the last half of this turbulent century.

This book has been designed to meet the needs of a wide variety of readers. Students of any of the diciplines covered will find it both a reliable guide to their own field of study and a stimulating introduction to related areas of knowledge. In this age of specialization most people find it impossible to keep fully abreast of developments in more than one or two fields of particular interest. Even the polymath sometimes needs to check a fact or clarify a concept. There is also a wider class of general reader who should welcome this book. Most of us who read (or skim) the arts pages of a newspaper will have been intrigued at one time or another by an unfamiliar reference and wanted further information or a fuller context. Even with access to a good reference library, it can be particularly difficult to find information about personalities and movements that have emerged in the last 20 years. Who, for example, is Anselm Kiefer and why is he considered significant? What nationality was Venedikt Erofeev and what are his principal works? What is postmodernism? What is IRCAM? To these, and many other, questions this Companion provides clear answers in unpretentious language.

As the compilers of this book are only too well aware, the terms 'European', 'culture', and 'contemporary' are all somewhat elastic. In order to define the scope of the present work a number of decisions had to be taken – some principled, others more pragmatic. 'European' has been taken to encompass both western and eastern Europe, including the European republics of the former Soviet Union, as well as the British Isles. Ancestry and place of birth have not been used as criteria to decide whether or not a person is European; Salman Rushdie and R. B. Kitaj both have a place in European culture, although they were born and brought up elsewhere. On the other hand, it was decided not to include the many important European-born figures who took US citizenship either during or immediately after World War II.

As for 'culture', a rough working definition of this notoriously slippery term had to be adopted in order to produce a coherent and useful book.

The majority of the articles here deal with the arts of painting and sculpture, architecture, music, literature, theatre, and cinema. Major figures and themes from science, philosophy, theology, and the social sciences have been included, when they are judged to have had a significant impact on the thought of the age. There has been no attempt to cover such wider 'cultural' phenomena as sport, cookery, fashion, and politics. A further decision, made largely for reasons of space, was that individual performers, such as musicians, actors, and dancers, should not be included unless they have also made a creative contribution. The most important conductors, choreographers, and theatre directors do appear, however.

It became clear at an early stage in the planning of this book that the overwhelming need was for a work that focused on cultural developments during the last 50 years. It was therefore decided to define 'contemporary' in this way, including biographical entries only for those figures who have emerged, or added significantly to their achievement, since 1945. With very few exceptions, major figures born more than a century ago (i.e. before 1892) have been excluded, even if they remained productive in their old age. Thus, no biographies of Picasso and Stravinsky – to take two of the most obvious examples – will be found in the Companion. Information on such figures is readily available elsewhere and it seemed better to devote the space to more truly contemporary figures whose careers are far less well documented. Movements, genres, and schools have not generally been included unless they originated during the post-war period; the same rule has been adopted for musical ensembles and theatre companies.

If a name or term is printed in small capitals, this means that the person or concept referred to has an entry in the book. As a general rule, titles of foreign-language works are given in English only. This rule has not been applied if a work (such as a film or an opera) is better known to English speakers by its original title. If the usual English title for a work differs significantly from the original title, both have been given (the latter in parentheses). Dates given are those of first publication in the original language for books and first performance for plays and musical works. If there was a significant interval between the date of writing and that of publication or performance, this is indicated.

J.L. 1993

ACKNOWLEDGMENTS

Editor

Jonathan Law BA

Editorial and computer staff

Amanda Isaacs BA
Anne Stibbs BA

Contributors

Richard Aczel PhD
Gilda Albano DLitt
Fran Alexander BA
Steven Brindle BA DPhil
Callum Brines
Sean Callery BA
Terence Charlston MA MMus FRCO LRAM
Ian Chilvers
John Daintith BSc PhD
Storm Dunlop FRAS FRMetS
Marie FitzPatrick MMus
Annette Fuchs MA PhD
Neil Harris
Elain Harwood Grad Dipl Cons (AA)
Louise Jones BA
Wolfgang Kienzler MA
Professor Arnold McMillin BA PhD
James Matson BA
Julia Norman MA
R. B. Peberdy MA
David Pickering MA
Michael Pursglove MA BPhil
Professor R. B. Pynsent MA PhD
Astrid Schleinitz MA
John Latimer Smith
Tanya Thresher MA
Peter Wickham RE ATC
John D. Wright MA PhD

A

Aalto, Alvar (1898–1976) Finnish architect, one of the leading figures of International Modernism. After training at the Helsinki Technical University, he established himself in independent practice in Jyväskylä, building up his reputation with a long succession of competition entries. His early work was a severe personal variant of the romantic-national style then prevalent in Scandinavia with an admixture of classical elements. By 1928 he had moved decisively towards modernism with the Turun Sanomat Newspaper Office in Turku, followed by the celebrated Tuberculosis Sanatorium in Paimio (1929–33). Aalto found ideal patrons in the paper magnates Harry and Mairea Gullichsen, for whom he built the Pulp Mill at Sunila (1933–34), the Workers Village there (1934–54), and the Villa Mairea at Noormarkku (1937–38). In the 1930s his personal style, combining modernism with an interest in natural materials and an overriding concern for the needs of the users, reached its maturity. The Finnish pavilions for the World Fairs in Paris (1937) and New York (1939) brought his work to international attention.

Aalto spent the lean years of the war in Finland, returning to the US to design a hall of residence at the Massachusetts Institute of Technology (1947–49). In the 1950s he became more interested in town planning and public buildings, designing the town hall at Säynätsalo (1950–52), the Vuoksenniska church at Imatra (1956–58), and the Technical Institute buildings at Otaniemi (1955–64). In their informal planning and varied profiles, these buildings exemplify Aalto's freedom from modernist orthodoxy and his interest in vernacular traditions.

Aalto continued to enter – and win – competitions, building flats at the Interbau exhibition in Berlin (1955), a cultural centre in Wolfsburg (1959–62), and offices in Bremen (1958–63). His most important work, however, continued to be in Finland, notably the Finlandia concert hall and conference centre in Helsinki (1962–75). He was not merely the most influential Scandinavian architect of his time but, with over 200 buildings to his credit in a career spanning 54 years, one of the most productive and eminent architects of the century and a vital force in the development and humanization of International Modernism.

Abakanowicz, Magdalena (1930–) Polish artist, weaver, and sculptor. She studied (1950–55) at the Academy of Fine Art, Warsaw, and since 1961 has concentrated on sculpture made from woven fabrics (typically using jute or sisal) – a field in which she is acknowledged as both the pioneer and the foremost exponent. "My intention was to extend the possibilities of man's contact with a work of art through touch and by being surrounded by it", she has written. "I have looked to those slowly growing irregular forms for an antidote against the brilliance and speed of contemporary technology." Abakanowicz has built up an international reputation and has won many awards, including the Grand Prize of the World Crafts Council in 1974. She exhibited at the Venice Biennale in 1968 and 1980. Her work has helped to dissolve barriers between 'art' and 'craft'.

Abbado, Claudio (1933–) Italian conductor noted mainly for his interpretations of romantic and 20th-century music. Born into a musical Milanese family, Abbado studied piano and composition at the Verdi Academy, Milan, and conducting in Vienna. Early competition successes included winning the Koussevitsky Award at the Berkshire Music Center (Tanglewood) in 1958 and the Mitropoulos prize in

1963. Abbado conducted the Vienna Philharmonic at the Salzburg Festival in 1965 and made his Covent Garden debut in 1968. He was principal conductor at La Scala, Milan, from 1968 until 1986 (musical director from 1972) and of the London Symphony Orchestra from 1979 until 1988 (musical director from 1983). He was musical director of the Vienna Staatsoper from 1986 until 1991. In 1989 he succeeded von KARAJAN as musical director of the Berlin Philharmonic Orchestra.

Abrahamsen, Hans (1952–) Danish composer. After studying the French horn at the Copenhagen Conservatory (1969–71), Abrahamsen pursued further studies in composition with Pelle Gudmundsen-Holmgreen and Per NØRGÅRD at the Arhus Conservatory, an establishment noted for its avant-garde connections. He has produced a considerable number of works since the early 1970s. His musical style makes frequent use of bitonality, savouring the effect of superimposing a melodic line against a harmonically conflicting background: in the concerto-like orchestral piece *Lied in Fall* (1988), for instance, the cello part clashes with dense orchestral accompaniment. Other orchestral works include *Foam* (1970), the *Symphony in C* (1972), the first symphony (1974), *Stratification* (1973–75), and *Nach und Trompeten*. He has also written a cello concerto (1987) and chamber music, including two string quartets (1973; 1981).

Absurd, Theatre of the A theatrical genre of the 1950s and 1960s, in which accepted stage conventions were largely abandoned in order to present a view of the world as meaningless and incomprehensible. The phrase was coined by the theatre critic Martin Esslin in 1961, who saw in the plays of BECKETT, IONESCO, and others a reflection of the philosophical concept of the Absurd popularized by existentialist writers such as CAMUS. IONESCO's one-act play *The Bald Prima Donna* (1950) is perhaps the earliest play to be recognizably absurdist in its style and preoccupations, while Beckett's *Waiting for Godot* (1956) is usually seen as the quintessential work in the genre. Other playwrights to be associated with the style included the Frenchman Arthur ADAMOV and the American Edward Albee. The impression of a coherent movement was largely the result of an accidental similarity of theme and treatment and by the 1960s the leading writers had already begun to take different paths – Ionesco and Albee adopting a more allegorical drama and Adamov imitating the EPIC THEATRE of BRECHT.

Academy of Ancient Music A chamber orchestra founded in London in 1973 by Christopher Hogwood to perform baroque and classical music in authentic playing styles on period instruments or modern copies of period instruments. It takes its name from an 18th-century London music society. The ensemble, the first British 'authentic' ensemble to gain widespread recognition, has a large repertory which includes works by Purcell, Handel, Vivaldi, J. C. Bach, Mozart, and Beethoven. Notable recordings have included the complete symphonies of Mozart. *See also* EARLY-MUSIC MOVEMENT.

Academy of St Martin-in-the-Fields An orchestra founded in London in 1959 by Neville MARRINER and a number of London's leading orchestral players to perform and record 18th-century music. Marriner organized and directed the Academy's activities until 1978. The current artistic directors are Iona Brown and Kenneth Sillito (with Sillito also directing the chamber ensemble): Marriner continues to conduct the larger orchestra, of which he remains musical director. The ensemble takes its name from the church in Trafalgar Square, London, in which its earliest performances were given. Its many polished recordings include 19th- and 20th-century works as well as the baroque and classical repertory. It has won many international awards: recent recordings include the soundtrack for Miloš FORMAN's film *Amadeus*, Handel's *Messiah*, and a complete cycle of Tchaikovsky's symphonies. Since 1991 the Academy has made regular tours of Europe, the US, and Japan. The Academy of St Martin-in-the-Fields Chorus, directed by Laszlo Heltay, was founded in 1975.

Achterberg, Gerrit (1905–62) Dutch poet. Achterberg worked for some years as a school teacher and a civil servant before devoting his life entirely to the writing of poetry. He took no role in the public literary life of his time, living in seclusion in a small Dutch village. The only spectacular event in his life occurred in 1937, when he killed the woman he was living with. He spent some time in mental institutions before returning to his writing.

Achterberg's first volume of poems, *Departure* (1931), introduces the theme that runs through all his subsequent writing: the death of the loved one and the search for a mystical reunion. In his poems the ideal of a closeness in love that transcends even death sometimes appears as a possibility to be effected through the power of poetry itself, while at other times the inadequacy of all human language is a cause of despair. Achterberg drew his vocabulary from a wide variety of sources, including the natural sciences as well as geography, philosophy, and economics. In doing so he created a wealth of new possibilities for poetic expression. Awarded the National Prize for Literature in 1949, Achterberg had a major influence on the younger Dutch poets of the following decades.

Action and Body Art A type of PERFORMANCE ART in which the artist uses his or her own body as the medium of expression. Such displays, generally involving nudity, self-mutilation, or an element of physical endurance, became fashionable in the late 1960s and early 1970s, when they often featured as part of a HAPPENING. The professed aim was usually to bring home some point about the violence or vapidity of contemporary life in a shockingly immediate way. Exponents of body art have included Josef BEUYS, who became famous for his bizarre ritual 'actions' in the 1970s, the Austrians Otto MUEHL and Hermann NITSCH, and Gina PANE.

Adami, Valerio (1935–) Italian painter and graphic artist, probably the best-known exponent of POP ART outside Britain and the US. After studies in Milan, Adami spent the early 1960s in London and Paris, before returning to Italy, where he has since chiefly worked. During this period his style evolved from abstraction towards a highly formal figurative style. Figures tend to be strongly outlined and painted in flat unmodulated colours, somewhat in the manner of a strip cartoon or animated film. His work shows a fascination with popular culture, especially advertising, and is notable for a strong element of wit and surrealistic fantasy.

Adamov, Arthur (1908–70) French playwright, born in Russia, who became a leading writer in the absurdist tradition of the 1950s (*see* ABSURD, THEATRE OF THE). His early plays were heavily influenced by Strindberg and tackle such themes as futility, obsession, and masochism, reflecting Adamov's own disturbed inner life. After *The Parody* (1950) and *The Large and the Small Manouevre* (1950), he scored a major success with *Professor Taranne* (1953), which remains his most frequently revived play and clearly owes a debt to the writings of Franz Kafka. In *Ping-Pong* (1955), a parable about capitalism in which the two main characters attempt to develop a new kind of pin-ball machine, he first explored the political themes that were to dominate his later work. Most of these subsequent dramas were satirical attacks on capitalist values; the more successful included the Brechtian *Paolo Paoli* (1957), which made political points while discussing the turn-of-the-century trade in ostrich feathers, *Spring of '71* (1962), an account of the Paris Commune, *Off Limits* (1968), and *If Summer Returned* (1970). Directors who championed Adamov's work included BLIN, PLANCHON, SERRAU, and VILAR.

Adamov's autobiographical writings *The Confession* (1946) and *Man and Child* (1968) provide a harrowing account of the private neuroses that fed the nightmarish world of his plays. He committed suicide.

Adorno, Theodor (Wiesengrund) (Theodor Wiesengrund; 1903–69) German philosopher and social theorist of the **Frankfurt School**. After taking a degree in philosophy at the University of Frankfurt, Adorno studied musical composition under Alban Berg in Vienna. In 1930 he returned to Frankfurt and taught at the Institute of Social Research until 1934, when he emigrated to Britain to escape Hitler's persecution of the Jews. In 1938 he moved to the US where he rejoined his colleagues HORKHEIMER and Herbert Marcuse and set up a version of the Frankfurt Institute in exile. When the University of Frankfurt reopened the Institute in 1950, Adorno and Horkheimer returned to Germany to become its joint directors.

Adorno's first major work, cowritten with Horkheimer in 1947, was *Dialectic of the Enlightenment*. In it he argued that the rationalism of the Enlightenment, once a powerful weapon against superstition and ignorance, had itself become a tool of oppression in modern technological societies. In *Negative Dialectics* (1966), an intensely obscure work that is nevertheless the most important statement of his thought, Adorno argued that all forms of systematic thought were potentially enslaving because of their dependence on false absolutes and their distortion of reality. Neither Marxism nor EXISTENTIALISM was excluded from this critique, while scientific empiricism was seen as perhaps the most dangerous delusion of all. Although these views proved popular with student radicals in the late 1960s, Adorno's most lasting work may well prove to be his writings on aesthetics and musicology. In *The Philosophy of Modern Music* (1949) he championed the music of Schoenberg and his followers.

Afro (Afro Basaldella; 1912–76) Italian abstract painter. After training in Florence and Venice, Afro worked briefly in Paris (1931) before settling in Rome (1937). During World War II he taught intermittently at the Venice Academy while serving in the Italian armed forces. In 1947–48 he associated with the young painters of the FRONTE NUOVO DELLE ARTI and when this broke up exhibited with the Gruppo degli Otto (Group of Eight), a splinter group dedicated to abstraction. By this time his style had developed from his cubist beginnings into a lyrical and expressionistic form of abstraction, characterized by flickering brushwork and a distinctive use of colour. In the mid 1950s he began to produce murals, including a series at Udine, his birthplace, and *The Garden of Hope* (1958) for the UNESCO building in Paris. Afro was awarded first prize for Italian painting at the Venice Biennale of 1956 and found increasing recognition in the US, where he sometimes taught. He spent his later years painting and teaching in Rome.

His brothers Dino and Mirko Basaldella were both sculptors.

Ahlin, Lars (1921–) Swedish novelist and literary critic. Born in Sundsvall, which provides the setting for much of his work, Ahlin is one of Sweden's greatest storytellers. Convinced that all men are created equal in the eyes of God, and that nobody has the right to judge another, Ahlin opposes all those who try to mould the world to fit their own dogmas.

His first novel, *Tåbb with the Manifesto* (1943), examines the socialist view of society and the way in which an individual can become dependent on his own ideals. In *If* (1946) the troubled relationship between a father and his son symbolizes the conflict between dogmatic authority and those who reject it. The novel is written with studied detachment, encouraging an intellectual, rather than a sentimental, response from the reader.

Night in the Market Tent (1957), Ahlin's most celebrated novel, is a sweeping philosophical-theological exploration of love. *Bark and Leaves* (1961), an exploration of the problems of the artist, was followed by over 20 years of silence. Ahlin returned in 1982 with *Hannibal the Conqueror*, a historical novel cowritten with his wife. *Your Fruit of Life* (1987) deals with a millionaire tax lawyer struggling to preserve the social-democratic ideals of his youth in an era of rising right-wing tendencies.

Ahlin has also written widely on ethics and aesthetics and is considered one of the few major theorists in Swedish literature.

Aichinger, Ilse (1921–) Austrian writer. Being half-Jewish, Aichinger led a precarious existence during the Nazi period and could only begin to study medicine after the war. She dropped her studies after five semesters to work for the publishers Fischer V in Frankfurt and married the German poet Günter EICH in 1954. She now lives in Vienna.

Aichinger's first novel *The Greater Hope* (1948), describes the terror of the Nazi period through the eyes of a group of children. Her protagonist Ellen has to confront both the fear of the adult world as well as her own 'fear of the fear' and comes to see the Star of David as a symbol of the 'greater hope'. Aichinger's collection of short stories *The Bound Man* (1953) influenced the development of the German short story by exploring themes of fear and alienation through parable and paradox. In her later short prose (*Eliza/Eliza*, 1965; *Bad Words*, 1976) and radio plays (*Auckland*, 1969) Aichinger abandons conventional plot and setting in favour of symbolic dream-like actions set in imaginary places. In 1978 she published her first volume of poems, *New Bond*. She has won many national and international awards.

Aix-en-Provence Festival An annual music festival held in Aix-en-Provence, France; founded in 1948, it lasts for a month each July. It is mainly an opera festival, with a particular emphasis on

Mozart's works, but includes a variety of concerts and recitals. It is possibly France's best-known music festival, with many performances held outdoors in the courtyard of the archiepiscopal palace and the cloisters of the Cathedral of St Sauveur. The town's other historical buildings are also utilized.

Akhmadulina, Bella (Izabella Akhatovna; 1937–) Russian poet. Of mixed Italian and Tatar descent, she numbers amongst her ancestors an Italian organ-grinder and A. M. Stopani, a close associate of Lenin. Born in Moscow, Akhmadulina attended the Gorkii Literary Institute until her expulsion in 1957. Her first poems were published in 1955, the year she married Evgenii EVTUSHENKO. Like him she is a brilliant reciter of her own verse, notably the poem *My Comrades*, dedicated to Andrei VOZNESENSKY. Married subsequently to Iurii NAGIBIN and then to the playwright and children's writer Gennadii Mamlin, she is now the wife of the artist and designer Boris Messerer. Her first collection, *String* (1962), demonstrated her ability to invest the commonplace with an air of mystery and surprise. This has been followed by *Chill* (1968), a volume that illustrates her preoccupation with the psychology of illness, *Music Lessons* (1969), the title poem of which is dedicated to Marina Tsvetaeva, *Blizzard* (1977), *Candle* (1977), and *Secret* (1983). Dogged by personal difficulties, she has written little in recent years. Her poetry, mostly consisting of short intensely personal lyrics and making subtle use of alliteration, assonance, and rhyme, is strongly influenced by Pushkin, Tsvetaeva, Akhmatova, and PASTERNAK. Unlike Pasternak, however, Akhmadulina concentrates largely on urban themes. She has written some longer poems, notably the popular *A Fairytale about the Rain* (1963) and the consciously Pushkinian *My Genealogy* (1964). She has also translated Georgian poetry.

Aksenov, Vasilii Pavlovich (1932–) Russian writer living in the US from 1980. Aksenov was brought up in Kazan and Magadan following the arrest of his parents on political charges. He trained as a doctor but by 1960 had devoted himself to writing; his work rapidly came to epitomize the new spirit of freedom in the post-Stalin years. In 1975–76 he was visiting professor at the University of California, Los Angeles, but four years later an attempt to publish an uncensored almanac, *Metropole*, led to his permanent expatriation. This move released several important novels for publication abroad, which further enhanced his reputation as a major writer. He now holds a senior professorship at George Mason University, Virginia.

Aksenov's best-known early work was a short novel about contemporary young people, *A Ticket to the Stars* (1961), notable for its brisk plot and racy dialogue. In later stories increasingly grotesque fantasy has come to play a part, particularly in his Kafkaesque allegory of Stalinism *The Steel Bird* (1965, published 1977). His major work to date is undoubtedly *The Burn* (1969–75, published 1980), a complex modernistic novel that presents a tragicomic picture of the author's generation. Other important works include *The Island of Crimea* (1980), a hilarious picaresque novel about Russian nationalism and self-delusion, *Paperscape* (1983), Askenov's first US novel, and *Say Cheese* (1980–83, published 1985), a coded version of the *Metropole* scandal. *In Search of the Melancholy Baby* (1987), a series of reflections on US life, is interesting for the light it throws on the problems of emigration and cultural adaptation.

Aktie Tomaat (Dutch: tomato action) An influential theatre campaign of the late 1960s that did much to rejuvenate Dutch drama and reflected changes in theatrical practice throughout Europe. The campaign developed from an incident during a performance by the Netherlandse Comedie in Amsterdam, during which drama students from the Amsterdam School of Drama threw tomatoes at the stage in protest against the theatrical establishment. They argued that the time had come for a more socially relevant theatre in which the director played a less autocratic role, allowing the creative energy of the actors to find expression. The campaign provoked much debate about the role of the theatre in modern society and led to the foundation of several new companies in which the new ideas could be tested; among the most important of these was Amsterdam's WERKTEATER. *See also* VORMINGSTONEEL.

Alberti, Rafael (1902–) Spanish poet of the 'Generation of 1927'. Born in Cadiz, Alberti moved in 1917 to Madrid, where an exhibition of his paintings was held in

1922. In 1923 he left Madrid for health reasons and began writing. His early work was steeped in the poetry of the 16th and 17th centuries; he particularly revered Góngora and also drew on traditional popular song. Alberti's extraordinary technical accomplishment and range were evident in his first book, *Sailor on Land* (1924), a tribute to the Andalusian sea, which won him the Premio Nacional de Literatura in 1925. The joyful *La Amante* (1925) again shows his mastery of many different styles. In *Quicklime and Song* (*Cal y canto*; 1927) he attempted to create images that 'succeed each other with cinematographic speed', but he confessed that his obsession with formal beauty in this work 'almost petrified my feelings'. A profound personal crisis, caused in part by an unhappy love affair, inspired *Concerning the Angels* (1928), a difficult but almost certainly his finest work. In 1927, Alberti was a prime mover in the tercentenary 'hommage' to Góngora organized by the so-called 'Generation of 1927', a group of writers that also included ALEIXANDRE, GUILLÉN, and García Lorca.

In the early 1930s Alberti became a committed communist, founding the left-wing journal *Octubre* (1934) and fighting with Republican forces in the Spanish Civil War. Following Franco's victory he fled (1940) to Argentina and subsequently travelled extensively, especially in communist countries. Alberti's later work contains much undistinguished political verse but *On Painting* (1945), a sequence of poems on the visual arts, and *Returns of the Living Distance* (1956) are of greater interest. His autobiography, *The Lost Grove*, was published in 1942 and his complete works in 1961; they include stories, essays, and plays. He returned to Spain in 1977 and was elected to the Spanish parliament as a communist the following year, resigning after a few months to devote himself to his work.

Albicocco, Jean-Gabriel (1936–) French film director noted for his lavish camerawork. Albicocco was born in Cannes, the son of the cinematographer Quinto Albicocco. He too began as a cinematographer before serving as an assistant director to Jules Dassin on *He Who Must Die* (1957), a version of the KAZANTZAKIS novel *Christ Recrucified*. Albicocco then directed a number of shorts before making his feature debut with an adaptation of a Balzac novel, *The Girl With the Golden Eyes* (1961), which starred his wife, Marie Laforêt. Albicocco's only film to make an impact outside France was *Le Grand Meaulnes* (*The Wanderer*, 1967), an adaptation of Alain-Fournier's much-loved classic of adolescent longing. His other films include *Le Rat d'Amérique* (1962), an episode in *L'Amour au féminin* (1968), *Le Cœur fou* (1970), *Le Petit Matin* (1971), and *Quint Jean-Baptiste, known as Quinto* (1982), a film about his father.

Albini, Franco (1905–77) One of the most influential Italian architects and designers of the post-war era. Born in Robbiate, near Como, he was trained at the Milan Politecnico. In the 1930s he emerged as an important designer of exhibitions and displays, for example with the Palace of Italian Civilization Project in Rome (1938). After World War II he carried out a number of important renovation projects on historic buildings, such as the Palazzo Bianco, Genoa (1952) and the Palazzo Rosso, Genoa (1957–61). His new museum for the Tesoro di San Lorenzo, Genoa (1952) and the Museum of Egyptian Art in Cairo (1963) combine simple geometrical shapes with dramatic lighting. He made a major contribution to furniture design, notably with his dining-room furniture of graded sizes, which packs away economically. His most important new building was the La Rinascente department store in Rome (1962–63), a controversial design with an exposed steel frame and near-windowless concrete walling. His later career saw more influential exhibition designs and more important renovation projects on historic buildings at Milan and Piacenza.

Aldeburgh Festival An annual British music festival held in Aldeburgh, Suffolk, for a fortnight in June. It was founded in 1948 by Benjamin BRITTEN, who settled in Aldeburgh during World War II, with the help of the English Opera Group, the singer Peter Pears, and Imogen Holst (daughter of the composer Gustav Holst). Britten wrote many pieces specifically for the festival. The programme has since diversified, becoming more international and often including film, literature, lectures, and exhibitions as well as music. The Maltings at Snape, a disused complex of industrial buildings, was converted by the festival directors in 1966–67, rebuilt in 1969 after a fire, and now provides a venue for large events and a home for the Britten-Pears School of Advanced Musical Studies.

aleatory music Music in which chance is allowed to dictate either the process of composition or aspects of the performance, or both. Typically, these procedures decide, for example, the order in which sections of a piece are to be performed. While aleatory works can use conventional musical notation, the possibilities for randomness can be further enhanced by using GRAPHIC NOTATION. The term was coined by Pierre BOULEZ (*musique aléatoire*).

Aleatory music is particularly associated with the US composer John Cage, whose 'chance music' (his preferred term) was influenced in part by the musical experiments of Charles Ives and Henry Cowell, as well as by Zen Buddhism. Aleatory techniques have been a significant force in avant-garde music since the 1950s; examples by Cage include *Music of Changes* (1952) and *Concert for Piano and Orchestra* (1958). Also noteworthy are STOCKHAUSEN's *Klavierstücke XI* (1956) and Boulez's *Third Piano Sonata* (1957) which, although not strictly aleatory works, allow the player to make various choices in performing them.

Alechinsky, Pierre (1927–) Belgian abstract painter and graphic artist of Russian extraction. Alechinsky studied the decorative arts at the Ecole Nationale Supérieure in Brussels, where he specialized in typography and book illustration. In 1947 he joined the avant-garde Jeune Peinture Belge group, painting at this stage in a post-cubist style influenced by Picasso. As a member of the COBRA group in 1949–51 he developed a turbulent expressionistic style characterized by fierce colours, agitated brushwork, and a vein of fantastic imagery that often approaches surrealism while remaining essentially abstract.

On the break-up of Cobra, Alechinsky settled in Paris, where he studied engraving under HAYTER at the celebrated Atelier 17. In 1955 a meeting with a group of Japanese calligraphers inspired him to visit the Far East, where he made the award-winning film *Japanese Calligraphy* (1956). The influence of eastern calligraphy is often apparent in his work of this period. The 1960s saw further travels in the US, Mexico, and the Canaries, and a growing reputation on both sides of the Atlantic. A major retrospective of his work was seen in Rotterdam, Paris, and Zürich in 1974–75, establishing him as one of the most audaciously original of post-war European painters. In addition to his savagely expressionistic work in oils and (from 1965) acrylics, he produced numerous book illustrations and other graphic works.

Aleixandre, Vicente (1898–1984) Spanish poet. Aleixandre was born in Seville, the son of a railway engineer. After studying law and business administration at Madrid University, he taught commercial law (1919–22) and worked for Andalusian Railroads (1921–25). He wrote his first poems while recovering from kidney failure in 1925, publishing his first collection in 1928. Poor health also prevented him from going into exile after the Civil War, during which he wrote in support of the Republic. His poetry was banned in Spain until 1944. After World War II he emerged as perhaps the leading influence on the poets of the rising generation. He was awarded the Nobel Prize for literature in 1977.

Aleixandre was a member of the so-called 'Generation of 1927', a group of writers that also included ALBERTI and García Lorca. His earlier poetry was much influenced by surrealism and sometimes incorporated an element of automatic writing. *Destruction or Love* (1935), Aleixandre's first major collection, demonstrates his mastery of free verse and his predilection for images drawn from dreams, the subconscious, and the natural world. In contrast to this volume, which presents a pantheistic vision of man in harmony with the cosmos, *Shadows of Paradise* (1944) presents man as an alienated being longing for a lost Eden.

In his post-war volumes *History of the Heart* (1954) and *In a Vast Domain* (1962) Aleixandre turned to more social and ethical themes. To accord with his new emphasis on human solidarity and the need for communication, he greatly simplified his style, consciously making his work more accessible. His last collections *Poems of Communication* (1968) and *Dialogues of Insight* (1974) are more intimate and philosophical. Aleixandre's best-known prose work is *The Meetings* (1958), a series of touching reminiscences of his fellow writers.

Alexander, Christopher (1936–) British architect, planner, and writer. Educated in both architecture and mathematics at Cambridge, Alexander took a doctorate in architecture at Harvard and has taught at Berkeley since 1967. The essence of his work is its criticism of crude rationalism in planning and its analysis of what makes a satisfying human environment. In two books, *Community and Privacy: Towards a New Architecture of Humanism* (1963, with Serge Chermayeff) and *Notes on the Synthesis of Form* (1964), he provided a coherent theoretical explanation of the shortcomings of modernism in planning and design and attempted to capture the elusive qualities of traditional planning. Alexander used mathematical analysis, rather than traditional art-historical methodologies, arousing intense interest and controversy.

Alexander has put his 'bottom-up' approach to planning into practice in master plans for communities in India, the US, Peru, Japan, France, Israel, Venezuela, and Brazil, but since the 1960s he has worked mainly in California. Latterly he has been an important influence on the growing self-build movement and in fostering the involvement of client groups in the design process. In the 1970s he developed his concept of Pattern Language as a medium for articulating users' needs and interests, thereby enabling architects to create environments in an adaptive and reactive manner rather than by imposition of monolithic ideas.

alienation effect A theatrical effect designed to prevent the audience from identifying too closely with the action presented on the stage in order that the political or other intellectual content of a play can be communicated with the greatest clarity. The theory of the a-effect, as it is sometimes called, was developed by Bertolt BRECHT both in his own plays and in his influential essays on the theatre. In contrast to the naturalistic method of Stanislavsky, the theory demands that the actor should maintain a certain detachment from his role and that the director should punctuate the action with songs, placards, direct speeches, etc., in order to remind the audience of the artificial nature of theatrical representation. *See also* EPIC THEATRE.

Almodóvar, Pedro (1949–) Spanish film director, who emerged in the 1980s as a leading and controversial figure in Spanish cinema. Born in Castile, Almodóvar moved to Madrid when he was 17 and has made almost all of his films there. While working for the national telephone company, he became interested in the new wave of Spanish cinema and began to write criticism; he later joined a theatre group. After teaching himself the rudiments of film-making, he made a series of underground films that earned comparisons with BUÑUEL. Such early films as *Dark Habits* (1983), a typically black farce about scandalous activities in a convent, were notable for their anarchic style and provocative concentration upon female sexuality. A recurring theme is the clash between traditional Spanish attitudes and the demands of liberated young women.

Almodóvar consolidated his reputation with such films as *What Have I Done to Deserve This?* (1984), an energetic comedy about a frustrated housewife, *Matador* (1985), *The Law of Desire* (1987), and *Women on the Verge of a Nervous Breakdown* (1988), all of which starred Carmen Maura. This last film, a frenetic farce with an absurd plot involving Islamic terrorists, won 50 awards and brought Almodóvar international fame. *Tie Me Up! Tie Me Down!* (1989), about a young actress who falls in love with her kidnapper, caused a furore among feminists who mistakenly thought it condoned rape. *High Heels* (1991) shows signs of greater seriousness; like its predecessor it starred Victoria Abril.

Alonso, Dámaso (1898–1990) Spanish poet, literary critic, and philologist. Alonso was educated at Madrid University, where he later held the chair of Romance languages (1939–68). He was a visiting professor at the universities of Berlin and Cambridge, as well as at several US universities.

Alonso first came to notice with his studies of the 17th-century poet Góngora, whose reputation he was largely responsible for restoring. His groundbreaking edition of Góngora's *Solitudes* appeared in 1927 and was followed by further important studies. The rediscovery of Góngora had an immense effect on contemporary Spanish writing. Other critical works include *The Poetry of St John of the Cross* (1942), *Six Examples of Spanish Literary*

Expression (1951, with C. Bonsoño), *Four Spanish Poets* (1962), and the landmark study *Spanish Poetry* (1950). His critical approach combined a respect for tradition and formal qualities with an emphasis on close reading derived from William Empson and I. A. Richards.

A member of the 'Generation of 1927', a group of poets that also included García Lorca and ALEIXANDRE, Alonso published four collections of original verse. His most important volume, *Children of Anger* (1944), startled its original readers with its anger and disgust at the modern world. *Man and God* (1955) shows the predominantly religious tenor of his work. Alonso translated the works of, among others, James Joyce, T. S. Eliot, and Gerard Manley Hopkins.

Alpengala *See* YEHUDI MENUHIN FESTIVAL OF MUSIC.

Alston, Richard (1948–) British choreographer, who found recognition as one of the most important choreographers of his generation in the 1980s. Much of his work bears the influence of the US choreographer Merce Cunningham and that of Sir Frederick ASHTON; his ballets have been much praised for their sensitivity and lyricism.

Educated at Eton, Alston studied at the London School of Contemporary Dance and made his debut as a choreographer shortly after joining the London Contemporary Dance Theatre in 1970. His work with the company earned him the 1972 Gulbenkian Award, which enabled him to found his own company, Strider. He choreographed and danced with this troupe until 1975, when he began studies in New York with Cunningham and others. Soon after returning to London in 1978 he won acclaim for *The Seven Deadly Sins*, which he created for the English National Opera. In 1980 he was appointed resident choreographer (artistic director since 1986) of the Ballet Rambert (*see* RAMBERT DANCE COMPANY). His most significant work with the Rambert company, from which he resigned in 1992, included *Bell High* (1980), *Soda Lake* (1981), which he created for Michael CLARK, and *Wildlife* (1984). Work for other companies includes *Dances from the Kingdom of the Pagodas* (1982) for the Royal Danish Ballet and *Midsummer* (1983) for the ROYAL BALLET.

alternative theatre *See* COLLECTIVE CREATION; COMMUNITY THEATRE; FRINGE THEATRE.

Althusser, Louis (1919–90) French Marxist philosopher. Born in Algeria, Althusser moved to France in 1930. As a philosophy student he initially took a position of militant Catholicism. After the war, most of which he spent in German prison camps, he enrolled at the Ecole Normale Supérieure in Paris, where he taught for the rest of his career. He joined the Communist Party of France in 1948. In the 1960s and 1970s Althusser's austere and highly theoretical reinterpretation of Marx made him one of the most celebrated figures on the intellectual left in France. After killing his wife in 1980 he spent the rest of his life in mental hospitals.

In his first collection of essays, *For Marx* (1965), Althusser attempted to free Marx from what he saw as the humanist and idealist distortions of some of his interpreters. Althusser insists that Marxism is not one philosophy among many but *the* science of history; alternative explanations of the world are dismissed as 'ideological', forms of false consciousness. His work is much concerned with the way in which intellectual concepts are (supposedly) produced by the material structures of society. These basic positions are elaborated with great sophistication in his major work *Reading Capital* (1965) and modified somewhat in his *Essays in Self-Criticism* (1976).

The importance of Althusser in the 1960s and 1970s was to a great extent based on the fact that he had opened a dialogue between STRUCTURALISM and Marxism. Ironically for a thinker who denied the importance of human subjectivity, he is likely to be remembered mainly for his autobiography, *The Future Lasts a Long Time*, in which he describes the events leading up to the killing of his wife. The book became a bestseller in France when published posthumously in 1992.

Amadeus Quartet British string quartet founded in London in 1947 and disbanded in 1987 on the death of its viola player, Peter Schidlof. Its other members were Norbert Brainin (first violin), Siegmund Nissel (second violin), and Martin Lovett (cello). Brainin, Nissel, and Schidlof came to Britain from Austria in 1938–39 and studied under Max Rostal during the 1940s; Lovett studied at the Royal College of Music in London. Schidlof changed from violin to viola in order to make the quartet possible and the group, after a successful London debut in 1948, rapidly established itself as the leading British quartet of its generation. Tours throughout Europe, North and South America, Japan, and Australia consolidated their international reputation as one of the finest postwar quartets. Their repertory was essentially rooted in the works of Haydn, Mozart, Beethoven, and Schubert, although they also performed and recorded works from the later 19th and 20th centuries, including BRITTEN's third string quartet, which was written for them.

Amis, Sir Kingsley (1922–) British satirical novelist and poet. Amis was educated at the City of London School and St John's College, Oxford, where Philip LARKIN became a close friend. A subsequent brief academic career provided the material for his first highly successful novel, *Lucky Jim* (1954), set in a provincial university. Its central character, Jim Dixon, was held to personify the social resentment of the newly educated lower-middle classes in the post-war era. Further novels such as *That Uncertain Feeling* (1955) and *Take A Girl Like You* (1960) continued to explore the frustrations of provincial middle-class life and the elusiveness of sexual satisfaction. With their somewhat unfocused satirical anger, these early novels led to Amis's being associated in the popular mind with such writers as John OSBORNE. During the 1960s he produced works in a variety of styles, including a ghost story, *The Green Man* (1969), and *The Anti-Death League* (1966), a spy story with a serious philosophical message. His later work, which includes *Ending Up* (1974), *Jake's Thing* (1978), *The Old Devils* (1986), *Difficulties with Girls* (1988), and *The Folks that Live on the Hill* (1990), is marked by an increasingly cantankerous tone and a hostility to most aspects of contemporary society. In several of these works Amis examines the failure, impotence, and anger of late middle age. Many of his books have been adapted for television and several have been made into successful films. His *Collected Poems 1944–1979* were published in 1979 and a volume of acerbic *Memoirs* appeared in 1991.

Amis was married (1965–83) to the novelist Elizabeth Jane Howard and is the father (by his first wife) of the novelist Martin Amis.

Amis, Martin (1949–) British novelist. The son of Sir Kingsley Amis, he studied at Exeter College, Oxford, gaining a first in English. He then worked as editorial assistant on the *Times Literary Supplement* and was also literary editor of the *New Statesman*. His first novel, *The Rachel Papers*, the tale of a precocious young intellectual's amorous encounters in 1970s London, was published in 1974, winning the Somerset Maugham Award. *Dead Babies* and *Success* followed in 1975 and 1978, both scabrous dissections of English social and sexual morality. After *Other People; A Mystery Story* (1981) came *Money* (1983), his most successful and popular novel to date. The story of an English pornographer's attempts to clinch a Hollywood film deal, *Money* depicts a world of frenzied greed and sleazy self-gratification; its narrator, the grotesque hedonist John Self, became a fitting anti-hero for the 1980s. Amis's most recent novels are *London Fields* (1989), in which the themes of social decay and urban pollution are continued, and *Time's Arrow* (1991) which controversially employs the conceit of reversing time to examine the life and morality of a Nazi concentration camp doctor. Other works include a collection of journalism *The Moronic Inferno and Other Visits to America* (1986) and *Einstein's Monsters* (1987), a collection of short stories dealing with the nuclear age. Amis's prose style – a pungent combination of street slang and literary cleverness overlaid with a laconic black humour – has become the most instantly recognizable in contemporary British fiction.

His work appears to both relish and condemn the decadence of the age.

Amis, Stanley F(rederick) *See* HOWELL, KILLICK, PARTRIDGE, AND AMIS.

Andersch, Alfred (1914–80) German novelist. Having experienced unemployment in the 1930s, he became an active member of the Communist Party in Bavaria. After being twice imprisoned in Dachau, Andersch broke his links with the Party choosing 'total introversion' as a reaction to the 'total state'. In 1943 he was sent to the Italian front, from which he deserted in 1944. After the war Andersch edited the journal *Der Ruf*, out of which developed GRUPPE 47. In 1972 he became a Swiss citizen.

Andersch's novels are influenced by EXISTENTIALISM and his rejection of all forms of historical determinism. His first novel, the autobiographical *The Cherries of Freedom* (1952), presents a soldier's decision to desert as a moment of achieved freedom and self-realization. In *Flight to Afar* (*Sansibar oder der letze Grund*; 1957) a group of social outsiders tries to save the sculpture of a reading nun, which serves as a symbol of freedom, from Nazi destruction; by deciding to flee from the Third Reich the characters realize their own freedom. In Andersch's later novels, such as *The Redhead* (1960) and *Efraim's Book* (1967), the characters similarly have to free themselves from an oppressive reality, often an emotional entanglement, in their 'decisive moment'. His novels, particularly *Winterspelt* (1974), explore the tension between the political and the private spheres. He has also written short stories and a number of radio plays.

Andersen, Benny (1929–) Danish poet and writer. Andersen's humorous and accessible style has made him the most popular contemporary poet in Denmark. His working-class background is reflected in his choice of language, while his interest in music has influenced his use of rhythm and metre.

Early collections such as *The Musical Eel* (1960) and *Camera with Kitchen Privileges* (1962) show the influence of the European symbolist tradition. His later work is more autobiographical but continues to explore social themes and the common experience of angst and nothingness. His explorations of modern life usually take typical everyday situations as their starting point. Amongst his concerns is the way in which personal development can be stultified by the structures of modern industrial society. His first novel, *On The Bridge* (1981), presents his ethical concerns more directly, without the comic exaggeration that characterizes his earlier work.

By playing with grammar, syntax, and metaphor, Andersen defamiliarizes normative speech habits and sets up disquieting undercurrents. This interest in language and wordplay has also led him to write popular children's stories, such as *Snøvsen, Egil and the Cat in the Bag* (1967), and to collect Danish and foreign nursery-rhymes. He has also worked in television and radio and produced a number of film scripts and records.

Anderson, Lindsay (Gordon) (1923–) British film and theatre director and critic, who established his reputation during the 1950s as a prominent figure in the FREE CINEMA movement. As a critic Anderson attacked the British film industry for its complacency, before making his debut as a director of documentary shorts. His first major film, *This Sporting Life* (1963), based on the novel by David STOREY, depicted the brutality of life in industrial northern England. After several years concentrating upon direction for the stage, Anderson returned to the cinema with *The White Bus* (1967) and *If...* (1968), a poetic, violent, and often funny fantasy about a rebellion in an English public school. Anderson maintained his criticism of the Establishment with such films as *O Lucky Man!* (1973), in which the hero of *If...* makes a spiritual journey through contemporary British society. Subsequent works, among them *In Celebration* (1974), *Britannia Hospital* (1982), and *Glory! Glory!* (1989), failed to recapture the appeal of his early work; *The Whales in August* (1987), starring the veterans Bette Davis and Lillian Gish, also roused comparatively little interest. As an actor, Anderson made a screen appearance in the film *Chariots of Fire* (1981). Anderson has been associate artistic director with the Royal Court Theatre (1969–75) and governor of the British Film Institute (1969–70).

Andrić, Ivo (1892–1975) Yugoslav (Bosnian) novelist and short-story writer. Born near Travnik, when Bosnia lay within the Austro-Hungarian empire, Andric studied in Sarajevo, Vienna, Cracow, and Graz. An ardent Yugoslav nationalist, he was interned by the Austrians during World War I. His first important work, *Ex Ponto*, appeared in 1918, the year that saw the emergence of an independent Yugoslavia. Andric continued to publish collections such as *Nemiri* (1921) while working in the diplomatic service; he was ambassador in Berlin in 1939. While held under house arrest in Belgrade during World War II he wrote the novels *Bosnian Story* (*Travnička hronika*), set in the Napoleonic era, *The Woman from Sarajevo* (*Gospodjica*), and his best-known work *The Bridge on the Dri a*, all published in 1945. They present a gallery of Balkan characters and racial types, drawn especially from the poor amongst whom he grew up, and dramatize the conflict between Eastern and Western outlooks. Andrić's attempt to reconcile man's noblest aspirations with his suffering and vulnerability found perhaps its deepest expression in the novella *The Damned Yard* (*Prokleta avlija*; 1954). He was awarded the Nobel Prize for literature in 1961. Andrić's vision of Bosnia as 'a country of hate and fear' provoked some criticism in Yugoslavia during his lifetime but appears to have been vindicated by recent developments.

Andriessen, Hendrik (1892–1981) Dutch composer, organist, and teacher. Andriessen studied piano, organ, and composition at the Amsterdam Conservatory, where he also taught harmony (1928–34). He held positions as an organist at St Joseph's Church in Haarlem (1916–34) and at Utrecht Cathedral (1934–49). He was director of the Utrecht Conservatory (1937–49) and of the Royal Conservatory in The Hague (1949–52) before becoming professor at the Catholic University in Nijmegen (1952–62). His compositions, mainly late-romantic in style but increasingly open to contemporary influences after World War II, include a major organ piece, *Sinfonia* (1939), the opera *Philomela* (1948), many religious and liturgical works, five symphonies, chamber music, and songs. His sons **Jurrian Andriessen** (1925–) and **Louis Andriessen** (1939–) are also composers, the latter being noted for such minimalist pieces as *Der Staat* (1976) for amplified women's voices, wind, and brass.

Andrzejewski, Jerzy (1909–83) Polish writer. Andrzejewski was born into a Catholic family in Warsaw and educated at the University there. His first novels, *Unavoidable Ways* (1936) and *Heart's Harmony* (1938), deal with the difficulties of reconciling Catholic morality with modern life and have been compared with the early works of Mauriac. During World War II he worked with the underground resistance to Nazi occupation and subsequently became a communist. His best-known novel, *Ashes and Diamonds* (1948), depicts the effects that the clash of Polish nationalism and communist idealism had on young Poles after World War II. A celebrated film version of the book appeared in 1958, codirected by the author and the Polish film director Andrzej WAJDA.

Andrzejewski was an officer of the Writers' Union and served in the Polish parliament from 1952 until 1956, when he left the Communist Party and began to criticize the policy of socialist realism in the arts. Subsequent works, such as *The Appeal* (1968), criticize totalitarianism and the abuses of power it inevitably breeds. The difficulties of the creative artist under a politically repressive system provide the theme of *He Cometh Leaping upon the Mountains* (1965) and *End of the Road* (1976). During the 1950s and 1960s many of his works were banned and he was eventually forbidden to publish. In 1976 he cofounded the Workers' Defence Committee (EOR), the organization that in 1980 became Solidarity.

The complexity of the ideas and attitudes in Andrzejewski's work is matched by the subtle intricacy of his prose, which exploits the rhythmic and poetic potential of Polish to the full. Among his other works are the plays *Winkelried's Day* (1945) and *Prometheus* (1972), the experimental novel *The Gates of Paradise* (1960), and *Pulp* (1972).

Angry Young Men A term applied by journalists to a number of young British novelists and dramatists in the later 1950s. The writers were not part of any organized movement but their work shared a number of characteristics, in particular an aggressive dissatisfaction with the social and moral values of post-war British society. Their concentration on the lives of the middle and working classes was something of a departure from the concerns of the previous generation of writers, who were generally from, and wrote about, the upper strata of English society. Principal figures associated with the term include Alan Sillitoe, Colin Wilson, and especially John Osborne, whose play *Look Back in Anger* (1956) is usually seen as the quintessentially 'Angry' work. Other representative works of the period include *Lucky Jim* (1954) by Kingsley AMIS, and Sillitoe's *Saturday Night and Sunday Morning* (1958). Stylistically there is an emphasis on naturalism and the language of ordinary people. *See also* KITCHEN-SINK SCHOOL.

Annigoni, Pietro (1910–88) Italian painter, best known for his portraits of the famous. Annigoni was born in Milan and trained at the Academy of Fine Arts in Florence. After World War II he exhibited with the FRONTE NUOVO DELLE ARTI, painting in the neorealist style that he maintained until his death. In the 1950s he moved to London and began to produce the society portraits that gained him his international reputation: these include famous images of Queen Elizabeth II (1955, 1969) and of President Kennedy (1961). Contrary to most modern practice, Annigoni's portraits were unashamedly idealized images of the sitter; he also courted ridicule through his wholesale imitation of the techniques of the Renaissance masters. While his work has been dismissed by many critics as shallow pastiche it proved unfailingly popular with the public: his second portrait of the Queen drew large crowds when it was exhibited in London in 1970. In the 1960s Annigoni became increasingly preoccupied with religious subjects, producing altarpieces and frescos for numerous Italian churches. He also attempted a number of large allegorical paintings. An autobiography, *An Artist's Life*, appeared in 1977.

Anouilh, Jean (1910–87) French playwright, who began his theatrical career as secretary to the director Louis Jouvet; he wrote the first of his many well-crafted plays, *Thieves' Carnival*, in 1932. The plays that followed are usually divided into the *pièces roses* (light comedies), the *pièces noires* (tragedies, sometimes based on Greek legend), the *pièces brillantes* (witty and sparkling comedies of manners), the *pièces grinçantes* (dramas with a harsher tone), and the *pièces costumées* (historical plays).

Although Anouilh attracted some attention with his earliest works, notably with *The Traveller Without Luggage* (1937), he established his reputation with the tragedy *Antigone* (1944), one of the most successful of his *pièces noires*. Based on the tragedy by Sophocles, but reaching different conclusions about the psychology of the main characters, the play soon acquired the status of a modern classic. Its ambiguous stance towards the rival claims of public and personal loyalty caused some controversy in the context of the German occupation of France.

After World War II, Anouilh consolidated his reputation with such plays as *Ring Round the Moon* (1947), an example of his *pièces brillantes*, which depicts an old lady who successfully manipulates all those around her; it is usually seen as a parable in which power is contrasted with purity. Many of his plays concern the sacrifices demanded of heroic figures, who refuse to make the compromises required of them by the world. Among the most admired of these are *Romeo and Jeanette* (1946), *Medea* (1953), *The Lark* (1953), which is a *pièce costumée* portraying the martyrdom of Joan of Arc, and *Becket, or the Honour of God* (1959), about the death of Thomas à Becket. The themes of his other dramas range from the clash between the ideal and the real, as in *The Waltz of the Toreadors* (1952), a *pièce grinçante* in which a man trapped in an unsatisfactory marriage reminisces about a girl with whom he once danced, to loneliness and old age.

Anouilh's later plays became increasingly whimsical and his reputation declined somewhat in the 1960s and 1970s. Nevertheless his plays continued to be performed all over the world.

antinovel Any novel that deliberately flouts the conventions of prose fiction, generally by dispensing with a coherent plot, intelligible characters, and a stable narrative voice. The term was first used by SARTRE in his introduction to Nathalie SARRAUTE's *Portrait of a Man Unknown* (1948) and was originally limited to discussion of the French NOUVEAU ROMAN. Since then, however, its use has been extended to cover almost any form of experimental prose fiction; it is even used retrospectively of such works as Sterne's *Tristram Shandy* (1759–67). Non-French writers particularly associated with the term include the German Uwe JOHNSON and the British novelist Christine Brooke-Rose.

Antonioni, Michelangelo (1912–) Italian film director, whose intense slow-moving dramas became highly fashionable in the 1960s. A student of economics and commerce at Bologna University, Antonioni subsequently found work as a film critic and graduated to the role of assistant to ROSSELLINI and Marcel Carné. He made his debut as a director in 1943 with *The People of the Po Valley*, following this with a series of other documentaries. He made his first feature film in 1950 with *Story of a Love Affair*, a brooding story of the guilt shared by two adulterous lovers when the husband of the woman dies in an accident.

Antonioni's reputation grew with *Love in the City* (1953), *The Lady Without Camellias* (1953), and *The Girl Friends* (1955), for which he won the Golden Lion at the Venice Film Festival. *The Cry* (1957) tells the story of the suicide of a man whose wife has left him. *L'Avventura* (1959), was the first part of a loosely linked trilogy completed by *La Notte* (1960) and *The Eclipse* (1962). The success of this sequence of films – all studies of emotional sterility and isolation in which narrative plays only a minor role – established Antonioni as a leading commentator upon contemporary social mores; it also made a star of the actress Monica Vitti (1931–), who was to appear in several of his subsequent films.

Antonioni experimented with the use of colour in *The Red Desert* (1964) and encapsulated the spirit of 'Swinging London' in *Blow-Up* (1967), an enigmatic thriller in which a photographer captures on film a murder that may not, in fact, have taken place. *Zabriskie Point* (1970), which was shot in California, was an attempted critique of modern materialism as seen through the eyes of a rebellious student, while *The Passenger* (1975), one of his most highly praised films, raised issues of personal identity through the story of a journalist (played by Jack Nicholson) who assumes the persona of a deceased gunrunner.

Antonioni's more recent works reflect his interest in the technical possibilities of video and include *The Oberwald Mystery* (1981), based on a story by Jean Cocteau, and *Identification of a Woman* (1982).

Appel, Karel (1921–) Dutch painter, sculptor, printmaker, and ceramicist. He studied at the Royal Academy of Fine Art in his native Amsterdam (1940–43), and held his first one-man exhibition in Groningen in 1946. In 1948 he was one of the founders of the experimental group Reflex, from which the more famous group COBRA developed. In 1950 he moved to Paris with two other members of Cobra – CONSTANT and CORNEILLE – and over the following decade built an international reputation, winning, for example, the UNESCO prize at the 1954 Venice Biennale and the 1960 Guggenheim International Award. In 1968 he began making relief paintings, followed by sculpture in painted wood and then in aluminium. Although Paris has remained his home, he has spent much of his time in the US.

In his early work Appel was an exponent of an extremely energetic expressive abstraction, using thick explosive brushwork and vivid colouring; Sir Herbert Read wrote that his pictures conveyed the impression "of a spiritual tornado that has left these images of its passage". His work usually retained figurative elements, however, often based on northern European myth or on children's art, in which he has a great interest. Later his handling became smoother (although still very vigorous). Some of his sculptures have a jokey character.

Arbuzov, Aleksei (Nikolaevich) (1908–86) Soviet playwright, actor, and theatre director, who established his reputation with *Tanya* (1939), a play about the character transformation of a weak and oppressed woman. A prolific writer for the stage, he went on to forge a distinctive style that combined the 'new lyricism' of the late 1950s with elements of sentimentalism, melodrama, fantasy, and romanticism. His most popular play was *It Happened in Irkutsk* (1959), a powerful romantic drama set in a half-built Siberian power station, which used various antinaturalistic techniques, including mime and direct speech to the audience. Subsequent successful productions included *My Poor Marat* (1965; also translated as *The Promise*), which was seen in Britain and the US and covered events in the lives of three people over a period of several years, the comedy *Tales of the Old Arbat* (1970; also translated as *Once Upon a Time*), and *An Old-Fashioned Comedy* (1978; also translated as *Do You Turn Somersaults?*).

Of Arbuzov's last plays, *Cruel Games* (1978) reflected the influence of Albee's *Who's Afraid of Virginia Woolf?*, while in *Remembrance* (1981) he returned to the romantic themes of his early work. He was also active in promoting the work of new playwrights and ran his own studio theatre.

Archigram An informal but highly influential group of British architects and designers; also a magazine produced intermittently by them (1961–73). It began with the meeting of Peter COOK, David Greene, and Michael Webb, who produced the first issue of Archigram in 1961. The following year they met Warren Chalk, Ron Herron, and Dennis Crompton, as they were all on the design team formed by Theo CROSBY to work on the new Euston Station. Archigram reacted against traditional notions of architecture as static and formal, arguing that modern manufacturing processes should be reflected in building and that construction should be merged with services such as power, light, and sanitation. The group published half-serious visions of an industrialized architecture, inventing such concepts as plug-in architecture, clip-on architecture, capsule dwellings, and mobile villages and illustrating them with collages and graphics. They argued for expendability in architecture as in car production, thereby making it more flexible. Internal streets, geodesic skins for communities, and controlled environments were among Archigram's other ideas. They produced a number of more finished designs as a group, including a competition-winning entry for an entertainment centre in Monte Carlo (1970). In 1973 the group mounted an exhibition covering its history at the ICA in London.

Architects' Co-Partnership (ACP) British architectural firm, established as the Architect's Co-operative Partnership by ex-students of the Architectural Association school in London in 1939. It was re-formed by eight of the partners in 1945 and changed its name to Architects' Co-Partnership in 1953. Enthusiastic proponents of Corbusian modernism (*see* LE CORBUSIER), they soon acquired an extensive practice, providing low-cost buildings for the post-war welfare state. Their first major building was the Bryn Mawr Rubber Factory in South Wales, designed in 1946 and built between 1948 and 1952. Analysing the factory processes, and housing them under concrete shell- and barrel-vaults, they created a new standard for industrial architecture. Buildings for the 1951 FESTIVAL OF BRITAIN brought their work to a wider public.

The big post-war programme of school building established ACP in the field of educational design; starting with Hertfordshire County Council's 'light and dry' building systems, they gradually evolved their own approach. As the educational building programmes of the 1960s and 1970s developed, ACP were much involved in university and polytechnic building, their largest undertaking being the master plan and most of the buildings for the University of Essex (1967–70). ACP have also been concerned with producing low-cost designs for developing countries, working extensively in Saudi Arabia, Nigeria, Jordan, Iraq, and Sudan.

Arden, John (1930–) British playwright and novelist who emerged as a leading theatrical influence in the 1950s, when several of his plays were staged at London's Royal Court Theatre. *Live Like Pigs* (1958), about an anarchic family, was followed by *Sergeant Musgrave's Dance* (1959), a poetic drama investigating themes of militarism and violence against a 19th-century background; this remains his best-known work (although it was at first poorly received).

Subsequent plays, among them *The Workhouse Donkey* (1964), an exuberant comedy about corruption in local government, and *Armstrong's Last Goodnight* (1964), which drew a parallel between 16th-century Scotland and the contemporary war in the Congo, consolidated his reputation for inventive and politically challenging theatre in the tradition of BRECHT. On several other plays, including *Ars Longa, Vita Brevis* (1965) and the musical *The Hero Rises Up* (1968) – a scathing reassessment of the life of Admiral Nelson – he has collaborated with the radical Irish playwright **Margaretta D'Arcy**, whom he married in 1957.

Arden's career in the theatre was interrupted in 1972 when he and D'Arcy clashed publicly with the Royal Shakespeare Company over the staging of their jointly written play *The Island of the Mighty*; since then Arden and D'Arcy have worked outside the theatrical mainstream, writing mainly for radio.

Arden's works of the later 1970s and 1980s include the pro-Republican *The Non-Stop Connolly Show* (1975), the adaptation *Gentleman Don Quixote De La Mancha* (1980), *Garland for a Hoar Head* (1982), and (with D'Arcy) *Whose is the Kingdom?* (1988), a long-running BBC radio series on the early history of Christianity. In the 1980s Arden began a second career as a novelist with *Silence Among the*

Weapons (1982), a picaresque tale set in the 1st century BC. Subsequent prose works include *Awkward Corners* (1988, with D'Arcy) and *Cogs Tyrannic* (1991), a collection of four novellas.

Ariès, Philippe (1914–84) French historian. After studying history in Paris, Ariès worked (1943–79) in the documentation centre of an institute dealing with tropical fruit. In 1980 he took an academic position at the École des Hautes Etudes en Sciences Sociales.

Himself the product of a traditionalist background (and at one time a member of the extreme right-wing Action Française), Ariès has investigated the impact of modernity and technological progress on older rural traditions. In his first book, *Social Traditions in the French Countryside* (1943), he stressed the public and social character of traditional rural life before the advent of modern notions of privacy. In *History of the French Peoples and Their Attitudes Toward Life Since the 18th Century* (1948) he showed that many 'timeless' rural traditions were themselves the result of historical development over a long period.

Centuries of Childhood (1960) describes the slow emergence of modern concepts of the family and of childhood since the late Middle Ages. In his study *The Hour of Our Death* (1977) Ariès shows how death itself has been deprived of its social context and removed into a purely private sphere.

Arman (Armand Fernandez; 1928–) French-born sculptor and painter, who became a US citizen in 1972. Born in Nice, he studied in Paris at the Ecole du Louvre and the Ecole Nationale des Arts Decoratifs. He relinquished his surname in 1947 and later adopted the form 'Arman' following a printing error in a catalogue. Between 1947 and 1953 he immersed himself in Japanese culture, studying Zen Buddhism and – like his friend Yves KLEIN – working for a time as a judo instructor. In 1963 he moved to New York.

Arman was one of the leading figures in the NOUVEAU RÉALISME movement and is best known for his assemblages of junk material (*see* ASSEMBLAGE). These began on a modest scale with accumulations of objects such as old spectacles but in 1982 he created what is probably the most physically imposing of all junk sculptures – *Long-Term Parking* (Marisa del Re Gallery, New York), consisting of 60 automobiles encased in concrete, forming a tower 60 feet high.

Armitage, Kenneth (1916–) British sculptor. Armitage studied at Leeds College of Art (1934–37) and then at the Slade School of Fine Art, London (1937–39). After service in the army in World War II, he taught sculpture at the Bath Academy of Art (1946–56) and was Gregory Fellow in Sculpture at Leeds University (1953–55).

In 1952 Armitage gave his first one-man show and exhibited at the Venice Biennale: he soon achieved international stature. Most of his works of this period consisted of groups of figures, often families or children, and were modelled in plaster over metal armatures before being cast in bronze. During the 1950s the figures became larger and more impersonal. In the 1960s he turned to single figures represented in a non-naturalistic manner. He later experimented with other materials: in the mid 1960s he worked in fibreglass and aluminium and from 1969 produced figures of wood, plaster, and paper that combined elements of drawing and sculpture.

Arnold, Sir Malcolm (1921–) British composer. After studying trumpet and composition at the Royal College of Music, Arnold pursued a playing career as a trumpeter with the London Philharmonic Orchestra and the BBC Symphony Orchestra. In 1948 he left the LPO to devote himself to composition and conducting.

Arnold's music is tonal and tends to be traditional in both style and form. He achieved early success in film music and several of his orchestral pieces have entered the concert repertoire. His music has ignored most contemporary trends and many critics have been disconcerted by its popularity. Works include nine symphonies, five ballets, two one-act operas, and numerous concertos. His score for the David LEAN film *The Bridge on the River Kwai* (1957), composed in ten days, was awarded an Oscar. He was knighted in 1993.

Aron, Raymond (1905–83) French sociologist and political commentator. Aron obtained his doctorate in letters in 1930 and subsequently taught in various universities and other institutions in France. After service with the Armed Air Force in 1940 he went into exile in London with General de Gaulle, where he became editor of the Free French journal *La France libre*. Following the liberation, Aron returned to Paris to teach sociology at the Sorbonne. From 1947 onwards he was a political columnist for *Le Figaro*, a role in which he acquired national prominence. Aron demonstrated his willingness to swim against the intellectual tide when he attacked SARTRE, formerly a close associate, and other left-wing thinkers for their uncritical support for the Soviet Union in *The Opium of the Intellectuals* (1955). He was an early advocate of French withdrawal from Algeria and a consistent supporter of the Western alliance during the Cold War period. These views made him a frequent critic of de Gaulle's policies in the 1950s and 1960s. Although best known for his political commentaries, he also wrote a number of academic works, notably *Main Currents in Sociological Thought* (1967).

Arpino, Giovanni (1927–) Italian novelist and journalist. A Piedmontese, he made his literary debut with the novel *You were Happy Giovanni* (1952) and the publication of a number of poems. Arpino's writings tend to focus on the relationship between an individual and his or her cultural background; his human sympathies are extremely wide. His prose style ranges from the elegiac to the ironic and grotesque. Outstanding amongst the novels is *Crime Passionnel* (1962), a bleak exploration of Italian machismo. The main character is a doctor who murders his peasant bride on discovering that she is not a virgin; only thus, he believes, can he restore his 'honour'. His other novels include *The Young Nun* (1959), *The Shadow of the Hills* (1964), *Darkness and Honey* (1964), *The Italian Brother* (1980), *The Secret Spouse* (1983), and *Farewell Step* (1986).

Arrabal, Fernando (1932–) Spanish playwright, writing in French, who was born in Morocco but now lives in Paris. Arrabal's traumatic childhood experiences during the Spanish Civil War – during which his strongly Catholic mother apparently turned his father over to his Nationalist enemies – are reflected in his plays, which deal with themes of violence, exile, and betrayal. He established his reputation as a leading figure in the absurdist tradition in 1958, when his first collection of plays was published (*see* ABSURD, THEATRE OF THE).

Arrabal himself labelled his distinctive and deliberately shocking combination of comedy and the grotesque *Théâtre Panique*. Several of his plays have a strong anti-Catholic element, among them *The Car Cemetery* (1964), which parodies the Crucifixion. Others draw directly on his memories of the Civil War, notably the widely admired *And They Put Handcuffs on the Flowers* (1969), a protest against political oppression, which was written after his own detention as a political prisoner in Spain in 1967.

His most experimental play is probably *Theatrical Orchestration* (1959), which contains no dialogue. Other plays include *Picnic on the Battlefield* (1959), *Fando and Lis* (1964), *The Architect and the Emperor of Assyria* (1967), *The Labyrinth* (1967), and *The Ballad of the Ghost Train* (1974). Among his other writing is the novel *Baal Babylone* (1959) as well as several volumes of poetry and essays. He has also directed and written the screenplays for several films.

Arrigo, Girolamo (1930–) Italian composer. After studying horn and composition at the Palermo Conservatory, Arrigo studied in Paris (1954–64) under the composer Max Deutsch, in New York (1964–65), and in Berlin (1967). He settled in Paris in 1968.

His first significant works, dating from the late 1950s and early 1960s – for example the string trio (1959) and *Fluxus* (1961) – show the influence of BOULEZ; works from the later 1960s continued to explore the same musical landscape. A decisive break occurred in 1969 with the anti-fascist theatre piece *Orden*, in which Arrigo demonstrated a new-found adherence to socially committed music: his musical language is here wholly adapted to the demands of the accompanying stage action. The later theatre piece *Addio Garibaldi* (1972), a political satire, makes notable use of musical quotation. Besides stage pieces and songs, his output includes instrumental and orchestral works of which *Shadows* (1966), *Thumos* (1965), and *Infrarosso* (1967) may be noted.

Art Brut (French: raw art, uncultured art). Unsophisticated art produced by people outside the cultural mainstream, such as solitary eccentrics, prisoners, children, and (especially) patients in psychiatric hospitals. The term was invented by the

French painter Jean DUBUFFET, who believed that such people, having to draw exclusively on their own inner resources, produced works that were in many ways more original and authentic than those of trained artists. Dubuffet began to collect examples of Art Brut in the immediate aftermath of World War II and gave his first exhibition of such works in Paris in 1947. With the Surrealist André Breton and others he founded (1948) the Compagnie de l'Art Brut to continue the work of collecting. Dubuffet and his followers also attempted to incorporate features of Art Brut into their own paintings. The Compagnie collapsed in 1951 for want of funds but was refounded in 1962 with the support of the painter Asger JORN and the writer Raymond QUENEAU. The collection was exhibited again in 1967; it was given to the city of Lausanne in 1972 and has been on public display at the Château de Beaulieu there since 1976. It now contains over 5000 works. Art Brut was one source of inspiration for those movements in postwar art that emphasized the free expression of the artist's emotions, unimpeded by the intellect or by tradition (such as ART INFORMEL). It was also a manifestation of an idea that became widespread in education: that individuals possess great powers of innate creativity that can easily be stifled by formal education and social controls.

Arte Povera (Italian: poor art) A movement in Italian art of the late 1960s and 1970s that rejected traditional media, materials, and content and reacted against the marketing of artworks as commodities. Instead, exponents of Arte Povera sought artistic outlets in spontaneous HAPPENINGS or in the creation of ephemeral works that defied collection and sale. The term was invented by the Italian critic Germano Celant, who organized an exhibition of Arte Povera at the Museo Civico in Turin in 1970 and produced an accompanying book.

More specifically, the term has been applied to the work of artists in Italy and elsewhere who have created works from cheap commonly available materials, such as sand, stones, or twigs. Notable exponents of this kind of Arte Povera include the Italians Mario MERZ and Michelangelo PISTOLETTO, the US sculptor Carl André, who has made many works from firebricks, and the British artist Richard LONG, who has worked with twigs and other natural objects.

Arte Povera has affinities with both CONCEPTUAL ART and MINIMAL ART.

Art Informel (French: art without form) A style of nongeometrical abstract painting that developed in Europe in the years after World War II. With its emphasis on subjective expression, improvisatory methods, and direct sensuous appeal, Art Informel is usually seen as a European equivalent to US abstract expressionism. The term was coined by the French critic Michel Tapié in the early 1950s; he organized the exhibition 'Signifiants d'Informel' in 1952. Pioneers of the style include the German-French artist Wols (1913–51), Henri MICHAUX, and Hans HARTUNG. Other artists associated with Art Informel include the Spaniard Antoni TÀPIES, the Italian Alberto BURRI, and the Frenchman Pierre SOULAGES.

Art Informel is also known as **Informalism**. The terms **expressive abstraction** and **lyrical abstraction** are used more generally to cover all forms of nongeometrical abstraction, including US abstract expressionism. *See also* TACHISME.

Arts Florissants, Les French early music ensemble, founded in Paris in 1978 by the US harpsichordist William Christie, who directs it from the keyboard. The ensemble was founded to perform and record French baroque music with special attention to French 18th-century vocal techniques, styles, and pronunciation (which Christie has described as being 'halfway between theatrical declamation and singing'). Their name is taken from the title of a *divertissement* by the French baroque composer Marc-Antoine Charpentier; the group has specialized in popularizing his oratorios and operas, as well as those of his contemporaries Lully and Rameau. Their pioneering recordings of Charpentier's opera *Médée* (1693) and Lully's opera *Atys* (1679) were well received. Notable recent performances have included Charpentier's pastorale *Actéon* (1683–85) and Rameau's opera-ballet *Les Indes galantes* (1735). The ensemble has expanded its repertoire beyond the French baroque, as is shown by their performance of Purcell's *Dido and Aeneas* on their London debut in 1990 and their involvement in the production of the same composer's *The Fairy Queen* at the 1990 AIX-EN-PROVENCE FESTIVAL.

Arup, Sir Ove Nyquist (1895–1988) British architect and engineer, born of Danish parents in Newcastle. Arup trained as an engineer in Copenhagen (1916–22) and was chief designer for the London office of the German engineers Christiani and Nielsen (1925–34) before joining the British firm of J. L. Kier in 1934. With a cousin he established a private consultancy, Arup and Arup Ltd, in London in 1938; in 1949 this became Ove Arup and Partners. Although more an engineer than an architect, Arup has been central to the development of modernism in Britain.

As chief designer with J. L. Kier, Arup was structural engineer of the innovative Highpoint I apartments in Highgate (1933) and the Penguin Pool in London Zoo (1939), both by the Tecton Group, and later of the Bryn Mawr Rubber Factory, Gwent (1946–47) by ARCHITECTS' CO-PARTNERSHIP. Ove Arup has remained at the forefront of design in reinforced and prestressed concrete, for instance in the FESTIVAL OF BRITAIN buildings (1951) and Sydney Opera House (by Jorn UTZON, 1957). Although the firm has developed a strong architectural arm under Sir Philip Dowson, engineering consultancy and design remain its core. With 2000 staff in ten offices in Britain and 1000 more in 40 offices around the world, it is Britain's most important structural engineering practice. Major recent jobs have included the engineering design for STIRLING's Stuttgart Staatsgalerie (1978–84), ROGERS's Lloyds building, London (1979–85), and FOSTER's HongKong and Shanghai Bank Headquarters in Hong Kong (1980–85).

Ashton, Sir Frederick (William Mallandaine) (1904–88) British choreographer, ballet director, and dancer, born in Ecuador. Ashton was first attracted to dance after seeing a performance by Anna Pavlova. He subsequently trained as a dancer with Marie Rambert in London and with Léonide Massine in Paris.

His first ballet, *A Tragedy of Fashion* (1926), in which he danced the role of a suicidal couturier, enjoyed considerable success. He went on to devise a further 20 ballets for Rambert over the next ten years, including *Capriol Suite* (1930) and *Façade* (1931), a comic one-act ballet to a score by WALTON. The work was much admired for its innovative use of popular dances, including the charleston and the tango.

Already established as the leading British choreographer of the day, Ashton transferred to Ninette DE VALOIS's Vic-Wells company in 1935. There he enjoyed success with such ballets as *Les Patineurs* (1937), in which the dancers imitated skaters, and *A Wedding Bouquet* (1937), based on the writings of Gertrude Stein. He also continued to appear as a dancer.

After World War II Ashton returned to the Vic-Wells company and consolidated his reputation with the *Symphonic Variations* (1946) and *Scènes de ballet* (1948) among other works. In 1948 he presented his *Cinderella*, the first full-length ballet by a British choreographer. The ballet was admired for its lyrical and atmospheric qualities, and for the elegance and wit of the choreography.

Subsequently Ashton remained with the Vic-Wells company (renamed the Sadler's Wells company and then the ROYAL BALLET), although he also created works for the New York City Ballet (1950) and the Royal Danish Ballet (1955). He was appointed director of the Royal Ballet in 1963. Major ballets of the latter part of his career included the full-length *Ondine* (1958), *La Fille mal gardée* (1960), *Marguerite and Armand* (1963), *The Dream* (1964), *Enigma Variations* (1968), *Death in Venice* (1973), *A Month in the Country* (1976), and *Rhapsody* (1980). He also choreographed and danced in the ballet film *The Tales of Beatrix Potter* (1971). Several of his later works provided roles for Margot Fonteyn and Rudolf NUREYEV, whose legendary partnership was largely a result of his influence. Other dancers to emerge under his directorship included Lynn Seymour and Anthony Dowell.

Many of Ashton's works remain in the repertory of the Royal Ballet and have almost come to define a British style of dance. He was knighted in 1962 and awarded the OM in 1977.

assemblage A work of art that incorporates preformed non-art objects, typically everyday items such as newspapers, refuse, etc; also the process of creating such a work. The practice originated in 1911–12 with the cubist collages of Picasso and Braque, which incorporated newspaper headlines and pieces of rope and canvas amongst other articles. By introducing an element of the three-dimensional these works blurred the distinction between painting and sculpture. The term 'assemblage' was first used by the French painter Jean DUBUFFET in 1953 for a set of lithographic prints that he made by cutting and pasting together sheets of paper. (The works were called 'assemblages d'empreintes'.) He used the term again in 1954 to describe a series of statuettes he made from scraps of wood, sponge, papier mâché, and other debris.

The term assemblage has since been applied to various types of unconventional artwork produced by futurists, Dadaists, pop artists, and conceptual artists, amongst others. In 1961 the Museum of Modern Art in New York was able to devote an entire exhibition to 'The Art of Assemblage'. Notable post-war exponents of assemblage include the British sculptor Richard Latham, the Italian Alberto BURRI, and the Frenchman CÉSAR.

Atelier 5 Swiss architectural practice, established in Bern in 1955. Housing has dominated their output, in particular public-housing projects in Switzerland and Germany. The firm's reputation was established by their Halen Housing Estate near Bern (designed in 1960), a self-contained community of dramatic concrete terraced blocks, sited in a forest clearing, and showing the influence of LE CORBUSIER. Subsequent experience as master planners for housing projects in existing communities has led to a more pragmatic approach; their winning competition entry for the Kaiser complex in the centre of Bern (1978) is based on principles of renovation rather than total replacement.

Attenborough, Sir Richard (Samuel) (1923–) British film director, producer, and actor, who became a major star of British cinema in the 1940s and subsequently emerged as a leading spokesman for the industry. His film debut playing a frightened sailor in Noël Coward's war epic *In Which We Serve* (1942) established him as the British audience's favourite coward – a role that he was to recreate in several subsequent films. In *Brighton Rock* (1947), from the novel by Graham GREENE, he played the villainous Pinkie, and subsequently he managed to diversify with a wide range of character parts. *Private's Progress* (1955), *The Angry Silence* (1959), *Seance on a Wet Afternoon* (1963), *The Great Escape* (1963), *Guns at Batasi* (1964), *Loot* (1971), and *Conduct Unbecoming* (1975) are some of the many films the ubiquitous Attenborough starred in during this period. He was also seen in occasional stage roles, which included a part in the original production of Agatha Christie's *The Mousetrap*, alongside his wife Sheila Sim (1922–).

In the late 1950s Attenborough began to interest himself in film production and set up two companies with the actor and director Bryan FORBES. Early successes included Forbes's *Whistle Down the Wind* (1962) and in 1969 Attenborough won numerous awards for his first film as a director, *Oh What a Lovely War!*, from the Theatre Workshop production by Joan LITTLEWOOD. *Young Winston* (1972) and *A Bridge Too Far* (1976) demonstrated his mastery of the epic adventure film and his ability to orchestrate huge numbers of extras, talents that brought him international acclaim for the biopic *Gandhi* (1982), which was 20 years in the planning and won eight Oscars. Subsequent films have included *A Chorus Line* (1985) and *Cry Freedom* (1987), based on the death in custody of the antiapartheid campaigner Steve Biko. His long-awaited film biography of Charlie Chaplin opened in 1992.

Attenborough was knighted for his services to the national cinema in 1976. He has chaired numerous cultural and charitable bodies, including the British Film Institute and Channel 4 television (1987–92), and has held the post of goodwill ambassador for UNICEF since 1987.

Aubertin, Bernard (1934–) French painter. Aubertin worked in an artist's studio for two years before studying at the Ecole des Metiers d'Art and the Ecole du Professorat de Dessin in Paris (1952–54). His earliest works were realistic landscapes, portraits, and still-lifes. Although aware of the latest artistic trends he found little stimulation in either figurative or abstract art.

In 1957 Aubertin met the French painter Yves KLEIN, who had been experimenting with the idea of monochrome paintings since the end of the war. Klein encouraged Aubertin to explore the same territory and between 1958 and 1960 the latter produced a series of red monochrome paintings, in which he worked the paint with various unconventional tools.

Aubertin, however, remained dissatisfied. In 1960 he threw nails onto a monochrome and saw new possibilities; a series of works followed in which nails were fixed into the canvas and paint was worked over and around them. He later experimented with other objects, including matches. In 1961 Aubertin lit the matches to create the first of many 'fire-paintings'. There followed works made from the remains of burnt telephone books. His works have been displayed in many European countries.

Audiberti, Jacques (1899–1965) French playwright, poet, and novelist, born in Antibes, who emerged as a leading writer for the French stage in the 1940s. Having been associated with the surrealist movement before World War II, he won attention as a playwright with such poetic dramas as *Quoat-Quoat* (1946), in which a young man has to choose between death and loss of identity. Of the 25 plays that followed most, in one form or another, depicted the struggle between good and evil; the plots frequently involved an element of the supernatural. The most successful amongst them included *Evil in the Air* (1947) and *The Falcon* (1956), which was an attack on the Church. His poetry collections included *The Race of Men* (1937) and *Tons of Seed* (1941); among his novels were *Abraxas* (1938) and *Monorail* (1964).

Auerbach, Frank (1931–) British painter. Born in Berlin, Auerbach came to Britain as a refugee in 1939 and became a British citizen in 1947. He studied at the St Martin's School of Art (1948–52) and at the Royal College of Art (1952–55). More importantly, Auerbach came under the influence of the British expressionist painter David Bomberg (1890–1957), whose evening classes he attended.

Although Auerbach's subjects have been traditional – mainly landscapes, townscapes, portraits, and nudes – his work achieves originality through its distinctive use of paint. In his earlier works Auerbach built up the paint on the canvas in layers to create thick impasto textures of an almost sculptural nature. In later years he has employed a wider range of colours, often returning to subjects he has painted many times before, such as favourite sitters and particular London scenes. The paint is now less dense but is still heavily worked. For long a somewhat neglected figure, Auerbach attracted renewed attention with the revival of figurative painting in the late 1970s. In 1978 he was given a major retrospective exhibition at the Hayward Gallery in London and in 1986 he represented Britain at the Venice Biennale.

Aurenche, Jean (1904–92) French screenwriter, whose best scripts were written in partnership with **Pierre Bost** (1901–75). "Screenwriters," he once remarked, "have made many a director believe he has talent." After working as a director of commercials and documentaries, Aurenche began writing films in the late 1930s, achieving his first great success with *Hotel du Nord* (1938) for Marcel Carné. Although he collaborated with such writers as ANOUILH and Marcel Achard, it is for his work with Bost, beginning in 1943, that he is mainly remembered. The pair wrote several memorable screenplays for the director Claude AUTANT-LARA, including *Devil in the Flesh* (1947), about a married woman's affair with a teenage schoolboy. Their other scripts include the macabre comedy *The Red Inn* (1951), which was banned in Britain, *Ripening Seed* (1953), a film about an older woman's seduction of an adolescent boy that was condemned by the Church, *The Red and the Black* (1954) adapted from the Stendhal novel, and the comedy *En Cas de Malheur* (1958). Aurenche and Bost's popularity declined somewhat in the wake of the NEW WAVE of the late 1950s, but they continued to produce excellent work, including a series of scripts for Bertrand TAVERNIER. These include the Simenon adaptation *The Watchmaker of St Paul* (1973), and *The Assassin* (1976); Aurenche and Tavernier also worked together on *Que La Fête Commence* (1975), about decadence at the court of Louis XV, and *Coup de Torchon* (1981), a black comedy about a murderous West African law officer. A year later, at the age of 78, Aurenche adapted another Simenon novel for the cinema as *L'Etoile du Nord*.

Auric, Georges (1899–1983) French composer. He studied first at Montpellier, then at the Paris Conservatoire with Caussade (1913), and later with Vincent d'Indy and Albert Roussel at the Schola Cantorum (1914–16). After World War I he was a member (with Durey, Honegger, Milhaud, POULENC, and Tailleferre) of the group Les Six, who aimed to rejuvenate French music through wit, brevity, and the avoidance of romantic excess. Other influences of this period include Satie, Stravinsky, and the aesthetic ideas of Jean Cocteau. Auric's first mature works were the ballets *Les Fâcheux* (1924), *Les Matelots* (1925), and *La Pastorale* (1926), commissioned by Serge Diaghilev for his Paris company. He is also well known for his scores for numerous French- and English-language films, such as René Clair's *A Nous la liberté* (1932) and Cocteau's *La Belle et le bête* (1946) and *Orphée* (1950). He was general administrator of the Paris Opéra and Opéra-comique (1962–68) and president of the French Union of Composers and Artists (1954–77). In addition to ballets and film scores, his considerable output includes piano music, songs, and chamber music.

Austin, J(ohn) L(angshaw) (1911–60) British philosopher, the leading exponent of linguistic philosophy in Britain after World War II. In 1933, after studying at Balliol College, Oxford, he became a fellow of All Souls, and in 1935 of Magdalen. After Intelligence work during World War II he returned to Oxford and in 1952 became White's Professor of Moral Philosophy, a chair he held until his death.

Austin considered linguistic analysis the major philosophical resource, advocating the use as a model of ordinary language, which he thought more subtle and revealing than the often unwieldy usages of traditional philosophical practice. He is particularly noted for his theory of speech acts (*How to Do Things with Words*, 1962). Here he classified speech items under three heads: locutions – meaningful sentences; illocutions – acts executed in speech, such as confession, statement, prayer; and perlocutions – results of speech, such as persuasion, fear. The distinction between locution and illocution has proved a continuing subject of dispute.

Philosophical Papers (1961) was published posthumously, as was *Sense and Sensibilia*, a critique of A. J. AYER's sense datum theory (which held that certain sensory objects exist only because and when perceived).

Autant-Lara, Claude (1901–) French film director, who won a wide audience for his elegant romantic dramas of the 1940s and 1950s. He entered the film industry in 1919 and worked as an assistant to René Clair on several of his popular stylish comedies. Autant-Lara emerged as a director in his own right with such films as *Fric-Frac* (1939), *Douce* (1943), a melancholy melodrama set against the background of the German occupation, and *Le Diable au corps* (*Devil in the Flesh*; 1947), an atmospheric tragedy about a schoolboy's affair with an older married woman. Of the films that followed the most successful included *Occupe-toi d'Amélie* (1949) and *The Red Inn* (1951), a black comedy about a hotel in which the guests are robbed and murdered by the owner and his wife. The Stendhal adaptation *The Red and the Black* (1954) starred Gérard Philipe as a priest who resorts to sexual intrigue for personal advancement, while *En Cas de malheur* (*Love is my Profession*; 1957) has Jean Gabin deserting his wife for Brigitte Bardot. His last films were a version of *The Count of Monte Cristo* (1961) and *The Red and the White* (1970).

auteur In cinema, a director who exercises authority over all aspects of the film-making process in order to convey his own personal message or vision. The auteur theory was adopted by a number of leading directors in the 1960s and 1970s, especially in France, where notable exponents included Jean-Luc GODARD.

Avignon Festival *See* VILAR, JEAN.

Axer, Erwin (1917–) Polish theatre director, born in Austria, who established an international reputation for his productions of important new works by leading contemporary Polish playwrights. He began his theatrical career at the National Theatre in Warsaw in 1938 and, after World War II, founded (1945) his own company at Łodz. Subsequently he became founder and director (1949–81) of Warsaw's Contemporary Theatre, where he presented the bulk of his most significant productions. As well as plays by such modern writers as MROŻEK, he also produced many classics, including works by BRECHT, Chekhov, and Shakespeare. The author of several books on the theatre, he has also directed plays at the ROYAL NATIONAL THEATRE and other prominent venues outside Poland.

Ayckbourn, Alan (1939–) British playwright and theatre director; currently one of the most successful writers for the commercial stage in Britain. His bitter comedies satirizing middle-class values and pretensions have mostly been premiered (at the rate of at least one play per year since 1959) at Scarborough's Stephen Joseph Theatre in the Round, of which he eventually became artistic director; many subsequently transferred successfully to the London stage.

Relatively Speaking (1967) was the first of his comedies to attract attention and established the themes that were to run through his subsequent work. At once hilarious and acutely sensitive to the frustrations and despair underlying English suburban society, his plays have also been admired for their technical inventiveness. In *Absurd Person Singular* (1973), for instance, the action takes place in the same setting on three consecutive Christmas Eves; in *Sisterly Feelings* (1980), the ending at each performance depends upon the toss of a coin; while *Way Upstream* (1982) requires a real riverboat floating on real water.

Ayckbourn's most popular plays have included the ingeniously constructed trilogy *The Norman Conquests* (1974), *Bedroom Farce* (1977), *Season's Greetings* (1980), and *A Chorus of Disapproval* (1985). In more recent works, such as *A Small Family Business* (1987), *Woman in Mind* (1988), *Man of the Moment* (1990), and *Wildest Dreams* (1991) – his 42nd play – he has continued to balance comedy with serious social observation, although the tone has noticeably darkened. As a director he has won praise for several productions at the ROYAL NATIONAL THEATRE and other venues.

Ayer, Sir A(lfred) J(ules) (1910–89) British philosopher. After graduating (1932) from Christ Church, Oxford, Ayer continued his studies in Vienna, where he became a convert to the logical positivism of the Vienna Circle. On his return to Oxford he worked as a lecturer and produced *Language, Truth, and Logic* (1936), a succinct and provocative statement of the logical positivist position that brought him fame at the age of 26. After work with the Intelligence service in World War II he became Grote professor of Philosophy at University College, London, before returning to a chair and a fellowship at Oxford in 1959. He retired in 1977.

Ayer remains best known for the abrasive brilliance of *Language, Truth, and Logic.* Central to his thesis was the so-called 'verification principle': all meaningful assertions must be either synthetic, that is, contingent on experience and therefore verifiable by empirical research, or necessary and analytic, that is, formulated in such terms that to deny such a statement would be self-contradictory. Utterances verifiable neither in experience nor by examination of their terms were, Ayer deemed, at best, expressions of emotion. This curt dismissal of religious and metaphysical assertions to the realms of nonsense provoked intense controversy.

Ayer's other important works are also in the field of epistemology; they include *Foundations of Empirical Knowledge* (1940) and *The Problem of Knowledge* (1956). In *The Central Problems of Philosophy* (1972) and the long introduction to the second edition (1946) of *Language, Truth, and Logic* he qualified some of the claims made in his first book. He also wrote on other philosophers (*The Origins of Pragmatism*, 1968; *Russell and Moore*, 1971; *Hume*, 1980; *Wittgenstein*, 1985), as well as producing several collections of essays and two highly readable volumes of autobiography (*Part of My Life*, 1977; *More of My Life*, 1984).

Aymé, Marcel (1902–67) French novelist, short-story writer, and playwright. Aymé was brought up in the rural Burgundy that provides the setting for most of his work. He began his career as a journalist, publishing his first novel in 1926 and finding success with *The Hollow Field* (1929) and the hugely popular *The Green Mare* (1933). Here as elsewhere in his work, Aymé's penchant for farcical plots and broad Rabelaisian humour masks considerable social and psychological insight. Aymé blends realism with the fantastic in stories like *The Dwarf* (1934), about a character who does not start to grow until the age of 30, *The Man Who Could Pass Through Walls* (1943), and *The Fable and the Flesh* (*La Vouivre*; 1943) in which the Vouivre (a serpent figure from regional folklore) falls in love with a farmer. The humour in his later works is generally more acrid and satirical. In *The Transient Hours* (1946) Aymé presents a family who ensure their post-war success by having one brother work for the Resistance while the other deals on the black market. Aymé also wrote a series of popular children's stories featuring talking farm animals (collected in *The Wonderful Farm*, 1951), as well as a number of plays, the best known of which is *The Head of Others* (1952), a satire on the French judicial system.

Ayres, Gillian (1930–) British abstract painter. Ayres studied at the Camberwell School of Art in London (1946–50) and taught at several art colleges from 1959 to 1981. While at the Camberwell School she became discontented with the realist ambitions of British painters of the Euston Road School (*see* COLDSTREAM, SIR WILLIAM) and during the 1950s adopted techniques developed by the US abstract expressionists. In 1957 she exhibited with other British exponents of lyrical abstraction (*see* ART INFORMEL) and in 1960 attracted considerable attention with her contributions to the 'Situation' exhibition of abstract art in London. In the late 1970s she returned to oil painting after more than a decade of using acrylics and began to model the paint on the canvas. At the same time her colours became richer, influenced by those of old masters such as Titian and Rubens. In 1981 she moved to North Wales and her paintings of the 1980s contain suggestions of mountain landscapes and the sea. Her exuberant and lyrical works have been included in exhibitions of abstract expressionism in many countries.

Ayrton, Michael (Michael Gould; 1921–75) British painter, sculptor, art critic, and writer. The son of the poet Gerald Gould, Ayrton spent much of his youth travelling in Europe. After brief wartime service in the RAF he became a teacher at the Camberwell School of Art at the age of 21. The turbulent melodramatic canvases for which Ayrton is still best known – these include his *Temptation of St Anthony* and *Skull Vision* (both 1943) – were produced in his early twenties. These much-disliked works typically feature distorted nude or seminude figures in phantasmagorical landscapes; the coloration is lurid and the general mood one of morbidity and anguish. During the 1940s Ayrton's provocative critical writings established him as the chief spokesman for the English neoromantics such as Graham SUTHERLAND and John Minton, while he also became known to a wider public as the youngest member of the radio Brains Trust.

In 1947 Ayrton visited Italy and began to paint in a more restrained fashion under the influence of the Renaissance masters. A decisive turning-point in his career came in 1954, when he largely gave up painting for sculpture. The work of his later years shows a developing obsession with classical myth, particularly the legends about the artificer Daedalus, his doomed son Icarus, and the Minotaur; for Ayrton all three figures symbolized aspects of the artist and his predicament. Besides producing numerous sculptures inspired by the legend – the best of which are considered his finest work – Ayrton used it as the basis of several books, including the novel *The Maze Maker*. His identification with the story even led him to construct a maze of stone and brick in the Catskill Mountains in emulation of the labyrinth built by Daedalus. The author of some 15 books, Ayrton also directed several documentary films and designed costumes and scenery for the ballet and drama.

B

Baaren, Kees van (1906–70) Dutch composer. He studied at the Hochschule für Musik in Berlin (1924–29) and then with the composer Willem Pijper in Rotterdam. He was director of the Amsterdam Music Academy (1948–53), of the Utrecht Conservatory (1953–57), and of the Royal Conservatory in The Hague (1958–70). His works, which show the influence of Pijper and the serialist procedures of Schoenberg and Webern, include the cantata *The Hollow Men* (1948), the important *Variazioni per Orchestra* (1959), piano pieces, string quartets, and organ music.

Babilée, Jean (Jean Gutman; 1923–) French dancer, choreographer, and actor. After training at the Paris Opéra Ballet School, he joined the Paris Opéra company as a dancer in the 1940s, emerging as *danseur étoile* of the Ballets des Champs-Elysées in 1945 and of the Opéra company in 1947. With his spectacular leaps and impeccable technique, he became one of the most celebrated dancers of his generation. Many of his most famous performances were in ballets created by such modern choreographers as CHARRAT, PETIT, and LAZZINI.

Babileée choreographed his first ballet in 1944. Many of his subsequent works were created for Les Ballets Jean Babilée, the international touring company that he founded in 1956. His other posts have included director of the Ballet du Rhin company (1972–73). His most admired works include *L'Amour et son amour* (1948), *Till Eulenspiegel* (1949), in which he also danced the main role, *Balance à trois* (1955), *Sable* (1956), *Cameléopard* (1956), *La Boucle* (1957), and *Haï-Kaï* (1969). He also appeared as an actor in several plays by GENET and in a number of films.

Bacewicz, Gra˙yna (1909–69) Polish composer, violinist, and writer. She studied music at the Warsaw Conservatory and then composition with Nadia Boulanger and violin with Carl Flesch at the Paris Conservatoire (1933–34). After returning to Poland she taught harmony and counterpoint at the Łódź Conservatory for brief periods (1934–35, 1945) but devoted most of her energies to her career as a professional violinist and composer. She retired from the concert stage in 1955 and in 1966 was appointed professor at the State Academy of Music in Warsaw. Her prolific output includes four symphonies, three ballets, a cello concerto, seven violin concertos, seven string quartets, as well as music for the theatre, radio, and cinema. Although her work is mainly neoclassical in style, later pieces show the influence of LUTOSŁAWSKI and the post-war avant-garde. She also wrote four novels, a television play, short stories, and essays.

Bachmann, Ingeborg (1926–73) Austrian poet. After spending her youth in Klagenfurt, Bachmann studied German, philosophy, and psychology in Innsbruck, Graz, and Vienna. In 1950 she received her doctorate for a thesis on the German philosopher Martin Heidegger. In the Vienna of the 1950s Bachmann met leading poets and writers, such as AICHINGER and Paul CELAN. Her poetry was widely acclaimed after her first major success with the GRUPPO 47 in 1952. After her relationship with the Swiss writer Max FRISCH ended, Bachmann lived in Berlin; in 1965 she moved to Rome, where she died in a house fire in 1973.

Bachmann is the best-known German-language woman poet of the post-war era. For her the driving force of poetry was suffering. The mythical-allegorical language of her poetry in *Time by the Hour* (*Die gestundete Zeit*; 1953) and *Invocation of the Big Bear* (1956) articulates a fundamental ambivalence: on the one hand man's relationship with nature has been ruined for ever through the destructive forces of history, particularly the murderous inhumanity of the Nazi past, yet on the other hand the poet still experiences isolated moments of overwhelming beauty and love. Partly because of this unresolvable tension Bachmann wrote only a few poems after 1956 and switched to prose. At the centre of her collections of short stories *The Thirtieth Year* (1961) and *Simultaneously* (1972) are female protagonists whose intellectual and human potential is destroyed by their egocentric male partners. Her short stories, together with her experimental novel *Malina* (1971), have become a paradigm for feminist writing in German.

Bacon, Francis (1909–92) British figurative painter. Born in Dublin of English parents, Bacon moved to London in 1925 and later worked as an interior designer. He taught himself to paint and was greatly influenced by his visit to an exhibition of Picasso's work in Paris in 1926. During the 1930s his work attracted some attention but made no major impact and he virtually abandoned painting. He resumed it after asthma led to his rejection for war service.

Bacon shot to prominence in 1945, when his triptych *Three Studies for Figures at the Base of a Crucifixion* (Tate Gallery, London) was exhibited in London. It shows three anguished contorted figures, half animal, half human, each of which is enclosed in a space with a low oppressive ceiling. This shocking work set the direction for most of Bacon's subsequent paintings, which continued to present hideously distorted figures trapped in claustrophobic interiors or spaces. Bacon often distorted his figures by smearing the paint with which he rendered their features, a technique that has a particularly repulsive effect. Influences on his works include magazines and films (such as Eisenstein's *Battleship Potemkin*), the scientific studies of motion made by the photographer Eadweard Muybridge (1830–1904), and medical books about wounds and disfigurement. Other works draw on paintings by old masters, such as the series of 'Screaming Popes' based on Veláquez's portrait of *Pope Innocent X*. On the whole, his later paintings relinquish the element of *grand guignol* in his early work in favour of a no less harrowing obsession with the loneliness and isolation of human beings.

Major retrospectives of Bacon's work were held in London in 1962 and 1985.

Bad Art *See* NEOEXPRESSIONISM.

Baertling, Olle (1911–81) Swedish abstract painter and sculptor. Born in Halmstad, Baertling studied business administration at the School of Economics and Trade in Stockholm (1928–29) and then worked as a branch manager for a bank (1929–55). For many years painting was a spare-time activity.

At first Baertling painted in an expressionist manner but around 1948 he came under the influence of the French artists Fernand Léger and André Lhote and began to paint in a geometrical abstract style. The works of the Dutch abstract painter Piet Mondrian were also an important influence. Where Mondrian, however, had worked with verticals and horizontals, Baertling (from 1953 onwards) began to produce works in which converging diagonal lines are used to separate fields of flat, usually harsh, colour. For many years he explored the possibilities of this simple basic idea, sometimes making the lines converge near the edge of the canvas (as in *Ardek*, 1963, Tate Gallery, London). Baertling also worked as a sculptor and from 1956 onwards created a series of metal works that explore triangular forms.

BAFTA *See* BRITISH ACADEMY OF FILM AND TELEVISION ARTS.

Baierl, Helmut (1926–) German playwright, born in Czechoslovakia, who emerged as a leading writer for the theatre while working with the BERLINER ENSEMBLE (1959–67). He first attracted attention while attached to the Deutsches Theater, which he joined in 1957, notably with his first play, *The Finding* (1958), in which he demonstrated his understanding of Brechtian technique. His successes with the Berliner Ensemble included an updated version of Brecht's *Mother Courage*, as *Frau Flinz* (1961). He entered politics in 1967.

Baird, Tadeusz (1928–81) Polish composer, whose music was firmly rooted in the 19th-century romantic tradition. He was most interested in the lyrical and dramatic in music and his scores are richly textured and much concerned with beauty of sound.

Baird studied composition at the Warsaw Conservatory where he cofounded Group 49, a society of young composers that also included Kazimierz Krenz. He began his career writing uncomplicated music that found favour with the musical and political establishment in post-war Poland. However, in his string quartet (1957) he turned away from his earlier conservative neoclassical style and began a period of experimentation with the 12-note techniques of Berg and Webern. At the same time his attitude to traditional forms and structures was also deepening, as demonstrated by his first and second symphonies (1950 and 1952) and the concerto for orchestra (1953). The later works are mostly for orchestra (oboe concerto, 1973) or combinations of instruments with voices (*Goethe Letters*, 1970). He also wrote much film and incidental music.

Bakema, Jacob *See* VAN DEN BROEK AND BAKEMA

Bakhtin, Mikhail (1895–1975) Russian literary critic and theorist. Bakhtin graduated from the University of St Petersburg in 1918 and moved to Vitebsk, where he produced a number of critiques of the Russian Formalists and their attempt to found a scientific description of literary language. He himself believed that language achieved meaning beyond its component parts and should not be analysed as if it were a piece of machinery. After moving to Leningrad in 1924 he turned his fire on psychoanalysis, arguing in *Freudianism: A Critical Sketch* (1927) that Freud used oversimplified rules of interpretation. Thereafter Bakhtin remained a maverick in literary circles, developing his belief that language and experience are inseparable in *Problems of Dostoevskii's Poetics* (1929). This explored the idea that the work of Dostoevskii, in contrast to that of Tolstoy, was 'dialogic' or 'polyphonic,' a vehicle for more than one outlook and voice. The book also introduced Bakhtin's key concept of the 'carnivalesque' – his term for the profane and subversive elements in popular humour, which he saw as a liberating influence on the literary tradition. Bakhtin later spent six years in internal exile and was unable to publish. However, his work on Dostoevskii brought him an international reputation in the early 1960s, leading to the publication of several earlier works on the novel. In *The Dialogic Imagination* (1981), consisting of two works written in the 1930s, he argued that the novel was the central focus of language and culture and not simply one of many literary forms.

Bakíc, Vojin (1915–) Croatian sculptor. Born at Bjelova, Bakíc studied at the Zagreb Academy of Fine Arts in the 1930s. During World War II he began to sculpt figures and heads, influenced principally by Rodin and the French sculptor Aristide Maillol. After the war he was commissioned to produce a sculpture of a resistance fighter to commemorate the Yugoslavian partisans. In the 1950s he turned to abstract sculpture. His works of this period, which are mainly organic rather than geometrical in form, show the influence of the Romanian sculptor Constantin Brancusi and the Franco-German artist Jean Arp. In the 1960s he produced a series of discus-like works with reflecting surfaces. He has had considerable influence on younger sculptors in the former Yugoslavia.

Balada, Leonardo (1933–) Spanish composer and conductor, based in the US since the late 1950s. After training as a pianist at the Barcelona Conservatory, Balada went on to study in the US at the New York College of Music (1956–57), the Juilliard School (1958–60), and at Mannes College of Music, New York (1961–62). His principal composition teachers were Vincent Persichetti, Norman Dello Joio, and Copland: he also studied conducting with Igor Markevitch in Paris. He taught at the UN International School in New York from 1963 to 1970, since when he has taught at the Carnegie Mellon University, Pittsburgh, becoming professor of composition there in 1975.

His music has developed beyond the Spanish nationalist models provided by his early training to a mature style that makes use of serialist procedures. His output, which is considerable, includes three operas: *Hangman, Hangman!* (1982), *Zapata!* (1984), and *Christopher Columbus* (1987), all notable for their musical variety and brilliant orchestration. He has also written a ballet, *La Casa* (1967). His concertos include a piano concerto (1964), the *Bandoneon Concerto* (1970), the concerto for piano, wind, and percussion (1974), the concerto for four guitars and orchestra (1976), and a violin concerto (1982). Other notable orchestral works include *Musica tranquila* (1960), *Guernica* (1966), *Sinfonia en negro: homage to Martin Luther*

King (1968), *Steel Symphony* (1972), *Fantasias sonoras* (1987), and *Alegrías* for flute and string orchestra (1988); he has also written chamber, solo, and choral pieces. Also noteworthy is *End and Beginning* (1970) for rock music ensemble.

Balcon, Sir Michael (1896–1977) British film producer, who was responsible for making many of the classic British films of the 1940s and 1950s. Balcon entered films in 1919, founding Gainsborough Pictures in 1928; he subsequently moved to Gaumont-British (1931) and MGM-British (1936), with which companies he made such films as *The Man Who Knew Too Much* (1934) and *The Thirty-Nine Steps* (1935). He was then appointed director and chief of productions at EALING STUDIOS, where he presided (1937–59) over the golden era in British film-making that saw the creation of a series of films known as the 'Ealing Comedies'; they included *Kind Hearts and Coronets* (1949), *Passport to Pimlico* (1949), and *The Lavender Hill Mob* (1952). In recognition of his achievements at Ealing he received a knighthood in 1948. Later films, in which he continued to insist upon the highest production standards, included the war epics *The Cruel Sea* (1953) and *Dunkirk* (1958), as well as the costume drama *Tom Jones* (1963). In 1964 he became chairman of British Lion Films. His autobiography, *A Lifetime of Films*, was published in 1969.

Ballek, Ladislav (1941–) Slovak novelist. After teachers' training college and military service, he worked in broadcasting, as a magazine editor, and in publishing. From 1977 onwards he held various posts in the cultural bureaucracy. He resigned from the Communist Party shortly before the 'Velvet Coup' and from his post as secretary of the Writers' Union in protest against police violence in November 1989.

Although he had published collections of polished short stories before and has published two meandering novels since, Ballek's most imaginative writing is contained in the novels *The Assistant* (1977) and *Acacias* (1981). The first covers the years 1945–46 in a South Slovak frontier town, a period of chaos, hope, and of the glorious hedonist greed embodied in the butcher's assistant, Volent Lančarič, who is one of the most vivid characters in post-war Slovak fiction. He also embodies Ballek's conception of Slovakness, for his name is South Slav and his culture is as Magyar as it is Slovak. Ballek's style is as sensual as the life of this sunny town surrounded by the acacia groves that give the second novel its title. *Acacias* covers the period from 1946 to the communist takeover in February 1948. It is an elegiac episodic narrative describing a socially, nationally, and politically variegated society, the complete opposite of the grey uniformity of socialist life. In *Acacias* man's life is governed not by the communist bureaucracy but by Nature. The dotty drunkard Filadelfi is almost as vivid as Lančarič in *The Assistant*. That the socialism he helped to maintain was wearing Ballek down as a writer is clear from his most recent novel, the cumbersome *The Strange Sleeper* (1990).

Ballet Gulbenkian A Portuguese-based ballet company, founded in Lisbon in 1965, which has gradually been recognized as one of the most important dance troupes to be formed in Europe since the war. The company was created with financial assistance from the Armenian philanthropist Calouste Gulbenkian and has attracted many of the leading figures in contemporary dance. Under Walter Gore the company presented a largely classical repertoire but subsequently it has diversified with works by numerous contemporary choreographers. Since 1977 native Portuguese dance has also been given priority under the leadership of Jorge Salavisa. Recent successes have included *Ghost Dances* (1981) by Christopher BRUCE and works by the resident choreographer, Vasco Wellenkamp.

Ballet of the 20th century An international ballet company founded in Brussels in 1960. The company is inseparably linked with the name of Maurice BÉJART, its founder and artistic director. Having performed on a regular basis at the Théâtre Royal de la Monnaie, the Cirque Royal, and the Forest National over a period of many years, the company finally left Brussels (1987) for a new home in Lausanne after conflict with the management of the Théâtre Royal. The company has toured throughout the world (visiting the US for the first time in 1971) and deliberately includes among its ensemble dancers from many different countries. The company's greatest triumphs have included performances of *Le Sacre du Printemps* (1959), *Bolero* (1960), *Les Noces* (1962), *Parade* (1964), *Baudelaire* (1968), *The Firebird* (1970), *Trionfi* (1974), *Petrushka* (1977), and *The Magic Flute* (1981). On relocating to Lausanne the company renamed itself the **Béjart Ballet Lausanne**.

Ballet Rambert *See* RAMBERT DANCE COMPANY.

Ballet-Théâtre Contemporain French ballet company, founded in 1968; one of the most important provincial dance organizations to have emerged since World War II. Established in Amiens as part of a campaign to promote links between the different arts, the company was subsequently seen at *maisons de culture* throughout the country, as well as overseas. It transferred to a new base in Angers in 1972 and attracted attention both with its employment of a wide range of choreographers and with its policy of collaboration with leading figures from the visual arts. Highlights of the company's history included programmes based on the music of Stravinsky and on STOCKHAUSEN's *Hymnen*. When the company broke up in 1978 several of the dancers formed the new Ballet Théâtre Français de Nancy.

Balthus (Count Balthasar Klossowski de Rola; 1908–) French painter. Born in Paris, Balthus was the son of a Polish painter and author of aristocratic background. He displayed an early flair for painting and was encouraged by his father and by the painters Pierre Bonnard and André Derain, who were friends of the family. He has lived and worked near Paris for most of his adult life. His early works were mostly interiors and street scenes, which combined elements of naturalism and surrealism.

Around 1950 Balthus changed direction: henceforth he has painted mainly pictures of adolescent girls in dimly lit and somewhat mysterious interiors. The girls are often naked or scantily dressed and appear to be absorbed in reverie, possibly erotic. The pictures have proved controversial among critics, some of whom have found them pornographic. In 1961 Balthus was appointed the director of the Villa Medici in Rome and later in the decade his works were shown in major exhibitions in France and Britain. In the 1970s and 1980s he also painted landscapes. Retrospectives of his work were held in Paris in 1983 and New York in 1984.

Bamberg Symphony Orchestra German orchestra. It was formed in Bamberg in 1946 from members of the Prague Deutsche Philharmonie, which was founded in Prague in 1939 but left Czechoslovakia for West Germany after World War II. The orchestra's principal conductors have included Herbert Albert (1947–48), Joseph Keilberth (1949–68), and Eugen JOCHUM (1948–49; 1969–73). Keilberth had previously conducted the Prague Deutsche Philharmonie (1940–45).

Banti, Anna (Lucia Lopresti; 1895–1985) Italian novelist and writer on the visual arts. Born and educated in Florence, Banti was a cofounder of the literary journal *Paragone*. The short stories collected in *Paolina's Itinerary* (1937) and *The Courage of Women* (1940) and the novel *Seven Moons* (1941) are mainly autobiographical.

The concern for the status of women in Italian society that informs all her work finds its most powerful expression in *Artemisia* (1947), a novel about the 16th-century painter Artemisia Gentileschi, depicted as one of the first women to fight for the rights of her gender. Other works include some major studies of painters (Angelico, Lotto, Velázquez) and more fiction (*The Bastard*, 1953; *The Golden Flies*, 1962; *The Burnt Shirt*, 1973; *A Piercing Cry*, 1981).

Barba, Eugenio (1936–) Italian theatre director, best known for his long association with the **Odin Teatret**, which he founded in Oslo in the 1960s. After graduating in Italy, he studied theatre in Warsaw and in 1961 became attached to GROTOWSKI's Laboratory Theatre. At the Odin Teatret – founded in Oslo but later transferred to Hostelbrö in Denmark – Barba pursued his ideal of a 'third theatre' occupying the middle ground between commercial but socially irrelevant theatre and obscure art theatre. The Odin Teatret promotes drama in remote areas not otherwise served by the theatre and hosts international conferences; particular successes have included the company's productions of *Ferai* from a work by Euripides, and *My Father's House*, from Dostoevskii. In 1979 Barba also founded the International School of Theatre Anthropology to coordinate theatre research. He has written extensively on drama theory, his books including *The Floating Islands* (1984) and *Beyond the Floating Islands* (1986).

Barbican Centre An arts complex in the City of London, which opened in 1982. One of Britain's most important cultural venues, it includes an art gallery, a concert hall, three cinemas, and the Barbican and Pit theatres. Among the many leading companies to visit the Barbican on a regular basis are the ROYAL SHAKESPEARE COMPANY, who have made the centre their London headquarters. The centre has its own resident orchestra, the London Symphony Orchestra, and has a close association with the neighbouring Guildhall School of Music and Drama. The controversial building was the work of CHAMBERLIN, POWELL, AND BON.

Barbirolli, Sir John (1899–1970) British conductor of Italian-French parentage. A cellist, he studied at Trinity College of Music, London and the Royal Academy of Music, London, making his debut as a concert soloist in 1917. During World War I he was a member of the Queen's Hall Orchestra and afterwards worked as a freelance cellist. In 1924 he formed his own string orchestra, which he also conducted. He was appointed staff conductor of the British National Opera Company in 1926 and from 1929 until 1933 was the principal conductor of the Covent Garden touring company. From 1933 until 1936 he conducted the Scottish Orchestra, Glasgow. After working with the New York Philharmonic, he returned to Britain in 1943 to become conductor of the Hallé Orchestra, Manchester, a post that he held until his death. He was also a regular guest conductor with several foreign orchestras, including the Berlin Philharmonic. He was known for a wide repertoire including music by Elgar, Vaughan Williams, Puccini, and Verdi; in his later years he won particular acclaim for his powerful interpretations of Mahler. He also arranged the music of Elizabethan composers for the orchestra and for his wife, the oboist Evelyn Barbirolli.

Bardem, Juan (Antonio) (1922–) Spanish film director and screenwriter. Born in Madrid, the son of an actor and an actress, Bardem joined the cinema section of the Spanish ministry of agriculture in 1946. He subsequently studied at the Spanish Institute of Cinema Research and Experimentation while writing film articles for magazines. In the late 1940s he worked with his former classmate Luis-Garcia BERLANGA on several unproduced scripts and the two codirected a short documentary, *Paseo Sobre una Guerra Antiqua* (1948). Three years later they had a major breakthrough with the cowritten *Welcome, Mr Marshall* (directed by Berlanga). One of Spain's few international film successes during the Franco years, it told the story of a poor village's attempt to woo visiting administrators of the Marshall Plan. The film was denounced by US officials.

In 1953 Bardem founded the cinema magazine *Objectivo* and directed his first solo film *Comedians*, which brought him international praise. He consolidated his reputation with two audacious political statements in the neorealist style (*see* NEOREALISM), *Death of a Cyclist* (1955), which won the Critics' Award at Cannes and *Calle Mayor* (*The Lovemaker*; 1956), a comedy about a young man who pretends to be in love with a spinster. The Spanish authorities, disturbed by Bardem's sordid picture of life under Franco, arrested him; he was in jail when the Cannes award was announced.

The government also banned *Objectivo* and heavily censored Bardem's next film, *The Vengeance* (1958), and many of his later offerings. His production company, Uninci, had its activity drastically curtailed after producing BUÑUEL's *Viridiana* (1961), an allegedly sacreligious film about a young novice who is corrupted by her uncle. Later films, which he continued to script, included *The Uninhibited* (1965), *The Last Day of the War* (1969), *The Corruption of Chris Miller* (1973), *The Mysterious Island of Captain Nemo* (1973), and *The Dog* (1977).

Barker, Howard (1946–) British playwright, whose work stands out from that of his contemporaries through its antinaturalistic style and dense, often scatological, rhetoric. Barker established his reputation with a series of harsh political plays at London's Royal Court Theatre in the 1970s. *Cheek* and *No One Was Saved* (both 1970) followed by *Claw* (1975) explored contemporary social and political issues from a broadly Marxist perspective. The preoccupation with violence and corruption recurs in Barker's later work where, however, the approach is more psychological than political.

Several of Barker's plays have a historical setting – *The Love of a Good Man* (1978), for instance, being concerned with the reburial of victims of World War I, while *Victory* (1983) recreates the ideological turmoil of the period following the Restoration of Charles II. Other plays include *The Castle* (1985), *Women Beware Women* (1986), from Thomas Middleton's 17th-century original, *The Last Supper* (1988), *Scenes from an Execution* (1989), set in 16th-century Venice, and *Seven Lears* (1989). His most recent works are the play *A Hard Heart* (1992) and the libretto for *The Terrible Mouth* (1992), Nigel OSBORNE's opera on the life of Goya.

Barnes, Peter (1931–) British playwright and theatre director, who first established his reputation for idiosyncratic political comedy with *The Ruling Class* (1968). An innovative combination of monologues, music, and ritual, *The Ruling Class* created a considerable stir with its assault on Establishment values. Subsequent plays, among them *Leonardo's Last Supper* (1969), *Laughter!* (1978), and *Red Noses* (1985), about a band of comics at the time of the Black Death, have also attacked abuses of power by the state and church. More recent works are *Women of Paris* (1987) and *Sunsets and Glories* (1990). Barnes is also the author of numerous adaptations of plays by Otway, Jonson, and other 17th-century playwrights as well as of several screenplays and many shorter works for radio.

Barraqué, Jean (1928–73) French composer. Barraqué studied at the Paris Conservatoire with Jean Langlais and MESSIAEN. Using the techniques of post-1945 SERIALISM, he evolved his own highly individualistic style, which he deployed within structures of large span and with grand neoromantic rhetoric. The early piano sonata (1952) and *Séquence* for soprano and ensemble (1950–55) are notable for their intensity, length, and expressive extremes. After a brief period of experimentation with MUSIQUE CONCRÈTE (*Etude*, 1954), Barraqué returned to acoustic instruments for *Au delà du hasard* (1959), the first of his works based on Hermann Broch's *The Death of Virgil*. Broch's novel, which examines the artist's urge to destroy his own creations, became the inspiration for a series of projects including Barraqué's last work, the concerto for clarinet (1968).

Barraud, Henry (1900–) French composer and critic. He studied at the Paris Conservatoire with Louis Aubert, Paul Dukas, and Caussade and in 1937 he was appointed director of music for the International Exhibition in Paris. During World War II he was active in the Resistance and after the liberation was appointed (1944) musical director of Radiodiffusion Française, where he encouraged young composers and strove to maintain musical standards. He retired in 1965 and in 1969 received the Grand Prix National de la Musique. Barraud eschewed innovation for its own sake and his compositions are basically diatonic in character. They include three symphonies, a piano concerto, chamber works, and vocal music including a cantata *Le Testament de François Villon* (1945), the oratorio *Le Mystère des Saints Innocents* (1946), and *La Divine Comédie* (1972).

Barrault, Jean-Louis (1910–) French actor, theatre director, and manager. Having trained as an actor under Charles Dullin and Étienne Decroux, he was subsequently associated with the playwright Antonin Artaud; he also studied mime and established himself as one of France's leading mime artists. He joined the Comédie-Française in 1940 and there met his future wife, the actress Madeleine Renaud. In 1946 Barrault and Renaud installed their newly founded Renaud-Barrault company in the Théâtre Marigny, where they remained for 10 years, gaining a reputation for performances of plays by Molière and Shakespeare as well as of more modern works by Claudel, Feydeau, and others. Productions at the Théâtre Sarah Bernhardt, the Palais-Royal, and the Odéon, to which the company moved in turn, included contemporary drama by such writers as BECKETT and IONESCO.

In the political upheaval of 1968 Barrault permitted rebellious students to use the Odéon as a headquarters; for this he was dismissed from his post. He and his company then returned to more experimental theatre and enjoyed immediate success with *Rabelais* (1969), Barrault's own adaptation of *Gargantua and Pantagruel*. Since 1980 he has been based at the Théâtre du Rond Point. He has appeared in many films, including Marcel Carné's

Les Enfants du Paradis (1944), in which he played the great mime Deburau, *La Ronde* (1950), and *The Longest Day* (1962). His writings include *Reflections on the Theatre* (1949).

Barthes, Roland (1915–80) French critic and semiologist. Barthes studied French and Classical literature and then grammar and philology at the University of Paris. He subsequently taught in a variety of institutions before becoming professor of literary semiology at the Collège de France in 1976.

Barthes developed his brand of structuralist semiology by drawing ideas from Saussure, BENVENISTE, and LÉVI-STRAUSS, as well as from Freud. In his first book *Writing Degree Zero* (1953) he argued that literary language is a closed and arbitrary system in which signs gather their meaning from the interplay with other signs. *Mythologies* (1957), his best-known work, extended this approach to the study of signs in the culture at large. In a series of short witty articles on subjects ranging from car advertising and wrestling to the eating of beefsteaks, Barthes set out to expose the process by which certain ideologically laden values and activities become accepted as 'natural' and universal. His work here has had an enormous influence on the analysis of popular culture.

Barthes came closest to giving a systematic exposition of his ideas in *Elements of Semiology* (1964). In *On Racine* (1963) he applied his method to the sign-world of classical French literature, provoking strong protests from academic experts on Racine and his times, while in *S/Z* (1970) he subjected a story by Balzac to a line-by-line analysis.

In later works such as *The Empire of Signs* (1970) and *The Pleasure of the Text* (1975) Barthes largely abandoned structuralist theory for a more subjective approach. Although these texts have not lacked admirers, many readers have found Barthes's later style infuriatingly mannered and his arguments elusive. In 1975 the autobiographical novel *Roland Barthes by Roland Barthes* became a surprise popular success. He died after a road accident. *See also* STRUCTURALISM; POSTSTRUCTURALISM.

Bartolozzi, Bruno (1911–80) Italian composer and theorist. Bartolozzi studied at the Florence Conservatory, returning there as a teacher in 1964. From 1941 to 1965, he was a violinist in the orchestra of the Maggio Musicale Fiorentino, an annual music festival held in Florence.

His works include serialist pieces – for example his string quartet of 1960 – written with the encouragement of DALLAPICCOLA. By the 1960s he had also devised the system for playing chords and microtones on woodwind instruments that he later expounded in *New Sounds for Woodwind* (1967), the book for which he is now best known. This development had already left its mark on his compositions, most famously on the *concertazioni* for bassoon (1963), written in consultation with the bassoonist Sergio Penazzi, but also on the later *concertazioni* for oboe (1965): both works introduce the new playing methods alongside traditional ones. Also noteworthy is his *Tres recuerdos del cielo* (1967), which uses quarter tones and *sprechgesang*. Other works include theatre pieces, orchestral and instrumental music, and some songs and solo instrumental pieces: particularly notable are the stage work *Tutto ciò che accade ti riguarda* (1972) and *The Solitary* (1976) for cor anglais and percussion.

Barton, Sir Derek Harold Richard (1918–) British organic chemist. Barton was educated at Imperial College, London. After a year as a visiting lecturer at Harvard (1950) he held professorships at Birbeck College, London, Glasgow University, and Imperial College (1957–78). He is currently professor of chemistry at Texas A and M University.

In 1950 he published the first of many papers on conformational analysis, in which he investigated the way in which the shape of molecules influenced the rate and course of their chemical reactions. His initial work was on the orientations of the rings of atoms in simple carbohydrates, following work by the Norwegian Odd Hassell, with whom he shared the 1969 Nobel Prize for chemistry.

Baselitz, Georg (1938–) German painter and sculptor, usually considered the leading figure in the expressionist revival of the late 1970s and 1980s (*see* NEO-EXPRESSIONISM). Baselitz began to study painting in East Berlin in 1956 but emigrated to the West a year later following official criticism of his work. In 1961 he published *Pandemonium*, an illustrated manifesto introducing the weird humanoid figures, often wounded or dismembered, that throng his earlier work. He first came to public attention in 1963 when his painting *The Great Piss-Up*, featuring a masturbating male figure, was seized by West German police and became the subject of an obscenity trial.

In 1969 Baselitz began his notorious practice of painting his subjects upside-down (the canvases are actually painted this way rather than being inverted when hung). This is apparently intended to draw attention to the gap between art and reality and – in Baselitz's words – to 'set imagination free'. During the 1980s his execution became wilder and his works assumed a semiabstract character. His turbulent aggressive style has its roots in prewar German expressionism while also showing the influence of primitive and prehistoric art.

By this time Baselitz had become a famous and controversial figure, widely credited with inspiring a revival in avant-garde figurative painting after the 1960s vogue for CONCEPTUAL ART and MINIMAL ART. He is one of the most prolific artists of his generation (recent estimates number his paintings at more than 600) and has become one of the most financially successful. In 1990 the Scottish National Gallery of Modern Art paid an unprecedented DM 750,000 for his unsettling wooden sculpture *Figure with Raised Arm*. While some critics now hail him as the greatest living European artist, others vehemently disagree, pointing to limitations in his technique and arguing that his angst often degenerates into *grand guignol*. A major retrospective of his work was held in Edinburgh in 1992.

Basov, Nicolai Gennadievich (1922–) Russian physicist. Basov was educated at the Moscow Institute of Physical Engineers, where he is now a professor. He was a member of the Presidium of the USSR Supreme Soviet (1982–89).

While working at the P. N. Ledebev Physical Institute on the microwave spectrum of gases, Basov and Aleksandr Prokhorov discovered that low-pressure beams of gas could be excited by microwaves so as to produce population inversion, in which a large proportion of the molecules in the beam were in an energetically excited state. Emission of radiation could be stimulated by a second source to give microwave amplification. In 1955 they produced the first working maser (microwave amplification by stimulated emission of radiation). In 1964 Basov and Prokhorov shared the Nobel Prize for physics with the US physicist Charles Townes, who had produced a similar device independently. In 1958 Basov went on to develop the laser from the maser and has since worked on the production of lasers using semiconducting crystals.

Bassani, Giorgio (1916–) Italian novelist and short-story writer. Born of Jewish parents in Bologna, he spent most of his early life in Ferrara, the setting for all his work. Bassani's novels reconstruct the life of the Jewish community of Ferrara in the years following the proclamation of the racial laws of 1938.

The central role of memory in his work is epitomized in his most famous novel, *The Garden of the Finzi-Continis* (1962), later adapted for the cinema by Vittorio DE SICA (1970). Here the secluded life of an aristocratic Jewish family is shattered by the realities of persecution and war; their idyllic walled garden becomes for the narrator a symbol of lost innocence and the fragility of happiness.

The early work in *Five Stories of Ferrara* (1956) was reissued in a much revised form under the title *Within the Walls* in 1973. Other works include *The Walk before Supper* (1953), the award-winning story *The Last Year of Clelia Trotti* (1955), *The Gold-Rimmed Spectacles* (1958), and *The Smell of Hay* (1972), all of which were included in *The Romance of Ferrara* (1974; revised 1980). *The Heron* (1968) deals with the lonely suicide of an Italian Holocaust survivor. He has also written a collection of critical essays, *The Prepared Words* (1966), and *Beyond the Heart* (1984).

Bastille, Opéra *See* OPÉRA BASTILLE.

Bataille, Georges (1897–1962) French philosophical writer. After a youth darkened by the serious illness of his father, Bataille became a librarian and worked in the Bibliothèque Nationale. He associated with the Paris Surrealists but was formally expelled from the movement in 1929. After undergoing a course of psychoanalysis he began to write. As the coeditor of one important journal (*Counter-Attack*) and the editor of another (*Acéphale*), he played a considerable role in post-war intellectual life. Despite this, his own work failed to find an audience and was almost forgotten when Roland BARTHES introduced his ideas into the theoretical discussions of the 1960s.

From his early pornographic novel *The Story of the Eye* (1928) onwards Bataille's work reveals an obsession with the idea that only by transgressing all moral and rational constraints can man seize life as a whole and transcend his limited nature. Extremes of evil and degradation must be investigated as part of this quest. Inspired by Nietzsche, de Sade, and surrealism he attacked conventional notions of good and evil and the concentration on utility in modern societies. 'Holy Eros', sexual desire in all its primitive and horrifying force, is seen as the chief agent of human liberation. Bataille developed his provocative ideas in works on literature (*Literature and Evil*; 1957), art (*Prehistoric Painting. Lascaux or the Birth of Art*; 1955), psychology (*Inner Experience*; 1947), philosophy (*A Method of Meditation*; 1947), economics (*The Accursed Sharp*; 1949), and law (*The Trial of Gilles de Rais*; 1967).

Bath International Festival A week-long arts festival held in Bath in May or June each year. Founded in 1948 as the Bath Assembly, it originally featured performances of 18th-century music in some of Bath's finest buildings. In 1956 it lapsed because of financial problems but was revived in 1959 by Yehudi Menuhin. The current artistic director is Amelia Freedman (until 1993) and the programme now incorporates newly commissioned works of contemporary music, as well as jazz, ballet, art, poetry, and theatre.

Baudrillard, Jean (1929–) French theorist of POSTMODERNISM. After taking a degree in German, Baudrillard became the assistant of the social historian Henri Lefèbvre and adopted his idiosyncratic Marxism. He subsequently taught sociology at the University of Nanterre from 1966 until 1987. He works as a journalist (contributing regularly to *Le Monde* amongst other publications) and is the editor of the journal *Traverses*.

Baudrillard's central thesis is that in an age dominated by the mass media traditional oppositions of the real and the unreal, substance and appearance, are no longer meaningful. In modern technological societies, Baudrillard argues, events only assume the aura of 'reality' when they have been refracted through the media; moreover, we find ourselves increasingly unable to understand our own experience except in terms dictated by television, advertising, and popular newsprint. Baudrillard goes so far as to assert that the 'real world' no longer exists; we live in a 'hyperreality' in which real things have been replaced by their media-generated 'simulacra'.

Although Baudrillard became a cult figure in the mid 1980s, his oracular style of argument, jargon-ridden prose, and taste for extravagant paradox – claiming for instance that the Gulf War of 1991 did not 'really' take place apart from its media representation – have more recently come in for severe criticism. His most important books are *The System of Objects* (1968), *Seduction* (1979), *Fatal Strategies* (1983), and *America* (1986).

Bauer, Wolfgang (1941–) Austrian playwright, who took a prominent role in the revival of the old folkplay tradition in the 1960s and 1970s. Based in Graz, he soon acquired a strong reputation with striking socially relevant plays written in local dialect, among them *Pig Transport* (1962), *Magic Afternoon* (1968), *Sylvester or the Massacre at the Hotel Sacher* (1971), and *Magnetic Kisses* (1976). Typically his plays take the form of farces in which the underlying seriousness of the subject is masked by stereotyped characters and a rapidly developing plot.

Bausch, Pina (Philippine Bausch; 1940–) German dancer, choreographer, and ballet director, whose work has had a profound influence on the development of European dance theatre since the mid 1970s. Her sombre but imaginative works tackle themes of emotional distress, despair, and human isolation against a background of failed relationships and brutality. They have been hailed as among the most significant works to be seen on the European stage since Diaghilev.

Born in Solingen, Bausch trained under Kurt Jooss at Essen and in New York at the Juilliard School, where she was coached by José Limón and Antony TUDOR. She subsequently joined the New American Ballet and danced at the Metropolitan Opera House under Tudor before returning to Germany in 1963 to join Jooss.

In 1973 Bausch began to work as a choreographer for the Wuppertal opera house;

her success led to an invitation to establish the **Wuppertal Dance Theatre,** of which she then became a long-term director. Since choreographing a version of Stravinsky's *Le Sacre du printemps* in 1975 she has presented a series of highly original works of her own creation, many of which combine elements of dance and dialogue. She has also conceived designs for many of the company's productions herself. Her most remarkable pieces have included the violent *Bluebeard* (1977), during which the performers dance on a leaf-strewn stage, *Café Muller* (1978), in which a sleepwalking woman (played by Bausch herself) rejects and is rejected by a series of characters from her imagination and memory, *Arien* (1979), which requires the stage to be flooded with water, *The Legend of Chastity* (1979), *Bandoneon* (1980), and *Nelken* (1982), in which the stage (ringed by uniformed guards with dogs) is covered with pink and white flowers, among which the dancers cavort in party frocks.

Bavarian Radio Symphony Orchestra German orchestra. It was formed in Munich in 1949, when Bavarian Radio expanded its operations: Eugen JOCHUM was engaged as its first conductor. Created to give public concerts and to make recordings and broadcasts, it was, from the outset, notably committed to contemporary music, with orchestral members playing in the MUSICA VIVA concerts under the composer Karl Amadeus Hartmann. Under Jochum the orchestra undertook tours throughout Europe; under Rafael KUBELIK, who succeeded Jochum as chief conductor in 1961, it has also toured the US and Japan.

Bazaine, Jean (1904–) French painter. Bazaine studied sculpture at the École des Beaux-Arts in Paris but was subsequently drawn to painting; his early figurative works attracted considerable attention. He gave his first one-man exhibition in 1932 and won the Prix Blumenthal in 1938. From 1932 onwards he began to move towards abstraction and by 1947 his work had become completely nonrepresentational, though he continued to draw inspiration from aspects of the natural world, such as the wind or the night. His early abstract work was rectilinear but this gave way to a freer more exuberant style in which the paint often appears ready to burst out of the paintings. After World War II he was recognized as one of the leading exponents of lyrical or expressive abstraction (*see* ART INFORMEL). Between 1948 and 1954 his work received several exhibitions in Paris and Bazaine became well known internationally. In subsequent decades he became more concerned with colour and experimented with combinations of tones. Bazaine was interested in Christian art and designed stained-glass windows and ceramic murals for churches; he also designed stained-glass windows for the headquarters of UNESCO in Paris.

BBPR (Banffi, Belgiojoso, Peressuti, and Rogers) Italian architectural partnership, formed by Gianluigi Banffi, Lodovico Belgiojoso, Enrico Peressuti, and Ernesto Nathan Rogers in Milan in 1932. The four had met as fiercely modernist students at the Milan Politecnico. Early projects included many competition entries, exhibition buildings, and a number of private interiors. Most of their work is in northern Italy, the best-known examples being their renovation of the Sforza Castle in Milan as a museum (1954–56) and the spectacular Torre Velasca, Milan (1957–60), which breaks with traditional skyscraper designs by having the top eight floors projecting out on giant brackets in a style reminiscent of medieval fortresses. Their office building for Chase Manhattan Bank in Milan (1969) likewise has a dramatically exposed frame, this time of steel. The firm's enormous output has included many town plans and renovations. Their modernism often uses the forms, shapes, and materials of historic buildings, a tendency that exposed the group to bitter criticism from purists in the 1950s; the sophistication of this approach is now recognized, however, and it has been widely influential.

Beaton, Sir Cecil (1904–80) British photographer and theatrical designer. After a privileged education at Harrow and Cambridge, Beaton began photographing the rich and famous, whom he relentlessly cultivated, for society magazines. After exhibiting in London in 1929, he worked for *Vogue* in the US, where his portraits of the British Royal Family made him much sought after in show-business circles. During World War II he documented the campaigns in Africa, India, and Burma and also worked in China, revealing an unexpected breadth to his talent and producing some of the most memorable images of the war. Beaton later concentrated on design for opera, theatre, and cinema, winning Academy Awards for the costumes in *Gigi* (1959) and for the sets and costumes in *My Fair Lady* (1965). Although elegant and meticulously composed, his portrait photographs remain essentially theatrical, revealing little of the inner nature of the sitter. Beaton's use of unconventional lighting and whimsical props and backdrops sometimes produces an effect that borders on surrealism. Beaton produced some 30 books, notably *The Book of Beauty* (1930), *The Glass of Fashion* (1954), and six volumes of diaries collected into *Self-Portrait with Friends* (1979).

Beauvoir, Simone de (1908–86) French writer and feminist. Born in Paris, Beauvoir studied at the Sorbonne, obtaining a degree in philosophy in 1929, the year in which she met her lifelong companion Jean-Paul SARTRE. This part of her life is recalled in *Memoirs of a Dutiful Daughter* (1958), the first volume of an extended autiobiographical sequence. *The Prime of Life* (1960) decribes her life as a school teacher and her early days with Sartre, while *The Force of Circumstance* (1963) recollects the post-war years when Beauvoir and Sartre were fêted as the leading intellectuals of France. The last volume of the sequence, *Adieux: A Farewell to Sartre* (*La Cérémonie des adieux*; 1981), gives a sometimes harrowing account of the philosopher's last years. The themes of old age and death are also explored in *A Very Easy Death* (1964), which concerns the death of Beauvoir's mother from cancer.

Beauvoir's first novel, *She Came to Stay* (1943), describes the destructive effect of a young girl on the life of the couple with whom she stays. *The Blood of Others* (1944) addresses the conflict between the existentialist concept of absolute freedom and the claims of political responsibility (*see* EXISTENTIALISM). *All Men Are Mortal* (1946) intends to show that only death gives meaning to life, while *The Mandarins* (1954) describes the difficulties faced by those post-war intellectuals who attempted to engage in political struggle.

Beauvoir's best-known theoretical work is *The Second Sex* (1949), a landmark of feminist literature; here she attacks not only the assumption of women's inferiority to men but also the idealization of marriage and motherhood and the concept of the 'eternal feminine'.

Becker, Jacques (1906–) French film director, known mostly for his elegant comedies of the 1950s. An assistant of Jean Renoir in the 1930s, Becker established himself as a director with *It Happened at the Inn* (1942), a melodramatic comedy about poaching, in which he showed his interest in characterization. Several of the comedies that followed dealt with Parisian society, among them *July Rendezvous* (1949), depicting the frustrations and despair of the young in post-war France, *Edward and Caroline* (1951), about discord between two newly-weds, and *Casque d'or* (1952), starring Simone Signoret and Serge Reggiani in a story about an ill-fated Parisian romance of the 1890s. Hailed as one of the great love stories, *Casque d'or* is a classic of the French cinema.

Honour Among Thieves (1953), starring Jean Gabin, was a unique gangster film that inspired many imitations by other directors; its success was largely owing to the depth given to its central character. Over the next six years Becker directed a number of less significant films before embarking on his last project, *The Hole* (1959), which is widely considered his best work. Like his earlier films, it is simple in style yet acute in its observation of character and relationships; it concerns an attempted escape by four prisoners and their betrayal by another prisoner.

Beckett, Samuel (1906–89) Irish playwright and novelist living in France from 1927 and writing in both French and English. Born in Dublin, he travelled in Europe before settling in Paris, where he became the friend and amanuensis of James Joyce. Under Joyce's influence he published poems, criticism, and the comic novel *Murphy* (1938). In World War II he took an active role in the French Resistance, earning the Croix de Guerre. While hiding in unoccupied France he wrote *Watt* (published 1953), a bizarre novel charting the title character's descent into total bewilderment in a world that refuses to make sense. Beckett's characteristic themes of physical decay, mental disintegration, and perplexed solipsism find their fullest expression in the post-war trilogy of novels *Molloy* (1951), *Malone Dies* (1951), and *The Unnamable* (1953). His depiction of the isolated human consciousness confronted with both the indifference of the external world and the engima of its own identity is often harrowing, but relieved by grotesque humour and passages of grave beauty. As a prose stylist in both French and English Beckett had few contemporary rivals.

Beckett found sudden fame with the production of his two-act play *Waiting for Godot* in 1953. This work, quickly identified as a cornerstone of the Theatre of the Absurd (*see* ABSURD, THEATRE OF THE), provoked extremes of bewilderment and admiration among audiences and critics. The symbolism of the two tramps waiting for the arrival of the mysterious Godot and their comic but despairing attempts to come to terms with the apparent futility of their existence is at once suggestive and opaque. The plays that followed showed a similar mastery of theatrical technique. In *Endgame* (*Fin de partie*; 1957) Hamm and Clov await death in a world that disintegrates around them. In *Krapp's Last Tape* (1958) the central character is barely able to comprehend the recordings he made earlier in his life and in *Happy Days* (1961) Winnie sinks slowly into the ground while keeping up a stream of trivial chatter.

Beckett's later plays became increasingly minimalist, abandoning any vestige of plot or even character. In *Acts Without Words* (1957 and 1959) he dispensed with dialogue altogether, while in *Not I* (1971) all that is visible to the audience is a woman's mouth that babbles semi-coherently. He wrote further monologues for women, such as *Footfalls* (1976), *Rockaby* (1980), and *Catastrophe* (1982), which was dedicated to Vaclav HAVEL. Late prose works, such as *Company* (1980), *Ill Seen Ill Said* (1982), and *Stirrings Still* (1988), are similarly austere.

Even those who find Beckett's vision repellent and his methods perverse are unable to deny the integrity and consistency with which he pursued his artistic ends. For others he is the major European writer of the post-war period. He was awarded the Nobel Prize for literature in 1969.

Bednár, Alfonz (1914–89) Slovak novelist. After reading languages at Prague and Bratislava Universities, he worked as a schoolmaster during World War II, in government service until 1948, and thereafter as a publisher's editor and literary adviser in the Slovak film industry. His first novel, *The Glass Mountain* (1954), marked the beginning of the thaw in Slovak literature. Though not an explicitly anticommunist novel, it describes the corruption and incompetence of the builders of socialism, especially the bullying and prejudices of Party officials; it also introduces the main theme of Bednár's prose, human violence, physical and moral. In his collection of novellas *The Hours and Minutes* (1956) he openly aligns Nazism with Stalinism. *The Thunderbolt* (1964), a picture of Slovak village life in flux between 1913 and 1923, is a study of human greed and restlessness and of 20th-century man's readiness to obliterate history for the sake of a dubious 'progress'. From *A Handful of Change* (1970–81) onwards, his attention turned ever more to modern consumerism, the attenuation of such values as fidelity, kindness, and common decency, and the political deformation of language. *Ad revidendum, Gemini* (1988) is an existentialist novel about isolation and the manipulation of language; it also constitutes a condemnation of the wartime Slovak fascist state, of communism, and of the mythologization of the Slovak village. Bednár is a powerful writer who seems to despair of human depravity, although in his later works he is able to treat his own despair with irony.

Behan, Brendan (Francis) (1923–64) Irish playwright, who joined the IRA at the age of 14, spent three years in borstal, and at the age of 19 was sentenced to 9 to 14 years in prison for attempted murder and various political offences, events he subsequently described in his autobiography *Borstal Boy* (1958).

Behan's works for the stage were as exuberant and blackly comic as his own life was turbulent and brief (he died an alcoholic). *The Quare Fellow* (1954), a tragicomedy set in an Irish prison on the eve of a hanging, was widely praised in a production by Joan LITTLEWOOD's Theatre Workshop, which subsequently transferred to London's West End; it is thought to have hastened the abolition of capital punishment in Britain.

The Hostage (1958; first produced in Gaelic as *An Giall*, 1957) was an equally provocative account of the murder of an English soldier held prisoner by the IRA in a brothel. The original production, featuring an exuberant combination of music, drama, and monologue, was remarkable for the series of direct addresses to the audience from the stage by the author. In his last years Behan's colourful personality and skill as a raconteur made him a celebrity on both sides of the Atlantic, but he added little to his literary achievement. A third play, *Richard's Cork Leg*, was unfinished at his death, although a completed version did reach the stage in 1972.

Behnisch, Gunther (1922–) German architect. Behnisch trained in Stuttgart and served in the German Navy in World War II. After working in partnership with Bruno Lambart in Stuttgart (1952–56), he practised on his own. From 1975 he lectured at the Technische Hochschule, Darmstadt. Obtaining commissions largely through competitions, Behnisch chose to concentrate on public-sector work, in particular housing and educational buildings. The most important work was the Olympia Park, the site for the 1972 Olympic Games in Munich. The spectacular tent roof over the main stadium was an early large-scale use of tension structures; the plan successfully integrated a site covering more than 4 sq km into Munich, and it remains the city's principal recreational area. In his designs for the new Assembly Hall and Parliament Buildings in Bonn (1974–80), Behnisch deliberately avoided monumentalism, aiming to produce an architectural expression of a free pluralistic society.

Béjart, Maurice (Maurice Berger; 1927–) French choreographer, dancer, and ballet director, who emerged as the most popular, if controversial, French choreographer of modern times during the 1950s and 1960s. Béjart's work has attracted mass audiences to the ballet but some critics have been estranged by his free adaptations of classical pieces and by the overt theatricality of much of his work.

The son of a philosopher, Béjart trained as a dancer in Marseilles, Paris, and London and made his stage debut in 1945. He gained experience under Roland PETIT and with the Royal Swedish Ballet (1950–52) before founding Les Ballets de l'Etoile in 1953 and serving as the company's star soloist and artistic director; the troupe developed in 1957 into the Ballet-Théâtre de Maurice Béjart.

In 1959 Béjart enjoyed enormous success with his powerfully sexual *Le Sacre du Printemps* (1959), presented in Brussels by a specially assembled company. The following year this ensemble became the BALLET OF THE 20TH CENTURY with Béjart as artistic director. During the 1960s the company toured widely, drawing huge crowds and establishing a reputation as one of the most exciting ensembles in the world. Among the ballets that Béjart himself created for the troupe were the highly theatrical *4 fils Aymon* (1961) and *The Merry Widow* (1963), *Romeo and Juliet* (1966), which was seen by no less than 300 000 people, the mystical *Mass for the Present Time* (1967) and *Bakhti* (1968); others included a series of ballets based on the music of Richard Wagner. Works for other companies included *The Journey* (1962), *The Damnation of Faust* (1964), and *Renard* (1965).

Béjart founded the dance school Mudra in 1970 and in 1974 set out his ideas of 'total dance' in *Ballet and Modern Dance*. His most successful work of the 1970s and 1980s has included *Firebird* (1970), an imaginative reworking of the original ballet, *Notre Faust* (1975), *The Magic Flute* (1981), and *Kabuki* (1986). Recent works include *Nijinsky, Clown and God* (1990). He moved the Ballet of the 20th Century to Lausanne in 1987 after disagreements with the management of the Théâtre Royal de la Monnaie in Brussels.

Béjart Ballet Lausanne *See* BALLET OF THE 20TH CENTURY.

Belfast Festival at Queen's An annual international arts festival, held in Queen's University and the Grand Opera House, Belfast, Northern Ireland. Founded in 1962, it is the largest festival in Ireland, with events taking place throughout November. The programme is diverse and has featured a remarkable range of artists, from Jimi Hendrix to James Galway. The festival is a focus for all types of cultural activity in Northern Ireland and includes dance, theatre, comedy, film, jazz, and folk music, along with a strong classical repertoire and a variety of events for children.

Bell Burnell, Jocelyn (1943–) British radio astronomer. Born in Belfast as Jocelyn Bell, she studied astronomy and physics at Glasgow University, graduating in 1965. She began working in radio astronomy with Antony HEWISH at Cambridge in 1965. She subsequently lectured and studied gamma rays at Southampton

University, moving to the Mullard Space Science Laboratory in 1974. At the Royal Observatory, Edinburgh, Bell Burnell was head of the James Clerk Maxwell Telescope millimetre-wavelength project. She is currently professor of physics at the Open University.

In 1967, while examining observational records for Hewish's project on the radio scintillation of quasars, Bell noticed an extraneous signal, which proved to be periodic, recurring at intervals of 1.3 seconds. Extensive investigations located additional similar sources and confirmed their stellar nature. The announcement of the discovery of these pulsars in 1968 generated great excitement. As pointed out by Thomas GOLD, they are evidence for the existence of neutron stars, ultradense objects a few kilometres in diameter, which had been predicted in the 1930s. Some pulsars rotate at very high speeds: the shortest periods are only a few milliseconds.

Bellmer, Hans (1902–75) German sculptor, painter, and graphic artist. Born in Katowice in Upper Silesia, Bellmer became interested in painting and drawing as a child. He studied engineering at the Technische Hochschule in Berlin (1923) and drawing with the painter George Grosz. In the 1920s Bellmer also became fascinated by the graphic works of the 16th-century German artists Albrecht Altdorfer and Hans Baldung-Grien. From 1926 until 1936 he worked in Berlin designing publicity material for industry.

In 1928 Bellmer and his wife gave lodgings to one of Frau Bellmer's cousins, who received a trunk from her mother containing, amongst other things, a number of broken dolls. Inspired by their macabre qualities, Bellmer began to construct female dolls and to photograph them, often in a broken or dismembered state. His photographs were greatly relished by the Paris Surrealists, who published a selection in their magazine *Minotaure*; in 1938 Bellmer moved to Paris and joined the group. With their overtones of violence and depraved sexuality, his doll sculptures and photographs are often seen as a response to the rise of Nazism. After the war, during which he was interned, Bellmer exhibited drawings and prints; many of these feature dolls or fantastic torsos. Bellmer also produced book illustrations and some moving self-portraits.

Bellocchio, Marco (1939–) Italian film director and screenwriter, who helped to launch the 'New Italian Cinema' of the 1960s. Bellocchio abandoned his philosophy studies at the Milan University of the Sacred Heart to enter Rome's Centro Sperimentale di Cinematografia and later attended the Slade School of Art in London. After directing shorts and documentaries, he borrowed money from his family to finance his first feature film *Fists in His Pocket* (1965). This powerful story of murder and incest within a family of epileptics made a number of points about moral decadence in contemporary society and collected an award at the Locarno Film Festival. Bellocchio, who often laces his films with leftist ideology, continued to challenge the social and political status quo in such films as *In the Name of the Father* (1971), in which a revolt against an oppressive father figure takes on a wider antiauthoritarian symbolism. His more recent offerings, many of which he coscripted, have been less striking and successful. They include the French-Italian *Les Yeux fertiles* (1977), *The Eyes, the Mouth* (1983), *Henry IV* (1984), *Devil in the Flesh* (1985), and *The Visions of Sabbah* (1987). His latest film is *The Sentence* (1990), which centres on a rape trial.

Bene, Carmelo (1937–) Italian theatre director, playwright, and actor, noted particularly for his acclaimed though sometimes eccentric interpretations of classic drama, many of which make striking use of modern technology. Bene began his career in the theatre with a series of relatively undemanding roles in commercial plays. Subsequently, however, he emerged as a flamboyant director and writer of considerable originality and went on to win a large and devoted following. In the 1970s he enjoyed success with many classic plays, including Shakespeare's *Hamlet* (1975), *Romeo and Juliet* (1976), and *Richard III* (1977). Other admired productions included *S.A.D.E.* (1974) and Manzoni's *Adelchi* (1984), which was also successfully adapted for television.

Benjamin, George (1960–) British composer and pianist. Born in London, he studied composition in Paris with MESSIAEN and with GOEHR at King's College, Cambridge. Other influences include

LIGETI and BOULEZ. The early promise shown by Benjamin's piano sonata (1978) was confirmed with his first major work, the orchestral piece *Ringed by the Flat Horizon*, first given at the proms in 1980. He carried out research at IRCAM from 1984 until 1987. Other pieces include *Altitude* (1977) for brass band, *A Mind of Winter* (1981) for soprano and orchestra, *At First Light* (1982) for chamber group, and the orchestral piece *Cascade* (1990).

Bennett, Alan (1934–) British playwright and actor. A star of the *Beyond the Fringe* revue at the 1960 Edinburgh Festival, he established himself as a playwright with the satirical *Forty Years On* (1968) and with *Habeas Corpus* (1973), an irreverent comedy reminiscent of Joe ORTON.

Bennett's extensive writing for television has consolidated his reputation as a keen observer of social mores, especially amongst the respectable working classes in his native north of England. His greatest resource as a writer is a shrewd ear for the linguistic oddities of everyday conversation. *Talking Heads* (1988), a series of monologues for TV, was particularly highly praised. As well as producing numerous screenplays he has also continued to write for the stage, often appearing in his own plays. His most recent dramas have included the double bill *Single Spies* (1988; *A Question of Attribution, An Englishman Abroad*), in which he played the British traitor Anthony Blunt, a new version of Kenneth Grahame's *The Wind in the Willows* (1990), and *The Madness of George III* (1991).

Bennett, Richard Rodney (1936–) British composer and pianist. Born in Broadstairs, Kent, Bennett studied at the Royal Academy of Music with BERKELEY and Howard Ferguson and then with BOULEZ in Paris. He had started composing before this, however, using the 12-note system by the time he was 16. His later works reflect such diverse influences as jazz, neoromanticism, and the expressionism of Berg. He has worked in a number of different spheres, composing over 35 film scores and working as a jazz pianist and an arranger of popular music. Principal works include the operas *The Mines of Sulphur* (1965), *A Penny for a Song* (1966), and *Victory* (1970), the ballet *Jazz Calendar* (1964), concertos, and choral works. Recent compositions include a clarinet quintet (1992). He now lives mainly in the US.

Benveniste, Emile (1902–76) French linguist. Born in Aleppo, Benveniste studied in Paris and taught comparative linguistics there from 1927. He was professor of comparative grammar at the Collège de France from 1937 until his retirement in 1969.

Benveniste counts among the structural linguists, being much influenced by Saussure, the founder of structural linguistics and a former occupant of his chair (*see* STRUCTURALISM). Much of his work consists of specialized studies in the field of comparative Indo-European linguistics, with particular attention to the Iranian languages. Works of this kind include *The Origin of Noun-formation in Indo-European Languages* (1935), *Nouns of Agents and Nouns of Action in Indo-European Languages* (1935), and *Indo-European Language and Society* (1969). Benveniste introduced historical and etymological research into the somewhat ahistorical structuralist method, as well as using structuralist concepts in traditional historical linguistics. His greatest intellectual achievement may well be his attempted reconstruction of the Indo-European social system from the evidence of the language.

Benveniste considered more general questions of language in *Problems of General Linguistics* (1969). Addressing himself to the question of the arbitrariness of linguistic signs, he concluded that in one respect they are arbitrary because there is no similarity between the sign and what it refers to, but that in another they are not because we accept the legitimacy of one sign rather than another and have good reasons for doing so. Benveniste's studies had a considerable influence on the younger French structuralists like BARTHES and KRISTEVA.

Bergen International Festival An annual arts festival, founded in 1953 and held over several weeks in May and June in Bergen, Norway. The programme includes a wide range of music, from church music to symphonies and jazz, as well as Norwegian and international folklore, art exhibitions, theatre, and ballet. Performances of chamber music are given at Grieg's former home.

Bergman, Ingmar (1918–) Swedish film and theatre director regarded as one of the most influential figures in post-war world cinema. The son of a Lutheran pastor, Bergman began as a trainee director in the theatre before becoming a film scriptwriter. His script for SJÖBERG's *Frenzy* (1944) won acclaim and a year later he made his debut as a director with *Crisis*. Such early films as *Prison* and *Thirst* (both 1949) established Bergman's characteristic territory, dissecting the tortuous workings of human relationships and touching on such philosophical themes as faith, purity, and death. After three bittersweet romance films in the early 1950s, Bergman established his international reputation with *Smiles of a Summer Night* (1955), a comedy of manners set in 1900 that won the Cannes Film Festival Award. *The Seventh Seal* (1956), awarded the Grand Prix at Cannes, was a sombre medieval tale; many of its remarkable images have passed into cinema legend. *Wild Strawberries* (1957) was acclaimed for its sympathetic portrayal of an elderly academic who is forced to come to terms with his own emotional sterility.

The films *Through a Glass Darkly* (1961), *Winter Light* (1962), and *The Silence* (1963), constitute a trilogy in which Bergman explores the meaning of religious belief in a world full of suffering and death. *Persona* (1966), *Hour of the Wolf* (1967), and *The Shame* (1968) investigate the relationship between art and reality. Tense relationships are again the focus of Bergman's interest in *A Passion* (1969), *The Touch* (1970), and – most successfully – the harrowing *Cries and Whispers* (1972). Charges of tax fraud forced Bergman into exile in 1976 but he returned to Sweden two years later to release *Autumn Sonata*, pairing Ingrid Bergman and Liv Ullmann in a mother-daughter conflict. Finally, the epic *Fanny and Alexander* (1982), a partly autobiographical family saga, was a successful compendium of Bergman themes and technical devices. He then retired from the cinema, his reputation firmly established. Recently he wrote the script for Bille Auguste's award-winning film *The Best Intentions* (1992); the story is based on the married life of Bergman's parents. The Ingmar Bergman Annual Prize is awarded in his honour to outstanding film-makers by the Swedish Film Institute.

Berio, Luciano (1925–) Italian composer, teacher, and conductor. After World War II he studied law at Milan University and music at the Milan Conservatory, taking lessons in composition from Giorgio Federico Ghedini and in conducting from Carlo Maria GIULINI. In 1950 he married the singer Cathy Berberian and travelled to the US, where he studied under DALLAPICCOLA at the Tanglewood Center. Critical for his future development were his meetings in 1954 with MADERNA, POUSSEUR, and STOCKHAUSEN – representatives of the serialist and electronic avant-garde. In 1955 his interest in electronic music, simmering since 1952, led to his opening (with Maderna) the Studio di Fonologia Musicale in Milan. He has since also worked with BOULEZ at IRCAM. The magazine and concert series *Incontri musicali* (1956–60) was another avant-garde development. From 1954 to 1959 he taught at DARMSTADT.

From 1963 until 1972 he worked in the US, teaching at Harvard University and at the Juilliard School (1965–71), where he founded and conducted the Juilliard Ensemble. In 1976 he became artistic director of the Accademia Filarmonica in Rome.

During the 1940s and 1950s his music developed from Stravinskian neoclassicism and Schoenbergian serialism, through a freer use of serialist procedures (*Nones*, 1954), to an assimilation of electronic techniques and aleatoricism. *Omaggio a Joyce* (1958) marks the end of his purely electronic music: *Differences* (1959) mixes live and recorded sound. From the same period the first *Sequenza*, for flute (1958), makes use of indeterminacy. His characteristic theatricality appears in, for example, *Circles* (1960), a setting of e. e. cummings, and in the well-known *Sinfonia* (1969) with its quotations from Mahler and others. Since the early 1960s many of his pieces have reworked material from earlier compositions (as in *Chemins IV*, 1975, based on *Sequenza VII*, 1969). Other significant works include the operas *La vera storia* (1982) and *Un re in ascolto* (1984), the ongoing *Sequenza* series of solo instrumental pieces, and such recent works as the string quartet (1990) and *Feuerklavier* (1989).

Beriozoff, Nicholas (1906–) Lithuanian-born dancer, choreographer, and ballet master, who stimulated a revival of the Stuttgart company in the late 1950s. Having studied ballet in Prague, Beriozoff danced with the company in Kaunas (1930–35) and with the René Blum Ballets de Monte Carlo (1935–38) and the Ballets Russes de Monte Carlo (1938–44). After World War II he was ballet master with Ballet International (1944), the Metropolitan Ballet (1948), La Scala (1950–51), the London Festival Ballet (1951–54), and the Grand Ballet du Marquis de Cuevas (1956) before accepting the role of director of the Stuttgart Ballet (1957–60).

In Stuttgart he concentrated on rebuilding the company's repertoire on traditional lines and raising performance standards; it was largely on the foundations laid by Beriozoff that John CRANKO, his successor, was able to make the company one of the most admired in the world. After leaving Stuttgart, Beriozoff worked with companies in Helsinki, Zürich, and Naples, among other cities. His work as a choreographer has included versions of many of the great classical ballets, among them *Romeo and Juliet* (1966) and *Cinderella* (1967). In recent years he has taught ballet in the US. He is the father of the popular dancer Svetlana Beriosova.

Berkeley, Sir Lennox (Randal Francis) (1903–89) British composer. Berkeley studied at Oxford and with Nadia Boulanger in Paris (1927–32), where he became friends with POULENC. During this French period he converted to Roman Catholicism (1928) and drew away from the English musical tradition towards the neoclassicism of Les Six and Stravinsky. His early music shows a natural flair for melody and texture somewhat akin to Fauré's. During World War II he worked for the BBC and afterwards taught (until 1968) at the Royal Academy of Music.

Berkeley's mature works include the full-scale opera *Nelson* (1954) and three chamber operas, *A Dinner Engagement* (1954), *Ruth* (1956), and *Castaway* (1967). He wrote concertos for piano (1947), two pianos (1948), flute (1952), piano and double string orchestra (1958), and four symphonies. His *Concertino* (1955) experiments with a 12-note theme and later works, such as the third symphony, use atonal and tonal material side by side. He wrote effectively for voices and produced a small body of deeply felt religious work, including *Four Poems of St Teresa of Avila* (1947) and the *Missa brevis* (1960).

Berkoff, Steven (1937–) British playwright, actor, and theatre director, who founded (1968) the London Theatre Group. His idiosyncratic productions with the company have included adaptations of Edgar Allan Poe and Franz Kafka, whose *Metamorphosis* (1969) Berkoff staged using a striking variety of techniques, including mime and acrobatics, to transform the piece into a metaphor for contemporary social ills. The play was subsequently seen on Broadway (in 1989) and is regularly revived at the EDINBURGH FESTIVAL with Berkoff in the main role.

East (1975), Berkoff's first completely original play, used blank verse and the conventions of high tragedy to portray life in London's East End; it was successfully transferred to the National Theatre. In *Greek* (1979) he interpreted the Oedipus myth in terms of feminist politics, while in *West* (1983) he translated the Beowulf story into a critical examination of British class structure. Subsequent plays have included *Sink the Belgrano!* (1986), a reworking of Shakespeare's *Henry V* based on a controversial incident during the Falklands War of 1982, and the award-winning *Kvetch* (1987), a bilious comedy about a neurotic Jewish salesman.

Berlanga, Luis (1921–) Spanish film director who made several films critical of life under the Franco regime. Born in Valencia, Berlanga studied in Switzerland and at Valencia University. He served on the Republican side in the Spanish Civil War and as a volunteer in World War II before enrolling (1947) in the Spanish Institute of Cinema Research and Experimentation. After collaborating with his classmate Juan BARDEM on a short, Berlanga directed their joint offering *Welcome, Mr Marshall* (1951), which gave a major boost to the Spanish cinema by winning high praise at the Cannes Film Festival. Berlanga, who was much influenced by the subversive social satires of Luis BUÑUEL, had forceful opinions and democratic ideals that often brought him into conflict with the Spanish censors, but he found some room for manoeuvre thanks to his continuing international success: *Plácido* (1961) was nominated for an Academy Award as best foreign film. Other films, many of which he coscripted, included *Not on Your Life* (1963), *Las Pirañas* (1967), *La Escopeta Nacional* (1978), *Calabuch* (1956), *The Executioner* (1963), and *Vivan los Novios* (1970). Two years after Franco's death, he again provoked the authorities when he shocked audiences at the Valladolid Festival with the erotic *Life Size* (1977), about a Parisian dentist who develops a fetish for a life-size doll.

Berlin, Isaiah (1909–) British philosopher, born in Latvia. A brilliant scholarship student at Oxford, Berlin remained there, as lecturer and professor, for the rest of his career. Since abandoning conventional philosophical studies in the 1940s he has concerned himself chiefly with the history of ideas. His main interest lies in the often unstated presuppositions that structure the thought and motivate the actions of both individuals and groups, and the way in which these presuppositions, apparently so absolute, change during the course of history. For Berlin, philosophical analysis always has historical implications.

In *Vico and Herder* (1976) and *Against the Current* (1979), a volume of essays on Machiavelli, Montesquieu, and Hamann, Berlin argued that fundamental changes in the conceptual infrastructure of European culture took place in the early 18th century. He argued that in the thought of these individuals pluralism, in knowledge as in ethics and aesthetics, began to replace a traditional belief in the unity of creation.

From his own acceptance of a pluralistic view arose the liberalism stoutly defended by Berlin in *Four Essays on Liberty* (1969). Here he attacked historical determinism and demanded freedom of action and of choice for each individual. Among his other works are *The Hedgehog and the Fox* (1953), an examination of Tolstoy's character through analysis of his historical theories, the anti-deterministic *Historical Inevitability* (1955), *The Age of Enlightenment* (1956), *Two Concepts of Liberty* (1958), and four volumes of *Collected Papers* (1975–80).

Berlin was knighted in 1957; from 1974 to 1978 he was president of the British Academy.

Berliner Ensemble The German theatre company founded by Bertolt BRECHT in Berlin in 1949. The company, established at the invitation of the East German Government, became the focus for much of the most important work then taking place in European theatre, not least in its productions of its founder's own plays and its assimilation of his theories of EPIC THEATRE. In 1954 the company moved from the Deutsches Theater to the Theater am Schiffbauerdamm; after Brecht's death in 1956, it was taken over by his widow, Helene Weigel and after her death in 1971 by their daughter, Barbara Brecht-Schall. Since then the Ensemble's reputation has declined sharply, apart from a period in the mid 1970s when it was revived by Manfred WEKWORTH; criticism has focused on the quality of the productions and on the interventionist style of Barbara Brecht-Schall and her actor husband Ekkerhard Schall. In 1992 five leading directors from the former West Germany (including Peter PALITZSCH and Peter ZADEK) were called in to save the company from collapse; it was also decided that the Ensemble, formerly funded by the East German state, should become a limited company.

Berliner Festwochen (Berlin Festival Weeks) A major festival of the arts held each September in Berlin. The festival was established in 1950 with the aim of reviving cultural life in Berlin after World War II. Following the erection of the Berlin Wall (1961) the main festival continued in West Berlin, with the eastern part of the city setting up its own equivalent (also held in September). The reunification of the city and falling attendance figures in recent years have led some to question whether the event should continue in its present form. Ulrich Eckhardt has been overall director of the festival since 1972.

Berlin Film Festival An international film festival founded in Berlin in 1951. The most prestigious prize awarded is the Golden Bear for Best Film. Winners since 1951, when Walt Disney's *Cinderella* took the prize, have included CLOUZOT's *The Wages of Fear* (1953), BERGMAN's *Wild Strawberries* (1958), CHABROL's *The Cousins* (1959), SCHLESINGER's *A Kind of Loving* (1962), POLANSKI's *Cul de Sac* (1966), DE SICA's *The Garden of the Finzi-Continis* (1971), SAURA's *Fast, Fast* (1981), FASSBINDER's *Veronika Voss* (1982), and David HARE's *Wetherby* (1985). In 1990 the Golden Bear was shared between MENZEL's *Larks on a String* and COSTA-GAVRAS's *Music Box*. The 1992 winner was

Lawrence Kasdan, for *Grand Canyon*. For many years films from the Eastern bloc countries were excluded.

Berlin Theatertreffen A German theatre festival held annually in Berlin. It was founded in 1963, partly with the aim of boosting morale in West Berlin following the erection of the Berlin Wall. The festival has traditionally been regarded as the most important showcase for the theatre of the German-speaking countries and regions. Each year a nine-person jury selects the best German-language productions of the past 12 months, which are then restaged in Berlin.

Bernhard, Thomas (1931–89) Austrian writer. After a childhood spent with his grandparents in Vienna and Seekirchen, Bernhard attended boarding school in Salzburg but left to become an apprentice in a grocer's shop. From 1949 onwards he suffered from a severe lung disease, as a result of which he had to spend long periods in sanatoriums and later to drop his studies of music and acting at the Akademie Mozarteum in Salzburg. In 1957 he became a full-time novelist and playwright.

Bernhard's first major success was his novel *Frost* (1963), which already maps out his future narrative landscape: the picturesque clichés of rural Austria are rudely assaulted and nature itself depicted as a perverse and inimical force. His protagonists in such works as *Gargoyles* (1967), *Correction* (1975), *Wittgenstein's Nephew* (1982), and *The Loser* (1989) are often failing artists or scientists, who are driven into suicide or madness. *Cutting Timber* (1984) and *Elimination* (1986) as well as his play *Heroes' Square* (1988) caused public scandals with their indictment of contemporary Austria as an unreformed Nazi state. Bernhard described himself as a 'destroyer of stories' and 'an artist in exaggeration'; certainly his highly rhetorical and hyperbolic narrative mode is closer to the baroque than the realist tradition. His five-part autobiography goes some way to explain the bitterness and negativity of his work. On his death Bernhard left an instruction in his will that for the duration of his publication rights no work of his may be published or produced in Austria and that his unpublished works must never be disclosed.

Berri, Claude (Claude Beri Langmann; 1934–) French film director and screenwriter, who has also starred in several of his own films. After experience as a film actor (1951–63), he won an Oscar for his direction of the short film *Le Poulet* (1963); he subsequently consolidated his reputation with *The Two of Us* (*Le Vieil Homme et l'enfant*; 1966), in which Berri, a Jew, drew on his experiences during the last months of World War II. *Marry Me! Marry Me!* (1968), a lively comedy in which Berri played a young Jewish bridegroom who falls for someone else shortly before his wedding, was equally well received.

During the 1970s Berri's films were less successful; *The Sex Shop* (1972) brought accusations of voyeurism, while *A Summer Affair* (1977) was said by the critics to be too bland. In the 1980s, however, he found a new audience with two films adapted from Marcel PAGNOL; *Jean de Florette* (1986), a beautifully observed story about a city-dweller's attempts to make a new life in the French countryside, starring Gérard Depardieu, and *Manon des Sources* (1986), in which the story is picked up ten years later. His most recent film, again starring Depardieu, is *Uranus* (1991), based on Marcel AYMÉ's novel about the ambiguities of wartime collaboration.

Berrocal, Miguel (1933–) Spanish sculptor. Born near Malága in Andalusia, Berrocal studied mathematics, chemistry, and architecture before deciding to become a sculptor. He trained at the School of Arts and Crafts and the School of Graphic Art in Madrid, later moving to Italy. More recently he has divided his time between Paris and his main base and foundry, the Villa Rizzardi di Negrar near Verona.

Berrocal's earliest work was in iron and shows the influence of the Spanish tradition of iron-working and the Spanish metal sculptor Julio González. His first works, produced in the mid 1950s, were abstract pieces of modest size with spiky elements but by the end of the decade his sculptures had become more massive. Since the 1960s his characteristic theme has been the human torso and his favoured material bronze. Some works refer to specifically Spanish subjects, such as *La Menina II* (1972), inspired by the painting *Las Meninas* by Velázquez. Berrocal has also designed sculptures with detachable sections that can be taken apart and reassembled by the spectator; some of these works have been produced in numerous copies, allowing them to find a wide ownership.

Bertolucci, Bernardo (1940–) Italian film director and poet, best known for such lavish epics as *1900* (1976) and *The Last Emperor* (1987). Bertolucci began his career as a poet, like his father, and won a major prize for his work while still at Rome University. However, an interest in film-making led him to become assistant director to PASOLINI on the latter's *Accattone* (1961). Pasolini wrote the script for Bertolucci's first film as director, *The Grim Reaper* (1962), a series of stylized reconstructions of the events leading up to the murder of a prostitute.

Bertolucci's second film, *Before the Revolution* (1964), was based on the writings of Stendhal; it attracted considerable attention with its analysis of the conflict between political conscience and the urge to bourgeois conformity. He returned to similar themes in *Partner* (1968), which was derived from Dostoevskii's *The Double*.

The Spider's Stratagem (1969) and *The Conformist* (1970), based on novels by Borges and MORAVIA respectively, explored the conflicts of loyalty created by the struggle against Fascism during World War II. Bertolucci's international reputation was enhanced by the success of *Last Tango in Paris* (1972), a brooding meditation on guilt, lust, and mortality, which created a sensation with its frank sexual scenes.

After the notoriety of *Last Tango*, Bertolucci indulged his taste for the epic with *1900* (1976), an extravaganza in which he attempted to trace the course of Italian history from 1900 to 1945; critics of the film questioned the coherence of its political content and the sacrifice of character to style. Similar criticisms were made of *La Luna* (1979), about an opera singer's love for her son, although *The Tragedy of a Ridiculous Man* (1982), a more political drama about a farmer's search for his missing son, was better received.

Bertolucci achieved his greatest popular success in 1987 with *The Last Emperor*, a lavish biopic about the last Chinese emperor, Pu Yi, emphasizing the contrast between his early years at court and his old age as a gardener under the communist regime. This film won no less than nine Oscars. *The Sheltering Sky* (1991), Bertolucci's latest film, was adapted from the novel by Paul Bowles.

Besson, Benno (1922–) Swiss theatre director and actor, who became a leading member of the BERLINER ENSEMBLE and subsequently emerged as one of the most admired directors in contemporary French, German, and Swiss theatre. He began his career working under SERRAU in Lyon before meeting BRECHT in Zürich and joining (1949) the Berliner Ensemble. He stayed with the Ensemble until 1958, winning acclaim for his adaptations of plays by Molière, Farquhar, and others. In 1960 he took over as director of the Deutsches Theater, transferring in 1969 to the Volksbühne, where he remained until 1977. In 1982 he became artistic director of the Comédie de Genève in Switzerland, where he consolidated his reputation for highly visual productions of both classics and new plays. Particularly successful productions in recent years have included revivals of several plays by Brecht, *Hamlet* (1977, 1983, and 1985), and *Rabbit Rabbit* (1986) by Elie Bourquin. He has also directed for the AVIGNON FESTIVAL.

Betjeman, Sir John (1906–84) British poet. Born in London to middle-class parents, he was educated at Marlborough and at Magdalen College, Oxford, where he mixed in fashionable circles and met contemporary poets such as W. H. Auden. He left university without taking a degree and taught in prep schools whilst beginning to publish his poetry. His first collection of verse, *Mount Zion*, appeared in 1932. This was followed by *Continual Dew* (1937), *Old Lights for New Chancels* (1940), *New Bats for Old Belfries* (1945), *A Few Late Chrysanthemums* (1954), *A Nip in the Air* (1974), and *High and Low* (1976). His *Collected Poems* appeared in 1958 (with an enlarged edition in 1962) and in 1960 he published a blank-verse autobiography, *Summoned by Bells*. With its adherence to traditional verse forms, its affectionate satire of the minutiae of provincial and suburban life, and its nostalgic Englishness, Betjeman's poetry has achieved widespread popularity in Britain. Although predominantly light in tone, there is an undercurrent of sadness and religious doubt and a marked preoccupation with death. Betjeman also wrote widely on architectural topics and helped to create an appreciation of Victorian and Edwardian architecture at a time when its merits were little regarded. Perhaps as a result of the apparent simplicity of his verse and its popularity with the general public, his work was neglected by serious critics in the 1950s and 1960s, but it has undergone a revival of interest in recent years. He was poet laureate from 1972 until his death.

Betti, Ugo (1892–1953) Italian playwright, poet, and short-story writer, whose plays drew heavily on his experience as a judge. Considered by many the natural successor to Pirandello, whose influence is discernible in several of the plays, Betti often explored themes of moral and religious belief in his work. He was recognized by critics as one of the most important modern Italian playwrights with his second play, *Landslide* (1936), which concerned an official inquiry into an accident. Several of his plays take the form of legal investigations or courtroom dramas: *Crime on Goat Island* (1948) and *Corruption in the Palace of Justice* (1949) are two examples. Other plays by Betti include the light comedy *Our Dreams* (1937), *The Burnt Flowerbed* (1942), *The Inquiry* (1947), and *The Queen and the Rebels* (1951), in which the life of a foolish queen is saved by the self-sacrifice of a prostitute.

Beuys, Joseph (1921–86) German sculptor and performance artist (*see* PERFORMANCE ART). Beuys served in the German air force during World War II and was badly injured when his plane crashed in the Crimea; according to his own account (which has been questioned) his life was saved by Tatars who wrapped him in felt and animal fat to prevent him from freezing to death. This supposedly explains the obsession with these materials shown in his art. After the war he studied at the Düsseldorf Academy of Arts (1947–52), where he later taught sculpture from 1961 until 1972, when he was dismissed for his left-wing political activities.

During the 1950s Beuys made cast bronze sculptures and also assemblages from refuse and other discarded items. From 1963 onwards he began to stage the 'actions' – ritualistic events with a strong element of the bizarre – for which he is best known (*see* ACTION AND BODY ART). In *How to Explain Pictures to a Dead Hare* (1965), for example, Beuys covered his head with honey and gold leaf and walked around an art gallery describing the pictures to a dead hare cradled in his arms. For *I Like America and America Likes Me* he spent a week locked in a cage with a wild coyote (and had 50 copies of the *Wall Street Journal* delivered daily), while for *Tallow* he arranged for 20 tons of molten animal fat to be poured into a void in a concrete bypass. While Beuys's early actions involved the creation, transformation, or destruction of works of art, he gradually abandoned formal artistic activity and concentrated on holding arguments and discussions, often in art galleries. Although Beuys came to consider the creation of art objects a reactionary activity some of the blackboards on which he wrote and drew during these later actions have been preserved. In the 1970s and 1980s Beuys became increasingly involved in radical and Green politics.

Biagi, Vittorio (1941–) Italian dancer, choreographer, and ballet director, who appeared widely throughout Europe before founding his own company. Born in Viareggio, Biagi studied dance in Genoa before joining La Scala in Milan in 1958. Two years later he was invited to join the BALLET OF THE 20TH CENTURY, where he won praise as a dancer in works by BÉJART and also made his debut as a choreographer with such pieces as *Jazz Impressions* (1964), *L'Aprés-midi d'un faune* (1964), and *Walpurgis Night* (1965).

In 1966 he transferred to the Opéra Comique in Paris but continued to choreograph for companies elsewhere, his works including steps for Ravel's *L'Enfant et les sortilèges* (1967) and Rameau's *Platée* (1968). He was appointed ballet director of the Lyons Ballet in 1969 and subsequently founded his own company, called Danza Prospettiva, in Italy. Ballets created by him for this troupe have included several works based on the music of Prokofiev and other pieces inspired by compositions by Berlioz, Beethoven, and Mahler.

Biermann, Wolf (1936–) German poet and singer-songwriter. Biermann was brought up in a working-class family in Hamburg. His childhood was scarred by the death of his Jewish and communist father in Auschwitz in 1943, an event that has had a formative influence on both his life and work. In 1953 Biermann chose to live in East Germany, where he studied political economics, mathematics, and philosophy at the Humboldt University, Berlin. From 1955 until 1957 he was an assistant producer with the BERLINER ENSEMBLE, where he became friends with BRECHT's widow, Helene Weigel, and the composer Hanns EISLER. Although a convinced Marxist, Biermann soon attracted official criticism for his satirical ballads, which voiced many of the frustrations of ordinary East Germans. He was banned from making public appearances in 1965 but his poetry and songs continued to circulate underground. His work was no less popular in West Germany, where the collection *Wire Harp* (1965) became the best-selling volume of poetry to appear since the war. The conflict with the authorities culminated in 1976 when Biermann was stripped of his citizenship while touring in the West. This caused a major upheaval among writers and intellectuals in both the Germanies. Biermann's political poems, songs, and essays are in the tradition of François Villon, Henrich Heine, Hanns Eisler, and Bertolt Brecht. Like Heine he combines the private with the public, the sensual with the political. His collections of words and music include *Germany. A Winter's Tale* (1972), *For My Comrades* (1972), and *The Prussian Icarus* (1978), in which poems written before and after his exile are separated by a blank page symbolizing the Berlin Wall. Since the coming down of the wall in 1989 Biermann has produced a running critical commentary on the process of German reunification.

Bill, Max (1908–) Swiss painter, sculptor, architect, and industrial designer. Bill was born at Winterthur, Switzerland, and trained as a silversmith at the Kunstgewerbeschule, Zürich. A lecture by LE CORBUSIER persuaded him to take up architecture, which he studied at the Bauhaus from 1927–28. Bill has worked mostly in Zürich, from 1929 as an abstract painter and sculptor, from 1936 as an architect, and from 1944 as an industrial designer. As a painter and sculptor, Bill practised a form of nonrepresentational abstraction based on mathematical principles that he himself termed 'concrete art' (borrowing a term invented by the Dutch painter Theo van Doesburg, 1883–1931). He organized exhibitions under the concrete art banner in Basle (1944) and Zürich (1960, 1964). His sculpture – for which he won a Grand Prix at the 1951 São Paulo Bienale – is sometimes seen as prefiguring MINIMAL ART. His architectural work does not fit readily into any school or category. Not a believer in system-building, he has conceived most of his 40-odd buildings from scratch. Temporary buildings, for example for the Swiss National Exhibition in 1939, the Swiss pavilions at the Milan Triennale and the Venice Biennale (1951–52), and for the Swiss National Exhibition in Lausanne (1961–64), helped Bill to develop techniques of prefabrication and increase building speeds. The buildings for the Hochschule für Gestaltung at Ulm (1951–55), where Bill served as director from 1951 until 1956, set a new standard in low-cost student accommodation. Bill was also a notable exhibition and theatre designer and did important work in advertising; his mastery of so many areas of design makes him a late exponent of the Bauhaus vision of *gesamtkunstwerk*.

Billetdoux, François (1927–91) French playwright, actor, and novelist, who trained under Charles Dullin and subsequently emerged as a highly original writer for the stage. His third novel, *Royal Garden Blues* (1957), attracted considerable attention although his early plays were not at first successful; *À la nuit la nuit* (1955) had to await a revival by BARRAULT in the 1980s before being noticed. *Tchin-Tchin* (1959), a tragicomedy about an affair between a bricklayer and a doctor's wife, established Billetdoux's reputation in the theatre and was translated into 19 languages. Among the plays that followed the most admired included *Chez Törpe* (1964), *How Goes the World, Sire? It Turns, Sire* (1964), depicting the meeting of two war heroes on release from concentration camp, the experimental drama *It is Necessary to Pass through the Clouds* (1964), and *Silence! The Tree Moves Again* (1967). Between 1974 and 1988 Billetdoux wrote nothing for the stage, concentrating instead on television screenplays. He returned to the theatre for the last time in 1988 with *Wake Up, Philadelphia*, in which a young girl finds herself trapped in an 84-year-old's body. He finished his final television screenplay, *Call from No-one to Nobody*, just 10 days before his death.

Bintley, David (Julian) (1957–) British choreographer and dancer. Bintley joined the Sadler's Wells Royal Ballet in 1976 and won praise as a dancer in ballets by MACMILLAN and other contemporary choreographers, as well as in classical works. He made his debut as a choreographer with the company in 1978 with *The Outsider*, based on the novel by CAMUS. Among the popular works that followed were *Take Five* (1978), set to the jazz music of Dave Brubeck, *Meadow of Proverbs* (1979), *Punch and the Street Party* (1979), *Homage to Chopin* (1980), *Adieu* (1980), *Polonia* (1980), and *Night Moves* (1981).

In 1983 he was appointed company choreographer with the Sadler's Wells Royal Ballet and in 1986 he became resident choreographer with the ROYAL BALLET (until 1993). His recent works have included *Metamorphosis* (1984), from the story by Kafka, *The Snow Queen* (1986), one of a series of three fairytales, *Allegri Diversi* (1987), the hugely popular *'Still Life' at the Penguin Café* (1988), in which the central characters were all representatives of endangered species, and *Tombeaux* (1993).

Birolli, Renato (1906–59) Italian painter. Born in Verona, Birolli studied briefly at the city's Accademia Cignaroli. He then moved to Milan, where he remained. Throughout his life he was involved with groups or movements of painters. From 1928 he was a member of the Comitato Direttivo del Novecento Italiano, a group that sought to maintain a naturalistic art rooted in Italian traditions. At this stage Birolli painted in an expressionist manner influenced by van Gogh but he later came under the influence of Picasso and adopted a more contemporary style. In 1938 he formed the Corrente, an association of artists that sought to uphold modern art at a time when Nazi opposition to modernism was becoming influential in Italy. The association was broken up by World War II, during which Birolli was persecuted and imprisoned.

In 1946 Birolli formed the FRONTE NUOVO DELLE ARTI, which brought together painters and sculptors interested in the newest artistic ideas, including US abstract expressionism. The group split in 1948 into those who upheld realism and those, like Birolli, who were comitted to expressive abstraction (*see* ART INFORMEL). In 1952 he became a member of a new group of abstract painters, the Gruppo degli Otto Pittori Italiani.

Birtwistle, Sir Harrison (Paul) (1934–) British composer. He studied the clarinet and composition at the Royal Manchester College of Music in the 1950s, where he was part of the Manchester New Music Group with GOEHR, Maxwell DAVIES, and John Ogdon. Subsequently he worked as a teacher and clarinettist. In 1967 he and Davies formed the Pierrot Players (later the FIRES OF LONDON) to perform chamber pieces with a theatrical element. In 1975 he was appointed music director of the National Theatre.

His own compositions are comparable with Stravinsky's in their use of ritual and with Varèse's in their violent subject-matter and imagery. Stylistically they are highly dissonant and make heavy use of ostinati. The preoccupation with ritualized violence is evident in the operas *Punch and Judy* (1968), based on the traditional puppet show, *The Mask of Orpheus* (1986), a complex examination of the classical myth, and *Gawain* (1991), an interpretation of the Middle English poem *Gawain and the Green Knight*. He was knighted in 1988. His other works include the opera *Yan Tan Tethera* (1986; libretto by Tony HARRISON), the dramatic cantatas *Down by the Greenwood Side* (1969) and *Bow Down* (1977), and the orchestral work *The Triumph of Time* (1972).

Bischof, Werner (1916–54) Swiss photographer. After studying in his native Zürich, Bischof worked for the Swiss picture magazine *Du* from 1942 to 1944. His most notable early works are a series of finely etched still lives in which shadow and light are used to subtle aesthetic effect. From 1945 onwards Bischof turned his technical prowess to the depiction of human misery in war-shattered Europe. His studies of life in France, Germany, the Netherlands, Italy, and Greece appeared in *Life*, *Picture Post*, *Paris Match* and many other journals. Bischof avoided ephemeral news photography but committed himself to covering major contemporary events; he covered the 1948 Olympic Games in London and joined the Magnum Photos cooperative agency in 1949. In the early 1950s, Bischof covered the Korean War for *Life* and travelled through India and Asia, publishing his last book *Japan* in 1954. He died in a motor accident in the Peruvian Andes.

Bitov, Andrei Georgievich (1937–) Russian prose writer. Born in Leningrad, he served in the army and studied mining before beginning to publish short stories in 1958. A disciple of Nabokov, he himself has considerably influenced the work of Tatiana TOLSTAIA. The majority of his stories, amongst the best collections of which are *The Big Balloon* (1963) and *Country Place* (1967), show a young, often lonely, urban man trying to come to terms with his life, fellow human beings, and natural surroundings. Somewhat Chekhovian in their fleeting moods of doubt and introspection, Bitov's stories make much use of psychologically subtle interior monologue. In their sinuous syntax they also recall something of the elegance of Nabokov, whose novel *The Gift* (1938, revised 1952) provides one of the keys to Bitov's *magnum opus Pushkin House* (1978), a fascinating novel which, like so much modern Russian fiction, is concerned with literature itself, in particular the classical tradition of Pushkin, Gogol, and Dostoevskii. Set in Leningrad, it paints a richly textured, entertaining, and unflattering picture of three generations of the Russian intelligentsia. First published in the US, *Pushkin House* appeared in Russia only in 1987, sixteen years after it was written.

Bjørneboe, Jens Ingvald (1920–76) Norwegian novelist, playwright, essayist, and poet; one of Scandinavia's most prolific and controversial writers. He made his literary debut in 1952 with *Before The Cock Crows*, a novel that uses the setting of a German concentration camp to explore the nature of evil, a subject Bjørneboe often returned to in his later works. His breakthrough came in 1955 with the novel *Jonas*, which attacked Norway's repressive educational system and examined Steiner teaching methods. A fierce polemicist, Bjørneboe constantly attacked authoritarian systems and oppressive social measures, leaving political and legal furore in his wake. He created a new kind of anti-novel in the trilogy *Moment Of Freedom* (1966), *The Powder Magazine* (1969), and *Silence* (1973), which explores man's inhumanity to man throughout history. Two of his novels, *Without a Stitch I* and *II* (1966 and 1967) were banned in Norway as pornographic.

Bjørneboe's best plays were written in the 1960s and were greatly influenced by BRECHT. *Today's The Day* (1965) is a hard-hitting attack on the dehumanization of prison inmates by the system. *The Bird Lovers* (1966) is an exposé of neo-Nazism and the power of money; it deals with an economic victory over a small Mediterranean village by Nazis who failed to capture it during the war. Bjørneboe's work revels in paradox and irony and constantly inverts accepted ideas of the truth. He had no time for courtesy or compromise and remained controversial until his suicide in 1976.

Bjørnvig, Thorkild (1918–) Danish poet, essayist, and literary scholar. Born in Århus, Bjørnvig studied literature before making his debut with the highly acclaimed collection of poems, *The Star Beyond the Gable* (1947). The following year he became coeditor of a new arts periodical, *Heretica*. A second poetry collection, *Eternal Springtime*, appeared in 1954 followed by *Anubis* (1955), a volume of intense love poems. The poems in *Figure and Fire* (1959) display greater formal complexity while *Vibrations* (1966) returns to a freer use of rhythm. *The Raven* (1968) is a cycle of poems on which Bjørnvig had worked for 30 years.

Several of Bjørnvig's collections deal with environmental concerns and attack the arrogance of the modern technological era. These include *The Dolphin* (1975), for which the author received the Danish Critics' Prize, *Ape Gods* (1981), and *Epimetheus* (1990).

Bjørnvig's doctoral thesis on the work of the Danish writer Martin A. Hansen caused considerable debate in the literary world when published in 1964. In 1974 he published a volume of reminiscences about his friend Karen Blixen.

He has published many essays in the field of literary research, notably those in the collection *Reality* (1973). He has also translated several foreign poets, including Rilke, into Danish.

Blacher, Boris (1903–1975) German composer and teacher, born in China of Russian-German parentage. He studied music in Irkutsk, Siberia, and Charbin, China, before moving to Berlin (1922), where he studied at the Musikhochschule and the University. After teaching at the Dresden Conservatory he became professor of composition and subsequently (1953–70) director at the Berlin Musikhochschule. He was president of the West Berlin Academy of Arts (1968–71).

Blacher's early compositions were influenced by Stravinsky and the music of Les Six, especially Milhaud. Another important influence was jazz, the rhythms of which helped Blacher to formulate his concept of 'variable metre', a technique he deployed for the first time in the piano piece *Ornamente* (1950). The same year saw his first significant use of 12-note procedures in the ballet *Lysistrata*. Most of Blacher's important works were for the theatre; they include *Romeo und Julia* (1943), *Die Flut* (1946), and *Zweihunderttausend* (1969) and the ballets *Hamlet* (1949) and *Tristan* (1965). He experimented with electronic sounds in the 1960s. Blacher's best-known piece remains the orchestral *Paganini Variations* (1947), the work that established his reputation.

Black, Sir James Whyte (1924–) British biochemist. Black graduated from St Andrews University in 1946 and later joined ICI as a pharmacologist (1958–64). After working with Smith, Kline and French he became professor of pharmacology at University College, London (1973–77), before joining Wellcome as Director of Therapeutic Research (1978–84). Since 1984 he has been professor of analytical pharmacology at King's College Hospital, London.

In his search for a drug to relieve angina he isolated the first beta-blockers, now widely used to treat hypertension and heart conditions. His subsequent work has been concerned with the control of gastric ulcers and his discovery of the drug cimetidine, which blocks the histamine receptors that stimulate the secretion of stomach ulcers. For this work and his work on beta-blockers he shared the 1988 Nobel Prize for physiology or medicine.

Blake, Peter (1932–) British pioneer of POP ART. Blake studied art at the Gravesend School of Art (1946–51) and at the Royal College of Art in London (1953–56). In 1956–57 he travelled on the continent, studying the folk art of western European countries. From 1960 to 1964 he taught at the St Martin's School of Art, the Harrow School of Art, and the Walthamstow School of Art in London and from 1964 to 1974 at the Royal College of Art.

In his early paintings Blake applied the 'naive' styles of folk art to subjects drawn from modern popular culture. He has shown a particular fascination with such ephemera as toys, comics, and pin-up photographs and with popular entertainers such as wrestlers and striptease artists. A characteristic work of 1957, *On the Balcony* (Tate Gallery, London), depicts children amidst photographs, tourist souvenirs, postcards, and magazine covers. Later works, many of them collages, show the influence of advertising and commercial design. His best-known work is undoubtedly the collage cover for the Beatles' LP record *Sergeant Pepper's Lonely Hearts Club Band* (1967). Blake's use of material from the commercial world made him one of the leading figures of the Pop Art movement of the late 1950s and 1960s. In 1975, however, he withdrew to the English countryside and helped to found the **Brotherhood of Ruralists**, a group of figurative artists who took their inspiration from Shakespeare and the Pre-Raphaelites. Several of his paintings from this period feature fairy characters from Shakespeare's *A Midsummer Night's Dream*. A retrospective of his work was held at the Tate Gallery in 1983.

Blaska, Félix (1941–) French dancer, choreographer, and ballet director, who emerged as one of the most dynamic and prolific French choreographers of the 1960s and 1970s. After training in Paris, Blaska danced with a number of leading companies, including that of Roland PETIT, for whom he did his first work as a choreographer in 1966. After success with such pieces as *Octandre*, *Les Affinités électives*, and *Die Wahlverwandtschaften*, he was invited (1968) to create further works for the newly founded BALLET-THÉÂTRE CONTEMPORAIN in Amiens. The company subsequently presented performances of Blaska's *Danses concertantes* and *Equivalences*.

In 1969 Blaska founded Les Ballets de Félix Blaska, which has been based at Grenoble since 1972; the company has regularly performed works by its founder both in France and abroad. Blaska has consolidated his reputation with works created for several other companies, among them the Marseilles Opéra, the

Royal Danish Ballet, and the Paris Opéra. His many ballets include *Electro-Bach* (1969), *Deuxième Concerto* (1970), *Arcana* (1973), and *Spectacle Berio* (1974). In 1981 he cofounded the US dance-theatre company Crowsnest.

Bleasdale, Alan (1946–) British playwright and novelist, who established his reputation in the 1980s with his screenplays for television. Throughout his career he has been closely associated with his home town, Liverpool, which featured prominently in *Boys from the Blackstuff* (1982), a bleak comedy about the city's unemployed, which first brought Bleasdale to notice and won him numerous prizes, including the Best British TV Drama of the Decade award. Among subsequent successes have been the stage musical *Are you Lonesome Tonight?* (1985), about the life of Elvis Presley, the screenplay for the film *No Surrender* (1986), and the television series *The Monocled Mutineer* (1986), which aroused controversy for its intermingling of fiction with historical events. *GBH* (1991), a return to contemporary Liverpool, was a complex tragicomedy about municipal politics.

Blier, Bertrand (1939–) French film director. The son of the film actor Bernard Blier (1916–89), he worked as an assistant to a series of leading directors and directed a number of documentaries in the CINÉMA VÉRITÉ style before graduating to feature films. After *Hitler? Connais Pas!* (1962) he enjoyed his first major success with *Les Valseuses* (1974), a deliberately shocking story featuring the then unknown Gérard Depardieu and Patrick Dewaere as two petty criminals with a cavalier disregard for everything except their own sexual pleasure. *Get Out Your Handkerchiefs* (1978) again starred Depardieu and Dewaere as loutish young men totally unable to comprehend the emotions of the women in their lives; it won an Oscar.

Buffet froid (1979), often considered Blier's best film, concerns the empathy between a confused psychotic (played by Depardieu), a mass murderer, and a callous police inspector (played by Bernard Blier). Subsequently Blier continued to explore the weaknesses of the male psyche in such films as *Stepfather* (1981), starring Dewaere as a widower tempted by his 14-year-old stepdaughter, *My Best Friend's Girl* (1983), *Our Story* (1984), and *Evening Dress* (1986), a biting comedy in which Depardieu excelled as a burglar who forms a ménage-à-trois with a frustrated housewife and her meek husband. Blier's recent films include *Trop belle pour toi* (1989), a black comedy about sexual obsession in which the influence of BUÑUEL is particularly apparent. It features Depardieu as a rich businessman who spurns his beautiful wife for a dowdy secretary. The film won a Special Jury Prize at the CANNES FILM FESTIVAL. Elements of surrealism also appeared in *Merci La Vie* (1991), a dark comedy about the activities of two promiscuous girls in a seaside town.

Blin, Roger (1907–84) French actor and theatre director, noted for his productions of plays by leading contemporary playwrights. For most of his career he was closely associated with the absurdists, often working in collaboration with Artaud and BARRAULT. His performance in and direction of the first production of BECKETT's *Waiting for Godot* (1953) won special praise; subsequently he also directed plays by ADAMOV and GENET. One hallmark of his distinctive style of production was his practice of designing his own sets, which he considered an integral part of a director's function.

Blom, Piet (1934–) Dutch architect. Born in Amsterdam, Blom trained at the Architecture Academy there under Aldo van EYCK (1956–62) and set up in private practice in Monickendam in 1967. Under van Eyck's influence he became a leading adherent of STRUCTURALISM in architecture, as opposed to the dominant modernist functionalism. Blom stressed the importance of the intermediate spaces between buildings and insisted on flexibility in building use, whether on a small or a large scale. He aimed to realize van Eyck's vision of the 'casbah organisée', allowing for individual variations and changes within an overall plan and designing with the consciousness that buildings change over time.

His first major work, the Boerderj Students Building at Twente Technical University (1962), was a conversion of farm buildings. The Spielhuis Leisure Centre in Helmond, Netherlands (1975–78), comprising a theatre, small halls, and dwellings, is based on the theme of a cube standing on one corner. Blom's most vigorous attempt to realize his programme was the 'Kasbah' housing development in Hengelo, although the communal areas were not completed as intended.

Blomdahl, Karl-Birger (1916–1968) Swedish composer and teacher. A pupil of Hilding Rosenberg from 1935, Blomdahl was a leading member of the Monday Group, an association of avant-garde musicians who met during the 1940s in Blomdahl's Stockholm flat to pursue their ideas for a new Swedish music. Their desire to fuse their new understanding of Bach and Renaissance composers with their knowledge of Hindemith is reflected in works such as Blomdahl's concerto grosso (1944). Following trips abroad in 1946 and 1947, Blomdahl's music began to show the influence of Bartók, Stravinsky, and Berg: his third symphony (*Facetter*; 1950) employs tonally oriented serialism within Bartókian structures. His 'space opera' *Aniara* (1958) remains his best-known work, its eclectic style encompassing jazz elements and electronics.

A crucial figure in the promotion of modern music in post-war Sweden, Blomdahl exerted a wide influence as a teacher and through his links with Swedish television and radio. He was a professor at the Royal Swedish Academy (1960–64) and director of the Swedish radio music department (1965–68). Later works include the orchestral piece *Forma Ferritonans* (1961) and the ballets *Minotaurus* (1957) and *Game for Eight* (1962).

Blumenberg, Hans (1920–) German philosopher. Blumenberg obtained degrees from Kiel University in 1947 and 1950 and subsequently taught philosophy in Hamburg, Giessen, Bochum, and Münster.

In *Paradigms Towards a Metaphorology* (1960) Blumenberg provides an outline of his general philosophical outlook and method. Traditional metaphors and stories, he believes, far from being mere literary figments, provide the only real means of interpreting the human situation. The proper task of philosophy is not to translate metaphors into some other form of discourse, but to assess them on their own terms. In *The Genesis of the Copernican World* (1975) and *The Legitimacy of the Modern Age* (1966) Blumenberg argues that it is misleading to see modern 'myths' – such as the ideas of progress or equality – as no more than secularized versions of older religious beliefs; they have their own legitimacy. In other books Blumenberg has explored the history of particular metaphors: *The Legibility of the World* (1981), for instance, investigates comparisons of the world to a book, while *Work on Myth* (1979) deals with the Prometheus story as a metaphor for the human condition. *The Laughter of the Maid* (1987) explores the story about Thales, the first philosopher, falling into a well while gazing at the stars, that was used by Plato to illustrate the relationship of the philosopher to the world around him. Blumenberg has been criticized for promenading endlessly around the great problems of philosophy rather than tackling them directly; but in his opinion this is all we can do.

Bobrowski, Johannes (1917–65) German poet and writer. Bobrowski abandoned his studies in the history of art to fight in World War II, serving in France, Poland, and the Soviet Union, where he was a prisoner of war from 1945 to 1949. On his return to Germany he worked in East Berlin as a publisher's editor.

Bobrowski is celebrated for his nature poetry, the importance of which for post-war German literature is now widely recognized. His poetry combines tradition and modernity, incorporating, for example, strikingly modern symbolism within conventional formal structures. The poems in *Shadow Lands* (1962) and *From the Rivers* (English translation 1975) evoke the landscapes and history of Sarmatia, an imaginary East European country haunted by its troubled past. His poetry articulates a sense of German as well as personal guilt. Bobrowski pursues similar themes in his novels *Levin's Mill* (1963) and *Lithuanian Pianos* (1966).

Bodor, Adam (1950–) Hungarian novelist and short-story writer. Born in Cluj, Romania, Bodor played a key role in the literary life of the Hungarian minority in Transylvania in the 1960s and 1970s. His first volume of short stories appeared in 1969 and he published four more collections before moving to Hungary in 1982. He now lives and works in Budapest. He won great critical acclaim with his sixth volume of stories, *The Euphrates at Babylon*, and is regarded by many as the most accomplished practitioner of the short story writing in Hungarian today. Set against the political and physical landscape of present-day Transylvania, Bodor's stories focus on the helplessness of the individual in a bleak and bizarre world of uncertainty, suspicion, and constant surveillance, but remain devoid of moral comment. Bodor's most recent work, a novel entitled *Sinistra District* (1992), grows directly out of the themes and concerns of his earlier stories; it describes the disturbing irrational world of a society of eternal outsiders somewhere among the Carpathians. *Sinistra District* has been widely received as the first masterpiece of post-communist Hungarian literature.

Body Art *See* ACTION AND BODY ART.

Bofill, Ricardo (1939–) Spanish (Catalan) architect. Born and trained in Barcelona, Bofill inherited something of the tradition of Catalan surrealism of Gaudí, Dalí, and Miró. He founded his firm Taller de Arquitectura in Barcelona in 1960, and it has built extensively in Spain and France. The practice has concentrated on mass housing, its peculiar characteristic being the use of giant and dramatic sculptural forms, together with the application of simplified or colossally inflated classical ornament. The most dramatic examples are all in France. The Le Viaduc housing scheme at St Quentin-en-Yvelines (1971–83), consists of 398 apartments in the form of a gigantic viaduct over a lake. In 1978–82 the even larger Palais d'Abraxas project, was built in Marne-la-Vallée near Paris, housing 441 apartments in Roman amphitheatre and theatre forms. A 288-apartment scheme, 'Antigone', rose in Montpellier between 1978 and 1985 and another, 'Les Echelles du Baroque', in Paris between 1979 and 1985. Since 1978 Bofill has also been involved in town planning in Algeria, notably with the Honari Boumedienne Agricultural Village.

Bohigas (Guardiola), Oriol *See* MARTORELL, BOHIGAS, AND MACKAY.

Böhm, Gottfried (1920–) German architect. The son of the church architect Dominikus Böhm (1880–1955), he has inherited his father's spiritual approach to the plasticity of form and space but has widened its application to municipal buildings, town planning, and offices. Based in Cologne, he is unusual in combining a strong regional identity with an international reputation.

Bohm's strong visual style evolved through a series of simple churches culminating in the dramatically rectangular Queen of Grace Church at Kassel-Wilhelmschohe (1958). Even more spectacular were his adaptations of ancient ruins into new buildings, beginning with his conversion of Bad Godesberg Castle into a restaurant and hotel (1956–57); heavy concrete forms now compliment the medieval remains. During the 1960s he continued this exploration of concrete, most remarkably at Bensberg Town Hall (1962–64), built on the foundations of a circular fortress and topped by a multifaceted tower. Another polygonal building was the massive Pilgrimage Church at Neviges (1962–64).

This use of historicism to inform adventurous new work continued in the 1970s. Bohm's Civic Centre at Bergisch Gladbach (1977–80) incorporated old houses and revitalized the market square, whilst at Bad Godesberg he linked the castle gardens and a dull 1950s development with an exciting walkway. His dynamism and sense of purpose produced much good public housing, notably in Cologne. Since the late 1970s Bohm has veered towards larger projects and away from concrete. Most acclaimed were his Zublin offices in Stuttgart, where a huge glazed atrium cuts the building to give views of the countryside beyond. Wholly modern, it shows the same love of space and landscape that flows through all his work.

Böll, Heinrich (1917–85) German writer. Böll was born in Cologne, the eighth child of Catholic parents. After secondary school he began an apprenticeship as a bookseller but abandoned it in 1939 in order to study German literature. During World War II he fought in the army and was briefly a Soviet prisoner of war. A founder of GRUPPE 47, Böll won the group's prestigious prize in 1951, becoming a full-time writer soon afterwards. In the 1960s and 1970s Böll became famous in West Germany not only for his writing but also for his dissenting views on a variety of public issues. Thus, for example, he attacked the tabloid press for its sensationalist coverage of the Baader-Meinhof terrorism, supported the antinuclear and peace movements, and championed the rights of minorities such as gypsies.

Böll's work constitutes a running moral and satirical commentary on post-war German history. His first novel to find international acclaim was *The Clown* (1963). Written from the viewpoint of the clown Hans Schnier, the novel attacks the political restoration of the Adenauer era and the collaboration of church and state in suppressing the guilt of the Nazi past. In *End of a Mission* (1966) and his most ambitious novel, *Group Portrait with Lady* (1971), Böll presents the conscience of the individual as the last line of defence for humanism. This was followed by *The Lost Honour of Katharina Blum* (1974) in which he attacked the abuses of the press and its power to destroy the individual. His novels have been criticized for their lack of formal innovation and for their moralism. But for Böll literature had to be anchored in reality as well as committed to a Utopian humanism. In 1972 he became the first post-war German writer to win the Nobel Prize for literature. Among other important works are *The Bread of our Early Years* (1957) and *Billiards at Half-Past Nine* (1959).

Bolognini, Mauro (1923–) Italian film director, whose work gives an optimistic picture of contemporary Italian life. Bolognini studied architecture at the University of France before training in set design at Rome's Centro Sperimentale di Cinematografia. He worked as an assistant director to ZAMPA and in France before making his directorial debut in 1953; international interest first came his way with *Wild Love* (1955). His successful stylish films, many of which he coscripts himself, include *Young Husbands* (1957), *From a Roman Balcony* (1960), *The Love Makers* (1960), *That Splendid November* (1968), *Black Journal* (1977), *The True Story of Camille* (1981), and *Goodbye Moscow* (1987).

Bolt, Robert (Oxton) (1924–) British playwright and screenwriter, whose works have encompassed a wide range of styles. He made his name in the theatre with *Flowering Cherry* (1957), in which Ralph Richardson took the lead, but received even greater praise for his play on the life of Sir Thomas More, *A Man for All Seasons* (1960), which reflected the influence of BRECHT. Subsequent plays included *Vivat! Vivat Regina!* (1970), about the relationship between Elizabeth I and Mary Queen of Scots, and his last work for the stage, *State of Revolution* (1977); his works for children – among them *The Thwarting of Baron Bolligrew* (1966) – have enjoyed similar success.

Bolt has also had a long association with the film director David LEAN, beginning with the screenplay for Lean's epic *Lawrence of Arabia* (1962) and continuing with *Doctor Zhivago* (1965), *Ryan's Daughter* (1970), and *A Passage to India* (1984). His screenplays for other directors have included those for *The Bounty* (1984) and Roland JOFFE's *The Mission* (1986). He has continued to write for both the stage and the screen in recent years, despite being severely disabled by a stroke. He is married to the actress Sarah Miles.

Bond, Edward (1934–) British playwright and theatre director, noted for his stark dramas of violence and injustice and his Marxist commitment. Many of Bond's plays have roused controversy, especially his second play *Saved* (1965), which – with its brutal stoning to death of a baby in its pram – had to be staged as a private performance at the Royal Court Theatre in order to evade censorship. The subsequent imposition of a small fine on the theatre fuelled the growing mood of protest that led to the dismantling of institutionalized censorship of the theatre in Britain.

Bond's other plays, among them *The Pope's Wedding* (1962), *Narrow Road to the Deep North* (1968), *Bingo* (1973), and *The Woman* (1978), have offered radical, often savage, reassessments of historical events and characters. *Black Mass* (1970) was written in support of the antiapartheid movement, while *Passion* (1971) was commissioned by CND, and *Stone* (1976) tackled homosexual issues. His most recent works for the stage have included the commercially successful *Restoration* (1981), which was revived by the RSC in 1989, *Derek* (1983), the trilogy *The War Plays* (1985), and *September* (1990).

Bond has also produced volumes of poetry, translations of Chekhov and Wedekind, libretti for HENZE's operas *We Come to the River* (1976) and *The English Cat* (1982), and screenplays for several films including ANTONIONI's *Blow-Up* (1967).

Bondarchuk, Sergei (1920–) Russian film director, screenwriter, and actor. A child actor, he learned the Stanislavsky Method at the Rostov Drama School. After entertaining Red Army troops during World War II, he studied at Moscow's All-Union State Institute of Cinematography. He made his film debut in GERASIMOV's *The Young Guard* (1948) and soon developed into a star of the Soviet cinema. Among his title roles were *Taras Shevchenko* (1951) and *Othello* (1956), in which he appeared opposite Irina Skobtseva, whom he subsequently married. Bondarchuk made an impressive debut as a director with *Fate of a Man* (1959), an intimate and realistic look at the way in which individuals cope with war; the film is unusually free from propaganda. He also played the leading role.

The crowning glory of Bondarchuk's career, and the most ambitious effort in Soviet cinema history, was his four-part screen version of Tolstoy's *War and Peace* (1966), which took five years to complete and cost up to $70 million; he again took the leading role. Bondarchuk followed this with another epic, the Soviet-Italian co-production *Waterloo* (1970), which culminated in a spectacular hour-long battle sequence. Since then, he has returned to Russian themes in Chekhov's *Uncle Vanya* (1974), *The Steppe*, which he also scripted, and *Ten Days That Shook the World* (1982), a remaking of the Eisenstein epic about the Bolshevik Revolution. Recent films include *Boris Godunov* (1987).

Bondi, Sir Hermann (1919–) British mathematician and cosmologist, born in Austria. Bondi studied at Cambridge University, where he later taught. In 1954 he moved to London to take up the chair in mathematics at King's College. Bondi has always been actively interested in the wider implications of science and the scientific outlook. He has served as chief scientific adviser to the British ministry of defence (1971–77) and chief scientist at the department of energy (1977–80). He was master of Churchill College, Cambridge (1983–90).

Bondi's most important work has been in applied mathematics and especially in cosmology. In collaboration with Thomas GOLD, he propounded (1948) a new version of the steady-state theory of the universe first suggested by Fred HOYLE. This, among other topics, forms the substance of Bondi's book *Cosmology* (1952). Bondi and Gold's model was innovatory in postulating that there is continuous creation of matter in order to maintain the universe's homogeneity despite the fact that it was known to be expanding. Although it enjoyed considerable popularity, the steady-state model is now considered to have been decisively refuted by observational evidence and the big-bang theory is favoured. Bondi's books include *Relativity and Commonsense* (1964), *Assumption and Myth in Physical Theory* (1967), and his autobiography *Science, Churchill and Me* (1990).

Bonet, Pep *See* STUDIO PER.

Bonnefoy, Yves (1923–) French poet and critic. Bonnefoy studied mathematics and philosophy at the Universities of Poitiers and Paris; he was briefly a member of the Surrealist group. Besides his poetry he has published numerous essays, the biography *Rimbaud* (1961), and translations of Shakespeare. In 1981 he was appointed professor of literature at the Collège de France, Paris.

Bonnefoy first came to the attention of the literary world with *On the Motion and Immobility of Douve* (1953), a poem sequence about the life of a loved woman that is at the same time an evocation of the river Douve and a meditation on poetry itself. In his poetry Bonnefoy turned away from his earlier surrealism, feeling that it paid insufficient attention to physical reality. His poems seek to evoke the reality of simple material things – such as a cloud, a stone, or a river – while simultaneously exploring their imaginative and metaphysical significance. Much of Bonnefoy's poetry is inspired by the barren landscape of the Haute Provence where he at one time lived. He writes mainly in traditional metrical forms. Bonnefoy's subsequent collections of poetry are *Yesterday the Desert Reigned* (1958), *Anti-Platon* (1962), *Written Stone* (1965), and *The Bait of the Threshold* (1975). He has also published a number of scholarly works on the history of art and literature, including *The Second Simplicity* (1961), *The Red Cloud* (1977), and *Conversations about Poetry* (1981).

Booker Prize (the Booker McConnell Prize for Fiction) British literary prize, founded in 1968 by the multinational company Booker McConnell Ltd and awarded for the best English-language novel published in the previous 12 months by a citizen of Britain, the Commonwealth, the Republic of Ireland, or South

Africa. The winner is chosen from a shortlist of about six books by a small jury of writers and critics. The aim of the prize, which is currently worth £20,000, is to stimulate public interest in the shortlisted writers and in quality contemporary fiction in general. The announcement of the jury's decision has been televised live since 1981 and the resulting publicity has had a substantial effect on the sales of all shortlisted books. Past winners include V. S. NAIPAUL, Iris MURDOCH, William GOLDING, and Salman RUSHDIE. The most recent winners are A. S. BYATT's *Possession* (1990), *The Famished Road* by Ben Okri (1991), and Michael Ondaatje's *The English Patient* and Barry Unsworth's *Sacred Hunger*, which shared the prize in 1992.

The first International Booker Prize was awarded to the Russian author Mark Kharitonov for his novel *Lines of Fate, or Milashevich's Casket* in 1992.

Boorman, John (1933–) British film and television director, regarded as one of the leading talents in the contemporary cinema. Boorman began his career as a critic before working on documentaries for television. His first full-length film, *Point Blank* (1967), attracted attention with its creative approach to the traditional thriller. The theme of self-discovery was further explored in *Hell in the Pacific* (1969), a World War II drama in which a US and a Japanese soldier pursue their own private version of the larger conflict on a desert island, in the less well-received *Leo the Last* (1970), and in the enormously popular *Deliverance* (1972), about four business executives who find their lives threatened by maniacal hillbillies while holidaying in a wilderness area of the US.

In contrast, such films as *Zardoz* (1974), a science-fiction epic, and *Excalibur* (1981), a departure into Arthurian legend, failed to please either critics or audiences, provoking accusations of pretentiousness and incoherence. More recent films such as *The Emerald Forest*, about a father's search for his son, who has been brought up by an Indian tribe in the threatened rain forest, and *Hope and Glory* (1987), a nostalgic recreation of London during the Blitz, have had greater success. In 1992 he launched *Projections*, an annual magazine intended as a forum for film-makers.

Borgen, Johan (1902–79) Norwegian novelist and literary critic. A product of the middle-class society he was later to portray as threatened by destruction, he began his career as a journalist for a national newspaper. His satirical attacks on the Nazis led to his arrest following the occupation and subsequent imprisonment in a concentration camp. He later wrote about this experience in the novel *Days at Grini* (1945).

Borgen made his literary debut in 1925 with the stylistically varied collection of novellas *Towards Darkness*, which explores human loneliness and confusion, often from the viewpoint of a child. His short stories, which appeared in a collected edition in 1961, are realistic with a strong vein of social comment; they are ironic, playful, serious, romantic, and above all lyrical. The stories often investigate the ways in which an individual's identity has been shaped by events in his or her past. Borgen's best-known work is the trilogy of psychological novels *Little Lord* (1955), *The Dark Springs* (1956) and *We Have Him Now* (1957), which traces the downfall of the protagonist, Wilfred Sagen, through his inability to balance the different sides of his character, especially in his relationships with others.

Borgen often experimented stylistically and was the first Norwegian writer to exploit Freud's theories of psychoanalysis. His subject matter reflects his experiences during the war, his work in journalism, and the political and social changes he witnessed. He remained highly productive until his death.

Bornkamm, Günther (1905–89) German Protestant theologian. Bornkamm began his career teaching theology in Königsberg and Bethel. After the Nazi authorities closed the theological school at Bethel in 1939 he worked as a pastor in Münster and Dortmund. He later taught theology of the New Testament in Göttingen (1946–49) and Heidelberg (from 1949).

The main theme of Bornkamm's work is the relation between history and religious belief in the New Testament, especially concerning the person of Jesus Christ. Bornkamm rejected the opinion of his teacher Bultmann that attempts to find the 'historical Jesus' were futile and that the entire New Testament had to be interpreted as an expression of faith alone. In his most widely read book *Jesus of Nazareth* (1956) he argued that although the nature of the sources makes a historical biography of Jesus impossible, there is still scope for a historical approach towards the events of the New Testament and their background.

In his study *Paul* (1969) Bornkamm again discusses the relation between history and belief, concluding that the story of Paul has to be interpreted theologically as well as biographically. Bornkamm's chief distinction lies in his introduction of a careful and balanced historical approach to the basic documents of the Christian religion.

Borowczyk, Walerian (1923–) Polish film director, living in France since 1959, who established a strong reputation with his animated films and dramas during the 1960s and 1970s. Having begun as an artist, Borowczyk made a series of animated shorts that demonstrated both his flair for the original and his taste for the cruel and macabre. He made his debut as a director of live action with *Goto, Isle of Love* (1969), a surrealistic tale of romance in a strange authoritarian state; once again, images of torture and oppression were pervasive.

In *Blanche* (1972), based on a story by Mazeppa, Borowczyk recreated life in a medieval French chateau, winning praise for his deft handling of the themes of betrayal and cruelty. Subsequent films have included *Immoral Tales* (1974), *The Story of Sin* (1974), *The Beast* (1975), and *Blood of Doctor Jekyll* (1981); latterly he has made a series of pornographic films.

Bortolotti, Mauro (1926–) Italian composer and teacher. He studied piano, organ, and composition at the Rome Conservatory (1944–56), where his teachers included PETRASSI. Subsequently he attended the DARMSTADT summer courses from 1957 to 1968, developing an interest in electronic music that was furthered by studies in Florence and Pisa during 1967. In 1961 he became a founder member of Nuova Consonanza, an avant-garde improvisation group based in Rome, where he teaches at the Accademia Nazionale di Danza.

His earliest work shows the influence of Bartók – especially the accessible Bartók of the *Concerto for Orchestra* – a composer on whom Bortolotti modelled himself on the advice of Petrassi. Attendance at Darmstadt was crucial for his acquisition of such modern techniques as serialism, aleatoricism, and the use of electronics. These rival influences have produced a noticeable tension in his work – between the approachable, romantic, and lyrical on the one hand and the determinedly unemotional and abstract on the other. He has written mostly for orchestra and instrumental groups. Important works include *Studio per e e cummings No. 2* (1964) for instrumental ensemble, *Sine nomine* (1974) for voice and instrumental ensemble, *Studio del vero* (1975) for orchestra and the stage work *E tu?* (1973).

Botta, Mario (1943–) Swiss architect. Born in Mendrisio in the Ticino region, Botta trained in Milan under Carlo SCARPA (1961–64), later working in LE CORBUSIER's office (1965) and with the US architect Louis Kahn (1969). Since then he has been associated with the informal grouping of Italian rationalist architects known as the Tendenza and has worked in private practice in Lugano. In his early work Botta concentrated on private houses, stressing simple geometric shapes executed in vernacular materials; a well-known later example is the Casa Rotunda at Stabio (1980), a load-bearing cylinder of brick with vertical and horizontal openings in the walls, which admit light and reveal the floor structure. Latterly Botta has moved into the public sphere with the municipal gymnasium at Balerna (1976–78) and the State Bank at Fribourg (1977–82). He unveiled his first furniture designs in 1983 and in 1988 received the commission for a new cathedral for Evry, outside Paris; the design consists of a brick cylinder cut off diagonally at the top. Asked whether his agnosticism was an obstacle to this project, he replied "you don't have to have a bank account to build a bank".

Boulez, Pierre (1925–) French composer and conductor. He studied music in Paris against his father's wishes, becoming a pupil of MESSIAEN at the Paris Conservatoire in 1944, where he also studied Viennese 12-note technique with René LEIBOWITZ. His early works combine these influences within standard forms (flute sonatina, 1946; first and second piano sonatas, 1946 and 1948) or are settings of René CHAR's highly charged poetry (*Le Visage nuptial*, 1946; *Le Soleil des eaux*, 1948). At the same time he was searching for a new means of order, especially for a serial technique to encompass rhythm (second piano sonata, 1948). By 1951 he had achieved a total SERIALISM of pitch, duration, timbre, and volume in such works as *Polyphonie X*, *Structures* (book I) for piano, and *2 Etudes* in *musique concrète*. Boulez quickly assumed the role of head of the post-war avant-garde and was a regular teacher at DARMSTADT.

His first undisputed masterpiece, *Le Marteau sans maître* (1954), returns to the poetry of Char while the middle movements of *Pli selon pli* (1962) are settings of Mallarmé's three *Improvisations*. Boulez also experimented with aleatoric principles in his third piano sonata (1957) and continued to supplement acoustic instruments with electronic sounds in such works as *Poésie pour pouvoir* (1958) for orchestra with tape.

Since the early 1960s Boulez has been in considerable demand as a conductor and his compositional output has diminished. In the mid 1970s he set up and directed the computer music studio IRCAM (Institut de Recherche et de Coordination Acoustique/Musique) in Paris. More recent pieces include a series of reworkings of early compositions entitled *Notations* (1980).

Boulting brothers The British twin brothers **John Boulting** (1913–85) and **Roy Boulting** (1913–), who are mainly remembered for their satirical comedies of the late 1950s and 1960s. The brothers set up their own independent film company in 1937 before serving in the forces during World War II. Subsequently, taking turns to fulfil the duties of producer and director, they made such films as *Fame is the Spur* (1946), Graham GREENE's *Brighton Rock* (1947), and *The Guinea Pig* (1949). Their next series of films targeted a number of British institutions for satirical attack. *Private's Progress* (1955) had Ian Carmichael making fun of the army, while the bar was the subject of *Brothers in Law* (1956). In 1958 they took a swipe at British diplomacy in *Carlton-Browne of the FO*, with Peter Sellers. Perhaps their most successful film was *I'm All Right Jack* (1959), which made a star of Sellers while lambasting the trade unions. Other films included *Lucky Jim* (1957), from the novel by Kingsley AMIS, and the *Family Way* (1966), starring Hayley Mills (who Roy later married). The brothers became directors of British Lion Films (1958–72) and of Charter Film Productions in 1973.

Bourbaki, Nicolas The collective *nom de plume* of a group of contemporary mathematicians. The precise membership of Bourbaki, which has changed over the years, is a closely guarded secret but it is known that most of the members are French.

Since 1939 Bourbaki has been publishing a monumental work, the *Elements of Mathematics*, of which over 30 volumes have so far appeared. This attempts to expound and display the architecture of the whole mathematical edifice, starting from certain carefully chosen logical concepts. The emphasis throughout the *Elements* is on the interrelationships to be found between the various structures present in mathematics. Consequently, Bourbaki's exposition cuts across traditional boundaries, such as that between algebra and topology.

The members of Bourbaki are all working mathematicians, rather than pure logicians, in contrast to other foundational enterprises (e.g. those of Gottlob Frege, Bertrand Russell, and A. N. Whitehead). Consequently the influence of Bourbaki's writings on contemporary mathematicians and their conception of the subject has been immense.

Bourdieu, Pierre (1930–) French sociologist. After completing his studies at the Ecole Normale Supérieure, Bourdieu worked as an anthropologist in Algeria, publishing his study *The Algerians* in 1958. He has taught sociology in Paris since the early 1960s.

Bourdieu's main interest is in the sociology of culture and education. His earlier works include the collaborations *A Middle Art; Essays About the Social Uses of Photography* (1965) and *Love of Art; European Museums and Their Public* (1966). In *Reproduction in Education, Society and Culture* (1970) Bourdieu developed his most fundamental idea, namely that power structures have a tendency to reproduce themselves in order to ensure their own survival. In the book he argues that the French education system is designed to give the children of those in power the best opportunities to reach similar positions of influence. The same line of thought is explored in *Homo Academicus* (1984), an anthropological study of the French academic elite. In *Distinction: A Social Critique of the Judgement of Taste* (1979) Bourdieu investigated the relationship between social class and lifestyle and the way in which questions of 'taste' are often invoked as a means of identifying and discriminating against outsiders. His recent publications include *Language and Symbolic Power* (1990).

Bourges International Electro-acoustic Music Competition A competition held in Bourges, France, since 1973. It was established by the French composers Françoise Barrière and Christian Clozier with the Groupe de Musique Experimental de Bourges to promote work by composers of ELECTRONIC MUSIC. The competition is now recognized internationally as an important platform for electronic and electro-acoustic composers.

Bradbury, Malcolm (Stanley) (1932–) British novelist and critic. A career academic, Bradbury has taught at several British universities and currently runs the well-known creative writing course at the University of East Anglia (former students include Ian MCEWAN and Kazuo Ishiguro). His critical works include *Possibilities: Essays on the State of the Novel* (1973) and *Modernism* (1976). His first two novels, *Eating People is Wrong* (1959) and *Stepping Westward* (1965), are both satirical campus novels, the former dealing with the academic and sexual adventures of a middle-aged professor in a red-brick university, while the second follows a naive young English lecturer on a tour of the US mid-west. In Bradbury's third novel, *The History Man* (1975), he began to experiment with such devices as interpolated footnotes and commentaries, while breaking the narrative down into short cinematic scenes. The novel satirizes 1970s radical chic through the activities of Howard Kirk, the manipulative and lecherous sociology lecturer at the fictional plate-glass University of Watermouth. Later works include *Cuts* (1987), a television screenplay that explores the different meanings of the title, and *Rates of Exchange* (1983), a witty examination of the place and meaning of culture that shows the influence of contemporary literary theory. Bradbury's most recent novel, *Doctor Criminale* (1992) concerns a journalist's attempts to discover the truth about a mysterious central European intellectual.

Branagh, Kenneth (Charles) (1960–) British actor and theatre and film director. Branagh was hailed as a successor to Laurence OLIVIER after winning a Society of West End Theatres' award for Most Promising Newcomer for his performance in *Another Country* (1982). As an actor he subsequently consolidated his reputation in a wide range of classical and modern roles on both stage and screen. In 1987 he revived the tradition of the actor-manager by founding the Renaissance Theatre Company, which quickly established itself as a leading force in the British theatre.

Branagh's work in the cinema has included screened versions of several of his stage successes, the best known being *Henry V* (1989), where he emulated Olivier by both directing and taking the leading role. More recently he directed and starred in the thriller *Dead Again* (1991) and *Peter's Friends* (1992), a comedy about the reunion of a group of college friends. His work for television has included the series *Fortunes of War* (based on the *Balkan Trilogy* and the *Levant Trilogy* by Olivia MANNING), in which he appeared with his wife, the actress Emma Thompson.

Brandt, Bill (1904–83) British photographer. Born in South London, Brandt worked in Paris from 1929 to 1931, spending a short period as assistant to the US photographer Man Ray. This experience taught him the creative use of experiment and laid the basis for his portraits of writers, actors, and painters. Returning to Britain, he contributed to *Weekly Illustrated* and *Picture Post*, developing his documentary work and revealing a love of shorelines and open countryside in his landscapes. Brandt was fascinated by the social contrasts of English society, producing memorable images of both London's affluent elite and the depression-hit cities of the north. *The English at Home* (1936) and *A Night in London* (1938) also exhibit the flair for creating surrealistic moods that he learnt in Paris. Brandt's wartime photographs of Londoners during the Blitz (commissioned by the government) confirmed his skill in blending telling reportage with an artistic eye for mood and composition. Brandt later concentrated on landscapes, portraiture, and the nude, receiving special acclaim for his experimental studies of the female body in *Perspective* *of Nudes* (1961) and *Shadow of Light* (1966). In many of these pictures lighting, setting, and the use of a wide-angle lens combine to transform the nude body into an almost abstract design. *Bill Brandt Nudes* was published in 1980.

Brassaï (Gyula Halász; 1899–1984) French photographer, painter, and writer, born in Hungary. His professional name means 'from Brassó', his birthplace. After studying in Budapest and Berlin he moved to Paris in 1924, where he worked as a journalist; he did not take his first photograph until the age of 30. Brassaï made his name in the 1930s with the collections *Paris at Night* (1932), a study of nocturnal low-life, and *Pleasures of Paris* (1934). Both evoke the Paris of cheap bars, lonely streetwalkers, and young gangs. Brassaï always encouraged the subject to evoke itself, rather than seeking to recreate it through complex composition: he believed that photography, unlike the other pictorial arts, could dispense entirely with interpretation. During the German occupation (1940–44), Brassaï complied with the ban on public photography and sketched and sculpted in the studio of his friend Picasso. He produced *The Sculptures of Picasso* (1948) and remained an avid portraitist of the leading artists and writers of Paris. But his passion remained the city itself in all its romance and sleaze. His later works include *Oeil de Paris* (1952) and *Graffiti* (1960). Brassaï travelled little but a visit to Spain resulted in *Holy Week, Seville* (1954). He strove to make his published collections into integrated studies of a single theme, rather than a series of separate glimpses.

Bratby, John (Randall) (1928–92) British painter and writer. Born in Wimbledon, South London, Bratby studied at the Kingston College of Art and at the Royal College of Art (1951–54). He won an Italian government scholarship and visited Italy (1954). He taught at the Carlisle College of Art (1956) and then at the Royal College of Art (1957–58).

During the 1950s Bratby was a member of the so-called KITCHEN-SINK SCHOOL of painters, who painted scenes from domestic working-class life (for example Bratby's *Still Life with a Chip Frier*, Tate Gallery, London) in a drably realistic style. In 1954 he gave his first one-man show and in 1956 and 1958 he won prizes at the Venice Biennale. Bratby displayed great versatility within the realist tradition, producing numerous portraits, still lifes, landscapes, flower paintings, and murals. He also provided the paintings for the film of Joyce Carey's novel of artistic life *The Horse's Mouth* (1958) and wrote several novels and books about painting and painters. From 1967 onwards he concentrated on producing portraits of the famous, whom he usually contacted by mailshot. A retrospective of his work was held at the National Portrait Gallery in 1991.

Braudel, Fernand (1902–86) French historian. After completing his studies in 1924, Braudel worked as a teacher in Algiers, Paris, and São Paolo until 1937. He spent most of World War II as a prisoner in Germany. Braudel belonged to the so-called 'Annales' school of French historians, which took its name from the journal *Annales d'histoire économique et sociale*. Led by the historians Marc Bloch and Lucien Febvre, the Annales school pioneered a new kind of historiography that drew widely on such disciplines as economics, geography, and statistical analysis.

In his most celebrated work *The Mediterranean and the Mediterranean World in the Age of Philip II* (2 vols: 1949, 1966) Braudel adopted such an approach to paint a comprehensive picture of the Mediterranean region in his chosen period, emphasizing slowly changing structures and patterns of social and economic life rather than political and military events. Braudel demonstrated the crucial importance of the early modern period from 1450 to 1750 for any understanding of modern capitalism.

In his essay *History and the Social Sciences* (1958) Braudel defended his interdisciplinary method, while at the same time drawing the line at the kind of STRUCTURALISM advocated by LEVI-STRAUSS, arguing that its attempts to describe atemporal structures of mind fall outside the proper domain of historical research. Braudel's other major works are *Material Civilization, Economy and Capitalism from the 15th to the 18th Century* (3 vols: 1967–1979) and the unfinished *The Identity of France* (2 vols: 1986, 1991).

Braun, Volker (1939–) German playwright, noted for his politically challenging dramas on contemporary issues. Braun began his career with the BERLINER ENSEM-

BLE but subsequently suffered greatly from the censorship imposed on his work by the East German authorities. *Tipper Paul Bauch* (1966), a provocative depiction of life in a modern factory, was banned by the state, as was *Lenin's Death* in 1970. In 1975 he aroused the interest of critics with *Guevara*, an innovative treatment of the life of the revolutionary in which the events leading to his death were related in reverse order. In 1979 the Berliner Ensemble enjoyed success with *The Big Peace*, an historical analysis of the progress of communism.

Brecht, (Eugen) Bertolt (Friedrich) (1898–1956) German playwright, theatre director, and poet, whose plays have had a profound influence upon world theatre since World War II. Brecht's first plays were written in the aftermath of World War I and reflect, in their mixture of exuberance and nihilism, the turmoil of German society at that time. *Baal* (1923) and *In the Jungle of the Cities* (1923) show the influence of the expressionists while introducing a brand of sardonic poetry new to German literature. *A Man's a Man* (1926) sees Brecht developing his theory of EPIC THEATRE and beginning to experiment with the highly innovative and controversial ALIENATION EFFECT, concepts of drama that were finally delineated in *A Little Organum for the Theatre*, an enormously important treatise published in 1949. Collaboration with Kurt Weill resulted in the classic musical productions *The Threepenny Opera* (1928), *The Rise and Fall of the City of Mahoganny* (1927), and *The Seven Deadly Sins* (1933).

Brecht's conversion to Marxism in the late 1920s led in the first place to a period of rather austere didacticism, typified by such works as *The Measures Taken* (1930). Following Hitler's rise to power in 1933, Brecht fled Germany with his wife, the actress Helene Weigel (1900–71); subsequently he moved from country to country before reaching the US in 1941. During this unsettled period he wrote most of his greatest plays, including *Galileo* (1943; written 1938), *The Good Person of Setzuan* (1943; written 1938–40) and *Mother Courage* (1941; written 1939). The chief work of his US sojourn was *The Caucasian Chalk Circle* (1948; written 1944–45). In 1947 Brecht was brought before the Committee for Un-American Activities but skilfully managed to avoid implicating others and in 1949 he and his wife returned to Germany, where they were invited to establish their own company (*see* BERLINER ENSEMBLE). Brecht died in 1956, leaving Weigel to take over the running of one of Europe's most influential companies.

Bregenz Festival A very popular and lighthearted music festival held in Bregenz, Austria, in July and August each year. Established in 1946, the festival focuses on two operas each year, one of which is usually performed outdoors on the spectacular floating stage on Lake Constance. The programme also includes operetta, recitals, and ballet.

Brel, Jacques (1929–78) Belgian singer, composer, and writer. Brel began singing at an early age and subsequently moved to Paris, where his talent was recognized by Jacques Canetti, who began to manage his career. His earthy, witty, and satirical songs, full of vitality and bitter romanticism, made him very popular in the 1950s. In 1967 he went into the theatre as producer, director, and actor but began to enjoy renewed success as a singer and songwriter after 1968 with the opening of a Broadway musical featuring his work, *Jacques Brel is Alive and Living in Paris*, which ran for 1800 performances.

Brenton, Howard (1942–) British playwright, whose controversial plays have been presented by both fringe and mainstream companies. His early works, including several one-act dramas and the full-length plays *Revenge* (1969), *Measure for Measure* (1972), and *The Churchill Play* (1974), were ferocious indictments of contemporary British society from a socialist viewpoint that earned their author a reputation as an uncompromising commentator on topical issues. Brenton's anti-imperialist drama *The Romans in Britain* (1980), became a *cause célèbre* with its depiction of the homosexual rape of a druid by Roman legionaries. A private prosecution on the grounds of indecency was threatened, but the case was dropped before it reached the courts.

Brenton's more recent works have included collaborations with other prominent playwrights, notably David HARE, with whom he wrote *Brassneck* (1973) and *Pravda* (1985), an attack on the British tabloid press. With Tariq Ali he wrote *Iranian Nights* (1989), a response to the Iranian death threat against Salman RUSH-

DIE, and *Moscow Gold* (1990), a somewhat heavyhanded treatment of political events in Gorbachov's Soviet Union. His most recent play, *Berlin Bertie* (1992), marks a move away from his earlier epic style to a more domestic mode.

Brenton has also written plays for television, translations of BRECHT and Büchner, and the novel *Diving for Pearls* (1989).

Bresson, Robert (1907–) French film director, one of the most influential European film-makers to emerge since World War II. Bresson had early aspirations to become a painter but entered films in the 1930s, writing screenplays for other directors. During World War II he spent a year as a prisoner-of-war, subsequently making his debut as a director with *Angels of Sin* (1943), about a young nun's determination to save the soul of a murderess, even at the cost of her own life. The film set the tone for much of Bresson's later work, exploring the concept of salvation with characteristic austerity.

Les Dames du Bois du Boulogne (1945), a tragedy about a spurned lover's revenge, with a screenplay by Jean Cocteau (based on a novel by Diderot), was acclaimed for the brilliant performances Bresson coaxed from its professional cast. In the films that followed, however, Bresson generally used amateur actors and wrote the scripts himself. *Diary of a Country Priest* (1950; from the novel by Bernanos), in which a priest comes to terms with his imminent death, *A Man Escaped* (1956), about a prisoner on the run from the Nazis, and *Pickpocket* (1959), concerning the redemption of a petty thief through love, established a recognizable Bresson territory: all are closely observed studies of human suffering and resilience.

Among his films of the 1960s were *The Trial of Joan of Arc* (1962), *Au Hasard Balthazar* (1966), depicting the cruelty of man through the sufferings of an ass, *Mouchette* (1967), about the miseries of an unloved peasant girl, and *Une Femme douce* (1969), concerning a broken marriage that ends in suicide. An increasingly pessimistic tone appeared in his films of the 1970s, which included *Four Nights of a Dreamer* (1971) and *The Devil Probably* (1977), both set in a bleak version of contemporary Paris, and *Lancelot du Lac* (1974), a violent excursion into Arthurian legend.

The most admired of Bresson's later films is *L'Argent* (1983), which traces the events linking a counterfeit 500-franc note with a motiveless axe murder; the film won the Grand Prix at the CANNES FILM FESTIVAL. Bresson, whose many awards include the Légion d'honneur, has also published *Notes sur le cinématographe* (1975).

Breuer, Marcel (1902–81) Hungarian-born architect and designer. Born in Pecs, Breuer studied in the furniture workshop at the Weimar Bauhaus, where he produced tubular steel furniture, including the famous 'Wassily chair' named for his friend Wassily Kandinsky. In 1925 he moved to Dessau with the Bauhaus, remaining there until 1928, when he began an architectural practice in Berlin. A further period of travel and study followed in the early 1930s, after which Breuer worked in London for Isokon Laminated Furniture. Moving with Walter Gropius to Harvard, Breuer became an associate professor there (1938–47) and had great influence on a generation of US architects. Marcel Breuer and Associates was founded in Cambridge, Massachussets, in 1937 and moved to New York in 1946. Until the early 1950s his output consisted largely of private houses in New England, but in 1958 Breuer (with NERVI and Bernard Zehrfuss) won the competition for the UNESCO headquarters in Paris. Important corporate commissions in the Netherlands, Switzerland, and Belgium followed, most notably the IBM Research Centre at La Gaude, France (1961). Giant blocks raised on *pilotis* (stilts), with deeply carved window walls of concrete, have become his hallmark, and he can be seen as an originator of the NEW BRUTALISM. Breuer was much concerned with the admission of natural light, an interest hinted at in the title of his major book, *Sun and Shadow: The Philosophy of an Architect*, edited by Peter Blake (1956). However, his most lasting influence is probably as the originator of mass-produced tubular furniture.

Brighton Festival A large international arts festival held in Brighton, East Sussex, for a month each May. It was first held in 1967 and is both cosmopolitan and wide-ranging in outlook. There is often a theme to the festival, which includes an extensive comedy programme, theatre, street theatre, children's theatre, and exhibitions, as well as music from opera to rock. It features peformers from around the world; the Drottningholm Opera from Sweden are regular guests.

British Academy of Film and Television Arts (BAFTA) A British film and television organization founded in 1946 as the British Film Academy and merged with the Society of Film and Television Arts in 1959. The organization presents the UK's most prestigious film and television awards, sometimes called the Stellas. Winners of the best film category before 1969, when only British films were eligible, included Carol REED's *Odd Man Out* (1948) and *The Third Man* (1950), and David LEAN's *The Sound Barrier* (1953), *The Bridge on the River Kwai* (1958), and *Lawrence of Arabia* (1963). Prizewinners since 1969 have included SCHLESINGER's *Midnight Cowboy* (1970) and *Sunday, Bloody Sunday* (1972), TRUFFAUT's *Day for Night* (1974), Milos FORMAN's *One Flew Over the Cuckoo's Nest* (1977), Richard ATTENBOROUGH's *Gandhi* (1983), Claude BERRI's *Jean de Florette* (1988), and BERTOLUCCI's *The Last Emperor* (1989).

Britten, Sir Benjamin (1913–76) British composer and pianist. Britten began composition studies with Frank Bridge at the age of 13, continuing at the Royal College of Music, London, where he also studied the piano. Plans to study with Alban Berg in Vienna came to nothing owing to parental opposition.

From 1935 he collaborated with W. H. Auden on documentary films for the GPO and various concert works, notably the symphonic song cycle *Our Hunting Fathers* (1936). The *Variations on a Theme of Frank Bridge* (1937) gained him greater public attention in Britain but in 1939 he followed Auden to the US. His companion on this journey, and for the rest of his life, was the tenor Peter Pears (1910–86), who interpreted many of his subsequent songs and operatic roles. Although the American period was creatively productive (*Seven Sonnets of Michelangelo*, 1940; *Sinfonia da Requiem*, 1940), Britten felt drawn back to his native Suffolk and returned to Britain in 1942.

Britten's first full-length opera, *Peter Grimes* (1945), established his reputation as a composer of international stature. He went on to write 12 more operatic works, including *Billy Budd* (1951), *Gloriana* (1953), *Owen Wingrave* (1970), and *Death in Venice* (1973) and the chamber operas *Rape of Lucretia* (1946), *The Turn of the Screw* (1954), and *Curlew River* (1964). In 1947 Britten helped to found the English Opera Group, which led in turn to the establishment (1948) of the ALDEBURGH FESTIVAL in the small Suffolk seaside town in which he and Pears had settled. In 1961 he composed his *War Requiem* for performance in the rebuilt Coventry Cathedral; the work combines chamber and large-scale operatic devices to express the private and public emotions arising from his text – the Latin of the requiem mass and the war poetry of Wilfred Owen. Britten's central position in post-war musical life in Britain was recognized by the award of a life peerage in 1976; he was the first musician to be so honoured.

Brno Festival A music festival held in Brno, in the Czech Republic, in September and October every year. It was founded in 1966 to promote the operas of Janáček and early Eastern European music. The programme also includes seminars and symposia on musicology.

Brodsky, Joseph (Iosif Aleksandrovich Brodsky; 1940–) Russian poet living in the US, considered by many the foremost Russian poet of his generation. Born in Leningrad of Jewish parents, he survived the three-year siege of that city during World War II. Between 1956 and 1962 he changed jobs 13 times, publishing his first poems in *samizdat* in 1960. In 1962 he met the poet Anna Akhmatova and remained her protégé until her death in 1966. Arrested in 1959, 1961, and 1962, Brodsky was placed in the Kashchenko Psychiatric Hospital in 1963 and a year later was sentenced to five years' hard labour for 'parasitism'. Following an international outcry against his sentence, he was allowed to return to Leningrad after spending a year in the Konoshsky district of Archangel Province. He emigrated to the US in 1972, becoming a US citizen in 1977.

Very little of his poetry was published in Russia until, in 1987, he was awarded the Nobel Prize for literature for his collections *Short and Long Poems* (1965), *A Halt in the Desert* (1966), *The End of a Beautiful Epoch* (1970), *A Part of Speech* (1977), and *Roman Elegies* (1982). A *Selected Poems* in English translation appeared in 1973, with an introduction by his friend W. H. Auden. Brodsky's interest in foreign poets, ranging from John Donne to T. S. Eliot and Robert Frost, was awakened by reading them in Polish translations; his knowledge of that language also explains the influence on his work of Czesław MIŁOSZ, whom he has translated into Russian, Zbigniew HERBERT, and Cyprian Norwid. Among Russian poets the main influences have been Gavriil Derzhavin, Evgenii Baratynsky, Osip Mandelshtam, Marina Tsvetaeva, and Boris PASTERNAK. Brodsky has made extensive use of Greek mythology in such poems as *Odysseus to Telemachus* (1972) and *To Lycomedes on Scyros* (1967). His longer poems include the celebrated *Gorbunov and Gorchakov* (1965–68), written in a style influenced by Samuel BECKETT.

Brodsky's collection of essays *Less than One* (1986) contains important assessments of Auden, Miłosz, and Akhmatova amongst others; he has also translated plays by Tom STOPPARD and Brendan BEHAN. He now writes in both English and Russian, serving as the US poet laureate (an annual appointment) from 1991 to 1992. *Watermark* (1992) was a series of prose meditations on Venice.

Broek, J(ohannes) H(endrik) van den See VAN DEN BROEK AND BAKEMA

Brook, Peter (Stephen Paul) (1925–) British theatre director and stage designer, who has created some of the most strikingly original productions of recent times. His first production, of Marlowe's *Dr Faustus*, immediately identified the 18-year-old Brook as a brilliant and original director. He consolidated his reputation with a series of highly successful productions of both classics and modern plays at Stratford-upon-Avon and elsewhere; in 1962 he became codirector at Stratford of the newly founded RSC. His 1970 production of *A Midsummer Night's Dream*, with its use of trapezes and a revolutionary white box set, remains one of the most celebrated RSC productions. Other major events included his staging of WEISS's *Marat/Sade* in 1964 and *Seneca's Oedipus* in 1968.

In 1970 Brook founded the INTERNATIONAL CENTRE OF THEATRE RESEARCH, with the aim of exploring techniques of expression outside the mainstream of Western theatre. The company travelled widely in the 1970s, presenting its experimental productions to tribesmen in Africa and Australia as well as to more conventional audiences. Brook's recent productions have included a nine-hour adaptation of the Indian epic *The Mahabharata* (1985) as well as a pared down production of the opera *Carmen* (1989). His films include *Lord of the Flies* (1962), *Marat/Sade* (1967), and *Meetings with Remarkable Men* (1979). He is also the author of the influential treatise *The Empty Space* (1968) and *The Shifting Point* (1988), a collection of his writings.

Brotherhood of Ruralists *See* BLAKE, PETER.

Bruce, Christopher (1945–) British choreographer and dancer, who established his reputation with his work for the Ballet Rambert (*see* RAMBERT DANCE COMPANY). His works are noted for their committed social stance and admired for their fusion of classical and contemporary dance techniques.

Bruce began his career as a dancer with the Ballet Rambert in 1963; in 1967 he was much admired in the title role of Glen Tetley's *Pierrot lunaire.* Subsequent roles have included Prospero in Tetley's *The Tempest* and the title role in *Petrushka* (1988).

Bruce's first ballet, *George Fridiric*, featured music by Handel and was performed by the Ballet Rambert in 1975. He was appointed associate director of the company in the same year and became associate choreographer in 1979. His other works for the Ballet Rambert have included *Girl in a Straw Hat* (1976), a tribute to Marie Rambert, *Ancient Voices of Children* (1975), and (in collaboration with the choreographer Lindsay Kemp) *Cruel Garden* (1977); both the latter were inspired by the writings of Federico García Lorca.

Bruce's most popular work for the company, however, was *Ghost Dances* (1981), a protest against political repression in the Third World that employed South American folk music. More recent works have included *Land* (1985) for the London Festival Ballet and *The Dream is Over* (1987), a tribute to John Lennon. In 1985 he accepted the post of associate choreographer with the London Festival Ballet.

Bruges Early Music Festival An annual music festival held in Bruges, Belgium, for a fortnight in July and August. As well as concerts and recitals of early European music, the festival hosts exhibitions of period instruments. *See also* EARLY-MUSIC MOVEMENT.

Brüs, Günter (1938–) Austrian graphic artist and exponent of PERFORMANCE ART. Born in Ardning, Brüs studied at the School of Arts and Crafts in Graz (1953–57) and at the Academy of Applied Art in Vienna (1957–60). In 1964 he was a founder of the **Vienna Actionists,** a group of artists who sought to use ACTION AND BODY ART as a vehicle for social revolution. He founded the Vienna Institute for Immediate Art with two of his fellow actionists, Otto MUEHL and Hermann NITSCH, in 1966. Brüs's 'actions', which included walking naked through Vienna with his body painted white (1965) and 'painting' with blood and excrement, were deliberately extreme and provocative. In 1969 he fled to West Berlin having been sentenced to six months in prison for insulting Austrian national symbols and committing immoral acts.

Thereafter Brüs concentrated on the production of poetry and graphic works, turning out thousands of drawings and many *Bild-Dichtungen* (poems with integral illustrations). Influenced by the English visionary poet and painter William Blake, children's book illustration, and the work of the Viennese expressionists of the early 20th century, these works show a rejection of mainstream modernism. In 1976, at the entreaty of Brüs's wife, his prison term was commuted to a fine. He subsequently revisited Vienna and in 1979 settled in Graz.

brutalism *See* NEW BRUTALISM.

Buero Vallejo, Antonio (1916–) Spanish playwright. A committed socialist, Buero Vallejo spent six years as a political prisoner under Franco. During his imprisonment he wrote his first play, *Story of a Staircase* (1949), which depicts events in the lives of the inhabitants of a dilapidated tenement over a period of 30 years and represents an attempt at a Spanish version of Socialist Realism. He consolidated his reputation with *In the Burning Darkness* (1950), set in a home for the blind, and *The Weaver of Dreams* (1952), which retold part of the story of Ulysses; by the mid-1950s he was recognized as one of the most significant writers for the contemporary Spanish stage. He has since produced works ranging from an historical trilogy (1959) and the tragedy *The Skylight* (1967) to *The Double Story of Dr Valmy* (1968), an attack upon the secret police that had to be given its first performance in Britain. Other plays, which have won many awards, have included *Today's a Holiday* (1956), *Myth* (1974), *Secret Dialogue* (1984), and *Lazarus in the Labyrinth* (1986). Buero Vallejo's other writing includes the essay *Three Masters before the Public* (1973).

Bufalino, Gesualdo (1920–) Italian novelist and writer. He was born in the Sicilian town of Comiso, where he taught until 1978. A self-defined 'secret writer', Bufalino did not begin his literary career until he was 60. His first short novel, *The Plague Sower* (1981; written in the 1950s), is semiautobiographical, reflecting his own sufferings in a sanatorium and during World War II. Here, as in all his fiction, Bufalino is preoccupied with themes of death, beauty, anguish, and the sense of nothingness; his style is highly literary with a tendency to the baroque and expressionistic.

Other works include *Bitter Michael* (1982), a collection of poems, *Museum of Shadows* (1982), a book of personal recollections, a second novel *Blind Argus, or the Dreams of Memory* (1984), and *The Evil Thinker* (1987), which is a volume of aphorisms. Recent publications include *The Man Possessed* (1988), a collection of stories featuring such mythological and historical figures as Eurydice, Noah, Baudelaire, and Jack the Ripper, *The Lies of the Night* (1988), an allegory set in an imaginary Kingdom of the Two Sicilies, and *The Naked Island* (1989). He has also translated works by Terence, Hugo, Baudelaire, and Giraudoux.

Buffet, Bernard (1928–) French figurative painter. Buffet studied at the École des Beaux-Arts in Paris from 1944. In 1949 he joined L'Homme-témoin, a group of figurative painters who aimed to uphold social realism against the prevailing fashion for abstraction. Buffet exhibited with the other members of the group but soon achieved a prominence beyond his colleagues. By the early 1950s his powerfully distinctive style had made him perhaps the best known of the younger painters in France. There were several exhibitions of his work during the 1950s.

Buffet's portraits, townscapes, still lifes, and religious subjects feature sharp, sometimes spiky, forms rendered in greys and other cold dark tones. The human figures in his work are emaciated, isolated, and alienated (for example, *Pietà*, 1946, Musée Nationale d'un Art Moderne, Paris). The paintings seemed to express SARTRE's pessimistic existentialist view of human life and to correspond to the desolate mood of post-war Europe (*see* EXISTENTIALISM). After achieving success Buffet received numerous commissions but the works that he produced rarely matched the power of his earlier paintings, becoming increasingly mannered and decorative. Buffet has also produced many drawings and book illustrations.

Building Design Partnership (BDP) A British architectural practice that is among the largest design consultancies in Europe. It was founded by G. Grenfell-Baines as the Grenfell-Baines Group in Preston in 1937, turning successfully into the Design Partnership and then BDP. The firm prospered in the 1960s and 1970s with large-scale public-sector commissions, such as the Nottingham University Hospital (planned 1965, built 1971–79), Blackburn town centre redevelopment (*c.* 1965–76), and the civil engineering department of Bradford University (completed 1970). If there is a BDP 'house style' it consists of a quiet, somewhat heavy, Corbusian manner (*see* LE CORBUSIER), most of their buildings having a strongly expressed reinforced concrete framework and long horizontal window-strips. Among their best buildings are the National Institute for Higher Education, Limerick, Ireland (1970–76), with brick cladding, bronze-tinted glass, and fenestration mildly reminiscent of Alvar AALTO, and the new headquarters of the Halifax Building Society, Halifax (opened 1973), with a giant main floor cantilevered out high above street level.

Buñuel, Luis (Luis Buñuel Portoles; 1900–83) Spanish film director, working mainly in Mexico after World War II, who became one of the most influential and controversial film-makers in European cinema. Buñuel was educated by the Jesuits in Zaragoza and subsequently at Madrid University, where he became friends with Salvador Dali and the writer García Lorca. He studied at the Académie du Cinéma in Paris and collaborated with Dali on his first film, the notorious *Un Chien Andalou* (1928). Another collaboration with Dali, *L'Age d'Or* (1930), was widely banned because of its anticlericalism and alleged blasphemy. After the Spanish Civil War Buñuel spent a number of years in relative obscurity in the US. Having settled in Mexico in 1946, he reclaimed his position as a leading film-maker with *The Young and the Damned* (*Los olvidados*; 1950), which earned him the Grand Prix at Cannes. Other films of this period included *El* (1952) and *The Criminal Life of Archibaldo de la Cruz* (1955).

Although *Viridiana* (1961) was filmed in Spain at the invitation of the Spanish government, a scene parodying the Last Supper led to the film being banned there. In *The Exterminating Angel* (1962) the conventional morality of a group of trapped dinner guests swiftly breaks down; in *Belle de Jour* (1966) Catherine Deneuve appears as a middle-class wife who takes up prostitution as an antidote to boredom; while in *Tristana* (1970) a young girl sets out to revenge herself on her seducer. His later films include two celebrated Oscar winners, *The Discreet Charm of the Bourgeoisie* (1972) and *That Obscure Object of Desire* (1977), an exploration of frustrated lust. Shortly before his death, Buñuel was awarded the Grand Cross of the Order of Isabella le Catolica as a gesture of reconciliation by the Spanish government. He published an autobiography, *My Last Sigh*, in 1983.

Buren, Daniel (1938–) French exponent of CONCEPTUAL ART. Buren studied at the Ecole Nationale Supérieure des Métiers d'Art in Paris (1956–60). In the early 1960s he became disillusioned with conventional art and the gallery system and began to produce deliberately ephemeral works that could not be installed in museums or galleries. Since 1965 his works have all featured vertical stripes in a single colour on a white background; the stripes are always exactly 8.7 cm wide. Buren seems to have chosen this motif for its total lack of content or suggestiveness.

In 1970 Buren attached white and orange stripes to billboards on 140 stations on the Paris Métro; photographs of the billboards were later published. In 1975 he undertook his so-called 'Wannsee Project', attaching striped sails to several boats in the Wannsee Regatta in Berlin. Afterwards the sails were exhibited in the Berlin Academy of Fine Arts, arranged in the order in which the boats finished the race. Buren has also created works for galleries, fixing coloured stripes to walls, ceilings, and windows to create striped environments. In 1987 his work *Deux Plateaux* ('Two Levels'), an arrangement of striped columns, was installed in the Cour d'Honour of the Palais Royal in Paris.

Burgess, Anthony (John Anthony Burgess Wilson; 1917–) British novelist and writer. Burgess was educated at the University of Manchester and served in the army during World War II. His first three novels, known as the *Malayan Trilogy*, were *Time for a Tiger* (1956), *The Enemy in the Blanket* (1958), and *Beds in the East* (1959). Set in the Far East, they were inspired by the time he spent in the Colonial Service in Malaya and Borneo. In 1962 he published the notorious *A Clockwork Orange*. A violent picture of a dystopian Britain of the near future, it is written in a fictional youth argot, 'Nadsat', combining cockney slang and Russian. Beneath the aggressive action, Burgess explores the dilemmas of moral choice and individual freedom. It was adapted for the cinema by the US director Stanley Kubrick in 1971. Other books include the Enderby series, *Inside Mr Enderby* (1963), *Enderby Outside* (1968), *The Clockwork Testament* (1974), and *Enderby's Dark Lady* (1984). The substantial *Earthly Powers* (1980) is arguably his most ambitious work. The narrative of an ageing homosexual writer, it presents a broad panorama of 20th-century society. *End of the World News* (1985) deals with an impending apocalypse from a number of perspectives, while *Any Old Iron* (1989) concerns the imagined rediscovery of King Arthur's sword in the late 20th century. He has recently published two volumes of autobiography, *Little Wilson and Big God* (1988) and *You've Had Your Time* (1990). *Homage to Qwert Yuiop* (1986) is a selection of his numerous reviews and essays. A prolific and erudite writer with a consuming interest in language, he has written several books on linguistics, including *Language Made Plain* (1964); *A Mouthful of Air* (1992) is an introduction to phonetics. Burgess has also composed many full-scale musical works for orchestra and other media; his third symphony was performed in the US in 1975.

Burra, Edward (John) (1905–76) British painter. Burra studied painting in London at the Chelsea Polytechnic (1921–23) and the Royal College of Art (1923–24). For most of his life he lived and painted in Rye, Sussex. In the 1920s and 1930s he also visited France, Spain, and the US, journeys that provided material for many paintings. From the mid 1920s until the mid 1930s he specialized in still lifes and scenes of low life in Mediterranean ports. In the 1930s, however, he came under the influence of European surrealism and contributed to two exhibitions of works by British surrealists (1936, 1938). By this time he had developed a highly individual style, which he was to maintain for the rest of his life.

From the late 1930s to the early 1950s Burra's paintings were full of the bizarre and the grotesque. His sense of evil, always strong, was intensified by the Spanish Civil War and World War II. Works from this period include *Death and the Soldiers* (1940) and *John Deth* (1952), in which a figure representing death intrudes on a group of dancers. Burra also painted new versions of traditional Christian subjects, such as *The Mocking of Christ* (1952, University of Dundee), and designed sets for six ballets, an opera, and a musical play. From the mid 1950s onwards he moved away from human subjects and focused on still life and the English landscape. The resulting paintings are dramatic with a strong element of the sinister.

Burri, Alberto (1915–) Italian artist. Born at Città di Castello, north of Perugia, Burri studied medicine (1934–39). During World War II he served as a medical officer with Italian forces in North Africa but was captured by the US army in 1943. He subsequently spent two years in Texas as a prisoner of war, during which time he began to paint. He returned to Italy in 1945 and in 1946 gave up medicine in favour of painting. He gave his first one-man exhibition in 1947 and won the International Critics' Prize in 1960.

Burri is one of the leading abstract artists to emerge from Italy since World War II. His work, which shows the influence of both cubism and Dada, combines oil painting in an abstract expressionist style with elements of collage. Its most distinctive feature is Burri's use of humble or discarded materials such as sackcloth, rags, or rusted metal, which he often burned or otherwise damaged before assembling on a dark (often a dark red) background. Some of the earlier works create an effect of blood seeping through cloth, which may reflect his experiences as a military surgeon. Burri has experimented with different materials over the decades; in the later 1950s he favoured burnt wood and plastic and in the 1960s hammered metal while in the 1970s his work featured 'cellotex' and incorporated networks of cracks. His use of unvalued materials anticipated Italian ARTE POVERA. *See also* ART INFORMEL.

Bussotti, Sylvano (1931–) Italian composer. Besides music he is involved with art, theatre, film, and journalism – a range which his family background (his brother and uncle are artists) and his musical training (conspicuous for its avoidance of formal academic study) render less surprising. He abandoned his instrumental studies at the Florence Conservatory, where his piano teacher was DALLAPICCOLA, to devote himself to composition, in which he is largely untaught, although he acknowledges the encouragement of Dallapiccola, BARTOLOZZI, and BOULEZ. Other influences on his early development were lessons in Paris with Max Deutsch (1957) and attendance at the DARMSTADT summer courses, particularly that of 1958 when he met John Cage. In 1963 he became a member of the Florentine Gruppo 70. Since then he has worked in the US (1964–65) and in Berlin (1972). He has taught at the L'Aquila Academy of Fine Arts and at the Milan Conservatory; in 1975 he became artistic director of the Teatro La Fenice, Venice.

His output falls into two categories: instrumental works and stage works. The instrumental pieces move from serialism (for example, *Nottetempo con lo scherzo e una rosa*, 1954–57) to works which make free use of aleatoricism (notably, *Fragmentation pour un joueur de harpes* (1962), and *Pièces de chair II* (1958–60), from which *Five Pieces for David Tudor* (1959) and *Pour clavier* (1961) are derived). Later works show a relative lack of interest in avant-garde techniques (such as the use of electronics), focusing instead on the creation of violent and often highly sensuous sound-worlds. In this they reflect Bussotti's flamboyant personality and lifestyle: his works are often autobiographical to the point of being exhibitionistic. A further change of style, noticeable in *Cinque frammenti all'Italia* (1967), resulted from his discovery of Renaissance music. Important among the stage works are *La Passion selon Sade* (1969), *Lorenzaccio* (1972), the ballet *Bergkristall* (1974), and *Le Racine* (1980). Other major works include *Torso* for voice and orchestra and *The Rara Requiem* (1970) for voice and instrumental ensemble.

Butler, Reg (1913–81) British metal sculptor. Butler trained as an architect at the Architectural Association School, London (1933–37) and worked in private practice until 1950. During World War II he worked as a blacksmith and began sculpting in wrought iron (1944). He gave up architecture for sculpture in 1950 and became the first Gregory Fellow in Sculpture at Leeds University (1950–53). He later taught sculpture at the Slade School of Fine Art in London.

One of the first British metal sculptors, Butler has produced both figurative and constructivist works, the latter often taking the form of tower-like structures. His early work was influenced by Henry MOORE, the US sculptor Alexander Calder, and the Spanish sculptor Julio González. In 1953 he achieved international recognition when he won first prize in a competition for a monument to 'The Unknown Political Prisoner'; his winning entry (Tate Gallery, London) features a tall metal structure standing on a mound with three small figures underneath. In later works figures are often enclosed within metal grids or boxes. Between 1967 and 1972 he made a series of female nude figures in bronze with realistically painted hair.

Butor, Michel (1926–) French writer and essayist. After studying literature and philosophy at the Sorbonne, Butor taught in Manchester, Thessaloníki (Greece), and Geneva. Since 1957 he has lived by his writing while continuing to appear as a visiting lecturer at various institutions in France and the US. With his earlier books Butor gained a reputation as a leading exponent of the NOUVEAU ROMAN. His first novel, *Passage from Milan* (1954), describes six hours in the life of an apartment house: the book takes its structure from the architecture of the building rather than from any conventional notion of plot. *Passing Time* (1956) is based on Butor's experience of killing time in Manchester. In *Second Thoughts* (1957) the narrator evokes the cities of Paris and Rome while travelling between the two by train.

In later books Butor abandons the novel form altogether, many of these works being best described as experimental travel books. *Mobile* (1962), subtitled 'Study for a Representation of the United States', uses a collage technique to evoke the experience of life in the US, while *6 810 000 Litres Per Second* (1965) describes Niagara Falls through the seasons; *Description of San Marco* (1964) describes the experience of standing in the great cathedral of Venice and *Boomerang* (1978) is about Australia. Butor has also written a large number of essays on a great variety of topics; those collected in the four volumes of *Répertoire* (1960–74) deal with individual writers and artists. Butor has compared his mode of writing to those Renaissance paintings in which an entire world is visible through a single archway or window. He is one of the most prolific and original French authors writing today.

Buxton International Festival A British music festival, founded in 1978, and held in Buxton, Derbyshire, from mid July to mid August each year. The restored Buxton Opera House is now the venue for some of the most striking productions of opera in Britain; the festival also includes jazz, films, lectures, and cabaret.

Buzzati, Dino (Dino Buzzati Traverso; 1906–72) Italian novelist and short-story writer. After taking a law degree (1928) from Milan University he worked as editor, correspondent, and art critic on the *Corriere della Sera.* He began his literary career with two short novels set in the mountains of northern Italy, *Bàrnabo of the Mountains* (1933) and *The Secret of the Old Wood* (1935); like a number of his other works, these are ostensibly for children but reveal a deeper meaning for adult readers. The influence of Kafka, which dominates all Buzzati's work, comes to the fore in *The Tartar Steppe* (1940), an acclaimed novel about a frontier garrison waiting in vain for an opportunity to show its courage. The novel carries an implicit anti-Fascist message. The collection of short stories *The Seven Messengers* (1945) has a gothic flavour. Buzzati's preoccupation with existentialist themes such as the mystery of human existence, man's obsession with death and guilt, and the problem of suffering, coexists with a love of the fantastic that pervades all his best short stories.

Other well-known works include the striking stories 'Fear of the Scala' (1949) and 'The Collapse of Baliverna' (1954) as well as the children's classic *The Bears' Famous Invasion of Sicily* (1945). Amongst Buzzati's later works are *A Love Affair* (1963), a realistic novel about a middle-aged man's infatuation with a young girl, *Cartoon Poem* (1969), an experimental retelling of the Orpheus myth, and *The Miracles of Val Morel* (1971). His plays *A Clinical Case* (1953) and *A Worm at the Ministry* (1960) are both satires on bureaucracy.

Byatt, A(ntonia) S(usan) (1936–) British novelist and critic. Educated at The Mount School, York, and Newnham College, Cambridge, she published her first novel, *Shadow of a Sun,* in 1964. This describes the difficult relationship between a writer and his daughter, while her second novel, *The Game* (1967), examines the lives of two literary sisters (Byatt's own sister is the novelist Margaret DRABBLE). *The Virgin in the Garden* (1978) and *Still Life* (1985) are the first two volumes of a planned series. The former, a vivid study of provincial intellectual life in the Coronation year of 1953, makes pointed historical and literary allusions to the first Elizabethan age. Her most successful novel, *Possession* (1990), similarly explores parallels between the past and the present as it follows the researches of two young academics into the lives and writings of two Victorian poets (whose 'works' Byatt herself supplies). Byatt explores the two relationships and the literary life of both ages in a way that is both intellectually stimulating and emotionally exciting. The novel won the BOOKER PRIZE in 1990. Her most recent publication is *Angels and Insects* (1992), a pair of novellas again set in the Victorian age.

Bykaw, Vasil (1924–) Belorussian war novelist. Born in a village in the Vitebsk region, he served as a young soldier in World War II, witnessing many of the reverses of the early campaigns. His first stories date from 1951 but were published only in 1956. Most of them are set in wartime and concern young soldiers caught between a ruthless and often incompetent Stalinist leadership and the German enemy. His first novel *The Cry of the Cranes* (1960) struck readers with its forthrightness and avoidance of the false heroics that have too often dominated Soviet war literature. Many of his short novels, such as *The Third Flare* (1962), *Kruhliany Bridge* (1969), and *The Ordeal* (*Sotnikaw*; 1972), are set in tense small-scale situations where difficult moral choices have to be made. Another recurrent theme is the relationship of wartime Stalinism to the present day, as, for instance, in *The Obelisk* (1971), *The Quarry* (1986) or in his longest work, for many years suppressed in the Soviet Union, *The Dead Feel No Pain* (1966). In these novels many of the cowards, bullies, and traitors of wartime are shown as flourishing in the years of peace. In the 1970s and 1980s Bykaw has continued to write about the war, dwelling especially on the atmosphere of suspicion and repression that greatly increased the sufferings of ordinary people in those years. Thought by many to be a Russian writer, Bykaw in fact makes Russian versions of his own Belorussian novels (having earlier suffered bowdlerization through translation). Respected throughout the former Soviet Union, in his native Belorussia he has for years been regarded as an almost lone independent voice and inspiration. He is now playing an active role in the country's struggle for genuine independence.

C

Cacoyannis, Michael (1922–) Greek film and theatre director, actor, and screenwriter. Born in Cyprus, he took a law degree in Britain and practised as a barrister; during World War II he produced Greek programmes for the BBC. After studying acting and directing, he made his stage debut in 1946 in *Salomé* at the Old Vic. He travelled in the US before returning to Greece in 1953 to direct his first film, *Windfall in Athens*. Two years later he won several international awards with *Stella*, starring Melina Mercouri, and followed this with *A Girl in Black* (1956), a film about a writer's love for an unsophisticated island girl and its tragic aftermath. In 1957 he scripted and directed another melodrama, *A Matter of Dignity*, about a poor woman who marries a millionaire for her parents' sake. There followed *Our Last Spring* (1959), *Eroica* (1960), and the Italian film *The Wastrel* (1961). Cacoyannis became a star in his own right with his performance in his filmed version of Sophocles's *Electra* (1961). He returned to the stage in 1963 with an off-Broadway production of *The Trojan Women*, which received excellent reviews.

Cacoyannis achieved his greatest commercial success with *Zorba the Greek* (1964; from the novel by KAZANTZAKIS), a celebration of the Greek spirit, which featured Alan Bates as a sensitive English writer in Crete who is befriended and overwhelmed by a local character (Anthony Quinn). Cacoyannis was nominated for Academy Awards for both his directing and screenwriting. Since then, he has made the British film *The Day the Fish Came Out* (1967), about radioactive fallout contaminating a Mediterranean island, a filmed version of *The Trojan Women* (1971), the documentary *Attila 74* (1975), *Iphigenia* (1977), and *Sweet Country* (1986) in black and white. In the late 1980s he directed operas by Mozart and Gluck. His *Collected Writings* were published in 1991.

Calvino, Italo (1923–85) Italian novelist, critic, essayist, editor, and translator. Born in Cuba, Calvino was brought up in Sanremo, where he lived until the age of 20. During World War II he joined the Resistance, an experience that inspired his first novel *The Path to the Nest of Spiders* (1947) and the stories in *Adam, One Afternoon and Other Stories* (1949). From 1945 onwards Calvino attended the University of Turin and became involved in left-wing politics (he remained a member of the Communist Party until 1957). After graduating in 1947 he worked for the publisher Einaudi, where he met PAVESE, the first to recognize his literary talent. In the 1960s and 1970s he spent long periods in France.

Calvino broke decisively with the prevailing NEOREALISM of post-war Italian fiction (including his own early work) in the trilogy *The Cloven Viscount* (1952), *The Baron in the Trees*, and *The Non-Existent Knight* (1959), subsequently collected in one volume as *Our Forefathers* (1960). With their combination of fantasy, satire, and erudition these sparkling philosophical fables remain amongst his most satisfying creations. *Cosmicomics* (1965; later enlarged as *Cosmicomics Old and New*, 1984) is an idiosyncratic collection of science-fiction stories. In later novels such as *Invisible Cities* (1972), in which Marco Polo describes 55 imaginary cities to Kublai Khan, *The Castle of Crossed Destinies* (1973), a series of linked stories based on the Tarot pack, and *If on a Winter's Night a Traveller* (1979), Calvino became increasingly preoccupied with the nature of narrative itself. His last completed novel was *Mr Palomar* (1983). *Under the Jaguar Sun*, an unfinished collection of stories based on the five senses, was published posthumously in 1992, as was *Six Memos for the Millenium*, a volume of lectures. Calvino will also be remembered for his collection of *Italian Folktales* (1956), a work of consummate scholarship and storytelling.

Camus, Albert (1913–60) French philosopher and writer. Born in poverty in Algeria, Camus studied philosophy at the University of Algiers and became for a short time a member of the Communist Party. In the 1940s he worked as a journalist and began to write. After World War II, during which he was active in the Resistance, he emerged as one of the leading intellectuals associated with the new ideas of EXISTENTIALISM. In 1957 he was awarded the Nobel Prize for literature. He died in a car accident.

According to Camus, the essential absurdity of the human condition proceeds from the conflict between the desire for eternity and the experience of transitoriness. *In the Myth of Sisyphus* (1942) he argued that the exclusion of metaphysical hope and an acceptance of life's meaninglessness can enlarge human liberty.

Camus's belief in the absurdity of life was brilliantly encapsulated in *The Outsider* (1942), the novel that brought him fame; the young protagonist is executed less for having committed a pointless murder than for his refusal to conform in matters of bourgeois etiquette. In *The Plague* (1947), an allegory of the Occupation, Camus revealed a sceptical attitude to political commitment. His rejection of communism in *The Rebel* (1953) led to a breach with SARTRE. *The Fall* (1957), Camus's third and final novel, is an anguished work of semiautobiography.

Candilis Josic Woods French-based architectural partnership. Georges Candilis (1913–), a Russian-born Greek, met the American Shadrach Woods (1923–73) in Paris; in 1951 they set up an office in Tangier for the Atelier des Batisseurs organization (ATBAT) and built a number of housing projects in French North Africa. On their return to Paris in 1955 they were joined by Alexis Josic (1921–), a Yugoslav. The practice concentrated on large-scale public commissions, in particular for housing projects. In the 1960s they moved away from the orthodoxy of isolated point blocks, towards the creation of a more traditional urban streetscape. The partnership was dissolved in 1969 with Woods's return to the US; Candilis and Josic remain in Paris but practise separately.

Canetti, Elias (1905–) Jewish writer in German. After spending his childhood and youth in Manchester, Lausanne, Vienna, Zürich, and Frankfurt he studied chemistry in Vienna from 1924, where he was influenced by Karl Kraus's lectures. In 1928–29 he met leading intellectuals and artists in Berlin, such as George Grosz, BRECHT, and Isaak Babel, while working as a translator. In the Vienna of the 1930s he met Hermann Broch, Alban Berg, Robert Musil, and Fritz WOTRUBA. Following Hitler's annexation of Austria in 1938, he emigrated via Paris to London. He is now a British citizen, living in Zürich and London.

Although the language spoken in the family was Spanish, Canetti writes in German, the 'love language' of his mother. His first major novel *Auto da fé* (*Die Blendung*; 1936) depicts a grotesque world inhabited by characters who live trapped in their own obsessions and use language merely as an instrument for projecting their manic fixations onto reality. The fate of his protagonist, Peter Kien, is a metaphor for the self-destruction of a culture blind to the social forces that threaten it. In *Crowds and Power* (1960) Canetti develops an anthropology of the crowd by interpreting socio-historical events in the light of myths and natural phenomena. Besides *Auto da fé* Canetti's most lasting work may well prove to be his three-part autobiography *The Tongue Set Free* (1977), *The Torch in my Ear* (1982), and *The Play of the Eyes* (1985), which describes the development of the mature writer from his childhood attempts to save his environment from destruction by telling tales. The form of the autobiography allows Canetti to combine his psychological and anthropological interests with personal recollection. Other major works are *The Conscience of Words* (1979), *The Human Province* (1973), *Ear Witness: Fifty Characters* (1974), and *The Voices of Marrakesh* (1967). In 1981 Canetti won the Nobel Prize for literature.

Cannes Film Festival An international film festival that takes place annually at Cannes in the South of France. Founded in 1946, the festival is regarded as the most important in Europe and attracts leading figures in the cinema as well as socialites and the world's press. Winners of the prestigious Palme d'Or award for best film have included Carol REED's *The Third Man* (1949), Vittorio DE SICA's *Miracle in Milan* (1951), FELLINI's *La Dolce Vita* (1960), BUÑUEL's *Viridiana* (1961), ANTONIONI's *Blow Up* (1967), OLMI's *The Tree of Wooden Clogs* (1978), WAJDA's *Man of Iron* (1981), Bille August's *Pelle the Conqueror* (1987), and Joel and Ethan Coen's *Barton Fink* (1991). There were no festivals in 1948, 1950, and 1968.

Cantiere Internazionale d'Arte a Montepulciano *See* MONTEPULCIANO FESTIVAL.

Capa, Robert (Andrei Friedmann; 1913–54) Hungarian-born war photographer. Born in Budapest, he trained as a photographer in Berlin; after the Nazis took power, he left for Paris and took his adopted name. Capa's coverage of the Spanish Civil War in 1936 won immediate acclaim. His work was rugged, vivid, and always compassionate to people in death, grief, and loneliness. His image of a Loyalist soldier shot in battle became a landmark of war photography. Moving unarmed in combat zones, Capa found poignancy besides brutality; his photographs are remarkable for conveying a sense of continuous action, before and after the shot was taken. From China, he covered the Japanese attack in 1938 and later emigrated to the US, where *Life* assigned him to the Normandy landings and other World War II campaigns. Capa took US citizenship and in 1947 helped to found the Magnum Photos cooperative agency with CARTIER-BRESSON and others. He published *Slightly out of Focus* (1947), *Russian Journal* (1948) with the US novelist John Steinbeck, and covered the early months of Israeli nationhood in 1949. Capa was killed by a landmine at Thai-Binh, Vietnam, during the Indo-China conflict in 1954. His work was collected in *Images of War* (1964).

Capogrossi, Giuseppe (1900–72) Italian painter. Born in Rome, Capogrossi trained as a lawyer but began to paint while living in Paris (1927–33). His earliest works were conventional realist paintings but exposure to surrealism – especially the works of Joan MIRÓ – led him to explore more contemporary styles. In 1933 he returned to Rome where he joined the Gruppo Romano (Roman School), who bravely advocated expressionist painting in the face of the dominant classicism of the Novecento Italiano group and the heroic realism favoured by Italy's Fascist government.

The most influential stage of Capogrossi's career began in 1949. In that year he left the Gruppo Romano and began to paint in a highly distinctive abstract style. His paintings no longer had titles but were numbered in sequence: most featured a personal symbol that looked like a comb or fork with 'teeth'. For a while he was exhibited with the Italian Concrete artists, who practised a form of geometrical abstraction, but his paintings also have strong affinities with post-war lyrical abstraction (*see* ART INFORMEL). They have influenced many younger Italian painters.

Caproni, Giorgio (1912–91) Italian poet and writer. He spent most of his life in Genoa. After World War II, during which he fought in the anti-Fascist Resistance, he moved to Rome, where he worked as a translator and contributed to journals and newspapers.

His first collection of poems *As an Allegory* (1936) was followed by *The Ball at Fontanigorda* (1938), *Chronicle* (1943), and *Rooms of the Cable Cars* (1952). In *The Passage of Aeneas* (1956) Caproni draws his subject-matter from classical legend and the life of his native Livorno. He expresses his overwhelming sense of the tragedy of human existence in a melodious language that combines the literary and the popular.

Later collections include *The Seed of Weeping* (1959), *The Wall of the Earth* (1975), *Free Hunter* (1982), and *The Count of Kevenhüller* (1986). His best-known prose writings are probably the short stories The Last Village (1980) and The Maze (1984).

Cardew, Cornelius (1936–81) British composer. Cardew studied the cello, piano, and composition at the Royal Academy of Music, London, electronic music in Cologne, where he assisted STOCKHAUSEN in the composition of *Carré* (1960), and composition with PETRASSI in Rome. After meeting John Cage in Germany he became attracted to the US composer's idea of musical indeterminacy and his mature works involve the performers in the creative process through improvisation and the use of aleatoric principles. Cardew also trained and worked as a graphic artist and became fascinated by the use of GRAPHIC NOTATION to extend the possibilities of interpretation. His 193-page graphic score *Treatise* (1967) is both a musical and an abstract visual composition, which lacks any precise performance directions.

In the early 1970s Cardew's Marxist sympathies led him to the writings of Mao Tse-tung and Chinese culture in general; several works from this period set revolutionary and Confucian texts. His political preoccupations are evident in such pieces as *The East is Red* (1973) for violin and piano and the *Vietnam Sonata* (1976). In 1974 Cardew repudiated his allegiance to the musical avant-garde in the notorious book *Stockhausen Serves Imperialism*; he subsequently devoted himself to political activism and the composition of agit-prop pieces in popular styles.

Cardew has also been highly influential as a performer, especially of free improvisation. In the 1960s he worked with experimental musicians with a jazz background and founded the group AMM with Keith Rowe, Lou Gare, Eddie Prevost, and Lawrence Sheaff. At Morley College he founded the Scratch Orchestra, a large ensemble of both trained and untrained musicians who performed both controlled and free improvisations. He was killed by a hit-and-run driver.

Carlstedt, (John) Birger (Jarl) (1907–75) Finnish abstract painter. Carlstedt studied at the Central School of Art in Helsinki before moving to Paris in the 1920s, where he came under the influence of the De Stijl group and Bauhaus teaching. After experimenting with constructivist styles he began to develop his own mode of abstract painting, characterized by the use of rich colours and intertwining forms.

Carlstedt gave his first one-man show as early as 1932 but only became influential in his homeland after 1945. He continued to paint in a powerful abstract style and received numerous commissions for murals in public buildings, such as the Television Building in Helsinki (1961). He was an important pioneer of abstract painting in Finland.

Caro, Sir Anthony (Alfred) (1924–) British metal sculptor. During school holidays Caro worked as an assistant to the sculptor Charles Wheeler. He subsequently studied engineering at Christ's College, Cambridge (1942–44) and served in the Royal Navy (1944–45) before studying sculpture in London at the Regent Street Polytechnic (1946) and the Royal Academy Schools (1947–53). Between 1951 and 1953 he was also a part-time assistant to Henry MOORE.

In the 1950s Caro worked by modelling figures in clay which he then cast in bronze. His development into one of Europe's leading sculptors followed a visit to the US in 1959, where he met, among others, the metal sculptor David Smith (1906–65). On his return Caro abandoned modelling and began to develop a new kind of sculpture using industrial metals – beams, sheets, tubes, and plates – which he welded and bolted together to create totally abstract works. Suddenly metal sculpture could emphasize lines and planes rather than simply mass. Caro often paints his works in bright colours, creating a strong sense of mood. They are intended to stand on the ground (rather than on plinths), positioned so that the viewer can walk around them and explore the numerous possible views. Though Caro uses a limited range of materials he has proved immensely resourceful and his works have great variety. In the early 1970s he sometimes left works unpainted and allowed them to rust; they were subsequently varnished. Later still he began to explore the possibilities of large sheets of steel. His works became larger in size (for example, the York works of 1974–75) and began to emphasize vertical rather than horizontal planes. He also returned to working in bronze. Caro's work has been exhibited in many countries and has been a powerful influence on younger sculptors. His students have included Richard LONG and GILBERT & GEORGE.

Carter, Angela (1940–92) British novelist and critic. Born in Eastbourne, she became a mature student at Bristol University and subsequently spent some time in Japan, the US, and Australia. Otherwise she spent most of her life in South London. Her first novel *Shadow Dance* (1965) was followed by *The Magic Toyshop* (1967), which won the John Llewellyn Rhys Prize. A third novel, *Several Perceptions*, won the Somerset Maugham Award in 1968. Her writings, which are often considered examples of MAGIC REALISM, show the influence of horror films, the Gothic novel, folk and fairy tales, Kleinian psychoanalysis and sexual fantasies; many contain surreal dream-like sequences. A principal theme in her work is the disruptive nature of female sexuality and its control and abuse by men. This emerges most clearly from her study of the writings of de Sade, *The Sadeian Woman* (1979), and the collection of short stories *The Bloody Chamber* (1974), which consists of macabre and sexual reworkings of traditional fairy tales. Her reimagining of the Little Red Riding Hood story was adapted into a film, *The Company of Wolves* (1984; directed by Neil JORDAN). Other works include *Heroes and Villains* (1969), *Love* (1971), *The Infernal Desire Machines of Dr Hoffman* (1972), *The Passion of New Eve* (1977) and *Nights at the Circus*, which won the James Tait Black Memorial Prize in 1985. Her final novel *Wise Children*, a richly comic work about two related theatrical families, was published in 1991. *Expletives Deleted*, a collection of her trenchant essays and reviews, appeared posthumously in 1992.

Cartier-Bresson, Henri (1908–) French photographer. Born in Chanteloup, near Paris, Cartier-Bresson studied painting (1927–28) under André Lhote. Turning to photography in 1931, he stuck almost at once on his characteristic method of taking photographs unobtrusively in everyday settings, usually carrying only a small 35-mm camera. His work was first exhibited in New York and Madrid in 1932–33. Three years later Cartier-Bresson joined the French film director Jean Renoir and worked as an assistant director on *Les Règles du jeu* (1939). During World War II Cartier-Bresson spent three years in a German prisoner-of-war camp, but escaped and worked for the French Resistance: in 1945 he directed *Le Retour*, a film of the return of French prisoners and deportees. Two years later, he became a founding member of the Magnum Photos cooperative agency and published *The Photographs of Henri Cartier-Bresson* (1947). His photojournalism appeared extensively in magazines around the world and, like his portraiture, aimed at a spontaneous unforced quality in which meaning arises naturally from the subject rather than being imposed by the photographer. In *The Decisive Moment* (*Images à la sauvette*; 1952) Cartier-Bresson expounded this ideal in terms that were to influence a generation of young photographers: photography should seek to capture the single instant when the inner nature of a subject is revealed most clearly through its outward appearance. He believed that photographers could be trained to recognize this moment by studying people in their natural surroundings as much as by technical experience. He refused to crop photographs. An inveterate traveller, Cartier-Bresson has published *Europeans* (1955), *Man and Machine* (1968), *The Face of Asia* (1972), *On the USSR* (1973) and *America in Passing* (1991). In recent years he has largely abandoned photography for painting and drawing.

Cascella, Pietro (1921–) Italian sculptor. Born in Pescara in the Abruzzi, Cascella studied at the Accademia di Belle Arti, Rome. Like many earlier Italian sculptors, Cascella was essentially a stone carver; nevertheless he developed a distinctive abstract style showing the influence of both primitive sculpture and European constructivism. He produced large-scale works, often featuring rounded feminine shapes, that are both simple and powerful. His style was particularly suitable for public monuments and in 1960 he won the competition to provide a monument at the Auschwitz death camp in Poland. He received many other commissions for monuments, including the Gate of Peace at Tel Aviv, the National Congress Monument at Strasbourg, and the monument to Giuseppe Mazzini in Milan.

Cassola, Carlo (1917–) Italian novelist and short-story writer. Cassola studied law in Rome before moving to Tuscany, where he served with the partisans during World War II and subsequently worked as a teacher. From 1962 he combined his writing with an academic career and work as a journalist.

Cassola's early short stories, collected in *From the Periphery* (1941) and *The Visit* (1942), present tiny incidents from the lives of simple unsophisticated people in a style of scrupulous objectivity. The influence of Joyce's *Dubliners* is evident. Despite the plainness of the prose and the lack of narrative interest, the stories convey a sense of the wonder of life that has made them remarkably popular in postwar Italy. The novels *Timber Cutting* (1954), *Fausto and Anna* (1952; revised 1958), and *Bube's Girl* (1960), which won the Strega Prize, reflect Cassola's experiences in the Resistance and the impact of post-war NEOREALISM. His treatment of the partisans in these and other works has drawn some criticism from the intellectual Left in Italy. After 1960 Cassola's writing reverted to the manner of his earlier work, but on the whole with less success. An exception is the novel *An Arid Heart* (1961), a study of isolation and loneliness that is sometimes considered his best work. More recent novels include *Portrait of Helena* (*Monte Maria*; 1973) and the antimilitarist *The Lesson of History* (1978). In the 1970s and 1980s Cassola was active in the antinuclear movement and produced a number of polemical works including *The Right to Survive* (1982) and *The Disarmament Revolution* (1983).

Casson, Sir Hugh (1910–) British architect. Educated at Cambridge and at the Bartlett School, London, Casson worked at the ministry of town and country planning, London (1944–46) and subsequently in private practice. The Casson Conder Partnership (with Neville Conder, 1922–) was established in 1952. Casson had already gained a reputation as a skilled planner with his work for the FESTIVAL OF BRITAIN.

Casson Conder's large output has included much work for the new universities and local authorities. The sculptural elephant house in hammered concrete at London Zoo (1964), the Assembly Rooms in Derby (1977), and the granite-faced Ismaili Centre in South Kensington (1984) illustrate the practice's range. Casson Conder has generally attracted work requiring specific solutions, rather than system-building projects. Casson has been an eminent public figure for 40 years, as trustee of the National Gallery and the Natural History Museum and, in particular, as President of the Royal Academy (1975–84). An accomplished watercolourist, he has published several volumes of paintings and held a number of exhibitions.

Castellani, Renato (1913–85) Italian film director and screenwriter. Castellani was raised in Argentina and Switzerland and later studied architecture in Milan. He began screenwriting for Italian films in the late 1930s, working with such directors as SOLDATI; his own debut as a director came in 1941 with *Un Colpo di Pistola*. After World War II his style shifted from NEOREALISM, as in *Under the Sun of Rome* (1948), to 1950s Hollywood elegance, as with the British production of *Romeo and Juliet* (1954). For the last 20 years of his career he made almost all his films for Italian television. He coscripted all of his own pictures and wrote numerous screenplays for other directors. His output includes *It's Forever Springtime* (1949), *Two Cents Worth of Hope* (1952), *Zaza* (1952), *Wild Wild Women* (1958), *Ghosts Italian Style* (1967), and *Leonardo da Vinci* (condensed from a five-part television special; 1972).

Castiglioni, Niccolò (1932–) Italian composer. He studied piano and composition at the Milan Conservatory, following this with studies at the Salzburg Mozarteum (1952–53) and at the DARMSTADT Institute. His career as a composer took off when his radio opera *Attraverso lo specchio* (from Lewis Carroll) won an Italia prize in 1961. Following his appointment as composer-in-residence at the State University of New York at Buffalo in 1966, he settled in the US, teaching at Michigan University (1967), the University of California at San Diego (1968), and Washington University, Seattle (1969). Since 1969 illness has restricted his ability to compose and he has returned to Italy.

His works are notable for their use of orchestral colour and their ability to absorb influences as diverse as BOULEZ on the one hand and Mahler and other late romantic composers on the other. Works such as *Elegia* (1957) and *Impromptus I–IV* (1958) combine serialism with tonal gestures and structures, while the use of aleatoric procedures in *Tropi* (1959) and *Aprèslude* (1959) reflects the influence of Cage and STOCKHAUSEN. The neoimpressionistic *Eine kleine Weihnachtsmusik* for chamber orchestra (1960) marked another change of direction. His output includes four operas, orchestral and instrumental music, and vocal and choral pieces. The operas *The Lords' Masque* and *Oberon*, both settings of 17th-century English masque texts, were premiered in Venice in 1980.

Caulfield, Patrick (1936–) British figurative painter and printmaker. Caulfield was born in London and studied at the Chelsea School of Art (1957–60) and at the Royal College of Art (1960–63). He subsequently taught at the Chelsea School (1963–71). His paintings soon attracted interest and were included in several exhibitions of work by young British painters in the 1960s. He gave his first one-man show in 1965.

Because his works often display the influence of popular printed illustrations, Caulfield is usually associated with the British POP ART movement of the 1960s. The influence of comic-strip art can be seen in the two most distinctive features of his work; namely, his use of flat bright colour and his tendency to surround his subjects with black outlines. Caulfield's subject matter and effects are, however, very different from those of other Pop artists. He favours traditional subjects, such as still lifes and interiors, and renders them in a highly stylized and decorative manner. A major retrospective exhibition of his work was held in Liverpool and at the Tate Gallery, London, in 1981. In the early 1980s he began to incorporate areas of illusionistic painting into his works and to abandon his characteristic black outlines. The resulting works have a complex and unsettling effect.

Cavani, Liliana (1936–) Italian film director, whose films have combined political and social concern with sex and violence. Born in Capri, she studied at the University of Bologna and subsequently at Rome's Centro Sperimentale di Cinematografia. She made 10 features and seven documentaries for Radiotelevisione Italiana before moving into feature films in the late 1960s. Her most striking film was *The Night Porter* (1974), which describes a sadomasochistic love affair between an opera conductor's wife and a hotel porter, whom she recognizes as the former commandant of a Nazi concentration camp in which she had been brutalized and raped. Although critics berated the film as crude and offensive it was a box-office success in the US. Cavani's films, which often draw their subject matter from history or myth, include *Francis of Assisi* (1966), *Galileo* (1968), *The Cannibals* (1969), which used the myth of Antigone as a symbol of Italian revolt against political authority, *Beyond Good and Evil* (1977) about Nietzsche, *The Berlin Affair* (1985), and *San Francesco* (1988).

Cayatte, André (1909–) French film director and screenwriter, noted for a series of courtroom dramas that probe the relationship between law and morality. Cayatte practised as a lawyer before becoming a full-time writer. After working as a journalist and novelist he turned to the cinema as a vehicle for his strong views on the injustices of French society. In 1942 he made his debut as a director with *La Fausse Maîtresse*, following this up with *The Lovers of Verona* (1949), an update of the *Romeo and Juliet* story.

Cayatte found international recognition in the 1950s, taking the Grand Prix at the Venice Film Festival with *Justice Is Done* (1950), a courtroom drama showing how jurors are personally affected by a mercy-killing case, the Special Jury Prize at Cannes for *We Are All Murderers* (1952), and the International Critics' Prize at Cannes with *Avant le Deluge* (1954). *Le Dossier noir* (1955) exposed shortcomings in the French judicial system. In the 1960s Cayatte directed *Anatomy of a Marriage* (1964), which looks at a strained marriage from the points of view of both partners, *The Crossing of the Rhine* (1960), a war film featuring Charles Aznavour, *Two Are Guilty* (1963), and *A Trap for Cinderella* (1965). Later work includes the screenplay for PONTI's *The Verdict* (1975), a melodrama starring Sophia Loren as a gangster's widow who kidnaps a judge. Cayatte, who continued to script all of his films, returned to the question of legal morality in *Justice* (1978).

Cayrol, Jean (1911–) French writer. After studying law and literature, Cayrol became a librarian. During World War II he participated in the Resistance and was sent to the Sachsenhausen concentration camp. After the war he worked as a literary consultant for the Editions du Seuil publishing house, which also published his own works.

Cayrol's concentration-camp experience led him to develop a radically new kind of prose writing, thereby greatly influencing the development of the NOUVEAU ROMAN. In a famous essay *Lazarus Among Us* (1950) he compared his own situation to that of Lazarus, who having once been dead can never return to normal life. His protagonists are isolated drifters who experience a profound incapacity to feel like other people (*Change of Residence*, 1956; *Foreign Bodies*, 1959). His other novels include the important trilogy *I Will Live the Love of Others* (1947–50), as well as *History of the Prairie* (1969), *History of the Desert* (1972), *History of the Forest* (1975), and *Exposed to the Sun* (1980).

Cayrol is considered one of the most important French writers of the post-war generation.

Cecchi D'Amico, Suso (Giovanna Cecchi; 1914–) Italian screenwriter, who played an important role in the development of post-war NEOREALISM. During her career she scripted almost 100 films. Born in Rome, the daughter of the screenwriter Emilio Cecchi, she studied classics and foreign languages before beginning a career as a journalist and translator of English-language plays. She began to write for the cinema after World War II, helping to define the neorealist style with her work for such directors as DE SICA (*Bicycle Thieves*, 1948; *Miracle in Milan*, 1951) and ZAMPA. She later worked with ANTONIONI and VISCONTI and had a long-running association (1949–66) with the director Alessandro Blasetti, for whom she scripted such films as *Too Bad She Is Bad* (1955). Her other scripts include *Rocco and His Brothers* (1960), about the problems of a peasant family who move to Milan, *Boccaccio '70* (1962), the US-Italian production of *The Leopard* (1963), the Elizabeth Taylor-Richard Burton version of *The Taming of the Shrew* (1967), and *Conversation Piece* (1975), about a professor who has to face up to both his homosexuality and his coming death.

Cela (y Trulock), Camilo José (1916–) Spanish novelist and writer. A controversial and iconoclastic figure, Cela has dominated the Spanish literary scene since the appearance of his first novel, *The Family of Pascal Duarte* in 1942. With its shocking brutality, black humour, and exaggerated style this savage tale of murder and revenge stands as the first novel of the *tremendista* school. His many works include short stories (*Those Passing Clouds*, 1945; *The Windmill*, 1956; and the 'black' *New Scenes from Madrid* in seven volumes, 1965–66), poetry (*Treading the Uncertain Light of Day*; 1945), and travel writings (*Journey to the Alcarria*; 1948). However, it is on his novels that his reputation ultimately rests. Among the most celebrated of these is *The Hive* (*La Colmena*; 1951), a panoramic work set in a sordid quarter of Madrid in the years after the Civil War. *Mrs Caldwell Talks with her Son* (1953) concerns a senile woman's grief for her dead son. *San Camilo, 1936* (1969), set again in Madrid, is another 'black' work, showing the influence of the French NOUVEAU ROMAN. *Mazurka for Two Dead* (1983), sometimes considered his masterpiece, deals with the horrors of the Civil War.

In 1968 Cela shocked readers again when he began publishing his *Secret Dictionary*, an erudite encyclopedia of sex. He became a member of the Spanish Academy in 1957 and was awarded the Nobel Prize for literature in 1989.

Celan, Paul (Paul Antschel; 1920–70) Romanian poet writing in German. Born in Czernovitz (now Chernovtsy in the Ukraine), Celan briefly studied medicine in France before returning home to study Romance languages and literature. A Jew, he was sent to a forced labour camp in World War II and worked on road construction; his parents were both killed by the Nazis. After the war he worked as an interpreter and a publisher's reader and began to publish his poems. From 1948 to 1950 he studied German literature in Paris and subsequently became a lecturer at the Ecole Normale Supérieure. Following a journey to Israel he committed suicide by drowning himself in the Seine.

Writing always in the shadow of the immense suffering of the Jewish people during the war, Celan developed a unique poetic style characterized by multiple metaphors, recondite allusions, and bewildering compressions of language and meaning. Influences include French surrealism and the Jewish mystical tradition. The poems struggle against any denial of the enormities that occurred and evoke the metaphysical loneliness that follows from a sense of God's abandonment. In the late 1950s Celan's poetry became more muted and fragmentary and began to show a preoccupation with the point at which language confesses its inadequacy before experience and lapses into silence. Arguably the most difficult poet in the German language, Celan has also proved one of the most influential; his work has had an enormous influence on post-war poetry. His major collections are *Poppy and Memory* (1952), *Speech-Grill* (1959), *Breath-Turn* (1967), and *Light-Constraint* (1970). Posthumously published volumes include *Snow-Part* (1971) and *Time-Farmyard* (1976).

Celaya, Gabriel (Rafael Múgica; 1911–) Spanish poet. The most prolific Spanish poet of the post-war era, Celaya belonged from 1944 to the Espadaña group, which embraced poetry as an agent of (socialist) social change. The quality of Celaya's work, however, does not generally match its quantity, or the level of his political courage, his poetry being too often verbose and diffuse. He varied his style and his pseudonyms with it (another pen name was Juan de Leceta). His 50-odd books include *Mazurkas* (1963), *The Muffled Lantern* (1964), and volumes of essays such as *Exploration of Poetry* (1971). His *Complete Works* were published in 1969 but several volumes have since appeared. Celaya also founded the publishing house North.

Celibidache, Sergiu (1912–) Romanian conductor, mainly of Russian music and Viennese classics. After studies at the Berlin Musikhochschule he conducted the Berlin Philharmonic Orchestra from 1945 until 1951, gaining an international reputation for his scrupulously researched but intensely vital performances. He spent much of his later career conducting radio orchestras in Stuttgart, Stockholm, and Munich. Celibidache has taught conducting in Siena and Philadelphia, US, and is the author of a study of Josquin Desprez. His own compositions include symphonies and piano concertos.

Centres Dramatiques *See* DÉCENTRALISATION DRAMATIQUE.

César (César Baldaccini; 1921–) French sculptor. Born in Marseilles, César studied sculpture at the Ecole des Beaux-Arts there (1935–39) and at the Ecole des Beaux-Arts in Paris (1943–48). Although his long training concentrated on classical figure sculpture César was anxious to find a more contemporary means of expression and from 1947 onwards he began to create figures in plaster and iron. In the early 1950s he began to use rubbish as his basic material, welding scrap iron, tin cans, and springs together to create seated figures and (from 1954 onwards) fantastic hybrid creatures. César gave his first one-man show in 1954. His works were subsequently exhibited in other countries, establishing his reputation as one of Europe's leading sculptors.

César is best known for his work of the early 1960s, when he crushed car bodies and parts of engines in a hydraulic press to create blocks of coloured crumpled metal (for example, *The Yellow Buick*, 1961, Museum of Modern Art, New York). These *compressions dirigées* or 'compressions' functioned both as abstract sculptures and as conceptual works (*see* CONCEPTUAL ART), inviting reflection on the nature of modern technology and the ways in which our society produces and disposes of material objects. From 1965 Cesar experimented with works cast in plastic (for example, *The Thumb*, 1965, Tate Gallery, London) and from 1966 with expanded polyurethane. In the late 1960s he organized a series of HAPPENINGS.

Chabrol, Claude (1930–) French film director, a leading member of the NEW WAVE. Chabrol trained as a pharmacist before working as a critic for the *Cahiers du Cinéma* and writing (with Eric ROHMER) a book on Alfred Hitchcock. He made his debut as a director of feature films in 1958 with *Le Beau Serge*, a beautifully shot study of rural France in which a young student attempts to redeem his childhood friend, now an alcoholic, at the cost of his own health. This film is now generally regarded as the first expression of the New Wave in French cinema.

The success of the film enabled Chabrol to set up his own production company, a move that allowed him greater scope in expressing his critical view of conventional bourgeois values. In *Les Cousins* (1959), about two cousins driven to violence by their desire for the same girl, *Les Bonnes Femmes* (1960), an exploration of the romantic daydreams of four Paris shopgirls (which included in the cast Chabrol's future wife, Stéphane Audran), and *The Third Lover* (1962), in which a journalist destroys a previously happy marriage when he informs the husband of the wife's adultery, Chabrol continued to explore his favourite themes of guilt, self-sacrifice, and redemption.

Over the next few years Chabrol produced only spy thrillers and other commercial projects, but in 1968 he returned to more serious films with *Les Biches*, a portrayal of the destructive effect of jealousy upon a lesbian love affair. Murder, and its ironically beneficial effects upon previously unstable relationships, was the central theme of *La Femme infidèle* (1968) and *Killer!* (1969). *Le Boucher* (1970) – possibly his most admired film – examined the impact of a child killer upon a small French village.

Chabrol's films of the mid 1970s were less remarkable and included several thrillers for television. More recently such films as *Violette Noizière* (1978), *Coq au Vin* (1984) and its sequel *Inspecteur Lavardin* (1986), as well as the futuristic thriller *Dr M* (1989) have pleased the critics.

Chadwick, Lynn (Russell) (1914–) British metal sculptor. Chadwick trained as an architectural draughtsman and served as a pilot during World War II. Between 1944 and 1946 he worked as an architectural and furniture designer but then moved to Gloucestershire, where he began to work as a sculptor. His earliest works, mobiles made of metal or of metal and coloured glass, show the influence of the US sculptor Alexander Calder (1898–1976) and the Spanish sculptor Julio González (1876–1942).

In the mid 1950s Chadwick began to work from steel skeletons, which he covered with skin or plaster and then cast in bronze. Although abstract, the resulting works often hinted at the shapes of humans or animals. Chadwick soon achieved international recognition, winning the International Sculpture Prize at the Venice Biennale in 1956. In the 1960s he reduced the figurative content of his work in favour of a greater emphasis on pure shape. Many of his works of this period were designed to be seen in the open air. In the 1980s he made figures of seated couples, walking figures, and standing forms.

Chailly, Luciano (1920–) Italian composer, teacher, and administrator. After studying the violin at the Ferrara Conservatory, Chailly took an arts degree at Bologna University and studied composition at the Milan Conservatory with Renzo Bossi. Subsequently he also studied with Hindemith, attending his courses at Salzburg in 1948. From 1950 to 1967 he was director of music programming for Italian Radio and Television: since then he has worked as artistic director and (from 1976) general director at the Teatro alla Scala, Milan. He has also worked as artistic director with opera companies in Turin and Verona and with Genoa Opera (1983–85). He taught composition at the Perugia Conservatory from 1968 to 1983 and at the Milan Conservatory from 1969.

Chailly's musical style is essentially neoclassical, although he has made use of both serialism and electronic effects. He has written 13 operas, of which *La cantatrice calva* (1985) is the most recent, and a number of ballets, including *Fantasmi al Grand-Hôtel* (1962), *Anne Frank* (1981), and *Es-Ballet* (1983). Among his instrumental pieces the 12-work series entitled 'Sonate tri tematiche' (1951–61) should be noted. He has also written a book on Italian opera during World War II. The conductor Riccardo Chailly is his son.

Chamberlin, Powell, and Bon (CPB) British architects. Peter Chamberlin (1919–78), Geoffry Powell (1920–), and Christoph Bon (1921–) formed a practice when Powell won the 1952 City of London competition with his designs for the Golden Lane Estate. This housing scheme, completed in 1962, established CPB's predilection for articulating the spaces between buildings as well as the blocks themselves, and gave Chamberlin the opportunity to propose a scheme of up-market housing and schools for the huge adjacent bomb-site. This became the Barbican, approved in 1959 and begun in 1963. It includes the tallest flats in Europe, set around a formal landscape where even the trees and fountains are part of a grid. As one of the schools they attracted was the Guildhall School of Music and Drama, CPB suggested providing a concert hall and theatre that the public could also use. In 1965 this idea was expanded into the present BARBICAN CENTRE, compressed onto the same site and not completed until 1982.

Chamberlin, Powell, and Bon's early work is recognizable for its witty use of bright colour, as seen at Golden Lane, Bousfield School, Kensington (1956), and Witham Seed Factory (1955, demolished). Their later work owes an admitted debt to LE CORBUSIER, seen in the finely finished forms of the Barbican and their expressive work at New Hall, Cambridge University (1962–66) and an extensive complex at Leeds University (1963–75).

Char, René (1907–88) French poet. Born in Isle-sur-la-Sorgue in southern France, René Char studied economics in Marseille and published his first poems in 1928. In Paris he befriended André Breton and the Surrealists and contributed to their journals. During World War II he led a Resistance group and met Albert CAMUS. After the war he returned to his native village and devoted himself to poetry.

In his nature poetry Char celebrates the earth and sun of Provence while also recognizing their demonic and destructive side. A critic of modern industrial civilization, he aimed to liberate intuition and restitute a lost wholeness through his writing. His most famous work, *Leaves from Hypnos* (1946), draws on his wartime experiences.

Although his compressed elliptical language makes his work difficult, Char is among the best-known poets of post-war France. His collections include *Search for the Base and the Summit* (1955) and *Common Presence* (1964); his *Collected Poems* appeared in 1983.

Charrat, Janine (1924–) French dancer, choreographer, and ballet director. Charrat began to dance as a child, performing in the film *La Mort du cygne* (*Ballerina*; 1937) at the age of 13 and going on to win acclaim with PETIT's company in the 1940s. She made her debut as a choreographer in 1945 with Stravinsky's *Jeu de cartes* and subsequently worked as dancer and choreographer with a number of different companies; notable successes included *Concerto No. 3* (1947) and *Abraxas* (1949).

In 1951 she founded Les Ballets Janine Charrat, her own ensemble, taking the dual roles of principal ballerina and choreographer herself. The company quickly attracted attention with performances of *Le Massacre des Amazones* (1951) and other works by Charrat. In 1953, now renamed the Ballet de France, the company staged the work that many consider Charrat's masterpiece as a choreographer, *Les Algues* (in which she also starred). Subsequently she worked alongside Maurice BÉJART in Brussels and enjoyed further success with such ballets as *The Seven Deadly Sins* (1956).

In 1961 Charrat's career was interrupted when she was severely burned in an accident in a television studio. She recovered sufficiently to take over as director of the Geneva Opéra in 1962 and continued to work as a dancer-choreographer. Her successes since then have included Stravinsky's *Firebird* (1969), *Casanova in London* (1969), and *Offrandes and Hyperprism* (1973). She opened her own ballet school in Paris in 1970 and in 1980 became director of the POMPIDOU CENTRE.

Cheltenham International Festival An annual music festival held in Cheltenham, Gloucestershire. Founded in 1945 as the Cheltenham Festival to promote contemporary British music, it broadened its scope in the 1960s and was renamed in 1974. The festival lasts for a fortnight each July. Fewer newly commissioned works are featured now; the programme includes orchestral and chamber music and many solo concerts.

Chéreau, Patrice (1944–) French theatre and opera director, who emerged as one of the most talented directors of the 1980s after early successes working under PLANCHON at the Théâtre National Populaire at Villeurbanne. He first came to attention by winning a competition for directors in 1967 with *The Soldiers* by Johann Lenz. He moved to Villeurbanne in 1972 and, after mounting an acclaimed production of Wagner's *Ring* cycle at Bayreuth (1976–80), subsequently transferred (1982) to the Théâtre des Amandiers at Nanterre. His most notable successes have included works by GENET, Ibsen, and Marivaux.

Chia, Sandro (1946–) Italian neoexpressionist painter. With Georg BASELITZ, Anselm KIEFER, and Francesco CLEMENTE, Chia was one of the leading European figures in the revival of expressionist styles in the late 1970s (*see* NEO-EXPRESSIONISM). Like his compatriots Clemente and Enzo Cucci, he moved to New York in the early 1980s, where their works became highly fashionable and began to command vast prices (the three painters becoming known in the art world as the 'three Cs').

Chia's paintings, most of which are very large and executed in rich swirling colours, typically feature heroic male figures who seem to be engaged in some kind of enigmatic quest (for example *Water Bearer*, 1981, Tate Gallery, London). With their exaggerated physique and heroic posturing these figures seem to derive partly from Italian Fascist art of the 1920s and 1930s. Other influences on Chia's work, which constantly flirts with pastiche and caricature, include the Italian surrealist Giorgio de Chirico (1888–1974) and his brother Alberto Savinio (1891–1952). Chia is usually considered the most technically accomplished of the neoexpressionist painters of the 1970s and 1980s. He has also sculpted in bronze.

Chillida (Juantegui), Eduardo (1924–) Spanish (Basque) sculptor. Born in San Sebastián in north-east Spain, Chillida studied architecture at Madrid University (1943–47). He began to sculpt in 1947. After studies in Paris (1948–51) he returned to Spain and settled in the Basque region, where he has since remained.

Chillida's earliest works were figurative but from about 1950 he began to experiment with abstract sculpture, working mainly in iron. He is best known for his work with wrought iron bars, which he generally fashioned into contorted shapes (for example, *Modulation of Space I*, 1963, Tate Gallery, London). The resulting works are entirely non-figurative with a very austere quality. In his later work he explored other materials, notably wood (from 1959), granite (from 1960), and alabaster (from 1964). He has also produced reliefs, drawings, and *papiers collés* (abstract paintings incorporating elements of collage). Chillida drew on the tradition of working wrought iron found in his native region and on the examples of the earlier Spanish metal sculptors Julio González and Pablo Gargallo. He gave several one-man shows in Paris in the 1950s and won a prize at the 1958 Venice Biennale, leading to an exhibition at the Guggenheim Museum in New York. Thereafter he was a figure of international stature.

Christensen, Inger (1935–) Danish poet, novelist, dramatist, essayist, and prose writer. Christensen is one of the most original poets working in Denmark today; her work is highly intellectual and draws heavily on the linguistic theories of Noam Chomsky.

Her first collection of poetry, *Light*, was published in 1962 and was followed by another, *Grass*, in 1963. Two novels, *The Eternity Machine* and *Azorno*, appeared in 1964 and 1967 respectively but it was not until the publication of the poetry collection *It* in 1969 that Christensen received her due recognition. The 'It' of the title is, on one level, the linguistic world that Christensen is at the same time creating and trying to transcend.

Partly owing to her dialectal background, her work is highly musical and she has been active in promoting the jazz-poetry genre in Denmark. Sometimes witty, her work is rarely entirely apolitical. In 1982 she published a collection of essays, *Part of the Labyrinth*, which provides a good introduction to her thought.

Christou, Jani (1926–1970) Greek composer, born and brought up in Egypt. Christou studied philosophy under Bertrand Russell and Ludwig Wittgenstein at Cambridge, while simultaneously taking private tuition in composition from Hans Redlich – a choice that reflects both the interaction of philosophy and music in his work and his uneasiness with academic musical training. Subsequently he studied music in Italy and spent time at the Jung Institute in Zürich. He returned to Egypt in 1950, settling finally in Greece in 1960. Just as his international reputation was growing, his career was cut short by his death in a car crash.

His freely atonal early works, typified by *Phoenix Music* (1949), are structured around short intense motifs. *Patterns and Permutations* (*Metatropes*; 1960), making use of Christou's technique of 'metaserialism', belongs to a second period in which his music has an overtly mystical purpose. The works of his third phase, most of which were labelled *anaparastasis* or 'reenactment' by the composer, are characterized by the use of taped sounds and an increasing abdication of the composer's conventional role in favour of improvisation. These works include a strong element of ritual and were intended to function as psychological therapy for the performers. His mammoth stage work *Oresteia* (1967–70) was left in fragmentary form at his death.

Chukrai, Grigori (1921–) Russian film director, noted for his state-approved attacks on Stalinism in the 1950s and 1960s. His studies at the VGIK, the Soviet state film school, were halted by World War II, during which he was wounded five times while serving in parachute and infantry units. He was decorated for valour. After the war Chukrai returned to school and made his debut as a director with *Nazar Srodolia* (1954), adapted from a play by Taras Shevchenko. He used his second offering, *The Forty-First* (1956), to poke mild fun at the idealized Stalinist hero; the film took the Jury Prize at the Cannes Festival. His compassionate antiwar film, *Ballad of a Soldier* (1959), also won an award at Cannes. Chukrai returned to his anti-Stalinist theme with more vigour in *Clear Skies* (1961). One of his later films, *There*

Was An Old Man and An Old Woman (1965) was shown widely in the West and he made an impressive documentary, *Battle of Stalingrad* (1970). More recent films include *Life is Beautiful* (1980) and *I Will Teach You to Dream* (1984).

Churchill, Caryl (1938–) British playwright, who emerged as a leading writer through her association with the Joint Stock Theatre Company in the 1970s. *Light Shining in Buckinghamshire* (1976) was the first of several plays treating historical subjects in the light of such topical issues as sexual identity and bureaucratic corruption. Her best-known plays since then have been *Top Girls* (1982), in which various famous women from history meet and exchange views, *Fen* (1982), set in historical East Anglia, *Serious Money* (1987), about business ethics in the City of London, the jazz-inspired *Icecream* (1989), *Mad Forest* (1990), concerning events in Romania following the overthrow of Ceauşescu, and *Lives of the Great Poisoners* (1991). Apart from her success in Britain, Caryl Churchill has a strong reputation in New York, and a production of her *Mad Forest* was particularly well received in Bucharest.

Cinecittà (Italian; cinema city) The sprawling Italian film studio complex whose 15 sound stages make it Europe's largest production centre. Built in 1937 six miles from the centre of Rome, Cinecittà became known as 'Hollywood on the Tiber' during the 1950s when US film-makers took advantage of Italy's low-cost facilities and cheap labour. By the 1970s, however, the boom had ended and the empty Cinecittà stages had come to symbolize the crisis within the Italian cinema.

In the last few years the complex has become more of a production centre in order to attract more features and television series to its full-service facilities. Recent productions have included three major films, Columbia's *The Adventures of Baron Munchhausen*, Paramount's *The Godfather, Part III*, and Tri-Star's *Hudson Hawk*. The state body now responsible for running the studios, Ente Gestione Cinema, has just updated and replaced equipment (with the assistance of Lucasfilm technicians).

cinéma vérité (French; truth cinema) A naturalistic style of film that came into fashion on both sides of the Atlantic in the 1960s. *Cinéma vérité* placed great emphasis upon the use of nonprofessional actors and unrehearsed dialogue in an attempt to convey a sense of real life. Cameras were generally lightweight and hand-held, allowing cameramen to 'eavesdrop' on conversations; sound was usually recorded synchronously and subsequent editing kept to the minimum. Notable examples of the genre included *Chronicle of a Summer* (1961) by Jean Rouch, in which the camera records a series of interviews designed to reveal the preoccupations of Parisian society in the early 1960s.

Cirici, Christián *See* STUDIO PER.

Ciulei, Liviu (1923–) Romanian theatre director and actor, who had an enormous impact upon contemporary Romanian theatre before moving to the US, where he worked (1981–85) in the Guthrie Theatre in Minnesota. As artistic director of the Lucia Sturdza-Bulandra Theatre in Bucharest from 1961, he became famous for his innovative and sometimes bizarre productions of a wide range of plays, which included such foreign works as DÜRRENMATT's *Play Strindberg* (1972). Ciulei was largely responsible for bringing the Romanian theatre into line with the mainstream of current European drama. In the US he consolidated his international reputation with striking productions of Ibsen, Shakespeare, and other classics, as well as the first performances of several important new US dramas. He is also an accomplished scene designer and film-maker.

Clark, Kenneth (Mackenzie) (Baron Clark of Saltwood; 1903–83) British art historian. Born in London, the son of a wealthy industrialist, Clark was educated at Winchester College and at Trinity College, Oxford (1922–25), where he read modern history. In 1925 he met the US art historian Bernard Berenson, who invited Clark to work with him on a revision of his corpus of Florentine drawings (1925–27). Clark later catalogued the Leonardo da Vinci drawings at Windsor Castle and helped to organize a major exhibition of Italian art at London's Royal Academy. In 1931 he was appointed Keeper of Fine Art at the Ashmolean Museum, Oxford, and in 1934 became director of the National Gallery, London, at the age of only 31. In 1945 he resigned. Thereafter writing was his main occupation, though he also served (1954–57) as the first chairman of the Independent Television Authority (which introduced commercial television to Britain) and as chairman of the Arts Council (1953–60).

Clark wrote many notable works on art history, including *Leonardo da Vinci* (1939) and *The Nude* (1956). He is best known, however, for his television series *Civilization*, first broadcast in 1969, in which he presented a personal history of the ideas expressed in the arts of Western civilization from the early Middle Ages onwards. The series achieved great success in many countries around the world and made Clark a celebrity. It remains one of the most successful documentary series ever made for television.

Clark, Michael (1962–) British choreographer and dancer, who became a leading figure in the alternative ballet movement of the 1980s. Clark's work sets out to challenge accepted notions of dance and is often deliberately controversial, employing eclectic musical scores and all manner of bizarre imagery .

Born in Scotland, Clark was invited to join the Royal Ballet School at the age of 13 and was soon acclaimed as one of the most talented dancers of his generation. In 1979 he joined the Ballet Rambert (*see* RAMBERT DANCE COMPANY) and danced in several works written especially for him by such leading contemporary choreographers as Richard ALSTON. He left the Rambert company in 1981 and in 1984 founded his own ensemble in order to develop his interest in choreography. His troupe soon acquired a reputation for their lively and imaginative style. Often the dancing itself was only one element of the whole entertainment. Such works as *No Fire Escape in Hell* (1986), *Because We Must* (1987), and *I Am Curious Orange* (1988) made innovative use of non-dancers and unusual costumes; the company has also attracted attention with its incorporation of nudity, loud rock music, and subversive sexual imagery. Clark has been commissioned to create works for the Paris Opéra Ballet, the Scottish Ballet, and the London Festival Ballet. His most recent works for the Ballet Rambert have included the acclaimed *Swamp* (1986). Clark's *Modern Masterpiece* (1992) was an eccentric reinterpretation of Stravinsky's *Le Sacre de printemps*.

Claus, Hugo (1929–) Belgian poet, novelist, playwright, and theatre director, who emerged as the most important figure in the Belgian theatre after World War II. Born in Bruges, Claus was educated at Catholic schools and worked as a housepainter and agricultural labourer before studying acting with Antonin Artaud in Paris. Of his early plays the best known are the family drama *A Bride in the Morning* (1953) and *Sugar* (1958) which depicted the brutality of the lives of seasonal farm labourers in France. Subsequent dramas have included *Friday* (1969), the film of which he subsequently directed himself, *Leopold II* (1970), an attack on Belgian colonial policy in the Congo, and various adaptations of classic texts, among them Seneca's *Oedipus* (1971) and *Phaedra* (1980), Jonson's *Volpone* (1972), and Euripides's *Orestes* (1976).

Claus's poetry includes the groundbreaking collection *Poems from Oostakker* (1955), which introduced a new experimentation to Flemish verse, and the long Poundian work *The Sign of the Hamster* (1969). His large and varied output of fiction includes *Sister of Earth* (*De Metsies*; 1950), the best-selling *The Year of the Cancer* (1972), a semiautobiographical love story, and *The Sorrows of Belgium* (1983), an attempted magnum opus that some critics found disappointing. His work is profoundly Flemish in both language and inspiration.

Clément, René (1913–) French film director, who established his reputation during the 1950s. He first attracted attention with *La Bataille du rail* (1946), an experiment in NEOREALISM depicting the involvement of French railway workers in the Resistance during World War II, and went on to win four major awards at the CANNES FILM FESTIVAL in the late 1940s and 1950s. In addition to these awards, he won two Oscars for *Au Dela des Grilles* (1949) and *Les Jeux interdits* (1952), in which a group of children create their own cemetery for animals in a perverse ritual mirroring the background horrors of World War II.

Knave of Hearts (1953) followed the romantic adventures of a Frenchman in London as he woos a succession of English ladies; the film's use of hidden cameras on London streets to capture the authentic life of the city caused a considerable stir when the film was shown in Britain. *Gervaise* (1955) was well received but few of his subsequent films repeated his earlier successes; they include *Tomorrow is Another Day* (1962), *The Love Cage* (1964), *A la Recherche du temps perdu* (1966), and *The Baby-Sitter* (1975).

Clemente, Francesco (1952–) Italian figurative painter, who emerged alongside Sandro CHIA and Georg BASELITZ as one of the most celebrated exponents of European NEOEXPRESSIONISM in the late 1970s. Clemente began his career in Rome but moved to New York in the early 1980s when his work became fashionable and began to command high prices there. Although best known for his spectacularly large works in oil on canvas (for example, the series *Fourteen Stations* from 1983), he has worked prolifically in a variety of media including watercolours, pastel, and fresco. More recently there has been something of a critical backlash against his work, with accusations of overproductivity, slapdash execution, and crude sensationalism in both style and content. Frequently lurid and grotesque in its imagery, his work draws heavily on the Tarot and other occult sources and shows a fascination with bodily functions that some have found childish; the figures in his paintings are often engaged in eating, excretion, or sexual activity. Another influence on his work is Indian art, particularly the sexually explicit art of the Tantric tradition; Clemente now spends part of each year working in Madras. In 1991 a major exhibition of Clemente's works representing the 'three worlds' of Rome, New York, and India was held at the Royal Academy, London.

Clementi, Aldo (1925–) Italian composer and teacher. Clementi studied literature at the Universities of Catania and Rome (1943–48) and acquired diplomas in piano and composition at the Accademia di Santa Cecilia in Rome, where his teachers included PETRASSI. Having studied piano in Siena for a further year, he attended STOCKHAUSEN's composition class at the DARMSTADT summer courses in 1961 and 1962. He had already experimented with electronic music at the Studio di Fonologia Musicale in Milan and adopted serialist procedures at the suggestions of MADERNA. He has taught at the Milan Conservatory and Bologna University.

Clementi's neoclassical works of the early 1950s, much influenced by PETRASSI and Stravinsky, were succeeded by pointillistic serialist pieces such as *Tre studi* (1957) and *Ideogrammi no. 1* (1959). Even these early pieces show a marked tendency to the non-developmental, with different phrases simply placed in collage-like juxtaposition. This tendency becomes more pronounced in his first fully characteristic works, the three *Informels*, completed in 1963. Like most of his subsequent works, these are highly indeterminate in structure, using a dense polyphonic technique in which individual intervals are, except for moments of attack, deliberately smothered. Though it also embraces dramatic, vocal, and electronic pieces, his large output concentrates on works for orchestra and instrumental ensemble: these include the violin concerto of 1977, the three *Varianti* (completed 1964), *Blitz* (1973) and *O, di selige* (1986).

Clergue, Lucien (1934–) French photographer and cinematographer. After a musical education, Clergue taught himself photography and staged his first individual exhibition in Zürich in 1958. Clergue has worked in both black-and-white and colour, showing a particular fascination with contrasts of motion and poise. His themes have encompassed bullfighting, life in Provence, nudes, seascapes, and studies of artists such as Picasso and Cocteau. His work has appeared in *Vogue*, *Harper's Bazaar*, and *Esquire* but he has never worked as a photojournalist. Clergue's many books include *El Cordobes* (1965), studies of the Spanish bullfighter, and *Mystique aux Doigts* (1976). He has worked as a cinematographer on several films, including the full-length *Picasso, War, Love and Peace* (1971), and lectured in photography at the University of Provence, Marseilles, the New School for Social Research in New York, and the École Nationale de la Photographie in his native Arles.

Clotet, Lluis *See* STUDIO PER.

Clouzot, Henri-Georges (1907–77) French film director and screenwriter, who established his reputation with a series of suspense thrillers in the 1940s. Clouzot began his career as a film critic and subsequently wrote several screenplays for French versions of German films.

He made his debut as a director in 1942 with the conventional thriller *L'Assassin habitué au 21* and the following year revealed himself as a major new talent with *The Raven* (1943), in which a small French town is torn apart by a campaign of poison-pen letters. The film's bitter view of provincial French life led to false accusations that Clouzot was working on behalf of the occupying Germans; for some years thereafter he was given little work.

In 1947 he reaffirmed his power as a director with *Quai des Orfèvres*, a traditional thriller in which an unhappily married couple face murder charges; the film was distinguished by its atmospheric sets and pervasive air of tragedy. Clouzot's best-known film remains, however, *The Wages of Fear* (1953), in which Yves Montand starred in a tense story of greed and danger set in a South American village. Similarly gripping was *The Fiends* (1955), about the murder of the sadistic headmaster of a down-at-heel boarding school. Other notable films included *The Picasso Mystery* (1956), *Les Espions* (1957), and *The Truth* (1960), an Oscar-winning murder mystery starring Brigitte Bardot.

COBRA An international group of artists, mainly from Scandinavia and the Low Countries, founded in Paris in 1948. The name derives from the initials of the members' home cities: Copenhagen, Brussels, and Amsterdam. The dominant figures in the group were the Dutchman Karel APPEL, the Belgian CORNEILLE, and the Dane Asger JORN; others who joined included Pierre ALECHINSKY, Constant, and Jean Atlan.

Characterized by violent brushwork, intense colours, and an emphasis on spontaneous expression, the painting of the Cobra group represented a reaction against the formalism of the prevailing styles in Paris after World War II. The group's paintings are semiabstract with an element of surrealistic fantasy; many feature strange distorted forms suggestive of mythical beings or fabulous beasts. Influences on the group included Nordic mythology and folk art and the art of children and primitive peoples. The group held major exhibitions in Amsterdam (1949) and Liège (1951) before disbanding; it also published a review (eight issues) and a number of monographs. Although shortlived, Cobra had an important influence on the development of expressive abstraction in Europe after World War II (*see* ART INFORMEL).

Coia, Jack *See* GILLESPIE, KIDD, AND COIA.

Coldstream, Sir William (1908–87) British figurative painter and educationalist. Coldstream studied at the Slade School of Fine Art in London (1926–29) and later worked for the General Post Office Film Unit (1934–37). In his early years as a painter he experimented with abstraction but later rebelled against it. In 1937 he founded the School of Drawing and Painting in Euston Road, London, with Victor PASMORE and Claude Rogers in order to encourage a return to naturalism in painting. The artists of the 'Euston Road School' are noted for their sombrely realistic work. The School closed at the outbreak of World War II but Coldstream adhered to its principles for the rest of his life in his landscapes, townscapes, still lifes, and numerous portraits. His obsession with accurate representation led him to paint according to a rigorous system of measurement (the measuring marks are often visible on his canvases).

After service as an official war artist, Coldstream taught at the Camberwell School of Art (1946–49). He was then appointed Slade Professor at the Slade School of Fine Art, where he remained until retirement in 1975. Coldstream was particularly concerned that artists should not become an isolated elite and that art should have a prominent place in Britain's national life. From 1958 to 1971 he served as Chairman of the Universities National Advisory Committee on Art Education, which encouraged the provision of more art courses as part of the expansion of higher education in Britain during the 1960s.

collective creation In the theatre, the collaboration of the members of a company in the creation of a new work of drama. Traditionally, texts were written by a single playwright and performers were warned against making substantial alterations to the script. Since World War II, however, such ideas have been questioned throughout European theatre and alternative methods of text creation have been explored. In the 1960s the increasing use of improvisation and new ideas about the relationship between the actor and his role, as promoted by the BERLINER ENSEMBLE among other companies, led to a new kind of drama in which all members of a company could have some creative input from the earliest stages of a theatrical project. Notable exponents of collective creation have included Joan LITTLEWOOD's Theatre Workshop.

Collegium Aureum German early-music ensemble. The Collegium was cofounded in 1964 in Cologne by Franz Josef Maier (violinist), who directs and leads it, to record baroque and early classical music on original instruments and authentic modern copies. They subsequently developed as a live performing group, touring Europe, the Soviet Union, and Japan. Their repertory originally concentrated on Bach (*Brandenburg concertos*, suites, cantatas), Handel (*Water Music*, *Music for the Royal Fireworks*), Haydn (symphonies and concertos), and Mozart (serenades, concertos, and symphonies), but their 'authentic' recording in 1976 of Beethoven's third symphony (*'Eroica'*) extended their repertory into the 19th century. *See also* EARLY-MUSIC MOVEMENT.

Collins, Cecil (1908–89) British painter. Born in Plymouth, he studied at the Plymouth School of Art (1923–27) and at the Royal College of Art, London (1927–31). He gave his first one-man exhibition in 1935 at the Bloomsbury Gallery, London, and in 1936 took part in the International Surrealist Exhibition in London, although he later repudiated surrealism. In 1938 he met the American artist Mark Tobey, who encouraged his interest in Oriental art and philosophy. In 1947 he published his book *The Vision of the Fool*, an account of his philosophy of art and life, in which he attacked the 'spiritual betrayal' of the modern world. From 1940 onwards he produced a long series of paintings and drawings originally called *The Holy Fool* but later retitled *The Vision of the Fool* in accordance with the book (an example is *Sleeping Fool*, 1943, in the Tate Gallery, London). For Collins the figure of the Fool represented spontaneity and purity in contrast to modern materialism and commercialism. He saw his work as an attempt to recapture the paradisiacal vision of childhood. His spiritual outlook led him to religious art, his work including an altarpiece for Chichester Cathedral (1973). A retrospective of Collins's life's work opened at the Tate Gallery, London, in the month before his death.

Comencini, Luigi (1916–) Italian film director and screenwriter, who in 1940 founded (with LATTUADA and Ferrari) the Cineteca Italiana film archives in Milan. He originally studied architecture but became a journalist and film critic. His directorial debut came in 1946 with the short documentary, *Bambini in Città* (1946). After a brief flirtation with NEOREALISM early in his career, Comencini turned to more conventional film-making with the Swiss production *Heidi* (1952) and the box-office success *Bread, Love and Dreams* (1953), a comedy about a policeman visiting a village to find a wife that starred DE SICA and Gina Lollobrigida. Its commercial success led to a sequel, *Bread, Love and Jealousy* (1954). Comencini continued to aim his work at the general cinema-going public with such offerings as *Everybody Go Home!* (1960), *Italian Secret Service* (1968), *The Sunday Woman* (1976), *They All Loved Him* (1980), *The Boy From Calabria* (1987), *La Bohème* (1989), *Merry Christmas, Happy New Year* (1990) and *Annabelle Partagée* (1993). Much of his most recent work has been for Italian television. He collaborates on scripts for his own films and those of other directors.

community theatre Any theatrical organization or form of drama that makes a special attempt to reach an audience that would not normally be attracted to the conventional theatre. Community theatre became a distinct theatrical phenomenon in the 1960s, when drama worldwide was seeking a new relevance in modern society. Some organizations identified particular subsections within the community that had been ignored by the established theatre and devoted themselves to filling the gap, specializing in drama that aired issues important to such groups as homosexuals, feminists, and racial minorities. Others sought to take drama to remote areas or to cater for the old and the handicapped. Inevitably such companies often adopted strident political views, which in some countries militated against substantial official support, but the genre did provide a new forum for discussion of difficult social issues as well as promoting the work of radical new playwrights.

A third variety of community theatre, which developed at much the same time, involves the creation and staging of documentary dramas based on the local history of a particular community. Local people are enlisted as performers and in technical roles, usually under the guidance of a professional director and with a professional playwright in attendance. This highly popular type of community play was pioneered by the writer and director Ann Jellicoe (1927–) in Dorset. Works commissioned by Jellicoe from well-known playwrights include Howard BARKER's *The Poor Man's Friend* (1981), set in Bridport, and David EDGAR's *Entertaining Friends* (1985), set in Dorchester.

Noteworthy examples of community theatre in recent years have included Peter BROOK's tours of Africa and India and the considerable achievements of the DÉCENTRALISATION DRAMATIQUE policy in France.

Comune, La *See* FO, DARIO; RAME, FRANCA.

Concentus Musicus *See* HARNONCOURT, NIKOLAUS.

conceptual art Art in which the ideas or concepts involved are more important than the objects used to convey them. Conceptual art has its roots in the Dadaist movement of 1915–1922, especially in the 'readymades' of Marcel Duchamp, who challenged ideas about what constitutes art by exhibiting ordinary objects, such as a urinal. Modern conceptual art developed in the 1950s with the work of such artists as Yves KLEIN, who in 1958 displayed *Le Vide* (*Emptiness*) – a gallery with windows painted blue and walls white, which was left empty.

From the mid 1960s onwards conceptual art became highly fashionable in Europe and the US. In part, this vogue was a reaction against the commercial nature of the art world. Conceptual artists often undertook actions that they then reported by means of photographs, drawings, texts, diagrams, etc; by doing so they hoped to avoid the creation of commercial art objects, though photographs and other items were often sold. Some conceptual art has also sought to make explicit political statements about the world (including the art world). For example, in 1974 Hans HAACKE devised his Manet Project for the Wallraf-Richartz Museum in Cologne, consisting of a Manet painting owned by the museum and a series of panels giving information about the social and economic status of the painting's owners; the final panel was to display information about the chairman of the Friends of the Museum. The museum banned the exhibit. Conceptual art became less fashionable in the late 1970s, though leading exponents continued to produce conceptual works through the 1980s. Conceptual artists usually intended their documentary material to be trivial; it remains an open question whether the ideas they meant to convey were generally any more valuable.

Constant, Marius (1925–) French composer and conductor, born in Romania. After graduating from the Bucharest Conservatory in 1944, Constant studied in Paris with MESSIAEN, Nadia Boulanger, and Arthur Honegger. He was director (1956–66) of the Ballets de Paris of Roland Petit and was appointed musical director of the Paris Opéra in 1971. He first attracted notice with his *24 Préludes* (1958) for orchestra but is perhaps best known as the founder, president, and musical director of the Ars Nova (1963–71), an ensemble specializing in new music. His works include the ballets *Cyrano de Bergerac* (1960), *Paradise Lost* (1967), and *Candide* (1970), *Turner* (1961) a symphonic hommage to the painter, *Piano Personnage* (1974), and music for radio.

Cook, Peter (1936–) British architect. Born in Southend, Cook was trained at the Bournemouth School of Art and the Architectural Association in London (1958–60). He was a founder member of the ARCHIGRAM group in 1960, coeditor of *Archigram* magazine (1961–70), and a partner, with Ron Herron and Dennis Crompton, in Archigram Architects (1969–75). He has been on the faculty of the Architectural Association since 1964 and was director of the Institute of Contemporary Arts (1973–74). Since 1978 he has been in partnership with Christine Hawley in Cook-Hawley Architects. In Archigram he helped develop the plug-in city and instant city concepts and has produced similar experimental concepts since, such as the Layer City (1981) and the Block City (1983). Cook Hawley have produced important designs for solar-powered housing but have built little. Peter Cook has held senior academic posts in New York, Oslo, Rhode Island, Frankfurt, Los Angeles, and elsewhere.

Co-op Himmelblau Austrian architectural practice, founded in Vienna in 1968 by Wolf D. Prix and Helmut Swiczinsky.

Identifying themselves firmly with the avant-garde, they declared "we wanted to built architecture like clouds. Architecture which responds to people, not the other way round." Most of their early projects were uncommissioned sculptures and designs; latterly substantial commissions have followed without diminishing the firm's radical, even confrontational, approach. The Hot Flat in Vienna (1979) "is a conflagration of rage. The great spike driven laterally through the building supports a flame-shaped glass roof. Architecture stands impaled in agony." Other schemes have included interiors for shops and cafes in Vienna, the Merz School in Vienna (1981–85), and the Funder Factory in Carinthia (1988–89). In 1987 they set up another office in Los Angeles and in 1988 their work was featured in the Deconstructivism exhibition in the New York Museum of Modern Art. Co-op Himmelblau won three major competitions in 1990; one for a town-planning project at Melun-Sénart near Paris, one for a renovation of a theatre in Vienna, and one for additions to the Hotel Altmannsdorf in Vienna.

Cork Jazz Festival An annual festival of jazz, lasting for a weekend in October. It is held in various venues – including the Opera House, several hotel ballrooms, and many pubs – in Cork, Ireland. Reputed to be Ireland's biggest music festival, it attracts some of the best-known international names in contemporary jazz as well as a host of local performers. The festival was founded in 1977 with the aim of involving the city and its inhabitants as much as possible; the central event each year is a large free concert. All types of jazz are featured, from jive to blues, along with a wealth of street music and busking. The festival is now sponsored by Guinness, the brewing company.

Corneille (Cornelis Guillaume van Beverloo; 1922–) Dutch abstract painter. Born in Liège, Belgium, Corneille emigrated to Holland in 1940 and subsequently became naturalized. He studied drawing at the Rijksakademie, Amsterdam (1940–43), etching under S. W. HAYTER at Atelier 17 in Paris, and ceramics with Mazzotti at Albisola Mare, Italy (1954–55) but was self-taught as a painter. He settled in Paris in 1953. In 1956 he received the Guggenheim Netherlands Prize and in 1966 held a retrospective exhibition at the Stedelijk Museum, Amsterdam.

In 1948 Corneille founded the Dutch Experimental Group with Karel APPEL and Constant. They published a short-lived magazine called *Reflex* before merging with the COBRA group, which aimed to allow the painters' unconscious free rein. He developed an individual style of expressive abstraction (*see* ART INFORMEL) using a contrasting outline around every facet of colour. In his later work he returned to figurative painting, while continuing to use his outlining technique.

Costa-Gavras, Constantin (1933–) Greek film director, living in France, who became well known for his political thrillers in the 1960s and 1970s. Of Russian descent, Costa-Gavras moved to Paris to study film and later became assistant to such directors as René Clair and Jacques DEMY. He made his directorial debut in 1965 with *The Sleeping Car Murders*, an accomplished thriller; this was followed by a second thriller, *Un Homme de trop* (1967).

In 1968 he established an international reputation with *Z*, the first of his thrillers to have a sharp political edge. The film's denunciation of government corruption and the abuse of human rights won Costa-Gavras recognition as one of Europe's most political directors. He continued to explore the official misuse of power in such films as *The Confession* (1970), about political trials in Stalinist Czechoslovakia, *State of Siege* (1972), about US involvement in atrocities in Uruguay, and *Special Section* (1975), which tackled wartime collaboration in Vichy France.

Costa-Gavras went to Hollywood to make his next film, which proved to be his most controversial work – *Missing* (1982). Starring Jack Lemmon and Sissy Spacek, it explored the role of the US in the coup against Allende in Chile in 1973; its open criticism of US foreign policy aroused the wrath of the US government.

Subsequently Costa-Gavras continued to court controversy, examining the Palestinian question in *Hannah K* (1983) and racism in the southern US in *Betrayed* (1988). *Music Box* (1991), a gripping thriller about the attempts of a US lawyer to defend her Hungarian-born father on war crimes charges, won the Golden Bear at the BERLIN FILM FESTIVAL.

Cousin, Gabriel (1908–) French playwright, one of the most important writers associated with the policy of DÉCENTRALISATION DRAMATIQUE. Seeing himself as a spokesman for the French working classes, from which he himself hails, Cousin has emerged as a provocative commentator on issues ranging from hunger and exploitation to racism and nuclear war. He made his name with *The Drama of the Fukuryu Maru* (1962), which dramatizes the experiences of fishermen who were accidentally harmed by a nuclear test in the Pacific in 1954; the play was much admired in its original production directed by Jean DASTÉ.

Cousin went on to consolidate his reputation with such plays as *Black Opera* (1967), a musical exploring the subject of racial prejudice, and *The Journey Behind the Mountain* (1966), which tackled the themes of poverty and old age. Best known of all his plays is *The Crab Cycle* (1975), set in a poor South American community; like many of his other works this makes effective use of music and dance to emphasize its message. He has directed an arts centre in Grenoble since 1972.

Cousteau, Jacques (Yves) (1910–) French oceanographer. Cousteau studied at the Ecole Navale in Brest and on graduation entered the French navy. During World War II he served in the French Resistance and was awarded the Légion d'Honneur and the Croix de Guerre. During the war he also designed and tested an aqualung. For this he adapted a valve (formerly used to enable car engines to work with cooking gas) into an underwater breathing apparatus. Using compressed air, the Cousteau–Gagnan aqualung allows long periods of underwater investigation at depths of more than 200 feet (61 m) and frees the diver of the need for a heavy suit and lifeline.

In 1946 Cousteau became head of the French navy's Underwater Research Group. In 1951–52 he travelled to the Red Sea in a converted minesweeper, the *Calypso*, and made the first underwater colour film to be taken at a depth of 150 feet (46 m). Later he helped Auguste Piccard in the development of the first bathyscaphes. Cousteau also designed and worked on a floating island off the French coast that enabled long-term study of marine life. He is the designer of an underwater diving 'saucer' capable of descents to more than 600 feet (183 m) and able to stay submerged for 20 hours. More significantly, he has worked on the future exploitation of the sea bed as a living environment for man, conducting various experiments on short-term undersea living. He was director of the Musée Océanographique in Monaco (1957–88).

Cousteau may be said to have made more significant contributions to undersea exploration and study than any other individual. His work has been brought to a wide audience through cinema and television, and a number of his films, for example, *The Silent World* (1956; with Louis MALLE), have won Academy Awards. His many books, such as *The Living Sea* (1963), *Dolphins* (1975), and *Jacques Cousteau's Amazon Journey* (1984), and his television documentaries in the series *The Undersea World of Jacques Cousteau* have captured the imagination of millions. In the 1980s he became increasingly active in ecological and antinuclear causes.

Cramér, Ivo (1921–) Swedish dancer, choreographer, and ballet director, born in Gothenburg, who emerged as one of the most influential figures in contemporary Swedish dance after World War II. Cramér began his career as a dancer with Birgit CULLBERG in 1944 and subsequently founded with her the avant-garde Svenska Dansteatern company, which toured Europe in the late 1940s. In 1948 he became ballet master of the Lisbon Verde Gaio company, after which he worked as a choreographer and director for a number of different troupes, including the Royal Swedish Ballet, which he directed from 1975 to 1980.

Cramér's most successful creations as a choreographer include the ballet *The Prodigal Son* (1958), which was first performed by the Royal Swedish Ballet, and more recently works for the Cramérballetten company, which he founded with his wife Tyyne Talvo in 1968. These include such pieces as *Good Evening, Beautiful Mask* (1971), based on the assassination of Gustav III and *Peasant Gospel* (1972).

Cranko, John (1927–73) British choreographer and ballet director, born in South Africa, who contributed to the revival of interest in ballet in the 1950s and 1960s. Cranko received his early training in South Africa and choreographed his first ballet, the suite from Stravinsky's *The Soldier Tale*, at the age of just 16. Subsequently he trained at the Sadler's Wells School and joined the Sadler's Wells Ballet under Ninette DE VALOIS. He became the company's resident choreographer in 1950 and enjoyed his first major success with *Pineapple Poll* (1951), a lively nautical comedy.

Cranko was widely praised for the vigour and dramatic intensity of his work and went on to create a further 30 or so pieces for Sadler's Wells and the ROYAL BALLET. The most notable of these included *Bonne-Bouche* (1952), *The Shadow* (1953), *The Lady and the Fool* (1954), and his full-length ballet *The Prince of the Pagodas* (1957), to a score by Benjamin BRITTEN. In 1960 he also directed the first production of Britten's opera *A Midsummer Night's Dream*.

Following a successful performance of *The Prince of the Pagodas* in Stuttgart in 1960, Cranko left the Royal Ballet to take the post of ballet director at the Stuttgart Ballet. Within a few years he had performed the 'Stuttgart Ballet Miracle', revitalizing the company and establishing its reputation as one of the best in the world. Ballets created for the company included *Romeo and Juliet* (1962), *Onegin* (1965), starring the fiery Brazilian dancer Marcia Haydée, *The Taming of the Shrew* (1969), *Carmen* (1971), and *Initials R.B.M.E.* (1972). Among classical ballets that he adapted the most successful was *Swan Lake* (1963).

Cranko died unexpectedly at the age of 45 while travelling back to Germany with his company after a successful tour of the US.

Crick, Francis (Harry Compton) (1916–) British molecular biologist. Crick graduated from University College, London, and during World War II worked on the development of radar and magnetic mines. Later he changed from physics to biology and in 1947 began work at the Strangeways Research Laboratory, Cambridge, transferring to the Medical Research Council unit at the Cavendish Laboratory in 1949. He remained in Cambridge until 1977, when he took up a professorship at the Salk Institute, San Diego, California.

In 1951 James Watson suggested to Crick that it was necessary to find the molecular structure of the hereditary material, DNA, before its function could be properly understood. Using existing knowledge of the chemical and physical nature of DNA and the X-ray diffraction data of Maurice Wilkins and Rosalind FRANKLIN, Crick and Watson had built, by 1953, a molecular model incorporating all the known features of DNA. Fundamental to the model was their conception of DNA as a double helix. The model served to explain how DNA replicates – by the two spirals uncoiling and each acting as a template – and how the hereditary information might be coded – in the sequence of bases along the chains. For their work, which has been called the most significant discovery of this century, they were awarded, with Wilkins, the 1962 Nobel Prize for physiology or medicine.

Crick, in collaboration with Sydney Brenner, made important contributions to the understanding of the genetic code and introduced the term 'codon' to describe a set of three adjacent bases that together code for one amino acid. He also formulated the adaptor hypothesis in which he suggested that, in protein synthesis, small adaptor molecules act as intermediaries between the messenger RNA template and the amino acids. Such adaptors, or transfer RNAs, were identified independently by Robert Holley and Paul Berg in 1956. Crick is also known for his formulation of the Central Dogma of molecular genetics, which assumes that the passage of genetic information is from DNA to RNA to protein. David Baltimore was later to show that in certain cases, information can actually go from RNA to DNA.

In 1966 Crick published the book *Of Molecules and Men*, reviewing the recent progress in molecular biology. Other books are *Life Itself* (1981) and *What Mad Pursuits: a Personal View of Scientific Discovery* (1988). He was appointed OM in 1991.

Crippa, (Gaetano) Roberto (1921–72) Italian painter and sculptor. Born at Monza in Lombardy, Crippa studied at the Accademia di Brera in Milan (1944–48). His teachers included Achille Funi, a leading member of the Novecento Italiano (a group that sought to uphold a figurative art based on Italian traditions) and Carlo Carrà, previously a leading futurist and Italian cubist painter.

Crippa began to paint in an abstract style with a hint of surrealism, apparently influenced by the Chilean surrealist Roberto Matta (1911–). In 1947 he became the first Italian painter to experiment with action painting but his works retained some surrealist features, often presenting objects hovering in space (paintings from this period include *Aurora Borealis*, 1952, Tate Gallery, London). In 1948 he joined Lucio FONTANA's Movimento Spazialismo, an avant-garde movement that specialized in the creation of three-dimensional 'environments'. Crippa's work continued to change and develop. From the mid 1950s onwards he produced paintings and cast-iron sculptures of totem-like figures. In 1956 he created a series of relief collages in an ART BRUT style; these were apparently influenced by his horror at the Soviet-led invasion of Hungary. In his later years he produced mainly collage-like paintings with brilliant colours. From the 1950s onwards Crippa's works were exhibited in the US and many European countries. Crippa was also a skilled aerobatic pilot; he died in a flying accident.

Cristaldi, Franco (1924–92) Italian film producer and cinema executive, who produced some of the most memorable films in post-war Italian cinema. He abandoned legal studies in Turin to set up his own production company, La Vides Cinematografica, at the age of 22. After several years making documentaries, he became Italy's youngest producer of features in 1953. During his career he worked with such key figures in modern Italian cinema as VISCONTI (*White Nights*, 1957; *Of a Thousand Delights*, 1965), FELLINI (*Amarcord*, 1974; *And the Ship Sailed on*, 1983) and BELLOCCHIO (*China is Near*, 1967; *In the Name of the Father*, 1971). He enjoyed a particularly successful partnership with Francesco ROSI, for whom he produced *Salvatore Giuliano* (1962), *Lucky Luciano* (1973), and the highly praised *Christ Stopped at Eboli* (1979; from the book by Carlo LEVI). Other important productions include GERMI's stylish black comedy *Divorce Italian Style* (1961), MONICELLI's *Persons Unknown* (1958), and PONTECORVO's *Kapo* (1960). In the 1970s he worked on a number of international coproductions including the British film *Lady Caroline Lamb* (1972) and became president of the International Federation of Film Producers Associations (IFFPA). Later successes included *The Name of the Rose* (1986; from the novel by Umberto ECO) and Giuseppe Tornatore's *Cinema Paradiso* (1988), which won an Oscar for best foreign film.

Crosby, Theo (1925–) British architect. Born in Mafeking, South Africa, Crosby was educated at the University of Witwatersrand and settled in Britain in 1947. He worked for FRY AND DREW (1947–52) and became technical editor of the magazine *Architectural Design* (1953–62) before working for Taylor Woodrow as supervising architect for the reconstruction of Euston station, London. In 1965 he was a founder-partner in Crosby/Fletcher/Forbes; in 1972 the firm was expanded and renamed Pentagram Design. Pentagram have established a leading role as designers of shops, exhibitions, and advertising, producing corporate identity programmes for companies such as BP, Reuters, and St Ivel. Their best-known work includes a complex remodelling of Ulster Terrace, one of the Nash Terraces in Regent's Park (1971–73), and the refurbishment of Unilever House, London (1978–83). Crosby has been an important critic of architects' monopoly over the urban environment, advocating a joint approach with designers.

Cruelty, Theatre of A theatrical movement of the 1950s and 1960s inspired by the theories of the French actor and director Antonin Artaud (1896–1948), as set out in his treatise *The Theatre and its Double* (1938). Influenced by surrealism and Eastern dance-drama, Artaud proposed that drama should return to its origins in ritual, making use of gesture, noise, incantation, and spectacle, rather than rational dialogue. The style would be deliberately shocking and violent in order to provoke a cathartic release of repressed emotions in its audience. Artaud's theories achieved great influence after World War II, affecting the work of the playwrights Jean GENET, Fernando ARRABAL, Joe ORTON, and Peter WEISS. Directors influenced by the Theatre of Cruelty have included Roger BLIN, Jean-Louis BARRAULT, Jean VILAR, Jerzy GROTOWSKI, and Peter BROOK, whose production of Weiss's *Marat/Sade* (1964) is usually considered the fullest embodiment of its ideas.

Cuixart, Modesto (1925–) Spanish painter. A native of Barcelona, Cuixart studied medicine before devoting himself to painting. His earliest works were sketches and paintings in an impressionist style but from 1946 onwards he painted in a surrealist manner. In 1948 Cuixart was a founder member (with Antonio TÀPIES) of the important group Dau al Set ('Seven on the Die'), an association of painters and writers who aimed to revive cultural life in Barcelona and to promote international artistic trends, especially surrealism, in Franco's Spain. The group's magazine, also called *Dau al Set*, featured Cuixart's drawings. The group lasted until 1953.

At about this time Cuixart abandoned painting. When he resumed, in 1956, he adopted an abstract style influenced by ART INFORMEL. His paintings of this period are notable for their rich colours, their use of metallic paints, and their impasto technique. In the late 1960s he returned to figurative painting and produced works featuring magical or sadomasochistic subject matter. Cuixart has won several major prizes for his work in Spain. From the late 1950s onwards his paintings were exhibited in Europe, the US, and Latin America.

Cullberg, Birgit (1908–) Swedish dancer, choreographer, and ballet director, born in Nyköping, who is widely regarded as the most important figure in contemporary Swedish dance. Having studied literature at Stockholm University, Cullberg trained as a dancer with such notable figures as Kurt Jooss in Britain and Martha Graham in the US. She founded her own company in 1939 and in 1946 cofounded the avant-garde Svenska Dansteatern touring company with Ivo CRAMÉR. She later joined the Royal Swedish Ballet as a choreographer (1952–57) before working with several companies throughout Europe and with the American Ballet Theatre in the US.

Cullberg's reputation was established with her dance version of Strindberg's *Miss Julie* (1950), in which she explored the possibilities of dance as psychological study, while combining modern and classical dance techniques. The ballet – much influenced by Roland PETIT's *Carmen* – has been revived many times and provided Erik Bruhn with one of his greatest roles, as the Butler. Subsequent successes included such ballets as *Medea* (1950), *The Moon Reindeer* (1957, which drew on Lapp folklore, *Lady from the Sea* (1960), based on Ibsen's play, *Eden* (1961), *Romeo and Juliet* (1969), *Bellman* (1971), *Revolte* (1973), and *War Dances* (1979). She has also devised numerous ballets for television, among them the award-winning *The Evil Queen* (1961), which was based on *Snow White*. Since 1967 she has worked primarily with the Cullberg Ballet. Her sons Niklas and **Mats Ek** have danced with her company and Mats has also been praised as a choreographer, like his mother drawing on folk legends and the theatre for inspiration. Among the successes enjoyed by their joint company, the Ek/Cullberg Ballet, is Ek's avant-garde version of *Swan Lake*.

Curtis, Jean-Louis (Louis Lafitte; 1917–) French writer. After studying literature at the Sorbonne, Curtis worked as a schoolteacher in Paris. During World War II he took part in the Resistance. After the war he taught and lectured widely in Europe, Africa, and the US while producing a series of novels, radio plays, and film scripts.

Written in a traditional narrative style, Curtis's novels tend to focus on the behaviour of individuals in situations that demand courage and determination. Nevertheless, his novel of occupied France, *The Forests of the Night* (1947), avoids idealizing the Resistance; it was awarded the Prix Goncourt. *Lucifer's Dream* (*Gibier de potence*; 1949) deals with the difficulties faced by young people in post-war Paris, while *The Side of the Angels* (*Les justes causes*; 1954) and *The Parade* (1960) explore the ways in which individual aspirations can lead to conflict with society. *The Silken Ladder* (1957) and *Wild Swan* (1962) are love stories. His writing blends pathos and irony. More recent publications include *The Beating of My Heart* (1981) and *The Temple of Love* (1990); he has also translated a number of Shakespeare's plays. Curtis was elected to the Académie Française in 1986.

D

Dallapiccola, Luigi (1904–75) Italian composer and writer. His early training as a pianist was interrupted by his family's internment in Graz (1917–18) during World War I, though he became acquainted there with Mozart's operas and a performance of Wagner's *The Flying Dutchman* (1917) inspired a wish to become a composer. In 1923 he entered the Florence Conservatory where he studied composition under Roberto Casiraghi and Vito Frazzi. By this time he had already absorbed two major influences: the music of the Italian Renaissance and that of Debussy. He was also greatly impressed by a performance of Schoenberg's *Pierrot Lunaire* in 1924. He taught piano at the Florence Conservatory from 1930, joining the staff full-time from 1934 to 1967. His knowledge of SERIALISM developed during the 1930s: he met Berg in 1934 and Webern in 1942. A long-standing opponent of Fascism, he was forced into hiding in 1943. After the war he resumed an active role in Italian musical life and *Canti di prigionia* (1941), his first important work, brought him international acclaim. Invited to teach at the Tanglewood Center in 1951, he began a series of visits to the US as well as continuing to travel throughout Europe. His opera *Ulisse* (1968) confirmed his international stature. Taken ill in 1972, he finished no further works.

Dallapiccola stands out from his generation of Italian composers for his early adoption of serialist procedures. Though essentially Schoenbergian, his use of these techniques revealed personal preferences and innovations from the outset; his liking for all-interval rows is evident in *Canti di liberazione* (1956). His concept of 'floating rhythm' – in which values are manipulated so as to obscure the rhythmic pulse – was developed during the 1950s.

Other significant works include the opera *Il prigioiniero* (1948) and the choral works *Requiescant* (1958) and *Tempus destruendi - Tempus aedificandi* (1971).

Dalwood, Hubert (1924–76) British sculptor. Born in Bristol, Dalwood served an apprenticeship at the Bristol Aeroplane Company before entering (1944) the Royal Navy as an engineer. From 1946 until 1949 he attended the Bath Academy of Art, where his teachers included the sculptor Kenneth ARMITAGE. Dalwood then travelled abroad and worked in Milan and Sicily. He was later Gregory Fellow in Sculpture at the University of Leeds (1955–58) and taught in London at the Hornsey College of Art (1966–73) and at the Central School of Art (1974–76).

Dalwood first came to public attention with a series of large female figures, which he produced in the mid 1950s. He then turned to the modelling of abstract reliefs and in the late 1960s produced abstract sculptures suited to exhibition outdoors in landscape settings. Dalwood gave his first one-man show in 1954 and won first prize in the John Moores Exhibition in Liverpool in 1959 and first prize for sculpture at the Venice Biennale in 1962. The Hayward Gallery in London gave a retrospective exhibition of his works in 1979.

Damiani, Damiano (1922–) Italian film director and screenwriter. He began a career as a director of documentaries in 1945, while still studying at Milan's Academia di Belle Arti; he went on to make some 30 shorts in 10 years. In the mid 1950s he became a screenwriter and assistant director of features. His debut feature film, *Lipstick* (1960), won a prize at the San Sebastian Film Festival. He coscripts most of his films. They have included *The Empty Canvas* (1963), from MORAVIA's novel about the tormented relationship between a painter and his promiscuous mistress, *Confessions of a Police Captain* (1971), *Assassins of Rome* (1973), *The Tempter* (1974), the British-Italian coproduction *The Devil Is a Woman* (1975), *The Genius* (1975), and *Goodbye and Amen* (1978).

Dantzig, Rudi van (1933–) Dutch dancer, choreographer, and ballet director, who is specially noted for his work with the DUTCH NATIONAL BALLET. He trained under Sonia GASKELL but was subsequently more influenced by the US choreographer Martha Graham; he made his first appearances with the Ballet Recital company in 1952. In 1954 he joined the Netherlands Ballet as a dancer and choreographer and five years later became a cofounder of the NETHERLANDS DANCE THEATRE. Since 1960 he has worked with the Dutch National Ballet – as codirector from 1969 and sole artistic director since 1971 – although he has also created works for such foreign companies as the Ballet Rambert (*see* RAMBERT DANCE COMPANY) and the Royal Danish Ballet.

Often working in close collaboration with the dancer, designer, and choreographer Toer van Schayk, he has established a reputation for intensely emotional and personal ballets incorporating both classical and modern techniques. He has also promoted the works of such contemporary choreographers as ASHTON and Balanchine. His works include *Night Island* (1955), to the music of Debussy, *The Family Circle* (1958), *Jungle* (1961), *Monument for a Dead Boy* (1965), which traced the tragic life of a homosexual, *Moments* (1968), *Epitaph* (1969), which was a sombre meditation upon death, *On the Way* (1970), *The Ropes of Time* (1970), created for Rudolf NUREYEV, *Coloured Birds* (1971), *Here Rests: A Summer Day* (1973), *Ramifications* (1973), *Blown in a Gentle Wind* (1975), *Four Last Songs* (1977), and *Life* (1974). His book *Ballet and the Modern Dance* (1974) traces the development of ballet in the Netherlands.

D'Arcy, Margaretta *See* ARDEN, JOHN.

Darmstadt A city in Germany (formerly in West Germany). In contemporary music circles it is important for the International Summer Courses for New Music (Internationale Ferienkürse für Neue Musik) started by Wolfgang Steinecke in 1946; they were held annually until 1970 and biennially thereafter. These courses – comprising classes in composition and interpretation, lectures, and first performances of new works – were particularly influential during the 1950s in disseminating knowledge of the techniques of SERIALISM. The courses have involved (whether as students or lecturers) most of those central to avant-garde music in the 1950s and 1960s, including MESSIAEN, BERIO, BOULEZ, Cage, MADERNA, NONO, POUSSEUR, STOCKHAUSEN, XENAKIS, and HENZE. The **Internationales Musikinstitute Darmstadt**, which runs the courses, is also an information centre and archive for contemporary music.

Dartington International Summer School and Festival An annual summer school and festival of music, held for a month in July and August in Dartington, Devon. It was founded in 1948 at Bryanston School, Dorset, but five years later moved to Dartington Hall, which is renowned for its fine medieval architecture and excellent acoustics. The programme has two main elements – the summer school, consisting of masterclasses, workshops, and coaching by British and international musicians, together with lectures and discussions on a variety of musical subjects, and the festival of concerts and recitals, which features chamber music, opera, and choral and orchestral works, as well as jazz improvisation and dance. The **Dartington Quartet** was formed for the summer school in 1958.

Dasté, Jean (1904–) French actor and theatre director, who took a leading role in implementing the policy of DÉCENTRALISATION DRAMATIQUE after World War II. Before the war Dasté had worked with the French director Jacques Copeau and had been a cofounder of the acclaimed Compagnie des Quatre Saisons (1936); he continued to tour with this company during the German occupation. In 1945 he formed a touring company in Grenoble that quickly established its reputation as one of the most significant to be founded under the new police of decentralization; the company moved to St Etienne in 1947, Dasté remaining there until he retired in 1971.

Under Dasté's leadership the company presented both classics by French writers and new plays by such authors as BRECHT and COUSIN in productions aimed specifically at a working-class audience. He also continued to pursue a career as a film actor, appearing in works by TRUFFAUT amongst others.

Dausset, Jean (1916–) French physician and immunologist. Dausset gained his MD from the University of Paris in 1945 following wartime service in the blood transfusion unit. He was associate professor of haematology (1958–68) and professor of immunohaematology (1968–77), at the University of Paris and professor of experimental medicine at the Collège de France (1977–87).

Dausset's war experience stimulated his interest in transfusion reactions, and in 1951 he showed that the blood of certain universal donors (those of blood group O), which had been assumed safe to use in all transfusions, could nonetheless be dangerous. This was because of the presence of strong immune antibodies in their plasma, which develop following antidiphtheria and antitetanus injections. Donor blood is now systematically tested for such antibodies.

In the 1950s Dausset noticed a peculiar feature in the histories of patients who had received a number of blood transfusions: they developed a low white blood cell (leucocyte) count. He suspected that the blood transfused could well have contained antigens that stimulated the production of antibodies against the leucocytes. Dausset went on to claim that the antigen on the blood cells, soon to be known as the HLA or human lymphocyte antigen, was the equivalent of the mouse H-2 system, described by George Snell.

The significance of Dausset's work was enormous. It meant that tissues could be typed quickly and cheaply by simple blood agglutination tests as opposed to the complicated and lengthy procedure using skin grafts. This work made kidney transplantation a practical medical option for the danger of rejection could be minimized by rapid, simple, and accurate tissue typing. Further confirmation of Dausset's work was obtained when the specific regions of the HLA gene complex were later identified by J. van Rood and R. Ceppellini as a single locus on human chromosome 6. Dausset later shared the 1980 Nobel Prize for physiology or medicine with Snell and Baruj Benacerraf.

Davičo, Oskar (1909–) Serbian poet, novelist, and essayist. Born in Šabac, Serbia, Davičo was educated in Paris and Belgrade, where he subsequently worked as a teacher. Davičo's early poetry, written during the late 1920s, was technically much influenced by French surrealism but also shows a keen social and political awareness. During the 1930s he became a vociferous communist and spent several years in prison. During World War II he was interned in Italy but escaped and joined the partisans.

A prolific writer, he established his reputation in the 1950s, when he emerged as an influential political journalist and published several fine collections of poetry, including *A Sour-Cherry Tree Behind the Wall* (1950), *Occupied Eyes* (1954) and *Tropes* (1959). At its best his work blends lyrical and subjective elements with wider political and philosophical interests. Davičo's first novel, *Poem* (1952), uses a variety of modernist techniques to describe the development of a young intellectual into a dedicated revolutionary. His much acclaimed tetralogy *Hard Labour* (*Silence*, 1963; *Hunger*, 1963; *Secrets*, 1964; *Escapes*, 1966) deals with the lives of a group of pre-war revolutionaries, both in and out of prison.

Although Davičo's works are often innovative and experimental in both style and content, his ideological outlook remains constant. Other works include the collection of essays *Before Noon* (1960) and the volumes of poetry *Flora* (1955), *Kairos* (1959) and *The Square M* (1968).

Davie, Alan (1920–) British painter, printmaker, jewellery maker, and jazz musician. Born at Grangemouth, Scotland, the son of a painter, he studied at Edinburgh College of Art (1937–40) before active service with the Royal Artillery during World War II. He had his first one-man exhibition at Grant's Bookshop in Edinburgh in 1946. In the late 1940s he made his living as a jazz musician (he plays several instruments) and as a maker of gold and silver jewellery; in 1950 he held the first of many exhibitions at Gimpel Fils, his London dealer. In 1956 he visited New York, where he had an exhibition at the Catherine Viviano Gallery and was awarded a Guggenheim prize. Since then he has consolidated his international reputation as one of the leading British artists of his generation and has won several prestigious awards, notably the prize for best foreign painter at the seventh São Paulo

Bienal in 1963 and first prize at the International Print Exhibition at Cracow in 1966.

Davie was one of the first British artists to respond to US abstract expressionism (he first encountered the work of Jackson Pollock in Venice in 1948). His paintings are very vigorously handled; although essentially abstract they often incorporate various enigmatic emblems that bear witness to his interest in such areas as magic and Zen Buddhism.

Davies, Sir Peter Maxwell (1934–) British composer. Davies studied at the Royal Manchester College of Music where he was part of the New Music group with BIRTWISTLE and GOEHR. In his early works he attempted to fuse the innovations of BOULEZ and STOCKHAUSEN with an understanding of medieval techniques and early English music. In 1957 he won an Italian government scholarship to study with PETRASSI in Rome, where his orchestral work *Prolation* (1958) won the Olivetti prize. On his return to Britain he taught at Cirencester Grammar School, an experience that stimulated an interest in children's music and led to his own work becoming more freely expressive. His works of this period include *O Magnum Mysterium*, a sequence of carols. In 1967 he and Birtwistle formed the Pierrot Players (later renamed the FIRES OF LONDON), an avant-garde chamber ensemble for which Davies subsequently composed over 50 pieces. These include *Eight Songs for a Mad King* (1969) and *Vesalii Icones* (1969), both savagely expressionistic works of music theatre. Similarly extreme is Davies's first opera *Taverner* (1970), concerning the religious apostacy of the Tudor composer John Taverner.

Davies's works of the 1970s and 1980s are strongly influenced by the history, landscapes, and legends of Orkney, where he has lived since 1970. In 1977 his opera *The Martyrdom of St Magnus* was premiered in St Magnus Cathedral, Kirkwall, as part of the first ST MAGNUS FESTIVAL of music, an event that he founded and continues to oversee. Other compositions include the operas *The Lighthouse* (1980) and *Resurrection* (1988), works of music theatre such as *Miss Donnithorne's Maggot* (1974), *Le Jongleur de Notre Dame* (1978), and *The no. 11 Bus* (1983), the choral pieces *Westerlings* (1977) and *Solstice of Light* (1979), and four symphonies (1976, 1980, 1983, 1989). He has also written two full-length ballets – *Salome* (1978) and *Caroline Mathilde* (1990) for the Royal Danish Ballet – as well as numerous music-theatre pieces for children. He is currently associate composer/conductor with the Royal Philharmonic Orchestra, the BBC Philharmonic, and the Scottish Chamber Orchestra, for whom he is writing a series of ten 'Strathclyde Concertos'.

Davies, Siobhan (1950–) British choreographer and dancer, who established a reputation as a leading choreographer with the London Contemporary Dance Theatre in the 1970s. Her works, which are characterized by restrained movement and emotional intensity, show the influence of Richard ALSTON, Merce Cunningham, and Robert Cohan. They have been much admired for their coordination of lighting (designed by Peter Mumford) and scenery (designed by her husband David Buckland) with the dance itself.

Davies began her career as a student at the London Contemporary Dance School and helped to found (1969) the London Contemporary Dance Theatre, becoming assistant choreographer with the company in 1974 and finally resident choreographer (1983–87). During this period she created 17 works for the company, among them *Relay* (1972), *Pilot* (1974), *The Calm* (1974), *Diary* (1975), *New Galileo* (1984), and *Bridge the Distance* (1985).

In 1981 she founded Siobhan Davies and Dancers, while in 1982 she was a cofounder of the Second Stride company, for whom she choreographed a further six dances. After work in the US she returned to Britain to found the Siobhan Davies Dance Company (1988). Her work for the BALLET RAMBERT has included *Celebrations* (1979) and *Embarque* (1988). Several of her pieces feature specially commissioned scores by such contemporary composers as Brian Eno. Recent works include *Make-Make* and *White Bird Featherless* (1992). She retired as a dancer in 1983.

Davis, Sir Colin (Rex) (1927–) British conductor; a major exponent of the works of Mozart, Berlioz, Stravinsky, Sibelius, and TIPPETT. After studying clarinet at the Royal College of Music and serving as a bandsman in the Household Cavalry he worked as a conductor with the Chelsea Opera Group, giving a series of well-received performances of Mozart in the early 1950s. He first achieved widespread recognition for a concert performance of *Don Giovanni* in London in 1959. He was associate conductor of the BBC Scottish Symphony Orchestra from 1957 until 1959 and musical director of the Sadler's Wells Opera from 1961 until 1965. From 1971 to 1986 he was chief conductor and musical director at Covent Garden. In 1977 he became the first British conductor to appear at the Bayreuth Festival, where he presented Wagner's *Tannhaüser*. He has worked widely in the US, making his debut at the New York Metropolitan Opera House with BRITTEN's *Peter Grimes* in 1966. His many acclaimed recordings include a complete cycle of the works of Berlioz with the Vienna Philharmonic. He is honorary conductor of the Dresden Staatskapelle and principal guest conductor with the English Chamber Orchestra. He was knighted in 1980.

de Beauvoir, Simone (1908–86) *See* BEAUVOIR, SIMONE DE.

De Broca, Philippe (1933–) French film director, who established his reputation with a series of stylish comedies during the 1960s. Among his most popular early films were *That Man from Rio* (1964), a spoof of the James Bond films starring Jean-Paul Belmondo and Dorléac Deneuve, the classic *King of Hearts* (1966), a whimsical story about the efforts of the hero (played by Alan Bates) to foil a World War I plot to destroy the inhabitants of an entire village, and *Louize* (1972), starring Jeanne Moreau as a divorcée who seduces a young Italian. De Broca has since maintained his reputation for brisk, witty, and stylish comedies; his more recent films have included *Dear Inspector* (1977) and *Psy* (1980).

De Carlo, Giancarlo (1919–) Italian architect. Born in Genoa, De Carlo trained at the Milan Politecnico, and has been in private practice in Milan since 1950. He was a leading member of Team X, the group of radical young architects who organized the tenth and last Congrès Internationaux d'Architecture Modern (CIAM) in 1956. As such he developed wide-ranging contacts abroad, resulting in many teaching and lecturing appointments. In 1975 De Carlo founded an International Laboratory of Architecture and Urban Design in Urbino, meeting each autumn. His most notable early works were in public housing, for example in the Comasina and Feltre quarters of Milan (1953–58). His most admired work is a succession of buildings for the University of Urbino (from 1962) with forms inspired by the shapes of Italian hill towns. Believing that good architecture is inseparable from regional planning, De Carlo has produced a succession of master plans for areas in Padua (1960), Volterra (1961), Rimini (1970–72), Siena (1976–79), Palermo (1979), and elsewhere.

Décentralisation Dramatique A national arts policy that was adopted in France after World War II in an attempt to revive the theatre and other cultural enterprises all over the country. With extensive government support, the policy stimulated many new ventures in the regions, which were organized on a local basis rather than from the capital, as they had been for many years previously.

In the theatre, regional activities were grouped under local **Centres Dramatiques**, which organized tours and individual productions by such new companies as the Comédie de Saint-Étienne in eastern France, the Grenier de Toulouse in southwest France, and the Comédie de l'Ouest in western France. The policy also saw the establishment of Troupes Permanentes (touring companies with their own home theatre) and continued support for the Théâtres Nationaux, which include the Comédie-Française and other famous national companies.

Other artistic groups were assisted on a similar basis by the **Maisons de la Culture**, which were intended to be interdisciplinary but which in practice were mainly active as promoters of drama. The political upheaval of 1968 entailed a loss of support for the 15 Maisons then in existence, although they revived somewhat in 1981, with financial aid from the socialist government. By the mid-1980s the number of Centres Dramatiques had grown to 29, stimulating renewed theatrical activity and fostering the careers of major new theatrical talents, including Marcel MARÉCHAL, Roger PLANCHON, Jean-Pierre VINCENT, and Antoine VITEZ. New playwriting to benefit from the movement has included the work of the Théâtre du Quotidien in the 1970s (*see* QUOTIDIEN; THÉÂTRE DU).

deconstruction *See* DERRIDA, JACQUES.

DEFA (Deutsche Film Aktien Gesellschaft) The former state-owned film organization of the German Democratic Republic (East Germany), which operated all the country's studios. Following World War II film-makers in East Germany set up Filmaktiv, an organization intended to renew the German cinema, under the auspices of the Soviet military administration. The first production from the Althoff Studios in Berlin was a newsreel, followed by documentaries and, in 1946, Germany's first post-war feature, Wolfgang Staudte's anti-Nazi film *The Murderers Are Among Us*. That same year Filmaktiv became DEFA and began an ambitious period despite poor facilities and equipment. By the end of the 1940s, however, it had fallen under the control of the Soviet Union's ministry of film production, which insisted on fewer entertainment films and more political dogma and also imposed strict censorship. This guaranteed limited distribution outside East Germany and drove the more creative film-makers to the West. The scant international approval that the East German cinema retained was mostly for its many straight documentaries and animated productions.

DEFA is presently in limbo following German reunification and the restructuring of state-run industries, with decisions being made by a privatization agency, Truehand. DEFA is to receive government funding for certain essential renovations but is then expected to become a holding company. Although the organization's equipment is outdated and in disrepair with up to $88 million needed for modernization, the studios occupy more than 500,000 square yards with more production capacity than any other German studio. If private investment is secured, DEFA could be a force in the German cinema of the future.

de Filippo, Eduardo (Eduardo Passacelli; 1900–84) Italian actor, playwright, and poet, who established an international reputation with his tragicomedies about family life. Influenced by Pirandello and often compared to the British playwright Alan AYCKBOURN, De Filippo was born into a theatrical family and founded his own company with his brother Peppino (1903–80) and his sister Titina (1898–1963), for which they acquired a permanent base in Naples. His extensive acting experience as a former member of the Scarpetta touring company and his familiarity with the commedia dell'arte tradition proved invaluable in writing the many successful plays he subsequently created for his own troupe; some 40 of his works were soon being translated and performed all over Europe.

An early success was *Filumena Marturamo* (1946), which revolves around the cunning ploys by which a businessman's mistress attempts to trap him into marriage; it was later filmed as *Marriage Italian Style*. Among those that followed were *Grand Magic* (1948), *Inner Voices* (1948; translated into English by N. F. Simpson as *My Darling and My Love* in 1955), and *The Son of Pulcinella* (1959).

Saturday, Sunday, Monday (1959), about a squabbling family coming together over a stormy Sunday lunch, was especially well received and remains De Filippo's best-known work. Subsequent plays became increasingly melancholy: they include *Napoli Milionaria* (1945), about wartime racketeering in Naples, which was highly successful in a film version, and *Ducking Out* (1982), depicting life in a lower-class Neapolitan family. *The Art of Comedy* (1964) was unusual in exploring themes outside the familiar De Filippo territory of domestic life; its subject is the state of the theatre in contemporary Italy.

Deineka, Aleksandr Aleksandrovich (1899–1969) Russian painter and sculptor. Born in Kursk, Deineka studied at the Kharkov art college (1915–17) and in Moscow at the Vkhutemas art school (1920–25). In the aftermath of the Bolshevik Revolution the school was the scene of fervent discussion of artistic aims and methods. In 1925 Deineka was a founder member of Ost, the 'Society of Easel Painters', which dedicated itself to the depiction of industry and Soviet man and woman. His paintings and illustrations of the 1920s reflect the experimental atmosphere of the period and the influence of German expressionism and surrealism.

In 1928 Deineka left Ost and joined the October Group, which advocated the creation of a new proletarian art. This emerged in the form of socialist realism, of which Deineka became a leading exponent. From 1928 onwards Deineka held a succession of posts in Soviet art schools. During World War II he painted war scenes, incuding the powerful *The Defence of Sebastopol* (1942, State Russian Museum, Moscow). After 1945 he returned to his prewar preoccupations, painting idealized scenes of life on collective farms, in the Red Army, and so on. In 1948, however, he came under suspicion and was forced to resign as director of Moscow's Institute of Applied and Decorative Art, probably because he had not enthusiastically supported the cult of Stalin. He painted little in his last years but his work continued to influence younger painters.

De Keersmaeker, Anne Teresa (1960–) Belgian choreographer, who emerged as a leading figure in contemporary dance in the 1980s. Her style combines minimalism with a powerful emotional content. Having studied dance at the Mudra School founded by Maurice BÉJART, she made her choreographic debut in 1980 with *Asch* before travelling to the US for further studies. *Fase* (1981) demonstrated both an interest in MINIMAL MUSIC and the extent to which she had been influenced by such US choreographers as Lucinda Childs.

On her return to Europe, De Keersmaeker founded her own company, Rosas, and explored a wider range of musical styles. Her successes included *Rosas Danst Rosas* (1983), *Elena's Aria* (1984), which incorporated dialogue and film, and *Bartók/Aantekeningen* (1986), all of which were highly energetic pieces danced by four women. Among her more recent works are the dance-theatre production *Verkommenes Ufer Medeamaterial Landschaft mit Argonauten* (1987), based on the writings of Heiner Müller.

De Laurentiis, Dino (1919–) Italian film producer who has enjoyed numerous international successes. The son of a Naples pasta manufacturer, De Laurentiis studied at Rome's Centro Sperimentale di Cinematografia while working in any casual cinema job: extra, propman, unit manager, and assistant director. By 1941 he had founded a production company, Real Cine, in Turin. After serving in World War II, he returned to producing and in 1948 won universal acclaim for the neorealist *Bitter Rice* (*see* NEOREALISM), about a thief's meeting with a girl in the rice fields of the Po Valley. This powerful film launched the career of the actress Silvano Mangano, who became De Laurentiis's wife a year later. In 1950 he and Carlo PONTI founded the Ponti-De Laurentiis production company, which in its seven-year existence was responsible for such box-office hits as FELLINI's *La Strada* (1954) and *The Nights of Cabiria* (1956), both of which won the Academy Award for best foreign film. Among other impressive early films were *Ulysses* (1954) and *War and Peace* (1956).

After this partnership dissolved, De Laurentiis in the early 1960s built Dinocittà, a sprawling studio complex near Rome, where he made several successful epics, including *Barabbas* (1961), *The Bible* (1966), and *Waterloo* (1970). Within ten years, however, he sold it to the Italian government and moved to California, where his De Laurentiis Entertainment Group now has its headquarters (in Beverly Hills). The company has produced numerous expensive and internationally popular films, including *King Kong* (1976), *Orca* (1977), *Hurricane* (1979), *Flash Gordon* (1980), *Ragtime* (1981), *Conan the Barbarian* (1982), *Fighting Back* (1982), *The Bounty* (1984), *Dune* (1985), *Blue Velvet* (1986), and *Crimes of the Heart* (1986).

Delblanc, Sven (Axel Herman) (1931–) Swedish novelist. Delblanc made his debut as a novelist with *Hermit Crab* in 1962. His main character, Axel, escapes from a totalitarian state to a society with no rules; he rejects both and dreams of a third alternative. *The Cassock* (1963), set in the 18th century, depicts the gradual disenchantment of the debauched hero, Hermann. In the later 1960s Delblanc's writing became more political in line with strong trends in Swedish literature. In *Homunculus* (1965) an idealistic inventor is disillusioned by superpower interest in the destructive potential of the perfect human being he has created. Between 1970 and 1975 Delblanc published a series of collective novels based on the community in which he grew up. In *Speranza* (1980), another novel set in the 18th century, Delblanc portrays the reality of oppression underlying the façade of Enlightenment civilisation; a parallel with contemporary Western society is clearly intended.

The Book of Samuel (1981) was the first of a series of novels following a Swedish-American family through several generations. The last volume, *Maria Alone*, was published in 1985. Other works include a diary, *Bridge of Asses* (1969), from the period Delblanc spent lecturing in the US, and *Dear Grandmother* (1979), in which the main character struggles to come to terms with the memory of his ruthless but spirited grandmother, now dead.

Delblanc's work has found a mixed reception from readers and critics in Sweden. While seeming to seek a return to earlier cultural values, he is essentially anarchic in his political and social ideas.

Del Mar, Norman (René) (1919–) British conductor and writer on musical subjects. After studying at the Royal College of Music, London, Del Mar played the horn in the Royal Philharmonic Orchestra under Beecham, becoming assistant conductor to the latter in 1947. As conductor of the Chelsea Symphony Orchestra, which he founded in 1944, he gave some of the first British performances of Mahler and Richard Strauss: the latter is the subject of a three-volume study by Del Mar (1962–72). As principal conductor of the English Opera Group (1949–54) he gave the first performance of BRITTEN's *Let's Make an Opera* (1949). Later appointments include conductor of the BBC Scottish Symphony Orchestra (1960–65) and of the Royal Academy of Music (1974–77). In recent years he has worked mainly as a freelance, guesting with many leading orchestras. He is particularly associated with the late romantic repertoire and with 20th-century British music.

Demy, Jacques (1931–90) French film director, best known for the lavish musicals and surreal romantic fantasies he made during the 1960s. Demy entered the film industry in the 1950s and found success with his first full-length feature, *Lola* (1960). A love story about the reunion of an American and a French cabaret singer, the film was particularly admired for its innovative camerawork and its emotional complexity. Like many of Demy's later works, the film revealed the influence of such directors as BRESSON, Cocteau, Ophuls, and Von Sternberg.

Bay of Angels (1962) featured Jeanne Moreau as a compulsive gambler and again testified to Demy's technical inventiveness, using the games of chance in the casino as a metaphor for the element of luck in his characters' lives. Perhaps the best known of all his films is the fantasy musical *The Umbrellas of Cherbourg* (1964), in which Demy turned a drab French seaside town into a Hollywood-style setting for high romance (ultimately deflated); the film was praised not only for the acting of Catherine Deneuve in the central role but also for its score and its camerawork.

Another musical, *The Young Girls of Rochefort* (1967), picked up some of the themes of *The Umbrellas of Cherbourg* but was criticized for poor choreography; few of Demy's later films equalled the success of his 1960s work. In 1970 Demy went to the US to make *Model Shop*, in which he successfully revived the character of Lola; he then returned to Europe and made a series of unpretentious comedies and fairytale adaptations before turning to more serious themes with *A Room in the Town* (1982), a sombre musical set against the background of a dockers' strike. His later films included *Parking* (1985).

He was married to the film director **Agnès Varda**, whose work includes *Le Bonheur* (1965) and *Vagabonde* (1985). In 1991 she released *Jacquot de Nantes*, a portrait of her husband's younger years.

Denny, Robyn (1930–) British abstract painter. Born in rural Surrey, Denny studied in London at St Martin's School of Art (1951–54) and the Royal College of Art (1954–57). He later taught in several art schools, including the Slade School of Fine Art in London.

As a student Denny was interested in theories of communication and produced collages and other works incorporating stencilled words. In the late 1950s, however, he developed his own distinctive abstract style in a series of large works, many 6–8 feet high. These usually featured a symmetrical design of bands or blocks of colour set against a colour ground (for example, *Life Line I*, 1963, Tate Gallery, London). In his numerous variations on this basic formula Denny explored the effects of different arrangements and combinations of colours with considerable subtlety. His early work in this vein was featured in the 1960 'Situation' exhibition in London, organized to promote the works of British abstract artists. Like many other works in the exhibition, Denny's contributions reacted against US and European abstract expressionism by eschewing any overt reference to states of mind or emotion. In 1973 Denny became the youngest artist to be given a retrospective exhibition at the Tate Gallery, London. In the late 1970s Denny's paintings became asymmetrical and used fewer colours.

Derrida, Jacques (1930–) French philosopher. Born in Algeria, Derrida studied philosophy at the Ecole Normale Supérieure, where he later taught, and at Harvard University. He is the originator of the philosophical method known as **deconstruction**. Through his teaching at Yale and Princeton he has disseminated his ideas widely in the US. In 1984 Derrida became director of research at the Centre des Hautes Etudes en Sciences Sociales. He holds a permanent visiting chair at the University of California in Irvine.

Derrida first emerged as the *enfant terrible* of the philosophical world with the publication in 1967 of three books – *Speech and Phenomena*, *Of Grammatology*, and *Writing and Difference*. His work is essentially an attempt to draw out the philosophical implications of the structural linguistics of Saussure – especially of Saussure's claim that meaning is generated by the internal differences within a language system rather than by any inherent connection between the linguistic sign and the thing or concept signified. For Derrida, this insight overturns the assumptions of the entire Western philosophical tradition, which has always sought a guarantee for meaning in such transcendental concepts as God, essence, truth, presence, origin, etc.

Crucial to Derrida's hermeneutics is his concept of *différence* – a neologism combining the senses of 'difference' and 'deferral'. According to Derrida, the endless play of differences within a text has the effect of endlessly deferring the possibility of determinate meaning. On close examination, all literary and philosophical texts will be found to refute the assumptions on which they proceed. The deconstructive method is, in practice, a strategy for reading such texts 'against the grain', so as to expose the internal contradictions that undermine their claims to coherence.

Derrida's work has provoked extreme reactions – not only for the tendency of his thought, which many have found nihilistic, but for the sometimes impenetrable manner in which it is expressed. His later work includes *The Margins of Philosophy* (1972), a collection of essays, *Post Card* (1980), two volumes about Freud, and *Of Spirit* (1987), a book on Heidegger.

De Santis, Giuseppe (1917–) Italian film director and screenwriter. De Santis studied literature and philosophy before enrolling at Rome's Centro Sperimentale de Cinematografia. He entered the film world as a critic for the magazine *Cinema*, where his calls for radical change in the style and content of Italian films anticipated many features of post-war NEOREALISM. He coscripted *Obsessione* (1942), VISCONTI's first feature film, and worked as an assistant director before making his own feature debut with *Tragic Hunt* (1947), which highlighted post-war Italy's desperate social conditions. He became famous with his second feature, the neorealist *Bitter Rice* (1949), which starred Silvana Mangano as a girl who tries to outwit a thief to escape her daily tedium. An even bleaker film was *Rome Eleven O'Clock* (1951), about the tragic collapse of a staircase under the weight of unemployed girls applying for a secretarial position. After the neorealist era, the director moved into less sensational films depicting personal relationships. His films include *Under the Olive Tree* (1950), *A Husband for Anna* (1953), *Days of Love* (1954), *Men and Wolves* (1956), the Soviet-Italian coproduction *Italiano brava Gente* (1964), and *Un Apprezzato Professionista di Sicuro Avvenire* (1972).

De Sica, Vittorio (1902–74) Italian film director and actor; one of the leading exponents of NEOREALISM.

His career as a director began with the comedies *Maddalena zero in condotta* (1941) and *Teresa Venerdi* (1941); these were followed by the neorealist *The Children are Watching Us* (1942), the first of several collaborations with the scriptwriter Cesare ZAVATTINI. The film introduced the style that characterized much of De Sica's subsequent work, employing nonprofessional actors and being shot on location to achieve the most naturalistic impact.

Of the collaborations that followed, the most important included *Shoeshine* (1946), about two shoeshine boys who fall foul of the law in wartime Italy, and the much-acclaimed *Bicycle Thieves* (1948), which won an Oscar among many other awards. This classic of neorealist cinema was a poignant examination of the injustices of Italian society, again seen through a child's eyes, as a young boy searches for the stolen bicycle that his father relies upon to get a job. Other influential films from this period included *Miracle in Milan* (1950), a fantasy in which the poor rise up against their oppressors, and *Umberto D* (1952), a pessimistic account of friendless old age.

Over the next few years De Sica abandoned neorealism and concentrated upon more commercial films featuring well-known professional performers. One of the most successful of these was *Two Women* (1960), starring Sophia Loren, who also featured in *Yesterday, Today and Tomorrow* (1963) and *Marriage Italian Style* (1964). After several more lightweight comedies and melodramas De Sica returned to more serious issues with *The Garden of the Finzi-Continis* (1971; from the novel by BUZZATI), about the treatment of the Jews in Fascist Italy; the film won an Oscar for best foreign language film.

Deutsche Film Aktion Gesellschaft *See* DEFA.

Deutsche Oper German opera company, established under this name in 1961, when the new Deutsche Oper theatre was opened in West Berlin. The company began its existence at the Deutsches Opernhaus in 1912 (renamed the Städtische Oper in 1925 when the Berlin city authorities took over its administration), remaining there until that building's destruction during World War II. It continued to perform in the Admiralpalast until 1945, when it transferred to the Theater des Westens. On moving to the Deutsche Oper, the company's resources were substantially increased in order to allow for an increase in personnel and a considerable enlargement of its basic repertory to over 75 works. The company has established a reputation for promoting new operas. Its musical directors have included Lorin Maazel (1965–75), Siegfried Palm, and Giuseppe Sinopoli; the German-Spanish conductor Rafael Frühbeck de Burgos takes over in 1993. Guest conductors have included Karl Böhm and Eugen JOCHUM. The company is sometimes referred to as Deutsche Oper, Berlin, to distinguish it from Deutsche Oper am Rhein, which is based in Düsseldorf and Duisburg.

Deutsche Staatsoper German opera company. It was formed in 1945 in East Berlin from members of the Staatsoper (the state opera company), which had replaced the court opera company in 1919. Its first *intendant* (chief administrator) was Ernst Legal, whose successors have included Heinrich Allmeroth, Max Burghardt, and Hans Pischner. The company gave its first world premiere in 1951 with Paul Dessau's opera *Die Verurteilung des Lukullus*: subsequent premieres of works by East German composers have included Ernst Hermann Meyer's *Reiter der Nacht* (1973) and Dessau's *Einstein* (1974). A repertory of over 50 works is maintained. The new opera house (replacing that destroyed during the war) was opened in 1955 with a performance of Wagner's *Die Meistersinger von Nürnberg*. Chief conductors have included Erich Kleiber, Horst Stein, and Otmar Suitner.

de Valois, Dame Ninette (Edris Stannus; 1898–) British dancer, choreographer, and ballet director, born in Ireland, who founded the ROYAL BALLET in 1956. She gained early experience as a dancer at Covent Garden and elsewhere, appearing with a company led by Léonide Massine in 1922 and subsequently with Diaghilev's Ballets Russes. Ultimately, however, she sacrificed her career as a dancer in order to lead her own companies.

In 1926 she founded the London Academy of Choreographic Art and went on to collaborate on a number of theatrical productions with Lilian Baylis at the Old Vic. In 1931 she moved to the Sadler's Wells Theatre, where she organized the Vic-Wells Ballet company with great success. The company, renamed the Sadler's Wells Ballet, transferred to the Royal Opera House in 1946, in which year de Valois also founded the Sadler's Wells Opera Ballet (later retitled the Sadler's Wells Theatre Ballet and merged with its sister company to form the Royal Ballet in 1956). She also won much praise for her work at the much-expanded Sadler's Wells Ballet School (subsequently renamed the Royal Ballet School).

By 1963, when she retired as director of the Royal Ballet, de Valois had (with Marie Rambert) laid the foundations of modern British ballet and established an international reputation for both the company and the ballet school. As a choreographer, she executed her most important work in the 1930s, using music by contemporary

British composers. Her most successful pieces included *The Rake's Progress* (1935), inspired by Hogarth's engravings, and *Checkmate* (1937), to a score by Arthur Bliss. Her writings include the memoirs *Invitation to the Ballet* (1937), *Come Dance With Me* (1957), and *Step to Step* (1977). De Valois was created a DBE in 1951.

Devine, George *See* ENGLISH STAGE COMPANY.

Djilas, Milovan (1911–) Yugoslav political philosopher. Born in Kolašin, Montenegro, Djilas studied law and philosophy at Belgrade University; he was imprisoned from 1933 to 1936 for communist agitation. A partisan leader in World War II, Djilas became chief propagandist in Tito's post-war government and a vigorous upholder of his country's independence from Soviet interference.

In 1953 he became one of Yugoslavia's vice-presidents but his increasingly outspoken criticisms of what he saw as abuses of power and political elitism led to his dismissal in 1954. Two years later he was jailed for his public defence of the Hungarian uprising. Djilas's critique of communism in practice soon spread to Marxist-Leninist theory as a whole. *The New Class* (1957), smuggled out of prison, argued that its precepts led inevitably to the replacement of one elite with another. Released in 1961, Djilas was jailed again for four years after publishing *Conversations with Stalin* (1962). In *The Unperfect Society* (1969) and *Memoirs of a Revolutionary* (1973) he developed his thesis that communist ideas were a vehicle of political oppression. More recent publications include *Tito* (1980), published in the year of the dictator's death. Djilas was formally rehabilitated in 1989.

Documenta A festival of the visual arts held every five years in Kassel, Germany. The first Documenta was held in 1947 and the event now constitutes one of the largest and most important exhibitions of contemporary art in the world, attracting international artists, dealers, and critics, and gaining much media coverage. Exhibitions are held in museums throughout the city, including the Fridericianum, and in many public places. The current artistic director is the Belgian curator San Hoet. In 1992 sporting and musical events were incorporated into the programme for the first time.

documentary theatre A type of factually based drama that emerged in Germany and several other European countries in the 1950s and 1960s. Also known as the **Theatre of Fact**, the genre placed a new emphasis on the reconstruction and analysis of real events in the theatre. Such writers as Rolf HOCHHUTH and Peter WEISS used official documents, court transcripts, newspapers, and other factual sources to interpret issues arising from recent history; the plays often aroused considerable controversy with their criticisms of national governments. Notable works of documentary theatre include Hochhuth's *The Representative* (1963), Weiss's *The Investigation* (1965), and KIPPHARDT's *In the Matter of J. R. Oppenheimer* (1967). Other exponents of the genre include Dario FO in Italy, Ariane MNOUCHKINE in France, and Howard BRENTON in Britain. The term is also used of the local history projects undertaken all over Europe by mixed groups of amateurs and professionals as COMMUNITY THEATRE.

Doderer, Heimito von (1896–1966) Austrian novelist. Doderer began to study law in Vienna in 1914 but was drafted into the army in 1915 and captured by the Russians a year later. In 1920 he managed to flee back to Vienna, where he took up the study of history and philosophy. After completing his doctorate in 1925 he wrote for journals and newspapers. He became a member of the Austrian National Socialist Party in 1933 but distanced himself from it in the late 1930s, converting to Roman Catholicism in 1940. In World War II he served as a Luftwaffe captain until his capture by the British in 1945. In 1946 he returned to Vienna, where he lived until his death.

Although the size and scope of Doderer's work has won comparisons with Proust and Musil, he is a far more traditional writer in both style and content. His most famous novels, *The Strudlhof Stairs* (1951) and *The Demons* (1956), are set mainly in the Vienna of the 1920s. Despite this historical background, Doderer concentrates on the inner development of his characters. Thus for example *The Strudlhof Stairs*, set in 1910–11 and 1923–25, suggests the continuity of everyday life in spite of the political and social changes since World War I. Similarly, at the climax of *The Demons* Doderer describes the burning down of the palace of justice in 1927 not in the light of its crucial political consequences, but with regard to the private fates of his characters. Doderer was later criticized for his tendency to marginalize history and to resolve conflicts in favour of idyllic endings; his work has even been seen as an expression of Austrian neo-Biedermaier. Another important work is *The Waterfalls of Slunj* (1963), the first part of a projected tetralogy.

Doisneau, Robert (1912–) French photographer. After studying lithography at the Ecole Estienne in Paris, Doisneau worked as an archivist photographer with Renault. During World War II he served in the French army and later as a forger in the Resistance, while making a living producing and selling tourist postcards. After 1945 Doisneau branched into fashion and portrait photography and began to take the pictures of Parisian street scenes for which he is best known. His work emphasizes the lighter, happier side of Parisian street life, attempting above all to capture the elusive ambience (or 'perfume' as Doisneau himself terms it) of a particular moment. His best-known single photograph is 'The Kiss at the Hotel de Ville', an image of two young lovers engaged in a passionate kiss and oblivious to all else that has been endlessly reproduced on posters and has come to epitomize the Bohemian glamour of Paris in the post-war years. Doisneau's compassion for factory workers and his fascination with heavy industry are apparent in works such as *La Pleine Lune du Bourget* (1946). The spontaneous quality of his best work reflects his belief in loitering in the streets and choosing his subjects as they present themselves. His work has been published in *La Rue de Robert Doisneau* (1974) and *Robert Doisneau* (1975). The largest ever retrospective of his work was held in Oxford in 1992.

Domela (Nieuwenhuis), César (1900–) Dutch painter and typographer. Born in Amsterdam, Domela lived and worked in various European cities before settling in Paris in 1933. After several years in Switzerland he moved to Berlin in 1923, where he exhibited with the Novembergruppe ('November group'), an association of radical artists who championed a variety of progressive art styles and sought closer relations between modern artists and the public.

In his early years as a painter Domela experimented with a series of figurative and abstract styles. In 1924–25 he met Theo van Doesburg and Piet Mondrian and joined the De Stijl group, which advocated 'plasticism' – an austere art based on straight lines, right angles, and primary colours. In the late 1920s he also came under the influence of the constructivism of Naum Gabo and produced some of his most notable works, a series of montages that explore contrasts of colour and materials. In 1933 Domela moved to Paris where he joined the group of abstract artists Abstraction-Creation. In the 1950s his works became looser and less rigidly geometrical. Domela's highly personal development of De Stijl principles in these later works represents an important link between the ideas of the 1920s and the art of the post-war world. His works have been exhibited in most western European countries and in Brazil, which he visited in 1954. He also did important work in typography.

Domin, Hilde (1912–) German poet. Of Jewish origin, Domin studied art history, law, sociology, and political economics before emigrating with her husband to escape the Nazi persecution. She subsequently lived in Florence, Oxford, and Santo Domingo, where she worked as a teacher and lecturer and began to write poems (in 1951). She was awarded several prizes and returned to Germany in 1954.

Influenced by her reading of the Spanish modernist poets, Domin developed a style of great simplicity and directness. Her poems draw on her experiences as an emigrant, being preoccupied with themes of loss, homelessness, and separation, which sometimes take on a metaphysical dimension (*Only a Rose for Support*, 1959; *The Return of the Ships*, 1962). In her critical essays she maintains that it is the duty of the poet to treat language as a precious heritage and the last defence of humanism (*Poetry Today, What For?*; 1968). By placing the relationships between human beings at the centre of her work she became one of the most popular poets in post-war Germany.

Donatoni, Franco (1927–) Italian composer. Born in Verona, he studied violin and composition at the Liceo Musicale there from the age of seven. He subsequently studied composition at the Milan Conservatory (1946–48), the Bologna Conservatory (1948–51), and the Accademia di Santa Cecilia in Rome (1952–53). The most decisive influences on his style, however, came from his meeting with MADERNA in 1953, his subsequent attendance at the DARMSTADT summer courses (1954, 1958, and 1961), and his friendship with the critic Mario Bortolotto. He became professor of composition at the Milan Conservatory in 1969, having previously taught at the Bologna and Turin conservatories; since 1970 he has given courses at Bologna University and the Accademia Chigiana, Siena.

The influence of PETRASSI and Bartók can be heard in student works such as the *Concertino* (1952) and the *Sinfonia* (1953). Following his first exposure to Darmstadt teaching he embraced Webernian SERIALISM in the *Composizione in quattro movimento* for piano (1955), later proceeding to a post-Webern style directly influenced by BOULEZ (*Tre Improvisazioni*, 1957) and STOCKHAUSEN (*Quartetto II*, 1958; *Puppenspiel*, 1961). Works such as *Per orchestra* (1962), in which Donatoni, following the US composer John Cage, attempted to ensure total indeterminacy, established his leading position among the younger generation of Italian composers. Important among his later works are *Quartetto IV* (1963), a Cagian work in which the performers react to stories in the day's newspapers, *Etwas ruhiger im Ausdruck* (1967), *Estratto II* (1970), *Voci* (1973), and *Arias* (1987). He has composed little since the 1960s.

Donaueschingen Festival A music festival held each October in Donaueschingen, Germany. The festival was inaugurated in 1921 to promote contemporary music but lapsed after nine years; it was successfully reestablished in 1950 and became one of the most important show cases for new avant-garde music in Europe. Works by BOULEZ, HENZE, MESSIAEN, and STOCKHAUSEN have all been premiered at the festival.

Donner, Jörn (1933–) Finnish film director, producer, and writer. Born in Helsinki to Swedish-speaking parents, he studied political science and Swedish literature at Helsinki University. After graduating he worked as a journalist and film critic and wrote poetry, fiction, and a book about post-war Germany, *Report from Berlin*. In 1954 he wrote and directed his first short, *Morning in the City*. He published a further travel book, *Report from the Danube*, before moving to Stockholm in 1961 to work as a film critic for a leading Swedish newspaper.

Donner made an impressive feature debut in 1963, winning a special prize at the Venice Film Festival for best first work by a director with *A Sunday in September*, a story about the breakdown of a marriage. He remained in Sweden to make such features as *To Love* (1964) and *Adventure Starts Here* (1965) and the documentary *Teenage Rebellion* (1967), but his flair for the unorthodox was not always appreciated and he returned to Finland in 1967. His subsequent work in Helsinki as a director, screenwriter, producer, and actor, has greatly invigorated the Finnish film industry. His later releases have included *Anna* (1970) which he coproduced, *Tenderness* (1972), and the documentary *The World of Ingmar Bergman* (1975). He also produced *The American Dream* (1976), *Home and Refuge* (1977), *Bluff Stop* (1978), and *Man Cannot Be Raped* (1978). He became chairman of the Finnish Film Foundation in 1981 and has served as an MP since 1987.

Doráti, Antal (1906–88) US conductor and composer, born in Hungary. Doráti studied at Budapest Academy and University and made his debut with the Hungarian Royal Opera in 1924. The early part of his career was spent working in opera in Budapest, Dresden, and Munster. From 1933 to 1945 he worked with ballet companies in Europe and the US, including the Ballet Russe de Monte Carlo. A US citizen from 1947, he held appointments with the Dallas Symphony Orchestra (1945–49) and the Minneapolis Symphony Orchestra (1949–60); more recently, he was principal conductor of the BBC Symphony Orchestra (1962–66) and of the Royal Philharmonic Orchestra (1976–). He was particularly noted for his interpretations of Bartók and Haydn and recorded all the latter's symphonies with the Philharmonia Hungarica.

Dorst, Tankred (1925–) German playwright, who won praise for his plays drawing on the techniques of BRECHT and the absurdists (*see* ABSURD, THEATRE OF THE). Dorst began his career in puppet theatre and first attracted interest as a playwright with *Great Vituperation at the City Wall* (1961), in which he employed Brechtian techniques to great effect. Most of his plays since then have eschewed political relevance, with the one notable exception of *Toller* (1968), a revue-style entertainment in which he traced the involvement of the playwright Ernst Toller (1893–1939) in left-wing politics. His more recent plays have ranged from *Ice Age* (1973), based on the life of the Norwegian writer and Nazi sympathizer Knut Hamsun, to *Merlin and the Wasteland* (1981), in which he reflects on the progress of modern society, and the fairytale *Ameley, the Beaver and the King on the Roof* (1982). Also notable is his multimedia epic on the history of modern Germany, a cycle of works consisting so far of the epilogue *On the Chimborazo* (1970), the novel *Dorothea Merz*, the film *Klara's Mother* (1978), one of several that he has directed, and the play *The Villa* (1984). He is also the author of several opera librettos.

Drabble, Margaret (1939–) British novelist and writer. Born in Sheffield, Drabble was educated at The Mount School, York, and at Newnham College, Cambridge. Her first novel, *The Garrick Year* (1964), deals with a young woman's attempts to cope with the simultaneous demands of marriage to an actor and her own career. This emphasis on the professional and marital difficulties of educated young women continued in such novels of the 1960s and 1970s as *The Millstone* (1965), *Jerusalem the Golden* (1967), *The Waterfall* (1969), *The Realms of Gold* (1975), and *The Ice Age* (1977). She has also written critical studies of the work of Wordsworth and Arnold Bennett, whose style of social realism has been an important influence on her own work. Her novels and stories are particularly successful in capturing the details of everyday middle-class life; a recurrent theme is the way in which ordinary women have coped with the changes in their lives since the late 1950s. *The Radiant Way* (1987), perhaps her most successful novel, describes the lives of three women of similar background as they approach middle age and begin to reflect on their youthful ambitions. The novel's sequels *A Natural Curiosity* (1989) and *The Gates of Ivory* (1991) were less well received by critics, some of whom felt that the social and thematic range of her work had become too narrow. Perhaps in an attempt to rebut such criticisms, the latter is set largely in Cambodia.

Margaret Drabble edited the 1985 edition of *The Oxford Companion to English Literature*. Her older sister is the novelist A. S. BYATT.

Drew, Jane *See* FRY AND DREW.

Drewermann, Eugen (1940–) German Roman Catholic theologian and psychoanalyst. After studying philosophy, theology, and psychoanalysis, Drewermann was ordained a priest in 1966. He subsequently worked as a teacher of theology and as a psychotherapist.

Drewermann's point of departure is man's fundamental feeling of fear and insecurity, something that he himself experienced intensely as a child during World War II. For him the purpose of religion is to give the individual a feeling of safety and acceptance rather than one of being a sinner with little hope of redemption. Drewermann argues that theology can achieve this only by applying all available contemporary knowledge, including the methods of psychoanalysis. In his first major work, *Structures of Evil* (1976), he interprets the story of the Fall, using sources from history and mythology besides the Biblical account, and takes it to be a story of the self-alienation of the human soul. Drewermann expounded and defended his methods in his book *Psychoanalysis and Exegesis* (1985), stressing that there are many sources of truth besides the Biblical tradition. He has been attacked for transgressing the limits of Catholic orthodoxy as well as for turning the religious believer from a responsible, if sinful, individual into a child seeking comfort from his or her fears. Drewermann's writings – including his psychoanalytical interpretations of Grimm's fairy tales – have been an enormous success with the public; in 1991 the Catholic Church cancelled his permission to teach theology and in 1992 he was suspended from his office as a priest.

Drottningholm Festival An annual festival of 18th-century opera and ballet held since 1953 at Drottningholm Palace, near Stockholm, Sweden. Performances are staged from May to September in the 18th-century Court Theatre in the grounds of the Royal Palace. The theatre was closed in 1792 following the murder of King Gustav II and remained neglected until 1921 when the historian Agne Beijer arranged for its restoration. The original sets and stage machinery are used in performances.

Druon, Maurice (1918–) French novelist. Maurice Druon was born into an upper-class background in Paris. During World War II he worked in London for the Free French information services; with his uncle, Joseph Kessel, he wrote the words to the Resistance song 'Le Chant des Partisans'. While working as a journalist Druon published his first novel, *The Last Detachment*: *The Cadets of Saumur* (1946), based on his own time at the Saumur cavalry school. In 1948 he was awarded the Prix Goncourt for his trilogy *The Curtain Falls*, which charts the decline of two upper-class families during the 1920s and 1930s and attacks the decadence of French society between the wars. He became famous for his sequence of historical novels *The Accursed Kings* (1956–62), based on the history of the French royal house in the 13th and 14th centuries. His books are known for their meticulously researched historical settings. In 1966 Druon was elected to the French Academy and in the 1970s he served for some years as the minister of culture, provoking fierce protests from French intellectuals with his conservative opinions.

Dubuffet, Jean (1901–85) French experimental artist, whose work anticipated many of the avant-garde trends of the last 30 years. Born in Le Havre, the son of a prosperous wine merchant, Dubuffet enrolled (1918) at the Académie Julian, Paris, but did not take his studies seriously. His circle of friends included André Masson, Joan MIRÓ, Suzanne Valadon, Raoul Dufy, and Fernand Léger. In 1924 he gave up painting to work in the family firm and in 1930 started his own wine business in Paris. Not until 1942 did he take up painting seriously. The deliberately unsophisticated paintings in his first exhibition, held in 1945 at the Galerie René Drouin, Paris, shocked the art world. In the immediate post-war years he produced numerous mixed-media works using rough materials such as plaster, concrete, asphalt, glue and putty, pebbles, and pieces of broken bottles. He was one of the first artists to abandon traditional materials in favour of discarded or humble materials. In 1957 he stated "my art is an attempt to bring all disparaged values into the limelight".

Drawing upon his awareness of the work of Klee and Miró and his reading of Prinzhorn's *Artistry of the Mentally Ill*, he arranged in 1947 an exhibition of art objects created by primitives, children, and the mentally ill, coining the term ART BRUT to describe such work. During the 1950s he continued to work in discarded material such as newspaper, tinfoil, dried flowers, etc., and held large retrospective exhibitions in Paris (1960) and at the Museum of Modern Art, New York (1961). His collected writings were published in 1967. *L'Hourloupe* (1962–74) was a series of drawings executed in ball-point pen while Dubuffet talked on the telephone.

Dudintsev, Vladimir Dmitrievich (1918–) Russian prose writer prominent during the THAW. After studying law in Moscow, Dudintsev wrote fairly conventional works in the socialist-realist mode until, in 1956, *Not by Bread Alone* brought him immense fame overnight. Stylistically no more adventurous than his earlier works, this novel describes the tribulations and eventual demise of an inventor who attempts to challenge the monopolistic and corrupt Soviet scientific establishment, and through it the entire legitimacy of socialist construction. There ensued a violent campaign against Dudintsev, which abated only in 1959 at the behest of Khruschev. In that same year he published *A New Year's Tale* which recast the novel in the form of a short fairy-tale, covertly acknowledging Khrushchev's assistance. After at one time epitomizing the struggle for greater freedom of expression in the Soviet Union, Dudintsev has been largely quiescent for the last three decades, though he is still respected for his earlier courage.

Duraș, Marguerite (Marguerite Donnadieu; 1914–) French writer. Duras grew up in French Indochina until she was 17, when she went to Paris to study law and politics. A member of the Communist Party until 1950, she remains committed to the political left (see, for instance, her political diary *Summer 80*, 1980). Duras began writing in 1942, achieving her first success in 1950 with *The Sea Wall*, a novel dealing with a poor family in Indochina. In 1958 she published *Moderato Cantabile*, like almost all of her books a bittersweet love story without a happy ending; it was filmed by Peter BROOK in 1960. In 1959 she produced an acclaimed screenplay for Alain RESNAIS's *Hiroshima Mon Amour*, beginning a long association with the cinema. Her novels and screenplays of the 1960s and 1970s are characterized by minimal plot, moody atmosphere, elliptical dialogue, and a preoccupation with the theme of hopeless love, often in a tropical setting (the resulting style has been dubbed the 'Duras effect'). Major novels of this period include *The Afternoon of Monsieur Andesmas* (1962), *The Rapture of Lol V. Stein* (1964), and *Destroy, She Said* (1969). The play *India Song* (1974) was made into a film scripted and directed by Duras herself.

Duras found worldwide success (and won the Prix Goncourt) with her novel *The Lover* (1984), a semiautobiographical story of a love affair between a young French girl and a rich young Chinese in the Indochina of the 1930s. Subsequent novels, such as *Blue Eyes, Black Hair* (1984) and *Summer Rain* (1991), have been somewhat poorly received.

Durrell, Lawrence (George) (1912–90) British novelist, poet, and travel writer. Durrell was born in India, the son of an engineer, and educated in Darjeeling and Canterbury. In his twenties he travelled widely before settling (1934) in Corfu; he also began to publish novels and poetry. Durrell spent World War II in Athens and Egypt, where he worked as a government press officer. After the war he held similar posts in a number of eastern Mediterranean countries, eventually becoming director of public relations for the government of Cyprus. He spent his later years in the South of France.

Durrell achieved a mild notoriety with the publication of his third novel, *The Black Book* (1938), a sexual fantasia that shows the influence of the US writer Henry Miller. Until the late 1950s, however, his literary reputation rested mainly on his poetry and his travel writings. *Prospero's Cell* (1945) about Corfu, *Reflections on a Marine Venus* (1953) about Rhodes, and the highly successful *Bitter Lemons* (1957) about Cyprus, all show the sensitivity to 'spirit of place' and flair for descriptive writing that mark his later novels.

Durrell is now best known for the *Alexandria Quartet* of novels, comprising *Justine* (1957), *Balthazar* (1958), *Mountolive* (1958), and *Clea* (1960). Written in an extravagant sensual style, the sequence traces the tangled liaisons of a cast of amoral and exotic characters in pre-war Alexandria. The city itself is powerfully evoked in all its beauty and squalor. The *Quartet* is famous for its dislocations of narrative sequence and its use of multiple perspectives; in the first three novels the same events are described from the viewpoints of three different characters, revealing new and startling aspects of the truth.

The element of gothic fantasy in Durrell's work became more pronounced in *Tunc* (1968) and its sequel *Nunquam* (1970), which were somewhat coolly received by English critics. His last major work was the *Avignon Quintet* of novels, consisting of *Monsieur* (1974), *Livia* (1978), *Constance* (1982), *Sebastian* (1983), and *Quinx* (1985). Set mainly in Provence, the sequence is structurally even more complex than the Alexandria books, involving a Russian-doll-like series of novels within novels. The content is a heady mixture of incest, gnosticism, psychoanalysis, and esoteric musings about the relationship between life and art. Durrell's other works include several verse plays and the 'Antrobus' books, a series of light satirical novels about diplomatic life. His *Collected Poems* were published in 1980.

Dürrenmatt, Friedrich (1921–90) Swiss playwright, novelist, and essayist, who became one of the most important writers in the German language in the second half of the 20th century. His first play, *It Is Written* (1947), was well received and demonstrated his indebtedness to the theories of BRECHT and the expressionists. Subsequently he established his reputation with a series of black comedies on such themes as human greed, hypocrisy, and cruelty, indicating his concern over the apparent breakdown of social concern in post-war Switzerland. *The Blind Man* (1948), *Romulus the Great* (1949), and *The Marriage of Mr Mississippi* (1952) shared the same sense of futility and desperation as other absurdist plays (*see* ABSURD, THEATRE OF THE), but were distinguished by their theatricality, which made them popular attractions in New York and London.

His best-known plays included *The Visit* (*Der Besuch der alten Dame*; 1956), about a rich old woman's revenge on her hometown for wrongs done to her many years before, and *The Physicists* (1962), a grotesque tragicomedy in which several fugitive scientists hide themselves in a lunatic asylum.

From the late 1960s Dürrenmatt turned increasingly to the novel, publishing a number of experimental works that combine speculative essays on politics, philosophy, and science with fiction. These include *The Conniver: a Complex* (1976) and *Connections: an Essay on Israel* (1976). Dürrenmatt's other writings include several treatises upon the theatre, plays for radio (published in a collected edition in 1961), and a number of detective novels.

Duruflé, Maurice (1902–86) French composer and organist. Duruflé entered the Paris Conservatoire in 1920, studying organ with Charles Tournemire and composition with Paul Dukas. He was appointed organist at the church of St Etienne-du-Mont in Paris in 1930 and later became professor of harmony at the Paris Conservatoire (1943–69). His works, which are relatively few in number, show the influence of Fauré and liturgical plainchant. His compositions include *Prélude et fugue sur le nom d'Alain* for organ (1947), a choral work *Cum Jubilo* (1966), and a requiem for organ, orchestra, and choir (1947), which has become his best-known work.

Dutch National Ballet One of the three foremost ballet companies in the Netherlands. Based in Amsterdam, it was formed in 1961 by the amalgamation of Sonia GASKELL's Netherlands Ballet and the Amsterdam Ballet. Gaskell eventually emerged as the head of the new company and established its international reputation with a wide range of classical works, including *Swan Lake* and *Romeo and Juliet*, consciously modelling the troupe upon the ROYAL BALLET in Britain.

In the 1960s such talents as Rudi van DANTZIG, Hans van MANEN, and Toer van Schayk also contributed to the development of the company, concentrating upon ballets by leading contemporary choreographers from abroad as well as staging their own creations. The company moved into the huge Het Muziektheater in 1987, after which it was under new management. It also undertakes regular foreign tours.

Dutilleux, Henri (1916–) French composer. Dutilleux studied (1933–38) at the Paris Conservatoire with the Gallon brothers and Henri Büsser and won the Grand Prix de Rome for composition (1938). He was director of singing at the Paris Opéra (1942) and worked intermittently with Paris Radio (1943–63). In 1961 he became professor at the Ecole Normale de Musique and in 1970 was appointed professor at the Paris Conservatoire. Although his early works show the influence of Debussy, Ravel, and Roussel, he soon developed a highly distinctive musical idiom of his own. Compositions include two symphonies (1950, 1959), *Cinq Métaboles* (1964) and *Timbres, espace, mouvement* (1978) for orchestra, a ballet *Le Loup* (1953), a piano sonata (1948), chamber music, film scores, and songs. Among his recent works are a violin concerto (1985) and *For Aldeburgh 85*, for oboe, harpsichord, and percussion.

E

Ealing Studios A small British studio complex in west London where many successful British films of the 1940s and 1950s were made. In this period the studios became virtually synonymous with British comedy under the guidance of Michael BALCON; the so-called 'Ealing Comedies' included *Whisky Galore* (1949), *The Man in the White Suit* (1951), one of several films starring Alec Guinness, *The Titfield Thunderbolt* (1952), and *The Ladykillers* (1955), again with Guinness. Other notable films made at Ealing included the chiller *Dead of Night* (1945), consisting of five short stories of the supernatural, *Mandy* (1952), about a deaf-and-dumb girl (Mandy Miller) and her teacher (Jack Hawkins), and the epic *Scott of the Antarctic* (1948). After the studios were closed for making major films they were occupied by the BBC.

early-music movement The resurgence of interest in early music (i.e. music written before the 19th century), especially as performed on period instruments using historical playing techniques, that has been a feature of musical life since the early 1970s. The pioneering work of scholars and period instrumentalists, once regarded as marginal and eccentric, has increasingly entered the musical mainstream, enlivening and broadening attitudes in the process. It has also opened up a philosophical debate concerning the aesthetics of performance and the notion of authenticity. More recently, the period instrument approach has been applied to 19th-century music, in direct competition with conventional modern instrument performance. Many contemporary composers have been influenced by the early-music movement and some have acknowledged a direct debt to it. It has also been argued that the diminishing audience for contemporary music is in part a reflection of the vogue for period instrument performances. Important early-music ensembles include the COLLEGIUM AUREUM, Les ARTS FLORISSANTS, the MONTEVERDI CHOIR, and MUSICA ANTIQUA KÖLN.

Earth art A form of expression in which untreated natural materials such as earth, stones, and wood are used to create works of art. This branch of art developed in the 1960s, partly as a reaction against the bland forms of MINIMAL ART and partly as a 'back-to-nature' expression of discontent with industrial culture. The term embraces a variety of activities, from excavating tons of earth to create huge new landscape features to arranging twigs in a gallery. Earth art has been mainly a US phenomenon (especially in its most spectacular manifestations), but the Dutch Conceptual artist Jan Dibbets (*see* CONCEPTUAL ART) and the British sculptor Richard LONG are among the well-known European artists whose activities are representative of the movement. There are also affinities with Italian ARTE POVERA. Earth art is sometimes known as **Land art**.

Eben, Petr (1929–) Czech composer. Eben's musical studies were interrupted by World War II, the last two years of which he spent interned in Buchenwald concentration camp. He resumed his studies in Prague, taking composition lessons from Pavel Bˇrkovec at the Academy and graduating in 1954. He has since combined the careers of composer, pianist, and educator.

Eben's music acknowledges a debt to the contrapuntal techniques of the Renaissance and baroque periods, especially the counterpoint of Bach, which he combines with overtly modern idioms. He has rooted his art in a humanist philosophy that is perhaps a response to his concentration-camp experience. His music is both archaic and powerfully expressive.

Works include the oratorio *Apologia Sokrates* (1967) and much other choral music, concertos for organ (1954) and piano (1961), chamber music, music for use in schools, and many extended organ pieces, such as *Faust* (1982).

Eck, Imre (1930–) Hungarian ballet dancer, choreographer, and ballet director, who emerged as one of the leading figures in Hungarian dance in the 1950s. Having joined the Budapest State Opera Ballet in 1947, he made his debut as a choreographer in 1958 with *Csonger and Tünde*; subsequently he won praise for such ballets as *Le Sacre du printemps* (1963), *Music for Strings, Celesta, and Percussion* (1964), and *Ondine* (1969). In 1960 he founded the influential Ballet Sopianae in Pécs, which went on to perform many more of his works (notably several set to the music of Bartók and other Hungarian composers).

Eco, Umberto (1932–) Italian novelist, literary critic, and professor of semiotics at Bologna University. He is an active contributor to academic and literary journals and has also written over the years for such papers as *Corriere della Sera*, *Manifesto*, and *L'Espresso*. He was a member of Gruppo 63, an avant-garde movement named after a convention held in Palermo in 1963 (the title also echoes the German GRUPPE 47).

Eco's remarkable energy has been expended chiefly in the fields of medieval philosophy, modern culture, the history of aesthetics, and mass communications. Though he has emerged as one of the most original figures in semiotics since Roland BARTHES, what shot him to fame was the novel *The Name of the Rose* (1980; later also a successful film). In this gothic murder mystery set in 1375 in a monastery in northern Italy, Eco explores a range of ideological and theological issues while providing an entertaining and highly complex plot.

His critical works include *The Open Work* (1962), *Apocalyptic and Integrated* (1964), *The Absent Structure* (1968), and *The Form of Content* (1971). Eco's systematic exposition of his ideas *A Theory of Semiotics* (1975) was first written in English. *Minimum Diary* (1963) is a collection of journalistic articles imbued with humour and wit. Other nonfiction works include *Domestic Customs* (1973), *From the Borders of the Empire* (1977), *Lector in Fabula* (1979), and studies of various aspects of popular culture (comic strips, the structure of the James Bond novels, Superman comics, etc). In 1988 he published *Foucault's Pendulum*, an idiosyncratic thriller about a modern academic's attempts to unravel a worldwide conspiracy with its roots in an underground tradition of esoteric teaching.

Edgar, David (1948–) British playwright, noted for such political plays as *Maydays* (1983), which explores the changes in British society from 1956 to the present. He established his reputation with *Destiny* (1976), a provocative examination of fascist and racist elements in British culture; it was the first of several of his plays to be produced by the ROYAL SHAKESPEARE COMPANY.

Edgar's greatest commercial success, his adaptation of Dickens's *The Life and Adventures of Nicholas Nickleby* (1980), was the fruit of a long collaboration with the cast of the original RSC production. Subsequently he worked with Ann Jellicoe on *Entertaining Strangers* (1985), a COMMUNITY THEATRE project in Dorset, and wrote the screenplay for Trevor Nunn's historical film *Lady Jane* (1986). Other stage plays by Edgar include *State of Emergency* (1972), *Blood Sports* (1976), *Wreckers* (1977), *Teendreams* (1979), and *That Summer* (1987). *The Shape of the Table* (1990), a drama set in an unidentified communist country during the political upheavals of 1989, was first presented at the National Theatre and later seen in Bucharest. Recent work includes the television play *Buying a Landslide* (1992), about US electoral politics.

Edinburgh Festival The best-known British cultural festival, which has taken place annually in Edinburgh since its foundation in 1947. Encompassing music, opera, drama, and other branches of the performing arts, the festival takes place in August and lasts three weeks. As well as visits by major professional companies, the festival's programme includes a host of events staged by less well-known performers (many of them amateur) under the aegis of the so-called **Edinburgh Fringe** (founded in 1949), which in recent years has attracted as much attention as the official festival itself. Over the years the festival has seen first performances of many major works, among them plays by T. S. Eliot,

Sean O'Casey, and Eugène IONESCO. The current director is Brian McMaster.

Edinburgh International Film Festival A film festival held in Edinburgh for a fortnight each August. Founded in 1947 to focus on documentary films, it is now the world's longest-running film festival and presents work in all genres from many countries. The festival's patron is the Scottish film actor Sean Connery. The programme includes children's cinema, masterclasses with famous actors and directors, and the presentation of several awards, including the Michael POWELL Prize for best British feature film and the Channel 4 Young Film-maker of the Year Award.

Egk, Werner (Werner Mayer; 1901–83) German composer and conductor. After studies in Munich with Carl ORFF, Egk worked as a conductor for theatre and radio. In the 1930s he conducted at the Berlin State Opera and from 1950 until 1953 was director of the Berlin Musikhochschule. Egk composed mainly for the theatre, supplying his own librettos, which are often ironic treatments of historical or legendary themes. His opera *Peer Gynt* (1938) was blacklisted by the Nazis for its satirical antiheroic spirit. His music combines the driving rhythms of early Stravinksy with harmonies derived from the French postimpressionists; the later work is often highly dissonant. Other important works are the operas *Die Zaubergeige* (1935), *Circle* (1948), *Irische Legende* (1955), *Der Revisor* (1957), *Die Verlobung in San Domingo* (1963), and *Abraxas* (1979). He also composed orchestral pieces, notably the *Olympische Festmusik* (1936) for the Berlin Olympics.

Egri, Susanna (1926–) Italian dancer and choreographer, who has also taught dance with several leading Italian companies. Having trained in Budapest, where she was born, Egri undertook further studies at the Hungarian State Institute for Choreography and Teaching and subsequently enjoyed an international career as a ballerina, appearing in Budapest, Paris, and in several major Italian opera houses.

In 1950 she settled in Turin, where she opened her own Ballet Academy; she is also ballet director of the company attached to the Turin opera house. She is particularly well known for her many appearances on Italian television, her televised version of *Cavalleria Rusticana* (1963) winning the PRIX ITALIA.

Eich, Günter (1907–72) German poet and radio playwright. After attending schools in Finsterwalde, Berlin, and Leipzig, Eich studied sinology and law in Berlin and Paris. From 1932 he lived as a writer in Berlin, working for the radio. He served as a soldier in World War II and was an American prisoner of war during the years 1944–45. A founder of GRUPPO 47, he married the Austrian writer Ilse AICHINGER in 1953.

Günter Eich was a leading figure in post-war German poetry as well as one of the founders of the radio play as a genre. The experience of World War II changed Eich's self-definition as a writer dramatically: in his first major post-war volume of poems, *Remote Farmsteads* (1948), Eich registers individual as well as collective disillusionment by stripping his language to the barest level. In *Underground* (1949) he focusses on aspects of everyday city life, such as the omnibus, a cigarette-selling woman, his walk to the station, etc. In the 1950s Eich's reached a wider audience with his radio plays, which became famous for their open endings. His later radio plays, as for example those in the collection *In Other Tongues* (1964), broke completely with the naturalist tradition. Eich's most avant-garde work may well be *Pigeons and Moles* (1970), a collection of highly intertextual prose poems full of hidden allusions and witty quotations.

Eiermann, Egon (1904–70) German architect. Born in Neuendorf near Berlin, he studied at the Berlin Technische Hochschule, (1923–27), establishing himself in private practice in 1930. His early work consisted largely of private houses but he also designed displays and films for Hitler's 'Give me four years' exhibition in 1936–37 and several large industrial buildings between 1936 and 1943. Eiermann became head of the Faculty of Architecture at Karlsruhe in 1947, moving his practice there at the same time. Germany's economic recovery in the 1950s and 1960s brought him many large corporate commissions, most of them carried out in collaboration with Robert Hilgers. Eiermann's work is firmly within the Miesian tradition of steel frames and glass surfaces. He came to international prominence with an apartment block at the Berlin Interbau exhibition (1958) and with the German pavilion at the 1958 Brussels World Fair. More controversial was his 'restoration' of the Kaiser Wilhelm Memorial Church in West Berlin; retaining just the massive bomb-damaged stone tower, he flanked it with immense prism-shaped towers faced with precast concrete panels, which have become popularly known as 'the egg crates'. In the 1960s he designed major high-rise buildings; the Bundestag offices in Bonn (1965–69), offices for IBM in Stuttgart (1967–72), and offices for Olivetti in Frankfurt (1968–72), in which fixed sun-screens serve to relieve the otherwise rectilinear outlines.

Einem, Gottfried von (1918–) Austrian composer, conductor, and administrator. Born in Switzerland of Austrian parents, Einem grew up in Germany, where he began his musical career as a repetiteur at Bayreuth and the Berlin State Opera. From 1941 until 1943 he studied composition with BLACHER in Berlin. On returning to Austria after World War II he became an administrator of the Salzburg Festival (1946–66); from 1963 until his retirement he taught composition at the Vienna Academy.

Einem enjoyed an early success with the ballet *Prinzessin Turandot* (1944) and subsequently came to international attention with the opera *Danton's Death* (1947). He composes mainly for the theatre in a dramatic dissonant style that shows the influence of Mahler, Stravinsky, and Blacher amongst others. His operas, which have enjoyed considerable success in Austria, include *The Trial* (1953, after Kafka), *Der Zerrissene* (1964), *The Visit of the Old Lady* (1971, after DÜRRENMATT), and *Jesu Hochzeit* (1980). He has also composed orchestral pieces such as *Capriccio* (1943) and *Hexameron* (1969).

Eisler, Hanns (1898–1962) Austro-German composer, noted for his politically committed work. Born in Leipzig, the son of the Austrian philosopher Rudolf Eisler, he grew up in Vienna, where he studied at the Conservatory and privately (1919–23) with Schoenberg. The older composer's serial technique is the dominant influence on all Eisler's early work (*see* SERIALISM). In 1925, however, he moved to Berlin where political developments in the Weimar Republic led him to repudiate his early style in favour of polemical songs in a straightforward diatonic idiom. During this period he formed a prolific partnership with Bertolt BRECHT, with whom he collaborated on such works as *The Measures Taken* (1930) and *The Mother* (1931).

In 1933 Eisler fled the Nazi regime, which ordered the destruction of his music; after some wandering he settled in the US, where he taught at the University of Southern California and worked on film scores for Charlie Chaplin amongst others. The anticommunist witchhunts of the post-war years led to his expulsion from the US in 1947. Following his return (1950) to East Berlin, Eisler devoted himself to producing 'applied' music for the socialist state, including the East German national anthem and many film scores and revolutionary songs. Other works by Eisler include the *Lenin Requiem* (1937), the opera *Johannes Faustus* (1953), and *Ernste Gesange* (1962). He was also important as an essayist and theoretician, his writings being much concerned with the function of music in society.

Ek, Matts *See* CULLBERG, BIRGIT.

electronic music Music involving the use of electronic equipment to alter natural sounds, to produce new synthesized sounds, or to record and reproduce sounds. The principal developments in electronic music have occurred since World War II. The arrival of the tape recorder (invented in 1935, but not widely available until the 1940s) was crucial, making possible both MUSIQUE CONCRÈTE and other experiments in electronic music carried out during the 1950s in newly established studios, often attached to radio stations. The first of these was the Studio für Elektronische Musik at Cologne (established in 1951); other important studios include the Studio di Fonologia at Milan (established 1955), the Columbia-Princeton Electronic Music Center in New York (established 1959), and more recently IRCAM in Paris. Tape recording made possible for the first time the transformation of sounds by, for example, editing, playing backwards, and mixing: since the mid 1960s the availability of synthesizers and computers has greatly extended the sophistication and flexibility of electronic sound production, a trend which the increasing use of MIDI (Musical Instrument Digital Interface) systems is likely to continue. *See also* GROUPE DE RECHERCHES MUSICALES.

Eliade, Mircea (1907–86) Romanian historian of religion and novelist. After gaining an MA in philosophy from Bucharest University, Eliade studied in Calcutta and lived for a while in an ashram. His doctoral thesis explored Indian mysticism and yoga. After World War II he settled in France and taught at the Sorbonne and other universities. From 1956 he was professor of the history of religion at Chicago University.

As a scholar of comparative religions and as a novelist alike, Eliade was preoccupied with the idea of the divine 'camouflaged in the banal'. He coined the term 'heirophany' for those manifestations of the sacred through the mundane that he saw as central to the religious understanding of the world. In *Treatise on the History of Religions* and *The Myth of the Eternal Return* (both 1949) he explored the rituals and belief systems of ancient societies in which the mundane world was regarded as deriving its reality and significance from a greater sacred realm. Eliade himself lamented the fact that modern Western societies had lost touch with such modes of thought by adopting a purely linear understanding of time. In *Shamanism* (1951) he celebrated the shamans, masters (and mistresses) of bringing divine or transcendent reality into the realm of the relative and mundane. Subsequent publications included *Yoga* (1954), *Autobiography* (1966), *The Quest* (1969), and *The History of Religious Beliefs and Ideas* (1976–81), a massive summation of his life's work. His most ambitious novel, *The Forbidden Forest* (1955), is a masterpiece of MAGIC REALISM dealing with Romanian society during World War II and its aftermath.

Elias, Norbert (1897–1990) German sociologist. Born in Breslau (today Wrocłau, Poland), Elias studied medicine, philosophy, and psychology in Breslau and Heidelberg. He worked with the sociologist Karl Mannheim in Frankfurt until 1933 when he, being of Jewish origin, fled Germany for Paris and then London. He later taught at the University of Leicester (1954–62) and for two years at the University of Ghana. In the 1970s he returned to Germany, living there and in Amsterdam. Elias's most important book, *The Civilizing Process*, appeared in 1939 but reached a wider readership only in the 1960s, when his work began to attract comparisons with that of the Annales school (*see* BRAUDEL, FERNAND). The book explores the relationship between the emergence of the nation state in Europe and the growing acceptance of greater restrictions on individual liberty and social behaviour during the same period. In *The Court Society* (1969) he selects as a key example of this process the growing importance of etiquette during the years that also saw the emergence of a centralized France. In his essay *What Is Sociology?* (1970) Elias explained his method of 'figurational sociology', arguing that changes within a complex society are more often the unforeseeable result of continually shifting social figurations than the product of struggle between fixed social classes.

Elytis, Odysseus (Odysseus Alepoudelis; 1912–) Greek poet. A Cretan, Elytis studied law at Athens University and later (1948–52) attended the Sorbonne. His pseudonym may derive from the Greek words for Greece, hope, and freedom, or from the Homeric epithet of Odysseus, which means the wanderer. His first works, written in an exuberant surrealist style, were published in the periodical *Nea Grammata* in the 1930s. During World War II he worked with the Resistance in Albania, his experiences there inspiring the long poem *An Heroic and Mournful Chant for the Lieutenant Lost in Albania* (1946). Since the war he has worked in a number of administrative and advisory roles for Greek National Broadcasting, the Greek National Theatre, the Greek Ballet, and other national cultural institutions.

Elytis's debt to French surrealism is most apparent in his first two collections of poetry, *Orientations* (1939) and *Sun the First* (1943), which also reveal his sensitivity to the Greek landscape. After a silence of nearly 15 years he published his greatest and most difficult poem *It is Worthy* (*Axion Est*; 1959), a complex work dealing with the struggle of the poet's creative spirit to transcend the turmoil of Greek history. The poem takes its structure from Byzantine liturgy. *Six and One Regrets for the Sky* (1960), *The Light Tree and the Fourteenth Beauty* (1971), and *The Monogram* (1972) are more personal and introspective. Among his more recent works are the long poem *Maria Nefeli* (1978), *Three Poems with Flags of Convenience* (1982), *Journal of an Unseen April* (1984), *Sappho* (1984), and *Private Way* (1991). He was awarded the Nobel Prize for literature in 1979.

English National Opera British opera company. Formerly the Sadler's Wells Opera (which itself developed from the Old Vic company), the company performed at the Sadler's Wells Theatre, London, before moving to the Coliseum in 1968. The present name was adopted in 1974. Recent music directors have included Stephen Arlen (1966–72), Lord Harewood (1972–85), and Peter Jonas (1985–). While having many established classics in its repertoire, the company has always had a commitment to innovation, performing BRITTEN's *Peter Grimes* for the first time in 1948, for instance, and introducing the works of Janáček to the British public. The company encourages experimental production styles and is committed to English-language productions. There is an emphasis on relatively low seat prices, in order to attract an audience who would not normally be exposed to opera. The general director is Peter Jonas (to be replaced by Dennis Marks in mid 1993), the music director Mark Elder (to be replaced by Sian Edwards in mid 1993).

English Stage Company British theatrical company, which was one of the most influential of all new theatre groups in the 1950s and 1960s; it was largely responsible for the post-war resurgence of the British theatre and the emergence of the so-called ANGRY YOUNG MEN.

Housed in the Royal Court Theatre, in London's Sloane Square, well away from the West End, the company was founded in 1955 by George Devine, who ran it until his premature death in 1966. It was mainly owing to the encouragement of Devine that such writers as OSBORNE, WESKER, ARDEN, BOND, STOREY, HAMPTON, and PINTER, were able to find a stage for their work. Osborne's *Look Back in Anger* (1956) was one of the English Stage Company's early successes. Devine also put on a number of plays by such contemporary foreign writers as IONESCO, BRECHT, and BECKETT. The company played an important role in the ultimately successful struggle to end state censorship of the British stage.

Enquist, Per Olov (1934–) Swedish novelist and writer. Since his debut in 1961 with *The Crystal Eye*, Enquist has been one of the most popular writers in Sweden; he is also well known in Europe and the US. He grew up in an isolated village in the Far North of Sweden and the pietistic attitudes he encountered there have left ambiguous traces in his works. The young Enquist was an excellent athlete and his interest in sport also shows in some works.

The Fifth Winter of the Magnetizer (1964), a novel set in the 1790s, explores the tension between faith and reality. *The Legionnaires* (1968) is a prize-winning documentary novel about the forcible repatriation of refugees in Sweden after World War II. Here, as in other works, Enquist is interested in language and how it relates to reality and truth. In *Stories from the Age of Cancelled Revolutions* (1974) Enquist studied the attempted social revolutions of the 1960s.

In 1978 Enquist, like many other Swedish authors of the time, returned to Sweden as his setting; *The March of the Musicians* depicts a rural community at the turn of the century, mixing history with fiction and exploring the relationship between individuals and society.

In 1981 Enquist published the triptych of plays *The Night of the Tribades*, *To Phaedra*, and *From the Life of the Rainsnakes*. He has also written several works in collaboration with other authors.

Ensemble InterContemporain French contemporary music ensemble. It was founded in Paris in 1976 at IRCAM (Institut de Recherche et de Coordination Acoustique/Musique). Its conductors are Pierre BOULEZ, the director of IRCAM (with whom the ensemble remains closely associated), and the Hungarian Peter Eötvös (1944–). It has given premieres of works by Boulez and other composers.

Ensemble Modern German contemporary music ensemble. It was founded in 1980 by members of the National Youth Orchestra of West Germany. It is associated with, among others, the composer Mauricio KAGEL, who has conducted the ensemble and written a number of works for it.

Enzensberger, Hans Magnus (1929–) German poet, translator, and editor. After spending his youth in Nuremberg and

Nördlingen, Enzensberger studied literature, languages, and philosophy in Erlangen, Hamburg, Freiburg, and Paris during the years 1949–54. In 1955 he received his doctorate for a dissertation on the Italian poet Clemens Brentano. Enzensberger has travelled widely, spending long periods in Norway, Italy, and in South and North America. In 1965 he became editor of the influential journal *Kursbuch* and in 1980 began to edit *Transatlantik*. Since the mid 1970s he has been a prolific translator of European, South American, and US writers, including Pablo Neruda, Octavio Paz, Lars GUSTAFSSON, and William Carlos Williams.

Enzensberger's own work can be divided into three phases. The political poetry of the 1950s and early 1960s established his reputation as a representative of a new radical generation of post-war writers. The three volumes of this period *Defence of the Wolves* (1957), *Natural Language* (1960), and *Braille* (1964) satirize the ideology of post-war West Germany during the so-called 'economic miracle'. This tendency became more pronounced in his second phase, which was dominated by editing *Kursbuch* and producing documentary literature, such as the play *The Havana Inquiry* (1970) and the novel *The Short Summer of Anarchy* (1972). In 1975 he published *Mausoleum: 37 Ballads from the History of Progress*, poems which explore the life and work of famous figures and examine the notion of historical progress. Finally the 1980s became the decade of essay writing: Enzensberger published *Political Crumbs* in 1982, *Europe, Europe* in 1987, and *Mediocrity and Delusion* in 1988.

epic theatre A form of drama developed by Bertolt BRECHT and the German theatre director Erwin PISCATOR from the 1920s onwards. The theory and practice of epic theatre – sometimes called the **Theatre of Reason** – derived from Brecht's central belief that drama should address itself to the intellect rather than to the emotions of the audience. Amongst other things, the theory advocates disregard for the unities of time and place in favour of a looser episodic structure, and the use of the ALIENATION EFFECT to prevent audiences from empathizing with the events portrayed. Songs, stylized acting, and third-person narrative are often used to remind the audience of the artificial nature of the action. Brecht's epic theatre proved a major influence on the politically committed playwrights of the 1950s and 1960s. Exponents have included John ARDEN in Britain, Peter WEISS in Germany, and Michel VINAVER in France.

Erofeev, Venedikt (1938–90) Russian dissident writer. Few biographical details are known about this tragic figure whose own alcoholism is reflected in his masterpiece *Moscow Circles* (also known as *Moscow to the End of the Line*: in Russian *Moskva-Petushki*: written 1969, published 1973). Describing a drunken journey up and down a godforsaken Moscow suburban railway line, this unique novel is saturated with literary and other cultural references, ranging from the Bible, Aeschylus, and Rabelais to Soviet politicians and hack writers. Mock-heroic in genre and lyrical in tone (it is described as a 'poem'), it is a hymn to the bliss of intoxication, incorporating a range of extraordinary (and disgusting) cocktails. Joyous, frequently scabrous, anecdotes and debates with other passengers (who may or not be real) gradually give way to a more sombre mood and the hero is eventually killed near the Kremlin walls by four KGB men. *Moscow Circles* is a truly modern masterpiece, brilliant in texture, wide-ranging in theme, and fascinatingly ambiguous.

Several works circulating in *samizdat* have also been attributed to Erofeev, including *Memoirs of a Psychopath* (1956–57) and *Dmitrii Shostakovich* (1972); an essay on the philosopher Rozanov was eventually published abroad in 1982. Of a planned dramatic trilogy, only the second part was completed: *Walpurgis Night* (1985) is set in a Soviet psychiatric hospital where, as in the novel, brilliant unfettered talk and orgiastic drinking give way to tragedy, as the carousing inmates poison and blind themselves with stolen hospital alcohol. Erofeev's early death from throat cancer deprived Russian literature of a great writer, although *Moscow Circles* should assure him of a lasting place.

Erró (Gudmundur Gudmundsson; 1932–) Icelandic painter. Born at Olafsvik in Iceland, Erró studied at the Academy of Art in Reykjavik (1949–51). His early works include frescoes at the Academies of Art in Oslo (1952–54) and Reykjavik (1955–58). Since then he has lived and worked in various parts of the world including Paris (1958–62), the US (1962–63, 1964), New York and Paris (1966–71), and Thailand and the Far East (1972–85).

Erró's paintings are often large and crammed with fantastic detail. Since the mid 1950s he has produced several groups of pictures on particular themes, usually to comment on aspects of modern life or politics. For example, between 1960 and 1962 he painted *Les Usines* ('Factories'), a series of about 30 works. One shows a large hall in which machines are dissecting human bodies on a production line – an attack on the division of labour and dehumanizing factory processes. In the 1960s he drew increasingly on material from advertising, comics, films, and television in the manner of pop artists (*see* POP ART). He also became involved in HAPPENINGS and films. His works often have a surrealist feel.

Erskine, Ralph (1914–) Anglo-Swedish architect. Erskine was born in London and educated at the Regent Street Polytechnic. A pacifist, he left Britain for Sweden shortly before the outbreak of World War II and continued his studies there, establishing a practice in Drottningholm in 1946. He designed a series of houses and housing projects, in which he responded to the harsh Scandinavian climate by treating the building as a wall with its back turned to the north. This idea of a 'wall-building' found its fullest expression in housing at Svappavaara in Sweden (1963), Resolute Bay in Canada (1973–74), and at Byker, Newcastle upon Tyne (1969–82). His enormous scheme at Byker, for 2400 council houses, followed a long campaign of local consultation and has been seen as the origin of 'community architecture' in Britain. Erskine had, however, been applying this consultative approach for some time in numerous housing projects in Scandinavia. With 'The Ark' in Hammersmith, London (1989–91), an immense oval office building with a bulging globular shape, Erskine was acclaimed as pioneering a 'green' approach to commercial architecture. He is currently working on projects in Botswana and Namibia.

Ervi, Aarne (1910–77) Finnish architect. Ervi studied at the Helsinki University of Technology and worked in Alvar AALTO's office before establishing his own practice in 1938. Influenced by Aalto's functionalism, he designed several industrial buildings, most notably the power stations at Pyhakoski (1949) and Jylhama (1950). His Porthania Building for Helsinki University (1950–57) was an early use of prefabricated reinforced concrete and led to work at Turku University. His major achievement was as planner and architect of the new garden-city of Tapiola, winning the competition for the overall plan in 1954, and designing the administrative and shopping centres (1961), the swimming pool (1964–65) and the main hotel (1974). As well as handling a large practice, Ervi was director of the Helsinki city planning office from 1965 to 1976.

Estang, Luc (Lucien Bastard; 1911–92) French poet, novelist, and critic. After an education in religious boarding schools and seminaries, Estang worked as a journalist on the Catholic newspaper *La Croix*, later becoming its editor in chief (1940–55). In 1955 he became one of the founding directors of the Editions du Seuil publishing house. He contributed to various literary magazines including the *Figaro littéraire*.

In his poems Luc Estang celebrated the mystery of creation and confronted the problem of original sin. Important collections include *Beyond Myself* (1938), *Moving the Flock* (1939), *The Mystery Tamed* (1943), *Time on a Leash* (1977), *Heart Body* (1982), and *Mémorable Planète* (1991). In his novels, notably the trilogy *The Cure of Souls* (1949–54), he explores the difficulties of faith in a depraved and cruel world and the enigma of grace. Like Graham GREENE he is preoccupied with the complexities of moral choice and the intricate movements of the human soul. Thus his novel *The Better Song* (1961) hinges on an act of adultery that gives the hero the only true happiness of his life. In later novels such as *The Apostate* (1968) and *The Deicides* (1980) he takes a more critical attitude to the Roman Catholic hierarchy than previously.

Esterházy, Peter (1950–) Hungarian novelist. A descendant of the famous aristocratic family, Esterházy graduated in mathematics from the University of Budapest in 1974 and published his first volume of short stories in 1976. His first novel, *A Novel of Production* (*Termelési-regény*; 1979), immediately established his reputation as the most challenging and experimental writer of his generation. The novel juxtaposes the story of a young computer technician's bizarre struggles against bureaucracy with an account of the author's everyday life given in a series of spoof footnotes that incorporate a wide range of literary styles and allusions. For the next seven years Esterházy devoted himself to a major creative undertaking in the form of a series of novels, stories, and other fictions given the umbrella title *An Introduction to Literature* (*Bevezetés a szépirodalomba*); these appeared in a single volume in 1986. The collection represents a powerful challenge to the various social and national roles imposed upon the Hungarian writer, not only by the dictates of post-war communism, but also by two centuries of didacticism in the native prose tradition. These texts combine satire and political criticism with an inexhaustible linguistic virtuosity that has become one of the hallmarks of Esterházy's style. Since *An Introduction to Literature*, Esterházy has published three further novels, including *Healing Verbs of the Heart* (1985), and two volumes of essays. He is widely considered to be the leading representative of Hungarian POSTMODERNISM.

European Film Awards An international film ceremony at which awards are given in a number of categories to outstanding European films and film-makers. The Awards were established in 1989 in an attempt to raise the profile of European cinema and were closely modelled on the Oscar awards presented annually in the US. Winners at the first European Film Awards ceremony included Theo Angelopoulos's *Landscape in a Mist*, which won the award for best film of the year, Géza Bereményi as best director for *The Midas Touch*, Ruth Sheen as best actress for *High Hopes*, and Philippe Noiret as best actor for *Life and Nothing But* and *Cinema Paradiso*. In 1992 the best film award was won by Gianni Amelio's *Il ladro di bambini*.

Evans-Pritchard, Edward Evan (1902–73) British social anthropologist. After graduating in modern history at Oxford, Evans-Pritchard studied anthropology under Bronisław Malinowski at the London School of Economics. In 1946, after a brief spell of teaching at Cambridge, he took a chair in social anthropology at Oxford, holding it until his retirement in 1970.

Evans-Pritchard made his name early on with two books on Sudanese tribal culture: *Witchcraft, Oracles, and Magic among the Azande* (1937) and *The Nuer* (1940), a study of a society without government, are regarded as classic case studies. He also coedited a hugely influential book of essays on African politics. After World War II his work became more theoretical; in particular, he came to reject Durkheim's benchmark 'scientistic' approach to the subject, arguing that anthropology should be classed with history as a humanity.

Always scholarly and literate, his later work was also often controversial. *Kinship and Marriage among the Nuer* (1951) explored the role of relationship taboos in Nuer society, while *The Sanusi of Cyrenaica* (1949) examined the disruptive effects of colonialism on a group of nomads. His last major work, *Nuer Religion* (1956), argued that the forms of religious belief cannot be accounted for entirely in sociological terms. A Catholic convert, Evans-Pritchard believed that the forms and language of tribal religion reflected an ineffable reality.

Evtushenko, Evgenii (Aleksandrovich) (1933–) Russian poet and novelist. Evtushenko was born in Stantsiia Zima, Siberia, of Ukrainian descent. After early ambitions to be a footballer, he made his name with the long autobiographical poem *Zima Station*, detailing the impact of the THAW on Russia in general and on the author in particular. In 1960 he visited the US with VOZNESENSKY and a year later published two of the most famous poems of the Thaw, *Babii Yar'* and *The Heirs of Stalin*. The first of these is always included in Evtushenko's public performances of his work, which are so accomplished that glaring deficiencies in the poems are sometimes hidden. The second was so devastatingly critical of latent Stalinism that it was not reprinted until 1987. Evtushenko's best poems have strongly marked rhythms (e.g. the dance rhythm of 'Weddings', 1955), achieved almost entirely through the use of traditional syllabo-accentual metres, and are characterized by verbal inventiveness, mordant wit and, at times, tender lyricism. Essentially a narrative poet, Evtushenko is far less convincing when writing in philosophical vein. His novel *Wild Berries* (1981) exemplifies both modes of his writing.

Evtushenko has always taken a high public profile, speaking out on topical issues and making frequent visits to the West. This has led to accusations that, during the Breshnev years, his role was that of licensed court jester. His defenders point to his unswerving support for poets repressed by Stalin, his espousal of ecological causes, and, most recently, his role in arranging for a monument to the victims of Stalinism to be placed outside the KGB headquarters in Moscow. During the abortive coup of 1991 Evtushenko declaimed his *August 19* outside the Russian parliament building, his own English translation of the poem appearing as early as August 22.

existentialism A movement in European philosophy that stressed the importance of personal experience and individual responsibility in the face of meaninglessness and death.

The existentialist thinker starts with the problem of being rather than the problem of knowledge, thereby sidestepping the debate between idealism and empiricism (both of which are seen as inadequate). Man is conceived of as a being with no fixed nature or essence, stranded in an 'absurd' universe without meaning or purpose. As such, he is forced to create his own values and meanings. By accepting the burden of his freedom man can authenticate his own existence; the alternative is the 'bad faith' of falling back on the readymade values offered by religion and social convention.

Existentialism emerged as the dominant trend in European thought in the immediate post-war years, when the writings of Jean-Paul SARTRE and Albert CAMUS in particular began to enjoy a wide currency. Key texts were Sartre's *Being and Nothingness* (1943) and Camus's *The Myth of Sisyphus* (1942). Other leading figures included Maurice MERLEAU-PONTY and Simone DE BEAUVOIR. Most of the important concepts of French existentialism can, however, be traced back to the pre-war work of the German thinkers Karl Jaspers (1883–1969) and Martin Heidegger (1889–1976), both of whom were preoccupied with the problem of being and questions of human freedom and authenticity. The emphasis on 'subjective truth' and the necessity of choice can be found earlier still in the radical Protestantism of Søren Kierkegard (1813–55).

The impact of existentialism was as much literary as philosophical, with several of the principal figures (notably Sartre and de Beauvoir) being important creative writers as well as thinkers. It has also had a major influence in such fields as psychology and Christian theology.

Eyck, Aldo van (1918–) Dutch architect. Van Eyck was educated in Britain and trained at technical schools in the Hague and Zürich before starting his career in Amsterdam's public works department. He has been in private practice in Amsterdam and the Hague since 1952, working in partnership with Theo Bosch (1971–82) and subsequently with his wife Hannie. An influential lecturer and teacher in Europe and the US, van Eyck has taught at the Delft Technical University since 1967. He was a participant in Team X, the group of radical young architects who organized the tenth and last Congrès Internationaux d'Architecture Moderne (CIAM) in 1956. He subsequently turned away from the rationalism of the Modern Movement, seeking new influences in the anthropology of LEVI-STRAUSS and the art of children and primitive tribesmen. In this he was an early proponent of architectural STRUCTURALISM, arguing that plans should be informed by anthropological rather than formal considerations. Nonetheless, modernism had a sufficient grip on Eyck for him to reject revivalism or any kind of expressionism. He is more important as a theorist than as a builder. His first major building was an orphanage in Amsterdam (1957–60); although it was built of plain industrial materials, Eyck declared that its complex plan based around small courtyards would 'untwist these little children'. It has recently been renovated. His 'Mothers' House', a hostel for single-parent families in Amsterdam (1978–81), carried these ideas further.

Eysenck, Hans Jürgen (1916–) British behavioural psychologist, born in Germany. Educated at the Universities of Dijon, Exeter, and London, Eysenck was director of the psychological department at the Maudsley Hospital, London from 1946 until 1950. In 1955 he became professor of psychology at the Institute of Psychiatry (London University), a post he held until his retirement in 1984. He was the chief editor of the journal *Behaviour Research and Therapy* from 1963.

A prolific writer, Eysenck has been the principal post-war popularizer of psychology in Britain. He has frequently been contentious, most notably in suggesting that interracial variations in performance in IQ tests could be due to genetic factors. He has also explored the relationship between personality types and the various kinds of neuroses, linking depression and anxiety neuroses to introversion and psychopathy to extroversion. In 1952 he wrote a controversial article claiming that the published evidence did not support the view that psychoanalysis did any better than no treatment in making neurotics well. In his own therapeutic work he attempted to alter undesirable behaviour patterns rather than to interpret them as symptoms of underlying causes. Unlike Freudian analysis, Eysenck's 'behaviour therapy', was based on statistical findings and subjected to experimental trial.

His numerous works include *Uses and Abuses of Psychology* (1953), *The Biological Bases of Personality* (1967), *Race, Intelligence and Education* (1971), *The Measurement of Intelligence* (1973), and *Decline and Fall of the Freudian Empire* (1986). In 1990 he published *Rebel With a Cause*, an autobiography.

F

Fabbri, Diego (1911–80) Italian playwright, best known for his poetic dramas on Catholic themes. Influenced by Pirandello, Fabbri sought to explore the relationship between religious faith and drama. Prior to World War II he attracted hostile attention from the Fascist authorities with *The Knot* (1935; rewritten as *The Swamp*, 1942); after the war he turned increasingly to religious topics in such acclaimed poetic dramas as *Inquisition* (1950), *Family Trial* (1953), and *The Trial of Jesus* (1955), further developing his thoughts on religion in the collection of essays *Christian Ambiguity* (1954). Other notable works for the stage included several comedies of manners, among them *The Seducer* (1951) and *The Liar* (1954), and adaptations of novels by Dostoevskii and others, some of which were also filmed for television and the cinema.

Fabre, Jan (1958–) Belgian theatre director, playwright, and artist, who emerged as a major theatrical talent in the 1980s. Fabre established his reputation with such pieces as *It is the Kind of Theatre One Could Expect and Foresee* (1982) and *The Power of Theatrical Madness* (1984), in which he demonstrated his commitment to expanding the boundaries of theatre; his works reject established dramatic conventions and combine elements of speech, mime, dance, and music. He is particularly noted for his preference for working with untrained actors and has toured internationally with nonprofessional casts. *Sweet Temptations* (1991) was jointly commissioned by theatrical organizations in Brussels, Amsterdam, Rotterdam, Frankfurt, and Vienna.

Fábri, Zoltán (1917–) Hungarian film director, who was a major force in Hungary's 'New Cinema' of the 1960s and 1970s. Born in Budapest, Fábri trained as a painter and set designer at Budapest's Academy of Fine Arts before transferring to the Academy of Dramatic and Film Art. He subsequently became an actor in the National Theatre (from 1941) and also directed. He spent much of World War II as a prisoner of war and returned to Hungary to direct films, also scripting and designing sets for many of them. His *Twenty Hours* (1964) won the Grand Prix at the Moscow Film Festival; more recent successes have included *The Fifth Seal* (1976), *The Hungarians* (1977), which dealt with expatriation, *Bálint Fábián Meets God* (1980), *Requiem* (1981), and *Name-Day Guests* (1984).

Faldbakken, Knut (1941–) Norwegian novelist, critic, and editor. Faldbakken has been a prominent cultural figure in Norway since the publication of *The Grey Rainbow* in 1967. After some years living in Paris, he returned to Norway to become editor of the literary magazine *The Window* (1975–79).

Many of Faldbakken's novels deal with introverted characters who fail to come to terms with external reality; he also shows a keen interest in the psychology of sex. A good example is the early novel *His Mother's House* (1969), in which a young man becomes involved in an incestuous relationship with his mother in an attempt to escape a problematic relationship with a girl of his own age. *The Sleeping Prince* (1971) deals with the fantasies of a middle-aged spinster, which eventually lead to tragedy. Faldbakken frequently questions traditional gender roles and shows the destructive influence they can have on a relationship. *Adam's Diary* (1978) is a good example of this, as is *The Honeymoon* (1982), which was a major success in the US. Faldbakken is best known outside Norway for the novels *Twilight Country* (1974) and *Sweetwater* (1976), both of which are set in disintegrating societies of the near future. Like several of Faldbakken's other works, both these books have been filmed.

Other novels include *Insect Summer* (1972) and *Life with Marilyn* (1987). Faldbakken has also published short stories and plays.

Fanon, Frantz (1925–61) French psychiatrist and political theorist, born in Martinique. Fanon served in the French Army during World War II. After studying medicine and psychiatry in Lyon he worked in a mental hospital in Algeria in 1953. In 1954 he joined the Algerian National Liberation Front and in 1956 he went to Tunisia to edit its illegal newspaper. In 1960 he served briefly as Algerian ambassador to Ghana.

Fanon is one of the most important theorists of anticolonialism. In his first book, *Black Skin, White Masks* (1952), he recounted his personal experience of racism, while in his best-known work, *The Wretched of the Earth* (1961; with a preface by Jean-Paul SARTRE), he argued that violence was a necessary tool in the struggle against colonial oppression. He opposed the French policy of colonial assimilation as well as the tendency of Third World urban elites to ignore the plight of the peasantry once independence was achieved. Combining elements of Freudian analysis with EXISTENTIALISM and Marxist-Leninism, Fanon sought to open up a way for the peoples of the Third World countries to develop collective and individual sovereignty.

Fassbinder, Rainer Werner (1946–82) German film director, actor, and screenwriter, who established his reputation with a series of provocative melodramas during the 1970s. He began his career as a theatre director with fringe groups in Munich and worked on shorts for the cinema in the mid 1960s, making his first feature, the gangster film *Love is Colder than Death*, in 1969. He first attracted attention, however, with *Katzelmacher* (1969), a film based on his own stage play, in which he exposed racial prejudice in modern Germany, as experienced by a Greek immigrant (played by Fassbinder himself). The film was notable for its stylized dialogue and its bleak view of modern society, traits which have become hallmarks of his work.

Fassbinder's concern for the oppressed lay at the heart of such films as *Why Does Herr R Run Amok?* (1969), in which a clerical worker is driven to mass murder, and *The Merchant of Four Seasons* (1971), which traces the decline of a fruit merchant into alcoholism and death. Similar themes were explored in *The Bitter Tears of Petra von Kant* (1972), about the lesbian relationship of a fashion designer with one of her models, and *Fear Eats the Soul* (1973), about a doomed love affair between a Moroccan immigrant worker and an older woman.

Fassbinder's pessimism about human relationships is also apparent from such films as *Effi Briest* (1974), in which a young woman is trapped in a marriage to an old aristocrat, *Fox* (1975), in which Fassbinder (a homosexual himself) played a young man drawn into the exploitative world of a group of homosexuals, and the less well-known *Satan's Brew* (1976).

For *Chinese Roulette* (1976) Fassbinder disbanded the team of actors he had previously used and experimented with innovative camera angles to explore the issue of collective German guilt arising from the Nazi era. After this *tour de force*, *Despair* (1978), a tale of obsession and schizophrenia starring Dirk Bogarde, found only muted praise. His next film, *In a Year with 13 Moons* (1978), drew on the suicide of one of his homosexual lovers. *The Marriage of Maria Braun* (1978) and *Lola* (1981) both concerned women who sacrifice their bodies to men in exchange for power, while in *Veronika Voss* (1982) Fassbinder delivered another attack on contemporary German society, this time through the story of the decline of a Third Reich movie star.

Fassbinder's career ended with *Querelle* (1982), a film version of GENET's novel; he died of a drugs and drink overdose.

Fehling, Hermann (1909–) German architect. Born in France of German parents, Fehling was educated in Lübeck and Hamburg and trained as a carpenter, later studying architecture in Hamburg. He worked in the offices of Erich Mendelsohn (1929–30) and Werner Issel (1930–37) and served in the German army in World War II before establishing his own practice in Berlin in 1945. Since 1953 he has been in partnership with Daniel Gogel; they came to prominence with the city of Berlin's pavilion and the glass industry pavilion at the Interbau exhibition in 1956–57.

Most of their work is in Berlin, the best-known examples probably being the Max Planck Institute for Educational Research (1965–74) and the Institute for Hygiene (1966–74).

Fellini, Federico (1920–) Italian film director. Born in Rimini, he began his career as a cartoonist, also writing for radio, before entering films in 1940 as a screenwriter for ROSSELLINI and others. His work on Rossellini's *Rome – Open City* and other films was highly praised and in 1950 he made his debut as a director with *Variety Lights*, a satirical story about a humble touring theatre (on which he worked with Alberto LATTUADA).

The White Sheik (1952) was a romantic comedy, while *The Young and the Passionate* (1953) reflected his love of the circus and his childhood experiences of street life. This motif reappeared in *The Road* (1954), a sentimental story about a young girl's travels with a circus; starring Fellini's wife, Giulietta Masina (1921–); the film won the director an Oscar.

Fellini continued to explore themes of personal identity and the conflict between sexuality and innocence, in such films as *Nights of Cabiria* (1957), which again starred Masina, and *La Dolce Vita* (1960), starring Marcello Mastroianni. This story of moral disintegration in contemporary high society was distinguished by Fellini's use of bizarre images and his highly stylized cinematography; the success of the film confirmed Fellini's international reputation.

Having contributed to the film *Boccaccio '70* (1962), Fellini went on to direct what many consider his masterpiece, *8½* (1963), in which Mastroianni again starred. The film had a strong autobiographical element and showed the director at his inventive best; it gathered several awards including first prize at the Moscow Film Festival. Fellini continued to indulge his taste for extravagant visual images in the somewhat less successful films *Juliet of the Spirits* (1965), *Fellini Satyricon* (1969), *The Clowns* (1970), *Fellini Roma* (1972), and *Amarcord* (1974), after which he attracted renewed interest with *Fellini's Casanova* (1976), a sombre portrait of the great lover in his declining years.

Few of Fellini's subsequent films have matched his earlier successes; his more recent works include *City of Women* (1980), which like *Ginger and Fred* (1986) starred Mastroianni, and the documentary-style *Intervista* (1987), in which Fellini develops themes suggested by his own career, even to the extent of incorporating scenes from *La Dolce Vita*. His writings on cinema include *Fellini on Fellini* (1976).

Felsenstein, Walter (1901–75) Influential Austrian opera and theatre director. After studies at the Vienna Burgtheater, Felsenstein worked as an actor in Germany, Austria, and Switzerland. From 1932 he directed operas in Cologne, Frankfurt, and Zürich, and at the Schiller Theatre in Berlin. In contrast to the highly artificial style of opera production favoured at the time, Felsentein aimed above all to present a convincing dramatic action that would allow the work's contemporary meaning to emerge. This unconventional approach caused some controversy in the music world and he found regular employment difficult to obtain. In 1947, however, he became director of the Komische Oper in East Berlin where he was able to further develop his ideas about integrating music with dramatic action. Felsenstein and his pupils have had a major influence on operatic production in the last 40 years. Amongst his important productions were Janáček's *The Cunning Little Vixen*, Mozart's *The Marriage of Figaro*, Bizet's *Carmen* (1949), and Verdi's *La Traviata* (1955).

Fenoglio, Beppe (1922–63) Italian novelist and short-story writer. After taking part in the Resistance he spent most of his life in Turin. His first collection of short stories, *The Twenty-Three Days of the City of Alba* (1952), the novel *Ruin* (1954), *Spring of Beauty* (1959), and his posthumous writings *A Day of Fire* (1963), *A Private Question* (1963), and *Johnny the Partisan* (1968), were all inspired by the harsh life of the peasants in the Langhe region of Piedmont and by the partisan experience. Their style shows the influence of the English and US writers whom he most admired, notably Shakespeare, Coleridge, Dos Passos, and Hemingway. The element of subjective lyricism in his work distinguishes it from other writing in the postwar tradition of NEOREALISM. His language combines literary Italian with dialect.

Ferencsik, János (1907–84) Hungarian conductor, noted especially for his performances of Hungarian music. After studies at the Budapest Conservatory he worked at the Budapest State Opera from 1927, becoming a conductor there in 1930. In 1953 he became musical director of the State Opera and chief conductor of the Hungarian State Symphony Orchestra. He made his debut at the Bayreuth Festival in 1930 and his British debut in 1957, later appearing widely around the world as a guest conductor.

Festival de Musique de Montreux-Vevey *See* MONTREUX-VEVEY MUSIC FESTIVAL.

Festival of Britain A celebration of British culture held ostensibly to mark the centenary of the 1851 Great Exhibition; in practice it was an attempt by the Labour government to raise Britain from its post-war doldrums. The main complex of 27 acres on the South Bank of the Thames was organized by Hugh CASSON and Misha Black, whilst the London County Council architects Robert Matthew, Leslie MARTIN, and Peter Moro designed the only building intended to be permanent, the Royal Festival Hall. Other architects devised individual exhibits, of which Ralph Tubbs's 'Dome of Discovery' and POWELL AND MOYA's 'Skylon', a cigar-shaped sculpture on wires, were the most eye-catching. There was a funfair in Battersea Park and part of the Lansbury neighbourhood in London's East End was rebuilt under the supervision of Frederick GIBBERD as a town-planning exhibit. Other parts of Britain staged smaller events, whilst buses and a ship carried the message of Britain's regeneration far and wide.

The South Bank exhibition opened on 3 May 1951 and was a huge success, only to be demolished by the incoming Conservatives soon after its closure in September 1951. Today only the interior of the Royal Festival Hall and parts of Lansbury survive. Yet the Festival was a landmark in British design and helped to establish many young architects; it affirmed the quality of British sculpture and was a particular success for Britain's designers of furniture and fabrics. Above all, it represented the triumph of a short-lived vogue for the picturesque characterized by bright colours, zany patterning, and informal planning – qualities which are now being reappraised.

Figini, Luigi (1903–84) and **Pollini, Gino** (1903–91) Italian architects, who trained together at the Polytechnic in Milan and worked together from 1926 until Figini's death. In 1927 they founded the Gruppo 7 with Giuseppe Terragni and four others, effectively launching modernism in Italy. Their first important commission was an office building (1931) that established their reputation for industrial architecture. In 1934 they began their long association with Adriano Olivetti, for whom they designed a factory at Ivrea (1934–57, in four stages). Also at Ivrea they built a nursery school (1939–41), housing (1940), and a social services centre (1954–57).

After World War II they built extensively in Milan, including elegant flats and offices in the Via Broletto (1948), offices in Via Hoepli (1955), and apartments in Via Cerco (1957). Less successful were their grid-like blocks of housing, such as those built for UNACASA (1951). Factories such as that for Pozzi ceramics at Sparanize near Naples (1963) continued to win them acclaim. Their most successful buildings, however, were two churches – firstly and most influentially the Madonna of the Poor in Milan (1954) and then the Church of St John and St Paul at Bergamo (1964). Here Figini and Pollini transcended their geometric repertory to create a series of steps and set-backs; in each case the fascinating play of angles is complemented by a campanile.

Pollini's last major building (with Vittorio GREGOTTI) was the Science Department at Palermo University (1978); it is more playful than any of his work with Figini.

figuration libre *See* NEOEXPRESSIONISM.

film noir (French; dark film) An expressionist style of film that enjoyed a considerable vogue on both sides of the Atlantic in the 1940s and 1950s. The term, reflecting both the dark nature of the subject matter and the sombre lighting effects employed, was coined in 1946 by French critics to describe a new type of Hollywood gangster thriller. Film noir productions were characterized by their bleak view of society, with plots focussing on murder, betrayal, corruption, and greed. Much of the action took place at night, contributing to the pervading atmosphere of menace and pessimism. An archetypical US example was *Double Indemnity* (1944) directed by Billy Wilder. Key directors of the style in Europe included Jean-Pierre MELVILLE.

Finlay, Ian Hamilton (1925–) Scottish sculptor, exponent of concrete poetry, garden designer, and publisher. Finlay was born in Nassau, Bahamas, of Scottish parents and studied at Mackintosh's School of Art, Glasgow. He now lives on his farm in Lanarkshire, Scotland, where for over 20 years he has dedicated himself to creating the remarkable sculpture garden 'Little Sparta', for which he is now best known. This work has been carried on in the face of considerable bureaucratic obstruction from the local council. The garden abounds in statues, carved sundials, typographic inscriptions, weathercocks, and other idiosyncratic features; its symbolism is intended to reflect both the ideals of the 18th-century Enlightenment and the violence of the French Revolution.

In 1960 Finlay founded the Wild Hawthorn Press to produce his own prints and cards, which are often of a highly individual and experimental nature. His poem 'XM', for example, resembles a Scottish burn undulating down the page with different typefaces used to suggest the changes in the surface of the water as the stream descends. Finlay has also made a series of 'standing poems' or 'poem-constructions' in glass and concrete. His work has influenced younger poets in the US and Canada.

Finlay's work as a sculptor shows a fascination with warfare and political violence that some have found disturbingly ambiguous. In 1988 his work provoked an international *cause célèbre* when his commission to design a 'revolutionary garden' in Versailles was withdrawn by the French government, following allegations that its symbolism was 'fascist'. A full retrospective of Finlay's work was held at the ICA, London, in 1992.

Finnissy, Michael (Peter) (1946–) British composer with a large and uncompromising output. Born in London, Finnissy studied at the Royal College of Music with Bernard Stevens and Humphrey SEARLE and then with Roman Vlad in Italy. He also formed the music department at the London School of Contemporary Dance. His works include the music theatre pieces *Medea* (1976), *Mr Punch* (1977), *Circle, Chorus and Formal Act* (1973), and *5 Mysteries* (1972–76), pieces for voices and instrumental ensemble, and much virtuoso piano music. Combining influences as varied as oriental music and English folk tunes, his music is complex and fiercely expressive.

Fires of London British chamber ensemble, specializing in contemporary music; it was founded as the Pierrot Players in 1967 and disbanded in 1987. The Pierrot Players (the name was taken from Schoenberg's *Pierrot Lunaire*) were jointly directed by the composers Peter Maxwell DAVIES and Harrison BIRTWISTLE. The name was changed to Fires of London in 1970, when Davies took sole charge. The ensemble concentrated on mixed-media works and music theatre, giving first performances of many contemporary works, including Davies's *Eight Songs for a Mad King* (1969) and *The Martyrdom of St Magnus* (1977).

Fischer, Fritz (1908–) German historian. In 1935 Fischer began teaching ecclesiastical history in Berlin, obtaining his degree two years later. He was appointed professor of history in Hamburg in 1942 but owing to war service and a period as a prisoner of war did not begin to lecture until 1947. He retired in 1971.

Fischer became known to a wider public through his book *Reaching for World Power* (1961), which triggered the so-called 'Fischer Controversy'. In the book Fischer tried to prove that far from blundering into World War I, the German military and political elite, including the Kaiser, had actively sought a major European war as a means of establishing Germany as the dominant power in Europe. In the ensuing controversy, in which Gerhard Ritter took a major part, Fischer was criticized for taking statements really expressing wishful thinking at face value. Fischer defended his position in his subsequent book *World Power or Decline* (1965), where he further explored German ambitions in the years before 1914. The same theme is expounded in *The War of Illusions. German Politics from 1911 to 1914* (1969). In 1979 Fischer extended the range of his studies while reemphasizing his original standpoint in *Pact of the Elites. On the Continuity of Power Structures in Germany 1871–1945*. Here he argued that there had been a high degree of continuity between the foreign policy objectives of Hitler and those of earlier German politicians. In forcing Germans to reassess the relationship between the Nazi period and the rest of their history, Fischer's work has had an importance that reaches far beyond the world of scholarly historical debate.

Flaiano, Ennio (1910–72) Italian novelist, screenwriter, journalist, art critic, and playwright. A fascinating and versatile writer, Flaiano depicts contemporary Italy and particularly Rome in satirical, often grotesque, colours.

In the 1950s and 1960s he worked as a scriptwriter on FELLINI's *La Strada*, *La Dolce Vita*, and *8½* and ANTONIONI's *La Notte*. Most of his published work takes the form of notes, sketches, travel diaries, and aphorisms such as those collected in *One and One Night* (1959), *The Game and the Massacre* (1970), and the posthumously published *Autobiography of Prussian Blue* (1974). His only novel, *Time to Kill*, appeared in 1974.

He also wrote for the theatre, publishing *The War Explained to the Poor* (1946), *The Woman in the Wardrobe* (1958), and *An Extraterrestrial in Rome and Other Farces* (1971).

Fleischmann, Adolf Richard (1892–1968) German abstract painter. Born at Esslingen in the Neckar Valley, Fleischmann studied at Stuttgart's Royal School of Art (1908–11) and Royal Academy of Art (1911–13). Badly wounded in World War I, he worked as a scientific draughtsman at a hospital in Zürich from 1917 until 1923. In 1921 he contributed to the Neue Sezession exhibition of expressionist works in Munich. In 1937 he settled in France, where he spent World War II; in 1943 most of his works were destroyed. In 1952 he moved to the US, where he again worked as a scientific draughtsman (1953–62).

Fleischmann was strongly influenced by the De Stijl movement, which advocated an austere art based on straight lines, right angles, and primary colours. Between 1934 and 1949 many of his paintings featured circles, squares, and triangles. In 1950, however, he began to build up his paintings from numerous small horizontal lines, blocks of which he painted in similar or contrasting colours before superimposing several longer vertical lines. The design was usually given an outline, often a circle or oval. The overall effect was a subtle impression of movement. In other words, Fleischmann was a notable exponent of constructivism who developed into a pioneer of OP ART.

Flindt, Flemming (1936–) Danish dancer, choreographer, and ballet director, who worked with the Royal Danish Ballet in the 1960s and 1970s. Born in Copenhagen, Flindt trained at the Royal Danish Ballet School and joined the senior company in 1955, becoming a solo dancer in 1957. Subsequently he performed with the London Festival Ballet, the Paris Opéra, and the ROYAL BALLET before returning once more to the Royal Danish Ballet in 1966, when he was appointed the company's director. As head of the company he built up a strong programme of both classical and modern pieces, among them ballets by leading US choreographers.

Having established a reputation as a dancer in both classical and modern works, he achieved his first major success as a choreographer in 1963 with a version of IONESCO's play *Le Leçon*, which he treated as a study of sexual obsession and rape. The ballet was created for television but was later presented by a number of leading companies, including the Opéra Comique in Paris. He consolidated his reputation as a choreographer with such ballets as *The Three Musketeers* (1966), *The Miraculous Mandarin* (1967), *The Young Man Must Marry* (1968), *Swan Lake* (1969), *The Nutcracker* (1971), *Felix Luna* (1973), and *Dreamland* (1974) before finally leaving the Royal Danish Ballet and forming his own troupe in 1978. His successes since then have included *Salome* (1978). He became artistic director of the Dallas Ballet in 1981, where he choreographed *Caroline Mathilde* (1990).

Fo, Dario (1926–) Italian actor, playwright, and theatre manager. One of Italy's best-known performers in the 1950s, he subsequently developed a worldwide reputation with a series of plays combining fierce political comment with delirious farce. Fo began his career in the theatre with appearances in Milan, but was soon performing in revue sketches and songs in cabaret with his wife Franca RAME. In 1957 they founded their own company, for which Fo wrote his first farces, among them *Archangels Don't Play the Pin-Tables* (1959), *Stealing a Foot Makes you Lucky in Love* (1961), and *Seventh: Thou Shalt Steal a Little Less* (1964). Although the company was one of the most successful in Italy, in 1968, prompted by the political upheaval then occurring throughout Europe, Fo and Rame set up a new company, the Compagnia Nuova Scena, with the support of the Communist Party.

In 1969 Fo presented his one-man play *Mistero Buffo*, a partly extemporized piece exploiting his own mastery of mime and comic gifts to the full. Incorporating an invented language called *grammelot*, which Fo claimed was first used by medieval actors to avoid censorship, the play satirized a range of Establishment institutions – ecclesiastical, political, and commercial. The act has been such a success that Fo has been able to revive it regularly throughout the 1970s and 1980s.

In 1970 Fo founded a further company in Milan – **La Comune** – to specialize in radical leftwing drama. The new enterprise's first success was Fo's play *Accidental Death of an Anarchist* (1970), a tragicomedy about the mysterious death in custody of an anarchist railway worker, based on a real incident; this has already achieved the status of a modern classic. Fo's more recent productions with La Comune have included *Can't Pay? Won't Pay!* (1974), in which high prices provoke public unrest, *Trumpets and Raspberries* (1981), and *The Open Couple* (1987).

Fontana, Lucio (1899–1968) Italian painter, sculptor, and potter. Born in Argentina of Italian parents, Fontana was taken back to Italy in 1905. He began to study sculpture with his father, a sculptor, and subsequently trained at the Accademia Brera in Milan (1927–29). In 1930 he gave the first exhibition of nonfigurative sculpture in Italy. During the 1930s his output was prolific and he joined the large Paris-based group of abstract artists, Abstraction-Création. He returned to Argentina for the duration of World War II, helping to found the avant-garde Accademia Altamira in Buenos Aires and publishing his famous *Manifesto Blanco* in 1946. This advocated the creation of a new art, using methods and materials supplied by modern technology, to meet the requirements of the scientific post-war age.

In 1947 Fontana returned to Italy and founded the Movimento Spaziale or **Spazialismo**, whose manifestos called for the creation of total artistic 'environments' combining colour, form, sound, and movement. His attempts to develop this idea in his own work anticipated many developments of the 1960s and 1970s, notably CONCEPTUAL ART and PERFORMANCE ART. He was perhaps the first artist to create such an environment with his 'black spatial environment' (a room painted black) of 1947. In about 1950 he began to create his so-called *Concetti* ('Concepts') – monochromatic paintings with holes in them; these were followed from 1958 by the better known *Atesse* – monochromatic paintings with slits (for example, *Spatial Concept 'Waiting'*, 1960, Tate Gallery London). During the 1950s he also worked in sheet metal, terracotta, and bronze, and experimented with neon lights. His work of the 1950s and 1960s was widely influential both in Italy and abroad. In 1966 he created an environment for the Walker Art Center, Minneapolis, and another in 1967 for the Stedelijk Museum in Amsterdam.

Forbes, Bryan (1926–) British film director, screenwriter, producer, and actor. Born in London, Forbes attended the Royal Academy of Dramatic Arts and began to act on the stage. After serving in Intelligence during World War II he appeared in minor film roles, including a part in *The Guns of Navarone* (1961). By the mid 1950s Forbes was scripting such war films as *Cockleshell Heroes* (1955) and *I Was Monty's Double* (1958). He also wrote the popular comedy *The Captain's Table* (1959), the trade-union drama *The Angry Silence* (1960), which he coproduced with Richard ATTENBOROUGH, and the Peter Sellers comedy *Only Two Can Play* (1962). He made his debut as a director with *Whistle Down the Wind* (1961), about three children who believe an escaped murderer to be Christ; he also won international acclaim with *The L-Shaped Room* (1962), a drama of London low-life that he also scripted. Other films include the melodrama *Seance on a Wet Afternoon* (1962), the US production *King Rat* (1965), *The Raging Moon* (1970), the US hit *The Stepford Wives* (1974), the comedy *Better Late Than Never* (1983), the mafia thriller *The Naked Face* (1985), and *The Endless Game* (1988) for television. He has also directed for the stage.

Besides films, Forbes has written short stories, novels, and *Notes for a Life* (1976), an autobiography. He served from 1969 to 1971 as managing director and chief of production for Associated British (EMI) and has been president of the National Youth Theatre since 1984.

Ford, Aleksander (1908–80) Polish film director, who greatly influenced the direction of post-war Polish cinema before settling in Denmark. Born in Łódź, Ford began directing in 1929, progressing within a year from shorts to documentaries and features. During World War II he lived in the Soviet Union, where he became head of the Polish Army's film unit. After the war he was appointed director of Film Polski, the state-run film industry, in which role he helped to train a new generation of film-makers. Ford left Poland for Israel in 1960 before moving on to Denmark (1962).

His early films include documentaries such as *Łódź – the Polish Manchester* (1929) and *Forward Cooperation* (1935). His best-known features, for which he also wrote the screenplays, were *Young Chopin* (1951), *Five from Barska Street* (1953), and *The Knights of the Teutonic Order* (1960). His later work included the documentary *Good Morning Poland* (1970), the Danish-German cooperation *The First Circle* (1975), and the German-Israeli co-production *The Martyr* (1975).

Forman, Miloš (1932–) Czech film director, living in the US since 1968. Forman lost both parents in German concentration camps. After training as a scriptwriter at the film college in Prague, he gained valuable experience with the Magic Lantern multi-media group and worked on semi-documentary shorts. He made his debut as a director with the short films *Audition* (1963) and *If There Was No Music* (1963), which were released together as *Talent Competition.*

His first full-length feature film was *Peter and Pavla* (1964), a wry depiction of the confusions faced by a trainee supermarket detective when he falls in love for the first time. Forman's use of nonprofessional actors and improvised dialogue earned him recognition as one of the leaders of the Czech New Wave; the film was awarded first prize at the Locarno Film Festival and the Czechoslovak Film Critics Prize. *A Blonde in Love* (1965), another mild satire on the confusions wrought by a love affair, was equally successful.

In *The Fireman's Ball* (1967), however, Forman's satire took a political turn, drawing parallels between the attempts of a small town's fire brigade to stage a beauty contest and the futile and corrupt management of the country by the Czech government. When Soviet troops invaded the country in 1968 Forman's film was banned and the director took up permanent exile in the West, subsequently concentrating on films that appealed to a mass audience.

Forman's US films have included *Taking Off* (1971), a subversive comment on the gulf between the generations, *One Flew Over the Cuckoo's Nest* (1975), a spectacularly successful version of the novel by Ken Kesey, starring Jack Nicholson as a rebellious inmate of a mental institution, and *Hair* (1979), a screen version of the stage musical. Among more recent films have been *Ragtime* (1981), *Amadeus* (1983), a much acclaimed version of the play by Peter SHAFFER that was awarded no less than eight Oscars, and *Valmont* (1989), based on Laclos's *Les Liaisons Dangereuses.*

Forsyth, Bill (1947–) Scottish film director and screenplay writer, who established his reputation in the 1980s with several comedies set in small Scottish communities. Forsyth worked with the Glasgow Youth Theatre in the 1970s and began his film career with a series of industrial documentaries, finally directing his first feature film, *That Sinking Feeling*, in 1980. This and his second film, *Gregory's Girl* (1980), about a young girl's attempts to join an all-male football team, established his style of understated comedy. *Local Hero* (1983) tackled the threat posed to a small local Scottish community by an oil company's plans for development. Forsyth's international standing was enhanced by the appearance of Burt Lancaster in this film.

Subsequent films have included *Comfort and Joy* (1984), about a Glasgow DJ who finds himself embroiled in a clash between rival ice-cream companies, *Housekeeping* (1987), Forsyth's first US film, about two sisters who have to come to terms with both the death of their mother and the eccentricities of the aunt who subsequently looks after them, and *Breaking In* (1990).

Forte, Dieter (1935–) German playwright, living in Switzerland, who established a reputation for challenging documentary drama in the 1970s. He made his name with *Martin Luther and Thomas*

Münzer or the Bookkeepers of the Reformation (1971), in which he combined documentary content with elements of farce in an attempt to undermine conventional attitudes to history. Subsequently he has applied the same comic-strip approach in such works as *Jean-Henri Dunant or the Introduction of Civilization* (1978) and *The Labyrinth of Dreams or the Separation of the Head from the Body* (1982), which attacked accepted views of Hitler's career. *See* DOCUMENTARY THEATRE.

Fortini, Franco (Franco Lattes; 1917–) Italian critic, poet, and writer. After his studies in law and literature, Fortini took part in the Resistance movement during World War II. Following the liberation he moved to Milan and embarked on a period of intense cultural and political activity, becoming editor of VITTORINI's journal *Il Politecnico*. He also contributed to the literary periodicals *Quarderni Piacentini* and *Paragone* and was one of the founders of the political-literary review *Ragionamenti*. From 1971 onwards he was professor of the history of literary criticism at the University of Siena.

His works include writings on politics and culture, as well as literary essays and a considerable corpus of poetry. He has translated French and German writers including Goethe, Éluard, BRECHT, and Proust.

Fortini is Italy's most important Marxist critic. His most significant contribution to post-war Italian culture has lain in his attempts to clarify the relationship between literature and politics, literature and life, and the role of the intellectual in the 'culture industry'. These explorations are also pursued in his poetry, which includes the collections *Expulsion Order* (1963), *Poetry and Error* (1959), and *This Wall* (1973). Collections of critical essays and other writings include *Ten Winters 1947–57* (1957), *Verification of Powers* (1965), *The Question of Demarcation* (1977), *Italian Essays* (1974), *Twentieth-Century Poets* (1977), and *Insistence* (1985).

Fortner, Wolfgang (1907–87) German composer, conductor, and teacher. After studies at Leipzig Conservatory with Hermann Grabner and at Leipzig University he taught composition at the Church Music Institute, Heidelburg from 1931 until 1954. He founded the Heidelburg Chamber Orchestra in 1935. Influenced initially by baroque music and the neoclassicism of Hindemith and Stravinsky, he began to adopt serialist procedures in the 1940s. His mature works include his symphony (1947) and the *Phantasie über B-A-C-H* (1950) for two pianos, nine solo instruments, and orchestra, which illustrates his virtuoso use of 12-tone technique. As composer and teacher Fortner became one of the most influential figures in post-war German music; his later teaching appointments included posts at the DARMSTADT Institute and the Freiburg Musikhochschule. Other major compositions include the operas *Die Bluthochzeit* (1957) and *Elisabeth Tudor* (1972), oratorios such as *Isaaks Opferung* (1952), and concertos for violin, cello, and piano.

Foster, Sir Norman (1935–) British architect. Born in Manchester, Foster was educated at Manchester University and the Yale School of Architecture, where he was a Henry Fellow. In 1963 he was a founder of **Team 4** (with Richard ROGERS). The firm achieved fame in 1966 with their elegant swiftly built factory at Swindon for Reliance Controls, a low-proportioned structure of rolled steel sections. When Team 4 ended in 1966 Norman and Wendy Foster founded Foster Associates. In the 1970s their work moved away from the formal expression of structure towards an emphasis on the building's skin, especially advanced curtain walls of glass, typified by the Olsen terminal at Millwall (1971, now demolished) and the Willis Faber building in Ipswich (1975). The late 1970s saw a renewed interest in expressing structure, with for instance the hangarlike design for the Sainsbury Centre for the Visual Arts at the University of East Anglia (1978; extended in 1991 by the new Crescent Wing) and the gigantic exoskeletal headquarters building for the HongKong and Shanghai Banking Corporation in Hong Kong (1979–85). In the 1980s Foster's output included examples of both the 'tight skin' approach (the ITN headquarters, London, 1990–91) and of the more structurally explicit manner (Renault Distribution Centre, Swindon, 1983; Stansted Airport, Essex, opened 1991). Foster remains one of the most important figures in the continuing modern movement, practising since 1991 as Sir Norman Foster & Partners. His ambitious master plan for the regeneration of the

King's Cross area of London waits on national political developments (1992).

Fotoform A school of German photography founded by Otto STEINERT in 1949 while teaching at the Staatliche School in Saarbrücken. Its cofounders were Peter Keetman, Toni Schneiders, Ludwig Windstosser, and Siegfried Lauterwasser. The group came together to pursue the possibilities of non-objective photography, producing startling abstract images through superimposition of negatives and other forms of technical manipulation. These attracted considerable attention when exhibited in Milan and Cologne in 1950. After this the group became a vehicle for Steinert's more elastic concept of 'Subjective Photography', holding exhibitions under this label in 1951, 1954, and 1958, when it disbanded. The group consistently emphasized photography's role as a means of personal expression rather than as a register of documentary truth. While not claiming originality of technique or achievement, Fotoform was an important restatement of pictorial values as Germany rebuilt itself after World War II.

Foucault, Michel (1926–84) French philosopher and social historian. Foucault studied philosophy, psychology, and psychopathology at the Ecole Normale Supérieure, where he was taught by ALTHUSSER. He worked in a mental hospital before taking a series of teaching posts abroad, in Uppsala (1955), Warsaw (1958), and Hamburg (1959). In 1967 he helped to found the Centre Universitaire Expérimental de Vincennes and three years later became a professor at the Collège de France, where he remained until his death. He supported political dissidents in the Soviet Union, Poland, and Brazil and was frequently involved in protests against French government policy.

Foucault's work as a historian of ideas involves a radical critique of the codes and conventions by which Western society defines itself. According to him, this self-definition hinges on the principle of exclusion. His work is preoccupied with the way in which certain classes of 'deviant' – the insane, criminals, sexual transgressors – are categorized and subjugated. His best-known writings are histories – or 'genealogies' as he prefers to call them – of the various 'discourses' employed in such specialized areas as medicine, politics, and criminology. For Foucault, these discourses function as instruments of social power, upholding an oppressive ideal of health and normality. His first book, *Madness and Civilization* (1961), examined historical attitudes to insanity, while *Discipline and Punish* (1975) gave a tendentious history of the process by which imprisonment became the main instrument of judicial punishment. The multivolume investigation *The History of Sexuality* (1976–84) remained unfinished on Foucault's death from AIDS. He attempted a more systematic exposition of his ideas in the theoretical works *The Order of Things* (*Les Mots et les choses*; 1966) and *The Archaeology of Knowledge* (1972). Foucault's work has been severely attacked for subjectivism and methodical inconsistency.

Fowles, John (1926–) British novelist. Fowles was educated at New College, Oxford, where he read French. He subsequently worked as a teacher, publishing his first novel *The Collector* in 1963. It is the story of a repressed working-class butterfly collector who uses his football pools winnings to abduct the young art student he is obsessed with, eventually causing her death. In 1965 it was adapted into a film directed by William Wyler. Other early works include *The Aristos* (1965), a collection of personal philosophy largely in note form, and *The Magus* (1966), an ambitious novel with an existentialist theme set on the imaginary Greek island of Phraxos. The latter became a cult book in the late 1960s, owing its popularity equally to Fowles's undoubted narrative skill and the book's somewhat confused philosophy. His next work, *The French Lieutenant's Woman* (1969), was an historical novel set a century earlier in Lyme Regis, Dorset (Fowles's home town). A powerful love story as well as a meditation on changing sexual mores, the book concerns a wealthy gentleman who breaks off his engagement after becoming obsessed with the apparently 'fallen' woman of the title. The novel is notable for Fowles's self-conscious narrative and his inclusion of alternative endings. A film was made of the book in 1981, directed by Karel REISZ and with a screenplay by Harold PINTER. Later works include *The Ebony Tower* (1974), a collection of novellas, *Daniel Martin* (1977), an experimental and partly autobiographical account of a screen writer's relations with his work and the Hollywood system, and *Mantissa* (1982), an erotic and mythical fantasy about a writer's relations with his muse. He has published no new work since *A Maggot* (1985).

Franju, Georges (1912–87) French film director and set designer, who made a series of idiosyncratic short documentaries before enjoying considerable success as a director of feature-length films. Having started as a critic, Franju cofounded the Cinématheque Française and in 1949 attracted attention as director of the documentary *Le Sang des bêtes*, a harrowing investigation into the fate of animals in a Paris abattoir. Other powerful documentaries included *Hôtel des Invalides* (1951), which expressed his pacifist sympathies by juxtaposing shots of the Hôtel des Invalides in Paris with images of crippled soldiers. Among his other early films was a tribute to the cinema pioneer Georges Méliès in *Le Grand Méliès* (1951).

Franju made his first full-length feature film, *The Keepers*, in 1958; concerning the incarceration of a middle-class dropout in a mental asylum, it marked its director out as a master of FILM NOIR with a poetic – if somewhat bizarre – insight into human diversity. *Eyes Without a Face* (1959), for example, was a horror story about a doctor who attempts to restore his daughter's beauty after an accident by grafting onto her face the skin of other girls, whom he has killed; the film was hailed for its challenging exploration of obsessive behaviour.

Films that followed included the thriller *Spotlight on a Murderer* (1961), *Thérèse Deyqueyroux* (1962), adapted from the novel by Mauriac, and *Judex* (1963), a highly surreal recreation of the adventure films of the silent era. Franju also adapted Cocteau's *Thomas the Imposter* (1964), about life in the trenches during World War I, and Zola's *The Sin of Father Mouret* (1970). His last major film for the cinema was *Shadowman* (1973), in which he explored the complex, often startling world of the pulp thriller. In his later years he directed films for television.

Frankfurt School *See* ADORNO, THEODOR (WIESENGRUND); HABERMAS, JÜRGEN; HORKHEIMER, MAX.

Franklin, Rosalind (1920–58) British X-ray crystallographer. After graduating from Cambridge University, Franklin joined the staff of the British Coal Utilisation Research Association in 1942, moving in 1947 to the Laboratoire Centrale des Services Chimique de L'Etat in Paris. She returned to Britain in 1950 and held research appointments at London University, initially at King's College (1951–53) and thereafter at Birkbeck College, until her untimely death from cancer at the age of 37.

Franklin played a major part in the discovery of the structure of DNA by James Watson and Francis CRICK. With the unflattering and distorted picture presented by Watson in his *The Double Helix* (1968) her role in this has become somewhat controversial. At King's, she had been recruited to work on biological molecules, specifically the structure of DNA. When she later learned that Maurice Wilkins, a colleague at King's, also intended to work on DNA, she felt unable to cooperate with him. Nor did she feel much respect for the early attempts of Watson and Crick in Cambridge to establish the structure.

The causes of friction were various, ranging from personality clashes to, it has been said, male hostility to the invasion of their private club by a woman. Despite this background Franklin did obtain results without which the structure established by Watson and Crick would have been at the least delayed. The most important of these was her X-ray photograph of hydrated DNA. Watson first saw it in 1952 at a seminar given by Franklin, and recognized that it indicated a helix. Franklin also appreciated, unlike Watson and Crick, that in the DNA molecule the phosphate groups lie on the outside rather than inside the helix.

Despite such insights it was Watson and Crick who first suggested that DNA has a double helix. By March 1953 Franklin had overcome her earlier opposition to helical structures and was in fact producing a draft paper on 17 March, 1953, in which she proposed a double-chain helical structure for DNA. It did not, however, contain the crucial idea of base pairing, nor did she realize that the two chains must run in opposite directions. She first heard of the Watson–Crick model on the following day.

Frayn, Michael (1933–) British playwright and novelist, who has enjoyed considerable success with a series of bitter stage comedies. After working with the Cambridge Footlights, he embarked on a career as a journalist and novelist before breaking into the professional theatre in 1970 with the quartet of short plays *The Two of Us*. His distinctive brand of tragicomedy developed with such plays as *Donkey's Years* (1976), *Clouds* (1976), and *Make and Break* (1980). The enormously successful *Noises Off* (1982) parodies the conventions of farce, portraying the chaotic events that occur with breathtaking rapidity both in front of and behind the set as a company of actors tours the provinces. His more recent work has included the plays *Benefactors* (1984) and the less well-received *Look Look* (1990) as well as the screenplay for the film comedy *Clockwise* (1986). His novels include *The Tin Men* (1965), *The Russian Interpreter* (1966), and *Towards the End of the Morning* (1967), one of several works to reflect his Fleet Street background. In the early 90s Frayn published his most considerable novels, *The Trick of It* (1990) and *A Landing on the Sun* (1991); both are comedies of disappointment, dealing with the inevitable frustration of hope. His most recent novel is *Now You Know* (1992). He has also translated several plays of Chekhov, a writer with whom he evidently feels an affinity.

free cinema A British film movement of the 1950s, which placed great emphasis on the social relevance of film-making and attempted to deal with topical issues neglected by the commercial cinema. Films made under the free cinema label tended to have a strong documentary component, although some aspired to art, notably those directed by Lindsay ANDERSON and Karel REISZ at the start of their careers.

Freud, Lucian (1922–) British painter. Born in Berlin, a grandson of Sigmund Freud, he came to Britain in 1932 and became a British citizen in 1939. His father was an architect who had painted earlier in his career. Freud showed a keen interest in drawing from a young age. He studied art in London at the Central School of Art (1942) and then part-time at Goldsmiths' College (1942–43). He taught at the Slade School of Fine Art from 1948 to 1958.

Freud has worked in a figurative style throughout his career, specializing in portraits of friends, interiors, and nudes. A distinctive feature of his work is its meticulous, sometimes merciless, observation of detail. His early paintings were predominantly linear, restrained in their choice of colours, and often seemed to capture a sense of tension and unease. His later work became more painterly and depicted bodies and faces in a more sculptural manner (for example, *Naked Portrait*, 1973, Tate Gallery, London). Freud's work was included in several exhibitions of work by young British painters in the 1950s. There were major retrospective exhibitions of his work at the Hayward Gallery in London in 1974 and 1988.

Fricker, Peter (Racine) (1920–90) British composer. Fricker studied at the Royal College of Music and later (1946–48) with the Hungarian composer Mátyás Seiber, through whom he absorbed the influence of Bartók. He was one of the first young British composers to come to prominence after World War II, winning the Clement's Prize with a wind quartet in 1947 and the Koussevitsky Award with his first symphony, which was first performed at the Cheltenham Festival under Sir John BARBIROLLI. His early works, in particular the first three symphonies (1949, 1951, 1960), reveal the influence of Hindemith, Berg, and Schoenberg as well as Bartók and their dissonant atonal style made a strong impact at a time when English music was still dominated by the native pastoral tradition. In 1964 he accepted a teaching post at the University of California. His later works, such as the choral pieces *Ave Maris Stella* (1967) and *Magnificat* (1968), are more concentrated in style. Other works include two violin concertos (1950, 1954), a piano concerto (1954), and four string quartets.

Fried, Erich (1921–88) Jewish Austrian poet. After his father's death at the hands of the Gestapo, Fried emigrated to London in 1938, where he worked for the Austrian Centre and the Jewish Refugee Committee, while earning his living as a manual worker, librarian, and editor. From 1952 until 1968 he was a commentator on the BBC German Service. His first-hand experience of fascism and anti-Semitism had a formative influence on his radical humanism: he supported the students' movement in the 1960s, criticized West Germany's handling of the Baader-Meinhof terrorism in the 1970s, and became an ardent supporter of the peace movement of the 1980s. He also attacked Israel for its treatment of the Palestinians.

Because of this radical partisanship, Fried has lacked neither admirers nor critics.

Fried published more than twenty volumes, including political poetry, radio plays, and prose. His first major success was *And Vietnam And* (1966), a volume of poems that both excited and shocked the public with its anti-lyrical style and its unconventional approach to contemporary political events. Fried used paradox, satire, and montage techniques to shock and agitate the reader. By employing phonetic puns and parodic quotations, he gave a new dimension to the genre of the didactic and political poem. Among his most controversial publications were *Listen Israel* (1974) and *That's How I Came Under the Germans* (1977). But Fried also wrote nature and love poetry (*Love Poems*; 1979) as well as translating Dylan Thomas, Sylvia Plath, T. S. Eliot, and more than 20 Shakespeare plays.

Friedman, Yona (1923–) Franco-Hungarian architectural thinker. Born in Budapest, Friedman was educated at the Budapest Technical University and in Israel; he settled in Paris in 1957 and has worked there ever since. He is a well-known theorist, having written several books and organized exhibitions, but has few buildings to his credit. Friedman was a cofounder of the Groupe d'Etude d'Architecture Mobile (GEAM) and has argued strongly for a mobile architecture, integrating functional planning, transportability, and flexibility. His first projects were published in Japan in the 1960s with the encouragement of the architect Kenzo Tange but the fullest statement came in *L'Architecture mobile* (1970) and *Pour une architecture scientifique* (1971). Most of Friedman's projects are based on a foundation of *pilotis* (stilts) supporting space frames, within which domestic, commercial, or public modules can be constructed to their users' requirements; the idea that the individual must assume responsibility for his environment is central to Friedman's thought.

Friel, Brian (1929–) Irish playwright, born in Northern Ireland. The product of a strongly Nationalist background, Friel moved across the border to Co Donegal when the troubles erupted in the late 1960s. Much of his work is concerned with the political conflict in the province, particularly with its historical origins and the questions of cultural identity it raises. In *Philadelphia, Here I Come!* (1965), *The Gentle Island* (1971), and *The Faith Healer* (1979), he explores the plight of those who feel driven to exile from Ireland in order to escape from the cycle of violence; *Freedom of the City* (1973) and *The Volunteers* (1975) depict the suffering of the innocent. *Translations* (1981) illustrates the clash of Irish and English cultures through the Royal Engineers' attempts to conduct a Survey of Ireland in the 1830s; by the end of the play it is clear that in this failure of communication lie the seeds of Ireland's future problems. Friel's subsequent works have included a translation of Chekhov's *Three Sisters* (1981) and *Making History* (1988). In 1980 Friel was a cofounder of the Irish cultural organization Field Day; he was later nominated to the Irish Senate but did not take an active role. Friel's masterpiece is *Dancing at Lughnasa* (1990), perhaps the most acclaimed English-language play of recent years. A poignant depiction of a family of sisters in pre-war Donegal, it is Friel's fullest treatment of his most distinctive theme – the supreme value but final untrustworthiness of memory.

fringe theatre Any form of drama that lies outside the mainstream theatrical tradition, usually because it adopts an extreme political stance or is experimental in terms of language, subject, style of performance, etc. The term derives from the so-called fringe events that grew up round the EDINBURGH FESTIVAL in the 1950s; these have encompassed everything from HAPPENINGs to the early plays of such writers as Tom STOPPARD and David HARE. Fringe events are now an integral part of arts festivals all over Europe – to the extent that some festivals have spawned 'fringes of fringes' as the original fringe has become too respectable. Fringe theatre represents the cutting edge of modern theatre and many notable works have transferred from venues specializing in such experimental drama to the commercial stage.

Frink, Dame Elisabeth (1930–93) British sculptor. Born in rural Suffolk, Frink studied at Guildford School of Art (1947–49) and then in London at the Chelsea School of Art (1949–53). In her early days she was taught by the sculptors Bernard Meadows and Willi Soukup. She was later influenced by GIACOMETTI's method of working. She taught at several London art colleges, including the Royal College of Art.

Frink gave her first one-woman show in 1951 and instantly captured public attention in Britain. Most of her works are expressionistic, her main subjects being the male figure, horses, and dogs. They are vigorously modelled and carved in plaster, then cast in bronze. She received numerous commissions for public sculptures, for example the *Walking Madonna* on the green outside Salisbury Cathedral. Major retrospectives of her work were held at the Royal Academy, London, in 1985 and at the National Museum of Women in the Arts, Washington, in 1990.

Frisch, Max (Rudolf) (1911–91) Swiss playwright and novelist, who emerged as one of the leading writers in the German language in the late 1940s. He wrote his first play, *Now You Can Sing*, an exploration of individual guilt during wartime, in 1945 while working as an architect in Zürich. The plays that followed, which established his reputation for witty and socially challenging drama, included *The Great Wall of China* (1946), *When the War was Over* (1949), *Overland* (*Graf Öderland*; 1951), and *The Fire-raisers* (*Biedermann und die Brandstifter*; 1958), a major contribution to absurdist theatre which remains his best-known work (*see* ABSURD, THEATRE OF THE). It attacks the moral complacency of modern society through the figure of Biedermann, a typical good citizen who nevertheless fails to prevent arsonists from starting a fire in his attic. Subsequent plays included *Andorra* (1961), which aroused controversy with its portrayal of the growth of anti-Semitism in a small and peaceful country, *Triptychon* (1979), and *Jonah and his Veteran* (1989), a drama about military service in Switzerland.

Frisch's novels, the best known of which are *Stiller* (1954), an exploration of the problems of personal identity, and *Homo Faber* (1957), have also been successful. More recent novels include *A Wilderness of Mirrors* (*Mein Name sei Gantenbein*; 1964) and *The Man in the Holocene* (1979). He has also published several volumes of diaries and literary sketchbooks.

Fronte Nuovo Delle Arti (Italian; New Art Front) An association of Italian artists formed in 1946 to promote the ideas of the European avant-garde in Italy. Founded as the Nuova Secessione Artistica Italiana, the group issued a celebrated manifesto (1946) calling for a new beginning in Italian art before adopting the name by which it is better known. The group brought together those younger Italian artists, previously working in isolation, who rejected both the aesthetic canons of Fascism and the traditionalism of the Novecento school, whose influence had been dominant throughout the 1930s. The Front also set out to combat the spirit of pessimism arising from the traumas of Fascism and military defeat. The original members of the group, which held its first exhibition in Milan in 1947, included Renato BIROLLI, its unofficial leader, Renato GUTTUSO, Guiseppe SANTOMASO, Emilio VEDOVA, and the sculptor Alberto VIANI. The very different aims and ideas of these artists became apparent when the group exhibited at the 1948 Venice Biennale, where a split developed between the neorealists on the one hand and those committed to exploring the possibilities of lyrical abstraction (*see* ART INFORMEL) on the other. A number of the latter subsequently formed a splinter group, the **Gruppo degli Otto Pittori Italiani**.

Frost, Terry (Terence) (1915–) British painter. Born in Leamington Spa, Frost joined the British army in 1939. He was a prisoner of war from 1941 to 1945 and began to paint during his captivity. On his release he took evening classes in painting and moved to St Ives in Cornwall, where he associated with the ST IVES SCHOOL of painters (1946–47). He then studied at the Camberwell School of Art (1947–49), where he was a pupil of Victor PASMORE. Frost subsequently taught at the Bath Academy (1952), was Gregory Fellow in Painting at the University of Leeds (1954–56), taught at the San José University, California (1964), was Fellow in Fine Art at the University of Newcastle (1964–65), and taught at the University of Reading (1965–81).

Frost produced his first nonrepresentational works in 1949 and soon found recognition as one of Britain's leading abstract painters. In his early works he explored harmonies of colour, showing a strong predeliction for yellows and oranges. Later works are simpler and more formal and often feature blue and black oval shapes against a white background.

His works have featured in several major exhibitions of British painting.

Fry, Christopher (Christopher Harris; 1907–) British playwright, who was a leading writer of poetic drama in the 1940s and 1950s. A former director of the Oxford Playhouse, Fry enjoyed a considerable vogue with his verse dramas *The Lady's Not for Burning* (1946), *A Phoenix Too Frequent* (1946), and *Venus Observed* (1950). These pieces demonstrated his linguistic dexterity and provided fine roles for such performers as John Gielgud, Edith Evans, and Laurence OLIVIER. Most of his plays have a historical background and reflect his Quaker beliefs. With the advent of the ANGRY YOUNG MEN of the 1950s and 1960s, poetic drama lost the ear of theatregoers and critics, and Fry's reputation never fully recovered – although he has since written a number of well received translations of plays by Anouilh, Giraudoux, and Ibsen. His other writing has included plays for television and screenplays for several Hollywood epics, among them *Ben-Hur* (1959) and *The Bible* (1966).

Fry and Drew British architectural partnership of Maxwell Fry (1899–1987) and **Jane Drew** (1911–). Fry was born in Wallasey, Cheshire. From 1920 to 1924 he studied at the Liverpool School of Architecture under Charles Reilly, imbibing traditional Beaux-Arts principles of design. Until 1934 he worked for the firm of Adams and Thompson, and for the Southern Railway's architects' department. His work there was neo-Georgian but Fry was already turning towards the continental Modern Movement when he left to found his own practice. The first major independent work, the Sun House, Hampstead (1935), bears a clear debt to Mies van der Rohe. From 1934–36 Fry was in partnership with Walter Gropius, their best-known work being the Impington Village College, Cambridgeshire (1936). Jane Drew was born in Thornton Heath, Surrey, and studied at the Architectural Association. After the break-up of her first marriage in 1939 she set up in private practice. She married Fry in 1942; at the time Fry was serving in the Royal Engineers while Drew became town planning adviser to the British West African colonies. In 1945 they established the firm of Fry and Drew. Drew's experience led to numerous commissions for housing and public buildings in Ghana and Nigera and in 1951 they were appointed joint architects for the new provincial capital of Chandigarh in India, inviting LE CORBUSIER to join them. Other important projects were University College, Ibadan, Nigeria (1953–59) and the Pilkington Head Office, St Helens, Lancashire (1963). Fry retired from practice in 1973, Drew the following year.

Fuller, Roy (Broadbent) (1912–91) British poet and novelist. Born in Lancashire, he was educated at Blackpool High School and trained and worked as a solicitor while contributing to a number of left-wing literary organs, such as *New Verse*. After wartime service in the Navy, he specialized in the law relating to building societies. He was professor of poetry at Oxford (1968–73).

Fuller's early poems were influenced by the work of Spender and Auden, with whom he shared political sympathies. His own first volume, *Poems*, was published in 1939; his *Collected Poems 1936–1961* appeared in 1962. With its mainly sardonic tone and conversational diction his poetry provides a link between the work of the radical poets of the 1930s and those associated with the MOVEMENT in the 1950s. His later poetry, including the volumes *From the Joke Shop* (1975), *Poor Roy* (1977), *The Reign of Sparrows* (1980), and *Available for Dreams* (1989) deals with more personal concerns, such as the approach of old age. He has also published many novels, including *Savage Gold* (1946) and *Image of a Society* (1956), drawn from his own experiences working in a northern building society. Later fiction includes *The Perfect Fool* (1963), *The Carnal Island* (1970), and *Stares* (1990). His three volumes of autobiography were collected as *The Strange and the Good* (1989), supplemented by *Spanner and Pen: Post-War Memoirs* (1991).

G

Gadamer, Hans-Georg (1900–) German philosopher. Gadamer received degrees in philosophy and classics from Marburg University in 1922 and 1928, his most important teacher being Martin Heidegger. In 1937 he obtained a professorship at Marburg and the following year he was appointed to a chair of philosophy in Leipzig, where he remained until 1947, when he moved to West Germany. From 1949 to 1968 Gadamer held a chair in Heidelberg (where he succeeded Karl Jaspers).

Gadamer's first book, *Plato's Dialectical Ethics* (1931), investigated the relationship between the dialogue form of Plato's writings and their philosophical and ethical content. His fame, however, rests almost entirely on one book that he published at the age of 60: *Truth and Method* (1960). In this book, Gadamer outlined a general hermeneutics – a method of understanding and interpreting both the human situation and literary texts. Man is defined as a being capable of interpreting the world around him and his chief means of doing this is to engage in the 'hermeneutical circle', a concept Gadamer found in Heidegger's *Being and Time*. We use our prejudices to interpret the new things we encounter, while new experience in turn causes us to modify our prejudices, and so on. Eventually this circular process may produce perfect understanding, as, for example, when we suddenly feel 'at home' in the presence of a work of art. This concept of an attainable truth in interpretation has more recently come under attack from deconstructionists led by DERRIDA, who entered into a well-publicized dispute with Gadamer.

Gadd, Ulf (1943–) Swedish dancer, choreographer, and ballet master, who has worked with the Gothenburg Ballet since the late 1960s. Having trained at the Royal Swedish Ballet School, Gadd joined the senior company in 1960, becoming a solo dancer in 1965. Subsequently he danced with the Harkness Ballet and in 1968 began his long association with the company in Gothenburg, where he worked intially with Conny Borg; his first major success as a choreographer, with Bartók's *The Miraculous Mandarin*, came while working here. Under the management of Borg and Gadd the troupe excited considerable interest as a focus for contemporary choreography, with such figures as Birgit CULLBERG, Ivo CRAMÉR, and Roland PETIT all working with them as guest choreographers.

Gadd cofounded the New Swedish Ballet with Borg in 1970 and established an international reputation touring abroad until 1972, when he became ballet master and principal dancer at Gothenburg. Since then he has choreographed numerous ballets both for the Gothenburg Ballet and other companies, his most successful works including *Tratto* (1972), *Choreographic Études* (1973), *Sleeping Beauty* (1974), and *Kalevala* (1975). In 1976 he was promoted to the post of artistic director of the Gothenburg Ballet.

Gadda, Carlo Emilio (1893–1973) Italian novelist, noted for his complex and innovative prose style. Born in Milan, he fought as a volunteer in World War I and was held as a prisoner in Germany. He subsequently trained as an industrial engineer and spent long periods working abroad, including a spell in Argentina. Back in Italy, he began to contribute short stories and other writings to the avant-garde journals *Solaria* and *Letteratura*. The latter also published his two main novels in instalments. The first, *Acquainted with Grief*, was serialized in 1938–41, appeared in a single volume in 1963, and was revised in 1970; it is a tragicomic story with a strong element of autobiography, set in an imaginary South American country resembling Gadda's native region of Lombardy. The second, *That Awful Mess on the Via Merulana*, serialized in 1946–47 and issued in a complete version in 1957, is an idiosyncratic detective story that also provides a broad canvas of Roman life during the years of Fascism. The novel's main point of interest, however, is its elaborately experimental prose style. Gadda's use of foreign language material, dialects and jargon, neologisms and puns, has earned comparisons with Joyce, as has his eclectic erudition. Other publications include the novel *Eros and Priapus: from Frenzy to Ashes* (1967) and *The Dreams and the Lightning* (1955), a collection of his earlier writings.

Gades, Antonio (1936–) Spanish ballet dancer and choreographer, who emerged as the most influential figure in Spanish dance in the 1970s. Born in Alicante, Gades danced in cabaret while still a child and had some experience as a matador before joining Pilar Lopez's Ballet Español at the age of 16. Nine years later he left the company to train as a choreographer in Italy and elsewhere, working with such leading international dancers as Anton Dolin.

He established his reputation in 1964, when his own company created a sensation at the New York World's Fair with its interpretation of flamenco; he has subsequently toured extensively. His work as a choreographer led to an invitation to collaborate with the film director Carlos SAURA on the dance films *Blood Wedding* (1981), *Carmen* (1983), and *A Love Bewitched* (1986), all of which put the dancers themselves very much in the foreground. Gades has done a great deal to transform flamenco into a modern dance form worthy of critical attention.

Galway Festival A festival of traditional arts held each July in Galway, Ireland. It features processions of elaborately costumed dancers, puppeteers, and musicians, representing faeries, monsters, and giants from Irish mythology, together with much Irish folk music and dance. European circus acts, dancers, and performers also appear. The festival culminates in the ceremonial crowning of the King and Queen of the Faeries, accompanied by fireworks and other celebrations.

Gaos, Vicente (1919–) Spanish poet and critic. Gaos's early poetry, collected in *Archangel of my Night* (1944) and *On Earth* (1945), was accomplished but derivative; major influences included 16th-century Spanish poetry and the writers of the so-called 'Generation of 1927'. *Light from the Dream* followed in 1947 but his best, and first genuinely original, work appeared in *Prophecy of Memory* (1956). Gaos is here at his most reflective and introspective, exploring his own mental states and perceptions and his religious difficulties. His criticism is more distinguished than his poetry and includes *Poetical Technique and Versification* (1955) and *Themes and Problems in Spanish Literature* (1959). Gaos taught in the US from 1945 until 1952 and thereafter in Spain.

Gardelli, Lamberto (1915–) Italian conductor, particularly admired for his interpretations of Verdi. After studies in Pesaro and Rome he worked as a repetiteur with Tullio Serafin in Rome, making his debut as a conductor with *La Traviata* in 1944. Gardelli worked with the Stockholm Opera from 1946 until 1955 and with the Danish Radio Symphony Orchestra from 1955 until 1961. He made his debut at Covent Garden in 1968. In 1983 he became principal conductor of the Munich Radio Symphony Orchestra. He has also composed four operas.

Gardiner, John Eliot (1943–) British conductor and organist, noted especially for his performances of baroque works with period instruments (*see* EARLY-MUSIC MOVEMENT). While still an undergraduate at Cambridge (where he studied Arabic and medieval Spanish) Gardiner conducted (1964) a groundbreaking performance of Monteverdi's *Vespers* and formed the MONTEVERDI CHOIR. He has continued to play a major part in the modern revival of interest in Monteverdi's work.

Gardiner's performances are based on an attempt to reconstruct the composer's original intentions from manuscripts and other historical material. He has specialized in editions of 18th-century French operas, in particular those of Rameau, whose *Les Boréades* received its stage premiere from Gardiner at the AIX-EN-PROVENCE FESTIVAL in 1982. He became artistic director of the Göttingen Festival in 1981 and musical director of the Lyons Opera in 1982. In recent years he has applied the same scholarly approach to works of the romantic era and later; his version of Debussy's *Pelléas et Mélisande* caused heated controversy when presented in 1985. He founded the Orchestre Révolutionnaire et Romantique in 1990.

Gardiner has continued to perform and record with the Monteverdi Choir and the English Baroque Soloists, a period instrument ensemble that he founded in 1978. The 25th anniversary of the founding of the Monteverdi Choir was celebrated with a special performance of the *Vespers* (also filmed and recorded) in St Mark's, Venice. In 1992 recordings by Gardiner won three *Gramophone* awards – a feat previously equalled only by von KARAJAN.

Gaskell, Sonia (1904–) Lithuanian-born dancer, choreographer, and ballet director, who has had a profound influence upon the development of the post-war ballet in the Netherlands. A former student of Diaghilev, she excelled as a teacher of dance, working in Paris (1936–39) and then in Amsterdam, where she founded the Ballet Recital group.

She was appointed director of the Netherlands Ballet in 1954 and went on to establish the Netherlands Ballet Academy in The Hague. In 1959 she became director of the Amsterdam Ballet, which merged with the Netherlands Ballet in 1961 to form the DUTCH NATIONAL BALLET, of which Gaskell was artistic director until 1969. Under Gaskell's leadership the company built up a large programme of classical works and became the most important Dutch troupe. As well as choreographing many productions herself, and continuing her work as a teacher, Gaskell fostered such new talents as Rudi van DANTZIG, Hans van MANEN, and Toer van Schayk; in doing so she effectively revitalized the Dutch dance tradition. Somewhat indirectly, she also stimulated the development of such innovative companies as the NETHERLANDS DANCE THEATRE, which concentrated on contemporary dance as a reaction to her classically based repertoire.

Gassman, Vittorio (1922–) Italian actor-manager and director, who founded the **Teatro Popolare Italiano** company in 1951. Gassman made his stage debut in 1943; since then his performances in Shakespeare (notably as Richard III and King Lear), Ibsen, and in many other classical roles have established him as one of Italy's foremost stage and screen actors. The Teatro Popolare Italiano became under his guidance Italy's best-known touring troupe, seating 3000 people at its shows. A popular film matinée idol, he has appeared in many films, including DE SANTIS's *Bitter Rice* (1948), *War and Peace* (1956), *Unidentified People* (1958), *The Devil in Love* (1962), and *Tempest* (1982).

Gatti, Armand (1924–) French playwright, poet, and writer of screenplays, who became a controversial figure in the 1960s with his radical political dramas. A survivor of the German concentration camps (an experience reflected in several of his works), Gatti established his reputation with the autobiographical play *Imaginary Life of August Geai* (1962), in which he set out his revolutionary political beliefs. He went on to develop his political theories in both straight drama and, in more recent years, in various mixed-media community projects (*see* COMMUNITY THEATRE) combining live action and the use of video. Much of his more recent work rejects the received theatrical conventions of time and place. His success as a documentary film-maker led to his appointment (1983) as head of the audiovisual Atelier de Création Populaire in Toulouse.

Gehlen, Arnold (1904–76) German philosopher and sociologist. After completing his philosophical studies in 1934, Gehlen held professorships in Leipzig, Königsberg, and Vienna. His membership of the Nazi Party led to his dismissal in 1945 but in 1948 Gehlen became professor at a technical college in Speyer, moving to the Technical University of Aachen in 1962.

Gehlen is one of the leading representatives of the school of philosophical anthropology, so-called because it tries to describe the 'essence' of man. His main work, *Man: His Nature and His Position in the World* (1940), defines man as a 'deficient being' lacking both the bodily strength and the sure instincts of wild animals. Man has to make up for these deficiences by constructing and handling tools and by building complex social structures. By prescribing the actions of the individual, conservative institutions such as the church and the state provide the only real substitute for the instincts man has lost in the course of evolution (*Primeval Man and*

Advanced Culture; 1956). The process of civilization and history is seen as a largely futile attempt to compensate for man's feeble nature. According to Gehlen, modern civilization removes man from the natural sphere, where nobility of action is still possible, into an artificial setting where conflicts are decided by petty procedure. Gehlen's pessimism and hostility to the modern world have provoked much criticism, but his image of man is still alive in philosophical discussion, as, for instance, in the work of LUHMANN.

Genet, Jean (1910–86) French novelist, playwright, and poet. Until the age of 30, Genet – illegitimate and abandoned as a child – was almost continually in reformatory or gaol on various charges of theft and other antisocial behaviour. His first novel, *Our Lady of the Flowers* (1943), a lyrical paean to crime and homosexuality written while the author was still in prison, brought Genet to the attention of SARTRE and other literary figures. *The Miracle of the Rose* (1946) draws on his prison experiences, while *The Thief's Journal* (1949) is a picaresque account of his early life. The novels are equally remarkable for their poetic prose and their nihilistic inversion of accepted moral values.

Like the novels, Genet's plays dwell obsessively on such themes as sexual perversion, violence, and corruption. *The Maids* (1946), which was first directed by Louis Jouvet, presents a ritual game that culminates in murder, while *Deathwatch* (1949) concerns the complex relationships that develop between fellow-prisoners. *The Balcony* (1956) uses the setting of a brothel in which clients act out their fantasies of power to attack the false values of society at large. *The Blacks* (1959) was another study in prejudice and exploitation and *The Screens* (1961) made specific comments about the Algerian struggle for independence from France. Genet's other writings include three screenplays and a ballet scenario.

Gerasimov, Sergei (1906–72) Russian actor, screenwriter, and film director, who became a key film executive in the Soviet system. Born in the Ural Mountains, he studied at the Leningrad Institute of Stage Art. He began acting in Soviet films in 1925 and continued his acting career after making his debut as a director in 1930. His first major film was the socialist-realist *City of Youth* (1938), glorifying communist youth. Other propagandist films, many of which he scripted himself, included *Fighting Film Album No. 1* (1941), *Film Concert for the Red Army's 25th Anniversary* (1943), *The Ural Front* (1944), the two-part *Young Guard* (1947, 1948), and the documentary *The New China* (1950). His other films included *The Country Doctor* (1952; from the novel by Bulgakov) and *The Journalist* (1967). Gerasimov came briefly to world notice in 1958 when he directed a successful two-part adaptation of Mikhail Sholokov's novel *And Quiet Flows the Don*.

In 1944, after joining the Communist Party, Gerasimov was named head of the documentary film studios. He was also vice-chairman of the Soviet Filmworker's Union, heading their acting-directing workshop at the State Institute of Cinematography. In 1949 he attacked US films for their violence and low morality at the Cultural and Scientific Conference for World Peace in New York.

Gerhard, Roberto (1896–1970) British composer, born in Spain, of mixed French and German descent. Gerhard studied with Granados and Felipe Pedrell in Barcelona and later with Schoenberg in Vienna and Berlin. He returned to Barcelona in 1929, becoming professor of music at the Ecola Normal de la Generalitat in 1932, an appointment that reflected his commitment to Catalan music. Following the Spanish Civil War, Gerhard settled in Cambridge, England (he became a naturalized British citizen in 1960). The success of his first symphony at Baden-Baden in 1955 led to an upsurge of interest in Britain and the US and prompted a spate of new works from the composer, including his principal orchestral and chamber pieces.

The Spanish influence, still apparent in the ballet *Don Quixote* (1941; revised 1950) and the opera *The Duenna* (1947; first staged 1991), is less obvious in his 'athematic' later works, which display a virtuosic use of orchestral and instrumental colour, an interest in sheer sound reminiscent of Varèse, abundant rhythmic energy, and a serialist approach to structural organization that increasingly encouraged single movement forms. This late output includes five symphonies (the fifth uncompleted), the concerto for orchestra (1965), electronic works, and a considerable amount of incidental music for films and plays.

Germi, Pietro (1914–74) Italian film director, screenwriter, and actor, whose career took him from post-war NEOREALISM to light comedy in the 1960s. Of working-class origin, Germi worked as a messenger and took nautical studies before enrolling at Rome's Centro Sperimentale di Cinematografia. He worked as an extra, writer, and assistant director before making his directorial debut in 1945 with *Il Testimone*, like most of his early films a neorealist social statement. He maintained an ambivalent relationship with Sicily and its poor uneducated people, portraying them as tragic figures in his earlier social dramas and then more lightly in his satirical comedies. He often returned to the theme of crime in such films as *Mafia* (1949), *In the Name of the Law* (1949), and *The Facts of Murder*.

Germi became internationally famous in 1961, when his *Divorce Italian Style*, a stylized comedy about a nobleman who arranges his wife's murder, won the Academy Award for best script. Two more box-office successes followed: *Seduced and Abandoned* (1963) and *The Birds and the Bees and the Italians*, which won the 1966 Grand Prize at the CANNES FILM FESTIVAL. Germi coscripted his films and acted in some of them.

Ghika, Nicolas (Nikolas Hadjikyriakos-Ghika; 1906–) Greek painter. Born in Athens, Ghika studied with a Greek painter and subsequently in Paris, where he lived from 1922 to 1934. He took courses in French and Greek literature at the Sorbonne and studied painting with Roger Bissière at the Académie Ransom. Ghika's early works were much influenced by cubism and by the post-cubist paintings of Picasso and Braque. He gave his first one-man show in 1927.

During the 1930s Ghika developed a growing interest in both classical and popular Greek art and also in Mediterranean landscape. He subsequently strove to achieve a synthesis between his Greek heritage and modern styles of painting. From 1940 to 1960 he was professor of painting at the School of Architecture in the National Technical University in Athens. He has also designed sets, costumes, and masks for theatre and ballet productions and helped to produce the magazine *The Third Eye*, which reviewed avant-garde art and culture. Ghika's works have been shown in exhibitions throughout Europe and in the US. In 1973 he became the first living Greek artist to be given a retrospective exhibition at the National Gallery of Athens.

Giacomelli, Mario (1925–) Italian photographer. Born in Senigallia, he left school at 13 and worked as a typographer. Giacomelli is best known as a recorder of the sombre passions often found beneath the gaiety of life in Italy. His work captures the traditional customs and attitudes of remote villages and explores the vivid effect of sunlight on the Italian countryside in both black-and-white and colour. It is renowned for its speed of execution. Giacomelli's method is to live reflectively with his subject while his insight matures and then to take only a small number of photographs, trusting in his own feelings rather than technical trial and error to secure the effect he seeks. His concern for human suffering has produced studies of old people's homes, the sick at Lourdes, and the victims of Ethiopian famine. His work was collected in *Mario Giacomelli* (1980).

Giacometti, Alberto (1901–66) Swiss painter and sculptor. The son of a successful painter, Giacometti showed considerable artistic talent as a boy. He studied painting at the École des Beaux-Arts in Geneva and sculpture at the École des Arts et Métiers (1919–20). He then lived in Italy (1920–21), where he was influenced by the pioneering cubist sculpture of Alexander Archipenko. In 1922 he settled in Paris, where he remained until his death (apart from the war years). Giacometti experimented with cubist sculpture in the mid 1920s before developing an interest in surrealism and the possibilities of drawing on the unconscious in art. From 1929 he was an active member of the Surrealist group in Paris and his works appeared in their exhibitions. At this time Giacometti specialized in creating cage-like structures, such as *The Palace at 4 a.m.* (1942–43).

Surrealism, however, took Giacometti too far from the representation of reality. In 1935 he broke with the Surrealists and returned to the modelling of figures. He now looked for new ways of representing reality outside the classical conventions. In 1937 he began to reduce the size of the heads of his figures and in 1947 he arrived at a frontal figure with an elongated emaciated body and small head. He continued to produce such figures until his death, modelling them in plaster of Paris over a wire foundation and then casting them in bronze. He produced individual standing figures (for example, *Man Pointing*, 1947, Tate Gallery, London), walking figures, and also groups. To many writing at this time, these figures seemed to correspond to the existentialists' view of man as an isolated and vulnerable being (*see* EXISTENTIALISM). Giacometti himself, however, was not so forthcoming about the meaning of his work. In the 1950s there were many exhibitions of Giacometti's sculpture, in Switzerland, Germany, Britain, and the US. He also continued to paint and draw.

Gibberd, Sir Frederick (1908–84) British architect, whose large output epitomizes post-war British modernism in both its successes and its failures. Born in Coventry, Gibberd trained at the Birmingham School of Architecture. His first well-known work was the Lansbury Estate market square, Poplar (1951). As a town planner and landscape architect, he received wider urban design briefs, such as new shopping precincts at Stratford-on-Avon, Bedford, and Banbury. Gibberd's largest work was the master plan and many of the individual buildings for the new town of Harlow, Essex (1946–72). He designed many of the most important buildings at Heathrow Airport (1950–69) and devised the architectural and landscape design for power stations at Hinkley and Didcot and reservoirs at Derwent, Kielder, and Llyn Celyn. Gibberd was acclaimed for pioneering a conservation-based approach to town planning, for instance in his treatment of Harlow Village and his façadist rebuilding of Coutts Bank on the Strand (1969). He won two rare opportunities to design grand religious buildings, the Regents Park Mosque and Liverpool Catholic Cathedral. Whereas the former simply represents the addition of a few Islamic motifs to a glazed box, the latter (1969) is a powerful piece of Corbusian sculpture (*see* LE CORBUSIER) and much his most original work. Frederick Gibberd and Partners, founded in 1965, has been one of the most prolific commercial practices in Britain; typical recent projects include Arundel Great Court on the Strand (completed 1975) and the Intercontinental Hotel at Hyde Park Corner (completed 1977).

Gilbert & George (Gilbert Proesch, 1943– , George Passmore, 1942–) British artists (Proesch is Austrian-born), who met in 1967 as students at St Martin's School of Art in London. Since 1968 they have lived and worked together as self-styled 'living sculptures' (they gave up 'living sculpture performances' in 1977 but still see themselves in these terms, considering their whole lifestyle a work of art). They have worked in various media, initially attracting attention as performance artists (*see* PERFORMANCE ART). In *Underneath the Arches* (1969), which they described as 'the most intelligent fascinating serious and beautiful art piece you have ever seen', they appeared dressed in their characteristic neat suits, collars and ties, with their faces and hands painted gold and mimed mechanically to the 1930s music-hall song of the title. More recently their most characteristic works have been large and garish wall-pieces made up of arrangements of photographs; these are often violent or aggressively homoerotic in content, with scatological titles.

Gilbert & George are without much doubt the best known avant-garde British artists of their generation. In 1986 they won the Tate Gallery's TURNER PRIZE for 'the greatest contribution to art in Britain in the previous 12 months'. At the same time they have attracted as much opprobrium as praise, representing to their critics all that is most pretentious and self-satisfied in contemporary art.

Gillespie, Kidd, and Coia Scottish architects. The established firm of Gillespie and Kidd had an unremarkable record until **Jack Coia** became a partner in 1927. Iacomo Antonio Coia (1898–1981) was born in Wolverhampton of Italian parents, moved to Glasgow as a child, and became the city's most maverick architect since Charles Rennie Mackintosh.

In the 1930s he designed a number of suburban churches for the Roman Catholic diocese of Strathclyde, such as St Columbkille, Rutherglen (1934–40). But it was in the 1950s that Coia's true talents as a designer of churches blossomed. He got the jobs through his Catholic connections and to design them he used two brilliant young assistants, Andy MacMillan (1928–) and Isi Metzstein (1928–). Their work shows a debt to LE CORBUSIER's expressive forms, with dramatic copper-clad roofs suspended over hidden clerestoreys and powerful massing. The breakthrough came with St Paul's, Glenrothes (1956–58), which anticipated the liturgical planning favoured by Pope John XXIII. The next ten years saw a prolific crop of churches across central Scotland as exciting as any in Europe. However, they are little appreciated. Contortion of space brings with it constructional problems: the outstanding St Benedict's, Drumchapel (1964), was ruthlessly demolished in 1991; St Bride's, East Kilbride (1961–64), has lost its tower through defective bricks; and the group's centrepiece, St Peter's Seminary, Cardross (1964–66), is derelict because the diocese no longer cares to find a use for it.

The practice's only English work was a few university buildings. Student accommodation in Hull (1963–68) was followed by Wadham College Library, Oxford (1971) and Robinson College, Cambridge (1974–81).

Ginzburg, Natalia (1916–91) Italian novelist and writer. Born Natalia Levi in Palermo, Sicily, Ginzburg was brought up in Turin, where her father was a professor of anatomy at the University. She began to publish short stories during the 1930s. Half Jewish and a known anti-Fascist, she spent World War II in internal exile in Abruzzi. Her husband, the academic and journalist Leone Ginzburg, was killed by the Nazis in 1944. After the war she worked for the publishers Einaudi in Turin (1944–49) and lived thereafter by her writing. She spent the late 1950s in London.

Ginzburg wrote her first novel, *The Road to the City* (1942), during her wartime exile. Like several of her later works, it describes a young girl's initiation into the adult world; the claustrophobia of provincial Italian life is tellingly evoked. Most of her earlier novels are set during the Fascist era. The lengthy *All Our Yesterdays* (*Tutti i nostri ìeri*; 1952) deals with the disintegration of a Piedmontese family under Fascism, while her most famous novel, *Family Sayings* (1963), draws still more directly on her own family's experience before and during the war. *Voices in the Dark* (1961), a novel written mostly in dialogue, also has a wartime setting.

The sombre tone of these novels became still more pronounced in her work of the 1970s and 1980s. There is a preoccupation with the breakdown of family and marital relationships and an underlying conviction that life is, for most people, a lonely and mostly futile affair. The influence of the British novelist Ivy Compton-Burnett (1892–1969) is often apparent. Later novels include *Families* (1977) and *The City and the House* (1984), perhaps her most despairing book. She also wrote plays, poems, essays and journalism, and *The Manzoni Family* (1983), in which she traces the ancestry of the writer Alessandro Manzoni.

Gischia, Leon (1903–) French painter. Born in the Landes region of south-west France, Gischia studied archaeology and literature before devoting himself to painting in 1927. He subsequently studied with several teachers, including the former Fauve Othon Friesz and the leading cubist painter Fernand Léger. In 1927 Gischia travelled to the US, where he temporarily gave up painting; he returned to France in 1930.

In 1936 Léger persuaded Gischia to begin painting again and in 1937 the two artists worked with LE CORBUSIER on the decoration of the French pavilion for the International Exhibition in Paris. Gischia generally favoured traditional subjects, especially still lifes. Although influenced by cubism and abstraction, his work remained representational. His still lifes are characterized by geometrical patterning and intense colours. He has also designed numerous stage sets and costumes for the Théâtre National Populaire of Jean VILAR. Examples of his work include *La Lanterne Japonaise*, 1938, and *Les Brioches, les toiles*, 1944, both in the Musée Nationale d'un Art Moderne, Paris.

Gisel, Ernst (1922–) Swiss architect. Gisel was apprenticed to a Zürich architectural practice and trained in interior design at the Zürich Technische Hochschule. In private practice since 1945, he has had an enormous output, nearly all of which is in Switzerland. At first most of his work was in private housing but since 1950 schools, civic buildings, and public housing have predominated. In his Park Theatre, Grenchen (1949) he used movable partitions to create a multifunctional building. The large Letz School at Zürich (1953) encloses a courtyard between two-storey blocks of reinforced concrete linked by pergolas. Gisel's works tend to be rectilinear, blockish, and severe and are mainly executed in concrete, glass, and metal.

Giudici, Giovanni (1924–) Italian poet. After graduating from Rome University he moved to Milan, where he worked for Olivetti as a copywriter. He now works as a translator, journalist, and essayist. Leading influences on his style and attitudes include MONTALE and T. S. Eliot; in his work of the late 1960s he moves towards an ironic critique of lower-middle class life, where autobiography is reduced to 'autobiology'. He has continued to develop his personal style, while also emerging as one of Italy's most outspoken critics of contemporary industrial society. His work includes *Life in Verses* (1965), *Autobiology* (1969), *O Beatrix* (1972), *The Evil of the Creditors* (1977), *The Restaurant of the Dead* (1981), and *Salutz* (1986). He has also published a collection of essays, *The Unwanted Dame* (1985).

Giulini, Carlo Maria (1914–) Italian conductor, chiefly of Verdi. He studied at the Accademia di Santa Cecilia, Rome, worked as a musical director for Italian Radio from 1946 until 1951, and made his theatrical debut conducting *La Traviata* in 1950. In 1953 he was appointed principal conductor at La Scala, Milan. He made his Glyndebourne debut with Verdi's *Falstaff* in 1955 and his Covent Garden debut with a revival of *Don Carlos* in 1958. He appeared regularly at Covent Garden until 1967, when he took the first of several orchestral appointments in the US. With SOLTI he became joint conductor of the Chicago Symphony Orchestra in 1969. He returned to opera with a revival of *Falstaff* in London in 1982.

Glasgow Mayfest One of the largest arts festivals in Britain, held in venues throughout Glasgow during the first three weeks in May each year. It was first held in 1990 to mark Glasgow's year as City of European Culture. Musical events range from classical performances to pop; the programme also includes theatre, puppetry, visual arts, dance, and cabaret as well as workshops and events for children.

GMW Partnership *See* GOLLINS, MELVIN, WARD.

Godard, Jean-Luc (1930–) French film director and screenwriter, one of the most important and innovative directors of the NEW WAVE. Godard worked as a critic for the influential journal *Cahiers du Cinéma* before directing a number of experimental shorts. His first full-length feature, *Breathless* (1959; with a script by TRUFFAUT) introduced the new techniques of cutting and shooting and the disconnected narrative style that characterize all his subsequent work. The film announced the arrival of both a major directorial talent and a new movement in European cinema.

Godard continued to develop his experimental style in such films as *The Virgin and the Soldier* (1960), in which a French secret agent suffers torture and betrayal, *It's My Life* (1962), depicting a girl's gradual descent into prostitution (which, like a number of his early films, starred Godard's wife Anna Karina), and *The Riflemen* (1963), a radical antiwar film about the exploits of two brainless soldiers who return home after service overseas.

Amongst Godard's major themes are the failure of human beings to communicate and the role of film itself. Both were central to *Contempt* (1963), concerning the personal conflicts between the members of a film crew; it remains one of his most admired works. Subsequent films adopted a more pessimistic tone, among them *Une Femme mariée* (1964), *Alphaville* (1965), and *Pierrot le fou* (1966).

After the breakdown of his marriage to Karina, Godard made a series of overtly Marxist films, such as *Made in the USA* (1966), *Weekend* (1967), and *One Plus One* (1969) before returning briefly to more commercial cinema with *Tout va bien* (1971), starring Jane Fonda and Yves Montand. Godard subsequently experimented with television and video for some years but revived his reputation in the cinema in the 1980s, notably with *First Name: Carmen* (1983), a modern reworking of the opera, and *Hail Mary* (1984), an updating of the Nativity story set in a petrol station that upset some religious groups. More recent films have included the thriller *Detective* (1985) and *King Lear* (1987), both of which were severely criticized as pretentious.

Goehr, Alexander (1932–) British composer, born in Germany. The son of the conductor Walter Goehr (1903–60), he was a contemporary of BIRTWISTLE and Maxwell DAVIES at the Royal Manchester College of Music in the 1950s. He subsequently studied with MESSIAEN in Paris. After working for the BBC and holding several posts in Britain and the US he became professor of music at Cambridge University in 1976. Goehr first came to notice as a composer with the cantatas *The Deluge* (1958) and *Sutter's Gold* (1960), which display a fierce expressionism greatly indebted to Schoenberg. His growing mastery of serial procedures is evident in the *Little Symphony* (1963). His first opera, *Arden Must Die* (1967), is almost Weillian in its didacticism while his second, *Behold the Sun* (1985), deals with social and intellectual turmoil in 16th-century Germany. In 1967 he founded the Music Theatre Ensemble for which he later composed *Triptych* (1968–70), a sequence of three dramatic pieces for speaker, mime, singers, and instrumentalists. Other important works include a violin concerto (1962), the *Deux Études* for orchestra (1981), and the oratorio *Babylon the Great is Fallen* (1979). In 1992 the choral work *The Death of Moses* was premiered in Seville Cathedral under John Eliot GARDINER. In 1987 he gave the BBC Reith lectures.

Gold, Thomas (1920–) British astronomer and cosmologist, born in Austria. Gold studied at Trinity College, Cambridge, and worked on naval radar during World War II. He then lectured at Cambridge, becoming a fellow of Trinity (1947), demonstrator in physics at the Cavendish Laboratory (1949), and chief assistant (1952–56) to Martin RYLE. He emigrated to the US in 1956, becoming professor of astronomy at Harvard University and then at Cornell University in 1959, when he also became director of the Center for Radiophysics and Space Research (1959–81).

Gold is best known for his proposal (1948), with Hermann BONDI and Fred HOYLE, of the steady-state theory of the universe. He has made significant contributions to solar-system studies with his work on the structure of the moon, the origin of the solar system, and the origin of life forms. In more recent years he has advanced controversial theories of the abiogenic origin of hydrocarbons and of the existence of hydrogen and helium in the earth's interior.

Goldfinger, Ernö (1902–87) Hungarian-born architect, who trained in Paris with the French neoclassicist Auguste Perret (1874–1954). He moved to London in 1934 but found few commissions, his only significant pre-war work being a terrace in Hampstead, including No 2 Willow Road for himself.

Goldfinger was in his fifties when he designed his first major buildings. These were two groups of offices for Imry Properties Ltd: Nos 45–46 Albemarle Street (1955–57) and Alexander Fleming House, a massive complex built between 1959 and 1966 that included a now demolished cinema. Both schemes played with projecting and receding planes (particularly in their glazing) structured around a classical grid formed in poured and bush-hammered reinforced concrete.

In the 1950s Goldfinger also began to work for the London County Council. Schools in Wandsworth, Hammersmith, and Haggerston were followed by the housing estates regarded as his masterpieces, the Brownfield Estate (1965–67) in Poplar and the Cheltenham Estate (1968–72) in Kensington. Both featured a huge tower block – respectively Balfron and Trellick Towers – just as these were going out of favour. Both owed a stylistic and ideological debt to LE CORBUSIER's unbuilt scheme for Algiers and his *Unités d'habitation*, whilst maintaining a rigorous grid and careful finishes worthy of Perret. Goldfinger combined the best of these two great 20th-century masters to give large buildings a strength of character and craftsmanship unique in Britain and rare elsewhere. He also gave his name to the James Bond character.

Golding, Sir William (1911–) British novelist and writer. Golding was educated at Marlborough Grammar School and Brasenose College, Oxford, after which he worked as an actor and producer with small theatre companies and as a schoolmaster. During World War II he served with the Royal Navy. His first novel *The Lord of the Flies* (1954), describes how a group of English schoolboys marooned on a desert island revert to savagery and paganism. An instant success, it found an even wider audience in the cinema. This was followed by *The Inheritors* (1955), another fable about the inherent cruelty of human nature; set in prehistoric times, the book describes how *Homo sapiens* extirpates the gentler Neanderthals. *Pincher Martin* (1956), describing the last hours of a naval officer clinging desperately to a rock in the ocean, was followed by the more realistic *Free Fall* (1959), and *The Spire* (1964), about the spiritual struggles of a medieval churchman. Golding's other novels include *The Pyramid* (1967), *The Scorpion God* (1971), and *Darkness Visible* (1979). His 1980 novel *Rites of Passage* (which won the BOOKER PRIZE) is set among a group of 18th-century passengers on the long voyage to Australia; it was followed by two sequels *Close Quarters* (1987) and *Fire Down Below* (1989). *The Paper Men* (1984), describing the plight of a world-famous author pursued by zealous academics, reflects Golding's own situation following the award of the Nobel Prize for literature in 1983.

Goldmann, Lucien (1913–70) Romanian Marxist literary critic and philosopher, living in France. Goldmann left Romania for political reasons in 1933 and settled in Paris a year later; he gained a PhD from Zürich University in 1944. For the last ten years of his life he was director of the Paris Practical School of Higher Studies.

Under the influence of the Hungarian literary critic Georg Lukács and the psychologist Jean PIAGET, Goldmann developed a type of literary criticism known as 'genetic structuralism'. This saw literary structure as deriving from the author's 'world vision', which in its turn is a function of the mental structures proper to the prevailing historical and social circumstances. Goldmann adopted this approach to brilliant and original effect in *The Hidden God* (1956), a study that relates the works of Pascal and Racine to the 17th-century religious movement Jansenism. The important study *Towards a Sociology of the Novel* (1964) includes an examination of Malraux's work. He also published *Humane Sciences and Philosophy* (1969), *Mental Structures and Cultural Creation* (1970), and many essays expounding the principles of genetic structuralism.

Gollins, Melvin, Ward A large British firm of architects, established in 1947 by **Frank Gollins**, **James Melvin**, and **Edmund Ward**; since 1975 their successors have practised internationally as the **GMW Partnership**.

In size and dynamics Gollins, Melvin, Ward are Britain's closest answer to the US firm SOM, and indeed their best work owes much to that practice's head designer Gordon Bunshaft. In the 1950s and 1960s no other British practice used curtain walling so well. Sheffield University was among the first to adopt a modern idiom for its expansion and between 1953 and 1974 Gollins, Melvin, Ward designed ten buildings there, of which the Arts Tower (completed in 1965) is the most dramatic. Commercial work followed. Their Castrol House of 1958–60 was London's first adaptation of the tower and podium design of Bunshaft's Lever House, New York; the idea was used more inventively in two linked blocks in the City for Commercial Union and P & O (1968–69). Whilst that for Commercial Union resembles SOM's Union Carbide building, that for P & O is more sculptural.

The practice has been a prolific one, designing large public buildings, such as the British terminal at JFK Airport, New York, and many buildings (in concrete) for the armed forces. But their subsequent commercial work has not matched the cool qualities of their curtain-walled buildings of the 1960s.

Gombrich, Sir Ernst (Hans Josef) (1909–) British art historian, born in Austria. Gombrich studied art history at Vienna University. In 1936 he came to Britain to take up a research post at the Warburg Institute in London, where he remained for most of his career. He was director of the Institute and professor of the history of the classical tradition at the University of London from 1959 until 1976. He also held many visiting fellowships, lectureships, and professorships in Britain and elsewhere and has received innumerable awards, prizes, and honours.

Gombrich's work falls into three main areas. First, he has been a gifted popularizer. In 1950 he followed his first published work, a *World History for Children* (1936), with *The Story of Art*, which has now been through over 15 editions and is probably the world's best-selling work of art history. Secondly, he has published many studies of the art of the Italian Renaissance, concentrating on the period's reworking of classical formulae. Thirdly, he has investigated the psychology of visual perception and its relation to artistic conventions (explored in *Art and Illusion*, 1960, *The Sense of Order*, 1979 and *The Image and the Eye*, 1982). Through his large body of publications and his teaching Gombrich has had enormous influence on art history in the Western world.

Gombrowicz, Witold (1904–69) Polish novelist and playwright, who spent most of his life in exile, chiefly in Argentina and France. The element of the fantastic and grotesque in Gombrowicz's imagination is well represented by *Ferdydurke* (1937), a novel about infantile regression that remains his best-known work. The disturbing unconventionality of his writing led to its being proscribed by both the Nazis and later the communists. Gombrowicz's best-known play, *Ivona, Princess of Burgundia* was written in 1938 but not seen in Poland until the cultural thaw of the late 1950s. A precursor of the Theatre of the Absurd, the play is now recognized as one of the most significant in the national repertory; later dramatic works include *The Marriage* (1947) and *Operetta* (1967).

The novels of Gombrowicz's post-war exile – *Trans-Atlantyk* (1953), *Pornography* (1966), and *Cosmos* (1967) – are remarkable for their experimental style and their exploration of such existentialist themes as freedom and the fear of freedom, nothingness, and absurdity. His work is also preoccupied with the question of artistic form and the problem of reconciling it with the intransigent complexity of life itself. Gombrowicz published three volumes of unconventional diaries (1957–66). *See* ABSURD, THEATRE OF THE.

Goossens, Sir Eugene (1893–1962) British conductor. The grandson and son of conductors (Eugene Goossens I and Eugene Goossens II), he studied at Bruges Conservatory, the Liverpool College of Music, and the Royal College of Music, London. Initially he was a chamber and orchestral violinist, but later he became a conductor of orchestral concerts, opera, and ballet. He went on to conduct the National Opera Company and the Russian Ballet and, like his father and grandfather, worked with the Carl Rosa Opera Company. He also worked with the orchestras of Sir Thomas Beecham. He worked extensively outside Europe, conducting the Symphony Orchestra at Rochester in the US and from 1947 to 1956 working as director and orchestral conductor of the New South Wales Conservatoire, Australia. He composed works in almost all forms, his operas *Judith* and *Don Juan* (with libretti by Arnold Bennett) being performed in London in 1929 and 1937. His oratorio *Apocalypse* was completed in 1951. His brother was the oboist Leon Goossens (1897–1988).

Górecki, Henryk (Mikołaj) (1933–) Polish composer. Górecki was brought up in Katowice and studied (1955–60) at the conservatory there under Bolesław Szabelski. He later pursued further studies in Paris (though not, as is often stated, with MESSIAEN). His earlier work belongs firmly in the tradition of the post-war avant-garde, being particularly influenced by Webern's brand of serialism. A radical change of direction occurred in the mid 1960s (apparently as the result of a friendly challenge to write a tune); since that time he has written in a radically simplified style showing the influence of Polish religious and folk music.

His three symphonies illustrate both the changes in his musical language and his continuing preoccupation with Poland's tragic 20th-century history. The first, scored for strings, percussion, piano, and harpsichord, is subtitled '1959' and reflects the mood of optimism prevalent in Poland during the 'thaw' of the late 1950s. The second (1973) is a much more sombre work written during a period of political repression; scored for soloists, chorus, and a large orchestra, the work sets texts from the psalms and from Copernicus. Górecki's current fame rests on his third symphony (1979), subtitled the 'Symphony of Sorrowful Songs'. It is an intense harmonically static work for soprano, strings, and piano, expressing a mood of mourning and deep religious yearning; the texts for the three movements (all slow) are taken from a medieval Polish prayer, a poem scrawled on the wall of a Gestapo cell in Zakopane, and a Polish folk song. A recording of the symphony released by the London Sinfonietta in 1992 became a surprise bestseller, entering the British top ten (an unprecedented feat for a work of modern classical music). Górecki himself, a reclusive figure who suffers from ill health, has appeared reluctant to embrace his sudden celebrity. His other works include the trilogy of chamber works *Genesis* (1963), a harpsichord concerto, and *Already in Dusk*, a string quartet. *See also* MINIMAL MUSIC.

Goretta, Claude (1929–) Swiss film director and screenwriter, noted for his compassionate studies of complex psychological relationships. Born in Geneva, Goretta obtained a law degree from the University of Geneva before enrolling at the British Film Institute in London, where he collaborated with another Swiss student, Alain Tanner, to make *Nice Time* (1957). During his time in Britain Goretta was briefly involved with the FREE CINEMA movement. He then worked in Swiss television for some years before writing and directing his first feature, *The Madman* (1970). This was followed by *The Wedding Day* (1971), *The Invitation* (1973), *The Wonderful Crook* (1975), and *The Lacemaker* (1977). The last was an intimate study of an 18-year-old girl's emotional withdrawal following the end of her first love affair. Later films included *The Girl from Lorraine* (1981), *The Death of Mario Ricci* (1983), about a Swiss television journalist's attempts to investigate the death of an Italian immigrant worker, *Orpheus* (1985), and *If the Sun does not Rise Again* (1987). His films are made in French.

Götz, Karl Otto (1914–) German painter. Götz studied art at the School of Arts and Crafts in his home town of Aachen (1931–34) and developed an interest in cubism. In the mid 1930s he experimented with photographic montages and abstract films. During World War II he was stationed in Norway and access to radar equipment enabled him to pursue his interest in the production of electronic pictures.

In 1948 Götz came into contact with the COBRA group of European artists, who championed the free expression of the unconscious in art. Götz himself became one of the leading action painters in Germany. Typically, he placed his canvases on the floor and worked over them in several stages, using various kinds of brushes, scrapers, and sponges. The resulting works, which are characterized by dynamic rhythms and the use of broad swathes of paint, have been exhibited widely in Europe.

Goytisolo, Juan (1931–) Spanish novelist. Goytisolo was born in Barcelona and educated at the universities of Barcelona and Madrid. His childhood was scarred by the experience of the Civil War, during which his mother was killed by a fascist bomb. He has since written angrily about the brutalizing effects of war and dictatorship on the Spanish people, especially children and the young. Overtly hostile to Franco, he cofounded the radical Turia group of writers in 1951. His first novel *The Young Assassins* (*Juegos de manos*; 1954) dealt with a group of delinquent drifters, the children of wealthy families, who plan a political assassination to give meaning to their empty lives. It immediately established Goytisolo in the forefront of Spanish novelists. *Children of Chaos* (*Duelo en el paraiso*; 1955) and *Fiestas* (1958) return to the theme of damaged youth.

In 1956, in a final repudiation of Franco, Goytisolo left Spain to settle in Paris, where he worked for the publishers Gallimard and in journalism. Since the mid 1960s he has gradually abandoned the social realism of his earlier work in favour of a fantastic and experimental style. This development can be seen in the course of the so-called Mendiola trilogy of novels, comprising *Marks of Identity* (1966), *Vindication of Count Julian* (1970), and *Juan the Landless* (1975), the last of which begins in Spanish but ends in Arabic. More recent novels include *Makbara* (1981), *The Landscape after the Battle* (1982), and *The Virtues of the Solitary Bird* (1988), perhaps his most difficult work. He has also published numerous critical and political essays in such collections as *Problems of the Novel* (1959) and *The Guard's Van* (1967). His collections of short stories include *To Live Here* (1960) and *End of the Fiesta* (1962).

Gracq, Julien (Louis Poirier; 1910–) French novelist. Gracq studied history at the Ecole Normale Supérieure and subsequently worked as a school teacher until his retirement in 1970.

Gracq is a highly individual writer whose work shows some affinities to that of the surrealists – he wrote a profound study of André Breton (1948) – while remaining uncategorizable. His books interweave dream and reality, history and myth. In his first two novels, *The Castle Argol* (1938) and *A Dark Stranger* (1943), both of which are set in Brittany, he creates a dream-like atmosphere largely by drawing on the Matière de Bretagne. Gracq's most famous book, *By the Shore of Syrtes* (1951), won the Prix Goncourt, which the author refused in protest against the 'business of literature' and attempts to put writing at the service of ideology and politics. In the book an imaginary empire tries to bring history to a standstill by celebrating its own past but in doing so becomes an easy prey for its neighbour.

Later works such as *A Balcony in the Forest* (1958) and the novellas in *The Peninsula* (1970) and *Narrow Waters* (1976) reveal a pessimistic, somewhat Spenglerian, view of history which is balanced by an acknowledgement of the beauty and richness of the natural world. Gracq's rejection of nihilism is apparent from the title of one of his essays, 'The Inhabitable Earth' (1946).

Graevenitz, Gerhard von (1934–) German sculptor and kinetic artist (*see* KINETIC ART). Born in eastern Germany, Graevenitz studied economics at Frankfurt University (1955–56) and art at the Academy of Arts in Munich (1956–61). He subsequently remained in Munich, where he became director of the Gallery Nota (1960–61) and gave his first one-man show in 1962. In 1970 he moved to Amsterdam.

Graevenitz's earliest works were white reliefs featuring regular rows of hollows or projections. In the early 1960s he co-founded the NOUVELLE TENDANCE ('New Tendency') movement, which championed a new kind of constructivism, using modern technologies and materials. Graevenitz himself began to construct kinetic objects in which electric motors were used to move simple geometrical shapes in unpredictable patterns. In the mid 1960s he began to use mobile aluminium pieces to create shifting patterns of reflected light; the mobile elements in his work also became considerably larger. Graevenitz has also made prints with the assistance of a computer. He sees his kinetic works as an attempt to create a wholly new art form rather than a development from traditional sculpture. An example of his work is the motorized relief *5 Black Rectangles* (1973) in the Tate Gallery, London.

Granada International Festival of Music and Dance An annual music festival held in Granada, Spain. Established in 1952, it features opera, orchestral works, chamber music, and ballet. It usually takes place over three weeks in June and July.

graphic notation A type of musical notation that uses new symbols and/or pictorial devices to sketch the desired shape of a musical structure, whether a phrase or an entire work; in this it differs from the conventional notation that specifies the pitch and duration of each note. Thus the graphic notation builds an element of indeterminacy into a work. One of several new notational approaches developed to cope with modern music, graphic notation has been widely used in ALEATORY MUSIC. Morton Feldman's *Projections* (1951) is generally considered the first graphically noted score: other composers to make use of graphic notation include STOCKHAUSEN, LIGETI, and Cornelius CARDEW.

Grass, Günter (1927–) German writer and graphic artist. Grass's boyhood in Danzig was marked by his family's Roman Catholicism and his own enthusiastic participation in the Hitler Youth movement. The shock of learning the truth about the Nazi crimes had a formative influence on his work, which is fundamentally sceptical towards all-encompassing systems of thought. From 1949 until 1956 Grass studied sculpture and graphic design in Düsseldorf and Berlin. In the 1950s he started to publish plays and poetry with the encouragement of GRUPPE 47. An outspoken commentator on public affairs, he campaigned for Willy Brandt's Social Democrats in the 1960s. More recently he has aroused controversy with his opposition to German reunification.

Grass achieved international recognition with his first novel, *The Tin Drum* (1958). The book depicts German history from the turn of the century to the 'economic miracle' of the 1950s through the eyes of Oscar Mazerath, a freak who is fully mentally developed at birth but stops growing physically at the age of three. Grass's invention of an autonomous, highly individualistic, and picaresque hero allowed him to satirize the whole of German society from the bottom up. The book's combination of fantasy and reality, of the grotesque and the historical, the ribald and the monstrous, has inspired Salman RUSHDIE amongst other writers. *The Tin Drum*, *Cat and Mouse* (1961), and *Dog Years* (1963) form Grass's *Danzig Trilogy*. His next major success was *The Flounder*

(1977). In nine chapters (nine months) the first-person narrator tells his pregnant wife the history of male power and domination from the stone age to the 1970s. Other works include *Local Anaesthetic* (1968), *From the Diary of a Snail* (1972), and *The Rat* (1986). His most recent novel *Toad Croaks* (1992) was severely criticized in Germany, where his reputation has come under growing attack from some younger writers and critics. Grass's talent as a graphic artist is increasingly recognized.

Grassi, Paolo (1919–81) Italian theatre director and actor, who cofounded the famous **Piccolo Teatro della Città di Milano** in 1947. In collaboration with Giorgio STREHLER, Grassi helped the company to become one of the most respected in Europe, staging a wide range of classic plays as well as modern works by such authors as BRECHT. *See also* TEATRO STABILE.

GRAV *See* GROUPE DE RECHERCHE D'ART VISUEL.

Graves, Robert (von Ranke) (1895–1985) British poet, novelist, and essayist. Educated at Charterhouse, Graves served in the army during World War I and suffered badly from shell shock for many years afterwards. His first collections, *Over the Brazier* (1916) and *Fairies and Fusiliers* (1917), contain a number of harsh war poems. After the war he attended St John's College, Oxford. His autobiographical *Goodbye to All That* (1924), an immediate commercial success, gives an account of his unhappy schooldays, his experiences in the trenches, and his life at Oxford. He subsequently spent most of his life on Majorca.

Graves saw himself primarily as a poet, who wrote fiction mainly for financial reasons. His first *Collected Poems* appeared in 1955 to widespread praise, with his love poetry being singled out for particular attention. Subsequent volumes of collected poems contain heavily revised versions of earlier work. His poetry is traditional in form but distinctive and personal; having shed the Georgian influences of his youth, he did not identify with any of the main strands in modern poetry. His obsession with the role of myth is clear from his most important nonfiction work, *The White Goddess* (1948), which explores the religious and erotic aspects of poetic inspiration. He also wrote a number of novels, most of which recreate historical or legendary figures. The most widely read were *I, Claudius* (1934) and its sequel *Claudius the God* (1934), comprising a fictional autobiography of the fourth Roman emperor. Other novels include *Antigua, Penny, Puce* (1936), and *Wife to Mr Milton* (1943). An original and provocative critic, he was professor of poetry at Oxford University (1961–66).

Greco, Emilio (1913–) Italian sculptor. Born at Catania in Sicily, Greco was apprenticed at 13 to a funerary stonemason and learnt to carve crosses and figures for cemeteries. For a short while he studied at the Academy of Art in Palermo (1934). He later moved to Rome, where he gave his first (highly successful) one-man show in 1946 and obtained a teaching post at the Liceo Artistico (1948–52). He has subsequently taught at the Academy of Fine Arts in Carrara (1952–55), the Naples Academy (1955–67), and the Rome Academy (from 1966).

Greco has worked mainly in bronze, producing portrait busts and elegant female nudes. His career has seen several changes of emphasis. Between 1939 and 1949 his figures seemed to express human dignity and hope, while for a brief period in 1949 they carry a strong hint of pathos. From 1950 onwards he strove to encapsulate a personal idea of female beauty in his nudes, some of which seem to parody classical statues (for example, his *Large Seated Figure*, 1951, Tate Gallery, London). In 1956 he won the City of Venice Sculpture Prize at the Venice Biennale for his *Large Bather I* (casts are in the Galleria Nazionale d'Arte Moderna, Rome; Tate Gallery, London; Middelheim Open-air Sculpture Park, Antwerp; and Shirokiye Foundation, Japan). Thereafter he received a number of important commissions, including three bronze doors for Orvieto Cathedral (1959–64) and a monument to Pope John XXIII for St Peter's Basilica in the Vatican (1965–67). More recent works include *Self-portrait* (1984), in the Uffizi Gallery, Florence.

Green, Julien (1900–) French novelist. Born of American parents in Paris and brought up there, Green spent three years at the University of Virginia, Charlottesville (1919–22), before returning to France. During World War II he served in the US Army. Green, who was brought up as a Protestant, converted to Catholicism at 15, lapsed some years later, and finally reconverted in 1939. The main theme of his novels is the struggle between good and evil in the human soul. Most of his books are tragedies in which the leading characters prove too weak to withstand the dark forces of hatred, fear, and despair that torment them. Green's first novel, *Avarice House* (*Mont-Cinère*; 1926), describes the mutual hatred of three women in a Puritan community, while in *The Closed Garden* (1928) a young woman fights against her father and the onset of insanity. *The Dark Journey* (1929), *The Dreamer* (1934), and *Midnight* (1936) similarly explore the darker side of the human psyche. The novels Green wrote after his second conversion (*Then Shall the Dust Return*, 1940; *If I Were You*, 1947) are somewhat less sombre; the earlier work is generally considered his most powerful. More recent publications include *The Other* (1971) and *The Stars of the South* (1989).

Green is also well known for his *Journal*, published in 14 volumes between 1928 and 1990. He was elected a member of the Academie Française in 1971.

Greenaway, Peter (1942–) British film director, who has enjoyed commercial success with a series of idiosyncratic and highly cerebral feature films. Greenaway began his career with a number of short enigmatic pieces in which he experimented with the complex imagery that was to characterize his best-known work. *The Draughtsman's Contract* (1982), in which the darker side of life in an English country house in 1694 is gradually exposed by the artist commissioned to draw the estate, was the first of Greenaway's films to attract widespread attention; it won him an immediate cult following, although many found the puzzle element in the film impossible to follow.

Since breaking into the commercial cinema Greenaway has refused to make any artistic compromises. *A Zed and Two Noughts* (1985) was a bizarre film about twins who become obsessed with decay after their wives die in a car crash caused by a flying swan. The film is typical of Greenaway's work in its visual references to Old Master paintings and its use of an elaborate formal structure (here derived from the alphabet). *The Belly of an Architect* (1987), in which a dying architect sees all his ambitions threatened, was similarly complex and macabre, as was *Drowning by Numbers* (1988), in which a coroner is gradually destroyed by three women with the same name, all of whom have murdered their husbands. *The Cook, the Thief, His Wife, and Her Lover* (1989) was a shockingly brutal film about a boorish gangster and his adulterous wife. *Prospero's Books*, which followed in 1991, made striking use of the visual possibilities afforded by modern video equipment and computers; a free adaptation of Shakespeare's *The Tempest*, it featured John Gielgud as Prospero. He has recently curated art exhibitions in Paris, Rotterdam, and Vienna.

Greene, (Henry) Graham (1904–91) British writer of novels, short stories, plays, and screenplays. Educated at Berkhamsted School (where his father was headmaster) and Balliol College, Oxford, he began his career as a journalist, becoming a full-time writer after the success of his second novel, *Stamboul Train* (1932), a thriller set on the Orient Express. Greene's earlier books, most of which he classed as 'entertainments', include *England Made Me* (1935) and *The Confidential Agent* (1939). *Brighton Rock* (1938) was the first of several books in which Greene explored the moral paradoxes posed by Roman Catholicism, to which he had converted in 1926. *The Power and the Glory* (1940) describes the struggles of a South American 'whisky priest' persecuted by his own guilt and the revolutionary fervour of the state, while *The Heart of the Matter* (1948) depicts the tragic dilemma of a British captain of police in an African colony, who believes that his moral lapses have brought about his damnation. *The End of the Affair* (1951) deals with the guilt resulting from a wartime love affair. The distinctive flavour of Greene's fiction owes much to his penchant for seedy (often Third World) settings and his fascination with antiheroic protagonists tortured by guilt, divided loyalties, or a sense of failure. *The Quiet American* (1955) is set in Vietnam, while the background in *A Burnt-Out Case* (1961) is a leper-colony in the Congo. *The Human Factor* (1973) examined the pressures of life in the British Secret Service. Even his more lightweight works such as *Our Man in Havana* (1958), about a vacuum-cleaner salesman turned reluctant spy, retain the moral dilemmas and run-down locations of his more serious works. In their imagery and narrative technique his novels show the influence of popular cinema and many of them have been adapted for the screen. Greene also wrote the screenplay for Carol REED's classic film *The Third Man* (1949). He has written many short stories (collected in *Twenty-One Stories* and *May We Borrow Your Husband*) as well as travel writings, plays, and two volumes of autobiography, *A Sort of Life* (1971) and *Ways of Escape* (1980). His last novel, *The Captain and the Enemy*, was published in 1988.

Gregotti, Vittorio (1927–) Italian architect. Born in Novara and trained at the Milan Polytechnic, Gregotti has been in practice in Milan with various partners since 1952. Although his built works are not very numerous, he has had great influence as an academic and teacher and, in particular, as editor of the magazines *Rassegna* (1979–) and *Casabella* (1982–).

His work of the 1960s, such as that for the Rinascente supermarket chain, was still modernist but since the 1970s he has been the most important figure in the development of a sophisticated historicism in Italian architecture. In the early 1980s he became the main apologist in Italy for the Art Nouveau revival. His design for the department of science at the University of Palermo (1984) unites Miesian modernism with references to Sicily's ancient past, in particular to Greek architecture.

Griffiths, Trevor (1935–) British playwright, whose writing for both stage and television reflects his commitment to revolutionary socialism. His first full-length play, *Occupations* (1970), was presented by the ROYAL SHAKESPEARE COMPANY, while other early one-act plays were produced by the 7:84 COMPANY. *The Party* (1973), a dramatized debate between representatives of various left-wing viewpoints, was first presented at the National Theatre with OLIVIER in the central role. *Comedians* (1975) his most highly praised play, explores the political implications of humour through the differing approaches of a group of would-be stand-up comics. There followed such varied work as *Deeds* (1978), on which he collaborated with Howard BRENTON, David HARE, and Ken Campbell, the television play *Oi for England* (1982), *Real Dreams* (1986), and the Chekhov adaptation *Piano* (1990). *The Gulf Between Us* (1992), Griffith's first wholly original stage work for 17 years, was a 'dream play' tackling the issues raised by the Gulf War of 1991.

In an attempt to reach a wider audience Griffiths has also written extensively for television, his work for the medium including episodes for *Doctor Finlay's Casebook*, an adaptation of D. H. Lawrence's *Sons and Lovers*, and his own drama series *Bill Brand*. His work for the cinema has included contributions to the screenplays for *Reds* (1981) and *Fatherland* (1987).

Grigorovich, Yuri Nikolaievich (1927–) Russian choreographer, dancer, and ballet director, who is widely regarded as the leading Russian choreographer of recent times. Born in Leningrad, Grigorovich trained at the Leningrad Choreography School before joining the Kirov Ballet, where he established a reputation in character roles. As a choreographer he first attracted serious attention with *Stone Flower* (1957), employing the music of Prokofiev to tell a traditional Russian folktale. The production proved so successful that he was asked to restage it at the Bolshoi Ballet in Moscow two years later, thus beginning his long and fruitful partnership with the company.

Legend of Love (1961), for the Kirov Ballet, consolidated Grigorovich's reputation and in 1964 he was appointed chief choreographer and artistic director at the Bolshoi, in which role he has since spent his entire career. After *Sleeping Beauty* (1965) and *The Nutcracker* (1966), he created what many consider the archetypal Grigorovich production, the highly successful *Spartacus* (1968). Making full use of the huge Bolshoi corps and of the epic possibilities offered by KHACHATURIAN's score, the ballet combined dance solos and duets with mass pageantry involving the whole company, the overall effect being one of spectacular grandeur. Especially influential has been his emphasis upon pure dance rather than mime and his rejection of the realist approach favoured by most of his predecessors in Soviet ballet.

His works since *Spartacus* have included *Swan Lake* (1969), a second *Sleeping Beauty* (1973), *Ivan the Terrible* (1975), which was on a similar scale to *Spartacus*, *Angara* (1976), *Romeo and Juliet* (1978), *Raymonda* (1984), and *Bayaderka* (1991).

Under Grigorovich the Bolshoi has known both good times and bad, the worst crises involving the defection of several of his stars to the West. In the early 1990s the company's presentation of 'suites' drawn from popular ballets, rather than whole works, provoked much criticism. His wife, the ballerina Natalia Bessmertnova, has interpreted many of the leading roles in his work.

Grotowski, Jerzy (1933–) Polish theatre director, whose production theories have had a major impact upon international theatre. He studied drama in Cracow and Moscow and as director of the 13 Rows Theatre in Opole (1959–64) established a reputation for experimental theatre involving a considerable amount of audience participation. Subsequently he worked with the same group, renamed the Institute for Research on Actor's Method Laboratory Theatre, in Wrocław and also abroad with companies in Britain, the US, France, and Scandinavia. His innovative use of sparse settings and strong ritualized movement, and his attempts to break down the conventional relationship between actors and audience, have won him disciples all over the world, among them such notable directors as Peter BROOK. His best-known productions have included plays by Calderón and Shakespeare, as well as many modern works; some plays he has returned to several times – notably Stanisław Wyspiański's *Acropolis*, which he has produced in three different versions. Since disbanding the Laboratory Theatre in 1976 he has moved away from the concept of staged performances altogether, preferring to continue his exploration of theatre as ritual, therapy, and spiritual exercise in a less formalized context. His revolutionary theories are set out in his book *Towards a Poor Theatre* (1968).

Group, the A loose association of British poets and other writers, founded in London in 1955 by Philip Hobsbaum. Meetings consisted of a reading followed by discussion. Key members during the early years included the poets Peter Redgrove, George MacBeth, Peter Porter, and the writer Edward Lucie-Smith; amongst those who joined later were Fleur Adcock and B. S. Johnson. Membership was by chairman's invitation. A first anthology of writings by Group members, *A Group Anthology*, was published in 1963. In 1965 it was superseded by a more structured setup called the Writers' Workshop.

Groupe de Recherche d'Art Visuel (GRAV) An association of artists founded in Paris in July 1960. It began with eleven members, but was soon reduced to six: Horacio García-Rossi, Julio Le Parc, François Morellet, Francisco Sobrino, Joel Stein, and Yvaral (Jean-Pierre Vasarely). Members of the group produced their own works and also collaborated on a number of projects in the early and mid 1960s.

The group was founded to pursue a programme of quasi-scientific research into the use of light, movement, and time in art. In practice this meant the creation of mobiles and kinetic objects (*see* KINETIC ART) and developing aspects of OP ART in its painting. GRAV was also interested in exploring the possibilities of new materials, such as plexiglass, and in producing works that required an element of spectator participation. Their work was exhibited in Paris, London, Germany, and New York. The group shared many aims with the wider NOUVELLE TENDANCE movement and in 1963 organized the major exhibition in Frankfurt entitled 'European Avant-Garde, Arte Programmata, Neue Tendenzen, Anti-Peinture, Zero'.

Groupe de Recherches Musicales An ELECTRONIC MUSIC studio, central to the development of MUSIQUE CONCRÈTE, founded in Paris in 1942 by Pierre Schaeffer as the Studio d'Essai. From 1950 to 1958 it was known as the Groupe de Recherche de Musique Concrète: during much of this time the group was headed by Pierre Henry, while Schaeffer was involved in setting up the French overseas broadcasting network. In 1958 Schaeffer, with the composer Luc Ferrari, reformed the organization as the Groupe de Recherches Musicales. Other composers who have worked at the studio include Varèse and XENAKIS.

Gruppe 47 The most influential German literary group of the post-war era, founded by Hans Werner RICHTER in 1947. The group began when the journal *Der Ruf*, edited by Richter and Alfred ANDERSCH, was banned by the Americans because of its socialist ideas. Richter and his team subsequently began to meet to read and discuss their manuscripts, inaugurating a tradition that influenced West German literature for the next 20 years. The group's annual meetings brought together leading critics, publishers, and authors who read their latest works. Major new writers discovered by the group include GRASS, BACHMANN, EICH, and BÖLL. The prize of the Gruppe 47 became perhaps the most prestigious post-war German literary award. Hans Magnus ENZENSBERGER described the group as the '*Zentralcafé* of a literature without a capital city.'

Gruppo degli Otto Pittori Italiani *See* FRONTE NUOVO DELLE ARTI.

Groves, Sir Charles (Barnard) (1915–92) British conductor. Born in London, Groves studied at the Royal College of Music before joining the BBC Music Productions Unit as a chorusmaster. He subsequently conducted the BBC Northern Orchestra (1944–51), the Bournemouth Symphony Orchestra (1954–61), and the Royal Liverpool Philharmonic Orchestra (1963–77). He also served as musical director of the Welsh National Opera, the ENGLISH NATIONAL OPERA, and as president of the National Youth Orchestra of Great Britain.

The first conductor to perform the complete cycle of Mahler's symphonies in Britain, Groves was especially well known for his interpretation of early 20th-century choral music and his promotion of the work of living composers.

Gsovsky, Tatjana (1901–) German choreographer, teacher, and ballet mistress, born in Russia, who became one of the most influential figures in post-war German ballet. Gsovsky trained under Isadora Duncan and leading Russian dance teachers before taking the post of ballet mistress in Krasnodar. Subsequently she moved to Berlin with her husband Victor Gsovsky, also a dancer and teacher, and opened a ballet school. She made her debut as a choreographer in the 1940s, with such works as Carl ORFF's *Catulli Carmina* (1943) and von Einem's *Prinzessin Turandot* (1944).

After World War II Gsovsky was appointed ballet mistress at the East Berlin State Opera (1945–52), the Buenos Aires Teatro Colón (1952–53), the West Berlin Municipal Opera (1954–66), and the Frankfurt Opera (1959–66); in 1955 she also founded the Berlin Ballet, with which she embarked on several international tours. Many of the most admired post-war German dancers emerged under her tutelage and she is widely recognized as one of the most important ballet teachers of her generation. Her original ballets include *Romeo and Juliet* (1948), *Der Idiot* (1952), *Menagerie* (1958), *The Seven Deadly Sins* (1960), and *Tristan* (1965).

Guillén, (Pedro) Jorge (1893–1984) Spanish poet. After graduating from the University of Madrid (1919), Guillén embarked on an academic career, teaching Spanish literature at the Sorbonne (1917–23), Oxford (1929–31), and Seville (1931–38). A supporter of the Republican side during the Civil War, he was jailed in 1936 and went into exile two years later. He subsequently lectured at numerous North American institutions, including Wellesley College, Massachusetts (1940–58). His many literary awards included the first Cervantes Prize (1976). He returned to Spain after Franco's death.

Guillén was a member of the so-called 'Generation of 1927', a group of writers that also included ALBERTI, ALEIXANDRE, and García Lorca. He owes his international reputation to *Cántico*, a volume of 330 poems on which he worked for some 25 years (progressively enlarged editions appeared in 1928, 1945, and 1950). Showing an unabashed optimism rare in serious 20th-century writing, the poems celebrate physical existence and the joys of erotic love, confidently proclaiming that 'the world is well made'. His style shows the influence of the French Symbolists and Jiménez and Góngora amongst Spanish poets.

Guillén went some way to answer the charge that he ignored the tragic side of existence in *Clamour* (3 vols; 1957–63), a series of poems in which he satirized various aspects of modern society and attacked political oppression. Together with *Homage* (1967), a volume paying tribute to his poetic forebears, the complete *Clamour* and *Cántico* were published as *Our Common Air* (5 vols; 1968). Several further collections appeared, including *Final* (1981). Guillén also wrote a considerable amount of journalism and literary criticism.

Gunn, Thom(son William) (1929–) British poet, resident in the US, where he teaches at the University of California (Berkley). Gunn was educated at Trinity College, Cambridge and later gained a fellowship at Stanford University, California, where he came under the influence of the

US poet and critic Yvor Winters. Other influences include US pop culture and the Beat writers of the 1950s. His first volume, *Fighting Terms*, was published in 1954, when he was still an undergraduate; later collections include *The Sense of Movement* (1957), *My Sad Captains* (1961), *Moly* (1971), *Jack Straw's Castle* (1976), and *The Passages of Joy* (1982). Terse, laconic, and intellectually incisive, his poetry shows a fascination with rebels and men of action, whose struggles are often seen in existentialist terms. His subject matter ranges from the freewheeling lifestyles of motorcyclists and other social outsiders ('On the Move', 'The Unsettled Motorcyclist's Vision of his Death') to the aesthetics of Caravaggio ('In Santa Maria del Popolo'). In the 1960s he was often linked in the public mind with his friend and contemporary Ted HUGHES, with whom he edited the volume *Five American Poets* (1962). In recent work he has been increasingly frank about his homosexuality. *The Man With Night Sweats* (1992) includes a sequence of elegaic pieces inspired by the AIDS epidemic.

Gustafsson, Lars (1936–) Swedish novelist, poet, and writer. Born in Västerås, Gustafsson studied philosophy at the University of Uppsala, where he was particularly influenced by the writings of Wittgenstein. Since making his literary debut in 1957 he has become well known as a writer in many different fields and literary forms.

He has published several collections of poetry and his novels are often very lyrical, for example, *The Poet Brumberg's Last Days and Death* (1959) and *The Actual Story About Mr Arenander* (1966). His novels of the 1970s are more experimental and are sometimes fragmentary in form. *Mr Gustafsson Himself* (1971) is a novel attacking what the author calls 'the public lie', which includes the public role of writers.

In the late 1970s Gustafsson produced a series of novels that form a single literary project while remaining independent works. *Sigismund* (1976) is an experimental prose work about contemporary Europe with science-fiction elements. The last in the series is *The Death of a Bee Keeper* (1978). *Bernard Foy's Third Castling* (1986) is an unusual spy story.

In all his work Gustafsson shows a preoccupation with the concepts of reality, identity, and freedom. Apart from his fiction and poetic works, he has made major contributions to philosophical, historical, and sociological study. He was editor of the influential *Bonniers Literary Magazine* in Sweden from 1962 to 1972 and is currently professor of philosophy at the University of Texas. Recent publications include the poetry collection *The Silence of the World before Bach* (1988).

Guttuso, Renato (1912–87) Italian painter, born in Bagheria, near Palermo, Sicily. He had little formal artistic training, abandoning legal studies to become a painter in 1931. His art is inseparable from his political beliefs and he is regarded as the leading exponent of social realism in 20th-century Italian art. In the 1930s he became ardently anti-Fascist and in 1940 he joined the Corrente, an association of anti-Fascist artists founded two years earlier by Renato BIROLLI. In spite of opposition from church and government, his work won official prizes in the early 1940s. In 1944 he joined the Resistance and in 1945 he published drawings attacking the Nazis. With Birolli and others he was one of the founders of the FRONTE NUOVO DELLE ARTI (1947) but he left in 1948 because of ideological differences. In the 1950s he began to achieve an international reputation and by the time of his death was one of the most celebrated of post-war Italian artists. He lived mainly in Rome but made frequent trips to Paris; his work includes some large paintings of the student riots there in 1968. He depicted other contemporary political events, sometimes in an allegorical manner, as well as scenes inspired by the hard lives of the Sicilian peasantry. His style was forceful and expressionistic.

Gyllensten, Lars (Johan Wictor) (1921–) Swedish writer. Gyllensten was born in Stockholm and studied medicine, thereafter working in scientific research until 1973 when he became a full-time writer. He has read widely, especially in philosophy, and his work can be formidably erudite.

Gyllensten made his debut in 1949 with *Modern Myths*, a collection of poems, sketches, and stories dealing with the problems posed by the decline in religious faith. *Infantilia* (1952) presents a conflict between erotic and spiritual love, using language that verges on the expressionistic. *The Senator* (1958) explores concepts of order and anarchy, themes that are further developed in *The Testament of Cain* (1963). In *Juvenilia* (1965) Gyllensten explores the idea of self-image, arguing that conventional concepts of personality are too limiting. His novel, *The Cave in the Desert* (1973), portrays three characters who have withdrawn from society both physically and philosophically.

Gyllensten's work is experimental in form, style, and content. Deeply affected by the atrocities of World War II and the use of atomic bombs against Japan, he rejects all ideologies and the concept of an objective reality.

Since the 1950s Gyllensten has been involved, often controversially, in public debate on subjects as diverse as nuclear power, medical ethics, and broadcasting. He has been a member of the Nobel Committee for Literature since 1968 and in 1977 became the permanent secretary of the Swedish Academy.

H

Haacke, Hans (1936–) German experimental artist. Born in Cologne, Haacke studied at the High School for Fine Arts in Kassel (1956–60) and HAYTER's Atelier 17 in Paris (1960–61). In 1962 he visited the US on a travelling scholarship. From 1963 to 1965 he held teaching posts in Germany and thereafter he taught in the US, holding a succession of posts at the Cooper Union in New York from 1967 onwards.

In the early 1960s Haacke began to create and exhibit natural systems, notably a series of plexiglass 'weather boxes' containing water that was heated to produce condensation and changing effects of reflected light. For the 1969 'Earth Art' exhibition at Cornell University he contributed a work called *Grass Grows*, in which rye was grown from seed and allowed to wither. In the 1970s his work became increasingly political. In 1971 his proposed exhibition at the Guggenheim Museum in New York was to include a series of 'Real Estate' works, featuring photographs of properties with captions giving information about the wealth and status of the owners; the director cancelled the exhibition and fired the curator responsible. In the 1980s Haacke incorporated texts from the publicity material of large corporations into his objects and screenprints. His work shows a preoccupation with the power of art to create and communicate awareness of systems and values. *See also* CONCEPTUAL ART.

Haas, Ernst (1921–86) Austrian photographer, one of the first important exponents of colour photograpy. After studying medicine and showing an early interest in painting, Haas took up photojournalism in 1947. He emigrated to the US in 1949, joining the newly formed Magnum Photos. For *Life* magazine he produced trenchant black-and-white photojournalism, such as *Returning Prisoners of War* (1949), before exploring the poetic effects of colour tones during the 1950s. The Museum of Modern Art in New York chose Haas's work for its first exhibition of colour photography in 1962, the year he wrote and directed *The Art of Seeing* for television. By using slow shutter speeds (rather than fast ones which produce clear detail without visible movement) Haas blurred colour to emphasize dynamic action in his studies of Spanish bullfights and motor racing. His interest in tonal quality is evident in *The Creation* (1971), a poetic treatment of Genesis, *In America* (1975), *In Deutschland* (1976), and *Himalayan Pilgrimage* (1978). Some of his later studies of US cities resemble POP ART paintings.

Haavikko, Paavo (1931–) Finnish poet, playwright, and prose writer. Born in Helsinki, Haavikko emerged as Finland's leading literary modernist with the publication of such collections as *The Roads that Lead Far Away* (1951), *On Windy Nights* (1953), and *Leaves are Leaves* (1958). He is celebrated for his precise, almost imagistic, use of language and his formal and stylistic innovations. Although much of Haavikko's inspiration is drawn from Finnish mythology and folk tradition, his work also reflects unusually wide cultural and historical interests. He has written works set in Ancient Rome, 16th-century Germany, and the Russia of Catherine the Great. His treatment of contemporary Finnish and Western society is often satirical. Major works include the poem sequences *Birthplace* (1955) and *The Winter Palace* (1959), a complex work in nine parts; both explore the nature of the creative process and the poet's role in the world. His other poetry collections include *The Trees, All Their Green* (1966), *In the World* (1974), *Wine, Writing* (1976), and *May, Eternal* (1988).

Haavikko's plays, many of which show the influence of European absurdism (*see* ABSURD, THEATRE OF THE), include *Münchhausen* (1958), about the legendary liar, and *The Dolls* (1960). His collected plays appeared in 1978 and *Five Small Dramatic Texts* in 1981.

The novel *Another Heaven and Earth* from 1961 deals with marital breakdown and suicide, while the short novel *The Years* (1962) portrays an alcoholic down-and-out. Haavikko's short stories, most of which are written in a bare objective style, were collected in *The Glass on the Table of Claudius Civilii's Conspirators* (1964). One of his more recent books, *Iron Age* (1982), a reworking of material from the *Kalevala*, was serialized on Finnish television. Haavikko has received several international literary prizes.

Habermas, Jürgen (1929–) German philosopher and social theorist of the **Frankfurt School**. After taking a degree in philosophy at the University of Frankfurt in 1954. Habermas became assistant (1956) to ADORNO at the Institute for Social Research in Frankfurt. He took his second degree at the University of Marburg in 1961 and subsequently taught philosophy in Heidelberg. Since 1964 he has held a chair of philosophy and sociology at the University of Frankfurt, with an interval from 1971 until 1983, when he was director of the Max Planck Institute in Starnberg.

Habermas's first major book, *The Structural Transformation of the Public Sphere* (1962), was an investigation in sociological history, dealing with the rise, transformation, and disintegration of the intellectual public in the 18th and 19th centuries. This combination of historical, sociological, and philosophical interests has characterized all his later work. In *Theory and Practice* (1963) and *Knowledge and Human Interests* (1968) he questioned the assumptions of modern scientific theory, arguing that far from being disinterested and value-free these served a number of social and political ends. Habermas's central philosophical project is the working out of his *Theory of Communicative Action* (1981). In the book he systematically and historically distinguishes between two forms of rationality by opposing 'technical' and 'communicative' rationality. Habermas attacks attempts 'to cut rationality in half' by reducing it to mere technical expertise. In his book *The Philosophical Discourse of Modernity* (1985) he defended his ideas against deconstructivist and postmodernist attempts to undermine rationality by reducing it to a cluster of loosely related language-games.

Hacks, Peter (1928–) German playwright and poet, who emerged as the most important writer for the East German theatre in the 1960s. Hacks began his career with the BERLINER ENSEMBLE, having been invited to join the company by BRECHT himself, and soon built up a reputation with his satires based on Brecht's concept of EPIC THEATRE, notably *The Chapbook of Duke Ernest* (1967; written 1953). Subsequently he concentrated on realistic dramas dealing with contemporary issues, including the problems of the East German economy, in such plays as *Anxieties and Power* (1960) and *Moritz Tassow* (1964).

In the late 1960s Hacks developed the highly poetic dramatic style for which he is best known, writing comedies derived from historical or mythological sources, as well as adapting plays by such authors as Aristophanes, Shakespeare, and Goethe. Such works as *Amphitryon* (1967), *Seneca's Death* (1978), and *Adam and Eve* (1973) became in Hacks' hands doubly relevant to contemporary audiences through the parallels he drew between his often archaic source material and the issues facing modern German society. The difficulty of translating the elaborate poetic language of his plays has, however, hindered the growth of his international reputation.

Haitink, Bernard (Johann Herman) (1929–) Dutch conductor. Haitink was born in Amsterdam and studied conducting under Felix Hupke, at the Amsterdam Conservatory before joining the Netherlands Radio Philharmonic Orchestra as a violinist. After further studies under Ferdinand Leitner he became the second conductor of the Netherlands Radio Union in 1955. He subsequently worked with the Concertgebouw Orchestra of Amsterdam, at first with Eugen JOCHUM but from 1964 as sole conductor and artistic director. He has worked with the Los Angeles Symphony Orchestra as conductor (1958), the London Philharmonic Orchestra as principal conductor and director (1967–79), and the Glyndebourne Festival Opera as musical director (1978–88). He became the musical director of the Royal Opera House, Covent Garden, in 1987. He is known for his interpretations of Mahler, Bruckner, Beethoven, and Liszt.

Halffter, Cristóbal (Jiménez) (1930–) Spanish composer and conductor. The nephew of the composers Rodolfo Halffter (1900–) and Ernesto Halffter (1905–), he studied at the Madrid Conservatory (1947–51), where he later taught (1960–67). In 1952 he began working for Spanish radio. By the mid 1960s he was internationally recognized as one of the leading Spanish composers of his generation. Among the orchestras which he has conducted is the Falla Ochestra (1955–63).

Halffter's earliest works, for example *Antifona pascual* (1952), show the influence of his uncles and of Falla, while *Dos movimientosi* and *Misa ducal* (both 1955) show the impact of Bartók and Stravinsky respectively. Radicalized by his contact with the music of the post-Schoenberg European avant-garde, he moved rapidly from the atonalism of the piano concerto (1953) to serialism (*Tres piezas* for string quartet, 1955; revised as *Concertino* for string orchestra, 1956) and to aleatoricism, (*Formantes* for two pianos, 1961). He has a decided preference for large-scale works: those from the late 1960s, such as *Anillos* (1968) and *Lineas y puntos* (1967), confirmed his foremost position amongst his Spanish contemporaries. His large output includes orchestral pieces, concertos for piano and for cello, instrumental pieces, electronic and vocal works, the ballet *Saeta* (1955), and the opera *Don Quixote* (1970).

Hall, Sir Peter (Reginald Frederick) (1930–) British theatre director and manager, who was director (1960–73) of the ROYAL SHAKESPEARE COMPANY and (1973–88) of the National Theatre (*see* ROYAL NATIONAL THEATRE). Hall built up a reputation for high standards of production at the Theatre Royal, Windsor and the Arts Theatre in London before founding his own company in 1957 and then moving to Stratford, where he founded the RSC as a permanent ensemble. He was quickly recognized as the foremost British director of Shakespeare's plays, *The Wars of the Roses* cycle of 1963 being particularly well reviewed.

Hall succeeded OLIVIER as director of the National Theatre in 1975 and was largely responsible for establishing the new company's reputation with a series of productions ranging from Shakespeare and Marlowe to PINTER and SHAFFER. On leaving the National Theatre he set up the Peter Hall Company in 1988 and continued to direct a wide range of classic and modern productions. He was also artistic director of the Glyndebourne (Opera) Festival from 1984 to 1990. Hall published his autobiography in 1993.

Hambraeus, Bengt (1928–) Swedish composer, teacher, musicologist, and organist. Born in Stockholm, he studied at Uppsala University (1947–56) and attended the DARMSTADT summer courses from 1951. Employed by the music department of Swedish radio from 1957, he became director of its chamber music section in 1965 and head of production in 1969, using his authority to promote modern composers. He became professor of composition at McGill University, Montreal, in 1972.

His output is large and includes works for orchestra, ensemble, voice, and electronic pieces. Important influences on his style include medieval music (which he studied at university), organ music (Hambraeus was the first organist in Sweden to play MESSIAEN's works), non-European music (especially Japanese), and the electronic and serial music of the Darmstadt group (his *Doppelrohr II*, produced in the Cologne electronic music studios in 1955, was the first electronic work by a Scandinavian composer). His music is notable for its stress on instrumental colour and its relative absence of pulse and of formal structural divisions. Other significant works include *Introduzione-Sequenze-Coda* (1959) for orchestra, *Rota* (1956–62) for orchestra and tape, *Rencontres* (1971) for orchestra, and the electronic piece *Intrada* (1975).

Hamilton, Richard (1922–) British painter and printmaker; a pioneer of POP ART. Born in London, Hamilton worked in the publicity department of an electrical company before studying art at the Royal Academy Schools (1938–40, 1946–47) and at the Slade School of Fine Art (1948–51) in London. As a student Hamilton developed an interest in the work of the French Dada artist, Marcel Duchamp.

During the war years he worked as a jig and tool draughtsman. He subsequently taught at the Central School of Art in London (1952–53), at King's College in Newcastle (1953–56), and at the Royal College of Art, London (1957–61).

Hamilton was one of the first serious artists to make use of images drawn from commercial art and popular illustration. His works have often incorporated sections of advertisements, prints, tickets, and other items in order to comment on the nature of contemporary life and values (for example, the well-known montage *Just What is it that Makes Today's Homes so Different, so Appealing?*, 1956). He has shown a particular interest in modern technology and the mass media. Recent work has generally been more sombre and political than his earlier output. The Gulf War of 1991 inspired him to produce *War Games*, a work criticizing the way media coverage had (allegedly) reduced the conflict to the status of a game. Major retrospective exhibitions of his work were held at the Tate Gallery, London, in 1970 and 1992. He represented Britain at the 1992 Venice Biennale.

Hampton, Christopher (James) (1946–) British playwright, whose reputation was established by his first play, *When Did You Last See My Mother?* (1964), which was produced at the Royal Court Theatre and then in the West End. Subsequently Hampton became resident playwright at the Royal Court, which presented his *Total Eclipse* (1968) and *The Philanthropist* (1970), a comedy inspired by Molière that launched the author as a commercial playwright. Successful plays that followed included *Savages* (1973) and adaptations of works by Ibsen, who profoundly influenced Hampton's subsequent dramas. *Treats* (1976) was an exploration of the tensions between the sexes, a theme that was central to Hampton's greatest success, *Les Liaisons Dangereuses* (1985). Based on the epistolary novel of sexual intrigue by Choderlos de Laclos, it was later filmed with Hampton's own screenplay. Other plays by Hampton have included *After Mercer* (1980), *Tales from Hollywood* (1982), and *White Chameleon* (1991), about the author's recollections of Alexandria during the Suez Crisis.

Handke, Peter (1942–) Austrian playwright and novelist, who established his reputation as a rebel against theatrical convention with his first play, aptly titled *Offending the Audience* (1966). Handke, whose plays explore the difficulties of communication and the ways in which language can influence personality, has attempted to dispense with conventional dialogue, replacing it with alternative forms of expression, including movement. In *Kaspar* (1968), for instance, the central character is totally unable to speak, while in *The Ride Across Lake Constance* (1971) the text consists entirely of clichés. These controversial experiments have earned Handke a notoriety that has overshadowed more recent plays such as *They are Dying Out* (1974).

Handke's novels are equally unconventional, stripping character and plot to the barest essentials and describing extreme mental states in a bald dispassionate style that has won comparisons with ROBBE-GRILLET. *The Goalie's Anxiety at the Penalty Kick* (1970), his best-known novel, is a bizarre thriller about a footballer who commits a pointless murder, while *The Left-Handed Woman* (1976) describes a woman's desperate attempts to cope with the departure of her husband. *Sorrow Beyond Dreams* (*Wunschloses Unglück*; 1976) is a memoir, later adapted for the stage, describing the life and suicide of the author's mother. More recent work includes the tetralogy *Slow Homecoming* (1979–82).

Hanka, Erika (1905–58) Austrian dancer, choreographer, and ballet director, who was the most prominent figure in the reconstruction of the Viennese ballet tradition after World War II. Having trained at the Vienna Academy and under Kurt Jooss, she appeared as a dancer with the Folkwang Ballet, which she joined in 1933. In 1936 she took the role of assistant ballet mistress with the company in Düsseldorf.

Hanka returned to Vienna in 1941 as a guest choreographer with the Vienna State Opera. Following the success of her production of Werner EGK's *Joan von Zarissa* (1942) she was appointed ballet mistress there, subsequently being promoted to ballet director. In the turmoil following the end of the war, Hanka managed to keep her company together and set about the task of rebuilding Vienna's reputation as a centre for dance with a series of dance-theatre productions. The most successful of these included Theodor Berger's *Homeric Symphony* (1950), Boris BLACHER's *The Moor of Venice* (1955), and Gottfried von EINEM's *Medusa* (1957). In 1955 she oversaw the State Opera's reopening in its rebuilt theatre on the Ringstrasse.

Hansen, Thorkild (1927–) Danish novelist, journalist, essayist, and historian. One of Denmark's most widely travelled writers, Hansen has been consistently popular since making his literary debut in 1947 with the novel *Weather-Wrapped Memories.* He is one of Europe's leading exponents of documentary literature, most of his works being either personal memoirs or reassessments of well-documented historical events.

Two early texts *Seven Seals* (1960) and *A Woman on the River* (1961) are written in diary form and give accounts of archaeological expeditions in Kuwait and Nubia, emphasizing the clash between the archaic indigenous way of life and Western European culture. His interest in the Middle East continued in *Happy Arabia* (1962), an account of an 18th-century Danish expedition to the Yemen.

In the late 1960s Hansen produced a trilogy describing the Danish slave trade in West Africa and the West Indies, *Slave Coast* (1967), *Slave Ship* (1968), and *Slave Island* (1970). The trilogy is based on personal memoirs and other historical documents.

In 1978 Hansen published *The Trial of Hamsun*, a provocative three-volume work analysing the case of the Nobel-Prize-winning Norwegian novelist Knut Hamsun, who was also a devoted admirer of Hitler. The book stirred up debate throughout Scandinavia. Hansen has also published travel diaries about Greenland, the Arctic, Africa, and Asia, and interviews with leading personalities.

happening An improvised or partly improvised artistic event of a type briefly popular in Europe and the US in the 1960s. Happenings generally combined elements of theatre, music, and the visual arts and tended to be deliberately outlandish or shocking in their content. They were often staged in a street or other public place, with a degree of audience participation being expected. In the atmosphere of the late 1960s, happenings were enthusiastically adopted as a means of breaking down the barriers between art and life. Since the early 1970s happenings have rarely been attempted outside theatre festivals. *See also* PERFORMANCE ART, ACTION AND BODY ART.

Hare, David (1947–) British playwright and theatre director, who emerged as one of the leading socialist dramatists of the 1970s. A joint founder of the Portable Theatre group and the JOINT STOCK COMPANY, he has also worked at the Royal Court Theatre as resident playwright and at the National Theatre. Many of his plays – several written with other socialist writers – are intended to highlight the failings of the capitalist system, although his recent works have concentrated upon questions of personal morality and belief. His more overtly political plays have included *Slag* (1970), *Lay By* (1971), *England's Ireland* (1972), *Fanshen* (1975), and *A Map of the World* (1982). *Plenty* (1978), the most celebrated of Hare's earlier plays, uses the long nervous decline of a former British Resistance heroine as a metaphor for the decay of idealism in British political life in the post-war era. Of his subsequent plays *Pravda* (1985), an exuberant satire about the dealings of two newspaper magnates, on which Hare collaborated with Howard BRENTON, was a great popular success, while *The Secret Rapture* (1988), a play about the nature of goodness, was especially well received. *Racing Demon* (1990), about upheavals in the modern Church of England, and *Murmuring Judges* (1991), a critique of the legal establishment, are intended to form the first two parts of a trilogy dealing with British institutions.

Hare became an associate director of the National Theatre for the first time in 1984. He has also written plays for television, among them *Licking Hitler* (1978) and *Saigon – Year of the Cat* (1983), and the screenplays for *Wetherby* (1985) and other films.

Harnoncourt, Nikolaus (1929–) Austrian conductor and cellist. Born in Berlin, Harnoncourt studied at the Academy of Music, Vienna, and played in the Vienna Symphony Orchestra from 1952 until 1969. In 1954 he founded the Vienna **Concentus Musicus**, an important early music group, which he has conducted in numerous period performances of Bach, Monteverdi, Handel, and other baroque and classical composers. The ensemble is led by his wife, the violinist Alice Harnoncourt. His fast tempi and idiosyncratic phrasing have sometimes proved controversial. Harnoncourt has also conducted the Zurich Opera and Amsterdam Concertgebouw Orchestra; he was appointed professor of the Mozarteum and institute of musicology at the University of Salzburg in 1972. In 1986 he founded the Styriarte, a music festival held annually in Graz. Recent recording projects include the complete cycle of Beethoven symphonies. *See also* EARLY-MUSIC MOVEMENT).

Harrison, Tony (1937–) British poet and playwright. Born to working-class parents in Yorkshire, Harrison was educated at Leeds Grammar School, where he showed a gift for languages. He subsequently worked as a teacher in Africa and Czechoslovakia, and travelled in the Soviet Union and the US, experiences which influenced his poetry. His earlier volumes include *Loiners* (1970) and *From 'The School of Eloquence' and other poems* (1978); the latter features an unfinished sonnet sequence (still in progress) about his relationship with his uneducated parents that is often considered his finest work. *Continuous* (1981) was followed by *V* (1985), a long poem about the state of modern Britain inspired by the vandalism of his parents' grave and set against the background of the 1984 miners' strike. When adapted for television, the poem provoked a furore in the tabloid press with its strong language. Several of Harrison's more recent works have also been televised, notably *In Loving Memory* and the *Blasphemer's Banquet*, a defence of Salman RUSHDIE. Harrison has translated and adapted a number of classical works for the British stage, including Molière's *The Misanthrope* (1973), Racine's *Phèdre* (*Phaedra Britannica*; 1975), and Aeschylus's *Oresteia* (1981). In *The Trackers of Oxyrhyncus* (1990), based on the only surviving fragment of a satyr play by Sophocles, Harrison attacked the separation of high and low culture. His most recent works are the poetry collection *The Gaze of the Gorgon* (1992) and *Square Rounds* (1992), a play about the German chemist Fritz Haber and his role in developing poison gases during World War I.

Hartung, Hans (1904–89) French abstract painter, born in Germany. Hartung studied at the academies of Leipzig (1924–25) and Dresden (1925–26). From 1927 to 1931 he lived mainly in Paris and subsequently spent periods in Minorca (1932–34) and Stockholm (1934–35). He returned to Germany in 1935 but was forced to flee from the Nazis; he spent the war years serving as a volunteer in the French Foreign Legion and became a naturalized French citizen in 1946.

Hartung began to paint abstract works in 1922 and remained devoted to the principle of total abstraction. His early works were influenced by the German Expressionist painters of the Brücke ('Bridge') group and by the abstract work of Kandinsky and Klee. After World War II Hartung, who had previously found little recognition, emerged as one of the leading Paris-based exponents of expressive abstraction (*see* ART INFORMEL). A major exhibition of his work was held in Paris in 1947 and in 1960 he won the Grand Prix at the Venice Biennale. His mature works characteristically feature swirling black lines on a coloured background. Hartung preferred to paint in an automatic manner after a period of meditation.

Harvey, Jonathan (Dean) (1939–) British composer of ELECTRONIC MUSIC. A cellist in the National Youth Orchestra, Harvey studied at Cambridge University and privately with Erwin Stein and Hans Keller. He subsequently (1969–70) studied with the US composer Milton Babbit at Princeton. His early compositions reflect the influences of BRITTEN, MESSIAEN, STOCKHAUSEN, and Maxwell DAVIES amongst others. In the 1970s he began to develop a more personal style in such pieces as *Inner Light I–III* (1973–77), which combine tapes and acoustic instruments; Harvey is now regarded as Britain's leading composer of electronic music. More recent pieces include *Mortuos Plango, Vivos Voco* (1980), *Bhakti* (1982) for small orchestra and tape, *Madonna of Winter and Spring* (1986) for orchestra, synthesizers, and electronics, and *Ritual Melodies* (1990) for tape. He has been professor of music at the University of Sussex since 1980.

Hauge, Olav Håkonson (1908–) Norwegian poet. A smallholder and gardener from the Hardanger region, Hauge made his debut as a poet at the age of 38 with *Embers and Ashes* (1946). Since then he has become one of Norway's most acclaimed poets. He writes in a western dialect of Nynorsk, the less common but more lyrical form of the Norwegian language.

Hauge's breakthrough came in 1956 with *Slowly Reddens the Forest in the Valley*. The harsh landscapes of the Hardanger region are a major source of inspiration in both this and the following collection, *Eagle Mound* (1961), which won the Critic's Prize.

In *Drops in the East Wind* (1966) Hauge moved away from his preoccupation with the natural world and began to produce his so-called 'object poetry', in which objects are presented without symbolism or rhetoric. Although *Ask the Wind* (1971) was more political than previous collections Hauge rejects the subjection of poetry to political purpose. He was nonetheless one of the few older poets to be respected by the young political writers of the 1970s. In his later work he has preferred to use free verse. Hauge's collected poems appeared in 1972; the third edition (1980) included new poems on the subject of old age.

Although self-educated, Hauge is exceedingly well read in European literature and has translated works by the French Symbolists and the British and US modernists. Even the most 'regional' of his work has a wider European significance.

Häusser, Robert (1924–) German photographer. Born in Stuttgart, he studied in Weimar and turned professional in 1950. His early work shows the influence of his teacher, Otto STEINERT, and of FOTOFORM. Häusser has consistently avoided literal documentation of the external world in his attempts to capture the inner truth of a place, an event, or a work of art. His first solo exhibition was staged in 1959 in Mannheim, his base for much of his career; the city forms the subject matter of his book *Mannheim* (1975). Other publications include *Heidelberg* (1961), *Alsace* (1962), *The Sculptor Hans Nagel* (1971), *The Painter K. F. Dahmen* (1972), and *The World of Opera* (1977). Many of his later landscape photographs border on abstract expressionism in their distortions of reality. Häusser has staged one-man exhibitions in several European cities and in the US and took a gold medal at the Venice Biennale in 1961. He also designed the scenery for a production of Pavel Kohut's play *So eine Liebe* (1973), performed at the Lucerne Festival and in Mannheim. His work, which covers many themes, shows sensitivity to mood as much as physical form. It has been collected in *Robert Häusser* (1972).

Havel, Václav (1936–) Czech playwright, essayist, and politician, who became president of Czechoslovakia (1989–92) following the collapse of the communist regime. Havel's plays reflect his longstanding political involvement, being largely concerned with such themes as the suffering of the individual in a totalitarian state and the fear, corruption, and dishonesty such a system inevitably engenders. Forbidden to study drama at university because of his *haute bourgeoisie* background, he became a stagehand, eventually working his way up to an appointment as resident playwright at Prague's Theatre on the Balustrade, for which he wrote such early absurdist plays as *The Garden Party* (1963), *The Memorandum* (1965), and *The Increased Difficulty of Concentration* (1968) (*see* ABSURD, THEATRE OF THE). After the Soviet invasion of 1968, it was impossible for Havel to have his plays staged in his own country, although they continued to be seen in the West.

In 1979 he was imprisoned for his association with the Committee for the Defence of the Unjustly Persecuted (VONS) and was not released until 1983, by which time he had become a symbol of resistance to state oppression in Czechoslovakia. Samuel BECKETT wrote *Catastrophe* (1982) in his honour and Havel was showered with international awards for his writing. In 1985 he wrote one of his best-known plays, *Largo Desolato*, in which a dissident academic tries to come to terms with his role as a figurehead for national unrest in an oppressive state; it was particularly well received in Britain in Tom STOPPARD's translation. *Temptation* (1985), a reworking of the Faust legend, constituted another scathing attack on the communist regime.

When the Communists finally lost power in 1989, Havel (who had once again been imprisoned) was the obvious choice for president. He continued to write prolifically, enjoying a unique reputation as both national hero and literary and moral thinker. Havel's political essays are, from the point of view of literary history, more important than his plays, and share many of the same themes. In *Towards Human Identity* (1984) he defines identity by responsibility, looks for a society whose goal is transcendental, not material, and analyses both the methods used by the socialist regime to destroy personal independence and the way individuals, often unwittingly, collaborate in their own oppression. In his essays and speeches as president he continued to emphasize personal responsibility and the need to restore standards of honesty and decency. He also consistently expressed opposition to illiberal laws introduced by the three Czechoslovak parliaments. Recent works include the play *Redevelopment* (1989) and the essays in *Summer Meditations* (1992). He resigned as president of Czechoslovakia in 1992, following his failure to prevent moves towards the break-up of the country; in 1993 he became president of the new Czech Republic.

Hawking, Stephen W(illiam) (1942–) British theoretical physicist. Hawking graduated from Oxford University and after being connected with various institutes and departments at Cambridge University was appointed to the chair of gravitational physics (1977–79). He became Lucasian professor of mathematics in 1979.

Hawking has worked mainly in the field of general relativity and in particular on the theory of black holes. He has objected to Einstein's treatment of gravity in his general theory since "it treats the gravitational field in a purely classical manner when all other observed fields seem to be quantized." A further objection, made with G. F. R. Ellis in their *Large Scale Structure of Space Time* (1973), was that the theory led inevitably to singularities that it could not describe adequately. Two such singularities they suggest are black holes and the big bang beginning the expansion of the universe. For these reasons Hawking has been one of the leaders in the search for a theory of quantum gravity. Such a search has yet to find any general success.

In the theory of black holes Hawking has been more successful, establishing a number of remarkable theorems. Black holes are celestial 'bodies' that having had a mass in excess of three solar masses have undergone a gravitational collapse so extreme that they contract below the critical radius at which light or any other signal can escape. At first it appeared that absolutely nothing could be known about such 'bodies' but Hawking has managed to construct many of their properties and show their relationship to more classical parts of physics.

Hawking showed that black holes could originate in other circumstances. There could be "a number of very much smaller black holes scattered around the universe, formed not by the collapse of stars but by the collapse of highly compressed regions ... that are believed to have existed shortly after the 'big bang' in which the universe originated." These 'mini black holes' could weigh a billion tons and yet be no bigger than a proton with a radius of 10^{-15} metres.

His most exciting result, published in 1974, was one that he confessed he found hard to believe. This was the claim that black holes are not 'black' but emit particles at a steady rate. This result has been repeatedly confirmed mathematically and Hawking is able to propose a physical quantum process that would produce the effect.

Since the early 1960s Hawking has been the victim of a progressive nervous disease. This has confined him to a wheelchair and has prevented him from writing or calculating in a direct and simple way. The bulk of his work, involving complex calculations, difficult mathematical proofs, and the introduction of new physical ideas, is thus interwoven into presentable form purely in his mind. His *A Brief History of Time* (1988) proved to be a worldwide popular bestseller.

Hayek, Friedrich (August von) (1899–1992) British economist, born in Austria. After graduating (1921) from the University of Vienna, Hayek worked as a civil servant before becoming director (1926) of the Austrian Institute for Economic Research. From 1931 until 1950 he was professor of economics at London University; subsequently he held professorships in Chicago, Freiburg, and Salzburg. He was a corecipient of the Nobel Prize for economics in 1974.

Although he had published a number of distinguished theoretical works in the 1930s and 1940s, Hayek remained little known outside academic circles until he drew out the political implications of his ideas in *The Road to Serfdom* (1944). Hayek here set out his passionately held belief in an absolutely free market as the only guarantee of individual liberty under the law. The book has been through 12 editions. His belief that economic and personal freedom are inseparable led him to reject even the most moderate and well-intentioned kinds of government intervention, arguing that such policies lead inevitably to slavery. This extreme libertarian position was further developed in such works as *The Constitution of Liberty* (1960), *Law, Legislation and Liberty* (3 vols: 1973–79), and *Unemployment and Monetary Policy* (1979). He even came to advocate individual freedom of choice with respect to the currency supply. In the mid 1970s much of his programme was embraced by the British Conservative Party and his ideas helped to shape the economic and social policies of the Thatcher governments of the 1980s.

Hay-on-Wye Festival of Literature and the Arts One of the largest annual literature festivals in the world, held over ten days in May in Hay-on-Wye, Wales. This small market town is Britain's principal centre for the second-hand book trade and the surrounding area has many literary associations, notably with the Victorian diarist Francis Kilvert. Although established as recently as 1987, the festival has attracted writers ranging from John OSBORNE to Jeffrey Archer, from Doris LESSING to Benjamin Zephaniah. The festival programme includes readings, discussions, lectures, and interviews.

Hayter, S(tanley) W(illiam) (1901–88) British printmaker and painter. Born in London, Hayter was the son of a painter, but did not originally intend to follow his father's career. He studied chemistry and geology at King's College, London (1917–21) and from 1922 to 1925 worked for the Anglo-Iranian Oil Company at Abadan in the Persian Gulf.

In 1926 Hayter moved to Paris, where he studied copper-engraving with Joseph Hecht. He also opened his celebrated studio on Rue Campagne-Première 17, known from 1933 as **Atelier 17**. Hayter's main aim was to teach and carry out research into printmaking techniques, but his studio also became an important meeting place for leading artists of the day, including Picasso, Dalí, Chagall, and GIACOMETTI.

Hayter was also a notable printmaker and painter in his own right, holding his first one-man show in London in 1928. In 1936 he helped to organize and contributed to the Surrealist Exhibition in London, though his works were not exclusively surrealist. In both his prints and his paintings Hayter reveals a fascination with the representation of movement, texture, and space. In 1940 he moved to New York, where he reestablished Atelier 17 and exerted a considerable influence on US printmakers. In 1950 he returned to Paris. In the 1970s and 1980s he produced numerous prints exploring the possibilities of new inks. His works are to be found in many public art collections in Europe. He received awards from both the French and British governments.

Heaney, Seamus (Justin) (1939–) Irish poet and critic. Born into a family of farmers in Northern Ireland, he was educated at Queen's College, Belfast and formed part of a group of young poets in that city in the 1960s. He lectured at Queen's until 1972 when he moved to the Republic of Ireland. In 1989 he was appointed professor of poetry at Oxford University, after earlier refusing the post.

Heaney's early poetry evokes his rural upbringing in language of great physical immediacy. The collections *Death of a Naturalist* (1966) and *Door into the Dark* (1969) also explore his family history and his own place within that heritage. His later poems are generally more complex in their explorations of Irish history and culture; a constant preoccupation is the role of language itself, especially as it relates to politics and violence. The collections *Wintering Out* (1972), *North* (1975), usually considered his strongest volume, and *Field Work* (1979) brought Heaney general recognition as the finest Irish poet since Yeats. The title sequence of *Station Island* (1984) is an autobiographical quest through the forces and events that have formed him as a poet. *Preoccupations* (1980) and *The Government of the Tongue* (1988) are collections of essays and lectures. He also edited *The Rattle Bag; an Anthology of Poetry* (1982) with fellow poet Ted HUGHES. His *New Selected Poems 1966–1987* were published in 1990 and the volume *Seeing Things* became a bestseller in 1991.

Heckroth, Hein (1897–1970) German art director, noted especially for his imaginative work on films featuring ballet and opera. Born in Giessen, Heckroth worked as a stage designer from an early age and came to specialize in set and costume design for German ballet productions. He travelled to Britain in 1945 to work on Gabriel Pascal's expensive film version of Shaw's *Caesar and Cleopatra* (1945) and remained to make a series of films with Michael POWELL and Emeric PRESSBURGER, including *Black Narcissus* (1947) and the ballet film *The Red Shoes* (1948), which won an Academy Award. His other films for Powell and Pressburger were *A Matter of Life and Death* (1946), featuring imaginative fantasy sets for the heavenly sequences, the suspense thriller *The Small Back Room* (1948), *The Elusive Pimpernel* (1950), *The Tales of Hoffman* (1951), an elaborate production involving ballet and opera sequences and described by *Punch* as 'an art director's picnic', *Oh Rosalinda!* (1955), an updating of *Die Fledermaus*, and *The Battle of the River Plate* (1956). Heckroth's design credits also include *The Story of Gilbert and Sullivan* (1953), the German film *The Girl and the Legend* (1957), which he also directed, the German-French *Threepenny Opera* (1963), and Alfred Hitchcock's *Torn Curtain* (1966).

Hegedušić, Krsto (1901–75) Yugoslav (Croatian) painter. Born at Petrinja in Croatia, Hegedušić grew up in the village of Hlebine near the Hungarian border. He studied art at the Academy of Art in Zagreb (1920–26) and in Paris as a French government scholar (1926–28).

Hegedušić's early paintings of peasant life were influenced by the work of Pieter Brueghel the Elder and intended as protests against the exploitation of the Croatian peasantry. On his return to Croatia, Hegedušić founded (1929) the Zemlja ('Earth') movement, an association of progressive Croatian painters who believed that their national art could be revived through contact with peasant culture. In 1930 they established an art school at Hlebine for peasant painters; its most notable student was the naive painter Ivan Generalić (1914–). Hegedušić's own work of this period includes *A Fair at Koprivnica* (1930, Tate Gallery, London). From 1936 onwards he taught at the Zagreb Academy of Art, though between 1931 and 1941 he was often arrested and during World War II he was interned. In 1945 he became a professor at the Academy. His post-war work remained predominantly realistic with a strong element of satire and the macabre that has prompted comparisons with the German artists Otto Dix and George Grosz. The influence of surrealism is sometimes apparent. He also produced book illustrations and designed theatre sets.

Heinesen, William (1900–) Faeroese novelist, short-story writer, and poet, writing in Danish. Heinesen draws heavily on his Faeroese background in his work but endows it with a universality that makes him one of the great international writers of the 20th century.

Born in Thórshavn, the capital of the Faeroe Islands, Heinesen was educated in Copenhagen, where he worked as a journalist before returning to his birthplace in 1932. During his time in Denmark he published several volumes of poetry in an elegaic symbolist style, including his debut, *Arctic Elegies* (1921). Later collections are written in a more contemporary idiom, with a strong vein of satire.

Much of his early prose explores the rapid changes in Faeroese society at the turn of the century. *The Lost Musicians* (1950) is a novel tracing the lives of a group of musicians in a society trying to enforce prohibition. *The Black Cauldron* (1949) takes a critical look at the British occupation of the islands during World War II and its subsequent moral impact upon Faeroese society; it is Heinesen's only real historical novel to date. *The Lively Hope* (1964), a complex work incorporating elements of fantasy, allegory, and stylistic pastiche, took its author some 40 years to complete.

Over the last 30 years he has concentrated increasingly on the short story, exploring a great variety of themes and approaches. *Let the Dance Go On* (1980), a collection of six stories, is considered by many his profoundest and most beautiful work.

Hélion, Jean (1904–87) French painter. Born at Couterne in Normandy, Hélion studied chemistry at Lille (1920–21) before moving to Paris, where he worked as an architect's draughtsman. He started to paint and sculpt in 1923, becoming a full-time artist in 1925. His early paintings were portraits, landscapes, and still lifes, but his work gradually became more abstract under the influence of cubism and the De Stijl movement, which advocated a geometrical art based on straight lines, right angles, and primary colours. In the early 1930s Hélion became an associate of De Stijl's leader, Theo van Doesburg, and a member of the large Paris-based group of abstract painters Abstraction-Création. He is best known for the abstract works he produced between 1929 and 1939. Most were geometrical (like the paintings of Mondrian and van Doesburg) but his composition became freer during the 1930s and often incorporated cubist-inspired forms.

In 1936 Hélion went to live in the US. During World War II he returned to France to serve in the French army but was captured by the Germans. He escaped, and made his way back to the US, returning to France in 1946. When he began to paint again in 1943 it was in a representational, even realistic, style. During the 1950s he painted mainly from nature, producing numerous colourful street scenes, figures, nudes, and landscapes. Towards the end of his life, in the late 1970s and early 1980s, there was a final flowering of his talent in a series of paintings showing himself as a young man with nudes and other figures.

Heller, Otto (1896–1970) British cinematographer, born in Czechoslovakia. Heller began his career as a photographer in Prague; in 1916, while serving in the Austrian army, he filmed the funeral procession of Emperor Franz Josef. After World War I he worked as director of photography on numerous Czech and German productions, often with the director Karel Lamac. He avoided Germany after Hitler's rise to power in 1933, working in his native country, as well as in France, Holland, and Britain. He fled Czechoslovakia for Britain in 1940 and joined a Czech air unit. After the war he became a British subject and continued to bring his artistic cinematography to successful British films for another 25 years.

Heller worked on more than 300 feature films. His early Czechoslovakian films included *The Czech Baby Jesus* (1918) and *The Kreutzer Sonata* (1926), while German work included *The First Kiss* (1928), *The Girl from the USA* (1930), and *Die Fledermaus* (1931). British films featuring his work include *The Winslow Boy* (1948), *The Ladykillers* (1955), OLIVIER's *Richard III* (1955), *Masquerade* (1965), *The Ipcress File* (1965), *Alfie* (1966), and *Funeral in Berlin* (1966).

Helsinki Festival An arts festival held in Helsinki, Finland, for three weeks during August and September each year. Founded in 1957 to promote the music of Sibelius, it now has a wide-ranging programme that includes dance, drama, exhibitions, and open-air rock concerts as well as classical music. The festival commissions new works and provides a platform for artists and orchestras from the Baltic region.

Henze, Hans Werner (1926–) German composer and conductor. Henze studied at the Brunswick State Music School and then, after service in World War II, with FORTNER at Heidelburg and LEIBOWITZ at DARMSTADT. He composed prolifically throughout his twenties, keeping his music open to such disparate influences as Stravinskian neoclassicism in his first symphony (1947), the 12-note method of Schoenberg in his second quartet (1952) and third symphony (1951), and even jazz. Whilst embracing SERIALISM he did not abandon traditional forms, composing ballets like *Jack Pudding* (1951) and *Labyrinth* (1951) and operas such as *Boulevard Solitude* (1952), his first major success.

In 1953 Henze settled in Italy and began to write in a looser, more eclectic, style in which a new lyricism and even lushness become apparent. Operas such as *König Hirsch* (1956), *Elegy for Young Lovers* (1961), and especially *The Bassarids* (1966), a reworking of the *Bacchae* of Euripides with a libretto by Auden and Chester Kallman, established Henze's claim to be considered the leading operatic composer of his generation. A third period began in the late 1960s, when Henze became committed to the politics of the extreme left; his sixth symphony, premiered in Cuba in 1969, incorporates revolutionary songs and makes use of amplified instruments. The operas *We Come to the River* (1976), an attack on war and social injustice, and *The English Cat* (1983) both have librettos by Edward BOND. Other works include the ballet *Undine* (1958), the operas *Der Prinz von Homburg* (1960), *Der Junge Lord* (1964), and a seventh symphony (1984). His latest opera, *Das verratene Meer*, was premiered at the Munich Biennale in 1992. *See also* MONTEPULCIANO FESTIVAL.

Hepworth, Dame Barbara (1903–75) British sculptor. Born in Wakefield, Hepworth studied at the Leeds School of Art

(1920) and at the Royal College of Art in London (1921–24), where her contemporaries included Henry MOORE. From 1924 until 1926 she lived in Rome and Florence where she studied Romanesque and Renaissance sculpture. During the late 1920s and 1930s she lived in London – from 1931 with her second husband, the painter Ben NICHOLSON. In 1939 she and Nicholson moved to St Ives in Cornwall, where she lived for the rest of her life (*see* ST IVES SCHOOL).

During the 1920s and 1930s Hepworth came to know many leading European artists, including Picasso, Brancusi, and Mondrian and was greatly influenced by their work. During this period she gradually moved from figure sculpture towards abstraction. Her first abstract works date from the early 1930s. Hepworth created and developed many new ideas in abstract sculpture. In 1931, for instance, she made *Pierced Form* (destroyed during World War II), which featured a hole cut through alabaster; Hepworth developed this motif in later works and it was also famously exploited by Henry Moore. From 1934 Hepworth began to include strings in her work, as a means of exploring tension and space. She also began to colour her sculptures. Many of Hepworth's sculptures have a lyrical quality, perhaps reflecting her love of the countryside and of the sea. After World War II she received many commissions from abroad including that for the memorial to Dag Hammarskjöld at the United Nations Building in New York. There was a major retrospective exhibition of her work at the Tate Gallery in London in 1968.

Herbert, Zbigniew (1924–) Polish poet. Born in Lvov, Herbert took separate degrees in economics, law, and philosophy and worked as an editor and critic for the literary review *Twórczośź* from 1955 until 1976. His poems, affirming personal sensibility and humour in the face of all dogma, appeared in magazines from 1948 but were not widely read until Poland's brief liberalization of 1956, when the collection *Cord of Light* (*Struna światla*) was published. Herbert reacted to the gloomy privations of communist life and the corrupting effect of official ideology by emphasizing the moral responsibility of the individual and the wider historical resources of European civilization. Many of the poems in *Hermes, a Dog and a Star* (1957) and *A Study of the Object* (1961) are cast as dramatic monologues, giving free play to the complex sense of irony that is perhaps the most distinctive feature of his work. In the 1970s Herbert wrote several dramas and a series of poems about the fictional character *Mr Cogito* (1974), in which he explores the plight of modern man, tormented by a vague awareness of a mystical dimension to life but unable to grasp it. Two volumes of *Selected Poems* (1968 and 1977) have appeared in English translation. The essays in *A Barbarian in the Garden* (1962) reflect his fascination with the history and culture of Western Europe.

Hermans, Willem Frederik (1921–) Dutch writer. Hermans published his first collections of poems while still a student of natural sciences and geography. He subsequently lectured in physical geography at Groningen University. In 1973 he emigrated to France after a serious disagreement with the university, an experience that provoked his satirical novel *Among Professors* (1975). He has refused several leading Dutch prizes.

Convinced that the essential modern experience is one of disorientation, Hermans presents characters who are a prey to chaotic inner and outer forces. The critiques of language offered by Nietzsche and Wittgenstein have also influenced his depiction of the difficulty of communication in books such as *Malice and Misunderstanding* (1948) and *Paranoia* (1953). His satirical novel *I Am Always Right* (1951) provoked a scandal with its anti-Catholic content. He became famous with *The Dark Room of Damocles* (1958), a novel about a photographer who becomes involved in a complex affair of espionage and counter-espionage. Hermans's preoccupation with the problems of personal identity comes to the fore in *Never Sleep Again* (1966), in which a young scientist comes to realize his own insignificance in the face of the overwhelming Norwegian landscape. Hermans, who has described the world as 'sadistic' (*The Sadistic Universe*; 1964), takes as his main theme the relationship between the individual and the impersonal world around him. His radical thought and original language make him the most important novelist in the Netherlands today.

Heron, Patrick (1920–) British painter and art critic. Born in Leeds, Heron studied part time at the Slade School of Fine Arts, London (1937–39), receiving no other formal training. In 1947 he made his first visit to the west of Cornwall, where he associated with the ST IVES SCHOOL of painters. He settled in the area in 1956 and, apart from a year teaching in the US, has remained there ever since. Since 1947 he has given over 60 one-man exhibitions of his work, including a major retrospective at the Barbican Art Gallery (1985).

Heron's work of the late 1940s is executed in a semiabstract style much influenced by the French cubist Georges Braque (an exhibition of whose work he had reviewed in 1946). In contrast to Braque's subdued palette, however, Heron painted from the first in brilliant colours. In 1956 Heron suddenly adopted a completely abstract style under the impact of US abstract expressionism. His most distinctive works of this period are his so-called 'colour stripe' paintings of 1957–58, composed of horizontal bands of strongly contrasting colours. He subsequently introduced verticals to create a 'tartan' effect. From about 1959 onwards Heron reduced the number of different colours in his paintings and abandoned stripes in favour of irregular rectangular and disk-like shapes. He has remained preoccupied with the experience of colour as "pure sensation", writing that colour is "both the subject and the means; the form, and the content, the image and the meaning in my painting". Many of his recent paintings, identified only by the date of composition, are inspired by his clifftop garden in Zennor.

Heron is also important as a writer on the visual arts. The articles he wrote for the *New Statesman* (1947–50) and other publications were collected in *The Changing Forms of Art* (1955), a book that had a wide influence on the rising generation of British painters. In the early 1960s he began to challenge the ascendancy of US abstract expressionism, questioning its reliance on grand oversimplified gestures. In 1966 he published a now celebrated article in *Studio International* proposing the heretical view that London, rather than New York, had produced most of the best painting of the post-war era.

Hertzberger, Herman (1932–) Dutch architect. Educated at Delft, Hertzberger has been in practice in Amsterdam since 1958. Much influenced by the STRUCTURALISM of Claude LÉVI-STRAUSS and by the architect Aldo van EYCK, Hertzberger's design arises as much from social as from architectural theory. His Diagoon Houses, Delft (1971), were intended as 'half-works' to be completed by the occupants. The Central Beheer Office Building, Apeldoorn (1972) is based on the idea of 'work-islands' for 16 employees each, the whole building being composed of cubic components on a gridiron plan. The De Drie Hoven Old People's Home, Amsterdam (1974) is organized around a central 'village square', with special attention paid to all the intermediate spaces.

Herzog, Werner (Werner Stipetic; 1942–) German film director, who emerged as one of the most original directors in German cinema in the 1970s. He began his film career while working as a welder, making his debut as a director of full-length features in 1967 with *Signs of Life*, about the mental disintegration of a German soldier during World War II. In its exploration of man's relationship with his surroundings and its sympathy with outcasts, the film anticipates Herzog's better-known works.

In *Even Dwarfs Started Small* (1970) and *Fata Morgana* (1971) Herzog further explored these themes, setting the first in a prison for dwarfs on a desolate island and the second on the edge of the Sahara desert, where a motley collection of eccentrics live amongst the debris of humanity. His next film, the documentary *Land of Silence and Darkness* (1972), was a sympathetic portrayal of a deaf and blind woman as she embarks on her first aeroplane trip. *Aguirre, Wrath of God* (1973), starring Klaus Kinski as a Spanish conquistador driven (like many of Herzog's central characters) to the edge of madness by his ambitions, won Herzog international attention. In *The Enigma of Kaspar Hauser* (1974) the inhabitants of a 19th-century German town are presented with the mystery of a stranger who can tell them nothing of his previous existence.

In *Heart of Glass* (1976) modern industrial society breaks down in a German town when the holder of the glass-making formula upon which local industry depends dies without communicating the secret, while in *Stroszek* (1977) three Germans decide to emigrate to the US, where their ambitions of wealth are predictably disappointed.

Nosferatu the Vampyre (1979), a remake of the classic silent horror film, acquired cult status and brought Herzog a mass audience. *Woyzeck* (1979) was a successful adaptation of the play by Büchner. *Fitzcarraldo* (1982), his most ambitious epic, concerns the efforts of a mad opera enthusiast (again played by Kinski) to bring opera to the natives of the Amazon basin. The bizarre plot and the sheer scale of the venture brought Herzog a reputation for eccentricity. Subsequent films have been similarly unusual, including *Where the Green Ants Dream* (1984), about the conflict between the Aborigines and the Whites over land rights in Australia, *Cobra Verde* (1988), about an outcast slave trader in West Africa, and *Lessons of Darkness* (1992), a documentary-style film about events in Kuwait following the Gulf War.

Heutling Quartet German string quartet. The Heutling made its debut in 1958 in Hannover. Its members are Werner Heutling (first violin), whose name the quartet takes, Oswald Gattermann (second violin), Erich Bohlscheid (viola), and Konrad Haesler (cello). Heutling, who studied at the Dresden Academy and at the Cologne Musikhochschule, is also a professor at the Hannover Musikhochschule and the leader of the Hannover State Orchestra. The quartet has toured extensively and has recorded complete cycles of Mozart's and Schubert's string quartets and all Mozart's quintets.

Hewish, Antony (1924–) British radio astronomer. Hewish studied at Cambridge University after wartime work with the Royal Aircraft Establishment, Farnborough. He lectured in physics at Cambridge for many years, becoming professor of radio astronomy (1971–89). In 1974 he was awarded the Nobel Prize for physics jointly with Martin RYLE.

One of Hewish's research projects was the study of radio scintillation using the 4.5-acre telescope. Radio scintillation is a phenomenon, similar to the twinkling of visible stars, arising from random deflections of radio waves by ionized gas. In 1967 a research student, Jocelyn BELL BURNELL, noticed a rapidly fluctuating but unusually regular radio signal. To determine the nature of the signal, Hewish first eliminated such man-made sources as satellites, radar echoes, and the like. Measurements indicated that it must be well beyond the solar system. It seemed possible that it had been transmitted by an alien intelligence and the LGM (Little Green Men) hypothesis, as it became known, was seriously considered at Cambridge, but was dropped when other similar sources emerged. They became known as pulsars.

Hewish was able to establish that the pulsar he was examining was extremely small, no more than a few thousand kilometres, and was situated in our Galaxy. His account of the first pulsar received wide publicity in the popular press and stimulated much thought among astronomers as to the possible mechanism. The proposal made by Thomas GOLD and others that pulsars were rapidly rotating neutron stars has since won acceptance.

Heyerdahl, Thor (1914–) Norwegian anthropologist. Heyerdahl caught the popular imagination with the voyages he undertook in support of his belief that similarities between the traditions of widely separated cultures could be accounted for by prehistoric migrations. This had hitherto been regarded as physically impossible, given the level of technology available to prehistoric man.

In 1947 the close resemblance of the Peruvian god Viracocha (also known as Kon-Tiki), who was said to have sailed away into the setting sun, to the Polynesian god Tiki, drove Heyerdahl to make his first and most famous voyage, from Peru to Polynesia on a balsawood raft (the *Kon-Tiki*) similar to those used by fifth-century Peruvians. The journey of 4300 miles took 101 days. Heyerdahl later (1970) sailed from the Mediterranean across the Atlantic Ocean to South America in a papyrus boat, the *Ra* (*Ra I* sank, but *Ra II* completed the journey). He also made similar voyages from Sumeria to Africa and from Iraq to Djibouti. In the late 1980s he organized a series of archaeological expeditions to Easter Island.

Heyerdahl's original premise is now generally accepted. His books include separate accounts of each expedition as well as more theoretical works on early civilizations and cultural diffusion.

Heym, Stefan (Hellmuth Fliegel: 1913–) German novelist. After a youth spent in Chemnitz, Heym emigrated to Prague in 1933, where he worked as a journalist. In 1935 he won a Jewish scholarship to the US, where he studied German literature and wrote for journals and emigré papers, fighting Nazi propaganda and expressing support for the Communist Party. He became a US citizen and participated in the invasion of Normandy as a press officer. He began to write novels on his return from the war, leaving the US for East Germany in 1951.

Heym's writing is influenced by his years of journalism and by the tradition of Anglo-American social realism. For Heym, formal criteria are not an end in themselves but only a means to expressing political and social ideas. His first novels were written and published in English. *Hostages* (1942), his first bestseller, is a political thriller centring on a group of hostages taken captive by the Nazis after the assassination of Heydrich in Prague. This was followed by *The Crusaders* (1948), which questioned American war motives and was sharply criticized in the US. After his return to East Germany he wrote *A Day Marked X*, which attacked the official interpretations of the workers' revolts in East Berlin (1953) put out by both the East and West German governments. The book was banned in East Germany. Although a convinced socialist, Heym maintained a critical attitude to the regime throughout the years of the GDR. Other works include *Lasalle* (1969), *Collin* (1979), *Ahasver* (1981, 1988) and *Schwarzenberg* (1984). A severe critic of German reunification – a process he has likened to 'a hedgehog being swallowed by a snake' – he recently helped to set up a pressure group to protect the interests of former East Germans in the united country.

Hierro, José (1922–) Spanish poet. Born in Madrid, he was imprisoned for several years after the Spanish Civil War. His work is at the same time highly personal and determinedly accessible. Hierro claims to be a man 'like many others' and employs a deliberately clear and direct style. His collections include *Earth Without Us* and the prizewinning *Happiness* (both 1947), *With the Stones, with the Wind* (1950), and *Drafted in '42*, which includes the well-known piece 'For an Aesthete', in which he demands a proper humility from the creative artist. He won the National Prize for Literature in 1953 and went on to produce *Reclining Statues* (1955), *What I Know about Me* (1957), and *A Book of Hallucinations* (1964). His *Collected Poems* appeared in 1960 and his *Complete Works* in 1962.

Like his contemporaries, Hierro was painfully aware of the brutality of the times he lived in and saw his work as having mainly documentary value. He asserted that, in times such as his own, when social wrongs overshadow individual grief, poetry should be epic in its ambitions. He identified two poetic modes: 'reporting', a direct narrative mode, in which the reader's emotional response is heightened by the use of hidden rhythms, and 'hallucinations' a more subjective 'mist-covered' style. Hierro himself used both styles but excelled in the former, where his fine sense of rhythm came into its own.

Hildesheimer, Wolfgang (1916–91) German Jewish writer and artist. After growing up in Hamburg, Berlin, Nimwegen, and Mannheim, Hildesheimer emigrated with his family to Palestine in 1933. In his early twenties he studied painting in London, returning to Tel Aviv in 1939, where he became an English teacher. From 1946 to 1949 he worked as a simultaneous translator at the Nuremberg Trials. In his later years he lived and worked in Poschiavo, Switzerland.

Hildesheimer's literary career began with the collection of short stories *Loveless Legends* (1952), in which he satirized the cultural rituals that serve to hide society's underlying lack of ethical values. In the 1950s he became well known as a radio playwright and as a writer in the tradition of the absurd (*see* ABSURD, THEATRE OF THE). His increasingly monologic radio plays, for example *Night Piece* (1963) and *Monologue* (1964), are parables of the incomprehensibility and absurdity of existence. Similar themes inform his novels *Tynset* (1965) and *Masante* (1973). He enjoyed a major success with the biography *Mozart* (1977), which was followed by the fictional biography *Marbot* in 1981. In 1975 Hildesheimer programmatically proclaimed 'the end of fiction'; he himself stopped publishing fiction in 1983 but continued to work as an artist, essayist, and translator.

Hill, Geoffrey (1932–) British poet and critic. Born and brought up in Worcestershire, the son of a policeman, Hill was educated at Keble College, Oxford, and published his first volume of poems, *For the Unfallen* in 1959. *King Log*, containing several of his best-known poems, was published in 1968 and won the Hawthornden prize in 1969. This was followed by *Mercian Hymns* (1971), a sequence of prose poems, *Tenebrae* (1978), and the long poem *The Mystery of the Charity of Charles Péguy* (1983), a complex meditation on the life and death in battle of the French poet. Hill's difficult and complex work is extremely resistant to paraphrase but a number of principal themes may be discerned. One is the violence of history, both ancient and modern, and the duty and inadequacy of the poet to respond to this ('Ovid in the Third Reich', 'September Song'). Another is the parodoxical nature of Christian experience and the strains this too puts upon human language. His style is compressed and allusive but often rises to effects of real grandeur. With Ted HUGHES and Seamus HEANEY, he is usually considered one of the three finest poets now writing in the British Isles. His *Collected Poems* appeared in 1985 and his critical essays have been collected in *The Lords of Limit* (1984) and *The Enemy's Country* (1991). He was professor of English literature at Leeds University (1976–80) and has been a professor at Boston University since 1988.

Hilton, Roger (1911–75) British painter. Born in Middlesex, Hilton studied at the Slade School of Fine Arts, London (1929–31) and subsequently in Paris with Roger Bissière (1931–39). After the war he gradually reduced the representational element in his work, which became entirely abstract from about 1950. He produced his most austerely geometrical work in 1953–54 following a visit to the Netherlands to see paintings by Piet Mondrian. From about 1955 onwards, however, he began to adopt a more lyrical and spontaneous style based on simple contrasting colours.

In 1956 Hilton made the first of many visits to the west of Cornwall, where he associated with the ST IVES SCHOOL of painters (he finally settled in the area in 1965). In his subsequent work a figurative element began to reappear, with suggestions of landscapes, atmospheric effects, and the human figure emerging from the essentially abstract compositions. Owing to his distinctive treatment of pictorial space, his forms often appear to be advancing out of the canvas towards the viewer. His best-known picture is probably the exuberant running nude *Oi yoi yoi* (1963, Tate Gallery, London).

Hitchens, Ivon (1893–1979) British painter, mainly of landscapes and flowers but also of nudes and decorative schemes. The son of a painter, he studied in London at St John's Wood Art School (1911–12) and the Royal Academy School (intermittently between 1912 and 1919). In 1920 he was a founder member of the Seven and Five Society (so-called because it originally included seven painters and five sculptors), the leading British association of progressive artists until its demise in 1935. In 1940 his London home was bombed and he moved to Lavington Common in Sussex, which remained his home for the rest of his life; many of his landscapes were inspired by the Sussex downs. From the 1950s onwards he produced several murals for public buildings, for example at Sussex University (1963).

In the 1930s Hitchens experimented with pure abstraction but by the time of his move to Sussex he had matured a highly distinctive style in which forms are extremely broadly and lushly painted and yet distinctly evoke the subjects that inspired them, most typically landscapes. Often these were painted on canvases that are very much broader than they are high. Apart from the fact that his colours became brighter and less naturalistic, Hitchens's style changed little in the last four decades of his life; despite this he maintained a remarkable freshness of vision and never became stereotyped. His reputation has grown considerably since his death.

Hjelmslev, Louis Trolle (1899–1965) Danish pioneer of structural linguistics. Hjelmslev studied at the University of Copenhagen, where he later (1937) became professor of comparative linguistics and the acknowledged leader of the so-called 'Copenhagen School' of linguistic thought. With his collaborators (notably Hans Jørgen Uldall) Hjelmslev developed the system of linguistic analysis known as 'glossematics', a glosseme being the smallest meaningful unit in a language. Like Saussure, he ascribed supreme importance to the formal patterns within a language system and held that they must be examined independently of semantic or phonetic content. Believing that language is a self-sufficient structure, he maintained that linguistic theory is not verifiable, but can only be assessed in terms of its consistency and thoroughness. His books include *Prolegomena to a Fundamental Theory of Language* (1943). Glossematics had an important influence on the development of European STRUCTURALISM.

Hjørth, Bror (1894–1968) Swedish sculptor, painter, and draughtsman, born in Marma. In the 1920s he lived in Paris, where he studied sculpture with Emile-Antoine Bourdelle (1921–24) and showed an interest in many aspects of modernism (cubism and the paintings of Chagall, for example). However, his roots remained in Swedish folk art and after his return to Sweden in 1930 his work became more traditional and naturalistic. He often depicted rustic subjects and his art has an earthy, at times almost primitive, vigour. As well as sculptures and paintings, he made polychrome wooden reliefs that combine elements of both; he was also an outstanding draughtsman. An influential teacher, Hjørth ran his own school of sculpture in Stockholm (1931–34) and was professor of drawing at the Stockholm College of Art (1949–59). He died in Uppsala; his studio there is now a museum dedicated to his work.

Hochhuth, Rolf (1931–) Swiss playwright, writing in German, who established his reputation with a series of controversial plays based on recent European history. *The Representative* (1963), a verse tragedy written in the style of Schiller, caused a considerable stir with its exploration of the Roman Catholic Church's passive role during the Holocaust in World War II. His second play, *Soldiers* (1967), created another furore with its allegation that Winston Churchill had been implicated in the death of the Polish leader Sikorski and its comments upon Churchill's role in the decision to firebomb Dresden. Hochhuth's mentor, the director Erwin PISCATOR, died in 1966 and his subsequent plays attracted less attention; they include *Guerillas* (1970), *Lysistrata and NATO* (1973), *Judith* (1984), and *Immaculate Conception* (1989), about surrogate motherhood. In 1992 Hochhuth caused fresh controversy with his play *Wessis in Weimar*, which accuses Western economic interests of exploiting the former East Germany following reunification. The play drew sharp criticism from Chancellor Helmut Kohl amongst others. Hochhuth's novels include *A German Love Story* (1980).

Hochwälder, Fritz (1911–) Austrian playwright, living in Switzerland and holding Israeli citizenship; he is noted for his dramas examining difficult moral issues, especially those concerning justice and personal responsibility. Born and educated in Vienna, he fled to Switzerland following the Anschluss and was interned in a labour camp for refugees. In 1940 he became the first dramatist to address the Nazi persecution of the Jews with his play *Esther*, which drew parallels between the biblical story of Esther and contemporary events in Europe. He employed similar historical parallels to explore the political issues facing post-war Austria in *The Public Prosecutor* (1947) and *The Command* (1968), both of which were set against the background of the French Revolution, while in *The Strong are Lonely* (1947) he used the experiences of the Jesuits in South America in the 18th century to discuss tensions between religion and politics in modern society. Several of his works have taken the form of modern mystery and morality plays and show the influence of the 19th-century playwright Franz Grillparzer; among the best known of these are *Donadieu* (1953), *Thursday* (1959), and *The Innocent Man* (1958). In *The Raspberry Picker* (1965), often considered his best play, Hochwälder mounts a direct attack on the older generation of Austrians for their ambivalent, even nostalgic, attitudes to the Nazi past. His more recent plays include *The Princess of Chimay* (1981).

Hockney, David (1937–) British painter, draughtsman, photographer, and designer. Born in Bradford, Hockney studied at the Bradford School of Art (1953–57) and then at the Royal College of Art in London (1959–62). He won several college prizes (including the Guinness Award for Etching) and began to attract national attention while still a student. In 1961 he won the junior section of the John Moores

Liverpool Exhibition. During the 1960s he taught at the Maidstone College of Art and at several US universities. Since the 1970s he has divided his time between California, New York, London, and Paris.

Hockney's first important works were the 16 etchings of *A Rake's Progress*. They were inspired by a visit to New York in 1961 and exhibited in 1963 – the year of Hockney's first one-man show. In the 1960s Hockney became associated with the British POP ART movement. Although many of his works from this period, such as his paintings of life in California, were notable for their cool quality and wit, they showed none of the fascination with popular commercial illustration found in the works of other Pop artists (such as Richard HAMILTON). In the 1970s Hockney became interested in realistic portraiture and painted a series of portraits of friends (for example, *Mr and Mrs Clark and Percy*, 1971, Tate Gallery, London). Throughout his career he has been fascinated by phenomena that are difficult to represent pictorially, such as water and reflecting glass. From the late 1970s onwards he experimented with new media. For example, in 1978 he began to work with liquid paper pulp and in the early 1980s he made collages ('joiners') from photographs. He has also experimented with colour photocopying and fax machines. Hockney is well known for his designs for plays and operas; his sets include those for Stravinsky's *The Rake's Progress* (1975), Mozart's *The Magic Flute* (1978), and Strauss's *Die Frau ohne Schatten* (1992).

Hoddinott, Alun (1929–) Welsh composer. Hoddinott studied at University College, Cardiff, and with Arthur Benjamin in London. After holding several teaching posts in Wales he became professor of music at University College, Cardiff, in 1967. He has been highly active in Welsh musical and artistic life, serving on the Welsh Arts Council, the council of the Welsh National Opera, and founding (1967) the Cardiff Festival of 20th-century music, which he directed until 1989.

His work is freely chromatic, drawing inspiration from Bartók and Hindemith amongst others. Amongst Hoddinott's best-known works are the orchestral pieces *the sun the great luminary of the universe* (1970), *Landscapes* (1975), and *Star Children*, a highly successful piece commissioned for the 1989 Proms. Recent works include *Noctis Equi* (1989), a 'poem for cello and orchestra' written for Mstislav Rostropovich, the song cycle for tenor and orchestra *Songs of Exile* (1989), and the cantata *Emynau Pantycelyn* (1990). One of the most prolific composers of his generation, Hoddinott has also written five operas, seven symphonies, concertos, chamber music, and songs.

Hodgkin, Sir Alan (Lloyd) (1914–) British physiologist. Hodgkin graduated from Cambridge University and became a fellow in 1936. He spent World War II working on radar for the Air Ministry. He then worked at the physiological laboratory at Cambridge, where he was appointed Foulerton Research Professor (1952–69) and professor of biophysics (1970–81). He was master of Trinity College, Cambridge from 1978 to 1984.

In 1951, with Andrew Huxley and Bernard Katz, he worked out the sodium theory to explain the difference in action and resting potentials in nerve fibres. Using the single nerve fibre (giant axon) of a squid, they were able to demonstrate that there is an exchange of sodium and potassium ions between the cell and its surroundings during a nervous impulse, which enables the nerve fibre to carry a further impulse. Hodgkin also showed that the nerve fibre's potential for electrical conduction was greater during the actual passage of an impulse than when the fibre is resting. For their work on the 'sodium pump' mechanism and the chemical basis of nerve transmission Hodgkin, Huxley, and John Eccles shared the Nobel Prize for physiology or medicine in 1963. He is the author of *Conduction of the Nervous Impulse* (1964).

Hodgkin, Dorothy Crowfoot (1910–) British chemist. Dorothy Crowfoot, as she was born, was educated at Somerville College, Oxford. After a brief period as a postgraduate student at Cambridge University, she returned to Oxford in 1934 and has spent her entire academic career there. She was Wolfson Research Professor of the Royal Society (1960–77).

At Cambridge Hodgkin worked for the physicist J. D. Bernal, who was keen to use the technique of x-ray diffraction analysis (introduced by Max von Laue in 1912) to investigate important complex organic molecules. Despite the demands of three young children and a busy political life, it was Hodgkin's persistence and talent that produced some of the first great successes of x-ray analysis. Her first major result came in 1949 when, with Charles Bunn, she published the three-dimensional structure of penicillin. This was followed by the structure of vitamin B_{12} (by 1956) and, in 1969, that of insulin. For her work on vitamin B_{12} she was awarded the Nobel Prize for chemistry in 1964.

Hodgkin, Howard (1932–) British painter. Hodgkin was born in London and studied at the Camberwell School of Art (1949–50) and at the Bath Academy of Art, Corsham (1950–54), where he subsequently taught. Since giving his first one-man show in 1962 he has held numerous exhibitions in Britain and abroad. He represented Britain at the 1984 Venice Biennale and was awarded the Tate Gallery's TURNER PRIZE the following year.

For over 30 years Hodgkin has produced a highly personal kind of semi-abstract painting based on his memories of particular times and places. During the process of composition Hodgkin seeks equivalents in form and colour for the sensual and emotional reality of the experience he is trying to evoke. Although the original circumstances are rarely apparent from the finished work, Hodgkin insists that he is not an abstract painter. Many of his paintings were inspired by social occasions (*Dinner at West Hill*, 1966) or suggested by exotic landscapes (*In Tangier*, 1987–90). His interest in domestic interiors has led to frequent comparisons with the French *intimistes* Bonnard and Vuillard. His paintings, which are usually executed in oils on wood or canvas, are particularly admired for their luscious colours. Despite their appearance of spontaneity, his works are the product of much deliberation and are often elaborated over long periods of time with much overpainting. In some of his more recent works, such as *Rain* (1985–91, Tate Gallery, London), he has attempted to work on a much larger scale than hitherto. He has also produced numerous prints in various media.

Hodrová, Daniela (1946–) Czech novelist and literary critic. After reading French, Russian, and comparative literature at Prague, she worked as a publisher's editor and subsequently in the Literature Institute of the Academy of Sciences. The main theme of her work of literary theory *Seeking the Novel* (1989) is the novel as labyrinth and the novel as a description of initiation; she appears to have applied these ideas to her own writing in the two parts of her fictional trilogy that have so far appeared. They constitute some of the most original writing in Czech since the war. The first part, *In Both Kinds* (1991), presents a world in which the living and the dead share the same space. Characters from early 19th-century Prague act and speak simultaneously with characters from the 1970s. Irony, wit, purity of style, melancholy, and an almost mystical spirituality come together to evoke the mysterious atmosphere of Prague, satirically to analyse the 'Czech character', and to express the sense of suffocation produced by the Soviet occupation. The second part (the Czech title is polysemic), *Masks/Pupae (Tableaux Vivants/Vivid Pictures)* is even more complex and the influence of esoteric thought explicit. The fate of the Czech Jews during World War II plays a major role, as does the Prague Uprising against the Germans. Prague is here a labyrinth through which the main character, Sofie (Wisdom) Syslová (Earthboundness), moves in her initiation into sexuality and spiritual knowledge. Irony, a tendency to the absurd, compassionate ridicule, and precision of emotional analysis make this a profound and funny book.

Hoel, Sigurd (1890–1960) Norwegian writer. As novelist, essayist, and critic, Hoel was one of the most influential literary figures in Norway in the years before and after World War II. He made his debut with a collection of short stories *The Road We Walk* (1922), written while he was the editor of a communist student paper *Towards Daybreak*. His breakthrough came in 1927 with the controversial novel *Sinners in Summertime*, about a group of young intellectuals who mistakenly believe themselves to be free of prejudice and repression. The novel was filmed in 1932. Other major pre-war novels include *One Day in October* (1931) and *The Way to the World's End* (1933).

Many of Hoel's later works deal with the inability to love and its consequences. Often his protagonist is a middle-aged man looking back on his life. In *Meeting at the Milestone* (1947) the 'blameless one', a former Resistance worker, is faced with the ghosts of his past and the realization that his betrayal of his lover led to his own son becoming a Nazi. Hoel's last novel *The Magic Circle* (1958), seen by many as his finest work, deals with similar themes of betrayal and guilt.

From 1929 onwards Hoel edited the 'Yellow Series' of foreign novels in Norwegian translation, introducing many major overseas writers to the public for the first time. He was active all his life in political and cultural debate, often in close alliance with his fellow authors and radicals Arnulf Øverland (1889–1968) and Helge Krog (1889–1962).

Hoffmann, Reinhild (1943–) German dancer and choreographer, whose work with the Bremen Ballet has made her one of the most prominent figures in modern German dance. Born in Sorau, Hoffmann trained at the Essen Folkwang School and later danced with the Folkwang Dance Studio and the Bremen Ballet.

Hoffmann was appointed joint choreographer of the Bremen Ballet in 1978 and created such works as *Solo with Sofa* (1977), featuring the music of John Cage, *Five Days, Five Nights* (1979), and *Unkrautgarten* (1980) for the company. She gave up the post in 1986 in order to transfer to the company at Bochum.

Hoflehner, Rudolf (1916–) Austrian sculptor, painter, and printmaker. Hoflehner studied mechanical engineering at the state technical college in his home city of Linz (1932–36) and architecture at the technical college in Graz (1936–38). He subsequently studied at the Vienna Academy of Arts (1938–40). After World War II he taught at the School of Arts and Crafts in Linz (1945–51) and at the Academy of Fine Art in Stuttgart (1962–81).

Hoflehner's earliest works were abstract sculptures made from large blocks of iron and steel. At this stage he was especially influenced by the work of Fritz WOTRUBA, in whose studio he worked from 1951 to 1954. In 1954 he visited Greece for six months and subsequent works show the influence of ancient Greek figure sculpture. He began to construct semi-abstract upright figures from steel components and, from 1963 onwards, reclining figures. Hoflehner gave his first one-man show in Vienna in 1963 and over the next few years his work was shown in several German cities and in New York. In 1967 he turned to painting and began to produce pictures of fantastic part-animal part-human creatures.

Holford, William (1907–75) British architect and town planner. Born in South Africa, Holford trained at Liverpool under Sir Charles Reilly. He began a long teaching career at Liverpool in 1933 and in 1947 became professor of town planning at University College, London. During World War II he was one of the main authors of the new planning legislation and administrative systems that have dominated the British architectural scene ever since. He also planned the vast Team Valley industrial estate near Newcastle upon Tyne, the first major scheme of its type and the model for dozens of others. At this time he was also involved in Ralph Abercrombie's Greater London Plan (1944). In the post-war period, Holford produced town plans for the City of London (1947), Pretoria (1949), and Corby (1951) and substantially revised the plan for Canberra (1957). Only in the late 1950s did he begin to undertake as much architectural as town-planning work, with work for Eton College and colleges at Oxford and Cambridge, bridges in Canberra, and several commercial buildings in Britain. However, it is for his influence on a generation of town planners that he will be remembered. Holford's style of comprehensive redevelopment – as seen in his plan for Paternoster Square in the City of London, or his unexecuted 1961 scheme to surround Piccadilly Circus with high-rise blocks – has become deeply unpopular and is hard to evaluate clearly at present. The Paternoster Square development itself is due shortly to be demolished.

Holland, Agnieszka (1948–) Polish film director, born in Warsaw. Her films include *Provincial Actors* (1979), about the problems of achieving a successful career in a socialist state, and *Fever* (1980), about the rising tide of opposition towards tsarist Russia that preceded the 1906 Polish Revolution; the latter film was clearly meant to reflect the growing resistance to Soviet influence in Poland at the time it was made. More recent films have included *Woman on Her Own* (1981), *Angry Harvest* (*Bitter Ernte*; 1985), and the US-French coproduction *To Kill a Priest* (1988), a story loosely based on the events leading up to the murder of the dissident priest Father Jerzy Popieluszko. The ambitious *Europa, Europa* (1991), about a Jewish boy who spends the war years masquerading as a Hitler Youth, and *Olivier, Olivier* (1993), about the effect on a family of a son's return six years after his disappearance, were also based on true stories.

Holland Festival A month-long festival held in cities throughout Holland each June. Originally set up in 1947 to provide a cultural focus for the Netherlands after World War II, it has staged the premieres of many operas and other works by contemporary Dutch composers; the outlook is, however, fully international. The programme include contemporary and classical music, drama, and experimental theatre productions.

Hollein, Hans (1934–) Austrian architect. After training at the Vienna Academy of Fine Arts, Hollein studied at the Illinois Institute of Technology and spent some years working for the US architects Mies van der Rohe, Frank Lloyd Wright, and Richard Neutra. He established a practice in Vienna in 1964. His first commissioned work, the tiny Retti candle shop (1965), is notable for its sculptural abstract form; Hollein designed two more shops in Vienna, for the jeweller Schullin (1975, 1982). Hollein has specialized in buildings that are consciously on public display, such as shops, exhibitions, and museums. His Austrian tourist office in Vienna (1978) is reminiscent of both John Nash and Otto Wagner with its vaulted ceiling and palm trees. His most important work has been the Municipal Museum at Abteiberg, Mönchengladbach, Germany (completed in 1982), which is informal in plan but also consciously grand, as an appropriate setting for fine objects.

Höllerer, Walter (1922–) German writer, critic, and literary organizer. After serving as a soldier in World War II Höllerer studied literature, obtaining degrees in 1949 and 1958. In 1958 he became professor of literature at the Technical University in Berlin.

Höllerer was mainly responsible for turning the formerly isolated West Berlin into one of the literary centres of Germany in the 1960s. From 1954 to 1967 he was joint editor of the important literary journal *Akzente* and in 1961 he founded his own periodical *Language in the Technical Age* to pursue his interest in the theory of literature and language. In 1963 Höllerer founded the Berlin Literary Colloquium, which organized regular discussions between writers and critics as well as issuing a series of publications. In 1972 he organized a major semiological exhibition in Berlin with the title *A World Made of Language*.

Höllerer's early poems (*The Other Guest*; 1952) are somewhat conventional and often recall the southern European landscapes he encountered as a soldier; he later moved towards an experimental style and a preoccupation with problems of political power and human communication (*Systems*; 1969). His only novel *The Elephant Clock* (1973) combines a satirical account of German intellectual life in the early 1970s with a semiological essay reflecting upon the problems of meaningful communication.

Holthusen, Hans Egon (1913–) German critic and poet. Holthusen obtained his doctorate in 1937 with a study of Rilke's *Sonnets to Orpheus*. He served in the army in World War II. After the war he began to publish poems and essays and taught literature in several institutions.

Holthusen first became known for poems dealing with the experience of the war in a style influenced by Rilke (*Lamenting the Brother*; 1947). Today he is known primarily for his literary essays. In his most celebrated volume, *The Homeless Man* (1951), the title of which became something of a catchphrase, Holthusen explored the way man is depicted as an alienated and godless creature in much modern literature, and declared his own opposition to this nihilism. In further books, *Yes and No* (1954) and *The Beautiful and the True* (1958), Holthusen continued this critique in a series of brilliantly written essays. In *The Avant-Garde and the Future of Modern Art* (1964) he declared the literary avant-garde dead and called for a more positive literature concerned with the actual problems of men. One of the most important conservative literary critics in Germany, Holthusen has also written biographies of the poets Rilke (1958), Eduard Mörike (1971), and Gottfried Benn (1983).

Holub, Miroslav (1923–) Czech poet, essayist, and immunologist. After medical studies in Prague and a year as a houseman in a pathology unit, he began work at the Biology Institute of the Academy of Sciences in 1954. As a blacklisted writer he was obliged to leave this post in 1971 but continued to work as an immunologist (he is the author of over 130 scientific papers). Although he recanted publicly in 1973, he was unable to publish any new book of verse until 1982. Holub is an intellectual poet, a writer of rationalist lyric verse in which he fuses the natural sciences with ancient and modern literary culture. In his early collections, such as *Achilles and the Tortoise* (1960), his rationalism involved a belief in progress and an apparently wholehearted support for socialism. Even here, however, he deals with such universal themes as human vanity, mortality, and the distortion of history, although his idealization of work is tainted by the socialist work-cult. The precise, almost brusque, imagery of this collection is refined in *Where Blood Flows* (1963), a cycle inspired by work in the operating theatre and experiments on animals. Here Holub adopts a form of EXISTENTIALISM; in these poems blood signifies pain, which constitutes the essence of human being. In *Although* (1969) his style is more complex, but pain remains a strong motif; the collection also contains lyrical impressions of the events of 1968 and tries to define the role of poetry in the contemporary political crisis. The title of the highly literary, philosophical, sometimes wryly humorous collection *On the Contrary* (1982) indicates the poet's main concerns – the ambiguity of existence and the fallibility of perception and knowledge. In *Vanishing Lung Syndrome* (1990) philosophy is replaced by anecdotal whimsy except in the political poems, which manifest something like anger at the authorities' reactions to the student demonstrations of January 1989, at the dictatorship of 'normality' in modern European civilization, and at socialism, which has become a destructive parasite. The essays in *The Jingle Principle* (1987) constitute an elegant commentary on everyday life. The main subjects are modern man's lack of decency and the nature of communication, especially verbal. Holub reveals himself as a master of Czech prose with his sophisticated, perspicuous, crisply simple style.

Horkheimer, Max (1895–1973) German philosopher and social theorist of the **Frankfurt School**. A student at the University of Frankfurt, Horkheimer obtained his final degree (1925) with a study of Kant. In 1930 he was appointed to the chair of philosophy in Frankfurt, becoming at the same time director of the Institute for Social Research, which he had helped to found in 1923. When the Nazis closed the Institute in 1933, Horkheimer moved it firstly to Geneva and subsequently to New York and California (1940). In 1949 he returned to Frankfurt to direct the newly reopened Institute.

Horkheimer's important essay *Traditional and Critical Theory* (1937) accuses traditional philosophy of neglecting social and material realities in its search for timeless truths. Horkheimer advocated a new kind of 'critical theory' that would combine detailed research into existing living conditions and the causes of oppression with a philosophical commitment to the struggle for freedom and justice. In 1947 Horkheimer and ADORNO published perhaps their most important work, *The Dialectics of Enlightenment*. Here the critique of capitalism has broadened into an assault on the whole intellectual tradition of the Enlightenment; in particular, technological progress is seen as an agent of social control rather than a means of emancipation. Horkheimer's *Eclipse of Reason* (1947) gives a rather pessimistic account of the weakness of reason in an age dominated by battling ideologies and an unexamined faith in technical progress. After his return to Germany, Horkheimer turned increasingly towards a Schopenhauerian pessimism while remaining highly critical of the society he lived in.

Hounsfield, Sir Godfrey Newbold (1919–) British engineer. Hounsfield was educated at the City and Guilds College, London, and the Faraday House College of Electrical Engineering, London. He worked for Electrical and Musical Industries (EMI) from 1951 and led the design effort for Britain's first large solid-state computer (EMIDEC 1100). Later he worked on problems of pattern recognition. He is now consultant to the medical research division of EMI (where he was formerly chief scientist). Although he had no formal university education he was granted an honorary doctorate in medicine by the City University, London (1975).

Hounsfield was awarded the 1979 Nobel Prize for physiology or medicine, together with the South-African-born physicist Allan Cormack, for his pioneering work on the application of computer techniques to x-ray examination of the human body. Working at the Central Research Laboratories of EMI he developed the first commercially successful machines to use computer-assisted tomography, also known as computerized axial tomography (CAT). In CAT, a high-resolution x-ray picture of an imaginary slice through the body (or head) is built up from information taken from detectors rotating around the patient. Introduced in 1973, early machines were used to overcome obstacles in the diagnosis of diseases of the brain, but the technique has now been extended to the whole body. Although Cormack worked on essentially the same technique, the two men did not collaborate, or even meet. Hounsfield has also explored the use of nuclear magnetic resonance (NMR) as a diagnostic imaging technique.

Howell, Killick, Partridge, and Amis (HKPA) British architectural practice founded in 1959 by **William G. Howell** (1922–74), **John A. Killick** (1924–72), and **John A. Partridge** (1924–) and joined in 1961 by **Stanley F. Amis** (1924–). They had all previously worked for the London County Council's architecture department, most notably on Alton West, a pioneering estate in the Corbusian manner (*see* LE CORBUSIER) and a testing ground for HKPA's ideas in lightweight concrete cladding. Additionally, Howell and Amis (with Gillian Howell) had in 1953–55 built a terrace in Hampstead that combined a double-height living space with a traditional London streetscape.

An early success for the practice was the faculty of commerce and social science at Birmingham University (1960–64), a concrete-clad rotunda with a sinuous terrace featuring brick cross-walls. The combination of traditional materials with strong concrete lintels and verticals became a feature of their best university work, as in their extensions to three Cambridge colleges, Sidney Sussex (1964–69), Darwin (1964–70), and (especially) Downing (1965–70), and to St Anne's College, Oxford (1965–69). St Anne's also shows their continuing preoccupation with projecting precast fenestration panels, used again at St Anthony's College, Oxford (1970–72). These dynamic shapes and hard materials compare with the more delicate construction of their private houses, such as the Cedar House, Keston (1958–60), and their brick public housing, as at Stonegrove (1964–68) and Lewisham (1973–78).

Howell, Killick, Partridge, and Amis have also built some exciting theatres, most famously the Young Vic Theatre, London (1968–71), and also the Arts Centre, Christ's Hospital School (1970–74). These also show HKPA's predilection for interiors expressive of their construction. Two large projects of the 1970s were the Medway Courthouse (1972–79) and a naval base at Devonport (1971–80); these led to a still-larger commission for new courts of justice in Trinidad (1978–85), and to a number of prison projects in Britain.

Hoyland, John (1934–) British painter. A native of Sheffield, Hoyland studied at Sheffield College of Art (1951–56) and at the Royal Academy Schools in London (1956–60). For many years he taught art: in London at Hornsey College of Art (1960–62), at the Croydon School of Art (1962–63), and at the Chelsea School of Art (1962–70); in New York at Colgate University (1972–74); then back in London at St Martin's School of Art (1974–77) and the Slade School of Fine Art (1974–77, 1980, 1983).

During his training Hoyland moved from painting still lifes and landscapes into abstraction. From 1957 onwards his work shows the influence of the colour-field paintings of the American Mark Rothko and the British painter William TURNBULL. In 1964 he visited New York, where he met the important colour-field painters Morris Louis and Jules Olitski. From 1963 onwards he worked by staining large canvases, which he then overpainted, seeking to achieve a unity of canvas and paint. He also produced works featuring large juxtaposed bands of colour (for example, *17.3.69*, 1969, Tate Gallery, London). Thereafter his works gradually became more painterly, often featuring runs of drip paint. Since the late 1970s his paintings have been dominated by diagonals.

Hoyle, Sir Fred (1915–) British astrophysicist. Hoyle studied at Emmanuel College, Cambridge, and worked on the development of naval radar during World

War II. He returned to Cambridge, becoming lecturer in mathematics (1946–58), professor of astronomy (1958–72), and director of the Institute for Theoretical Astronomy (1967–73).

Hoyle proposed the steady-state theory of the universe with Hermann BONDI and Thomas GOLD in 1948. Despite the general acceptance of the rival big-bang theory, he has remained a staunch advocate of modified versions of the steady-state model. In the 1960s Hoyle, with William Fowler and others, had a major success in explaining the processes within stars by which helium is converted into the elements up to and including iron; they also explained how the still heavier elements are created in supernova explosions. In recent years Hoyle has advanced a number of highly controversial theories, including ideas about the nature of quasars, the existence of bacteria in space, and the arrival of diseases from space. None of these has received general acceptance. He has written numerous popular works on science and, more recently, science fiction. His autobiography, *The Small World of Fred Hoyle*, was published in 1986.

Hrabal, Bohumil (1914–) Czech novelist and short-story writer. After reading law in Prague, he had a variety of jobs ranging from commercial traveller to platelayer and steelworker. Since 1962 he has devoted himself entirely to writing; he was blacklisted after the Soviet occupation but recanted in 1975 and thereafter was allowed to publish. Although a collection of his stories appeared privately in 1956, his first freely published work was the collection of absurd, scurrilous, somewhat amorphous short stories, *Pearl in the Deep* (1963). Satire, parody, nostalgia, and a boundless love for humanity are communicated in an earthy conversational style, which often includes occupational slang. Hrabal's tendency to sentimentalize all but disappeared in the more sophisticated *Bletherers* (1964), where the anecdotes have a tighter structure and parody has more clearly become part of a quasisurrealist method. *Dancing Classes for Elderly and Advanced Pupils* (1964) is the rambling monologue of an old man who is speaking, mainly about sex, to a girl under a cherry tree; it is both high comedy on the human condition and an elegantly vulgarized account of Czech national mythology. Subsequent publications, such as *Closely Observed Trains* (1965) or *Cropping* (1976), were far more conventional, until the appearance of *I Waited on the King of England* (1977), his masterpiece. Previously the characters in his works were one-dimensional, but here the hero, a diminutive waiter who longs to be a millionaire, is a flesh-and-blood character with his own perverted psychology – by which, however, the reader forgets to be repelled because of the profundity of Hrabal's humour. The author has interpreted his hero as representing 'the Czechs' indomitable capacity to adapt to any regime'. *Too Loud a Solitude* (1980; written 1976) is a history of Stalinist cultural oppression embodied in a wastepaper pulper who reads all the banned books he has to compress in his machine and so becomes the owner of all knowledge, almost God, in a society of cultural penury.

Huber, Klaus (1924–) Swiss composer. He studied violin and composition in Zürich and Berlin and went on to teach violin at the Zürich conservatory, music history at Lucerne, and composition in Freiburg, where he directed the Institute for New Music. As a teacher he has been a champion of younger composers; his pupils have included Brian Ferneyhough, Michael Jarrell, Younghi Pagh-Paan, and Wolfgang RIHM.

Huber's music uses a wide and often esoteric range of styles, including medieval music and post-Webern serial techniques; material from older compositions (Lutheran chorales, Hindemith, Bartok, Bach, and Machaut) is sometimes incorporated. His literary inspiration likewise spans both old and new. *Seht den Boden, Blutgetrankt* (1983) is a setting of Chilean revolutionary songs, while other works draw on the German Renaissance mystics and the poetry of Günter GRASS. Since the 1960s Huber has received international recognition for his scores, which include large-scale vocal and orchestral works (*Erniedrigt*; 1983) and one opera, *Jot* (1973).

Huchel, Peter (1903–81) German poet. After studying literature and philosophy Huchel moved to France, where he lived as a farm labourer and began to contribute to literary journals. After World War II he worked in radio in the Soviet Zone of occupied Germany and became editor-in-chief of the important literary journal *Sinn* *und Form*. In 1972 he left the German Democratic Republic for the West after a decade of restrictions on his ability to publish.

In his poems Huchel evokes the natural world as a magical realm of both joy and fear. Familiar objects are rendered mysterious and wonderful. While his earlier work is mostly traditional in style, the poems in *Highroads* (*Chausseen, Chausseen*; 1963) and *Counted Days* (1972) adopt a more original and contemporary idiom. As the editor of *Sinn und Form* Huchel had an enormous influence on the literary and intellectual climate in the German Democratic Republic. He also counts amongst the most important nature poets in modern German literature.

Huddersfield Contemporary Music Festival An annual festival of new music founded in 1978 by Richard Steinitz, a music lecturer at Huddersfield Polytechnic. Held in November, it features works by a wide range of international composers.

Hughes, Ted (1930–) British poet. Hughes was born in Yorkshire and educated at Pembroke College, Oxford, where he met the US poet Sylvia Plath, whom he married in 1956; she committed suicide seven years later. He became poet laureate in 1984.

Hughes's poetry is largely preoccupied with the beauty and terror of the natural world. In the late 1950s the violent physicality of his work set him apart from most of his British contemporaries, in particular those associated with the MOVEMENT. His early collections, which contain some of his best-known animal poems, include *The Hawk in the Rain* (1957), *Lupercal* (1960) and *Wodwo* (1967). Hughes's interest in mythology came to the fore in *Crow* (1970; illustrated by the US artist Leonard Baskin), a sequence that draws on the creation myths of a number of primitive cultures. The sequence is probably Hughes's most savage work, the title character representing (in the poet's own words) 'the horror of creation'. Later volumes include *Season Songs* (1976), *Cave Birds* (1978), *Moortown* (1979), and *Flowers and Insects* (1987). Several of his volumes have been published with accompanying nature photographs: *Remains of Elmet* (1979), a sequence of poems about the Calder Valley, is illustrated by the work of Fay Godwin while *River* (1983) features the photographs of Peter Keen. In recent years Hughes has become increasingly associated with environmental issues. He has also written many books for children.

Huillet, Daniele *See* STRAUB, JEAN-MARIE.

Hundertwasser, Fritz (Friedrich Stowasser; 1928–) Austrian abstract painter. Born in Vienna, Hundertwasser showed talent as a draughtsman and painter at a young age. He attended the Vienna Academy of Art for three months in 1948 but was largely self-taught. His idiosyncratic work shows the influence of Austrian baroque art and Art Nouveau, the works of Gustav Klimt and Egon Schiele, and Persian and Indian miniature paintings.

During a visit to Paris in 1949 Hundertwasser came into contact with ART INFORMEL and subsequent works show him developing a personal style of expressive abstraction. From about 1953 onwards his work is dominated by spiral shapes, a motif to which he attached an esoteric symbolic significance. Hundertwasser liked to claim that the artistic urge was essentially religious and that his works – full of rich colours and silver and gold – could transport the observer to a paradisiacal world of peace and happiness. A somewhat grandiose figure with a gift for self-publicity, he exhibited widely in the 1960s and travelled extensively in Europe, the US, and the East. In the 1970s and 1980s he was in great demand as a poster artist, producing work for the Munich Olympics of 1972 and an antinuclear campaign in the United States in 1980.

I

Illyés, Gyula (1902–83) Hungarian poet, dramatist, and essayist. Born into a poor peasant family in Western Hungary, Illyés became active in the Hungarian labour movement at an early age. He enrolled at the University of Budapest but left the Hungarian capital in 1922 to visit Vienna, Berlin, and Paris. In Paris he spent several years attending lectures on literature and psychology at the Sorbonne and familiarizing himself with the literary avant-garde, which exercised considerable influence on his early poetry. After his return to Hungary in 1926, Illyés grew increasingly interested in the plight of the Hungarian peasantry and in the 1930s became a leading figure in the Hungarian 'populist' movement. The populists drew their literary inspiration from the traditional values of the Hungarian peasantry and strove to improve the social conditions of that class. Illyés's *People of the Puszta* (1936), a semi-autobiographical depiction of life on the great Hungarian plain, is one of the most celebrated works of inter-war Hungarian populism. It fuses autobiography, social criticism, and cultural anthropology into a passionate and richly lyrical work of literary art. In the post-war Stalinist period, Illyés withdrew from public life. In 1956 he published perhaps his most celebrated poetic work, *One Sentence on Tyranny* (written in 1950), a powerful indictment of totalitarianism, over fifty stanzas in length. In the 1960s and 1970s Illyés was once again a key figure in Hungarian literary and intellectual life. His essays on the situation of the Hungarian minorities living in neighbouring countries and on national character in general were particularly influential.

Independent Group An informal discussion group of painters, architects, photographers, and critics that met in London in the 1950s. It was founded in 1952 and met during the winter of 1952–53 to discuss themes for public lectures at the Institute of Contemporary Arts (ICA) in London. Originally convened by the architectural writer Reyner Banham, the group was reconvened in 1954 by John McHale and the critic Lawrence Alloway, with Alloway as the moving spirit.

The group's members, including the artists Eduardo PAOLOZZI and Richard HAMILTON, were fascinated by the mass media and US popular culture – especially cinema, advertising, and popular music. Their discussions gave impetus to the emergence of British POP ART, a term that was invented by Alloway. The group organized the notable 'This is Tomorrow' exhibition at the Whitechapel Art Gallery in London in 1956; works shown included Richard Hamilton's celebrated collage painting *Just What is it that Makes Today's Homes so Different, so Appealing?*

Informalism *See* ART INFORMEL.

Institut de Recherche et de Coordination Acoustique/Musique *See* IRCAM.

International Centre of Theatre Research A theatrical organization founded by Peter BROOK and Jean-Louis BARRAULT in 1970 to facilitate contact between different branches of world theatre. With regular visits to Africa, India, and other distant parts of the world, the Centre represents one of Europe's most direct links with other theatrical traditions. Productions staged under the Centre's auspices have included several by Brook himself and works assembled using the techniques of COLLECTIVE CREATION. The Centre moved to its present base in the **Théâtre des Bouffes du Nord** in Paris in 1974; this is now recognized as one of the most important venues for experimental drama in France. As a matter of policy the Centre invites performers from many different countries to participate in its productions, the most celebrated of which have included Brook's version of the Indian epic *The Mahabharata* (1985).

Internationales Musikinstitute Darmstadt *See* DARMSTADT.

International Federation of Theatre Research A research organization founded in London in 1955 to provide a focus for the study of contemporary theatre in a number of member countries. Established under the auspices of the British Society for Theatre Research, the Federation helps to coordinate the activities of national research organizations and publishes its own journal. It also manages an institute for theatre research in the Casa Goldoni in Venice.

International Flanders Festival An annual music festival founded in 1964; events are staged in Flanders, Limburg, Bruges, Brussels, and other Belgian towns between April and October. The extensive programme includes concerts, recitals, opera, and dance. The emphasis is on Flemish culture and local artists and performers are featured alongside those from other countries.

International Theatre Institute An organization founded under the auspices of UNESCO in Prague in 1948 to promote contact between the world's theatrical traditions. With a base in Paris, the Institute is active in fostering cultural exchanges between national theatres and offers various facilities at its centres in each country.

Ionesco, Eugène (1912–) French playwright, born in Romania, whose first play, *The Bald Prima Donna* (1950), effectively launched the Theatre of the ABSURD, of which Ionesco was to become a leader. The play, which was inspired by the author's reading of English phrase books, was initially greeted with incomprehension. It was later heralded as announcing the arrival of a new form of post-war drama in which everything, from the meaning of existence to the adequacy of language as a means of communication, was open to question.

Other preoccupations included the relationship between the real and the conceptual, as in *The Lesson* (1951), in which a girl is killed by the word 'knife', and *The Chairs* (1952), in which the stage is dominated by the presence of a large number of empty chairs. In *Amédée or How to Get Rid of It* (1954) two lovers are obsessed by the idea that there is a huge dead body in the next room, while in *The New Tenant* (1957) the central character is gradually overwhelmed by his own furniture.

Ionesco's full-length plays are generally less highly regarded than his one-act pieces. However, the antifascist *Rhinoceros* (1960) was a notable exception; it depicts the plight of the hapless Élie Bérenger, whose discovery that all his friends are turning into rhinoceroses forces him to choose between making the same transformation for the sake of conformity or rebellion. Bérenger was introduced in *The Killer* (1959) and reappeared in *Exit the King* (1962) and *A Stroll in the Air* (1963), representing in each play the archetypal bewildered individual in a remorselessly confusing world. More recent works have dwelt on dreams, visions, and other facets of the subconscious; they have included *Thirst and Hunger* (1966), *Killing Game* (1970), *Macbett* (1972), a reworking of Shakespeare's play, *A Hell of a Mess* (1975), and *Journey Among the Dead* (1982).

Ionesco's other writing has included a radio play, short stories, screenplays, a novel, a ballet scenario, and numerous essays and journals in which, among other things, he has revealed his right-wing political views.

Iovine, Francesco *See* JOVINE, FRANCESCO.

Ipoustéguy, Jean (1920–) French artist who has worked in various media but principally as a sculptor. Born at Dun-sur-Meuse, he studied painting in Paris at evening classes. In 1947–49 he carried out frescoes and stained-glass for the church of St Jacques at Montrouge and in 1949 settled at Choisy-le-Roi. In about 1954 he turned to sculpture, giving his first one-man exhibition of sculptures at the Galerie Claude Bernard, Paris, in 1962. Initially he experimented with various materials and worked in an abstract vein, but he found his métier as a figurative sculptor in bronze. Characteristically, his figures have a black or very dark patina with smooth surfaces shattered at various points. There is a strong sense of tradition in his work (sometimes he takes his subjects from history or myth) but his expressionistic handling of his themes is personal and original.

Ipoustéguy is regarded as one of the outstanding figurative sculptors in post-war French art. The awards he has won include the David E. Bright prize at the 1964 Venice Biennale.

IRCAM An electronic music studio, attached to the POMPIDOU CENTRE in Paris, founded in 1969 and opened in 1977. It is primarily associated with its director Pierre BOULEZ and the ENSEMBLE INTERCONTEMPORAIN; others who have worked there include Luciano BERIO. The studio provides, through its four departments, facilities for research and training in composition, electronic and computer techniques, acoustics, and the development of new (electronic) instruments. Following Boulez's resignation from IRCAM in 1992 its future looks uncertain.

Italia Prize *See* PRIX ITALIA FESTIVAL.

Iuren'en, Sergei Sergeevich (1948–) Russian writer living in Munich. Born the son of an army officer stationed in Germany, Iuren'en studied in Minsk and Moscow before working as an editor on the journal *The Friendship of Peoples*. An early story about student life, 'The Bread Winner' (1975), was awarded a prize and after the appearance of a collection of stories, *On the Way Home* (1977), he was admitted to the Writers' Union. In the same year, however, he married a foreigner and took the opportunity of emigrating to France. His novel *The Marksman* (1984) first appeared in French (*Le Franc tireur*; 1980) and won considerable critical praise. Somewhat unbalanced in form and inconsistent in characterization, it concerns an émigré writer who feels drawn back to Russia but then falls into the clutches of an ambiguous KGB agent with whom he travels around the former East Prussia; brutal interrogations are interspersed with frequent and heartless sex scenes and, above all, endless monologues and debates on the nature of the East-West divide and Russian national identity and destiny. More successful was Iuren'en's second novel, *Escape across the Frontier* (1984), again about young people (now in the period of Brezhnevian disillusion) looking for either revolution or escape. *The Son of Empire, an Infantile Novel* (1986) is a nostalgic account of childhood, free from the sexual obsession seen elsewhere and far more coherent than, for instance, *The Marksman*. A recent collection of 15 stories from different years, *Petersburg Express* (1991), provides unglamorous but often hauntingly memorable cameos of many aspects of Soviet and émigré life. Iuren'en is a gifted writer who is still developing in both style and technique.

J

Jacobsen, Arne (1902–71) Danish architect and designer. His buildings are as cool and understated as the Danish landscape and consummately crafted. Graduating in 1927, he began a series of houses at Ordrup that continued with increasing sophistication into the 1950s. He also worked extensively at Bellevue, producing the Bellavista estate in the 1930s and in 1952–56 the Søholm estate; the latter included a staggered terrace of brick houses, one of them for himself. The fusion of old and new materials, monopitched roofs, odd levels, and clerestory lighting found here are all typical of Jacobsen's best housing.

Jacobsen's evolution from the craft tradition of Gunnar Asplund, with whom he corresponded in the 1930s, to the simplicity of Mies can be seen most clearly in his series of town halls. The Århus Town Hall (1937–42, with Eric Møller) was followed by those for Søllerød (1939–42), Glostrup (1954–59), and Rødovre (1954–56), the last consisting of two curtain-walled slabs at right angles masking a top-lit council chamber.

Jacobsen's only war-time work was a herring-smoking plant at Sjællands Odde, an oddly expressionistic building to which he added a circular manager's house in 1956–57. In 1943 he fled to Sweden where he designed textiles and wallpaper; his furniture later won international fame. Owing to his mastery of curtain walling, his post-war commercial projects could be of huge proportions. Yet for the massive SAS hotel and headquarters in Copenhagen (1958–60) he even designed the ashtrays. By contrast, two factories in Aalborg (1957) and Ballerup (Tom's Chocolate Factory; 1961) achieved elegance with factory-made components. He also built many fine schools, most famously at Munkesgårds (1955), where the design comprises a grid of single-storey classrooms with steep roofs and set-back clerestorys that open onto enclosed courtyards.

In the 1960s Jacobsen's international reputation earned him many foreign commissions, several uncompleted at his death. The best was arguably St Catherine's College, Oxford (1960–65), for Nikolaus PEVSNER 'a perfect piece of architecture'.

Jacobsen, Rolf (1907–) Norwegian poet. Jacobsen, who made his literary debut in 1933 with the collection *Earth and Iron*, has been one of the most consistently popular poets in Norway this century.

His first two collections were innovative both stylistically and thematically, the modern industrial world being his main subject. Jacobsen did not publish any further works for 16 years; his third collection *Long Distance Train* appeared in 1951. A sense of the spiritual emptiness of the mechanized world, only hinted at earlier, now becomes overt in his work. In *Secret Life* (1954), considered by many his best collection, machines are seen as destructive and dehumanizing. Not all technology is negative to Jacobsen, however, and a more positive side is shown in *The Summer in the Grass* (1956).

Since 1956 Jacobsen has published seven further collections with similar themes but showing a great variety of style. His collected works were published between 1977 and 1982 and he has been translated into about 20 languages. *Night Open* (1985) was a bestseller in Norway – a rare achievement for a collection of poetry.

Unlike many other Scandinavian authors, Jacobsen has never been a very public figure.

Jahnn, Hans Henry (1894–1959) German novelist and playwright. Born in

Hamburg, Jahnn refused military service in World War I and emigrated to Norway. On his return to Germany he worked as an organ-builder and founded (1920) the spiritual community 'Ugrino' in Hamburg. In the 1930s his work was banned in Germany and he lived as a farmer in Bornholm, Denmark, while writing his magnum opus *River Without Banks*. Always an outsider, he was nevertheless elected the main director of the PEN centre after World War II and enjoyed great esteem among avant-garde writers.

In his novels and plays Jahnn created a demonic world of passionate love, desire, fear, pain, violence, and obsession. His first play *Pastor Ephraim Magnus* (1919), which describes how the three children of a pastor bring mutilation and death on themselves by trying to live like Christ, provoked intense controversy. Later plays included *Medea* (1926) and *Thomas Chatterton* (1935). His best-known work, the trilogy of novels *River Without Banks* (1949–50), describes the close friendship that develops between a composer and a murderer in a wild and beautiful part of Norway. Their attempts to reconcile the destructive and creative forces in man end in failure. Jahnn's passionate and experimental prose shows the influence of Joyce and the metaphysical poetry of the 17th century. Although little known outside his own country, Jahnn is arguably the most original and profound novelist of post-war Germany.

Jakubowska, Wanda (1907–) Polish film director. Born in Warsaw, Jakubowska survived imprisonment in Auschwitz and Ravensbrück concentration camps during World War II. She studied art history at Warsaw University before becoming a documentary filmmaker; in 1948 she made the harshly realistic *The Last Stop* about life in the Nazi camps. Her later films, which had a major impact on the direction of Poland's post-war cinema, included *Soldier of Victory* (1953), *It Happened Yesterday* (1960), *The End of Our World* (1964), *The Hot Line* (1965), and *Ludwik Warynski* (1978).

Janáček Quartet Czech (Moravian) string quartet, formed in Brno in 1947 and making its debut under this name in 1949. The current members are Bohumil Smejkal (first violin), Adolf Sýkora (second violin), Ladislav Kyselak (viola), and Bretislav Vybiral (cello). The original members were Jiří Trávníček (first violin), Miroslav Matyáš (second violin), Jiří Kratochvíl (viola), and Karel Krafta (cello), who were all classmates at the Brno Conservatory. Matyáš was replaced by Adolf Sýkora in 1952 and Trávníček died in 1973; the other members of the original quartet (Kratochvíl and Krafta) have been replaced more recently. Since 1969 the quartet's members have been lecturers in chamber music at the Brno Academy.

The quartet chose its name in homage to the composer Leoš Janáček, who spent most of his working life in Brno, and specifically in response to his first string quartet. They are particularly noted for their performances of music by Janáček and other Czech composers.

Jancsó, Miklós (1921–) Hungarian film director, who emerged as one of Hungary's leading film-makers in the 1960s. Having begun as a director of documentary shorts, Jancsó directed his first full-length feature film, *The Bells Have Gone to Rome*, in 1958. His reputation was established by *Cantata* (1963) and *My Way Home* (1964), the revolutionary fervour of which continues through much of his later work. International recognition came with *The Round-Up* (1965), a detailed account of atrocities perpetrated against the peasant population during the days of the Austro-Hungarian Empire. The film was particularly admired for Jancsó's handling of huge set-pieces. In *The Red and the White* (1967), an epic recreation of the Russian Civil War, the two opposing armies are locked in a futile struggle to dominate a vast empty landscape.

Jancsó drew on memories of his own youth in *The Confrontation* (1968), while in *Agnus Dei* (1971) he portrayed the conflict between religion and revolution. *Red Psalm* (1971) was praised for its sympathetic analysis of the plight of the Hungarian peasantry at the turn of the century. In the 1970s Jancsó also filmed outside Hungary, making *The Pacifist* (1971) in Italy, for example. In *Elektreia* (1975) he adapted Greek myth to further explore the concept of revolution, while in *Private Vices and Public Virtues* (1976) he interpreted the Mayerling scandal as a consequence of youthful rebellion against patriarchal tyranny.

Jancsó's most recent works have been somewhat coolly received, partly owing to changes in the political climate; they have included *Hungarian Rhapsody* (1979).

Janni, Joseph (1916–) British film producer, born in Italy. Janni attended Milan University and Rome's Centro Sperimentale di Cinematografia before moving to Britain in 1939. He entered the cinema two years later and founded his own production company in 1947. His output includes an impressive number of films that have been both critically acclaimed and commercially successful. Several of these were directed by John SCHLESINGER, including the international hit *Sunday Bloody Sunday* (1971), about a designer who divides his sexual life between a homosexual doctor and a woman executive; it won Academy Award nominations for Schlesinger and the stars, Glenda Jackson and Peter Finch. Among other successes have been *A Town Like Alice* (1956), a drama of women prisoners of the Japanese in Malaya, the quintessentially British comedy *The Captain's Table* (1958), the melodramatic *A Kind of Loving* (1962), *Billy Liar* (1963), *Darling* (1965), *Far From the Madding Crowd* (1967), and the coproduced *Yanks* (1979) about the personal lives of GIs stationed in Lancashire during World War II.

Jansson, Tove (Marika) (1914–) Finnish writer and illustrator, writing in Swedish, who became internationally famous as the author of the Moomin books for children.

Born in Helsinki, Jansson studied art in Stockholm, Helsinki, and Paris. She made her debut as a writer with *Little Trolls and the Great Flood* (1945), followed by *Comet in Moominland* (1946). Over the next 25 years she wrote and illustrated a further eight Moomin books including *Finn Family Moomintroll* (1948; *Trollkarlens Hatt*), *The Exploits of Moominpappa* (1950), *Tales from Moominvalley* (1962; *Det Osynliga Barnet*) and *Moominvalley in November* (1971). The Moomin stories have been widely translated and turned into strip cartoons and films. In her characters, Jansson captures the idiosyncracies of the middle-class society in which she grew up.

In the late 1960s Jansson turned to writing for adults. The story of *The Sculptor's Daughter* (1968) has similarities with her own life although it is not an autobiography. *The Listener* (1971) is a collection of short stories showing a preoccupation with the power of the imagination and the potential danger of fantasy worlds. *Sun City* (1974), set in an old people's home, portrays the effects of old age and loneliness on the personality. The title story of the short-story collection *The Dolls House* (1978) similarly depicts an old man trapped in a fantasy world of his own creation.

Tove Jansson has won many prizes, including the 1966 Hans Christian Andersen medal. As well as writing novels and stories, she has published plays and strip cartoons and illustrated numerous books.

Jarman, Derek (1942–) British film director, artist, and writer, whose experimental films have established him as one of the most original and controversial directors in contemporary cinema. Jarman began his career as a designer working under Ken RUSSELL on such films as *The Devils* (1971) and *Savage Messiah* (1972); he made his own first full-length feature, *Sebastiane*, in 1975. Like much of his subsequent work, this film was preoccupied with themes of sexual identity and personal power, presented with wit and striking photography. In *Jubilee* (1977), Elizabeth I tours a futuristic punk-style Britain, while in *The Tempest* (1979) Jarman set Shakespeare's play in a crumbling mansion populated by strange camp figures.

Jarman won the best notices of his career with *Caravaggio* (1986), an account of the turbulent life of the Renaissance painter shot in a chiaroscuro style imitating the paintings themselves. His other films have included *The Last of England* (1987), a bitter analysis of English society, *War Requiem* (1989), a sequence of images inspired by Benjamin BRITTEN's work, *The Garden* (1991), a highly personal statement about Jarman's life filmed in the garden he has created at Dungeness, *Edward II* (1991), an idiosyncratic adaptation of Marlowe's play, and *Wittgenstein* (1993). A recurring theme in all Jarman's films is that of his own homosexuality; in *The Garden* he contemplates his own mortality, having been diagnosed HIV positive. He has published two volumes of memoirs, *Dancing Ledge* (1984) and *Modern Nature* (1991).

Jeanneret, (Arnold André) Pierre (1896–1967) Swiss-born architect whose principal works were in France and India. From 1921 to 1940 Jeanneret was in partnership with his distant cousin, Charles-Edouard Jeanneret, LE CORBUSIER; whilst the latter gained independent fame from his theoretical writings, many of the texts and all the buildings of the 1920s and 1930s were jointly credited. In 1968 *L'Architecture d'Aujourd'hui* wrote that 'Le Corbusier had the genius, Pierre the talent'.

During World War II Jeanneret worked independently on prefabrication in Grenoble and participated in the Resistance; in 1944 he set up his own office in Paris. His many unbuilt projects included a sophisticated antecedent of Le Corbusier's famous Unité d'Habitation in Marseilles, revealing an interest in the practicalities of prefabrication and rationalization greater than his cousin's. A year in New York designing Knoll furniture was followed in 1951 by an invitation to join Le Corbusier in work on the new provincial capital of Chandigarh, India.

India revealed Jeanneret's talent for working with low-cost materials (often brick) and local technology in a difficult climate. He stayed on after Le Corbusier's departure in 1954 to oversee the latter's projects as well as his own and to train local architects. He produced the city plan for Chandigarh, designed hospitals, schools, housing, the state library and town hall, the deputy minister's house and governor's palace, and the University campus, where he taught at the school of architecture. He also produced city plans for Pandoh, Sundernager, Slapper, and Agmedabad, and designed new towns for Beas-Sutlej and Talwara. His most famous work, however, is a simple memorial to Mahatma Gandhi (c. 1960). Jeanneret's own memorial is Chandigarh itself; in 1970 his ashes were scattered in its lake.

Jelinek, Elfriede (1946–) Austrian novelist. Jelinek was brought up in Mürzzuschlag and Vienna, where she studied history of art, music, and drama. Her youth was overshadowed by the insanity of her father, a Jewish scientist who had been forced to work for the Nazis. She was a member of the Austrian avant-garde literary group Forum Stadtpark, out of which developed the influential journal *Manuscripts*.

Jelinek is one of the most radical of Austrian feminist writers and her work is unsparing in its attacks on Austrian provincialism, traditionalism, and conservatism. *The Lovers* (1975) describes the fate of two working-class women in the Austrian provinces, whose lives are totally dominated by male power. The novel is a vigorous assault on the unreformed patriarchal structure of Austrian society. This is also a dominant theme of *The Outcasts* (1980), a novel that exposes the social myths of the 1950s. In *The Pianist* (1983) Jelinek returns to the problem of female repression: years of domination by her mother have turned the novel's main character, the pianist Erika Kohut, into a masochist who is sexually and emotionally exploited by men. Jelinek explores sexual and emotional repression further in *Lust* (1989), her most notorious work. Apparently intended as a satirical attack on pornography, the book has been widely condemned as itself pornographic; it became a bestseller in several European countries largely on the strength of this reputation. In her novels the battle between the sexes is always lost by women, mainly because they have been educated into passivity and masochism. She is renowned for her sharp wit, her distanced point of view, and her ferocious sarcasm. Jelinek has also written plays – including *What Happened after Nora Left her Husband*, a continuation of Ibsen's *A Doll's House* – and film scripts.

Jens, Walter (1923–) German writer, critic, and orator. After completing a degree in classical studies in 1949 Jens began a teaching career in Tübingen. Since 1962 he has been professor of classical studies and rhetoric there.

A popular media personality in Germany, Jens has written plays for radio and television as well as an important column of television criticism. He is a brilliant orator and has spoken on many public occasions, including Protestant church services. In addition to writing several novels, the last of which appeared in 1963, and a number of plays for the theatre (often modern adaptations from ancient Greek drama), he has translated several books of the Bible into contemporary German. A popularizer rather than an original thinker, Jens has drawn his ideas from three main sources; firstly, the classics, which according to Jens could still serve as a common foundation for the intellectual life; secondly, the New Testament, which Jens views as a manual of spiritual resistance to any kind of unjust power; and lastly, such great figures of the German Enlightenment as Lessing, Lichtenberg, and Heine. For Jens, these writers represent the better German tradition of liberal, yet Christian, republicanism as opposed to the militaristic Prussian tradition of Bismarck and Hitler. Collections of Jens's speeches have appeared as *Of German Speech* (1969) and *Republican Speeches* (1976). He has also written a history of the University of Tübingen from 1477 to 1977.

Jersild, Per Christian (1935–) Swedish novelist. Formerly a physician, Jersild became one of Sweden's most popular novelists with his satirical descriptions of bureaucracy. His first novel, *To Warmer Climes*, appeared in 1961 but it was not until 1965 and the publication of *Calvinol's Journey Through the World* that his career took off. The novel places the Rabelaisian Dr Calvinol in various situations throughout history in order to ridicule pompous patriotism and the glorification of war.

The Pighunt (1968) takes the form of a diary kept by an official given the task of eradicating all the pigs on Gotland; the effect is to ridicule his blind acceptance of the system. *The House of Babel* (1978), Jersild's most realistic work, deals with life in a Stockholm hospital. The allegation that patients had become incidental, almost irrelevant, to the workings of the public health system caused much public debate in Sweden. *A Living Soul* (1980) documents the thoughts of a human brain as it is being experimented upon in a laboratory: efficiency and the profit motif have triumphed over ethics. *After the Flood* (1982), Jersild's starkest warning to date, is set 30 years after a nuclear accident in a harsh brutal society, which is paradoxically wiped out by a virus-carrying flock of white doves.

Jochum, Eugen (1902–87) German conductor. Born into a musical family (his two brothers were also conductors) in Babnenhausen, Germany, he studied at the Akademie der Tonkunst, Munich. He was principal conductor at the Kiel Opera House (1926–29) and musical director of Berlin Radio and conductor of the Berlin Philharmonic Orchestra from 1932 to 1934. While director of the Hamburg State Opera (1934–49) he continued to perform works by 20th-century composers such as Bartók, Stravinsky, and Hindemith, which the Nazis had banned elsewhere. In 1949 he became musical director of Bavarian Radio and established the Bavarian Symphony Orchestra. He has been a guest conductor throughout Europe and the US and was chief conductor (1961–64) of the Amsterdam Concertgebouw Orchestra with Bernard HAITINK. He was renowned for his interpretations of Bruckner.

Joffe, Roland (1945–) British film director, who is also noted for his work in television. Joffe made his cinema debut with *The Killing Fields* (1984), a harrowing depiction of the horrors of Pol Pot's Kampuchea, as experienced by a US journalist. The film was nominated for Academy Awards for best director and best film. Joffe also received an Oscar nomination for the $22 million epic *The Mission* (1985), a beautifully photographed story about the attempts of Jesuit priests to resist the colonial exploitation of the natives in 18th-century South America. *Fat Man and Little Boy* (1989) was a controversial film about the development of the atomic bomb during World War II, a theme Joffe returned to in the television film *Shadow Makers* (1990). His other work for television has included *Spongers* (1978), an indignant account of poverty in modern Britain that won the PRIX ITALIA, *No Mama No* (1980), *United Kingdom* (1981), and a version of the Jacobean revenge tragedy *'Tis Pity She's a Whore* (1980).

Johanides, Ján (1934–) Slovak prose writer. After abandoning his course in Fine Arts at Bratislava University he held jobs varying from factory psychologist to cultural *apparatchik*. His first publication, the short-story collection *Privacy* (1963), bears the stamp of French EXISTENTIALISM, but by the beginning of the 1980s that influence had been partly superseded by that of Jewish and Renaissance esoteric thought. The main theme of his work is guilt – the guilt inherent in being alive (*The Basis of the Quarry*, 1965; *Ballad of a Savings Account*, 1979), inherited guilt (*The Saddest Ballad of Orva*; 1988), political guilt (*Elephants in Mauthausen*; 1985), and political guilt combined with sexual guilt (*The Crime of the Shy Lesbian. Black Frost*;

1992). Johanides's most complex work is the historical novel *Marek, Master of Horse and the Hungarian Pope* (1983), an evocation of the violent early 16th century in Hungary. The hero, Marek de Molnay, is one of Johanides's 'knowers', like the policeman in *The Crime of the Shy Lesbian*. Marek understands men as well as he does horses and, as he travels off at the end of the novel, it is clear that he knows what the modern age will bring. For Johanides it was the Renaissance that started the vulgarization of modern man; 'the Renaissance invented chewing gum.'

Johnson, Eyvind (1900–76) Swedish novelist and writer. Born in poverty in the far north of Sweden, Johnson was to become one of Sweden's most internationalist writers. Almost entirely self-educated, he left Sweden to escape unemployment and spent the 1920s mainly in France and Germany.

In 1924 he made his literary debut with the short-story collection *The Four Strangers*. The novel *Timans and Justice*, based on his experiences in Paris, followed a year later. *Town of Darkness* (1927) returns to northern Sweden and depicts the attitudes and achievements of two men from different classes.

Johnson's works of the 1920s and 1930s often portray characters who have difficulties in coming to terms with their backgrounds. Between 1934 and 1937 he produced a tetralogy of semiautobiographical novels, beginning with *Now It Is 1914* (1934). Class conflicts feature prominently in these novels, as does the conflict between the individual and society.

During World War II Johnson attacked Swedish neutrality in the major allegorical trilogy *Krilon's Group* (1941), *Krilon's Journey* (1942), and *Krilon Himself* (1943). These novels depict man's struggle against evil, represented most potently by Nazism. *Dreams of Roses and Fire* (1949), about a witch-trial in 17th-century France, is the first of three historical works showing how the lives of ordinary people are ruined by war and oppression. *The Days of His Grace* followed in 1960 and *Life's Long Day* in 1964. In *Favel Alone* (1968), a novel about the meeting in Britain of four refugees from the Nazis, Johnson returns to his themes of idealism and human evil.

Johnson was a member of the Swedish Academy and joint winner of the Nobel Prize for literature in 1974.

Johnson, Uwe (1934–84) German novelist. After a youth spent in Mecklenburg, Johnson studied German in Rostock and Leipzig (1952–56). In 1954 he left the communist youth organization in protest at their campaign against the Christian youth community. In 1959 he left East Germany after experiencing difficulties in publishing his work and lived in West Berlin until 1974, when he moved to Sheerness-on-Sea in England.

Johnson's main theme is the post-war division of Germany. *Speculations about Jakob* (1959) describes the fate of the railway worker Jakob Abs who crosses the border twice because he can live neither in the East nor in the West. This was followed by *The Third Book about Achim* (1961) and *Two Views* (1965), both of which explore the difficulties East and West Germans had in understanding each other. Johnson's novels are highly self-reflexive in that they articulate an ongoing process of perceiving and interpreting reality; syntax is often dislocated and grammatical rules are freely flouted. His major work is *Anniversaries – From the Life of Gesine Cresspahl*, the four volumes of which were published in 1970, 1971, 1973, and 1983. Set in the 12 months August 1967 to August 1968, the novel concerns Gesine Cresspahl, an interpreter working in New York, and her attempts to provide an account of her youth in Mecklenburg to her daughter. The book is a highly complex structure of spontaneous impressions, quotations, reflections, dialogue, and stream-of consciousness, which artfully interweaves memories of Mecklenburg during the Weimar Republic and the Nazi dictatorship with the public events of the late 1960s. Johnson is one of the most determinedly avant-garde of post-war German writers.

Johnson-Marshall, Sir Stirrat *See* ROBERT MATTHEW JOHNSON MARSHALL AND PARTNERS.

Joint Stock Company British theatre company, considered the most important touring fringe theatre group currently working in the UK. The company was founded in 1974 to foster greater cooperation between performers and writers. Praised for its ensemble playing and creative use of improvisation, it had an early success with David HARE's *Fanshen* (1975). Other leading playwrights associated with the group include Caryl CHURCHILL and Howard BRENTON.

Jolivet, André (1905–74) French composer. He was a pupil of Le Flem (1928–33) and also of Edgard Varèse (1930–33), whose innovative ideas had a radical influence on Jolivet's compositional style and technique. One of Jolivet's first mature works, *Mana* (1935), is a suite of six piano pieces, each of which is dedicated to an object (chosen in each case by Varèse), whose essence is supposedly conveyed in the music. In 1936 he founded the group La Jeune France, together with Yves Baudner, MESSIAEN, and Daniel Lesur, with the aim of rehumanizing French music by reconnecting it to ordinary human life and aspirations. He was conductor and musical director of the Comédie-Française (1943–59), president of the Concerts Lamoureux (1963–68), and professor of composition at the Paris Conservatoire (1965–70). His output also includes a comic opera *Dolorès* (1942), ballets, the oratorio *La Verité de Jeanne* (1956), *Songe à nouveau rêve* for voice and orchestra, concertos for various instruments, three symphonies, chamber and piano music, and songs.

Jones, Allen (1937–) British painter, printmaker, designer, and teacher. After studies at Hornsey College of Art and the Royal College of Art, Jones emerged at the memorable 'Young Contemporaries' show of 1961 as one of the most original, and most painterly, of the second wave of British Pop artists (*see* POP ART).

Jones's early work, which shows an interest in visual puzzles and ideas from dreams and the unconscious, reflects his reading of Freud, Jung, and Nietzsche. His interest in metamorphoses and visual as well as sexual ambiguities led to the 'Hermaphrodite' series, in which male and female images merge one into another. Irregularly shaped canvases and grouped panels were used to create an impression of movement that contrasted with the static images. By his own account, the figurative elements in Jones's work are secondary to the abstract visual qualities. His use of colour was influenced by Matisse and Robert Delaunay.

The hard strident style and markedly sexual content of Jones's later work developed during his visit to the US in 1964–66. In New York he became fascinated by commercial fetishist wear and adopted a new style setting elements of three-dimensional illusionism against monochrome areas on the canvas or print surface. This erotic illusionist fantasy is seen at its most extreme in the sculptures *Hat Stand* and *Table Sculpture* (both 1969), both of which incorporate female figures in fetishistic garb. This aspect of Jones's work has been fiercely criticized by feminists and others. Jones has designed for West German television and created an advertising mural at Basel railway station (1978). In 1982–83 he was guest professor at the Hochschule der Künste, West Berlin.

Jordan, Neil (1950–) Irish film director and writer. Modern Ireland provided the setting for Jordan's first film, *Angel* (1982), in which a saxophone player sets out to avenge a sectarian murder he has witnessed; like his subsequent films this thriller, influenced by BUÑUEL and Scorsese, has a surreal and apocalyptic edge. He established his name in the cinema with *The Company of Wolves* (1984), an adaptation of Angela CARTER's reworking of the Little Red Riding Hood story. The film, which blends elements of fairytale with horror and sexual fantasy, was much praised for the quality of its photography and its special effects.

Jordan enjoyed even greater commercial success with his third film, *Mona Lisa* (1986), which follows the developing relationship between a small-time villain and a prostitute in London's underworld. Less successful was the supernatural comedy *High Spirits* (1988), starring Peter O'Toole, although the special effects were once again remarkable. *The Crying Game* (1992) is a powerful story of love and murder set in Northern Ireland and London.

Joris, Charles (1935–) Swiss theatre director and actor, who in 1961 founded the influential French-speaking Théâtre Populaire Romand company. Joris began his career as an actor in Strasbourg (1958–61) before establishing his famous touring company, which has since won acclaim for its productions of new works by contemporary playwrights, mostly Swiss. Under Joris the company, which has toured in France, has also presented such plays as *Man is Man* (1968) by BRECHT, *Through Towns and Villages* (1984) by HANDKE, and

BECKETT's *Waiting for Godot* (1985), as well as doing much to encourage amateur groups and to organize local drama festivals. Although recognized as the foremost training institution for the Swiss theatre, the company has suffered from lack of official support.

Jorn, Asger (Asger Oluf Jørgensen; 1914–73) Danish painter and printmaker. He adopted the name Jorn in 1945. His main periods of study were at the Académie Contemporaine, Paris (1936–37), where he was taught by Léger, and the Royal Academy, Copenhagen (1938–40). During the German occupation of Denmark (1940–45) he produced an underground magazine. He travelled widely in the decade following World War II and in 1954 settled in Paris. However, he regularly spent the summer in Albisola Marina in northern Italy and it was here that he made a large ceramic mural (1959) for a school at Aarhus in Denmark. His varied output also included experimental films and recordings as well as occasional sculptures and a number of publications on art theory. He donated a large number of works of modern art, including many of his own, to the museum at Silkeborg in Denmark.

Jorn was one of the founders of the COBRA group in 1948. Like the other members of the group he painted in an expressionistic semiabstract style, characterized by unrestrained brushwork and intense colour. He summed up his approach when he wrote: "I believe that colour immediately and totally transmits the content of a painting."

Josephson, Brian (David) (1940–) British physicist. Josephson was educated at Cambridge University where he obtained his PhD in 1964. He remained at Cambridge and in 1974 was appointed to a professorship of physics.

His name is associated with the Josephson effects, which he described in 1962 while still a graduate student. The work came out of theoretical speculations on electrons in semiconductors involving the exchange of electrons between two superconducting regions separated by a thin insulating layer (a Josephson junction). He showed theoretically that a current can flow across the junction in the absence of an applied voltage. Furthermore, a small direct voltage across the junction produces an alternating current with a frequency that is inversely proportional to the voltage. The effects have been used in making accurate physical measurements and in measuring weak magnetic fields. Josephson junctions can also be used as very fast switching devices in computers. For this work Josephson shared the 1973 Nobel Prize for physics with Leo Esaki and Ivar Giaever.

More recently, Josephson has turned his atention to the study of the mind and the relationship between science and religion. In 1980 he coedited *Consciousness and the Physical World*.

Jovine, Francesco (1902–50) Italian novelist. Jovine was born into a modest background in the Abruzzi region of southern Italy, which provided the inspiration for most of his work. His first novel, *A Temporary Man* (1934), provoked strong opposition from the Fascist regime; it was followed by *Seeds in the Wind* (*Signora Ava*; 1942) and a series of short stories. But his reputation rests mainly on his last novel, *The Estate in Abruzzi* (*Le terre del Sacramento*; 1950); its title refers to Church lands expropriated by the newly formed government of unified Italy (1860). The novel revolves around the heroic figure of Luca Marano, a peasant whose death in a fight with the Fascists makes him a symbol of the peasantry in its eternal struggle against the landowners.

Acutely sensitive to social injustice, Jovine portrayed lives dominated by misery, ignorance, and resignation with realism and sympathy. His work skilfully blends historical events with myth.

Jyväskylä Festival An annual arts festival held in Jyväskylä, Finland, for a week each June. All areas of cultural activity are included and there is a special emphasis on the breaking down of traditional boundaries between the different arts. Different themes are highlighted and explored each year, with the influence of science and politics on cultural life receiving particular attention. The festival features artists and performers from around the world, but especially those from the Baltic states and Russia.

K

Kabalevsky, Dmitry Borisovich (1904–87) Soviet composer, conductor, pianist, and writer on music. He studied the piano at the Scriabin Musical Institute in Moscow (1919–25) and worked as an accompanist and piano teacher before entering the Moscow Conservatory, where he continued his piano studies with Goldenweiser and studied composition with George Catoire and Nikolai Miaskovsky. He was an assistant professor of composition at the Moscow Conservatory from 1932 and was appointed full professor in 1939. As a composer, Kabalevsky skilfully combined creative integrity with political rectitude to achieve popular acclaim within the nationalistic Russian idiom. His prolific output includes operas, operettas, symphonies, piano music, ballets, chamber works, choral music, patriotic songs, and film scores. He became well known internationally through such works as the second piano concerto (1935), the operas *Colas Breugnon* (1938) and *The Taras Family* (1947), the classically structured second symphony (1933), and the three concertos for violin, cello, and piano (1948–52) written for young musicians. After World War II he made several visits to western Europe and the US as a guest conductor; he also became increasingly prominent within the Soviet Union as an administrator, writer, and teacher. He was the principal editor of *Soviet Music* during the 1940s and in 1972 he was awarded an honorary degree by the International Society of Musical Education.

Kadár, Ján(os) (1918–79) Czechoslovakian film director. Born in Budapest, he abandoned his legal education to study at the Bratislava Film School; World War II intervened, however, and Kadár was forced into a Nazi labour camp. After the war, he returned to Bratislava to direct his first film, *Life is Rising from the Ruins* (1945), a documentary short; he subsequently joined the Barrandov Studios in Prague as a screenwriter and assistant director. In 1950 he directed his first feature, *Katya*, a comedy that displeased the state authorities. Two years later he began a rewarding 17-year collaboration with **Elmar Klos** (1910–), with whom he codirected and coscripted a string of documentary and feature films that have been much praised for their technical brilliance. Several won international prizes, notably *The Shop on Main Street*, a sentimental tale about a carpenter's disastrous attempt to protect a Jewish woman during the German occupation, which won the 1965 Academy Award for best foreign film. Other films included *Kidnap* (1952), *The House at the Terminus* (1957), *Three Wishes* (1958), the documentary *Youth* (1960), *Death is Called Engelchen* (1963), and *The Accused* (1964).

Kadár and Klos were often called in by the communist authorities to answer questions about the submerged political content of their films. This resulted in one suspension of two years, while the Soviet invasion of Czechoslovakia in 1968 delayed the release of their Czech-American coproduction *Adrift* for three years. Kadár emigrated to the US in 1969 and a year later made his first American film, *The Angel Levine*, a parable about an elderly Jewish tailor's visitation by a black angel. In 1975 he made *Lies My Father Told Me*, a sentimental Canadian film about a poor Jewish boy and his grandfather in 1920s Montreal. In his last years Kadár worked mainly for television, making such documentaries as *The Other Side of Hell* (1977) and *Freedom Road* (1978).

Kadare, Ismail (1936–) Albanian novelist living in France. Born in Gjirokastër, he studied at the University of Tiranë and the Gorkii Institute of World Literature in

Moscow. Kadare's boyhood observation of his homeland as a World War II battle zone inspired *The General of the Dead Army* (1963), an account of the mental collapse of an Italian general searching for his soldiers' remains that is generally regarded as the first great Albanian novel. A scholar of Albanian folklore and myths, Kadare explored the conflict between these traditions and communist values in *The Wedding* (1968) and *The Three-Arched Bridge* (1978), a novel set in the Middle Ages. *Chronicle in Stone* (1971) describes the experiences of a young boy in an Albanian mountain village occupied by opposing armies, while *Le Crépuscule des dieux de la steppe* (1981) satirizes student life in the Soviet Union in the 1950s. An opponent of totalitarianism, Kadare analysed the cohesive power of such systems as well as their brutality in the allegorical *The Palace of Dreams* (1982). More recent works include the collection of short stories *Invitation to an Official Concert* (1985) and the novel *Albanian Spring* (1991). He has also published several volumes of poetry. He was granted political asylum in France in 1990.

Kagel, Mauricio (1931–) Argentinian composer, conductor, and teacher, working in Germany. Kagel worked in Buenos Aires as a choral coach and a conductor of film music before moving to Cologne in 1957. In Europe he completed his first characteristic work, *Anagrama* (1958) for voices, speaking chorus, and instruments. Like other works by Kagel this incorporates elements of the absurd and the deliberately incongruous within a formal structure of great rigour and sophistication. Subsequent works, such as *Match* (1964) for two cellists and percussionist, *Antithese* (1962) for actor, electronic sounds, and audience, *Diaphonie* (1962–64) for two projectors, chorus and orchestra, became increasingly theatrical, employing visual and performance elements in mixed-media presentations. His compositions include the unconventional 'operas' *Staatstheater* (1970) and *Die Erschöpfung der Welt* (1985) and other works of music theatre such as *Tremens* (1965) and *Kantrimusik* (1975). Kagel's radical and totally idiosyncratic work is intended to prompt a reexamination of the roles music has traditionally played in Western society.

Kalatozov, Mikhail (Mikhail Kalatozishvili; 1902–73) Soviet film director and executive. After studying economics, he joined the Georgian Studios in 1925 and worked variously as an actor, cutter, and cameraman. His second feature as a director, *Salt for Svanetia* (1930), was a dreamlike portrait of the daily life of a rustic Caucasian village. Soviet censors criticized its negative view and were more harsh with Kalatozov's next offering, *A Nail in the Boot* (1932), which was banned. For the next five years he was an administrator in the Georgian film industry; during World War II he was chief administrator of feature film production and spent a period in Hollywood as a cultural representative. After the war he became deputy minister of Soviet film production and in 1950 returned to directing.

Kalatozov's one international success, *The Cranes Are Flying* (1957), was a moving story of a woman's refusal to believe official war reports of her lover's death. Its blend of romanticism and realism (and its avoidance of propaganda) earned critical plaudits in the West and it shared the 1958 Cannes Festival Best Picture award. Later films, such as *I Am Cuba* (1966), made little impact. The Soviet-Italian coproduction *The Red Tent* (1969) was a spectacular retelling of a fatal 1928 dirigible expedition to the Arctic with an all-star cast headed by Sean Connery and Peter Finch.

Kantor, Tadeusz (1915–) Polish theatre director, actor, and artist, who began his theatrical career organizing underground productions in Cracow during World War II. He became known internationally for his work at the Stary Theatre in Cracow (1945–55); in 1955 he founded Cracow's Cricot 2 Theatre, where he specialized in highly experimental productions, including a number of HAPPENINGS. His work has been seen at several international theatre festivals and he has been praised for his direction of and designs for such plays as *Cuttle Fish* (1956), *Dead Class* (1975), *Wielopole-Wielopole* (1980), and *Let the Artists Die* (1985), as well as works by the Polish playwright Stanisław Witkiewicz. Kantor's preoccupation with themes of death, memory, and time led to his work of the 1970s being popularly labelled the 'Theatre of Death'.

Kantor's paintings, which include *The Line of Division* (1965), *Rembrandt's Anato-*

my Lesson (1968), and *Cambriolage* (1971), have been shown at exhibitions all over the world.

Kapoor, Anish (1954–) British abstract sculptor, born in India, the son of a Jewish mother and Hindu father. He came to London in 1973 and studied at the Hornsey School of Art and Chelsea School of Art. Apart from a preference for bright colours in some of his early sculpture, his work is not obviously indebted stylistically to his Indian heritage, but he feels a deep affinity with the spirituality of Indian art and has said; "I don't want to make sculpture about form...I wish to make sculpture about belief, or about passion, about experience that is outside of material concern." In the late 1980s he turned from predominantly fairly lightweight materials (wood and mixed media) to stone, this change coinciding with the acquisition of a large ground-floor studio where he could handle heavy materials. Typically, his most recent pieces are extremely hefty and rough-hewn, sometimes consisting of an arrangement of several large blocks. In 1990 he was Britain's representative at the Venice Biennale and in 1991 he received the TURNER PRIZE.

Karajan, Herbert von (1908–89) Austrian conductor. Born in Salzburg, Austria, Karajan was a gifted child pianist and he studied at the Salzburg Mozarteum while still at school. He subsequently studied conducting at the Vienna Conservatoire under Franz Schalk. He conducted for the State Theatre in Ulm (1927–34) and then at Aachen, where he joined the Nazi party. His first major appointment was in 1937 when he became conductor of the Berlin State Opera. After World War II his association with the Nazis almost brought about the end of his career. Following his exoneration by an Allied tribunal, he was appointed conductor of the Vienna Symphony Orchestra in 1947, becoming concert director for life in 1949. He was also artistic director of the Berlin Philharmonic Orchestra in 1955–56, remaining closely associated with the orchestra until a disagreement in 1983. An earlier dispute had brought about his resignation from the Vienna State Opera, which he directed from 1956 until 1964 (he returned in 1977). He directed the Salzburg Festival (1956–60; 1964) and founded the Salzburg Easter Festival in 1967. Karajan also conducted the New York Philharmonic Orchestra, L'Orchestre de Paris (1969–70), and at La Scala, Milan. His style emphasized precision and objectivity.

Karol Szymanowski Philharmonic Polish music society. Founded in Cracow in 1945 as the Cracow Philharmonic, the society was renamed in honour of the Polish composer Karol Szymanowski (1882–1937) in 1962. Its functions include organizing the different ensembles which meet under its auspices – notably the Cracow Philharmonic Orchestra and various choirs (including children's choirs) – and giving around 700 concerts a year.

Kasack, Hermann (1896–1966) German novelist and poet. Born in Potsdam, Kasack studied German literature and philosophy before starting (1920) a career in publishing in Berlin. After World War II he settled in Stuttgart and became a full-time writer. In 1953 he was elected president of the German Academy for Language and Poetry. Kasack became famous with his novel *The City Beyond the River* (1947), which enjoyed a huge success in the Germany of the immediate post-war years. The novel describes a twilight city through which people are travelling between life and death – a setting inspired by the Egyptian Book of the Dead and Germany's bombed-out cities. The city features a huge and omnipresent bureaucracy and two factories, one baking artificial stones from powder and the other making powder from artificial stones. The element of Kafkaesque absurdity is also present in Kasack's story *Falsifications* (1953), which develops the notion that all material objects are falsifications, and in his novel *The Great Net* (1952), in which a film company stages the end of the world in miniature, using a real bomb to get a more realistic effect. Kasack's work had great resonance in the atmosphere of 1945–50 but has not worn well when compared to the work either of Kafka or of Kasack's contemporary and friend, NOSSACK. Kasack's works include several volumes of poetry in a rather traditional style and a number of plays; he was also active as an editor, mainly of poetry.

Kasatkina, Natalia Dmitrievna (1934–) Russian ballet dancer and choreographer, who established her reputation with the ballets she created with her husband, the dancer **Vladimir Vasiliov** (1931–). She trained at the Bolshoi Ballet School in Moscow and in 1954 became a soloist with the Bolshoi company. She made her choreographic debut (with her husband) in 1962, with *Vanina Vanini*; later works have included *Geologist* (1964), *Le Sacre du printemps* (1965), *Preludes and Fugues* (1968), which employed the music of Bach, *Creation of the World* (1971), *The Magic Cloak* (1982), *Pushkin* (1986), *The Fairy's Kiss* (1984), and *Don Quixote* (film ballet; 1990). In 1977 she and her husband took over the direction of the Moscow State Ballet Theatre; among their most significant productions with the company have been the first joint Anglo-Russian staging of *Swan Lake*.

Kaschnitz, Marie-Luise (1901–74) German poet and writer. Kaschnitz was born in Karlsruhe, but spent her youth in Berlin and Potsdam. After training as a bookseller in Weimar she lived and worked in Rome, Königsberg, Frankfurt, and Marburg. In the 1930s she travelled widely with her husband, the archaeologist Guido Freiherr von Kaschnitz-Weinberg; their visits to classical sites in the Mediterranean inspired her book *The Greek Myths* (1943) and contributed a vein of imagery to her poetry. Although she published two novels in the 1930s, it was for her writings of the immediate post-war era that Kaschnitz became famous. The poetry in *Dance of Death and Poems of the Times* (1947) and *Utopian Music* (1950) declares her belief in humanity in the face of indifference, brutality, and the omnipresence of death. Her later poetry is characterized by the combination of a subjective and a more distanced voice; the tone of her poems became increasingly laconic in, for example, *New Poems* (1957) and *No Magic Spell* (1972). The poems in *Your Silence, My Voice* (1962) deal movingly with the death of her husband. Among her outstanding volumes of novellas and short stories are *The Big Child* (1951), *Long Distance Calls* (1966), and *Description of a Village* (1966). In later life she concentrated on autobiographical writing as, for example, in *Days, Days, Years* (1968). Kaschnitz won many literary prizes.

Käsemann, Ernst (1906–) German Protestant theologian. After completing his theological studies in 1931 Käsemann worked as a pastor in the industrial city of Gelsenkirchen. A member of the Confessing Church (a German Protestant movement that refused any accommodation with Nazi ideology), in 1938 he wrote *God's Wandering People*, in which he described the Church as a community of believers in opposition to the organized powers of the world. Käsemann was imprisoned several times during the Nazi era. After World War II he taught theology of the New Testament in Mainz, Göttingen, and Tübingen.

Käsemann is an important advocate of ecumenicism, arguing in his theological writings that the Christian religion has been manifold from its inception and that the New Testament offers a variety of spiritual perspectives rather than a single dogmatic faith. The person and teaching of Christ provide a point of origin for several possible Christian denominations. (*Essays on New Testament Themes*; 1960).

Consequently Käsemann has opposed any kind of Church hierarchy or bureaucracy. In *Jesus Means Freedom* (1968) he sees Christianity as a source of political as well as spiritual freedom. Käsemann has taken a strong interest in the Christianity of Third World countries, arguing that the new perspectives on the teachings of Jesus opened up in poorer nations have profound implications for the future of the Church in the West.

Kaütner, Helmut (1908–1980) German film director and screenwriter. Born in Düsseldorf, Käutner studied at the University of Munich and became a film actor in the early 1930s. He worked as a screenwriter before directing his first features, *Kitty and the World Conference* and *Die acht Entfesselten* (both 1939) and continued to script most of his films. After the war Käutner found his strength with a series of warm innovative films that attracted an international audience: *The Original Sin* (1948), *The Last Bridge* (1954), a World War II melodrama about a German nurse captured by Yugoslavian partisans, *The Devil's General* (1955), about a German airman who decides to help a Jewish couple, *Ludwig II* (1955), *Sky Without Stars* (1955), and *The Captain from Koepenick* (1956), an antimilitarist fable about a sham Prussian officer who takes over a government office in a Berlin suburb.

Käutner made no great impression during his brief period with Universal in Hollywood. His two US films were *The Wonderful Years* (1958) and *Stranger in My Arms* (1959), a slow-moving romance (spread across Cinemascope) about a test pilot who falls in love with his friend's widow. His later German releases were *The Rest Is Silence* (1959), *A Glass of Water* (1960), *The Redhead* (1962), *The House in Montevideo* (1963), *Lausbubengeschichten* (1964), and *Die Feuerzangenbowle* (1970). From the mid 1960s he directed mostly for German television.

Kavanagh, Patrick (1905–67) Irish poet and writer. Born in rural Co. Monaghan, Kavanagh worked on the land for nearly 20 years before travelling to Dublin to seek work as a journalist. Although entirely self-educated, he had already published the poems in *Ploughman and Other Poems* (1936) and an early autobiography, *The Green Fool* (1939). Later publications include *A Soul for Sale* (1947), *Come Dance with Kitty Stobling* (1960), and the novel *Terry Flynn* (1948). Kavanagh's claim to be more than an entertaining minor poet depends mainly on his long poem *The Great Hunger* (1942), an angry sardonic work that exposes the gulf between the idealized images of rural Ireland current in much Irish literature and the reality of life on the land as he had experienced it. However, he was also able to show a genial nostalgia for his rural upbringing in such poems as 'Kerr's Ass' and 'Memory of My Father'. In 1952 he produced the shortlived periodical *Kavanagh's Weekly*, notorious for its vituperative attacks on all aspects of Irish life, with his brother Peter. His *Collected Poems* appeared in 1964 and his *Collected Pruse* (sic) in 1967.

Kawalerowicz, Jerzy (1922–) Polish film director and screenwriter, born in the Ukraine. After graduating from the Cracow Film Institute, he worked as an assistant director and screenwriter before codirecting his first film, *Commune*, in 1950. Five years later he became artistic director of the KADR production unit, whose members have included such directors as WAJDA, MUNK, and KONWICKI. Kawalerowicz, who has created some of the most visually memorable scenes in Polish cinema, also collaborates on his films' scripts and often uses the talents of his actress wife, Lucyna Winnicka. His greatest success came with *Mother Joan of the Angels* (1961), a historical drama about demonaic possession in a convent; scripted by Tadeusz Konwicki, the film won a prize at the Cannes Festival in 1961. Other films include *Night Train* (*Poriag*; 1959), *The Pharaoh* (1964), and *Death of the President* (1978).

Kazakov, Yurii Pavlovich (1927–82) Russian short-story writer, playwright, and translator. Born in Moscow of provincial parents, he showed an early talent for architecture and music before switching to literature. He graduated from the Gorkii Literary Institute in 1957 and became a member of the Writers' Union in 1958, the year in which his first collection of short stories *Man'ka* was published in Archangel. Between then and 1969 Kazakov published 35 short stories in eight collections. His last collection, *You Cried Bitterly in Your Sleep*, appeared in 1977 and was largely retrospective. A victim of alcoholism and depression, Kazakov published nothing more.

Kazakov's work marks a transitional stage in the development of the Russian short story. On the one hand, it looks back to earlier masters of the genre, notably Chekhov, whom Kazakov evokes in *The Cursed North*, Ivan Bunin, and Mikhail Prishvin, to whom Kazakov dedicated perhaps his best story, *Arcturus the Hound*. On the other hand it looks forward, particularly in its preoccupation with provincial Russia, notably the White Sea area, to the 'Village Prose' writers of the 1970s. Kazakov's stories often feature heroes and heroines who are self-possessed yet emotionally vulnerable. Above all they are isolated, either by geography, circumstance, or psychological make-up. Criticized in its day by the Soviet literary bureaucracy for alleged 'pessimism', Kazakov's work has attracted growing interest since his death.

Kazantzakis, Nikos (1885–1957) Greek writer. Born in Iráklion, Crete, Kazantzakis was educated at a French Catholic school on Naxos and at Athens University, where he studied law. A keen traveller with an equally restless mind, he read widely in philosophy, literature, politics, and religion. His early writing consisted mainly of essays and translations of works including Dante's *Divine Comedy* and texts by Nietzsche, Bergson, and Marx.

Much of Kazantzakis's philosophical and religious thought was incorporated into *The Odyssey* (1938), a 'modern sequel' to the *Odyssey* of Homer. With 33 333 lines – a number to which Kazantzakis ascribed a mystical significance – it is one of the longest poems ever written.

Most of Kazantzakis's novels were written in his later years, when he lived mainly in the South of France. They tend to be grand in scale and theme and full of flamboyant energy. Two have been made into successful films; *Zorba the Greek* (1952) was filmed by Michael CACOYANNIS in 1964 and *The Last Temptation of Christ* (1960) became a controversial film in 1988, directed by Martin Scorsese. *Christ Recrucified: A Greek Passion* (1954) similarly deals with the relationship between man and God. An understanding of psychology and an interest in politics also inform Kazantzakis's work, but his main emphasis is on man as a religious being. His other works include travel writings, plays, poems, the biography *God's Pauper – Saint Francis of Assisi* (1962), and the posthumously published autobiographical novel *Report to Greco* (1965). He campaigned persistently for the official acceptance of demotic Greek as his country's national and literary language.

Kempe, Rudolf (1910–76) German conductor, best known for his performances of Wagner and Richard Strauss. Kempe began his musical career as an oboist, initially in Dortmund and then with the Leipzig orchestra. From 1935 to 1942 he worked as repetiteur with the Leipzig Opera, making his debut as a conductor in 1935 with Lortzing's *Der Wildschutz*. He became musical director at the Dresden Opera in 1949 and at the Bavarian State Opera in 1952. He made his Covent Garden debut in 1953 with the Munich Company and performed the complete *Ring* cycle there on several occasions in the late 1950s. From 1960 he conducted regularly at Bayreuth. He became chief conductor of the Royal Philharmonic Orchestra in 1961, artistic director from 1964, and principal conductor for life from 1970. He also had a long association with the Zürich Tonhalle Orchestra.

Kertesz, Istvan (1929–73) German conductor born in Hungary. After studies at the Liszt Academy in Budapest and in Rome, he worked as a staff conductor at the Budapest Academy and then at the Budapest State Opera. Following the uprising of 1956 he moved to Germany, becoming musical director at Augsburg (1958–63) and of Cologne Opera (1964–73). He made his London debut in 1960 with the London Symphony Orchestra, serving as that orchestra's principal conductor from 1965 until 1968. He was known for a wide repertoire including many 20th-century works.

Khachaturian, Aram Il'yich (1903–73) Armenian composer. Khachaturian studied at the Gnesin Music Academy before entering the Moscow Conservatory at the age of 26, where his composition teacher was Myaskovsky. By the time he graduated in 1937, he was already an established composer with several large orchestral works to his credit. Thanks largely to Prokofiev, his music was widely performed abroad and his piano concerto (1936) brought him international recognition. He soon achieved office in the newly formed Union of Soviet Composers and his patriotic songs and cantatas found favour during World War II. Although his own style was conservative, his association with SHOSTAKOVICH and Prokofiev caused him to be officially reprimanded in the 1948 Stalinist reaction to musical modernism. After Stalin's death in 1953 he spoke out for greater artistic freedoms and achieved a major international success with the ballet *Spartacus* (1954; revised 1968).

In general, Khachaturian found favour with the Soviet authorities and his music embodies the populist ideals of socialist realism. At the same time he was able to achieve his own original synthesis of the Russian tradition of Rimsky-Korsakov with the folk music of his native Armenia. His film scores and incidental music for the stage contain much of his finest writing while his orchestral works, which include three symphonies and several concertos for violin and cello, are never less than craftsmanlike.

Kiefer, Anselm (1945–) German artist, one of the leading figures in the revival of expressionist styles (*see* NEOEXPRESSIONISM) in the late 1970s and 1980s. Kiefer studied at the Düsseldorf Academy under Josef BEUYS, who has remained a major influence. His densely allusive works explore the largest subjects from European history, literature, and philosophy. In particular, he has shown a preoccupation with the German romantic and nationalist tradition and its ambiguous relationship with the moral catastrophe of Nazism. His work also draws on sources as diverse as alchemy, occultism, and Egyptian mythology.

Kiefer first came to public attention in the earlier 1970s with a series of paintings of ravaged German landscapes. Another series sought to reinterpret German myths, such as the Parsifal legend, in the light of Nazism and the post-war division of Germany. *Shulamite* (1983), a sinister painting of a vast crypt blackened by fire with an altar at the far end, is one of a number of works to allude obliquely to the Holocaust. Kiefer generally works in subdued monotonous colours on very large canvases; the prevailing mood is mournful and elegiac with a strong suggestion of menace. Besides paint, his works make use of materials such as tar, straw, sand, molten lead, and gold leaf.

Since the mid 1980s Kiefer has also attracted attention with a number of large-scale installations, most notably *The High Priestess* (1989), two gigantic steel bookcases filled with huge books made of lead. Equally enigmatic and disturbing was *The Women of the Revolution* (1992), consisting of 14 iron beds with lead sheets, each having a water-filled cavity in its centre; names of female protagonists of the French Revolution were also displayed in the room. Kiefer's fascination with dereliction comes to the fore again in his recent paintings of ruined buildings, which he has festooned with dried and decaying vegetation.

Kieslowski, Krzysztof (1941–) Polish film director. Kieslowski was born in Warsaw and attended the School of Cinema and Theatre in Łódź. His *First Love* (1974) won the Golden Dragon at the International Festival of Short Films in Cracow while the light comedy *Camera Buff* (1979) won the Moscow Film Festival Grand Prix despite its implicit antiauthoritarian message. In 1988 Kieslowski came to international attention with *A Short Film about Killing*, a grim piece about a man who commits a motiveless murder and is then – equally pointlessly – executed. The film won an Academy Award for best foreign film and a Special Jury Prize at the CANNES FILM FESTIVAL. It also inaugurated Kieslowski's momentous film series *Decalogue*, each episode of which is based on one of the Ten Commandments. *A Short Film about Love* (1988), the second in the series, is a bleak film about a teenage voyeur. Other films include *Blind Chance* (1982), *No End* (1984), and *City Life* (1990).

The Double Life of Veronique (1992), which he also scripted, consolidated Kieslowski's reputation as perhaps the most imaginative and accomplished director in Europe. It tells a story of two parallel lives: Veronica, a singer, sees a double among a busload of French tourists in a Cracow square; she dies early in the film from a mysterious illness, while her French double, Véronique, lives on. The film received rapturous reviews and took the International Critics' Jury award at Cannes. In 1993 he released *Blue*, the first film in a planned trilogy. Kieslowski has also made many documentaries, shorts, and films for television.

Killick, John A(lexander) *See* HOWELL, KILLICK, PARTRIDGE, AND AMIS.

kinetic art Art objects that move or appear to move or depend for their effect on a moving observer. In its loosest sense, the term is very wide-ranging, embracing – for example – motion pictures and PERFORMANCE ART, but in normal parlance it is generally restricted to sculptures that are either driven by motors or set in motion by air currents. The word 'kinetic' was first used in connection with the visual arts in 1920 in the *Realist Manifesto* of the Russian Constructivists Antoine Pevsner and Naum Gabo; and there were various works in the 1920s (such as Marcel Duchamp's *Rotative Plaques*) that incorporated movement. However, it was not until the 1950s that the phrase 'kinetic art' became critically established. The exhibition 'Le Mouvement' held at the Denise René Gallery in Paris in 1955 was one of the key events in establishing a distinct genre of kinetic works.

The 'mobiles' (a word coined by Duchamp in 1932) of the US sculptor Alexander Calder are probably the best-known examples of kinetic art. Other exponents have included Gerhard von GRAEVENITZ, TAKIS, Jean TINGUELY, and the members of the ZERO GROUP. The Israeli artist Yaacov Agam has produced kinetic artworks that depend on spectator movement (and sometimes participation).

King, Phillip (1934–) British abstract sculptor. Born in Tunisia, he came to England in 1946 and studied modern languages at Christ's College, Cambridge (1954–57). He subsequently (1957–58) studied sculpture at St Martin's School of Art, London, where he was taught by Anthony CARO, and in 1959–60 he was assistant to Henry MOORE, an experience that was of particular value in giving him confidence in working on a large scale. He gave his first one-man exhibition in 1964 at the Rowan Gallery, London, and in 1965 was one of nine young British sculptors whose work was shown at the 'New Generation Sculpture' exhibition at the Whitechapel Gallery, London. This was a showcase for a type of sculpture influenced by Caro – large-scale, coloured, and with smooth surfaces (as opposed to the more expressive textures common in the 1950s) – and King has emerged as the most illustrious of this 'New Generation'. His work has been related to POP ART (because of its bright colours and zaniness) and to Hard-Edge abstraction and MINIMAL ART (because of its simple shapes). He uses modern materials such as plastics and fibreglass and his work often has an impersonal factory-like finish.

King has won numerous awards for his work and in 1980 he was appointed professor of sculpture at the Royal College of Art.

Kipphardt, Heinar (1922–82) German playwright, who is chiefly remembered for his pioneering work in DOCUMENTARY THEATRE. Having trained in medicine, Kipphardt subsequently became resident playwright for the Deutsches Theater in Berlin, for which he wrote such plays as *Wanted Urgently: Shakespeare* (1954) and *In the Matter of J. Robert Oppenheimer* (1964), his first important work to employ documentary techniques. Intended originally for television, the play broke new ground in its handling of recent historical facts, especially when produced by PISCATOR, who turned it into a multimedia investigation of the McCarthyist intrigues surrounding the US nuclear physicist.

Joel Brand – the History of a Deal (1965) applied similar techniques to the subject of Nazi attempts to exchange Jewish prisoners for military equipment. Kipphardt's later documentary dramas included *The Life of the Schizophrenic Poet Alexander März* (1981) and *Brother Eichmann* (1983), which drew parallels between the beliefs of the notorious Nazi fugitive and military thinking in Cold War Europe. Among his other plays was the black comedy *The Night the Boss was Slaughtered* (1967).

Kirsch, Sarah (1935–) German poet. Having studied biology, Sarah Kirsch worked in a sugar factory before beginning to study literature. Since 1965 she has produced poems, short prose pieces, and children's stories. In 1978 she left the German Democratic Republic for West Berlin, moving subsequently to the north German countryside. After Hilde DOMIN she is the best-known woman poet in Germany today.

Her early poetry is characterized by a playful laconic style and the use of simple rhythmic forms derived from nursery rhymes and children's verse. Elements from fairy tales and legend are often present (*A Stay in the Country*, 1967; *Tailwind*, 1977). Other poems explore the ever-changing relations between the poet, with her various feelings of love, desire, melancholy, pain, and anger and the natural world (*Magic spells*, 1973; *A Cat's Life*, 1984). Recent collections of poems and prose poems are dominated by a mood of obstinate resignation; in the end nature becomes more familiar and comforting than human companionship (*Warmth of Snow*, 1989; *Swinging Lawn*, 1990). Owing mainly to their freshness of language Kirsch's poems enjoy a great reputation in today's Germany. Her best-known pieces are collected in the volume *Conjurations* (1985).

Kitaj, R(onald) B(rooks) (1932–) US painter and printmaker, resident mainly in Britain since 1958. Kitaj studied art at the Cooper Union, New York (1950–51) and the Academy of Fine Art, Vienna (1951–52) before working as a merchant seaman and serving in the US army in Germany. He came to Britain on a GI scholarship and studied at the Ruskin School, Oxford (1958–59) and the Royal College of Art, London (1959–61), where his contemporaries included David HOCKNEY and Allen JONES. Following his first one-man exhibition at the Marlborough Gallery, London, in 1963 he was widely regarded as one of the leaders of British POP ART, although he has dissociated his work from this label. He also attracted attention as a champion of figurative art, laying stress on the traditional practices of drawing and painting from the life; in 1976 he organized an Arts Council exhibition of figurative art entitled 'The Human Clay' at the Hayward Gallery in London.

Unlike other artists associated with the Pop movement, Kitaj has shown more interest in serious intellectual matters than in popular culture, his subjects reflecting his wide literary, historical, and pictorial interests. His pictures often have a comic-book look, however, with broad areas of flat colour within a strong linear framework. Recent work has shown a growing interest in his Jewish background.

Kitchen-Sink School A group of British social realist painters who held a number of joint exhibitions at the Beaux-Arts Gallery, London, in the mid 1950s. The group, which included John BRATBY, Derrick Greaves, and Edward Middleditch, specialized in drab working-class interiors and still-lifes featuring the debris of ordinary domestic life (cornflake packets, milk bottles, chip pans, etc.). The 'kitchen-sink' label was first used in a review of their work in 1954. Owing to their choice of subject matter and harsh vigorous style the painters were often associated with their literary contemporaries, the so-called ANGRY YOUNG MEN.

In the later 1950s the term **kitchen-sink drama** was applied (often disparagingly) to the new wave of plays that dealt realistically with the domestic lives of working or lower-middle class characters. The use of humdrum or seedy settings in such plays as OSBORNE's *Look Back in Anger* (1956), Shelagh Delaney's *A Taste of Honey* (1958), and WESKER's *Roots* (1959), represented a decisive break with the elegant drawing-room comedies of (for instance) Nöel Coward or Terence RATTIGAN. *Roots* actually begins with a character washing up at a kitchen sink.

Kleihues, J(osef) P(aul) (1933–) German architect. After training at the Technical Universities of Stuttgart and Berlin, Kleihues established a private practice in Berlin in 1962. His work is modernist, informed by the neoclassicism of Claude-Nicolas Ledoux and Karl Friedrich Schinkel. His output, all in Germany, is dominated by housing, such as the Wohnblock 270 in Berlin (1972–76) and the houses at the centre of Wulfen New Town (1975–80), where he also provided shops. His Municipal Refuse Collection Depot, Berlin (1975–79) has three big nave-like unloading areas. Kleihues has been influential through his Dortmund Architecture Days, an international symposium held in Dortmund annually since 1975.

Klein, Yves (1928–62) French artist. In the course of his brief but spectacular career, Klein became one of the most influential neo-dadaists of the late 1950s and 1960s. A pioneer of PERFORMANCE ART, he emphasized the symbolic nature of his actions, the ritualized process of creating rather than the completion of an object. His most impressive creation was his own personality; Klein was also a jazz musician, a judo enthusiast (visiting Japan to develop his skill), and a Rosicrucian.

In 1947 Klein conceived the idea of paintings in monochrome. Blue became the favoured hue for these works and Klein even took out a patent for 'International Klein Blue'. His 1958 exhibition at the Galérie Iris Clert, Paris, consisted of a bare room painted white; the blue exterior was guarded by blue-uniformed Garde Republicaine. In *Anthropométries*, first performed in 1960, Klein directed the actions of naked girls smeared with blue paint as they imprinted canvases on the floor by rolling on them. This was accompanied by a performance of Klein's *Monotone Symphony*, a work consisting of a single repeated note. The film *Mondo Kane* records the making of these 'imprints'. *Cosmogonies* (1960) exploited the effects of natural weathering on canvases while for *Fire Paintings* Klein used a blowlamp. In the early 1960s Klein sold his so-called 'Zones of Pictorial Sensibility' to members of the public for gold leaf, which the artist threw in the river Seine while the purchasers burnt their receipts.

In 1960 he was a founder of the avant-garde Nouveau Réaliste group with Christo, ARMAN, TINGUELY, and the critic Pierre Restany (*see* NOUVEAU RÉALISME).

Klimov, Elim (Germanovich) (1933–) Russian film director, who emerged as a leading spokesman for the Soviet film industry in the 1980s and is now regarded as one of his country's most prominent film-makers. Having trained as an aviation engineer, Klimov began his career in the cinema with a series of allegorical films satirizing the Soviet system; they were consequently banned. *Agony* (1975), a fantastic portrayal of the relationship between Rasputin and the Romanov family (and the first Soviet film to depict the mad monk), remained unshown for several years. Klimov did not make another film until *Larisa* (1980), a tribute to his wife **Larisa Shepitko**, also a noted film director, who had been killed in a car accident in 1979. Klimov then completed his wife's film *Farewell* (1981), a haunting account of the destruction of a Siberian village to make way for a new dam. The film was received in the West as a masterpiece.

Further praise came in 1985 with *Come and See*, in which Klimov dwelt upon the atrocities committed during the Nazi invasion of Byelorussia in World War II. Klimov's films found a wider audience in the West in the late 1980s and the director was appointed first secretary to the Film-Makers' Union.

Klos, Elmar *See* KADÁR, JÁN(OS).

Kluge, Alexander (1932–) German film director and writer, who emerged as a leading figure in the NEW CINEMA movement of the 1960s. Kluge practised as a lawyer and joined the literary association GRUPPE 47 before becoming involved in film. A signatory of the 1962 Oberhauser Manifesto that launched the New Cinema, Kluge made his debut as a director of feature-length films in 1966 with the bleakly humorous *Yesterday Girl*, which starred his sister Alexandra as a bewildered East German refugee; the film won eight prizes at the Venice Film Festival, becoming the first post-war German film to earn a major international award.

Kluge soon acquired a reputation as a maker of intellectually complex films that nevertheless gained a wide audience with their ironic wit. *Artistes at the Top of the Big Top: Disorientated* (1968) was a political allegory about the impossibility of achieving a Utopian society. After two science-fiction stories, Kluge returned to his exploration of contemporary angst with *Occasional Work of a Female Slave*, a politically radical comedy starring his sister as a part-time abortionist. *Strongman Ferdinand* (1976) made telling points about the corrupting nature of power, while *Germany in Autumn* (1978) was an impassioned attack on state repression. His other films include *The Patriot* (1979), which re-examines German attitudes to the country's recent past, and *The Candidate* (1980).

Knipper, Lev (Konstantinovich) (1898–1974) Soviet composer. Born in Georgia, he served with the Red Army before studying the piano and composition with Reinhold Glière in Moscow, Phillip Jarnach in Berlin, and Julius Weissmann in Freiburg. Although his works of the 1920s were influenced by modern European styles, he later devoted himself to the study of the folk traditions of the diverse national groups within the Soviet Union. His considerable output includes 20 symphonies, the operas *The North Wind* (1930) and *On the Baikal Lake* (1948), violin, oboe, and cello concertos, orchestral suites on folk melodies, chamber music, and songs.

Knussen, (Stuart) Oliver (1952–) British composer and conductor. Born in Glasgow, he studied in London with John Lambert and subsequently with Gunther Schuller at the Tanglewood Center, Berkshire, US, where he later served as coordinator of contemporary music (1986–90). Knussen is best known for the opera *Where the Wild Things Are* (1983), based on the children's book by Maurice Sendak; the original Glyndebourne production featured stage sets and costumes designed by the author. *Higglety Pigglety Pop* (1985) was also based on a book by Sendak and premiered at Glyndebourne. Knussen's other works include three symphonies (1967, 1971, 1979), *Ophelia Dances* (1975) for chamber ensemble, and *Coursing* (1980) for small orchestra. He has been an artistic director of the ALDEBURGH FESTIVAL since 1983. His *Songs Without Voices* for celeste and small ensemble were premiered at Aldeburgh in 1992.

Koestler, Arthur (1905–83) British writer, born in Hungary. After studying engineering in Vienna, Koestler worked as a foreign correspondent, travelling to the Soviet Union and the Middle East as well as throughout Western Europe. He was an undercover member of the Communist Party from 1932 until 1938. While reporting the Spanish Civil War he was captured and held prisoner by the Nationalists, an experience described in his *Spanish Testament* (1937). He came to Britain during World War II.

Koestler's best-known works of fiction are *Darkness at Noon* (1940), dealing with Stalin's show trials and drawing on Koestler's own experiences of imprisonment during the Spanish Civil War, and *Thieves in the Night* (1946), about Palestine. He also contributed to *The God That Failed* (1949), a collection of essays by disillusioned ex-communists.

After the war Koestler produced a steady stream of nonfiction books on political, scientific, cultural, and psychological topics. *The Act of Creation* (1964) investigates the nature of the creative process, while *The Ghost in the Machine* (1967) examines the effect of evolution upon the formation of the human brain, in particular the separation between left- and right-brain functions. *The Roots of Coincidence* (1972) – its title an allusion to Jung's notion of 'synchronicity' or meaningful coincidence – examines the claims of parapsychology, a subject with which Koestler became increasingly preoccupied in his last years. He also published several volumes of essays and memoirs. An advocate of euthanasia, he and his wife committed suicide when he was suffering from leukaemia and Parkinson's Disease.

Koestler was a prolific and versatile author, who is likely to be remembered mainly as a popularizer of complex and eclectic ideas.

Kokkonen, Joonas (1921–) Finnish composer and teacher. Although a student at the Sibelius Academy, Helsinki, and subsequently at Helsinki University, Kokkonen is virtually self-taught as a composer. His central position in Finnish musical life since 1960 rests on his work as a teacher (at the Sibelius Academy from 1950 to 1963) and the influence that he has exerted as a member of various important musical organizations.

The music of Sibelius (especially his acerbic fourth symphony) has proved a lasting influence on Kokkonen's work, particularly as regards structural reliance on motivic development. The *Music for String Orchestra* (1957) marks the emergence of his individual style, a personal synthesis of the contrapuntal techniques of Bach, Bartók, and Hindemith with SERIALISM. The 12-note technique which he used in his works of the late 1950s, such as the first symphony and the first string quartet, soon gave way to the freer chromatic idiom, tolerant of tonal gestures, that is found in his second symphony (1961). His opera *The Last Temptations* (1975) has attracted much critical acclaim and comparisons with Bartók's *Bluebeard's Castle.* His orchestral output includes four symphonies, *Symphonic Sketches* (1968), and a cello concerto (1969): he has also written chamber music, including three string quartets, and a requiem mass.

Kolakowski, Leszek (1927–) Polish philosopher. Born at Radom, he used his professorship at the University of Warsaw to expound a liberal Marxism within the Communist Party. His writings steadily catalysed dissent across eastern Europe and in 1956 helped to pave the way for the Polish nationalist Władysław Gomulka to take power. When Gomulka reverted to orthodox communism, Kolakowski concluded that doctrinaire Marxism was ultimately incompatible with political freedom. He was expelled from the party in 1966 and lost his chair two years later. After teaching in the US and Canada, he settled at Oxford University in 1970. In his collection of essays *Towards a Marxist Humanism* (1970), he affirmed the duty of the individual to make moral choices, dismissing both Marxist determinism and collectivist ethics. Kolakowski's concern for ethical principles finds expression in the three volumes of *Main Currents in Marxism* (1978) and *Religion* (1982), which explored Christian notions of grace and sin as a source of human action. He has also published three volumes of short stories and written a number of plays.

Koltai, Ralph (1924–) British stage designer, born in Germany, whose designs for theatrical productions throughout Europe and the US have been widely admired. A graduate of the Central School of Art and Design in London, Koltai subsequently joined the ROYAL SHAKESPEARE COMPANY (1963–66 and 1976–) and produced a series of bold designs employing a wide range of modern materials for a varied programme of plays from Shakespeare to BRECHT. His work for the National Theatre consolidated his reputation; he has also produced designs for opera and dance events throughout the world, including productions of *The Flying Dutchman* (1987) and *La Traviata* (1990) for the Hong Kong Arts Festival. Other productions to have attracted attention include *The Love Girl and the Innocent* (1981), *Cyrano de Bergerac* (1983), and *They Shoot Horses, Don't They?* (1987) for the RSC, and *Brand* (1978) and *Man and Superman* (1981) for the National Theatre.

Konchalovsky, Andrei (Andrei Mikhalkov-Konchalovsky; 1937–) Russian film director, living in the US, who emerged as a leading young director in the 1960s. Konchalovsky began his career in the cinema writing screenplays for TARKOVSKY, subsequently making his debut as a director of full-length feature films in 1965, with *The First Teacher*. This story of a young soldier's attempts to reeducate a rural community in revolutionary theory marked Konchalovsky out as one of the most promising new talents in Soviet cinema. However, his second feature, *Asya's Happiness* (1967), about life on a collective farm, fell foul of the Soviet censors and was banned for 20 years; thereafter he was obliged to tackle less challenging and relevant subjects.

After directing a number of uncontroversial adaptations of works by such writers as Chekhov and Turgenev, Konchalovsky settled in the US. Here, he revived his reputation with *Maria's Lovers* (1984), a moving portrayal of the difficulties faced by veterans of World War II on their return home. Also well received was *Runaway Train* (1985), a thriller starring Jon Voight as a convict on the run who sacrifices himself to prevent another young man from turning to crime. Subsequently Konchalovsky's reputation has declined somewhat owing to a series of misjudged ventures intended to attract a mass commercial audience. *The Inner Circle* (1992), a film about Stalin and his coterie as seen through the eyes of his personal projectionist, was the first US film to be shot inside the Kremlin and the former KGB headquarters. Konchalovsky's brother, Nikita Mikhalkov, is also a film director.

Konrád, György (1933–) Hungarian novelist, essayist, and sociologist. After studying Hungarian literature at university, Konrád spent six years as a social worker in Budapest. This experience informed his first novel, *The Case Worker* (*A látogató*; 1969), which won Konrád international critical acclaim. The novel examines the psychology of the social reformer and questions the value of state intervention in the life of the individual. Konrád's next two novels, *The City Builder* (*A városalapító*; 1977) and *The Loser* (*A cinkós*; 1983), examine the different options – complicity, compromise, or criticism – open to the individual in a totalitarian state.

Of Konrád's sociological and political works the best known internationally are *The Intellectuals on the Road to Class Power* (with Iván Szelényi; 1979) and *Antipolitics* (1984). The latter is an extended essay on the post-war division of Europe and stresses the role of civil society and the 'autonomous intellectual' in resisting the tendency to hostile polarization built into power structures in both East and West. Owing to Konrád's active involvement in the Hungarian democratic opposition, many of his works were banned in Hungary until recently, being published either by foreign or *samizdat* presses. He is particularly well-known in Germany. His most recent work is *A Feast in the Garden* (1991), a semiautobiographical novel that is also a meditation on the fate of the 1956 generation of Hungarian intellectuals.

Konwicki, Tadeusz (1926–) Polish novelist, film director, and screenwriter born in Lithuania. He fought as a partisan during World War II while still a teenager and was awarded three medals. His major post-war novels include *Wladza* (1954), *The Marshes* (1956), and *A Dreambook of Our Time* (1963), all of which reflect his war-time experiences in the marshes and forests of Lithuania. Later books such as *Ascension* (1967), *The Calendar and the Sand-Glass* (1976), and *A Minor Apocalypse* (1979) have been criticized for their mannered prose style.

Konwicki wrote cinema criticism in the late 1940s and turned to screenwriting in the 1950s, scripting such films as *Winter Twilight* (1957), KAWALEROWICZ's *Mother Joan of the Angels* (1961) and *Pharaoh* (1964), and Janusz Morgenstern's *Jovita* (1967). He made an impressive directorial debut in 1958 with *The Last Day of Summer*, a warm intimate film about the war's aftermath that he codirected, cowrote, and cophotographed with Jan Laskowski. His subsequent films, which have remained melancholy and intensely personal, include *Halloween* (1961), *Salto* (1965), *How Far and Yet How Near* (1972), and *Lawa* (1989).

Koolhaas, Rem (1944–) Dutch-born architect and writer. He abandoned a career in copywriting to study at the Architectural Association in London (1968–72) under Peter COOK, whose experimental ARCHIGRAM projects made a deep impression. Subsequent study in New York prompted *Delirious New York* (1978), an exhibition and book that assessed Manhattan life through film and advertising as well as architecture and planning.

Koolhaas's idiosyncratic style owes much to Russian constructivism, the Dutch architect J. J. P. Oud, the hard forms of International Modernism, and the panache of advertising imagery. In 1975 he founded the **Office for Metropolitan Architecture** with Elia and Zoe Zenghelis and Madelon Vriesendorp; this now operates as a network with bases in Rotterdam, Berlin, Athens, and London. Its programme is to define new ways in which modern architecture can align itself with contemporary culture. So far theoretical projects outweigh those built in both number and importance, the most influential being a successful competition entry for the Parc de la Villette in Paris (1982–83). That OMA have built at all is a credit to Dutch patronage; buildings include a police station at Almere-Haven (1984–86), the redevelopment of the IJ-Plein shipbuilding yards (plan 1981–82, housing 1983–87), a bus-station in Rotterdam, and a hotel, concert hall, and dance theatre in The Hague (1980–87) that best exemplifies their 'functional fairyland' imagery. Since then they have designed a new commercial centre for Lille, a Centre for Art and Media Technology in Karlsruhe, and a ferry terminal for Zeebrugge shaped like a colossal head.

Korsholm Festival *See* MEA FESTIVAL OF CHAMBER MUSIC.

Kosintsev, Grigori (1905–73) Soviet film director, one of the most innovative new directors to emerge following the 1917 Revolution. In collaboration with Leonid Trauberg, Kosintsev founded FEX (Factory of the Eccentric Actor) and subsequently ventured into cinema with *The Adventures of Oktyabrina* (1924), a Marxist propaganda film. *The Devil's Wheel* (1926), an energetic adventure story set in Leningrad, illustrated the director's flair for visual effects and characterization. He continued to develop these talents in such films as *New Babylon* (1929), an historical adventure set during the fall of the Paris Commune in 1870 with music by SHOSTAKOVICH; this was the first of many collaborations with the composer.

Kosintsev and Trauberg made their first sound film, *Alone*, in 1931 and then embarked on the celebrated 'Maxim' trilogy, tracing the experiences of a revolutionary hero through *The Youth of Maxim* (1935), *The Return of Maxim* (1937), and *The Vyborg Side* (1939). The two then pursued their own careers, Kosintsev winning new praise with a series of much-admired literary adaptations. *Don Quixote* (1957), a brilliant reworking of Cervantes's tale, was followed by versions of Shakespeare, among them *Hamlet* (1964) – in a translation by PASTERNAK – and *King Lear* (1971), a highly atmospheric and political film in which Kosintsev allowed his visual imagination full rein.

Koudelka, Josef (1938–) Czech photographer. Koudelka was born in Buškovice and educated at the University of Prague, where he took a degree in engineering (1961). He is self-taught as a photographer. From 1962 until 1970 he worked as a photographer for the Divadlo Theatre in Prague and in 1971 became a freelancer for the Magnum Photos agency. He is now based in Paris.

Koudelka first came to notice in the West with his poignant images of the Soviet-led invasion of Czechoslovakia in 1968. He is now better known, however, for the earlier photographs collected in *Gypsies* (1975), the product of several years travelling with the Romanies in central Europe. The photographs are both a valuable documentary record of a disappearing lifestyle and mysterious and fascinating images in their own right. Many remain oddly inscrutable to the viewer, who is obliged to construct his or her own interpretation of what is taking place.

Since settling in the West, Koudelka has shown a greater interest in abstract design. Much of the recent work collected in *Exiles* (1988) also has a surrealist flavour. He became a naturalized French citizen in 1987. In 1993 he was invited back to Prague to record the inauguration of Václav HAVEL as president of the Czech Republic.

Koun, Károlos (1908–) Greek theatre director, who distinguished himself as a director of classical plays in Athens during the 1930s. After World War II his name became closely associated with the Greek National Theatre company, which has been seen in cities all over Europe, including Paris and London. His productions with this and other companies have also included numerous plays by more modern writers, among them Pirandello and Tennessee Williams. In 1967 he directed a highly successful production of *Romeo and Juliet* for the ROYAL SHAKESPEARE COMPANY.

Kounellis, Jannis (1936–) Greek experimental artist and sculptor, who has lived in Italy since 1956. Kounellis studied at the Academy of Fine Arts in Rome and gave his first one-man exhibition at the Galleria La Tartaruga, Rome, in 1960. The works shown there featured letters, numbers, and symbols stencilled on canvas but later in the 1960s he abandoned painting, which he considered anachronistic in the modern world, and turned to installations, becoming one of the leading figures of the ARTE POVERA movement. Typical works make use of such materials as steel, coal, wool, and live animals; one of his best-known pieces, *Cavalli* (1969), involved stabling horses in a Rome art gallery. He has exhibited in many European cities and in 1986 there was a large retrospective of his work at the Museum of Contemporary Art in Chicago. Recent work has placed an emphasis on the texture and smell of natural materials.

Krejča, Otomar (1921–) Czech theatre director, who founded Prague's famous **Theatre Behind the Gate** in 1965, having been chief director and head of drama at Czechoslovakia's National Theatre since the late 1950s. Krejča built up an international reputation with productions of plays by both classical and modern writers, among them Chekhov, Shakespeare, and BECKETT, many of which were presented at leading European theatre festivals. In most of his earlier productions he worked in partnership with the designer Josef SVOBODA, with whom he shared an enthusiasm for bold interpretations of powerful plays. Productions that attracted particular praise included *The Seagull* (1960), *Romeo and Juliet* (1963), and Krejča's own *Oedipus-Antigone* (1971). Krejča lost his post at the Theatre Behind the Gate in 1971 and the theatre itself was closed shortly afterwards. In 1976 he was banned from working in Czechoslovakia; subsequently he worked as a director in Belgium and elsewhere. He returned to Prague to found a new theatre company in 1990.

Krier, Leon (1946–) Luxembourgeois architect and theorist. Krier was born in Luxembourg, the brother of Rob KRIER, from whom he received his earliest architectural education. He attended the University of Stuttgart, subsequently working as an assistant (1968–70) to James STIRLING. Krier has held academic posts at the Architectural Association, Princeton and the University of Virginia. Although his list of built works is short, he has wielded great influence as one of the most powerful critics of modernist rationalism, in both planning and design. A vigorous opponent of modernist zoning, Krier has argued for a return to a more traditional type of urban planning, stressing the importance of mixed uses in promoting a democratic anti-monopolistic environment. Krier has been a forceful critic of the break with the past inherent in much modernist design and planning and seeks to reconnect today's civil life to European tradition. His own designs are Greek Revival, bearing the stamp of Boullée, Ledoux, Soane, and Loos. His projects for Royal Mint Court, London, Spitalfields Market, London, and the La Villette quarter in Paris have had a wide influence despite remaining unexecuted. His most important built work has been the master plan and a number of individual buildings for Sea Side, a holiday resort in Florida (1983). Latterly, Krier has been an architectural adviser to the Prince of Wales and is involved with the Prince's new School of Architecture (1992).

Krier, Rob (1938–) Luxembourgeois architect, brother to Leon KRIER. Rob Krier studied architecture at the Technical University, Munich, (1959–64), and worked in the offices of O. M. Mungers and Frei OTTO (1965–70). He has been in private practice in Vienna since 1976. His output has consisted largely of social housing in Berlin and Vienna. Krier is a major figure in the reaction away from the rationalism of LE CORBUSIER and other modernist planners towards a more organic and traditional approach to city planning, as argued for in his book *Urban Space in Theory and Practice* (1975).

Krips, Josef (1902–74) Austrian conductor known mostly for performances of Mozart and Schubert. Krips studied at the

Vienna Academy, where he made his debut as a conductor in 1921. After working in Dortmund, Karlsruhe, and Vienna in the 1920s and 1930s he became conductor of the Vienna State Opera in 1935. After World War II, during which he was banned from conducting by the Nazis, he played an important role in reestablishing Viennese cultural life, conducting the first opera performance in post-war Vienna and reopening the Salzburg Festival in 1946. He made his Covent Garden debut with the Vienna Philharmonic in 1947 and was principal conductor of the London Symphony Orchestra from 1950 until 1954. He also held posts in the US with the Buffalo Philharmonic Orchestra and the San Francisco Symphony Orchestra.

Kristeva, Julia (1941–) French literary theorist, born in Bulgaria. In 1965 Kristeva travelled to Paris, where she studied linguistics, literature, and psychology. In the late 1960s she joined the group of semioticians associated with the journal *Tel Quel* and worked as an assistant to Claude LÉVI-STRAUSS. Following Jacques LACAN, she postulated a link between psychoanalysis and the philosophy of language in her first book *Semeiotike* (1969). Here she argues that subjective identity is itself a product of language. These ideas were developed further in *The Revolution of Poetical Language* (1974). With her husband Philippe Sollers and Roland BARTHES she made a journey to Mao's China in 1974 and published the study *About Chinese Women*. In her later work Kristeva has investigated the complex relations between sexuality and text and the way in which language seems to exclude the idea of women as intellectual beings (*Polylogue*, 1977; *Love Stories*, 1983; *Strangers to Ourselves*, 1988). Her preoccupation with the concept of the feminine and the relationship between language and the body made Kristeva a vogue figure amongst feminist theorists in the 1980s. In 1991 she published *Les Samourais*, a *roman à clef* in which many leading French intellectuals of the 1960s and 1970s appear in lightly disguised form.

Kroetz, Franz Xaver (1946–) German playwright, noted for his hard-hitting dramas written in the form of the traditional German folk play. His first work, *Wild Game Crossing* (1969), was directed by FASSBINDER and reflected the influence of the folk plays of such writers as Ödön von Horvath. Kroetz first attracted widespread attention, however, in 1971 when riots greeted the first performances of *Homework* and *Stiffnecked*, which depicted the realities of peasant life in all their coarseness and brutality. Equally uncompromising was his next double bill, *Dairy Farm* and *Ghost Train* (1972), which dealt with the seduction and pregnancy of a mentally retarded young woman in similarly unsympathetic rural surroundings. Like Kroetz's other works, these plays are populated with repressed and virtually inarticulate characters, who face emotional humiliation and hardship on a daily basis.

In *Oberosterreich* (1972) and *The Nest* (1975) Kroetz turned his attention to the lives of similarly deprived characters in urban society. He subsequently adopted a more stylized approach in such works as *Neither Fish nor Flesh* (1981). His other plays include *Maria Magdalena* (1973), based on the play by Hebbel, *Fear and Hope in the FRG* (1984), and *Help Wanted* (1986). In 1991 he published four volumes of essays and poetry.

Kroll, Lucien (1929–) Belgian architect. Born in Brussels, Kroll studied there before entering practice with Charles Vandenhove. In the 1950s he designed private houses, thereafter obtaining a number of ecclesiastical projects. His first independent commission was the creation of craft workshops out of a barn in the Abbey of Maredsous (1957). His chapel in Linkebeek (1960–63) was a communal project, designed in consultation with the congregation and partly built by them. From 1962 to 1970 he was engaged on government buidings for the new state of Rwanda. Kroll used the commission for housing on the medical campus of Louvain University as another occasion for a democratic consultative approach to planning, organizing committees of the students who were to use the buildings (1969–72). Further church projects have followed those at Woluwe Saint Lambert (1969) and Biesmerée (1976).

Krolow, Karl (1915–) German poet. Born in Hannover, Krolow studied German, art history, philosophy, and Romance languages; he began to publish his poems in the early 1940s. As a member of numerous literary academies (Akademie der Wissenschaften und der Literatur,

Mainz; Akademie für Sprache und Dichtung, Darmstadt), he has effected a considerable influence on post-war writing. He has been awarded several prizes for his own work.

Beginning as a nature poet writing in a somewhat conventional style, Krolow later adopted a more contemporary idiom that shows the influence of Spanish modernism and French surrealism. His laconic manner often masks a deep-rooted melancholy. The poems celebrate the momentary triumph of language over a world that is seen as chaotic and absurd but nevertheless beautiful. Krolow is one of the most powerful poets in modern Germany. His most important publications are: *Days and Nights* (1956), *Passing of Time* (1972), *Mortal* (1980), and *The Other Side of the World* (1987).

Kubelik, (Jeronym) Rafael (1914–) Czech conductor and composer who became a Swiss national in 1973. The son of the violinist Jan Kubelik, Rafael Kubelik was born in Býchory, Czechoslovakia, and educated at the Prague Conservatorium. He first conducted the Czech Philharmonic Orchestra in 1934 and two years later was officially appointed conductor, a position he held until 1948, with a two-year break directing the Brno Opera (1939–41). Following World War II he emigrated first to Britain (conducting the Glyndebourne Opera in 1948) and then to Switzerland. He has also conducted the Bavarian Radio Symphony Orchestra (1961–79) the Metropolitan Opera, New York (1973–74), and the Chicago Symphony Orchestra (1950–53), a position from which he was forced to resign following a dispute over his inclusion of at least 60 modern compositions in the orchestra's repertoire. He was musical director of the Royal Opera House, Covent Garden, from 1955 to 1958. His own compositions include symphonies, operas, string quartets, and a violin concerto. He is also known for promoting Czech music.

Kundera, Milan (1929–) Czech poet, novelist, dramatist, and essayist, living in France. He began studies at the Arts Faculty in Prague but was forced to leave and took a film course at the Academy of Performing Arts, where he subsequently taught world literature. After the Soviet occupation (1968) he was prevented from publishing, but eventually (1975) allowed to travel to France, where he took up a teaching post at Rennes. In 1979 he was deprived of his Czechoslovak citizenship; he subsequently moved to Paris, where he also taught.

Kundera's early verse includes *The Last May* (1955), notorious for its comparison of the communist hero Julius Fučik (1903–43) with Christ and his Gestapo interrogator with the Devil. However, the tension between the socialist realist theme and the well-nigh absurdist form of his first play, *The Owners of the Keys* (1962), makes it one of the most original Czech post-war dramas. *Cock-Up* (1969), a blend of black comedy and erotic farce, demonstrates his unexploited skill as a satirist, whereas his third play, *Jacques and His Master* (1975) is a vacuous 'metadrama' about sex and writing. The first two volumes of *Laughable Loves* (1963 and 1965) show his ability to present embarrassment with pithy irony; the theme of humiliation is also the mainspring of the novel that made Kundera's name, *The Joke* (1967). His most accomplished novel is his quasi-confessional *Life Is Elsewhere* (1973), a work concerning deception and self-deception, which shows a pompous young socialist poet dying after moral and sexual humiliation. The intellectualism of *The Book of Laughter and Forgetting* (1979) becomes somewhat overbearing in *The Unbearable Lightness of Being* (1984), in which the characters – apart from the dog – are little more than pegs for the author's philosophical ideas. *Immortality* (1990) does have one real character, the beautiful victim Agnes. Apparently new here, though probably latent as early as *Laughable Loves*, is a brand of dualism; Kundera seems to suggest that man's identity is only recognizable in pain, and pain is evil. His books have enjoyed considerable success in the West.

Küng, Hans (1928–) Swiss Roman Catholic theologian. Küng studied philosophy and theology in Rome and was ordained a priest in 1954. He obtained his doctorate in Paris and in 1960 was appointed to a chair of theology in Tübingen. In his earlier writings Küng investigated the relationship between the Catholic hierarchy, headed by the Pope, and the Catholic Church understood as a community of believers, past and present; for Küng the latter, rather than the former, is the true basis of Catholic religion (*The Church*; 1967). In 1970 Küng applied this approach to the question of Papal infallibility, concluding that the Church as a whole cannot err but that the Pope as its head may (*Infallible? An Enquiry*). The book provoked worldwide discussion in Catholic circles and marked the beginning of Küng's conflicts with the Roman Catholic hierarchy.

In his book *On Being a Christian* (1974) Küng insisted that the person and teaching of Jesus Christ, as presented in the New Testament, must be the final touchstone of authentic Christianity. In Küng's view, the frequent failure of Catholic doctrine to acknowledge this has been one of the main reasons for the permanent disunion of the different Christian denominations. In *Does God Exist?* (1979) Küng answered his own question in the affirmative, while accepting (against the traditional Catholic position) that there cannot be any rational proof of this.

In 1979 Küng was stripped of his licence to teach in the name of the Catholic Church. Subsequently he has taught in Tübingen under secular auspices while insisting on his continuing right to speak out for the community of Catholic believers. More recent works include *Eternal Life?* (1984) and several important contributions to the developing debate about the relationship between Christianity and the other world religions.

Kylián, Jirí (1947–) Czech dancer and choreographer, who emerged as one of the most influential new talents of the 1970s, particularly through his association with the NETHERLANDS DANCE THEATRE. Having studied dance at the Prague Conservatory and at the Royal Ballet School in London, Kylián joined John CRANKO's Stuttgart Ballet as a dancer in 1968. He executed his first works as a choreographer in 1970. Rapidly attracting attention for both the vitality and musicality of his creations, he was soon being acclaimed as the most important choreographer to emerge from central Europe since Kurt Jooss.

In 1975 Kylián left the company to become artistic director of the Netherlands Dance Theatre (sole director from 1978) and soon established the troupe as one of the finest companies in Europe, concentrating largely on his own ballets. His mastery of both classical and modern dance techniques ensured the success of such works as *Return to the Strange Land* (1975), *Symphony of Psalms* (1978), *Sinfonietta* (1979), *Soldier's Mass* (1980), a trilogy based on Australian aboriginal culture, *L'Enfant et les sortilèges* (1984), about the fantasy world of a child, and *Kaguya-Hime* (1988), based on Japanese mythology.

L

Lacan, Jacques (1901–81) French psychoanalyst and philosopher. After studying medicine Lacan became a psychiatrist, publishing his thesis on female paranoia in 1932. At the 14th International Congregation of Psychoanalysts (1936) he presented his famous study of the narcissistic 'mirror-stage' in the development of the child. Lacan's unconventional methods and his highly original interpretation of Freud led to a quarrel with the Association of French Psychoanalysts and he was excluded from the International Society of Psychoanalysts in 1963. In 1964 he founded his own school, the Ecole Freudienne de Paris.

Lacan's chief contribution to modern thought was his reinterpretation of Freudian psychology in terms provided by the structural linguistics of Saussure and Roman Jakobson (*see* STRUCTURALISM; POST-STRUCTURALISM). In particular, he rejected any notion of a stable autonomous ego, arguing that the human subject is constituted by the 'symbolic order' of language, law, and custom and is inherently unstable and neurotic. The experience of alienation begins when the infant achieves self-definition by separating him or herself from the not-self. Despite their frequent obscurity, Lacan's ideas have had an immense influence on French intellectual life since the late 1960s. His principal publication was *Writings* (1966), a collection of articles and lectures.

Lagerkvist, Pär (1891–1974) Swedish novelist, poet, and playwright. Lagerkvist was born and brought up in Växjö, a small town largely cut off from the social, economic, and cultural changes of the time. The conflict between the pietistic values of his youth and the demands of the modern sceptical intellect is the mainspring of all his work; Lagerkvist asks fundamental questions about the purpose of human life, finding mainly ambiguous answers.

Lagerkvist's early works are intensely pessimistic, reflecting his loss of religious faith. The poems in *Anguish* (1916) and the short expressionist plays in *The Difficult Hour* (1918) present human life as largely without hope or meaning. A more positive and humanistic vision emerges in *The Triumph over Life* (1927), a book of prose meditations.

Although Lagerkvist's poetry and drama have helped to shape the development of these genres in Sweden, his international fame rests upon his prose fiction. *The Hangman* (*Bödeln*; 1933) is an acclaimed short story dealing with human brutality and evil in the light of contemporary events in Germany. Lagerkvist's most completely successful works are probably the short novels *The Dwarf* (1944), a sombre tale with a Renaissance setting, and *Barabbas* (1950), which investigates the significance of Christ's crucifixion to the thief released in his place. Barabbas emerges as an unattractive Everyman figure torn between his desire to trust in God and his inability to do so. The novels *The Sibyl* (1956), *Death of Ahasuerus* (1960), *Pilgrim at Sea* (1962), and *The Holy Land* (1964) together form a pentalogy in which the relationship between God and man is debated at great length and from a variety of different positions. Lagerkvist was awarded the Nobel Prize for literature in 1951.

Laing, R(onald) D(avid) (1927–89) British psychiatrist. Born in Glasgow, Laing worked as a psychiatrist with the British army from 1951 until 1953. After further training he joined London's Tavistock Institute in 1957 and from 1962 until 1965 directed the Langham Clinic. It was during this period that he began to specialize in the study of psychiatric illness in the context of the family. In 1964 Laing founded the Philadelphia Association, which organized a number of communities in which deeply disturbed people could take refuge without being labelled 'psychotic'; they were subjected to neither medical treatment nor 'analysis'.

Laing first came to public attention with the publication of *The Divided Self* (1960), a book that set out to demystify madness and questioned the validity of the very terms 'sane' and 'insane'. Laing argued that 'insane' behaviour is often a reasonable response to intolerable pressures. In *The Self and Others* (1961) and *Sanity, Madness and the Family* (1964; with Aaron Esterson) he argued that the main source of such pressures was the nuclear family itself. In *The Politics of Experience/The Bird of Paradise* (1967) these ideas acquired mystical and sociopolitical overtones; the book established him a guru for the radical student 'generation of 1968'. The psychotic is here seen as the sacrificial victim of an insane society and conventional psychiatry is denounced as a mechanism of social control.

Knots (1970) is a collection of aphorisms exploring ontology, consciousness, and relationships. In the early 1970s Laing, a tireless self-educator, studied Oriental philosophy and meditation in the East under Buddhist and Hindu masters. His exploration of the roots of madness in contemporary society continued in such works as *The Facts of Life* (1976), which attacks modern medical attitudes to the birth process. He also continued to practise as a healer of the mentally disturbed, favouring the use of psychedelic drugs in carefully selected doses.

Laing's ideas had considerable appeal in the artistic and political culture of the late 1960s and early 1970s but have made little impact on psychiatric practice. His later years were clouded by long periods of alcoholic depression.

Lamorisse, Albert (1922–70) French film director, best known for his short fantasy films. Born in Paris, Lamorisse worked as a photographer before beginning to direct short subjects such as *Djerba* (1947) and *Bim* (1949). He gained worldwide praise for *White Mane* (1952), which earned a Grand Prize at the Cannes Film Festival, and *The Red Balloon* (1956), which took the same prize and an Academy Award. The latter is a delightful fantasy about a lonely boy and his encounter with a balloon, which eventually lifts him above Paris. Lamorisse made several feature films in the 1960s, including *Fifi la Plume* (1964), a fantasy about a burglar who learns to fly and is mistaken for an angel. He soon returned to shorts, however, including such notable documentaries as *Versailles* (1967) and *Paris jamais vu* (1968). He died in a helicopter crash while filming *The Lovers' Wind*, a documentary about Iran. It was completed and edited according to his outlines and received an Academy Award nomination for best feature documentary in 1978.

Lampedusa, Giuseppe Tomasi di (1896–1957) Italian novelist. A wealthy Sicilian aristocrat, Lampedusa served as an artillery officer in World War I, during which he escaped from a Hungarian prison camp and made an adventurous return to Italy on foot. After suffering a nervous breakdown he devoted himself entirely to intellectual pursuits. He achieved posthumous fame when his only novel *The Leopard*, written in the last years of his life, was discovered and published by BASSANI in 1958. An immediate bestseller, it reached a still wider audience through VISCONTI's film version (1963).

The novel depicts upper-class Sicilian life in the 1860s during the upheavals of the Risorgimento and the overthrow of the Bourbon Kingdom of the Two Sicilies. A bitter picture of an immobile and 'irredeemable' Sicily emerges. The psychological focus of the book is the proudly aristocratic Don Fabrizio, prince of Salina, who, faced with a choice between resisting the new order or reaching an accommodation, finds his own solution. With its penetrating characterization, evocative atmosphere, and its highly literary style, *The Leopard* is recognized as one of the very greatest of post-war Italian novels. Lampedusa's other works, all published posthumously, include a volume of short stories and reminiscences (1961), a collection of critical essays on Stendhal (1971), and his *Invitation to Sixteenth-Century French Literature* (1979).

Land art *See* EARTH ART.

Lander, Harald (Alfred Bernhardt Stevnsborg; 1905–71) Danish-French designer, choreographer, and ballet director, who revitalized Danish ballet while serving as director of the Royal Danish Ballet in the 1940s; he later embarked on a successful international career. Having trained at the Royal Danish Ballet School, he joined the senior company in 1923 and emerged as one of the star dancers of his generation, touring the Soviet Union, Mexico, and the US before returning to Denmark in 1929. He was appointed ballet master of the Royal Danish Ballet in 1930 and took over as director of the Royal Danish Ballet School in 1932. Over the next 20 years he transformed the company into one of the most prestigious in Europe, reviving many of the ballets of August Bournonville and adding some 30 ballets choreographed by himself.

The company's greatest successes of the 1930s and 1940s included Lander's *Football* (1933), *The Little Mermaid* (1936), *The Denmark Ballet* (1939), *The Sorcerer's Apprentice* (1940), and the one-act *Études* (1948), which he subsequently revived with other companies on several occasions. In 1952 Lander moved to Paris, where he eventually became director (1956–57 and 1959–63) of the Paris Opéra School, at the same time working as a choreographer for companies all over the world. His most popular works of the 1950s included *Printemps à Vienne* (1954), *Concerto aux étoiles* (1956), and *Vita Eterna* (1958). He returned to Copenhagen in 1962, where further successes included *Les Victoires de l'amour* and revivals of some of his earlier ballets.

Landolfi, Tommaso (1908–79) Italian novelist, short-story writer, and poet. Landolfi's fiction was influenced by his friendship with poets of the hermetic school such as LUZI and MONTALE and with Roman writers such as MORAVIA and Brancati. He was a distinguished translator of 19th- and 20th-century French and Russian authors (Pushkin, Gogol, Merimée) and a contributor to the avant-garde magazines *Campo di Marte* and *Letteratura*. An eccentric, an inveterate gambler, and an incurable dandy, Landolfi remained an enigmatic figure in the literary world.

His *Dialogue Concerning the Two Chief World Systems* (1937) was followed by several collections of short stories, notably *The Moon Stone* (1939), *The Sword* (1942), and *The Autumn Tale* (1947). The elements of the grotesque and the surreal in his shorter fiction have led to comparisons with CALVINO and Jorge Luis Borges. Landolfi also produced science-fiction novels such as *Cancerqueen* (1950), fables for children such as *The Unhappy Prince* (1954), and Pirandellesque plays such as *Faust 67* (1969). His poetry is collected in *Death Violet* (1972) and his final publication, *Inadvertently* (1975).

Lanyon, Peter (1918–64) British painter and sculptor. Lanyon studied at the Euston Road Art School in 1938 and from 1939 in his native St Ives with Ben NICHOLSON and the Russian sculptor Naum Gabo. During World War II he served in the RAF.

One of the ST IVES SCHOOL of painters, he produced mainly Cornish landscapes, initially in a somewhat traditional manner but later in a more abstract style influenced by ART INFORMEL. Under Gabo's influence he also made three-dimensional constructions from such materials as perspex, stained glass, and wire; these sometimes incorporated found objects such as driftwood or rope. Although usually intended as preparatory studies for paintings, these constructions are of great interest in their own right. His best-known paintings include the monumental *Porthleven* (1951), commissioned for the FESTIVAL OF BRITAIN. Later work shows the influence of the US abstract expressionists de Kooning and Rothko.

Lanyon taught at the Bath Academy of Art, Corsham (1950–57). In 1963 he was visiting painter at the San Antonio Art Institute, Texas, and he lectured for the British Council in Czechoslovakia the following year. A keen glider, he died in a flying accident.

Lapicque, Charles (1898–) French abstract painter. Lapicque studied civil engineering and only took up painting as a hobby in 1925. He exhibited at the leading Paris salons in the 1930s and in 1937 created the interior decorations for the Palais de la Découverte at the Paris Exposition Universelle. In 1939 he became a Doctor of Science with a dissertation on optics and the perception of contours.

In 1940 he made contact with the young abstract painters BAZAINE, MANESSIER and Esteve, and became part of their Jeunes Peintures de la Tradition Français group. His post-war paintings combine abstract techniques derived from the cubists, Fauves, and Orphists with a continuing interest in natural appearances. In his most characteristic works fragments of recognizable scenes – a landscape, a regatta, or horse race – appear through a grid of crisscrossing lines. According to Lapicque, his colourful and rhythmic paintings were intended to appeal directly to the emotions in the same way as a piece of music.

Larkin, Philip (Arthur) (1922–85) British poet and novelist. Born in Coventry, he was educated at St John's College, Oxford and subsequently became a librarian. In 1955 he was appointed librarian of Hull University, where he remained for the rest of his life. His early poems, which are much influenced by Auden and Yeats, appeared in the anthology *Poetry from Oxford in Wartime* (1944) and his own first collection *The North Ship* (1945). Larkin's personal voice emerged in his second volume *The Less Deceived* (1955), where such poems as 'Toads' established his characteristic tone of melancholy leavened by stoicism and deadpan humour. His use of the rhythms of everyday speech and his choice of topics from ordinary life led him to be identified with the MOVEMENT; several of his poems appeared in the anthology *New Lines* (1956). In 1964 he published *The Whitsun Weddings*, continuing his preoccupation with the frustrations and ironies of provincial and suburban life. His final volume, *High Windows* (1974), explores themes of old age and death, with Larkin ironically but regretfully accepting his own and his generation's sense of being left behind. He also published two novels *Jill* (1946) and *A Girl in Winter* (1947). The former deals with a lonely undergraduate at Oxford and his fantasies about the privileged girl of the title, while the latter records a day in the life of a provincial librarian. Larkin also published a volume of essays on jazz, *All What Jazz?* (1970), and edited *The Oxford Book of Twentieth Century English Verse* (1973). His *Collected Poems*, containing much previously unavailable material, appeared posthumously in 1988. A volume of *Selected Letters* was published in 1992.

Larrieu, Daniel (1957–) French dancer and choreographer, who emerged as a leading exponent of dance theatre in France in the 1980s. He began his career as a dancer, forming his own small company (called Astrakhan and initially consisting of just three dancers) in 1982; he subsequently attracted attention with a series of witty pieces in which he played on provocative juxtapositions of music, images, and movement.

Larrieu's *Un Sucre ou deux* (1982), an innovative series of dance movements set to the music of Prokofiev's *Romeo and Juliet*, was widely praised. More recently, he created *Waterproof* (1986) for the Centre National de Danse Contemporaine in Angers, in which nine dancers perform in a huge water-filled swimming pool, their movements being relayed to the audience on large video screens. He has also created works for other major companies, including the LONDON CONTEMPORARY DANCE THEATRE and the NETHERLANDS DANCE THEATRE.

Lasdun, Sir Denys (1906–) British architect responsible for many major buildings in Britain in the 1960s. His first postwar work, the Hallfield Estate and School, Paddington (1947–55, with Lindsay Drake) was inherited from Lubetkin's Tecton practice. Housing in Usk Street, Bethnal Green (1955–58) followed during his partnership with FRY AND DREW (until 1960). A shop for Peter Robinson's (1959), luxury flats in St James's Place (1960), and Fitzwilliam College, Cambridge (1961–67) were his first independent works. Major projects soon followed: the Royal Institute of Physicians (1961), the University of East Anglia (1962–68) and the National Theatre, London, (1965–76), which was originally intended to include an opera house. Lasdun acknowledges a debt to LE CORBUSIER but has developed a distinctive love of strong horizontal planes that play with projecting and receding space, a theme also exploited in the National Theatre interiors. The Royal Institute of Physicians and St James's Place flats show his skill with good materials, but the poor concrete of some of his public buildings has provoked fierce criticism. It is unfortunate that his largest public commissions should have suffered from severe financial constraints.

Lattuada, Alberto (1914–) Italian film director and screenwriter, best known for his contribution to post-war NEOREALISM. Born in Milan, he was the son of a composer, Felice Lattuada, who later provided the music for many of his films. Lattuada studied architecture while working as a cinema set decorator. In 1940 he joined Ferrari and COMENCINI in setting up the Italian film archives, Cineteca Italiana, and in 1942 he directed his first film, *Giacomo l'Idealista.* After World War II he became swept up in the neorealist movement, directing and coscripting such impressive films as *The Bandit* (1946), *Without Pity* (1948), *The Mill on the Po* (1948), *Variety Lights* (1950; in collaboration with FELLINI), and *Il Capotto* (1952). His greatest box-office success was the sentimental *Anna* (1951), starring Silvana Mangano as a novice nun who recalls her former life. His later films, which ranged from dramas to spectacles, included *The Adolescents* (1961), *The Love Root* (1965), *The Betrayer* (1968), *Stay As You Are* (1978), and *A Thorn in the Heart* (1986).

Lausanne International Festival A music festival held in Lausanne, Switzerland, in May and June each year. It was established in 1956. The programme includes opera, concerts, ballet, and jazz.

Lavant, Christine (Christine Habernig; 1915–73) Austrian poet and short-story writer. Born in Carinthia, she endured a childhood blighted by illness and poverty. Almost entirely self-educated, she began to write poems while working as a knitter. Her poems present the world as a place of permanent struggle between good and evil and are much preoccupied with the problems of unrequited love and loneliness. An heir of the romantics and the expressionists, she developed a dark hermetic style full of mysterious imagery. She presents the inner life as both attractive and dangerous, because it is permeable to the demonic and destructive forces in nature and in man himself; in her view, these perils can only be overcome with the help of divine love. Her work received several prizes and was widely admired in post-war Austria. Her major collections are: *The Beggar's Cup* (1956), *Spindle in the Moon* (1959), and *The Cry of the Peacock* (1962).

Lavrovsky, Leonid Mikhailovich (1905–67) Soviet dancer, choreographer, and ballet director. Born in St Petersburg, Lavrovsky danced with George Balanchine in the 1920s and subsequently developed his career as a choreographer, his first full-length ballet being *Fadetta* (1934). After *Katerina* (1935) he was appointed ballet director at the Maly Theatre (1935–38) and then of the Kirov Theatre (1938–44), during which period he created *Romeo and Juliet* (1940). This ballet is considered one of the best interpretations of Prokofiev's score and firmly established Lavrovsky as the most important Soviet choreographer of the early post-war period. It was highly praised when it came to London in 1950.

After this success, Lavrovsky became chief choreographer and artistic director of the Bolshoi Ballet (1944–56 and 1960–64). His later works included productions of *Giselle* (1944), *The Red Poppy* (1949), *Paganini* (1960), and *Pages of Life* (1961). His son, Mikhail Lavrovsky, became one of the Bolshoi's principal dancers, often appearing opposite Natalia Bessmertnova.

Laxness, Halldór Kiljan (Halldór Kiljan Gudjónsson; 1902–) Icelandic novelist, playwright, and short-story writer. Born in Reykjavik, Laxness is modern Iceland's most famous writer. As a young man he travelled widely and showed an equal intellectual restlessness. His first important work, *The Great Weaver from Kashmir* (1927), reflects both his conversion to and later disenchantment with Roman Catholicism. Laxness spent the following three years in the US, where the glaring social inequalities led him to embrace the socialism that informs the major novels of his middle phase. He made his name internationally with *Salka Valka* (1931–32), two linked novels set in an Icelandic fishing village, and *Independent People* (1934–35), about a stubbornly individualistic hill farmer. These ambitious novels were followed by works on a still larger scale – the tetralogy *World Light* (1937–40) and the trilogy of historical novels *Iceland's Bell* (1943–46), concerning the attempts of a wrongly convicted man to clear his name. *Atom Station* (1948) was a satirical novel that criticized US influence in post-war Iceland. A growing scepticism towards socialism is apparent in the equally satirical *Paradise Regained* (1960), which is set partly in the US. Outstanding amongst Laxness's later novels is *Christianity below the Glacier* (1970), which depicts the rich human oddity to be found in a remote Icelandic village.

Laxness has also written a number of successful plays, including *The Silver Moon* (1954), about the US military presence in Iceland, which caused much debate when first produced. The social comedies *The Chimney Play* and *The Sun Knitting Works* followed in 1961 and 1962, although the latter was not performed until 1966. The same year saw the appearance of *The Pigeon Banquet*, considered by many to be Laxness's best play, which was a great success both in Iceland and abroad. His collections of short stories include *Seven Signs* (1964). In the 1970s Laxness produced several volumes of autobiography.

Although most of Laxness's works are set in rural Iceland and are strongly nationalist in feeling, his characteristic themes – notably the conflict between the individual conscience and external authority – are of universal relevance and he has found a wide international readership.

Lazzini, Joseph (1927–) French dancer, choreographer, and ballet director, who attracted particular attention for his work with the Ballet de Marseille in the 1960s. Lazzini studied dance in Nice and began his performing career with the Nice Opéra Ballet in 1945. Subsequently he danced with several Italian companies and directed troupes in Liège (1954–57) and Toulouse (1958), before taking over the Ballet de Marseilles in 1959.

Over the next ten years, Lazzini made the company the most prominent in France after the Paris Opéra Ballet, with a series of spectacular productions in which he enlisted the services of leading performers and designers. His greatest successes with the troupe included *Hommage à Jérôme Bosch* (1961), *E=MC²* (1964), *Lascaux* (1965), *Eppur si muove* (1965), and *Ecce Homo* (1968). When Lazzini left the company in 1968 to found another troupe of his own he was replaced by Roland PETIT, who maintained the company's high reputation. Lazzini has also created works for the Metropolitan Opera House, La Scala, and the Paris Opéra.

Leach, Bernard (1887–1979) British studio potter. The son of a colonial official, Leach spent his early years in Japan and the Far East. After studying as a painter and etcher at the Slade School of Fine Art (1903–08), he returned to Japan. He took up pottery in 1911, becoming apprenticed to the sixth generation of Japanese potters working in the tradition of the noted 17th-century maker of *raku* ware, Ogata Kenzan. He and Tomimoto Kenkichi (1886–1963) were later awarded the title of Kenzan VII, marking the seventh generation of Kenzan potters.

He returned to England in 1920 and established the Leach Pottery at St Ives, Cornwall, with his friend and fellow potter Shōji Hamada (1894–1978). From here he produced ceramics in the oriental (and particularly *raku*) tradition, becoming especially well known for his simple sturdy tableware and flower vases decorated with subtle glazes. His style has had a great influence on contemporary ceramic design throughout the world.

Leach published *A Potter's Book* (1940), containing much personal philosophy, as well as biographies of Kenzan and Hamada. He was largely responsible for the acceptance of potters as artists rather than simply craftsmen.

Leakey, Mary (1913–) British palaeoanthropologist. Mary Nicol first made contact with the world of the professional palaeontologist through her skill as a draughtswoman. After marrying the palaeontologist **Louis Leakey** in 1936 she spent the next 36 years working with him on his East African field trips and collaborating with him as excavator, author, and palaeontologist. She was director of research of the Olduvai Gorge Excavations. She is also the mother of Richard Leakey, director of the Wildlife and Conservation Management Service in Kenya.

Many of the more dramatic discoveries associated with the Leakeys were in fact made by Mary and not by her better-known husband. Thus, it was Mary who discovered in Kenya in 1947 the skull of *Proconsul africanus*, the first fossil ape skull ever to be found. It was also Mary, at Olduvai in 1959, who found the skull of *Zinjanthropus boisei*, a 1.75 million-year-old new species of Australopithecus, and claimed by the Leakeys as the true ancestor of man. Working in northern Tanzania in the Laetoli beds near Lake Eyasi, she made (1976) what she has described as 'the most remarkable find' of her whole career. Still preserved in the volcanic ash she had found footprints of hominids, clear evidence that man's ancestors had alredy adopted an upright posture some 3.75 million years ago.

Lean, Sir David (1908–91) British film director, whose epic productions have included some of the most successful and acclaimed works of the post-war European cinema. Lean began his career as a studio teaboy, gradually working his way up to become an editor for such directors as Paul Czinner, Anthony Asquith, and Michael POWELL. In 1942 he codirected with Noël Coward the propaganda adventure *In Which We Serve*. Subsequently he worked with Coward on *This Happy Breed* (1944), *Blithe Spirit* (1945), and *Brief Encounter* (1945), one of the best-loved romances of the British cinema.

In 1946 Lean made *Great Expectations*, from the novel by Charles Dickens, the first of the large-scale productions with which his name is usually associated. A further Dickens adaptation, *Oliver Twist*, followed in 1948. During the 1950s he made a number of relatively small-budget films, such as *The Sound Barrier* (1952), which costarred Lean's wife Ann Todd, and *Hobson's Choice* (1953), featuring Charles Laughton and John Mills. The lavish romance *Summertime* (or *Summer Madness*; 1955), with Katharine Hepburn, followed. This led to arguably his most successful film, *The Bridge on the River Kwai* (1957), starring Alec Guinness as an obsessive British officer in a Japanese prisoner-of-war camp who transforms the building of a bridge for the enemy into a morale-boosting exercise for his own men. This moving and highly polished classic of the cinema earned Lean his first Oscar.

During the 1960s Lean continued to make spectacular larger-than-life movies including *Lawrence of Arabia* (1962), with Peter O'Toole as T. E. Lawrence, *Doctor Zhivago* (1965; from the novel by PASTERNAK), starring Omar Sharif and Julie Christie in a love story set in post-revolutionary Russia, and *Ryan's Daughter* (1970), where the intimate story of adultery in an Irish village in 1916 was somewhat swamped by Lean's epic treatment.

After the failure of *Ryan's Daughter*, Lean retired from the cinema for ten years, but returned with *A Passage to India* (1984), based on the novel by E. M. Forster. This epic of India under the Raj again demonstrated Lean's competence with huge casts and largely reestablished his earlier reputation.

Leavis, F(rank) R(aymond) (1895–1978) British literary critic. Leavis was born and educated in Cambridge, reading history and then English at Emmanuel College. On graduating he became a lecturer and continued to teach at Cambridge until 1964. From 1932 until 1953 he was the principal editor of the critical quarterly *Scrutiny*. Here, as in his teaching, he developed a new approach to literary criticism that combined close reading of the text with a vigilant moral awareness. In *New Bearings in English Poetry* (1932) he championed the work of Eliot and Pound, while in *Revaluation* (1936) his attempts to redraw the map of English poetry led him to attack such revered figures as Milton and Shelley. Leavis brought a similarly rigorous approach to discussion of the novel in *The Great Tradition* (1948), where he declared that the great English novelists were Jane Austen, George Eliot, Henry James, and Conrad. For Leavis, the only true successor to this tradition was D. H. Lawrence, whose work he brought to greater prominence in *D. H. Lawrence: Novelist* (1955).

In his cultural writings, which include *For Continuity* (1933), and *Education and the University* (1943), Leavis argued for the creation within the universities of an intellectual elite capable of preserving the values embodied in the literary tradition in an age of technology and mass culture. Although his uncompromising views and abrasive style made him a controversial figure, his influence over the teaching of English grew steadily after World War II and remained dominant until the 1970s. He was married to the critic Q. D. Leavis, with whom he collaborated on a number of works, notably *Dickens the Novelist* (1970).

Le Corbusier (Charles-Edouard Jeanneret; 1887–1965) French architect and city planner, born in Switzerland, whose ideas dominated international architecture for nearly 50 years. His pre-1945 work consisted largely of private houses; it did, however, include the Pavilion Suisse in the Cité Universitaire, Paris (1930–33), with robust *pilotis* (or stilts) and varied surface treatments, as well as communal housing, as in the Cité de Réfuge, Paris (1929–33).

More important was his writing. *Vers une architecture* (1923) established his idea of a cityscape of tall blocks on *pilotis* that liberated the ground for traffic and parks. This saw eventual fruition as his first Unité d'Habitation in Marseilles (1945–52). No other building was so influential in postwar architecture: it is a vast block of flats on stilts, built of rough concrete or *béton brût* because of steel and labour shortages, with deep balconies that gave a shadowplay termed *brise-soleil*. Each flat had a double-height living room; the block included a shopping street half-way up and a roof garden with sports facilities and a nursery. Later Unités were less successful away from a Mediterranean climate and communities used to living in flats.

Other major works were the Maisons Jaoul (1951–55), the monastery of La Tourette (1953–59), and the church of Notre Dame du Haut, Ronchamp (1950–55). This is a small sculptural building with a great prow and curved roof, whose dark interior makes moving use of tiny panes of coloured glass. In 1951 Le Corbusier was invited to help build the new city of Chandigarh in India with Albert Mayer, Jane Drew, Maxwell Fry (*see* FRY AND DREW), and his cousin Pierre JEANNERET. Here he designed the Secretariat (1951–58), a long Unité-like block that allowed breezes through its *brise-soleil* grid, and the Palace of Assembly (1951–62).

Le Corbusier was an idealist, more interested in sculpting space than in the practicalities of architecture. That his ideals have been devalued by their repetition in lesser hands and in unsuitable locations does not diminish the power of his best work.

LeFanu, Nicola (Frances) (1947–) British composer. The daughter of the composer Elizabeth MACONCHY, she studied at Oxford University and the Royal College of Music; she has also been a pupil of PETRASSI and of Egon Wellesz. She won the Cobbet chamber music prize in 1968 and first prize in the BBC composers' competition in 1971. After teaching at Morley College she was appointed senior lecturer in music at King's College, London in 1977; in 1979 she was composer-in-residence at the New South Wales Conservatorium, Sydney. Her compositions, which reflect a wide range of influences, include orchestral pieces such as *Columbia Falls* (1975) and *Farne* (1979), music-theatre such as *Dawnpath* (1977), vocal pieces like *The Same Day Dawns* (1974) and *The Little Valleys* (1975), and many works of chamber music. She has been active in the antinuclear and women's movements and in environmental campaigns. Her opera *Blood Wedding*, based on Lorca's play, was staged by the Women's Playhouse Trust in 1992.

Leibowitz, René (1913–72) French composer, teacher, and musicologist, born in Poland. Leibowitz was a pupil of Arthur Schoenberg and Anton Webern in Berlin and Vienna (1930–33) and became a leading exponent of the 12-tone method (*see* SERIALISM). After settling in Paris in 1945 he founded (1947) the International Festival of Chamber Music, which has featured premieres of works by Schoenberg, Webern, and Alban Berg. His own compositions include operas and orchestral, chamber, choral, and piano music, although he is best remembered as a teacher and for his theoretical writings, notably the expository study *Schoenberg and his School* (1949).

Lelouch, Claude (1937–) French film director. Lelouch made his debut as a director in 1960 and scored his biggest success in 1966 with *A Man and a Woman*, a love story employing a wide range of technical effects; the film won him both the Palme d'Or at the CANNES FILM FESTIVAL and an Oscar. *Life for Life* (1967), a more melodramatic treatment of similar themes set in New York and Vietnam, was less well received. Critics have generally found his subsequent films sentimental and old fashioned. He was one of the directors to collaborate on *Far From Vietnam* (1969), a protest against the Vietnam War. In 1973 he presented a variant upon the themes of *A Man and a Woman* in *Happy New Year*, about the relationship between a jewellery thief and an antique dealer. Lelouch's more recent films have included *And Now My Love* (1975), the western *Another Man, Another Chance* (1977), *Bolero* (1981), *Edith and Marcel* (1983), a not very well-received biopic sentimentalizing the affair between Edith Piaf and the boxer Marcel Cerdan, *A Man and Woman...20 Years Later* (1986), and *The New Bandits* (1987).

Lenz, Siegfried (1926–) German novelist. In 1943 Lenz was drafted into the navy but deserted shortly before the end of the war. After a spell as a British prisoner of war he returned to Germany, where he studied philosophy, English, and literature in Hamburg. From 1948 onwards he published short stories and essays and in 1951 his first novel. Since 1952, when he became a full-time writer, he has lived in Hamburg and Denmark.

Lenz is one of the best-known contemporary novelists in his own country. His novels, most of which are set on the north

German coast or in the east Prussian region of Masuren, focus on the moral responsibility of the individual. His first international success was *The German Lesson* (1968), a psychological study of the authoritarian character set during the Nazi period. Siggi Jepsen, an inmate of a borstal, remembers his father, a local policeman and Nazi, who tried to persecute and undermine the painter Nansen (a character based on Emil Nolde). Lenz's second bestseller was *The Heritage* (*Heimatmuseum*; 1978), in which the narrator Zygmunt Rogalla justifies setting fire to the local museum; the novel is a critique of the conservative interpretation of local history. Other novels include *The Lightship* (1960), *The Survivor*, and *An Exemplary Life*. He has also written short stories and radio plays. His works have been translated into many languages.

Leonard, Hugh (John Keyes Byrne; 1926–) Irish playwright and critic, whose plays use farce and bitter humour to explore such serious topics as Anglo-Irish tensions, broken relationships, exile, and terminal illness. His best-known works include *The Big Birthday* (1956), first seen at the Abbey Theatre, *The Patrick Pearse Motel* (1971), *Da* (1973), which reached Broadway and was subsequently filmed, *A Life* (1978), and *The Mask of Moriarty* (1986). His many adaptations include *The Passion of Peter Ginty* (1961), from Ibsen's *Peer Gynt*, and *Stephen D.* (1962), from the writings of James Joyce. Leonard has been programme director of the Dublin Theatre Festival since 1978. He has also written screenplays, two volumes of autobiography, the television series *The Irish R.M.*, and the novel (also televised) *Parnell and the Englishwoman* (1990).

Leone, Sergio (1929–89) Italian film director, who established his reputation in the 1970s with his popular SPAGHETTI WESTERNS. Leone began his career in the cinema as an assistant to other directors, also working as a screenwriter on various adventure epics; he made his debut as a director in the late 1950s. His first major success came with *A Fistful of Dollars* (1964), a reworking of Kurosawa's *Yojimbo* in which the action was relocated to the Wild West. Unlike many earlier westerns, the film avoided sentimentality by combining brutality with black humour; it was also notable for its striking musical score by Ennio Morricone.

Leone repeated this success with two further instalments in what became known as *The Man with No Name* trilogy, all featuring the US actor Clint Eastwood in the role of the tight-lipped fast-shooting antihero. Both *For a Few Dollars More* (1965) and *The Good, The Bad and The Ugly* (1967) became cult films.

Once Upon a Time in the West (1969), another epic, was hailed by some critics as the best western ever made for its reinterpretation of the myth of the Wild West. *A Fistful of Dynamite* (1972), a variant on the spaghetti western theme, traced the involvement of an exiled IRA terrorist with a bandit at the time of the Mexican Revolution.

After several years in which he made no further films, Leone (in collaboration with BERTOLUCCI) directed the highly praised *Once Upon a Time in America* (1983), a gangster epic incorporating themes of betrayal, guilt, and self-discovery to avoid glamorizing the sordid US underworld.

Le Roy Ladurie, Emmanuel (1929–) French historian. Since obtaining his doctorate with the study *The Peasants of Languedoc* (1966) he has taught history at the Sorbonne, the University of Paris, and the Collège de France. He is one of the most popular and prolific of contemporary French historians. In *Times of Feast, Times of Famine. A History of Climate Since the Year 1000* (1967), a study of climatic change in the spirit of the Annales school of historiography (*see* BRAUDEL), he made pioneering use of computers to analyse data. In his collection of essays *The Territory of the Historian* (1973) Le Roy Ladurie proclaimed the 'quantitative revolution in history', meaning the application of mathematical and statistical techniques to historical evidence. In his most successful books he chose subjects where a great mass of evidence could be shaped to yield a vivid picture of the past. *Montaillou. Cathars and Catholics in a French Village* (1975), an international bestseller, used the records of the Inquisition to reconstruct everyday life in a small village in the Pyrenees around 1300. In a similar manner *Carnival. A People's Uprising at Romans 1579–80* (1979) reconstructed the social and economic background of a small community in the south of France in the late 16th century.

More recent publications include *Money, Love and Death in the Pays d'Oc* (1980) and *Pierre Prion, Scribe* (1987).

Lessing, Doris (May) (1919–) British novelist and short story writer. Born Doris May Tayler in Persia (now Iran), she was brought up in Rhodesia (now Zimbabwe), which provided the setting for her first novel *The Grass is Singing* (1950). In 1949 her communism and involvement in Black politics forced her to leave Southern Africa and she settled in London. There she embarked on her *Children of Violence* quintet, a semiautobiographical series of novels that follows the life of the significantly named Martha Quest from childhood in Rhodesia to a final apocalypse in Britain in 2000 AD. The quintet comprises *Martha Quest* (1952), *A Proper Marriage* (1954), *A Ripple From the Storm* (1958), *Landlocked* (1965), and *The Four-Gated City* (1969). Perhaps her most highly praised work is *The Golden Notebook* (1962), which deals with the emotional, creative, and political life of a feminist writer, Anna Wulf. Written in a variety of different styles, it describes her attempts to achieve independence and fulfilment in a male-dominated society. Other experimental works include *Briefing for a Descent into Hell* (1971), a technically audacious depiction of a mental breakdown, and the series *Canopus in Argus: Archives*, which uses the conventions of science fiction to explore themes from psychology; the sequence comprises *Colonised Planet 5, Shikasta* (1979), *The Marriages Between Zones Three, Four and Five* (1980), *The Sirian Experiments* (1981), *The Making of the Representatives for Planet 8* (1982), and *Documents Relating to the Sentimental Agents in the Volyen Empire* (1983). *The Good Terrorist* (1985), a highly praised novel that scrutinizes the morality of political activism, won the W. H. Smith Literary Award in 1986; her latest novel, *The Fifth Child* (1988), explores the philosophical questions raised by innate and apparently motiveless evil. She has also published two volumes of *Collected Stories* (1978).

Levi, Carlo (1902–75) Italian physician, journalist, painter, and writer. After graduating in medicine in 1923, he devoted himself mainly to literature and art. He became an active anti-Fascist which led to his internal exile (1935–36) in the southern Italian region of Basilicata. In 1942 he fled to France, where he took part in the Resistance; following the collapse of Fascism he worked for the Italian press. A lifelong campaigner for social justice, he sat as an independent communist senator from 1963 until 1972.

Levi's most widely acclaimed work is *Christ Stopped at Eboli* (1945), a documentary novel inspired by his time in Basilicata. He portrays, with the sympathetic eye of an anthropologist, poverty and superstition in a remote and barren corner of Italy that Christ, symbolizing civilization, has yet to reach. While Levi offers an effective analysis of the beliefs, mores, and behaviour of preindustrial rural society, the narrative is closer to fiction than reportage in its poetic use of metaphor and myth.

His nonfiction works include *Of Fear and Freedom* (1946), *The Watch* (1950), a depiction of political intrigue in Rome immediately after the war, *Words are Stones* (1955), a study of the social condition of Sicily and the Mafia, and travel books on Russia (*The Future has an Ancient Heart*); on Germany (*The Linden Tree*; *La doppia notte dei tigli*, 1959), and on Sardinia (*All the Honey is Finished*; 1964).

Levi, Primo (1919–87) Italian novelist, poet, and writer. After graduating (1941) in chemistry from Turin University, he worked for a pharmaceutical firm in Milan. In 1943 Levi, a Jew, was arrested with a group of partisans and sent to Auschwitz, where he owed his survival to working as a chemist in the I.G. synthetic rubber factory. Liberated by Soviet troops in 1945, he returned to Italy after an epic journey through eastern Europe. From 1961 onwards he was technical director of a paint factory in Turin. He retired in 1977 and devoted himself to writing. Ten years later he committed suicide.

Levi gives an account of his Auschwitz experience in *This Is a Man* (1947) while its sequel *The Truce* (1963) describes his return to Italy. Both have come to be regarded as classics of concentration-camp literature. In *Natural Histories* (1966), a collection of science-fiction stories published under the pseudonym of Damiano Malabaila, Levi expressed doubts about the future of humanity. *The Periodic Table* (1975) is a volume of 21 semiautobiographical sketches, each of which is given the title of a chemical element. In *The Wrench* (1978) he emphasizes the importance of meaningful work in a person's life, using the device of a series of fictional interviews between the author and a skilled but otherwise uneducated construction worker.

Levi's other works include *If Not Now, When?* (1982), a fictional account of Jewish Russian and Polish partisans during World War II, an anthology *The Search for Roots* (1981), the poetry collections *The Tavern of Brema* (1975) and *At an Uncertain Hour* (1984), a volume of essays *Other's People's Trades* (1985), and the autobiographical *The Drowned and the Saved* (1986).

Lévi-Strauss, Claude (1908–) French anthropologist, born in Belgium. After completing his philosophy studies at the Sorbonne, Lévi-Strauss taught sociology in São Paulo. During this period he undertook various ethnological expeditions into central Brazil. From 1942 to 1945 he worked for the New School for Social Research in New York. In 1947 he became one of the directors of the Musée de l'Homme in Paris and in 1960 he was appointed professor of anthropology at the Collège de France. He was elected to the Académie Française in 1972 and awarded the Légion d'honneur in 1991.

Lévi-Strauss was the founder of structural anthropology and the central figure in the development of the wider structuralist movement (*see* STRUCTURALISM) that dominated intellectual life in Europe and the US in the 1960s and 1970s. By applying the principles of structural linguistics to the study of societies and cultures, Lévi-Strauss effected an intellectual synthesis that had profound repercussions for all the humanities. The main characteristic of his work is its attempt to analyse complex social phenomena – such as religion, mythology, and kinship – in terms of a few simple structures that he held to underlie all human thinking. (The best known of these is the principle of binary opposition, which Lévi-Strauss borrowed from phonology.) He insisted on the fundamental similarity between scientific thinking and the thinking of primitive peoples. His individual studies include *The Elementary Structures of Kinship* (1949), *The Savage Mind* (1962), and the four volumes of *Mythologies* (1964–71). In spite of his search for a universal code, Lévi-Strauss retained a respect for the otherness of foreign cultures.

Lewerentz, Sigurd (1885–1975) Swedish architect and designer, whose career spanned every movement of the 20th century, from the arts-and-crafts movement through classicism to modernism. Lewerentz built relatively little but devoted many years to designing and manufacturing light fittings, metal windows, and shop-fronts. He is perhaps best known for his association with Gunnar Asplund (1885–1940), with whom he broke away from Royal Academy teaching in 1910. He built several cemetery chapels, outstanding among which was his neo-classical Chapel of the Resurrection, Stockholm (1925), and crematoria. His fascination with glazing is revealed in a series of churches built in the 1950s and 1960s, in Stockholm (1956–60), Skarpnäck, and Klippan (1963–66), all of which feature windows set directly into expressionist brickwork of high quality and elegance.

Lewis, C(live) S(taples) (1898–1963) British scholar, religious apologist, and writer of science fiction and children's books, born in Northern Ireland. Apart from service in World War I, Lewis spent the whole of his adult life in academia; he was a fellow of Magdalen College, Oxford from 1925 until 1954 and professor of medieval and Renaissance English at Cambridge University thereafter. His works of literary scholarship, which include *The Allegory of Love* (1936) and *English Literature in the Sixteenth Century* (1954), are notable for their clarity of exposition and for Lewis's delight in attacking received ideas. The same qualities distinguish the popular religious works with which Lewis reached a much wider audience in the 1940s and 1950s, although the arguments are here far less subtle. These include *The Problem of Pain* (1940), *Mere Christianity* (1952), and *The Screwtape Letters* (1940), in which an experienced devil instructs a younger colleague in the best ways of snaring human souls.

Lewis's theological ideas also inform the science-fiction trilogy that begins with *Out of the Silent Planet* (1938) and the Seven Chronicles of Narnia, a sequence of fantasy novels for children that opens with *The Lion the Witch and the Wardrobe* (1950). The latter have remained enduringly popular with children, most of whom seem little bothered by the underlying Christian allegory. With his friends J. R. R. TOLKIEN and Charles Williams, Lewis formed the Inklings, an Oxford literary group that met to share their interest in fantasy literature and theological discussion.

Lidman, Sara (1923–) Swedish novelist and writer. Born in Västerbotten in the Far North of Sweden, Lidman is one of the most innovative writers in Sweden today. Her first four novels, *The Tar Still* (1953), *Cloudberry Land* (1955), *The Rainbird* (1958) and *Carry Mistletoe* (1960) are set in the remotest part of Norrland and deal with personal relationships in a community struggling for survival under harsh conditions.

In the 1960s Lidman turned away from the mainstream novel in an attempt to express her radical political views more directly. *Conversations in Hanoi* (1965), written after a visit to war-torn North Vietnam, uses interview material and conversations with local people to make her point against US intervention in the region. Her next work *Mine* (1968) provides probably the best example of her documentary method. A collection of transcripts from interviews with iron miners, it reveals the harsh working conditions they face and the exploitation they suffer.

In the late 1960s and 1970s Lidman's political activities took over completely from literary production but she has since returned to writing with a series of novels about Västerbotten. *The Servant Heareth* (1977), *Child of Wrath* (1979), *Naboth's Stone* (1981), and *The Wonderful Man* (1983) all depict life in the Far North in precise ethnographic detail, from the days of the early settlers struggling to eke an existence from the land to the advent of the railway at the turn of the century. The sequence shows an idealistic comunity subjected to ruthless pressure from big business.

Ligeti, György (1923–) Hungarian composer. Ligeti studied with Ferenc Farkas at the Kolozsvár Conservatory (1942–43) and then with Sándor Veress in Budapest (1945–49). From 1950 to 1956 he taught at the Budapest Conservatory and published a number of pieces in the officially approved style of Kodály, while also writing more daring scores that could not be performed in Hungary at the time. After the Soviet invasion of 1956 he moved to the West and worked alongside the major figures of the post-war European avant-garde, especially STOCKHAUSEN and BOULEZ. The orchestral work *Apparitions* (1960) brought Ligeti international recognition and established his position within the DARMSTADT circle. In *Atmosphères* (1961) and the organ piece *Volumina* (1962) Ligeti developed a technique of cluster composition that eschewed precise notation of melody, harmony, and rhythm. The juxtaposition of frenetic music with interludes of calm is a feature of the works of his next phase, such as the requiem (1965) for voices and orchestra and *Lux Aeterna* (1966) and *Lontano* (1967) for orchestra. These and subsequent works reintroduce defined harmony and rhythm while melodic elements return in *Melodien* (1971). His most recent large-scale work is the opera *La Grand Macabre* (1977) while the horn trio (1983) draws together his preoccupations with time, harmony, and texture in a 'homage' to Brahms. Ligeti has also produced some amusing minor pieces that satirize the performance aesthetics of John Cage; these include the *Poème symphonique* (1962) for 100 metronomes.

Limonov, Eduard (1943–) Russian poet and novelist. Born and brought up in Khar'kiv, a period described luridly in a quasiautobiography, *The Adolescent* (1983), he became known as a minor *samizdat* poet in Leningrad before emigrating to the US in 1974. A book of his poems, *Russianness*, appeared in 1978 and various prose pieces also came out around this time. In 1979, however, his novel *It's Me Eddy* created a scandal that split the Russian emigré community on account of its coarse language, open descriptions of sexual adventures with partners of both sexes, and above all its author's highly critical, utterly ungrateful, attitude to his host country. He subsequently moved to Paris. *Diary of a Failure or a Secret Notebook* (1982) consists of erotic and scatalogical jottings, which accentuate the self-obsession evident in *It's Me Eddy*. *L'Histoire de son serviteur* (1984) and *The Executioner* (1986) provide further evidence of the author's interest in sadomasochism. Though no-one would claim Limonov to be a second Henry Miller or Jean GENET, several scholars have taken *It's Me Eddy* seriously, praising its ebullience and freshness, as well the topographical precision of the writing.

Limonov returned to Russia following the collapse of the Soviet Union. Since then he has shocked many of his former admirers by becoming involved in extreme nationalist politics. In 1992 he fought as a volunteer with Serbian forces in Bosnia.

Lindgren, Astrid (1907–) Swedish writer. Best known abroad for her children's fiction, Lindgren is also celebrated in Sweden for her active role in politics. A prolific writer, she has published 70 books in 47 years.

Lindgren's most popular works are probably those about the fiercely independent Pippi Longstocking, which appeared from 1945 onwards. These have been widely translated and filmed. Other titles that have appeared in translation include *Little Brother and Karlsson on the Roof* (1955), *Madicken* (1960) about the naughty little girl of the title and her well-behaved sister Lisabet, the *Bullerby* books (1947–52), and *Mio, My Son* (1954). The naughty but loveable Emil arrived in *Emil in the Soup Tureen* (1963) with *Emil and the Clever Pig* following in 1970. *The Lionheart Brothers*, a more serious work, appeared in 1973; it deals with children's attitudes to death. *Ronia, the Robber's Daughter* (1981) was turned into an internationally successful film.

Astrid Lindgren has also been an active campaigner in Swedish social and political life. Her successful fight against factory farming culminated in an act named after her (the *Lex Astrid*) ruling that animals had rights to grazing and bedding. Her stance against Swedish membership of the European Community has again taken her into the headlines following Denmark's rejection of the Maastricht treaty in 1992.

Now in her eighties, Astrid Lindgren has recently decided to stop writing because of her failing eyesight.

Lindsay Quartet British string quartet founded in 1965, when its original players were all students at the Royal Academy of Music in London. Its members are Peter Cropper (first violin), Ronald Birks (second violin since 1971), Robin Ireland (viola since 1985, when he replaced Roger Bigley) and Bernard Gregor-Smith (cello). The quartet is noted for its commitment to widening the audience for chamber music through educational work and imaginative presentation as well as through their energetic performances. The Lindsay takes its name from the founder of Keele University, where it was quartet in residence (a position it now holds at Manchester University). The quartet is noted for its performances of music by Haydn, Beethoven, and Bartók. It also performs works by contemporary British composers, notably Alexander GOEHR, Peter Maxwell DAVIES, and Michael TIPPETT. Since 1984 they have promoted an annual chamber music festival in Sheffield.

Littlewood, (Maudie) Joan (1914–) British theatre director, whose direction of the Theatre Workshop in the 1950s and 1960s had a profound effect upon the development of modern European drama. Littlewood's first theatrical experience came through her collaboration with the left-wing Theatre of Action, run by the folksinger Ewan McColl (who became her husband) in Manchester. This group formed the basis for what was to become the Theatre Workshop after World War II. The company took over the Theatre Royal, Stratford East, in 1953, where they subsequently presented a series of innovative productions. Littlewood was much influenced by the theories of BRECHT and in 1955 was permitted to stage the British premiere of his *Mother Courage*. She was the first British director to make significant use of improvisation and COLLECTIVE CREATION. The company's most successful productions included BEHAN's *The Quare Fellow*, Shelagh Delaney's *A Taste of Honey*, Lionel Bart's *Fings Ain't Wot They Used T'Be*, and *Oh, What a Lovely War!*, their own irreverent and critical presentation of the brutality of World War I. Many of these productions were so successful that they transferred to the West End, meaning that the company had to be continually rebuilt. Littlewood finally disbanded the group in 1973 and in 1975 moved to France. During the 1960s she also pursued varied theatrical projects in Africa and India.

Liubimov, Iurii (Petrovich) (1917–) Russian theatre director, the most influential (and controversial) director in the Soviet theatre since World War II. His production of BRECHT's *The Good Woman of Setzuan* (1962) at the Vakhtangov Theatre, where he had been trained, caused a sensation. As a result, in 1964 he was given the post of artistic director at the ailing TAGANKA THEATRE, where he consolidated his reputation with a long series of avant-garde productions guided by the principles of Meyerhold, Stanislavsky, and Vakhtangov.

Characteristics of Liubimov's productions include complex lighting plots and precisely timed technical effects, as well as the interpolation of songs, speeches, and other extraneous material into the text. His productions have included John Reed's *Ten Days That Shook the World* (1965), EVTUSHENKO's *Under the Skin of the Statue of Liberty* (1972), and works by Chernyshevsky, Trifonov, and Boris Mozhaev. Among his productions of plays from the classical repertoire have been Molière's *Tartuffe* (1969) and Shakespeare's *Hamlet* (1974), as well as, more recently, plays by Bulgakov, Gogol, and Dostoevskii.

Liubimov's reputation as 'the conscience of Soviet theatre' and his challenging programme ultimately led to his removal from the directorship of the Taganka Theatre and to his expulsion from the country. In 1989, however, he was back in his post at the Taganka and celebrating his return with his own version of Pushkin's *The Plague-Time Feast* and a revival of Mozhaev's *Alive*, banned in 1968 because it recalled the bureaucratic blunders of the 1930s. In 1992 he directed *Electra*, his first venture into classical Greek drama, in Athens.

Liverpool Poets The British poets Adrian Henri (1932–), Roger McGough (1937–), and Brian Patten (1946–), who emerged from Liverpool in the mid 1960s; their rise to national prominence owed much to the general excitement surrounding the Mersey scene at that time following the extraordinary success of the Beatles. Their work was published in several joint anthologies, notably *The Mersey Sound* (1967) and *The Liverpool Scene* (1967). Perhaps influenced as much by the US Beat Poets as by the contemporary music scene, they envisaged poetry as a popular performance art and held frequent informal readings of their work in local venues. The poetry was deliberately antiacademic in style, mixing humour with sentimentality and drawing most of its imagery from popular culture and contemporary urban life. Individual collections include Henri's *City* (1969) and *From the Loveless Motel* (1980) and McGough's *Watchwords* (1969) and *Waving at Trains* (1982).

Lizzani, Carlo (1917–) Italian film director and screenwriter, who was an early theoretician of NEOREALISM. Born in Rome, Lizzani was a film critic for the magazines *Cinema* and *Bianco e Nero* before starting a career as an assistant director and screenwriter in 1946. He carried out both duties on DE SANTIS's *Tragic Hunt* (1947), in which he also acted, and assisted with the direction of *Bitter Rice* (1948), ROSSELLINI's *Germany Year Zero* (1947), and LATTUADA's *The Mill on the Po* (1948). After making several documentaries, he directed his first feature film, *Achtung! Banditi!* (1951), a story about the Italian Resistance movement that gave Gina Lollobrigida her first starring role. Lizzani then directed the important *A Chronicle of Poor Lovers* (1954), a romance set against the struggle between the Fascists and their political opponents in the 1920s. He has coscripted most of his films, which generally reflect his Marxist views. His other notable films include *The Hunchback of Rome* (1960), *The Hills Run Red* (1966; directed under the pseudonym of Lee W. Beaver), *The Violent Four* (1968), the US-Italian *Crazy Joe* (1974), which depicts the life of a Mafia gangster in New York, and *The Last Four Days* (1974), about Mussolini's death.

Llangollen International Eisteddfod One of the most important musical events held in Wales, the Eisteddfod takes place in Llangollen each June and lasts for a week. The daily musical competitions, originating from the meetings of Welsh bards in the Middle Ages, make up the majority of the performances. The Eisteddfod was founded in 1947 to promote peace and international understanding by bringing people from different countries together to share in music and dance. This international flavour distinguishes it from more traditional Eisteddfods, as does the fact that the proceedings are conducted in English. There is a particular emphasis on folksong and dance. The Royal International Pavilion, an innovative tent-like structure featuring hi-tech PVC membranes, was opened on the site in 1992.

Loach, Ken (1936–) British film director, who established his reputation directing documentaries for television and subsequently became known for his harshly realistic films about social problems in Britain. Loach's work belongs to the FREE CINEMA tradition of British film-making, combining striking imagery with radical political comment. His early productions for television included *Up the Junction* (1965) and *Cathy Come Home* (1966), a play about homelessness in British cities that caused a considerable stir. He made his first feature film, *Poor Cow*, in 1967 and won high praise for *Kes* (1970), a sympathetic account of a young boy's attempts to train a kestrel, which becomes a symbol of his own desire to escape from the brutality and hopelessness of life in the industrial north of England.

Family Life (1972; screenplay by David MERCER) is a harrowing depiction of the mental breakdown of a young girl in which her schizophrenia is seen as a response to her stifling environment. Loach continued to express his political views in the television films *The Price of Coal* (1977), about the mining industry, and *The Gamekeeper* (1979), which explored class division in modern British society, and the film *Looks and Smiles* (1981), about a doomed teenage romance in Thatcherite Britain.

More recent films include *Fatherland* (1987), which compares capitalist West Germany and communist East Germany, finding faults with both, and *Hidden Agenda* (1990), a highly controversial drama about the British presence in Northern Ireland. *Riff-Raff* (1991), a comedy about workers on a building site, initially failed to find a distributor in Britain; it was subsequently given a limited release after winning the International Critics' Award at the CANNES FILM FESTIVAL.

Lodge, David (John) (1935–) British novelist and critic. Lodge was educated at University College, London, and after holding several academic posts became professor of modern English literature at the University of Birmingham in 1976 (honorary professor since 1987). His critical works include *The Language of Fiction* (1966), *The Novelist at the Crossroads* (1971), *The Modes of Modern Writing* (1977), and *Working with Structuralism* (1981). These works have helped to introduce the writings of continental literary philosophers, such as BARTHES and DERRIDA, to mainstream English literary thought. More recently, Lodge has contributed a weekly column to the *Independent on Sunday*, called *The Art of Fiction* (published in book form in 1992).

His career as a novelist began in 1960 with *The Picturegoers*, which was followed by *Ginger You're Balmy* (1962) and *The British Museum is Falling Down* (1965). *Changing Places* (1975) is a campus novel that contrasts academic life in Britain and the US. *How Far Can You Go?* (1980) deals with the religious, social, and sexual changes that beset a group of educated Roman Catholics in the 1950s and 1960s. *Small World* (1984) follows the US academic Morris Zapp and his British counterpart Philip Swallow (characters introduced in *Changing Places*) as they travel from one international conference to the next. It has been serialized for television, as has *Nice Work* (1988), which wittily explores the relationship between industry and academia. His latest novel is *Paradise News* (1991). Lodge's novels combine naturalism with an intellectual playfulness influenced by his critical ideas; his use of such devices as an intrusive narrator and his references to other media enable him to explore the conventions of realism with skilful irony.

Lohse, Richard (1902–) Swiss painter and graphic artist. After studies at the School of Arts and Crafts in his native Zürich, Lohse worked (1922–27) in an advertising studio. In 1937 he was one of the founders of Allianz, an association of progressive Swiss artists. From 1948 to 1955 he edited the journal *Building and Living* and from 1958 to 1965 he was co-editor of the journal *New Graphics*. His work was widely exhibited from about 1950 onwards and in 1958 he won the Guggenheim International Prize.

In his early work Lohse experimented with various subjects (including landscapes, portraits, and still-lifes) and a number of styles (including cubism and surrealism). In the 1940s, however, he emerged as one of the leading exponents of concrete art – a type of abstraction employing only the most basic geometric forms. His paintings are mathematically planned, with gridlike or chequer-board-type patterns spread more or less evenly across the canvas. Far from being cold or analytical, however, his paintings are distinguished by extraordinary subtlety and sensitivity of colour and are among the most lyrically beautiful of all abstract works.

London Contemporary Dance Theatre British ballet company, founded in London in 1967 (as the Contemporary Dance Group). Based in London at The Place, the company specializes in modern dance and enjoys close links with the Martha Graham School in New York. Major works presented by the company have included pieces by Graham herself, Anna Sokolow, Alvin Ailey, Richard ALSTON, Siobhan DAVIES, and Robert North. In 1992 the founding director Robert Cohan was recalled to fill the gap left by the resignation of Nancy Duncan, the company's director since 1991.

London Festival Ballet British ballet company, founded in London in 1949 as the Festival Ballet (in reference to the forthcoming FESTIVAL OF BRITAIN). The original company was assembled around Dame Alicia Markova and Anton Dolin with Julian Braunsweg as manager; early performances featured guest appearances by such major international stars as Massine and Riabouchinska. The company was motivated from the beginning by a desire to reach a mass audience by staging accessible popular works. It has continued to tour extensively despite repeated financial crises. Dolin stepped down as artistic director in 1962 and was followed by a succession of directors until Peter Schaufuss took over in 1984. The company's repertory continues to be based largely on classical ballets, although works by Glen Tetley, Michael CLARK, and other contemporary choreographers have also been successfully performed; particularly notable in recent years have been NUREYEV's productions of *The Sleeping Beauty* (1975) and *Romeo and Juliet* (1977) and Schaufuss's *La Sylphide* (1979). The company has two London bases, the Royal Festival Hall and (since 1968) the Coliseum.

London Film Festival One of Europe's leading festivals of cinema, the London Film Festival has taken place annually since it began in 1958. The festival was founded by the critics Derek Prouse and Dilys Powell; among the 15 films seen at the opening were premieres of Kurosawa's *Throne of Blood* and BERGMAN's *The Seventh Seal*. By the 30th anniversary of the festival in 1988 the programme had grown to include 150 films (by 1992 this figure had increased to over 200 films from 40 countries). In recent years the festival has attempted to shed its somewhat elitist image by presenting films in leading commercial cinemas in London, as well as in its home base at the NATIONAL FILM THEATRE.

London Sinfonietta A chamber orchestra founded in London in 1968 by David Atherton, specifically to perform 20th-century music. It has given first performances of works by BERIO, STOCKHAUSEN, and Elliott Carter: it also regularly commissions and performs new works. The orchestra presents an annual series of concerts in London and is now resident on the South Bank. Associated with it are the Opera Factory, which performs opera and music theatre, and the London Sinfonietta Voices.

Long, Richard (1945–) British artist; a leading exponent of EARTH ART. Long was born in Bristol and studied at St Martin's School of Art, London. Since the mid 1960s all his artistic activities have arisen from the long solitary walks he takes in the countryside, often in remote and inhospitable areas. Sometimes he brings found objects such as stones, twigs, or mud into the gallery, where he arranges them into designs but otherwise leaves them untreated (*Slate Circle*, 1979, Tate Gallery, London). These constructions are generally either circular or based on other simple geometrical forms. Long has also created and photographed such works in their original landscape settings, where they sometimes take on the portentous quality of prehistoric remains (*A Circle in Ireland, County Clare*, 1975).

While this aspect of Long's work has affinities with the sculpture of MOORE and CARO, in other respects his approach is nearer to CONCEPTUAL ART. He has written: "The knowledge of my actions, in whatever form, is the art. My art is the essence of my experience, not a representation of it." He has often chosen to document his walks with photographs, maps, and brief texts, rather than by the creation of works with more obvious aesthetic claims. Long's work can be seen as a development of the English romantic landscape tradition using the procedures of the post-war avant-garde. A major exhibition of his work entitled *Walking in Cir-*

cles was held at the Hayward Gallery, London, in 1991.

Lorenz, Konrad (Zacharias) (1903–89) Austrian zoologist and ethologist. Widely regarded as the father of ethology (the study of animal behaviour under natural conditions), Lorenz studied medicine in the US and Vienna, graduating from Vienna in 1928. In the late 1930s he founded, with Nikolaas TINBERGEN, the ethological school of animal behaviour, a group whose views differed widely from the US school of experimental psychologists, based on the ideas of J. B. Watson. The opposite approaches of the two schools – the Americans concentrating on studying learning using laboratory animals, and the Europeans investigating instinctive behaviour by watching animals in the wild – led to some sharp exchanges between the two sides.

Following war service as an army physician, Lorenz became the head of the Institute of Comparative Ethology at Altenburg. In 1950 he established a department of comparative ethology at the Buldern Max Planck Institute and in 1955 cofounded the Institute for Behaviour Psychology at Seewiesen (director 1961–73).

Lorenz's studies of wild or semiwild animals, such as geese and jackdaws, have led to a deeper understanding of behaviour patterns. For example, a very young animal, separated from its natural parents, may come to regard foster parents, even humans, as its true parents through a process termed 'imprinting', in which stimuli from the parent bring about a following response. Lorenz's work is of considerable value in advancing appreciation of how such patterns of behaviour may have evolved as a result of evolutionary adaptation to environment. In *On Aggression* (1963) Lorenz maintained that while aggressive behaviour in man is inborn it may be modified or channelled into other forms of activity, whereas in other animals it is purely survival-motivated. Lorenz was the recipient, with Karl von Frisch and Tinbergen, of the Nobel Prize for physiology or medicine in 1973. He was the author of a number of other books, which have enjoyed wide popularity. They include *King Solomon's Ring* (1949), *Man Meets Dog* (1950), and *Evolution and Modification of Behaviour* (1961).

Løveid, Cecilie (1951–) One of Norway's most innovative writers, Løveid made her literary debut in the anthology *Eight from Bergen* (1969), although her real breakthrough came in 1972 with the novel *Most*. She has since produced six novels and two collections of dramatic works that deal mainly with women's search for identity in the modern world. The characters in Løveid's plays often appear to lack clear identity or logical motivation and the relationships between them sometimes change inexplicably from one scene to the next. Social and linguistic taboos are freely transgressed. Løveid consciously seeks to give her work a plurality of meaning, often fusing several genres in one piece and experimenting freely with language, as in her most popular novel, *Sea Swell* (1979).

Løveid was awarded the PRIX ITALIA in 1983 for her radio play *Seagull Eaters* (*Måkespisere*) and remains one of only two women to have had works performed successfully in Norway's theatres.

Lovell, Sir (Alfred Charles) Bernard (1913–) British radio astronomer. Lovell received his PhD in 1936 from the University of Bristol and in the same year was appointed as a lecturer in physics at the University of Manchester. In 1945, after war service on the development of radar, he returned to Manchester and became professor of radio astronomy (1951–80) and the director of Jodrell Bank Experimental Station, now the Nuffield Radio Astronomy Laboratories (1951–81).

Lovell's first research was in the field of cosmic rays. In the course of his war work he realized that radio waves were a possible tool with which to pursue his studies. Thus in 1945 two trailers of radar equipment that had been used in wartime defence work were parked in a field at Jodrell Bank in Cheshire to begin radio investigation of cosmic rays, meteors, and comets. Lovell soon produced worthwhile results on meteor velocities and other topics and began to feel that a more permanent and ambitious telescope should be built.

Lovell then began a ten-year struggle to finance a 250-foot (76-m) steerable radio telescope with a parabolic dish that would be able to receive radio waves as short as 30 centimetres.

The Jodrell Bank telescope came to public notice when it was used to track the first Sputnik in 1957. It was not just an adjunct to the space program, however, but a major tool for astronomical research, of which Lovell has given a full account in his *Out of the Zenith* (1973). The steerable Jodrell Bank telescope could observe objects for as long as they were above the horizon; of the 50 pulsars discovered in the northern hemisphere before 1972, 27 were detected at Jodrell Bank. Lovell also used his telescope to make important discoveries relating to quasars. His books, other than those about Jodrell Bank, include *In the Centre of Immensities* (1978) and his autobiography *Astronomer by Chance* (1990).

Löwith, Karl (1897–1973) German philosopher and historian of ideas. Löwith fought in World War I as a volunteer, then studied biology and philosophy. In 1928 he obtained his final degree under the guidance of Martin Heidegger. Of Jewish origin, Löwith fled Germany in 1934, spending two years in Rome before taking up an appointment as professor of philosophy in Sendai, Japan. In 1940 he wrote an account of *My Life in Germany Before and After 1933* (published posthumously in 1986). In 1941 Löwith moved on to the US, returning to Germany in 1952 to accept a chair at Heidelberg.

Löwith's writings are chiefly concerned with man's various attempts to find a meaning in history, an endeavour that he considered both futile and harmful, preferring the ancient concept of a stable unchanging universe to Christian, Marxist, or Hegelian philosophies of progress. In *Nietzsche's Philosophy of Eternal Recurrence* (1933) Löwith interprets Nietzsche as denying any possibility of real progress in history, while in his chief work, *From Hegel to Nietzsche* (1941), he traces the dissolution of the Hegelian concept of meaningful history in the course of the 19th century. The story up to Hegel is told in Löwith's most popular book, *Meaning in History* (1949), in which two thousand years of attempts to find a positive meaning in human history are presented as largely worthless. In 1953 Löwith published *Heidegger, Thinker in Dark Times*, criticizing his former teacher for his philosophy of history. Löwith's negation of history has been much condemned but his highly original approach continues to arouse considerable interest.

Lucebert (Lubertus Jacobus Swaanswijk; 1928–) Dutch poet and painter. Born in Amsterdam, Lucebert studied briefly at the Institute for Arts and Crafts there (1938). After World War II, during which he carried out forced labour in Germany, he lived as a vagabond, painting on walls and producing numerous poems and drawings. Following his first exhibition in 1948 he joined the Dutch Experimental Group of painters, which merged with COBRA in 1949. He published his first book of poems in 1951. His poetry won a series of major prizes in the 1960s and 1970s and he has continued to hold exhibitions of his paintings and drawings.

Lucebert made his name in the early 1950s as the literary iconoclast *par excellence*, rejecting traditional forms and even the conventions of punctuation as useless and corrupt. With its bizarre images, exuberant experimentation, and reliance on subconscious associative processes, his work shows the influence of Dada and surrealism. His poetry has been a major influence on avant-garde writing in Germany and France. The principal collections of his poetry are: *Triangle in the Jungle followed by the Animals of Democracy* (1951), *Apocrypha. The Analphabetical Name* (1952), *The Amsterdam School* (1952), *A Trap for the God of Flies* (1959), and *Poems 1948–1963* (1965). In the 1960s and 1970s he seems to have become disillusioned with literature and concentrated mainly on painting. His later collection *Harvesting in the Maze* (1981) shows a greater sobriety than his early work.

Luhmann, Niklas (1927–) German social theorist. After completing his law studies Luhmann worked (1954–62) in the public administration of Lower Saxony. Subsequently he taught in several social research institutions before his appointment (1968) to a chair of sociology at the new University of Bielefeld. The main question Luhmann tackles in his writings is the origin and change of meaning within social systems. According to Luhmann, this question should be answered not at the level of the autonomous subject or individual but rather at the level of the social structure itself. Luhmann attacks traditional philosophical conceptions of subjectivity and free will as naive. In a highly complex world dominated by technology, social structures offer the individual a 'reduction of complexity' that is necessary to his very survival. Here Luhmann takes up an idea of GEHLEN.

Luhmann's principal work is *Social Systems* (1984) but he has also applied his approach to a number of specific fields in *Sociology of Law* (1972), *The Function of Religion* (1974), and in his most popular book, *Love as Passion* (1982). Here he argues that the language used to speak of love is a symbolic code that determines the individual's experience of 'being in love'.

Luhmann has been attacked by liberal critics as an antihumanist technocrat but the influence of his ideas has continued to grow.

Lund, Kjell (1927–) and **Slaatto, Nils** (1923–) Norwegian architects who have been in partnership since 1958. Their forms are precisely structured and owe a debt to Norway's tradition of timber framing, especially in their smaller works, such as houses at Kragerø (1961), Biri (1974), and Lillehammer (1978). Even when using such modern materials as steel, their work fits harmoniously into older streetscapes: the gleaming white Skagen Brygge Hotel (1986–88) enlivens the waterfront at Stavanger, while the Cultural Centre (1979–87) provides the same town with an exciting new hub without disturbing the old pattern of streets.

Lund and Slaatto's use of concrete and brick, respectively at Asker Town Hall (1958–64) and Akerhaus Agricultural College (1961–70), Arnes, also reflects this structural formalism. The mass of both buildings is broken down by a careful arrangement of volumes while their roofs appear to float above continuous glazing. Their logical approach to space is best seen at their two laboratories for Norske Veritas at Høvik of 1972–76 and 1981–83, the latter being their most refined building. In Oslo this sensitivity has been made use of in the restoration of Eidsvon Square (1977–80), with its open-air restaurants, and the Bank of Norway (1974–87).

Lund and Slaatto's traditional houses and elegant commercial buildings contrast sharply with their churches. St Halvard church and cloister (1958–61), Oslo, an oval church set in a brick cube with a concave concrete roof, is their best-known work but its dim interior is not typical. Eidsvåg church (1969–85), Bergen, is white and light in accordance with ideas of liturgical renewal, while St Magnus (1987–89), Lillestrøm, owes something to Jørn UTZON.

Lundqvist, Evert (1904–) Swedish painter. Lundqvist studied at the Academy of Art in Stockholm and visited France and Germany in his twenties. His early work places him firmly in the tradition of northern European expressionism, with the influence of Munch being particularly apparent. At the same time his composition reveals a debt to the French classical tradition of Corot and Ingres.

In the 1940s he began to give less emphasis to individual motifs and more to the general composition of his work, which became increasingly abstract and emotive. His mature work is characterized by rich glowing colours and a heavy impasto technique.

In the 1950s Lundqvist supported Swedish neoexpressionism in its struggle with the predominant fashion for geometrical abstraction. By this time he was generally recognized as Sweden's most impressive living painter. He created a stained glass mosaic for the Town Hall in Skellefteå (1955) and in later years produced much graphic work.

Lurçat, Jean (1892–1966) French painter and designer, best known for his role in reviving the art of tapestry making. After training to be a doctor, Lurçat studied art under Victor Prouvé in Nancy and subsequently attended the Académie Colarossi in Paris, where he worked with the graphic artist Bernard Naudin (1876–1946). He was involved in the launch of the magazine *Feuilles de Mai* in 1913 and began to study tapestry two years later. He was wounded during World War I. Lurçat travelled widely in the 1920s, visiting Spain, North Africa, Greece, and the Middle East. He settled in Switzerland in 1931, but continued to travel extensively, making a trip to China in 1955. In his later years he lived in Paris.

After an early impressionist period, Lurçat came under the influence of cubism, largely through his friendship with Picasso and Louis Marcoussis. In the 1920s his travels inspired a fresh approach to his art and he began to paint desert landscapes and imaginary architecture, often with a surreal flavour. This aspect of his work emerged even more strongly in his tapestries. Here surreal depictions of animals and plants are blended with traditional tapestry stylizations to produce an innovative and distinctive style. His first such design was *Illusions d'Icare* in 1936; among many subsequent important works is *The Apocalypse*, a series of tapestries for the choir of the church of Assy (1948). Lurçat also designed stage sets and costumes and produced numerous illustrations for books. Towards the end of his life he returned to painting.

Lutosławski, Witold (1913–) Polish composer. As a child Lutosławski displayed a prodigious talent and went on to study piano and composition at the Warsaw Conservatory (1932–37). His musical development was curtailed by World War II, which Lutosławski spent playing piano duets with PANUFNIK in cafés. During the Stalinist years Lutosławski's work remained largely unperformed except for a few children's works in the style of Bartók. Lutosławski's search for a personal musical style bore fruit in his first acknowledged masterpiece, the *Concerto for Orchestra* (1954), which marks the summit of his early achievement. The works of his maturity begin with the *Funeral Music* (1958), in memory of Bartók, which experiments with serial techniques, and *Venetian Games* (1961), which was inspired by the aleatoric principles of John Cage's concerto for piano and orchestra. A similar freedom can be felt in Lutosławski's confident but playful applications of his new-found musical language in subsequent works, such as the cello concerto (1970) and the *Preludes and Fugue* for 13 strings (1972). Random procedures and extemporization continue to figure in his recent music (double concerto for oboe, harp, and strings, 1980; *Chain 1* for chamber orchestra, 1983; *Chain 2* for violin and orchestra, 1985; *Chain 3* for violin and symphony orchestra, 1986).

In the 1980s Lutosławski publicly allied himself with the Solidarity movement. In 1989 he served on the committee of intellectuals who supervised Poland's first free elections for 40 years. The latest of his four symphonies was premiered in Los Angeles in 1993.

Lutyens, (Agnes) Elisabeth (1906–83) British composer. The daughter of the architect Sir Edward Lutyens, she studied at the École Normale de Musique, Paris, and at the Royal College of Music, London, under Henry Darke. Lutyens was one of the first British composers to make use of 12-tone techniques, notably in her chamber concerto for nine instruments (1939). Despite physical and mental ill-health (including alcoholism) she kept up a prolific output and became highly influential as a teacher. Her works include the operas *Infidelio* (1954) and *Time off? Not a Ghost of a Chance* (1972), 13 string quartets, an acclaimed motet on a text by Wittgenstein (1954), numerous settings of contemporary English poetry, and a setting of Rimbaud's *O Saisons, O Chateaux!* (1946) for soprano and strings. She also wrote nearly 100 scores for films and carried out a similar number of commissions for radio. In 1931 she helped to found the Macnaghten-Lemare concerts of contemporary British music in London and in 1954 founded the Composers' Concourse. She published her autobiography, *A Goldfish Bowl*, in 1972.

Luzi, Mario (1914–) Italian poet. Born near Florence, Luzi studied literature at the University there (1930–36) and began to contribute to avant-garde journals associated with the hermetic movement in Italian poetry. His early collections *The Ship* (1935), *Nocturnal Advent* (1940), and *A Toast* (1946) are typical of the Florentine hermeticism of the 1940s in their introspection and their fastidious use of language. Important influences included Ungaretti, MONTALE, and the French Symbolists.

After World War II Luzi worked as a teacher before being appointed professor of French literature at Florence University in 1955. In later volumes such as *Gothic Notebook* (1947), *First Fruits of the Desert* (1952), *Respect for the Truth* (1957), *In the Magma* (1963), and *On Invisible Foundations* (1971) his style became far more explicit and direct as his range of interests grew wider. His mature poetry shows an increasing preoccupation with religious and philosophical themes and a familiarity with the mystical traditions of both East and West. Existential themes such as man's isolation and alienation, and the conflict between mortality and timelessness, are treated with a combination of sadness and serenity. Following the publication of his collected poems in 1979 and the death of Montale in 1981, Luzi was recognized as the most important living Italian poet.

Luzi has also contributed important critical essays on Mallarmé and French Symbolism, as well as translations of Coleridge, Shakespeare, and Racine.

Lyons, Eric (1912–78) British architect, who outraged his profession by designing private-enterprise housing estates with the builder Leslie Bilsby and the developer Geoffrey Townsend (and later with Ivor Cunningham). Their Span Developments Ltd proved that speculative low-cost housing could be exciting if designed well, with careful attention to layout, landscaping, and estate management. His estates at Parkleys, Ham (1954–6), Blackheath Park (1956–), and New Ash Green, Kent (1965–70, subsequently taken over by Bovis) are not considered inferior to the public housing championed by his contemporaries and, by contrast, remain popular, with their elegant landscaping well maintained. Lyons also designed public housing in Harlow and at the World's End in Chelsea (1969–77). For the latter he produced a series of towers whose brick cladding was an early reaction to the aesthetics of the NEW BRUTALISM.

Lyotard, Jean Francois (1924–) French philosopher of POSTMODERNISM. After studying philosophy Lyotard worked as a teacher in Algeria and joined a radical Marxist group. In 1972 he was appointed professor at the University of St Denis. Together with Jacques DERRIDA he founded the Collège International de Philosophie. He has taught at Berkeley, São Paulo, and Quebec and holds a permanent visiting chair at the University of California in Irvine.

Lyotard achieved his first recognition as an original thinker with his analysis of *The Postmodern Condition* (1979). Here Lyotard argued that the conditions of knowledge in the postindustrial world make the search for any kind of coherence – whether this be political, religious, or scientific – untenable. The idea of an absolute monolithic truth must be replaced by a recognition of the many 'narratives' about the world that can be devised. For Lyotard, however, postmodernism involves not only the end of classical modernism – seen as beginning with the French Revolution and ending with the dominance of technology and the mass media in the late 20th century – but also the idea that modernism can be completed and improved (*The Differend*; 1983). Lyotard argues that the aesthetic category of the sublime, which provokes both admiration and fear, should serve as a model for philosophers and artists as they attempt to renew the artistic and scientific ideas of the avant-garde in the early 20th-century. Although he has been reproached for irrationalism, Lyotard's concept of postmodernism has provided a focus for subsequent worldwide discussion.

lyrical abstraction *See* ART INFORMEL.

M

MacCaig, Norman (Alexander) (1910–) Scottish poet. MacCaig was educated at Edinburgh University and worked as a schoolteacher for nearly 40 years before becoming a lecturer at the University of Stirling. His first volume, *Far Cry*, was published in 1943 but he did not find his distinctive voice until *Riding Lights* (1955). Later collections include *The Sinai Sort* (1957), *Rings on a Tree* (1968), *The White Bird* (1973), *The Equal Skies* (1980), *A World of Difference* (1983), and *Voice-Over* (1988). Editions of his collected poems appeared in 1985 and 1990. He has also edited two anthologies of Scottish poetry, *Honour'd Shade* (1959) and *Contemporary Scottish Verse 1959–1969* (1970). His own verse deals with Edinburgh life and the landscape and history of Scotland in a restrained but sometimes highly metaphorical style that shows the influence of the English metaphysical poets. The author of some particularly fine love poems, he is widely considered the most accomplished English-language poet now writing in Scotland.

McCullin, Don(ald) (1935–) British photojournalist. Born in London, McCullin studied design and took up photography in 1958. His studies of the Berlin Wall won a national press award three years later. In the late 1960s his photographs of the war in Vietnam and Cambodia for *The Sunday Times* uncompromisingly depicted the horror of battle and the anonymity of its heroes and victims. These stark melancholy images caught the prevailing mood that war was more futile than glorious and played a role in turning British public opinion against US policy in Asia. McCullin also documented the conflicts in Biafra, Northern Ireland, Congo, Israel, Cyprus, and Lebanon; his collection *The Destruction Business* (1971) evoked the hardships of war and its aftermath in the suffering faces of its victims. Preferring black-and-white, McCullin perfected his stark tonal qualities in the darkroom and insisted on clear exposure readings even in combat zones. His other works include *The Homecoming* (1979), a study of the Palestinians, *Hearts of Darkness* (1980), and *Perspectives* (1987). In recent years he has turned increasingly to landscape photography, as in the collection *Open Skies* (1988). He published the autobiography *Unreasonable Behaviour* in 1990.

McEwan, Ian (Russell) (1948–) British novelist and writer. He was educated at the Universities of Sussex and East Anglia, where he studied creative writing under Malcolm BRADBURY, and subsequently worked as a journalist. In 1976 he won the Somerset Maugham Award for *First Love, Last Rites* (1975), a collection of macabre stories exploring such taboo subjects as incest, child abuse, and masturbation. It was followed by a similar collection, *In Between the Sheets* (1978). His early novels also show a penchant for the gruesome and the bizarre. In *The Cement Garden* (1978) a group of children keep a deadly secret, while in *The Comfort of Strangers* (1981) a young English couple are first befriended and then terrorized by an older couple in Venice. His third novel, *The Child in Time* (1987), shows a great broadening of range and won the Whitbread prize for fiction in 1988. A poignant account of the efforts of an estranged young couple to come to terms with the disappearance of their young daughter, the book also embraces an element of fantastic political satire and a meditation on the implications of post-Newtonian physics. *The Innocent* (1990), the story of a naive Englishman stranded in Cold War Berlin, achieved a certain notoriety for a scene in which the dismemberment of a murdered corpse is described in graphic detail. His most recent novel,

The Black Dogs (1992), uses a modern couple's chance encounter with the Nazi past to explore the nature of evil and the conflict between the religious and the non-religious views of the world. McEwan has also written *The Imitation Game* (1981), a series of plays for television, and *The Ploughman's Lunch* (1983), a screenplay.

McGrath, John (Peter) (1935–) British playwright and theatre director, who in 1971 founded the influential **7:84 Theatre Company**. A committed socialist, he began his professional career with the Royal Court Theatre and then moved to television, where he worked on such popular series as *Z Cars* as well as helping to direct new plays. As artistic director of 7:84, he was able to direct his own work and present his radical political ideas all around the country. His plays with the group included *The Cheviot, the Stag, and the Black, Black Oil* (1973), concerning the 19th-century Highland Clearances and subsequent issues relevant to Scottish identity, *Blood Red Roses* (1980), *The Baby and the Bathwater* (1984), *Mhàri Mhór* (1987), and *John Brown's Body* (1990). He has also produced adaptations of many classic plays, among them works by Chekhov and BRECHT. His screenplays include *The Bofors Gun* (1968) and *The Virgin Soldiers* (1969). He became a director of Channel 4 Television in 1989.

Mack, Heinz (1931–) German sculptor and exponent of KINETIC ART. Mack attended the Academy of Art in Düsseldorf (1950–53), following this with a degree in philosophy at Cologne (1953–56). Two years later, with Otto PIENE, he founded the ZERO GROUP of experimental artists and began to coedit its magazine. He won the Marzotto Prize in 1965 and first prize for sculpture at the Paris Biennale the following year.

In the late 1950s Mack began to use polished metals to create his so-called 'light reliefs' and soon expanded the concept to include an element of motion. These 'dynamic structures' or 'light dynamos' often incorporated curved glass or plexiglass in addition to metal plates; an electric motor moved these at irregular intervals to produce changing patterns of reflected light. In the 1960s he worked on a series of large-scale outdoor projects, the best known of these being his *Sahara Project*, in which the desert sunlight was reflected to startling effect. Mack also created an 11-m-high light column for a television film.

Mackay, David *See* MARTORELL, BOHIGAS, AND MACKAY.

MacMillan, Sir Kenneth (1929–92) British choreographer, dancer, and ballet director. MacMillan began his career as a dancer and appeared with the Sadler's Wells Theatre Ballet from 1946 onwards. His first ballet as a choreographer, *Somnambulism*, was seen in 1953. He subsequently attracted attention for his innovative approach to classical dance forms, pushing the boundaries of movement and drama further than any of his contemporaries. Among his early successes was *The Burrow* (1958), a piece inspired by the diary of Anne Frank; many of his later works were similarly based on historical characters and events.

The Invitation (1960), featuring Lynn Seymour, established MacMillan as the most promising young British choreographer of the period and introduced his characteristic themes of betrayal, social disintegration, and sexual conflict. An original interpretation of Stravinsky's *Le Sacre du Printemps* (1962) consolidated his reputation, while his first full-length ballet – *Romeo and Juliet* (1965) – provided Rudolf NUREYEV and Margot Fonteyn with two of their finest roles.

In 1965 MacMillan visited Stuttgart to direct *Song of the Earth*, one of several pieces he created for John CRANKO's company there. A year later he and Seymour moved to Berlin, where he assumed the artistic directorship of the Deutsches Oper ballet company; his successes there included *Concerto* (1966), *Anastasia* (1967), *Sleeping Beauty* (1967), *Olympiad* (1968), *Cain and Abel* (1968), and *Swan Lake* (1969).

In 1970 MacMillan succeeded his mentor ASHTON as artistic director of the ROYAL BALLET. His subsequent work with the company included the full-length *Anastasia* (1971) and *Manon* (1974) and the comic *Elite Syncopations* (1974), set to the music of Scott Joplin. He returned to Stuttgart in 1976 to present the *Fauré Requiem* in memory of Cranko and soon afterwards resigned his post at the Royal Ballet to concentrate on choreography (he remained chief choreographer with the company).

Mayerling (1978), a powerful depiction of the relationship between Crown Prince Rudolf and his 17-year old mistress, was much praised for its combination of high drama and brilliant choreography. Subsequent works included *My Brother, My Sisters* (1978), a tale of incest and murder, *Gloria* (1980), which employed the music of Poulenc, *Isadora* (1980), about the life of Isadora Duncan, *Wild Boy* (1981), *Different Drummer* (1984), and *Sea of Troubles* (1988), which was based on Shakespeare's *Hamlet*.

MacMillan also choreographed works for the American Ballet Theatre (from 1984). His most recent productions include his sixth full-length ballet for the Royal Ballet, *The Prince of the Pagodas* (1989). Also a director of stage plays by IONESCO, Strindberg, and Tennessee Williams, he was knighted for his services to dance in 1983. He died suddenly while attending a revival of *Mayerling* at Covent Garden.

Maconchy, Dame Elizabeth (1907–) British composer of Irish extraction. She studied (1923–29) at the Royal College of Music with Charles Wood and Vaughan Williams and subsequently with Karel Jirák in Prague. The influence of Bartók and other central European composers is evident in the driving rhythms and free chromaticism of much of her work. Her piano concerto was first performed with the Prague Symphony Orchestra in 1930, the same year that her suite *The Land* was given at the proms in London. She is best known as a prolific composer of chamber music, her 14 string quartets having found particular acclaim. Other works include settings of Hopkins, Donne, and Dylan Thomas and the one-act operas *The Sofa* (1967), *The Three Strangers* (1967), and *The King of the Golden River* (1975) for children. Amongst her most successful works is *Ariadne* (1970), a cantata for soprano and chamber orchestra. She continued to compose into the 1980s, producing such works as the wind quintet (1982), *Still Falls the Rain* (1984) for double choir, and *Life Story* (1985) for string orchestra. Her daughter is the composer Nicola LEFANU.

Maderna, Bruno (1920–73) Italian composer, conductor, and teacher. A leading figure in post-war Italian music, he greatly influenced, among others, BERIO, NONO, Aldo CLEMENTI and Franco DONATONI. A child prodigy, he studied composition at the Rome Conservatory and at the Venice Conservatory under Malipiero. Later he studied conducting with Hermann Scherchen who steered him towards serialism. From 1947 to 1950 he taught composition at the Venice Conservatory. In 1951 he first attended DARMSTADT, a visit which profoundly affected his career. He settled in Darmstadt during the 1950s and from 1954 onwards taught composition, conducting, and musical analysis at the summer schools there. In 1954 he founded, with Berio, the electronic Studio di Fonologia Musicale in Milan. As a teacher he has also worked at the Milan Conservatory, the Salzburg Mozarteum (1967–70) and the Rotterdam Conservatory (from 1967). His conducting career has specialized in contemporary music: besides being conductor of the Darmstadt International Chamber Ensemble, he has been chief conductor of the Radio Milan Symphony Orchestra and Director of the Tanglewood Music Center, Massachusetts (1971–72).

Typical of his early Schoenbergian serialist works is *Studi per 'Il Processo' di Kafka* (1950), while his *Musica in due dimensioni* (1952; revised 1963) is acknowledged as the first work to combine live and recorded sound. Works such as *Composizion in tre tempi* (1954), which borrows from folksong, and the string quartet of 1955, which is constructed in mirror form, use total SERIALISM. Following the decline of total serialism in the late 1950s, Maderna disregarded most avant-garde trends. Instead the first oboe concerto (1962) and subsequent works blend elements of neoclassicism, expressionism, and aleatoricism. Important pieces such as *Grande aulodia* (1970) for orchestra and *Giardino religioso* (1972) for orchestra combined aleatoric and notated elements.

His output includes stage works, notably *Hyperion* (1964), and *Satyricon* (1973), orchestral and ensemble works, piano, oboe and flute concertos, vocal music, and electronic pieces.

Madsen, Svend Åge (1939–) Danish novelist and prose writer, noted for his experimental works. Madsen made his literary debut in 1962, when his short story 'The Eighth Day' was published in the Danish periodical *The Wind Rose*. In his first novel, *The Visit*, which appeared the following year, Madsen's protagonist desperately tries to create order in the world around him but ends up paralysed by his neurosis. The problematic relationship between the individual and his environment remains a major theme throughout Madsen's work.

In 1964 Madsen published the ANTI-NOVEL *Pictures of Desire*, which explores the relationship between victim and tormentor in various situations. *Assuming the World Exists* (1971) gives a fragmented view of the world through the individual experiences of five characters. The novel stresses the importance of accepting different viewpoints. Madsen's most experimental text, *Days with Diam* (1972), has a contents page in diagram form; the reader must chart his own way through the book, following the story to one of several different conclusions. This indeterminate form reflects the doubts of the central character.

In 1965 Madsen returned to the short-story form with the collection *Eight Times Orphan*. He has also written radio plays such as *Presentations* (1970) and *In Reality* (1971); he won the Radio Play Prize for 1973 and returned to the genre in 1982 with *Kaspar Seeks an Existence*.

Madsen's most recent works include *The Laveran Family* (1988), *To Tell the People* (1989), and *Between Heaven and Earth* (1990). He was awarded the main Danish Academy Prize for 1972.

magic realism A type of writing in which fantastic events are described in a matter-of-fact style normally associated with realism. The term was originally coined to describe the work of the German Neue Sachlichkeit painters of the 1920s, who sometimes rendered phantasmagoric scenes in a sharply realistic style. It was later used of a minor trend in the German literature of the 1950s but did not become widely current until the 1970s, when it was applied to the work of certain Latin American writers – notably Gabriel García Márquez and Jorge Luis Borges – who combined the everyday with the miraculous and supernatural. In the 1980s this manner of writing was imitated by many younger novelists, who drew upon myth, dreams, and fairy tales while retaining many of the conventions of naturalism. European writers whose work has been characterized as magical realist include Elsa MORANTE in Italy, Günter GRASS in Germany, Milan KUNDERA in the former Czechoslovakia, and Salman RUSHDIE and Angela CARTER in Britain.

Magritte, René (1898–1967) Belgian surrealist painter. Born in Lessines, Magritte took painting lessons from the age of 10. His youth was overshadowed by the suicide (1912) of his mother, an event alluded to in many of his paintings. He attended the Académie des Beaux-Arts in Brussels for two years from the age of 18. As part of an avant-garde circle that included Pierre-Louis Flouquet (1900–67) and E.L.T. Mesens (1903–71) he showed an interest in such movements as futurism and Orphism. In 1922 he married Georgette Berger, who was to model for him throughout her life, and took a job as a designer in a wallpaper factory. The same year a viewing of Giorgio de Chiroco's enigmatic *Le Chant d'Amour* led him towards a new vision of what his art should be.

In 1925 Magritte conclusively embraced surrealism and became a full-time painter; two years later he moved to Perreux-sur-Marne, outside Paris, to be near the French Surrealists. During his years in France Magritte produced some of his most menacing works; he returned to settle in Brussels in 1930. Although his work featured in surrealist exhibitions throughout the 1930s he did not achieve an international reputation until relatively late in life. In the 1950s and 1960s he painted murals for the Casino of Knokke-le Zoute, the Palais des Beaux-Arts, Charleroi, and the Palais de Congrès in Brussels.

Magritte's style was the essence of surrealism: his work creates a fantastic world in which familiar objects are brought together in incongruous or paradoxical combinations to produce an unsettling dreamlike effect. His realist technique hardly changed apart from a brief flirtation with late impressionism after World War II (his 'Renoir' period) and some experimentation with an aggressive style known as *'vache'* in 1948. A small number of images – clouds, torsos, men in bowler hats – recurs obsessively throughout his work. In the 1960s his painting had a major influence on the emerging POP ART style; it has also been widely imitated in advertising and the mass media.

Makavejev, Dušan (1932–) Yugoslavian (Serbian) film director, who attracted much attention in the 1960s with his challenging films on political and sexual themes. Born in Belgrade, Makavejev made shorts and documentaries before releasing his first feature film in 1965; *Man is Not a Bird* is a provocative portrayal of the doomed love between a girl and a factory worker. His reputation continued to grow with *Switchboard Operator* (1966), an exposé of contemporary sexual mores that also raised questions about political freedom. Both films were admired for their wit and unconventional editing.

Makavejev adopted the documentary form for *Innocence Unprotected* (1968), a humorous but sensitive depiction of the making of the first Serbian talkie during the German occupation, for which he reunited the original actors and film crew. The radical political and sexual theories of Wilhelm Reich were the subject of the equally free-form *WR: Mysteries of the Organism* (1971), after which Makavejev made a widely banned film about the Miss World competition. His next film, *Montenegro*, a witty depiction of the sexual liberation of a frustrated housewife, did not appear until 1981. Subsequent films have been less well received, with the political and sexual themes of *The Coca-Cola Kid* (1985) and *Manifesto* (1988) failing to arouse the interest that they did in the 1960s.

Makovecz, Imre (1935–) Hungarian architect. Born in Budapest and educated at the Technical University there, Makovecz has been the prime mover in an extraordinary revival of romantic-vernacular architecture in Hungary. Until the fall of communism he worked in the face of considerable official disapproval and often found it hard to get his designs built.

The son of a carpenter, Makovecz helped his father in the repair of war-damaged buildings, gaining a deep understanding of the use and potential of timber. Many of his buildings make striking use of wood or other natural materials: some incorporate whole trees. His expressionist supermarket at Saropspataki (1971), with its concrete walls battered outwards and long horizontal lighting strips, reflects the influence of Eric Mendelsohn and Frank Lloyd Wright's Guggenheim Museum. Perhaps his most remarkable building is the funerary chapel (1977) at the Farkasret Cemetery in Budapest. The huge timber roof has great curved roof ribs – reminiscent of the inside of a giant ribcage. After leaving the state architecture bureau in 1977 (under some pressure) Makovecz worked in the forestry commission. During this period he designed a series of remarkable cultural centres for villages in rural Hungary, including one at Bak in the shape of an eagle's wings. Despite their extravagantly romantic forms, his buildings have proved highly functional. Makovecz said of his apartment houses (1982) at Sārospatak in Budapest that they "represent the formal entry of nature and prehistoric culture into our present day".

Maksimov, Vladimir Emel'ianovich (Lev Alekseevich Samsonov; 1932–) Russian poet, dramatist, novelist, and editor, living in France. Brought up in orphanages and schools for juvenile delinquents, Maksimov first worked as a labourer but began to publish poetry as early as 1952. In 1961 he first came to notice as a prose writer with a long short story 'We Make the Earth Feel Homy'. Another story, 'Man Keeps on Living' (1962), attracted great attention when dramatized in 1965. Maksimov served as an editor of the journal *October* until 1971, when his novel *The Seven Days of Creation* was published abroad; a second novel, *Quarantine* (1973), circulated widely in *samizdat*. Maksimov was expelled from the Writers Union before being exiled in 1974.

Settling in Paris, Maksimov has continued to write novels while editing the leading conservative émigré journal *Continent* (1974–). Amongst his major works are *Farewell from Nowhere* (1973, revised 1982), *Ark for the Uncalled* (1976) and *To Gaze into the Abyss* (1986). A lonely figure, at odds with many fellow émigrés and Western Slavists (whom he attacked for weak liberalism in *Saga of the Rhinoceroses*, 1981), Maksimov writes in a realistic manner but with a variable, even eccentric, grasp of time and place and using shifting points of view. His characters are mostly drawn from the proletariat and display fierce, often violent, passions. A believer himself, he presents religion in his novels as generally no more than an awareness of evil; nearly all his characters behave immorally in one way or another. In his best novels, particularly *The Seven Days of Creation*, Maksimov offers a memorable vision of Soviet life in the raw.

Malle, Louis (1932–) French film director of the NEW WAVE. After studying at the Sorbonne and the Institute of Advanced Cinematographic Studies, Malle worked as an assistant to the director Robert BRESSON. His first film was the documentary *World of Silence* (1956), codirected with the oceanographer Jacques COUSTEAU. This was followed by the imaginative thriller *Lift to the Scaffold* (1957). In 1958 Malle's second feature *Les Amants*, an exploration of bourgeois sexuality, achieved international success and made a star of its lead, Jeanne Moreau. Other early successes included *Zazie dans le metro* (1961), adapted from the novel by Raymond QUENEAU, and the much acclaimed *Le Feu follet* (*The Fire Within*; 1963), a sombre depiction of the last hours in the life of a suicidal playboy. *Dearest Love* (1971) aroused controversy with its scenes of incest between a son and his mother, while the acclaimed *Lacombe, Lucien* (1974) probed the then equally taboo subject of collaboration during the German occupation. In 1978 Malle directed his first US-made film, *Pretty Baby*, the story of a 12-year-old girl growing up in a New Orleans brothel. *My Dinner with Andre* (1981) was a film consisting almost entirely of a cerebral dinner-party conversation between two characters. Other US films have included *Atlantic City* (1980), starring Burt Lancaster as an ageing petty criminal and *And the Pursuit of Happiness* (1986). In 1987 *Au revoir les enfants*, a semiautobiographical film about a young French boy's friendship with a Jewish boy hiding in a Roman Catholic school during the Nazi occupation, proved a great critical and popular success. Malle's most recent film is *Damage* (1992).

Mallet-Joris, Françoise (Françoise Lilar; 1930–) French novelist and writer. Born in Antwerp, the daughter of a Belgian cabinet minister and the dramatist Suzanne Lilar, Mallet-Joris was educated in Philadelphia and at the Sorbonne. She is married to a Frenchman and lives in Paris.

In her first book, a volume of poems (*Sunday Poems*; 1947), Mallet-Joris described her search for peace and order through the power of words. Her novels focus on the relationships between people and the gap between the real self and the social mask. With her novel *Into the Labyrinth* (*Le Rempart des Béguines*; 1951), the story of a lesbian love affair between a young girl and her father's mistress, she provoked a scandal similar to that caused by SAGAN's *Bonjour Tristesse* a few years later. This was followed by the family stories *The Red Room* (1953), and *House of Lies* (*Les Mesonges*; 1957), both of which feature independent young heroines in revolt against their backgrounds. In *Café Celeste* (1958) she evokes the atmosphere of a Montmartre café and describes its clientele. The autobiographical *A Letter to Myself* (1963) described her religious conversion and later publications such as *The Paper House* (1970), *Allegra* (1976), and the stories in *The Wink of an Angel* (1983) show a growing preoccupation with spiritual matters. As a novelist Mallet-Joris owes more to 19th-century tradition than to any of her contemporaries. She has also written biographies, children's books, and song lyrics.

Malraux, André (1901–76) French writer. In his youth Malraux chose to mix with figures from the literary and artistic worlds rather than to further his formal education. At the age of 20 he married a German and travelled to the Far East, where he became committed to the liberation of the French colonies. His disillusionment with Western culture is clear from *The Temptation of the Occident* (1926). In 1933 he was awarded the Prix Goncourt for his novel *The Human Condition*, set during the political upheavals in China. In the 1930s Malraux was involved in several antifascist committees and organized the Republican Air Force in the Spanish Civil War. During World War II he led a brigade of the Resistance. After the war he became increasingly involved in French politics as a follower of de Gaulle. He served as minister of culture from 1958 until his death.

Malraux's refusal to separate political commitment from art is apparent from his novels *Days of Contempt* (1935) and *Days of Hope* (1937), both of which concern the antifascist struggle of the 1930s, and *The Walnuts of Altenburg* (1943–45), his last novel. His main characters are mostly communists. Malraux's insistence on the complexity of the human situation and the necessity of struggling against terror and death even when there is no guarantee of victory brought him close to the ideas of

EXISTENTIALISM. As intellectual and man of action Malraux provided a powerful image for a generation of younger French writers. Most of his post-war writings, such as *The Voices of Silence* (1951) and *Museum without Walls* (1952–54), dealt with the philosophy of art. Other late writings include his *Antimémoires* (1967) and a collection of speeches.

Mandel'shtam, Nadezhda (Nadezhda Yakovlevna Khazina: 1899–1980). Russian writer and critic. Born in Saratov, she studied art in Kiev and worked as a translator in several European languages. In 1922 she married the great Russian poet Osip Emil'evitch Mandel'shtam (1891–1938), whom she followed into two periods of internal exile during the Stalin years. He died alone during his third exile in 1938, probably in a labour camp. Nadezhda was largely responsible for preserving her husband's poetry from oblivion by assiduously collecting copies and memorizing long passages. This devotion to his poetry, and her open contempt for communism, provided the main impetus for *Hope Against Hope* (*Vospominaniya*; 1970), a harrowing chronicle of the fate of the Russian intelligentsia under Stalin and of her own marriage. It revealed her perspicacity as both literary critic and political observer, showing the dehumanizing tortures of conscience suffered by Russian artists and thinkers. She argued that the intelligentsia capitulated with the 1917 Revolution itself and not, as widely held, only after Stalin replaced Lenin. *Hope Abandoned* (*Vtoraya kniga*; 1972), a panoramic view of Russian life from peasants to literary figures, documented the more than 20 years she spent in rootless wanderings across Russia after her husband's death, a semi-exile teaching English for tiny sums. Her two volumes have been described by Joseph BRODSKY as 'a Day of Judgement on earth for her age and for its literature'.

Manen, Hans van (1932–) Dutch dancer, choreographer, and ballet director, who emerged as one of the foremost choreographers associated with the NETHERLANDS DANCE THEATRE in the 1960s. Having studied under Sonia GASKELL, van Manen joined her Ballet Recital company in 1951 and subsequently worked with the Amsterdam Opera Ballet and with Roland PETIT. Unhappy with the predominant classicism of Gaskell's company he left it in 1960 to become a founder member of the Netherlands Dance Theatre, with whom he first established his reputation as a choreographer and eventually served as artistic director. Notable successes with the company included his own ballets *Symphony in Three Movements* (1963), *Five Sketches* (1966), and *Mutations* (1970); in collaboration with Rudi van DANTZIG and Toer van Schayk he also promoted the work of such contemporary choreographers as Balanchine and ASHTON.

In 1970 van Manen left the company and in 1973 moved to the DUTCH NATIONAL BALLET as choreographer and ballet master. Subsequently he abandoned the energetic jazz rhythms of his earlier work in favour of more formal compositions, among them *Twilight* (1972), *Adagio Hammerklavier* (1973), and *Four Schumann Pieces* (1975), which was created for Anthony Dowell and the ROYAL BALLET – although in contrast, *5 Tangos* (1977) was a lively and immediately accessible entertainment based on South American dance. He returned to the Netherlands Dance Theatre in 1988.

Manessier, Alfred (1911–) French painter and designer of stained glass. Manessier was born in Saint-Ouen, Somme, and studied architecture at the Ecole des Beaux-Arts in Amiens before moving to Paris in 1929. Here he studied informally and copied old masters in the Louvre. After an early figurative period, he passed through surrealist and cubist phases during the 1930s. In 1940–41 he studied with the French painter Roger Bissière (1888–1964), whose style of abstraction derived from natural appearances became a major influence on his work. He exhibited in the celebrated 'Jeunes Peintres de la Tradition Française' show in Paris, in 1941. Major exhibitions of Manessier's work were held in Paris in 1949 and in Brussels two years later; he won the painting prize at the São Paulo Biennale in 1953.

After World War II Manessier emerged as a major exponent of expressive abstraction (*see* ART INFORMEL). Important influences on his work of this period include the art of Paul Klee and medieval stained glass. It was in his commissions from churches for stained-glass windows that his art found its most perfect expression. A visit to the monastery at La Trappe in 1943 deepened the religious aspects of his work, though it retained its abstract character. He produced a striking series of lithographs on the theme of Easter in 1949. Manessier also designed a number of tapestries, including that for the National Center of Art in Ottawa.

Mangiarotti, Angelo (1921–) Italian architect and designer. Born and educated in Milan, Mangiarotti became professor of design at the Illinois Institute of Technology, Chicago (1948–55) and produced fine plywood furniture and household items. From 1955 to 1962 he was in partnership with Bruno Morassuti, whose organic forms complemented Mangiarotti's experimental rationalism.

Mangiarotti's work as an architect includes a number of elegant private houses with great slab roofs and split-level plans, as well as a large number of flats, mostly around Milan. But his most spectacular work is his simplest. His Matris Misericordiae Church in Baranzate (1957, with Morassuti) used a rectangular plan with just four columns supporting a prefabricated concrete roof. It is clad in shimmering opaque glass; otherwise its form prefigures the industrial buildings that dominate Mangiarotti's independent work. He has produced a variety of post-and-beam systems for prefabricating warehouses and factories, some in steel, as at Mestre (1962), Lusone (1964), and the exciting Snaidero Industrial Complex in Udine (1978), others in reinforced concrete (Alzate Brianza, Como, 1969). At times his severe forms approach a primitive classicism, with precast orderless capitals. Mangiarotti has also researched cladding systems, using glass, aluminium, zinc, and local hemp resin (SIAG Industrial and Housing Complex, Caserta, 1962).

Since 1982 Mangiarotti has been designing new stations linking Milan's railway and underground systems. He has produced a suspension structure equally adaptable to open-air and underground sites.

Manning, Olivia (1908–80) British novelist. Born in Portsmouth, Manning married R. D. Smith, a lecturer for the British Council, in 1939 and travelled with him to Romania at the outbreak of World War II. She had already written one novel, *The Wind Changes* (1937), set in Dublin, but her reputation now rests on a sequence of works based on her experiences in Romania, Greece, and the Middle East during the war. These comprise *The Balkan Trilogy*, consisting of *The Great Fortune* (1960), *The Spoilt City* (1962), and *Friends and Heroes* (1965), and *The Levant Trilogy*, consisting of *The Danger Tree* (1977), *The Battle Lost and Won* (1978), and *The Sum of Things* (1980). The sequence traces the fluctuating relationship of the newly married Guy and Harriet Pringle as they are repeatedly separated and reunited by the larger currents of the war. Although *The Battle Lost and Won* contains a celebrated set-piece description of the Battle of El Alamein, the conflict is mainly seen from the viewpoint of civilians caught up in events beyond their control or understanding. The books are notable for their many colourful minor characters and are strongly evocative of both place and period.

Manzoni, Giacomo (1932–) Italian composer, musicologist, and critic. Born in Milan, he studied piano and composition at the Liceo Musicale in Messina (1948–50) and at the Milan Conservatory; he also attended the DARMSTADT summer courses in 1956 and 1957. He has worked as music critic for *L'unità* (1958–66) and *Prisma* (1968), as editor of the music journal *Il diapason* (1958), and on the editorial staff of *Musica Realta* since 1980. His teaching appointments have included professor of composition at the conservatories of Milan (1962–64; 1974–) and Bologna (1969–74). He has translated the musical writings of Schoenberg and ADORNO.

Manzoni first gained widespread attention as a composer when his *Parole da Beckett* for double chorus, instrumental groups, and tape won a UNESCO prize in 1973. His style developed from the free atonalism found in the two little suites for violin and piano (1952) to the use of serialism and electronics found in the stage work *Atomtod* (1965); thereafter, works such as *Ombre (alla memoria di Che Guevara)* (1968), *Per M. Robespierre* (1975), and *Hölderlin (frammento)* (1972) have attempted to create new post-serialist techniques and structures. As some of these titles suggest, his left-wing political commitment has had an important influence on his work. His output includes stage works, orchestral music (notably *Multipli*, 1972, and *Variabili*, 1973), chamber works (notably the string quartet of 1971), and electronic and vocal pieces. Recent works include the *Scena Sinfoniche per il Dr Faustus* (1984).

Manzoni, Piero (1933–63) Italian experimental artist. Manzoni studied at the University of Milan, his native city, and began to paint in a traditional figurative style. In the mid 1950s, however, he came under the influence of the *spazialismo* of Lucio FONTANA, which argued for the abandonment of traditional easel painting. Another major influence was Yves KLEIN, whom he met for the first time in 1957. In the same year Manzoni exhibited the first of his *Acromes*, white monochromes produced by dipping the canvas in lime and kaolin. He later tried using glass fibre, cotton wool, and polystyrene to achieve similar effects. In the last years of his life he concentrated mainly on PERFORMANCE ART and such neo-Dadaist stunts as selling a balloon full of his own breath. His 'sealed lines' were a series of works consisting of lines drawn on paper and sealed in metal canisters; the longest of the lines extended 7200 m. He was a founding member of Milan's Galerie Azimuth in 1959 and helped to start its magazine. His early death was caused by cirrhosis. Manzoni's work anticipated both ARTE POVERA and CONCEPTUAL ART.

Manzù, Giacomo (1908–91) Italian sculptor. Born in poverty in Bergamo, Manzù was apprenticed to local craftsmen who taught him how to work wood, metal, and stone. He trained in sculpture at the Accademia Cicognini in Verona during intervals in his military service (1927–28). His seated nude *Francesca* won the Grand Prix at the Rome Quadrennale in 1942 and six years later he was awarded first prize for sculpture at the Venice Biennale. From 1943 to 1954 he was professor of sculpture at the Academy of Fine Arts in Milan.

In 1950 Manzù gained a commission to produce a set of monumental bronze doors for St Peter's in Rome, reviving the ancient tradition of bronze doors for ecclesiastical buildings. He went on to produce doors for Salzburg Cathedral (1958), the Church of Sankt-Laurents in Belgium (1969), and the relief *Mother and Child* for the Rockefeller Center in New York City. He also produced numerous sculptures (in widely divergent sizes) of Roman Catholic cardinals. In this and other work, Manzù brought a new vitality to figurative bronze sculpture.

In the 1930s Manzù was influenced by Rodin and the impressionist style of Medardo Rosso (1858–1928) but after World War II he returned to classical principles. His style blended realism with flowing movements to produce works which vary from austere severity to the deeply sensuous. He allowed tiny irregularities into the texture of his work to offset its general air of tranquillity. His reliefs, most of which are religious in theme, are characterized by delicate modelling and full rounded contours.

Marceau, Félicien (Louis Carette; 1913–) French writer, born in Belgium. After training as a lawyer, Louis Carette worked for Belgian radio, continuing in this role during the German occupation in World War II. To escape punishment as a collaborator he fled to France in 1946, adopting French nationality and the name Félicien Marceau.

After writing such satirical novels as *The China Sheperdess* (1953) and *The Flutterings of the Heart* (1955) Marceau found success with his sardonic play *The Egg* (1956), which suggested that the world itself was a rotten egg. His next play *The Good Soup* (1958) was also a big success in France, striking a popular balance between the theatre of the ABSURD and boulevard comedy.

In 1969 Marceau won the Prix Goncourt for his novel *Creezy*, the story of a doomed love affair between an ambitious politician and a beautiful model; the failure of the relationship exposes the unbridgeable gap between appearance and reality in the world of advertising. In 1975 Marceau was elected to the Académie Française. His more recent works include the novels *Call Me Mademoiselle* (1984) and *A Bird in the Sky* (1989); he has also published essays and memoirs.

Maréchal, Marcel (1937–) French actor and theatre director, who emerged as one of France's leading contemporary directors in the 1960s. He established his reputation while director of the experimental Théâtre du Cothurne in Lyon in the 1960s, winning particular acclaim for his revivals of important absurdist plays from the 1950s. He founded the Théâtre de Huitième in 1968 and subsequently directed lively productions of major works by such authors as BRECHT, Jean VAUTHIER, and Peter WEISS. He was appointed head of the Théâtre National de Marseille in 1975.

Marin, Maguy (1951–) French choreographer. Her powerfully atmospheric pieces, often on an epic scale and with a significant political content, have won her a reputation as perhaps the most important choreographer working in France today.

Marin trained in Toulouse and began her career with the Strasbourg Opéra Ballet. Subsequently she studied under BÉJART and made her choreographic debut with the BALLET OF THE 20TH CENTURY, for whom she created *Yu-ku-ri* (1976). In 1978 she established her own company, now known as the Compagnie Maguy Marin, installing it in 1981 in the Parisian suburb of Créteil. Her successes with the new company included *May B* (1981), inspired by the writing of Samuel BECKETT, and *Babel Babel* (1982), an epic work tracing the development and disintegration of human society.

Other influential works by Marin have included *Jaleo* (1983) and *Leçon de ténèbres* (1988), which were commissioned by the Paris Opéra Ballet, and the hugely popular *Cinderella* (1985) and *The Seven Deadly Sins* (1987), which were first performed in collaboration with the Lyon Opéra Ballet. She has also produced several pieces for the DUTCH NATIONAL BALLET.

Marini, Marino (1901–80) Italian sculptor and painter. Born in Pistoia, he studied painting and sculpture at the Academy of Fine Arts in Florence. He initially concentrated on graphic art but from 1930 onwards devoted himself almost exclusively to sculpture. He visited much of Europe and the US in the 1930s, living in Switzerland from 1942 until 1946 and afterwards mainly in Milan. Marini won first prize for sculpture at the Rome Quadriennale in 1935 and two years later was awarded a prize at the Exposition Universelle, Paris. The 1952 Venice Biennale awarded him its sculpture prize.

Marini is best known for his many variations on the theme that dominated his work from 1935 onwards: the horse and rider. He progressed from early works in which the two forms have separate identities (for example *Waiting Rider*, 1937), to works in which they are as one. He later focused on the drama of a rider about to topple from a rearing horse, as in *Monumental Rider* (1958), commissioned for the Bouwgelust estate in The Hague. This is noticeably more abstract than his earlier more classically influenced pieces. Marini often completed his sculptures by using a chisel on the bronze cast and applying corrosive dyes to introduce blemishes and colouring. An example is the bronze *Dancer* (1949–54) at the Städt Mus, Duisburg. He also produced a number of brilliant portrait sculptures, such as that of *Igor Stravinsky* (1951).

Marker, Chris (Christian François Bouche-Villeneuve; 1921–) French film director, screenwriter, and photographer of didactic films with a Marxist message. Much influenced by the documentaries of the Soviet director Dziga Vertov, Marker played a major role in developing the film essay form and has been called 'the one true essayist of the French cinema'. He was born in Neuilly-sur-Seine and, after service with the Resistance in World War II, became a prolific writer of articles and essays, also publishing a novel and a collection of poems. He entered cinema in the early 1950s with a series of medium-length CINÉMA VÉRITÉ documentaries which he used to express his sociopolitical concerns. These include *Sunday in Peking* (1955), *Letter from Siberia* (1958), the Israeli short *Description d'un combat* (1960), and *Cuba Si!* (1961). In 1967 Marker founded the film cooperative SLON (Société pour la Lancement des Oeuvres Nouvelles) to produce his antiwar film *Far From Vietnam*. His later films have included *The Battle of Chili* (1975–76), a two-part documentary, and *Le Fond de l'air est rouge* (1977), also in two parts.

Marriner, Sir Neville (1924–) British conductor and violinist. Born in Lincoln, he studied the violin at the Royal College of Music, London, where he later (1946–59) taught. He also studied under René Benedetti at the Paris Conservatoire and played in the London Philharmonia (1952–56) and the London Symphony Orchestra (1956–68). Marriner is best known for his association with the ACADEMY OF ST MARTIN-IN-THE-FIELDS, an ensemble specializing in baroque music, which he founded in 1959. He continued to organize and direct the Academy until 1978 and remains its musical director. He has also directed the Los Angeles Chamber Orchestra (1969–78), the Minnesota Orchestra (1979–86), and the Stuttgart Radio Symphony Orchestra (1984) as well as organizing the South Bank Festival of Music (1969–78) and the Barbican Summer Festival (1985–87; *see* BARBICAN CENTRE).

Martin, Frank (1890–1974) Swiss composer, pianist, and harpsichordist. Born in Geneva, Martin studied in his birthplace and later in Zürich, Paris, and Rome. In early works such as the first piano concerto (1934) and the symphony (1937) the influences of French impressionism and Schoenberg are somewhat uneasily combined; a more convincing fusion was achieved in the oratorio *Le Vin herbé* (1941), where Martin's distinctive voice emerges for the first time. Martin taught at the Geneva Conservatory and was director of the Technicum Moderne de Musique, Geneva, from 1933 until 1939; he travelled widely as a performer and was president of the Swiss Musicians Union (1943–46). After World War II he spent long periods in the Netherlands and in Germany, where he taught at the Cologne Musikhochschule (1950–57). His mature works include the *Petite Symphonie concertante* (1945), probably his best-known piece, the operas *Der Sturm* (1956) and *Monsieur de Pourceaugnac* (1962), the oratorios *In Terra Pax* (1944) and *Golgotha* (1948), and the *Sechs Monologue aus 'Jedermann'* (1943) for voice and orchestra. Later works include a second piano concerto (1969) and a requiem (1972).

Martin, Kenneth (1905–) British constructivist painter and sculptor, best known for his mobiles. Born in Sheffield, he studied (1921–29) at the School of Art there and at the Royal College of Art in London. Although he produced mainly naturalistic landscapes during the 1930s, over the next decade he steadily reduced the representational element in his work.

By 1948 he and his wife **Mary Martin** (*née* Balmford; 1907–69) were producing totally abstract works. With Victor PASMORE, Anthony Hill, and Adrian Heath they formed a new British constructivist movement, dedicated to the idea that art should be entirely nonrepresentational and nonexpressive. In 1951 Martin began to produce wire mobiles, designed to create constantly changing spatial forms and patterns of light as they revolved. The largest and best known of these were the *Screw Mobile* series, made from brass rods with rectangular plates attached. He also assembled small, usually brass, freestanding constructions which, like the mobiles, created intricate configurations from a few simple elements. Martin likewise applied his constructionist theories to his painting, using mathematical formulae as a basis for his mostly linear designs. After 1969 he introduced an element of chance into these works, thus combining the arbitrary with the rational.

Martin, Sir (John) Leslie (1908–) British architect. Trained at the University of Manchester, and subsequently a lecturer there, Martin was later head of the school of architecture at Hull (1930–39). In 1939 he became assistant architect to the London Midland and Scottish Railway but reached the peak of his career as deputy architect (1948–52) and then architect (1952–56) to the London County Council. Subsequently he was professor of architecture at the University of Cambridge (1956–72) and held a private practice in the city. Martin produced a moderate and very English kind of modernism, influenced by Scandinavian as much as French or German types and best exemplified by the Royal Festival Hall, London (with Robert Marshall; 1951; *see* FESTIVAL OF BRITAIN). Since then most of his work has been in educational building. He produced general layout designs for the universities of Hull and Leicester and the Royal Holloway College. His Zoology and Psychology Building, and his Law and English Faculty, both at Oxford, are big blocks carved into deep steps and terraces, with wide entrance steps and podiums and horizontal bands of windows. His most recent major work is a cultural complex in Glasgow, containing several concert halls and a new home for the Royal Scottish Academy of Music and Drama (with Ivor Richards; 1981–91).

Martinon, Jean (1909–76) French conductor and composer. Martinon studied composition with Albert Roussel and conducting with Charles MÜNCH at the Paris Conservatoire, graduating in 1928 with the first prize in violin. In the 1930s he appeared as a soloist and conductor with various orchestras before producing his first distinctive works, the *Sinfonietta* (1935) and first symphony (1936). After 1945 he became one of the country's leading conductors; as director of the Concerts Lamoureux in Paris (1951–57) he established a reputation as an outstanding interpreter of the works of Ravel, Roussel, and especially Debussy, whose complete orchestral music he recorded. He was director of the Israel Philharmonic Orchestra (1958–59), musical director of the Chicago Symphony Orchestra (1963–69), and from 1969 musical director of the Orchestre National Française. His compositions include *Stalag IX, ou musique d'exil* (1941), reflecting his experiences as a prisoner of war, the opera *Hécube* (1949–54), four symphonies, concertos, including two for violin, and choral and chamber music.

Martorell, Bohigas, and Mackay Spanish architectural partnership. **José Oriol Bohigas (Guardiola)** (1925–) was born and educated in Barcelona, graduating from the School of Architecture in 1951. **Josep Martorell (Codina)** (1925–) graduated in the same year and established an office with Bohigas in 1952. **David Mackay** (1933–) was born in Eastbourne, England, and joined the practice in 1962. The bulk of their work has been in the Barcelona area, with public housing and school building predominating. The severity of their earlier modernist style later developed into a more eclectic approach in the pursuit of 'poetic realism'. The Meridiana housing complex in Barcelona (1959–65) is an irregular wall of housing pierced with apertures. At the Secretario Coloma Housing, Barcelona (1960–65), the flat windows have wooden awnings and screens, producing a somewhat Japanese effect. More recent work has emphasized exposed industrial materials, for example, in the Piher Factory, Barcelona (1968–72) and the Thau School (1972–74), with its long staircase glazed up one side. Oriol Bohigas was appointed master planner for the 1992 Barcelona Olympics, a major feature of which was the regeneration of the waterfront, with the construction of a great esplanade and new apartment towers.

Massine, Léonide Fedorovich (Leonid Miassin; 1895–1979) Russian ballet dancer, choreographer, and ballet master, who was one of the leading figures in 20th century dance. Massine's long career began with the Bolshoi Ballet before World War I. In 1914, when still a teenager, he was invited to join Diaghilev's company in Paris. He enjoyed immediate success dancing in *The Legend of Joseph* and was then coached by Diaghilev to become Nijinsky's successor.

As a choreographer, Massine made his debut in 1915 with *Soleil de nuit* and subsequently created numerous pieces for the Ballets Russes de Monte Carlo, the most notable including *Parade* (1917), *La Boutique fantasque* (1919), and *The Three-Cornered Hat* (1919), (which – like *Parade* – featured innovative sets by Picasso. He left the company in 1928. After staging *Le Sacre du printemps* (1930) in New York, with Martha Graham dancing the main role, he returned to Europe to lead one of the splinter groups into which the Ballets Russes broke up after Diaghilev's death. In this period he choreographed a series of grandiose symphonic ballets that were much admired in their day and led to Massine being hailed as the most significant contemporary European choreographer. These included *Les Présages* (1933), to Tchaikovsky's Fifth Symphony, and *Symphonie fantastique* (1936), to the music of Berlioz.

In 1938 Massine joined the Ballets Russes de Monte Carlo and enjoyed almost immediate success with the comic ballet *Gaîte Parisienne*. After further triumphs he left the company in 1943 and subsequently worked chiefly in Europe with such companies as the Sadler's Wells Ballet and the ROYAL BALLET. His post-war works included *Clock Symphony* (1948), *Harold in Italy* (1951), *Don Juan* (1959), and – for the Ballet Europeo company that he set up in 1960 for the Nervi Festival – *La Commedia umana*. He also taught at the Royal Ballet school and left a permanent record of his work as a choreographer in the films *The Red Shoes* (1946), *Tales of Hoffmann* (1951), and *Carosello Napoletano* (1954).

Matthew, Sir Robert *See* ROBERT MATTHEW JOHNSON MARSHALL AND PARTNERS

Mattsson, Arne (1919–) Swedish film director and screenwriter, noted for his thrillers in the Hitchcock vein. Born in Uppsala, Mattsson entered films in 1942

and trained as an assistant to the director Per Lindberg. He came to international attention in 1951 with the success of *One Summer of Happiness*. His prolific output includes *And All These Women*, *Dangerous Spring* (1948), *Woman in White* (1949), *Enchanted Walk* (1954), *A Little Place of One's Own* (1956), *Mannequin in Red* (1958), *Rider in Blue* (1959), *The Doll* (1962), *The Yellow Car* (1963), *Two Vikings* (1965), *I the Body* (1965), which he coscripted, *Woman of Darkness* (1966), *The Murderer* (1967), *Anne and Eve* (1970), the Swedish-Yugoslavian coproduction *The Truck* (1976), and *Black Sun* (1978), which he scripted.

Maurstad, Toralv (1926–) Norwegian actor and theatre director, who has been manager of the Nationaltheatret since 1978. Born into one of Norway's most distinguished theatrical families, Maurstad studied at Uppsala University and the Royal Academy of Dramatic Art in London, making his stage debut in Trondheim in 1947. Subsequently he won acclaim in a wide range of roles, from Shakespeare to BRECHT, often directing the plays himself. In 1967 he became manager of the Oslo Nye Teater, a venue with which he had enjoyed a long association as an actor. Recent successes have included productions at the Nationaltheatret of Shakespeare's *Much Ado About Nothing* (1981) and *Hamlet* (1983); he has also appeared in several films.

May, Ernst (1886–1970) German architect and town planner. Born in Frankfurt-am-Main, May studied in London and worked with the town planner Ramond Unwin before returning to his birthplace as city architect in 1925. There he designed the Römerstadt Housing Estate, combining low-cost modern structures with Garden City principals. In 1930 he went to the Soviet Union to advise on town planning only to leave, frustrated, in 1934 for East Africa. He stayed there until 1952, spending as much time farming as designing buildings.

Returning to Germany, he produced a number of huge plans for housing in Aachen, Neu Altona, Bremen, Wiesbaden, Hamburg (Die neue Heimat), Stuttgart, and Mainz. Yet May was primarily a creative architect who never lost sight of his early ambition to create a decent environment for healthy living, and he became increasingly concerned that the modern planner had the power to make an environment wholly lacking in human qualties. He himself never surpassed his early work in Frankfurt.

Medawar, Sir Peter Brian (1915–87) British immunologist. The son of a Lebanese businessman, Medawar graduated in zoology from Oxford University in 1939, continuing at Oxford to work under Howard Florey. His first researches concerned factors affecting tissue-culture growth but during World War II he turned his attention to medical biology. He subsequently developed a concentrated solution of the blood-clotting protein fibrinogen, which could be used clinically as a biological glue to fix together damaged nerves and keep nerve grafts in position.

The terrible burns of many war casualties led Medawar to study the reasons why skin grafts from donors are rejected. He realized that each invididual develops his own immunological system and that the length of time a graft lasts depends on how closely related the recipient and donor are. He found that grafting was successful not only between identical twins but also between nonidentical, or fraternal, twins. It had already been shown in cattle that tissues, notably the red-cell precursors, are exchanged between twin fetuses. This led to the suggestion by Macfarlane Burnet that the immunological system is not developed at conception but is gradually acquired. Thus if an embryo is injected with the tissues of a future donor, the animal after birth should be tolerant to any grafts from that donor.

Medawar tested this hypothesis by injecting mouse embryos, verifying that they do not have the ability to form antibodies against foreign tissue but do acquire immunologic tolerance to it. For this discovery Medawar and Burnet were awarded the 1960 Nobel Prize for physiology or medicine.

Medawar was professor of zoology at Birmingham University (1947–51) and at University College, London (1951–62). He then became director of the National Institute for Medical Research, London (1962–71) and head of the Division of Surgical Sciences at the Clinical Research Centre (1971–84). He wrote many influential books including *The Future of Man* (1960 Reith Lectures), *The Art of the Soluble* (1967), and *The Limits to Science*

(1984). He was paralyzed by a brain haemorrhage in 1969, a fact alluded to in the title of his autobiography, *Memoirs of a Thinking Radish* (1986).

Melos Quartet German string quartet, formed in Stuttgart in 1965. Its members are Wilhelm Melcher (first violin), Gerhard Voss (second violin), his brother Hermann Voss (viola), and Peter Buck (cello). Before joining the quartet Melcher, Gerhard Voss, and Buck were members of the Württemberg Chamber Orchestra in Stuttgart (as leader, coleader, and principal cellist respectively), while Hermann Voss was principal violist with the Stuttgart Chamber Orchestra. Melcher had previously been leader of the Hamburg Symphony Orchestra.

Following successes in 1966 at the Geneva International Competition and at the Villa-Lobos String Quartet Competition in Rio de Janeiro, the members gave up their orchestral jobs in favour of full-time quartet-playing. They have toured extensively and acquired an international reputation with their recordings, which include complete cycles of the Beethoven, Schubert, and Mendelssohn quartets.

Melville, Jean-Pierre (Jean-Pierre Grumbach; 1917–73) French film director, noted for his original gangster films, which often transcended their US models in terms of symbolic content. Having fought with the Free French during World War II, Melville (who renamed himself after his favourite author) made shorts with his own production company before embarking upon a career as a director of feature films. His first full-length film was *Le Silence de la mer* (1947), about the love-hate relationship between a German officer and the two French people with whom he is billeted. This was followed by an adaptation of Jean Cocteau's *Les Enfants terribles* (1948), in which he explored for the first time the themes of loyalty and betrayal that dominate his later films.

His first gangster thriller was *Bob the Gambler* (1955), in which the conventions of US gangster films of the 1940s and 1950s were translated to nighttime Paris with enormous success; the effectiveness of his Parisian night scenes influenced several directors of the NEW WAVE. Over the next few years Melville continued to explore a range of subjects. In *Leon Morin, Priest* (1961) he examines the moral issues arising when a priest attempts to convert a young girl who is in love with him. In this film he developed the austere stylized manner that was to characterize all his subsequent work.

Second Breath (1966), a striking poetic FILM NOIR in which Melville once more probed the complex loyalties of the gangster world, consolidated the director's reputation and remains one of his most admired works. Similar themes of friendship and honour among thieves and outlaws resurfaced in *The Samurai* (1967), a moody thriller starring Alain Delon as a contract killer, and *Army in the Shadow* (1969), about the French Resistance.

Melville's last films, *The Red Circle* (1970) and *Dirty Money* (1972), are among the best examples of the distinctive French gangster genre he had created. They were noticeably less optimistic than his earlier films, being somewhat bleak in both style and philosophy. Melville's reinterpretation of the Hollywood gangster tradition has since had a pronounced effect upon such US film makers as Martin Scorsese.

Melvin, James *See* GOLLINS, MELVIN, WARD.

Meneghello, Luigi (1922–) Italian writer. Born in Malo, a village near Vicenza, Meneghello graduated in philosophy from the University of Padua. During World War II he took part in the armed Resistance against the Fascists and the Germans. In 1947 he left Italy for England, where he founded the Italian department at Reading University, teaching there until 1980. He now divides his time between London and Thiene near Vicenza.

Meneghello is one of Italy's most original and interesting contemporary writers. His first narrative, *Deliver Us From Evil* (1963; the Italian title, *Libera Nos a Malo*, contains a pun on the name of his native village), is based on his memories of childhood. Here the clash between literary Italian and the author's local dialect is the source of endless verbal invention and helps him to explore the distance between the past and the present. His vivid and elegant prose combines syntactical precision with lexical richness.

His other books include *The Outlaws* (1967), *Pomo Pero* (1974), *Italian Flowers* (1976), the essay collection *Jura* (1987), *Bau-Sette* (1988; the title is equivalent to the English expression 'peep-bo!'), and

Maradè maradè... (1991), a series of reflections on his local dialect.

Menotti, Gian Carlo (1911–) Italian composer, living in the US. Menotti was born in Cadegliano, Italy, and wrote his first opera, *The Death of Pierrot*, when he was 11 years old. He was educated at the Milan Conservatory from 1924 until 1927, when (at the suggestion of Toscanini) he went to the US to study under Rosario Scalero at the Curtis Institute of Music, Philadelphia. During his time at the Institute, Menotti befriended the US composer Samuel Barber; he later wrote the libretto for Barber's opera *Vanessa* (1958).

Menotti's own operas have combined 20th-century themes and settings with music in the Italian operatic tradition of Puccini and Verdi. The composer writes his own librettos, generally in English. His first successful opera, *Amelia Goes to the Ball* (1937), satirizes behaviour in high society, while *The Consul* (1950) is about a woman's attempts to escape a totalitarian regime. The chamber operas *The Medium* (1945) and *The Telephone* (1946) were performed as a double-bill on Broadway and *The Medium* was later made into a successful film. The 'madrigal fable' *The Unicorn, the Gorgon and the Manticore* (1956) combines orchestral and choral music with dance, while the opera *Tamu-Tamu* (1973), with a text in both English and Indonesian, condemns war. Keen to bring opera to a wider audience, he wrote *Amahl and the Night Visitors* (1951) and *The Labyrinth* (1963) specifically for television and has created many operas for children, including *Martin's Lie* (1964), *Help! Help! the Globolinks!* (1968) and *A Bride from Pluto* (1982).

In 1958 Menotti founded the SPOLETO FESTIVAL OF THE TWO WORLDS, which he directed until 1967, with the aim of bringing together musicians from Europe and the US; in 1977 he established a US counterpart in Charleston, South Carolina. Amongst his other works are operas, symphonic poems, concertos, chamber pieces, cantatas, and ballets. His most recent compositions include the operas *St Teresa* (1982) and *Goya* (1986).

Menzel, Jiří (1938–) Czech film and theatre director and actor, who was a leading figure in the brief 'liberal spring' of the Czech cinema in the late 1960s. A graduate of FAMU, the Prague film school, he made a striking feature debut with *Closely Observed Trains* (1966), which established his often theatrical static camera style and won the 1968 Academy Award for the best foreign film. Menzel also coscripted and acted in the film, a sometimes black comedy about wartime saboteurs. His eye for the ridiculous in socialist society hindered his career after the 1968 Soviet invasion: his *Larks on a String* (1969) was banned and he retreated for a while to the stage. Later films were less controversial; he chose nostalgia in 1979, directing, scripting, and acting in *Those Wonderful Film Cranks* (1979), a charming comedy about the early days of filmmaking in Prague.

Menzel has received a number of honours since the fall of communism in Czechoslovakia: his *End of the Old Times* (1990) took the Grand Prize of the International Film Producers' Meeting in Cannes and he received the 1990 Akira Kurosawa Prize for Lifelong Merit in Cinematography. *Larks on a String* was finally released in 1991 to commercial and critical success, winning the Czech Film Critics' Prize and a Berlin Festival award. He was appointed head of the department of film directing at the Film Academy of Performing Arts, Prague, in 1990.

Mercer, David (1928–80) British playwright, whose work for the cinema, television, and the stage shows a preoccupation with the uneasy relationship between the individual and society. Mercer established his reputation with a series of television plays that were amongst the first to reveal the possibility of the medium for the serious writer. His first full-length work for the stage, *Ride a Cock Horse*, depicting a writer's emotional breakdown after a sequence of sexual disasters, was produced in 1965. Of the theatrical pieces that followed, the most successful included *After Haggerty* (1970), about a Marxist theatre critic, *Flint* (1970), which considered the life of a renegade Irish priest, *Cousin Vladimir* (1978), and *No Limits to Love* (1980). Perhaps his most admired work was, however, his screenplay for Karel REISZ's film *Morgan! – A Suitable Case for Treatment* (1965), in which an artist faces the onset of insanity. Mercer suffered a breakdown himself in the late 1950s and mental instability is a recurring theme in his work. It is treated again in the screenplay for Ken LOACH's film *Family Life* (1971), in which the ideas of R. D. LAING are a major influence. His other screenplays included *Providence* (1977).

Merleau-Ponty, Maurice (1908–61) French philosopher and phenomenologist. After studying philosophy at the Ecole Normale Supérieure, Merleau-Ponty worked as a schoolteacher until World War II. In 1945 he and Jean-Paul SARTRE founded the left-wing journal *Les Temps modernes*. He was an assistant professor at the University of Lyon (1945–49) and a professor at the Sorbonne, where he taught child psychology and pedagogics. In 1952 he was appointed professor at the Collège de France. In the early 1950s he quarrelled publicly with Sartre over the Korean War and the role of the Communist Party.

In his major work, *The Phenomenology of Perception* (1945), Merleau-Ponty analyses the relationship of man, as an embodied consciousness, with the physical world he perceives and attempts to conceptualize. Rejecting both extreme empiricist and idealist positions, he proposes a more complex model of interaction whereby man both receives from his environment and helps to construct it mentally. The most important influences on his work are EXISTENTIALISM and the phenomenology of Edmund Husserl, but the insights of anthropology, psychology, and linguistic theory are also drawn upon. In late work such as *Signs* (1960) he can be seen moving closer to a structuralist position (*see* STRUCTURALISM).

Merz, Mario (1925–) Italian artist, born in Milan and active in Turin. During World War II he was a member of an anti-Fascist group and in 1945 he was imprisoned for his activities. His first one-man exhibition at the Galleria La Bussola, Turin, in 1954, featured work in the spontaneous abstract style known as ART INFORMEL. In the 1960s, however, he turned from painting to experimental art and became associated with the ARTE POVERA movement. He is best known for his installations, which have incorporated found objects, everyday items, and neon lettering. Since 1969 they have often been arranged according to the Fibonacci series – a mathematical sequence in which each number (after the first two) is the sum of the previous two numbers: 0,1,1,2,3,5,8,... In 1979 he returned to painting, favouring exotic subjects, including wild beasts and vegetal forms.

Messiaen, Olivier (1908–92) French composer and teacher. One of the most important composers of the 20th century, Messiaen has remained independent of all schools and groupings. His Roman Catholic faith lies at the heart of all his work and has influenced his attitude toward the language and structure of music. From his earliest works onwards Messiaen rejected the 19th-century symphonic tradition by adopting an essentially static and nondevelopmental style. In general, his music is imbued with a meditative, almost mystical, quality and his works often assume very large proportions. His musical technique derives from many sources including the music of other cultures (Greek and oriental especially), birdsong, scales of his own creation, plainsong, complex harmonies, and even total SERIALISM.

Messiaen studied at the Paris Conservatoire (1919–30) with Marcel Dupré and Paul Dukas, becoming organist of La Saint Trinité in Paris thereafter. His early works are for organ (*La Nativité du Seigneur*; 1935), orchestra (*Les Offrandes oubliées*; 1930), and voice (*Poèmes pour Mi*; 1936). He spent part of World War II in a prisoner-of-war camp where he composed and performed his *Quatuor pour la fin du temps* (1941). On his release he returned to Paris and began his teaching career, which brought him into close contact with such major figures of the post-war period as BARRAQUÉ, BOULEZ, and STOCKHAUSEN. He was greatly influenced by his pupils' ideas and formulated his own serial technique in the piano piece *Mode de valeurs et d'intensités* (1950), which became a seminal text for the composers of the DARMSTADT school. His epic *Turangalîa Symphony* (1948), for orchestra, solo piano, and ondes martenot, dates from this period.

The music of the 1950s makes use of birdsong to enliven rhythm, melody, and timbre (*Oiseaux exotiques*; 1956). He also began using large-scale structuring principles, such as medieval isorhythm. After a series of abstract impressionistic works in the early 1960s (*Chronochromie*, 1960; *Couleurs de la cité céleste*, 1963) he returned to the symmetrical and liturgical forms of his earlier works. The resulting style juxtaposes ideas rather than attempting a synthesis and the diversity of material requires very large structures. The later works include the oratorio *La Transfiguration de Notre Seigneur Jésus Christ* (1969), *Des Canyons aux étoiles* (1974) for orchestra, his only opera *St François d'Assise* (1983), and the organ work *Le Livre du Saint Sacrement* (1984).

Mészöly, Miklós (1926–) Hungarian novelist. After completing his studies in law and political science at the University of Budapest, Mészöly was drafted into the Hungarian army and fought in World War II; he was captured on more than one occasion and spent time as a prisoner of war. He published his first collection of short stories in 1948 but this did not meet with the approval of the Stalinist regime. His second volume of stories did not appear until after the 1956 revolution. It was with his first novel, *The Death of an Athlete* (1966), however, that Mészöly established his reputation as an outstanding innovator in Hungarian prose fiction. In this novel the widow of an athlete is asked to write a biography of her deceased husband. Her thoughts on, and investigations into, her husband's life are presented without any identifiable hierarchy and both life (as narrative) and character remain open-ended concepts. The narrative techniques of *The Death of an Athlete* and of the two novels that followed it – *Saulus* (1968) and *Film* (1976) – have been compared to those of the NOUVEAU ROMAN.

In recent years Mészöly's focus has returned to the short story. The location of his stories is most frequently the small central European town, surviving precariously on the borderlines of history, with the narrator functioning as a kind of archivist faced with the impossible task of piecing together the disconnected fragments of an ambiguous past. Mészöly's most powerful story in this vein is *Forgiveness* (1983). Mészöly's work has exerted a major influence over the younger generation of Hungarian prose writers who began their careers in the mid 1970s.

Metzger, Gustav (1926–) German experimental artist, who settled in Britain in 1939 as a refugee from Nazism. He studied at various art colleges, including a period (1950–53) at Borough Polytechnic, London, where he was taught by David Bomberg; until 1957 he was a painter. However, as he told Bomberg, he was searching for something 'extremely fast and intense' and in 1960 he began 'painting' with acid on nylon, thus becoming a pioneer of autodestructive art, for which he has remained the chief spokesman. He has written and lectured a good deal on the subject, as well as 'painting' with acid in front of audiences; in 1966 he was secretary of the Destruction in Art Symposium (DIAS) sponsored by the Institute of Contemporary Arts in London. His work has been seen as a protest against consumerism and the destructive nature of technology. Those influenced by his ideas are said to include Pete Townshend of the pop group The Who, whose stage act used to include the smashing of musical instruments.

Michaux, Henri (1899–1984) French writer and painter, born in Belgium. A solitary introspective child, Michaux developed an early interest in poetry and mysticism. After abandoning his medical studies he joined (1920) the French merchant marine and travelled to South America and the Far East. He settled in Paris in 1924 but continued to travel widely. Michaux began to write in the 1920s and to paint seriously in the years before World War II. In the 1930s he edited the mystical journal *Hermès*.

Michaux's poetry is highly original and almost impossible to categorize; it has some affinity with the work of both the symbolists and the surrealists. His main preoccupation was the conflict between the inner world of dreams, hallucinations, and spiritual experience and the outer world of everyday 'reality'. His eccentric humour came to the fore in *A Certain Plume* (1930) and *Elsewhere* (1948), a trilogy of pieces about imaginary countries. In the mid 1950s he began to experiment with hallucinogenic drugs, reporting his experiences in *Exploration through Drugs* (1961) and other works. He also published several volumes of travel writing (*Ecuador*, 1929; *A Barbarian in Asia*, 1932) and the autobiography *The Major Ordeals of the Mind and Countless Minor Ones* (1966).

Michaux was equally original as a painter. His early abstract paintings, mainly executed in gouache, evoke a world of myth and dream and make him an important precursor of ART INFORMEL. In the early 1950s he produced turbulent drawings in Indian ink and later in the decade he drew and painted while under the influence of mescalin. His work has been widely exhibited.

Michelucci, Giovanni (1891–1991) Italian architect and planner. Michelluci was born in Pistoia, near Florence, and most of his work is in this area. His astounding success came in 1933, when he won a competition for St Maria Novella Station in Florence with the only modern design in a field of 98. Remarkably, Mussolini allowed it to be built; it has since been hailed as Italy's masterpiece of 1930s rationalism.

Michelucci's first post-war work was in Pistoia, where he converted the stock exchange into a bank (1949–50) and built a new central market (1950). Further bank commissions followed in Florence, earning him a reputation for sensitive modern designs in historic cities. He also built several churches, including the Collina di Pentolungo, Pistoia (1946–54). But his great churches date from the 1960s, when he rediscovered expressionism as a vehicle for his humanist philosophy. First came the 'Church of the Autostrada', St John the Baptist at Campi Bisenzio, Florence (1960–64), featuring "a breathtaking curved sail ceiling and tall branching pillars with light filtering down as through the trees of a forest". So wrote LE CORBUSIER. It was followed by Borgo Maggiore Church in San Marino (1961–67), where the same love of tree formations is apparent, and the church at Longarone (1966–76), which has an amphitheatre on its roof reached by a winding ramp.

Michelucci's endeavour to create a humane architecture is nowhere better expressed than in his last work, a garden for prisoners and their visitors. He was also a popular teacher, firstly at the University of Florence and then, from 1948, as director of the Insitute of Technical Architecture, Bologna.

Mickery-theater A Dutch theatre institution that promotes visits to the Netherlands by leading foreign companies. Founded in 1965, the organization has attracted numerous important troupes to Amsterdam, where the Mickery-theater has been based since 1970. The organization has provided an invaluable stimulus for Dutch drama, notably in furthering the development of multimedia theatre and innovative seating arrangements. More recent work includes *Fairground '84*, produced for the HOLLAND FESTIVAL.

Millares, Manuel (1926–72) Spanish painter. Born in Las Palmas, Millares was self-taught as a painter. His first exhibition (1945) revealed a talented figurative artist but he soon moved in the direction of surrealism, being particularly influenced by Joan MIRÓ. The 1950s saw a shift towards a more abstract style of ART INFORMEL; he helped to organize the Valencia Salón de Arte Abstracto in 1956. The following year Millares became a founding member of the El Paso group of abstract artists (with Antonio SAURA).

In the late 1950s Millares began to incorporate elements of collage into his work. From 1959 onwards he produced a series of highly dramatic works, often on ripped canvases, dominated by the colours red, white, and black. The series *Antropfaunas* (from 1969) incorporated painted rags and other textiles with wild scribbles and theatrical daubs of paint. Millares's work has been widely exhibited in Europe and has also been shown in North and South America.

Mills, Edward David (1915–) Prolific British architect who began practising in 1937 after working with Walter Gropius and Maxwell Fry (*see* FRY AND DREW). His work may be divided into two main categories: a large number of inexpensive churches, mostly for the Methodist movement, and an equal number of large factories and warehouses. His factory at Dagenham for May and Baker (1943–58) included Britain's first shell-concrete construction. He also designed public housing, most notably for Hackney, London, and the administrative buildings for the FESTIVAL OF BRITAIN.

The National Exhibition Centre (1972–76, with Frank Turner) is Mills's most public building. It is neatly detailed, but has no pretensions to be more than a warehouse for exhibitions; the combination of neat finishes, practicality, and dullness seems common in Britain's larger public buildings since 1970.

Miloslavskii, Turii Georgievich (1946–) Russian writer living in Israel. Having left the Soviet Union in 1973, Miloslavskii published two cycles of stories, *Urban Romances* (1979) and *Love* (1980), but made the greatest impact with his powerful novel

Fortified Cities (1980). Here he portrayed Soviet dissidents, and in particular Jewish emigrants, as a motley and unsavoury crowd with none of the saintly aura bestowed on them by the Western media. Corrupt, criminal, and pathetic types abound, depicted in a dispassionate semi-expressionist manner that arouses in the reader less sympathy than voyeuristic curiosity. The author is as forthright about physical intimacy as about violence and cruelty; indeed, he seems to revel in sex scenes of all kinds. *From the Noise of Horsemen and Archers* (1984), a collection of short stories published in the US, also concentrates on the delinquent dregs of society struggling to survive in a world devoid of decency or justice. For all the controversy surrounding his works, Miloslavskii is one of the most popular Russian writers in Israel.

Miłosz, Czeslaw (1911–) Polish poet, living in the US. Born in Szetejnie, Lithuania, Miłsoz was brought up as a Roman Catholic and studied law at the University of Vilnius. His early collection *Poem of Frozen Time* (1933) castigated social conditions in Lithuania in a manner that he later dismissed as journalistic. In the 1930s he was a leading representative of 'catastrophism', a literary movement that prophecied doom for mankind. In Warsaw when the Nazis invaded in 1939, he went underground, working with the Resistance and editing an anthology of anti-Nazi verse. *Rescue* (1945) was a mature collection that evoked Poland's wartime ordeal and his own guilt at surviving but also expressed alarm at the new emerging order. Though not a Communist Party member, Miłosz served as second secretary to the embassy in Washington and cultural attaché in Paris. He sought exile in 1951 rather than write in conformity with communist propaganda. Despite his own commitment to pure creativity, his famous book of essays *The Captive Mind* (1953) shows an understanding of the seductive appeal that the Marxist view of 'historical necessity' has exercised over writers. Major poetry collections of the 1950s were *Daylight* (*Światło dzienne*; 1953) and *The Poetic Treatise* (1957), which contains reflections on Polish history since 1918 and a defence of poetry. A gifted linguist and prolific translator, Miłosz moved to the US in 1960 and became a professor of Slavic languages and literatures at the University of California. The metaphysical views expressed in Miłosz's poetry have been variously characterized as Catholic, Pantheist, Gnostic, and Manichaean; influences include the thought of T. S. Eliot, Blake, and Simone Weil. His later works include the autobiography *Native Realm* (1968), a history of Polish literature (1969), and the poetry collection *Bells in Winter* (1978). In 1980 Miłosz was awarded the Nobel Prize for literature.

Milstein, César (1927–) British molecular biologist, born in Argentina. Milstein graduated in chemistry from the University of Buenos Aires in 1952, obtaining a doctorate in biochemistry in 1957. He moved to Britain in 1958 to work at the University of Cambridge. He returned to Argentina to head the molecular-biology division of the National Microbiological Institute but later (1963) moved back to Britain to the Medical Research Council's laboratory of molecular biology at Cambridge, where he is head of the division of protein and nucleic acid chemistry.

Milstein has conducted research into the structure, evolution, and genetics of immunoglobulins and phosphoenzymes. He is best known for his work on monoclonal antibodies. In 1975 he and his colleagues managed to multiply mouse antibody-secreting cells (lymphocytes from the spleen) by fusing them with mouse myeloma cells and cloning the resultant hybrid myeloma. This work has many potential applications, for example in passive immunization and in tumour therapy. It proved difficult to extend the technique to human cells but success was eventually achieved by a team of scientists from the universities of Glasgow and Strathclyde.

minimal art or **minimalist art** A type of art characterized by extreme simplicity of form, minimal differentiation, and a deliberate lack of expressive content. It developed during the 1950s and 1960s, chiefly in the US, as a reaction to the subjectivity and emotionalism of abstract expressionism. However, the roots of the style go back much earlier, to the first experiments with geometrical abstraction early this century. The first minimal painting was arguably Kasimir Malevich's *Black Square on a White Ground* (1915). The style also has antecedents in Dada and the 'readymades' of Marcel Duchamp.

The concept of minimal art was taken to its limit in the all-white and later all-black canvases of Robert Rauschenberg and the monochromes of Yves KLEIN. Minimalist sculptures consist mainly of simple geometric forms in plastic, metal, or fibreglass; many are produced industrially with little or no intervention by the artist. Practitioners include the Americans Carl André and Robert Morris. Minimal painting places an emphasis on hard edges, precise geometrical forms, pure colours, and immaculate surfaces. There are elements of minimalism in POP ART, KINETIC ART, and much CONCEPTUAL ART.

minimal music or **minimalist music** Music created from deliberately simple and restricted musical material. Typically, such music uses consonant harmonies, a limited variety of pitches, and relatively straightforward rhythms, which are used to build repetitive and slowly evolving works; it provides a deliberate contrast to the complexity of, for example, SERIALISM. Minimal music developed in the 1960s and 1970s. Well-known works of this era include *In C* (1964) by Terry Riley, *Drumming* (1971) by Steve Reich, and *Einstein on the Beach* (1976) by Philip Glass. More recently the so-called 'religious minimalism' of such composers as GÓRECKI, PÄRT, and TAVENER has enjoyed a considerable vogue. Minimal music has proved readily accessible to audiences nurtured on pop and rock music.

Minotis, Alexis (1906–90) Greek actor and theatre director, who won acclaim through his long association with the Greek National Theatre. Minotis made his first stage appearance in 1925 and joined the National Theatre in 1930, where he soon graduated to leading roles and established himself as a major director of plays by both classical and contemporary playwrights. He married the actress Katina Paxinou in 1940 and was seen overseas on tour with the National Theatre company on many occasions. From 1939 to 1967 he served as artistic director of the company, subsequently becoming its general director (1974–81). His work included a highly successful production of Cherubini's opera *Medea* and regular visits to the drama festivals at Epidaurus and Athens. He formed his own company, with Paxinou, in 1967. His later work included plays by O'Neil, O'Casey, Strindberg, BRECHT, and Shakespeare. In 1976 he toured the Soviet Union, playing Sophocles' Oedipus, while in 1980 he toured Japan and China. In 1986 he established a new experimental theatre; he continued to act and produce until his death.

Miró, Joan (1893–1983) Spanish (Catalan) painter and sculptor. Born into an artisan family in Barcelona, Miró studied at the Francisco Galí School of Art and the Barcelona École des Beaux-Arts. His early pictures – mainly landscapes, portraits, and nudes – show the influence of Catalan folk art in their expressive gestures and dark heavy colours.

Miró visited Paris in 1919, where he met and was influenced by Picasso. He settled in Paris in 1920 and joined the Dadaists, later switching his loyalty to the surrealists; another important influence at this time was the work of Paul Klee. Miró's personal style, characterized by fantastic semifigurative forms (usually either spiky or amoeba-like) set against largely plain backgrounds, began to emerge in 1923–24. A visit to Holland and a study of the Dutch 17th-century painters led him to add substance to his figures in the late 1920s, but his work continued to become more abstract. A new vein of terror and savagery appears in the 'wild' pictures he produced in response to the Spanish Civil War.

By contrast, when Miró returned to Spain in 1940 he created a series of dream-like gouaches on paper, called *Constellations*, in which man and the cosmos appear to be united in harmony. In the 1940s he began to produce ceramics and terracotta work with the potter Llorens Artigas. He concentrated on this medium for most of the 1950s, producing two large ceramic wall designs for the Unesco Building in Paris (1950–58). He won the Grand Prix for graphic art at the 1954 Venice Biennale.

Miró's work features magical images of occasionally frightening ambiguity. With Picasso and Juan Gris (1887–1927) he is one of the three most influential Spanish painters of the 20th century. The largest ever exhibition of his work was held in Barcelona in 1993 to mark the centenary of his birth.

Mnouchkine, Ariane (1938–) French theatre director and playwright, whose long association with the **Théâtre du Soleil** has established the company as one of the most respected in Europe. A founder of the Théâtre du Soleil in 1964 and subsequently its manager, Mnouchkine fostered the company's enthusiasm for COLLECTIVE CREATION. Despite early successes with the plays of Gorkii and WESKER, among others, the troupe is best known for its own collaborative efforts, notably *1789* (1970), an epic treatment of the French Revolution using five stages and multiple casting, its sequel *1793* (1972), and *The Golden Age* (1975), all of which employed a wide range of theatrical techniques, including puppetry and tumbling skills. More recently the company has staged Mnouchkine's adaptation of Klaus Mann's novel *Méphisto* (1979), several Shakespeare plays using traditional Japanese theatre devices, and work by the feminist writer Hélène Cixous – notably *Norodom Sihanouk* (1985), on the subject of modern Cambodia. Mnouchkine has also directed a successful film about Molière, in which she explored the mechanics of a theatre company at work. Since 1972 her company has occupied somewhat dilapidated premises in a former munitions factory in Vincennes; it is still run on a strictly egalitarian basis. In 1992 she presented *Les Atrides*, a cycle of Greek tragedies comprising Euripides's *Iphigenia in Aulis* and the three parts of Aeschylus's *Oresteia*. Her typically imaginative staging drew freely on non-Western theatrical traditions.

Moltmann, Jürgen (1926–) German Protestant theologian. Moltmann served in World War II and remained a prisoner of war until 1948. He was a professor of philosophy in Wuppertal from 1958 to 1963, when he took up a similar appointment in Bonn; since 1967 he has been professor for systematic theology in Tübingen.

Moltmann is one of the most prominent liberal theologians in Germany today; his work addresses itself directly to the religious, social, and political life of the present. In 1964 he published *Theology of Hope; Justification and Consequences of Christian Eschatology*, in which he argued, from eschatological premises, that the Church should play an active role in social affairs and that it must be ready to sacrifice obsolete religious forms where these are an obstacle to growth. In *The Crucified God* (1972), his best-known book, Moltmann grappled with the idea that God Himself experienced suffering and death at the Crucifixion. In this light, the passion and death of Christ is interpreted as a sign of hope for all history's victims. In *God in Creation* (1985) he developed a doctrine of creation that is fully in accord with modern ecological concerns.

Mompou, Federico (1893–1987) Spanish (Catalan) composer. Born in Barcelona, where he began to study the piano, he subsequently (1911) travelled to Paris for further study on the recommendations of Granados. He returned to Barcelona at the outbreak of war in 1914, went back to Paris in 1921, and stayed there until 1941, when he once more settled in Barcelona.

He initially expected to be a concert pianist but his exceptional shyness ruled that out and he concentrated instead on composition. His arrival in Paris in 1911 brought him into contact with the new French music of Debussy, Ravel, and Satie. All strongly influenced Mompou, Satie in particular affecting his choice of genres, titles, and, more fundamentally, his idea of 'primitivism' (*'recomençament'*). This attitude appears most obviously in Mompou's refusal to develop material, relying instead on ostinato and repetition to sometimes hypnotic effect: it also lies behind his use of such simplified notational practices as repeating accidentals before any notes requiring them.

Most of his music consists of salon-type piano pieces reminiscent of Satie, though the influence of Catalan folk music can also be heard in, for example, the collection *Música callada* (1959–67). There are also a few larger-scale works such as the *Improperios* (1963) and *Cantar del alma* (1966) and some songs.

Moneo (Vales), José Rafael (1937–) Spanish architect, writer, and teacher. Born in Tudela, Navarre, Moneo trained in Madrid (1956–61) under Saenz de Oiza and then worked (1961–62) for Jørn UTZON on the Sydney Opera House. This was followed by a period in Italy (1963–65) that introduced him to the work of Aldo ROSSI, an influence that proved decisive on his career. Moneo's built work exhibits a highly disciplined classicism carefully adapted to give an understated presence to historical sites. Examples include the Bankinter offices in Madrid (1975), Longroño Town Hall (1976–81), and a huge office building for La Previsión Española in Seville (1982–87).

Moneo's reputation as one of Spain's most important architects rests equally on his theoretical writings, many of which first appeared in the journal *Architecturas-Bis*, which he cofounded in 1974. He has also taught extensively, in Barcelona, Madrid, and New York; in 1985 he became chairman of the department of architecture at Harvard.

Monicelli, Mario (1915–) Italian film director and screenwriter, noted for his comedy films. Born in Rome, he attended the University of Pisa and studied literature and philosophy at the University of Milan. He wrote film criticism and worked as an assistant director and screenwriter before starting to direct features in the late 1940s. In the early 1950s Monicelli made his mark with a series of light comedies starring the popular performer Totò, such as *Totò e le Donne* (1953) and *Totò e Carolina* (1956). He won international praise for *Persons Unknown* (1958), a satirical comedy about a gang of incompetent robbers. A year later he won an award at the Venice Film Festival for his skilful satire on World War I, *The Great War* (1959). Other films have included the crime capers *Cops and Robbers* (1951) and *The Passionate Thief* (1960), *The Organizer* (1963) about Italian trade unions, *Casanova '70* (1965), *Girl With A Gun* (1968), *Travels With Anita* (1979), and *Il Marchese del Grillo* (1980).

Monod, Jacques Lucien (1910–76) French biochemist. Monod graduated from the University of Paris in 1931 and became assistant professor of zoology there in 1934. After World War II, during which he served in the Resistance, he joined the Pasteur Institute, becoming head of the cellular biochemistry department in 1953.

In 1958 Monod began working with François Jacob and Arthur Pardee on the regulation of enzyme synthesis in mutant bacteria. This work led to the formulation, by Monod and Jacob, of a theory explaining gene action and particularly how genes are switched on and off as necessary. In 1960 they introduced the term 'operon' for a closely linked group of genes, each of which controls a different step in a given biochemical pathway. The following year they postulated the existence of a molecule, messenger RNA, that carries the genetic information necessary for protein synthesis from the operon to the ribosomes, where proteins are made. For this work Monod and Jacob were awarded the 1965 Nobel Prize for physiology or medicine, which they shared with André Lwoff, who was also working on bacterial genetics.

In 1971 Monod became director of the Pasteur Institute and in the same year published the best-selling book *Chance and Necessity*, in which he argued that life arose by chance and progressed to its present level as a necessary consequence of the pressures exerted by natural selection.

Montale, Eugenio (1896–1981) Italian poet. Born in Genoa, Montale served in World War I and worked as a librarian until 1938, when he was dismissed for his anti-Fascism. After World War II he worked as a journalist and translator. Widely recognized as the major Italian poet of the 20th century, he was awarded the Nobel Prize for literature in 1975.

Montale's first collection of poems, *Cuttlefish Bones* (1925), marked a decisive break with the rhetorical tradition of 19th-century Italian poetry. His style blends sophisticated literary language with the prosaic; the tone is often harshly pessimistic. Montale's next volume, *The Occasions* (1939), was widely attacked on its first appearance for its forbiddingly hermetic style. A more relaxed diction emerges in *The Storm and Other Things* (1956), a mainly tragic collection dealing with themes of war, genocide, and personal suffering. *Satura* (1971) is mainly notable for the poem sequence 'Xenia', a series of poignant lyrics written after the death of his wife. *Diary of 1971 and 1972* (1973) is more sardonic and discursive than his earlier work. His last collections were *It Depends; a Poet's Notebook* (1980) and *Other Poems* (1981).

Montale also published several volumes of essays, including *Auto-da-fé* (1966) and *On Poetry* (1976), and *The Butterfly of Dinard* (1969), a collection of autobiographical prose sketches.

Monteiro, Luís de Stau (1926–) Portuguese playwright and novelist, who enjoyed great success in the theatre during the 1960s. Well known as a left-wing journalist, he made his theatrical debut in

1961 with *Luckily We Still Have the Moonlight*, a historical play about the end of British rule in Portugal after the Peninsular War that draws clear parallels with contemporary affairs. He followed up this notable success with *The Statue* (1966), in which he lampooned the personality cult surrounding the dictator Salazar without actually naming him. His other plays have included a reworking of Vicente's *Auto da barca do inferno*, which became in his hands a critique of capitalist values.

Montepulciano Festival (Cantiere Internazionale D'Arte a Montepulciano) An annual music festival held in Montepulciano, Italy, and lasting for a fortnight in July. It was established in 1975 by the German composer Hans Werner HENZE. The programme features mainly new compositions, performed largely by young artists. The emphasis is on local involvement and accessibility, rather than on the involvement of famous figures. Workshops, masterclasses, and community projects are featured as well as concerts and recitals. In 1992 Henze walked out of the festival in protest at cuts in public funding; although some private sponsorship has been obtained, the future of the event looks uncertain.

Monteverdi Choir A British chamber choir founded in 1964 by its conductor John Eliot GARDINER. Associated in the first instance with Renaissance and baroque works, the choir, made up of selected amateur and professional singers, quickly gained a reputation for vivid, rhythmic, and idiomatic singing in works by such composers as Monteverdi, Purcell, Schütz, Rameau, and Bach. This remains true of their performances of later works, as is indicated by their recent prizewinning recordings of Beethoven's *Missa Solemnis* and Mozart's *Idomeneo* (both 1991), and by their acclaimed world premiere of Alexander GOEHR's *The Death of Moses* at Expo '92 in Seville. The choir has completed a number of successful European tours. Its many recordings include projects jointly undertaken with the English Baroque Soloists and the Orchestre Revolutionnaire et Romantique, also conducted by Gardiner.

Montreux Festival An annual festival of international television held at Montreux in Switzerland. The **Golden Rose of Montreux**, the most senior award given at the festival, is Europe's most prestigious prize for a television programme; silver and bronze Roses are also awarded.

Montreux-Vevey Music Festival (Festival de Musique de Montreux-Vevey) An international music festival, held in Montreux-Vevey, on the shores of Lake Geneva, Switzerland. Founded in 1945, the festival comprises a month of concerts and recitals held each year during September. Many leading international orchestras and performers are featured, and new compositions as well as traditional works make up the programme.

Montsalvage, Xavier (1912–   ) Spanish (Catalan) composer, teacher, music critic, and editor. A student of the Barcelona Conservatory (1923–36), Montsalvage has taught there since 1970, having previously worked at other musical institutions in Barcelona. After graduating he developed an interest in ballet: this led during the 1940s to work with the Goubé-Alexander ballet company, for whom he wrote over 20 scores including *La Venus d'Elna* (1946).

Like his contemporaries GERHARD and MOMPOU, Montsalvage has shown a continuing allegiance to his Catalan heritage; in his case this is tempered, at least in his early works, by an attraction to neoclassicism. An abiding interest in rhythmic procedures ensured that Stravinsky would be a long-term influence. His magic opera *El gato con botas* (1948) was very successful; later operas include *Una voce in off* (1962) and *Babel-1948* (1968). In several works Montsalvage consciously acknowledges the Spanish component in Afro-Caribbean musical styles; typical is *Cinco canciones negras* for voice and piano (1945; orchestrated 1949). His works for orchestra include concertos ranging from the *Peoma concertante* for violin and orchestra (1951) and the *Concierto breve* for piano and orchestra (1953) to the *Concierto per un virtuoso* for harpsichord and orchestra of 1977. Notable among his chamber music is the string quartet *Cuarteto indiano* (1952). His considerable output also includes film scores and incidental music.

Moore, Henry (1898–1986) British sculptor and graphic artist. Born in Yorkshire, Moore studied at Leeds School of Art and then at the Royal College of Art (1921–23). Early influences on his work included the French sculptor Gaudier-Brzeska, the frescos of Masaccio, and the primitive (especially pre-Columbian) art he studied at the British Museum. A one-man show in 1928 led to his first public commission – a relief carving of the *North Wind* for London Transport's new headquarters. During the 1930s Moore absorbed such contemporary influences as Picasso, surrealism, and abstraction while continuing to develop a personal style based on biomorphic forms and the scooping and piercing of large masses. He left London for Hertfordshire during the Blitz but returned to the city as an official war artist to produce some evocative sketches of citizens sheltering in underground stations.

Such major commissions of the 1940s as the *Madonna and Child* in St Matthew's church, Northampton (1943), and *Three Draped Standing Figures*, Battersea Park, London show a renewed emphasis on the human form. During this period his international reputation blossomed and he was awarded the 1948 sculpture prize at the Venice Biennale. Moore's post-war work is characterized by a concentration on the reclining figure, always a favourite theme, and an increasing monumentality of scale. He also abandoned the direct carving of wood or stone in favour of casting in bronze. Examples include a huge reclining figure for the Unesco headquarters in Paris (1958) and a two-piece reclining figure for the Lincoln Art Center in New York (1963–65). Although some critics bemoaned Moore's failure to develop in a more avant-garde direction after the war, his standing as Britain's best-known and most popular contemporary artist remained unchallenged until his death. He was awarded the OM in 1963. The principal collections of his work are at his Much Hadham, Hertfordshire, home and the Henry Moore Sculpture Center in Toronto.

Morandi, Giorgio (1890–1964) Italian painter and etcher. Morandi lived all his life in his native Bologna, generally staying aloof from modernist developments and concentrating with single-minded devotion on his chosen theme of still life, in which he was one of the 20th century's greatest masters. He studied at the Bologna Academy (1907–13), taught drawing at the city's elementary schools (1914–30), and was professor of engraving and etching at the Bologna Academy (1930–56). After World War II he acquired an international reputation, his awards include the City of Venice prize for an Italian painter at the 1948 Venice Biennale and the Grand Prix at the 1957 São Paulo Bienal.

Morandi revered Giotto, Piero della Francesca, and Uccello among the Italian old masters (all three renowned for the grandeur and nobility of their compositions) and Cézanne was his ideal among modern artists. His paintings usually feature simple arrangements of bottles and pots, devoid of any literary or symbolic associations and depicted with great sensitivity and beauty.

Morandi, Riccardo (1902–89) Italian engineer and pioneer of prestressed concrete, who explored its structural and expressive qualities when scaled to gigantic proportions. Having completed his training in Rome in 1927, he first challenged conventional engineering solutions in his work in the earthquake region of Calabria and in the building of cinemas. In 1936 he worked with the French architect Eugène Freyssinet (1879–1962) and began to explore the possibilities of prestressed concrete, patenting Italy's first system in 1948.

Thus evolved his preoccupation with massive motorway bridge construction, beginning in 1950–51 with that over the Elsa in Siena, followed by those at Arenzano (1952) and at Storms River, South Africa (1953). Morandi's bridges are no less visually romantic and delicately wrought for being so challenging in scale – indeed, they are frequently more so. His most powerful designs include the viaduct over the Polcevera at Genoa (1958–67) and the bridge over the Maracaibo Lagoon in Venezuela (1957–62). These pioneered a new form of suspension bridge, the *strallato* with oblique connecting rods to guide loads onto a reduced number of piers. Morandi's sometimes symbolic use of form found particular expression in his non-bridge projects, such as the Boeing 747 hangar at Fiumicino Airport, Rome (1962), with its great sail roof, the basilica of the Garligliano Nuclear Establishment (1971), and the vast gentle curve of his Central Railway Station, Baghdad (1980).

Morante, Elsa (1918–85) Italian novelist, poet, and writer. Born in Rome, Morante began her literary career as an essayist (*The Secret Game*; 1941) and a writer of children's stories (*The Marvellous Adven-*

tures of Kathy Pigtail; 1941). In 1948 she produced her first novel, *House of Liars*, which depicts the attempts of the orphaned heroine, Elisa, to reconstruct the story of her family's dramatic decline by sifting fact from fiction, truth from legend.

Morante's preoccupation with the relationship between fantasy and reality and her highly poetic and allusive style make her an early exponent of MAGIC REALISM. These characteristics are seen most clearly in *Arturo's Island* (1957), the story of an adolescent's gradual awakening from the fantasy world of his childhood into the disenchantment of adulthood. Similar themes are explored 25 years later in Morante's novel *Aracoeli* (1982).

The poems in *The World Saved by Little Children* (1968) present a bitter vision of a world organized for the oppression of the weak; only a few free spirits escape this fate, the *'ragazzetti celesti'* capable of love and salvation. This vision also informs her best-known work, *History* (1974), a novel that depicts the turmoil and suffering of Italy and Europe in the 1940s through the fortunes of one eccentric family. The book aroused intense political debate on its publication and went on to become the best-selling Italian novel of the century. Morante was married to the novelist Alberto MORAVIA.

Moravia, Alberto (Alberto Pincherle; 1907–90). Italian novelist, playwright, journalist, and literary and film critic. The son of a Jewish architect, Moravia became famous overnight with the publication of his first novel, *The Time of Indifference* (1929), written during a prolonged bout of tuberculosis of the bone. The book shows signs of the voracious reading of major European writers undertaken by Moravia during nine years in which private study had replaced formal education. It was immediately banned by the Fascist censorship, its cynical analysis of the contemporary Italian bourgeoisie being perceived as subversive and damaging to the regime. In the 1930s his anti-Fascist activity and Italy's racial laws forced him to travel extensively both in and outside Europe. After World War II he became a regular contributor to major literary journals and newspapers. He was married three times, to the writers Elsa MORANTE, Dacia Maraini, and Carmen Llera.

In his fiction Moravia explored a number of preoccupations with great thoroughness and consistency: the superficiality of middle-class existence, the pivotal role of sex and money in human and social relations, and man's isolation and alienation. Fundamentally a realist writer, Moravia was a master of plot and concise description; his spare narrative style emphasized dialogue and action rather than analysis of the inner life. His most significant novels include *The Wheel of Fortune* (1935), *Agostino* (1948), *Luca* (1948), *Conjugal Love* (1949), *The Conformist* (1951), *A Ghost at Noon* (1955), *The Empty Canvas* (1960), and *The Man Who Observes* (1985). Collections of short stories include *Roman Tales* (1954), *Life is a Game* (1969), *Paradise* (1970), *Boh* (1976), and *Friday's Villa* (1990). He also published several volumes of essays, criticism, and travel writings. His work has been translated into some 40 languages.

Morselli, Guido (1912–73) Italian novelist. Morselli spent most of his adult life as a solitary recluse in the same villa in northern Italy. During his lifetime his novels were rejected by many publishers; only after his suicide was his entire work published by Adelphi.

Morselli's novels are generally set in a fantastically imagined future or past, and place a strong emphasis on the paradoxes of history, politics, and human behaviour. *Rome without the Pope* (1966) depicts a Rome of the near future that has lost its role of *Caput Mundi* and become a low-ranking small capital owing to Pope John XXIV's decision to move the Holy See. In *Counter-Perfect* (1975) the author suggests a different ending for World War I. *Entertainment 1899* (1975) is an account of an amorous adventure of King Umberto I that nostalgically evokes the close of the 19th century. *The Communist* (1976) describes the political disillusionment of a communist MP, while his last novel *Dissipatio H. G.* (1977) depicts the suicide attempt of a man who discovers that the human race has abandoned the world, leaving him as the only survivor.

Mössbauer, Rudolph Ludwig (1929–) German physicist. Mössbauer studied physics at the Munich Technical University. He did postgraduate research at the Max-Planck Institute for Medical Research in Heidelberg (1955–57) gaining his doctorate from the Technical University in 1958. He was professor of physics at the California Institute of Technology (1962–64) and has been professor at the Munich Technical University since 1964.

From 1953 he had been studying the absorption of gamma rays in matter, in particular the phenomenon of nuclear resonance absorption. Normally, when an atomic nucleus emits a gamma ray, it will recoil, and this recoil action will influence the wavelength of the gamma ray emitted. Mössbauer discovered that at a sufficiently low temperature the nucleus can be locked into position in the crystal lattice, and it is the lattice itself that recoils, with negligible effect on the wavelength. The result is that the wavelength can be defined with extremely high precision. As with emission, so it is with absorption; a crystal of the same material under similar conditions absorbs gamma rays at the same highly specific wavelength. If, however, the conditions are slightly different, the small changes in wavelength can be accurately compensated and thus measured using the Doppler effect (by moving the source relative to the receiver).

This phenomenon of recoilless nuclear resonance absorption, now known as the Mössbauer effect, has been used to verify (1960) the prediction of Einstein's general theory of relativity that the frequency of an electromagnetic radiation (in this case gamma rays) is influenced by gravity. The Mössbauer effect is now commonly employed as a spectroscopic method in chemical and solid-state physics (Mössbauer spectroscopy).

In 1961 Mössbauer shared the Nobel Prize for physics with Robert Hofstadter, who had advanced knowledge of the nucleus by electron-scattering methods.

Mott, Sir Nevill Francis (1905–) British physicist. Mott studied at Cambridge University where he subsequently lectured before moving to Bristol University as a professor of theoretical physics (1938–48). He returned to Cambridge as Cavendish Professor of Experimental Physics (1954–71).

Mott's work in the early 1930s was on the quantum theory of atomic collisions and scattering. With Harrie Massey he wrote the first of several classic texts, *The Theory of Atomic Collisions* (1934). Other influential texts that followed included *Electronic Processes in Ionic Crystals* with R. W. Gurney (1940). Mott then began to explore also the defects and surface phenomena involved in the photographic process (explaining latent-image formation), and did significant work on dislocations, defects, and the strength of crystals.

By the mid 1950s, Mott was able to turn his attention to problems of disordered materials, liquid metals, impurity bands in semiconductors, and the glassy semiconductors. In 1977 Mott shared the Nobel Prize for physics with Philip Anderson and John Van Vleck for their "fundamental theoretical investigations of the electronic structure of magnetic and disordered systems."

Mounier, Emmanuel (1905–1950) French philosopher. After studying philosophy in Grenoble and Paris, Mounier worked as a school teacher in France and Belgium. An admirer of the poet Charles Péguy and his idiosyncratic blend of socialism, Christianity, and patriotism, Mounier wrote *The Thought of Charles Péguy* (1931) and founded the journal *Esprit* in order to continue Péguy's work. In 1941 the Vichy government banned the journal and Mounier spent some time in prison. After the war, he returned to Paris and the editing of *Esprit* and wrote several books explaining his philosophy of 'personalism'. In his basic work *What is Personalism?* (1947) he argues that man's essential task is to communicate with others in pursuit of mutual understanding. He criticized Descartes for founding modern philosophy on a solipsistic basis, claiming that the original human experience is not the experience of the self but of the other and of the 'we'. Mounier also attacked the cult of the autonomous individual in economic life. For Mounier, a real person is directed towards fellowship with other persons. Personalism was in many ways close to post-war EXISTENTIALISM but drew a much more positive image of man as a being living in communication with others.

Movement, the A journalistic term first used in 1954 by J. D. Scott of *The Spectator* to describe a group of young writers that included Philip LARKIN, Kingsley AMIS, D. J. Enright, John Wain, Elizabeth Jennings, Donald Davie, and Robert Conquest. Most of these writers had been at Oxford together and contributed to the anthologies *Poets of the 1950s* (1955) and *New Lines* (1956). Although the group had no common programme, the writers were all to some extent reacting against the modernism of Pound and Eliot and the rhetorical excesses of the poets of the 1940s, favouring instead a poetry of clear disciplined statement and ironic detachment. Other attitudes associated with the group were a dry antiromanticism and a suspicion of the highbrow and the foreign (although the last is only really true of Amis and Larkin). The writers concerned developed in different directions and by the late 1950s the Movement had lost any coherence it may once have possessed.

Moya, Hidalgo *See* POWELL AND MOYA.

Moynihan, Rodrigo (1910–90) British painter. Born on Tenerife in the Canary Islands (his mother was Spanish), he moved to Britain in 1918 and travelled widely before enrolling at the Slade School of Fine Arts, London, in 1928. In the early 1930s he was in the forefront of abstract painting in Britain but in 1937 he became associated with the Euston Road School (*see* COLDSTREAM, SIR WILLIAM) and began to paint in the sober figurative style of art adopted by its members, becoming particularly well known as a portraitist. From 1948 to 1957 he was professor of painting at the Royal College of Art; his most famous work is the large *Portrait Group* (1951, Tate Gallery) showing himself and the eight other members of the teaching staff of the painting school there. In 1956 he returned to abstract art under the influence of US abstract expressionism. After leaving the Royal College of Art in 1957 he lived mainly in France, although he also had a studio in New York from 1968 to 1971. In the 1970s he once more concentrated on figurative painting, notably portraits and still lifes. There was a major retrospective exhibition of his work at the Royal Academy, London, in 1978.

Mro˙ek, Sławomir (1930–) Polish playwright, essayist, and short-story writer, who is one of the best known Polish writers outside his own country. After protesting against the occupation of Czechoslovakia by the Soviet Union, he was obliged to flee (1963) to Paris, where he has remained. In the West he consolidated his reputation as playwright in the absurdist tradition (*see* ABSURD, THEATRE OF THE) and as a satirist upon totalitarianism. Such plays as *Charlie* (1961), *The Party* (1962), and *The Enchanted Night* (1963) were well received in translation in several countries, while *Tango* (1964) – a complex and funny play about power struggles within an anarchic family – was particularly highly praised in a translation by Tom STOPPARD. More recent plays have included *Emigrés* (1975), in which an academic and a worker exchange views on New Year's Eve, *The Hunchback* (1976), and *A Summer's Day* (1983), in which two potential suicides compare their lives. Typically, his plays employ a variety of styles, including the conventions of vaudeville and revue, to lampoon Polish national myths. His short stories, most of which are satirical with an element of fantasy, are collected in such volumes as *The Elephant* (1957), *The Rain* (1962), and *The Ugupu Bird* (1968). He has also published two books of satirical drawings, *Poland in Pictures* (1957) and *Progressive Man* (1960).

Muehl, Otto (1925–) Austrian performance artist, one of the so-called **Vienna Actionists**. Muehl saw active service in World War II (winning the Iron Cross in 1944) and afterwards studied at the university (1947–52) and Academy of Fine Art (1952–57) in Vienna. Interested in psychoanalysis, he worked as a drawing therapist in the 1950s as well as teaching mathematics. In the 1960s he turned from more traditional means of expression to the performance of ritual actions; with his fellow Actionists Günter BRÜS and Hermann NITSCH, Muehl came to represent the most unsavoury and masochistic trends in PERFORMANCE ART. In *Libi*, for example, a broken egg was dripped into his mouth from the vagina of a menstruating woman. Muehl has now renounced art, declaring that 'it is the assignment of the artist to destroy art.' *See* ACTION AND BODY ART.

Müller, Heiner (1929–) German playwright, who in the 1960s emerged (with Peter HACKS) as one of the two leading dramatists in East Germany. Müller was born in Saxony, the son of a social democrat who was removed to a concentration camp soon after Hitler's rise to power. After the war Müller became a convinced supporter of the GDR. He began his career with the BERLINER ENSEMBLE and subsequently built up a reputation with plays written in several different styles. His early play *The Scab* (1950) was strongly socialist in doctrine, as were such subsequent works as *The Correction* (1958), *Tractor* (1961), and *Cement* (1972). Quite different in style but equally acclaimed was a series of plays using classical legends to draw political parallels with modern society; these included *Hercules 5* (1966) and the highly accomplished *Philoktet* (1968). Other plays, such as *Germania – Death in Berlin* (1971), are historical studies of German society; these freely structured, often violent, meditations on political issues frequently incurred the displeasure of the East German censor. His recent works include *Quartet* (1982), an exploration of sexual psychology. Other works by Müller have included translations and adaptations of such plays as *Macbeth* (1972) and *Medea* (as *Depraved Shore*, 1982). His best-known piece is probably *Hamletmaschine* (1977), a brief reworking of Shakespeare's play in which Hamlet declines to kill Claudius. Müller revived the piece in the autumn of 1989, adding new lines each night in response to the rapidly developing situation on the street as the East German state collapsed. In 1992 his memoirs *War Without a Battle* provoked some controversy about his somewhat ambiguous relations with the communist authorities. A year later he was exposed as a former agent of the East German security police.

Münch, Charles (1891–1968) French conductor. He studied the violin and composition with Hans Pfitzner in Strasbourg, Lucien Capet in Paris, and Carl Flesch in Berlin. He became professor of composition at the Strasbourg Conservatory in 1919 and made his conducting debut in 1932 with the Paris Symphony Orchestra; in 1935 he founded the Orchestre de la Societé Philharmonique and in 1938 became principal conductor of the Paris Conservatoire Orchestra. During the German occupation he remained in Paris and was active in the Resistance. After the liberation he was regarded with great affection by the French public, toured extensively, and also became very popular in the US, serving as director of the Boston Symphony Orchestra (1948–62). In this capacity he became a leading interpreter of the works of modern French composers such as Roussel, Milhaud, Honegger, and DUTILLEUX, many of whose works he premiered. In 1967 he founded the ORCHESTRE DE PARIS, with which he was on tour in the US when he died.

Munk, Andrzej (1921–61) Polish film director, who contributed greatly to the New Wave of Polish cinema in the 1950s. Born in Kraków, he was a Resistance fighter with the Warsaw underground during World War II. After the war he studied architecture, law, and economics at university before transferring to the Łódź film school, where he learned directing and camerawork, graduating in 1950. After several years directing documentaries, he turned to feature films with *Men of the Blue Cross* (1955), *Eroica* (1957), and *Bad Luck* (1960). His films present a cynical view of state bureaucracy and other oppressive aspects of Polish life under communism. Munk's death in a car accident occurred before the authorities' crackdown on artistic freedom in the 1960s. The film he was shooting at the time, *Passenger*, was completed by his associates and released in 1963.

Murdoch, Iris (Jean) (1919–) British novelist and philosopher, born in Dublin of Anglo-Irish parents. She was educated at Somerville College, Oxford, and has lectured in philosophy in Cambridge, Oxford, and London. After World War II she spent two years working with the UN refugee programme in Europe; during this period she met and came under the influence of SARTRE, the subject of her first book *Sartre, Romantic Rationalist* (1953). Her principal philosophical works are *The Sovereignty of Good* (1970) and *Metaphysics as a Guide to Morals* (1992), in which she defends Platonism and the concept of 'the Good'. Philosophical issues, complex ethical dilemmas, and questions of religious faith and doubt also loom large in her 23 novels. The first of these, the picaresque *Under the Net* (1954), shows her interest in EXISTENTIALISM, while *The Sandcastle* (1957) deals with the sexual and political dilemmas of the quiet schoolteacher Bill Mor. This was followed by *The Bell* (1958), set in a lay community in a large country house and dealing with questions of personal and public morality. Major novels of the 1960s and 1970s include *A Severed Head* (1961), *The Unicorn* (1963), *The Nice and the Good* (1968), *Bruno's Dream* (1969), and *The Black Prince* (1973), which won the James Tait Black Memorial Prize. *The Sacred and Profane Love Machine* won the Whitbread Prize in 1974 and in 1978 she won the BOOKER PRIZE for *The Sea, The Sea*, a novel about a theatre director and his childhood love, which uses *The Tempest* as a model. Her later novels, beginning with *Nuns and Soldiers* (1980), are longer and more loosely structured than earlier work. *The Philosopher's Pupil* (1983) was followed by *The Good Apprentice* (1985) and *The Book and the Brotherhood* (1987), both of which were shortlisted for the Booker Prize. Her latest novel is *The Message to the Planet* (1989).

Musgrave, Thea (1928–) Scottish composer. She studied with Hans Gál at Edinburgh University and then in Paris (1950–54) with Nadia Boulanger; she subsequently taught at the Universities of London and California. Musgrave began to adopt serial procedures in the late 1950s, at first somewhat cerebrally but achieving a new vigour and expressiveness in her first opera *The Decision* (1967). Her other operas are *The Voice of Ariadne* (1973), *Mary, Queen of Scots* (1977), *A Christmas Carol* (1979), and *Harriet, the Woman called Moses* (1985). Musgrave is also notable as a writer of concertos, her output including the three chamber concertos (1963–66), a concerto for orchestra (1967), and works for clarinet (1968), horn (1971), and viola (1973). Several of these – most notably the clarinet concerto – allow the soloist an element of freedom and experiment with spatial ideas (*see* SPATIAL MUSIC). Musgrave's recent works include *For The Time Being* (1986), to a text by W. H. Auden, and the orchestral pieces *The Seasons* (1988) and *Rainbow* (1990).

Musica Antiqua Köln German early music ensemble. It was founded in 1973 by Reinhard Goebel (violinist), who directs and leads it, to perform Italian and French early baroque music in period playing style on original instruments and modern copies. Goebel is a former pupil of Franz Josef Maier, the founder of the COLLEGIUM AUREUM. Like other early baroque music ensembles, Musica Antiqua Köln has extended its range into the mainstream baroque repertory and now specializes in the music of J. S. Bach and his immediate predecessors. Their work includes a recording (1990) of Telemann's *Tafelmusik*. The group has toured extensively in Europe, North and South America, Asia, and Australia.

Musica Viva An important festival of contemporary music held annually in Munich, Germany. It was founded by the composer Karl Amadeus Hartmann in 1946 to reintroduce music that had been banned by the Nazis. The festival was a focal point for the German musical revival after World War II and became a model for other festivals.

musique concrète Music consisting of natural or machine-generated sounds (such as voices, animals, trains, and cars) recorded, assembled, and modified on tape. It was the earliest example of ELECTRONIC MUSIC, having been invented in Paris in 1948 by Pierre Schaeffer, a sound technician at French National Radio, with the help of Pierre Henry. The term was coined to distinguish the 'concrete' (real-life) sounds used in such compositions from the 'abstract' sounds produced by conventional instruments. In *musique concrète*, unlike later forms of electronic music, the original sound is not generated electronically, a restriction that caused it to be rapidly superseded. Examples of *musique concrète* include Schaeffer and Henry's *Symphonie pour un homme seul* (1950), Varèse's *Déserts* (1954), which alternates *musique concrète* with sections for live instruments, and XENAKIS's *Bohor* (1962). *See also* GROUPE DE RECHERCHES MUSICALES.

Muti, Riccardo (1941–) Italian conductor. Born in Naples, Muti studied the piano at the conservatory there while still a child. He subsequently studied conducting (under Antonino Votto) and composition (under Bruno Bettinelli) at the Giuseppe Verdi Conservatory in Milan. In 1968 he made his debut with the Italian Radio Symphony Orchestra, becoming conductor of the Florence Maggio Musicale the following year. The New Philharmonia Orchestra, London, made him their principal conductor in 1973, musical director in 1979, and conductor laureate in 1982. From 1977 to 1992 he also conducted the Philadelphia Orchestra (principal conductor and musical director from 1980). In 1986 he became musical director at La Scala, Milan. He has been a guest conductor for numerous European orchestras and has conducted many successful opera productions, notably revivals of Verdi's *Attila* and *I Masnadieri*.

N

Nádas, Péter (1947–) Hungarian novelist and essayist. For most of the 1960s Nádas worked as a reporter and photojournalist, publishing his first volume of short stories in 1967. His first novel, *The End of a Family Novel* (1977), was a major critical success and soon appeared in several languages. It is a highly compressed and lyrical account of a Jewish-Hungarian childhood in the 1950s; the book questions the significance of tradition and family history and closes with a crisis of personal and historical identity. Nádas seems to suggest that the genre of the family (or genealogical) novel is no longer viable for the central European writer at the end of the 20th century. Nádas's second novel, *A Book of Memoirs* (1986) – on which he worked for 11 years – is regarded by many as the masterpiece of post-war Hungarian fiction. Like *The End of a Family Novel*, *A Book of Memoirs* tackles themes of memory, personal identity, and historical continuity. It consists of three apparently separate narratives, or memoirs: the story of a Hungarian student in East Berlin in the 1970s, that of an adolescent boy growing up in Budapest in the 1950s, and that of a German novelist living and writing at the turn of the century. Only at the end of the novel do we learn that the first and second narrators are one and the same person, while the third is his fictional creation. Since completing *A Book of Memoirs*, Nádas has concentrated primarily on a form of essay writing that fuses discursive and imaginative prose.

Nagibin, Iurii Markovich (1920–) Russian prose writer. Born in Moscow, he studied briefly at medical school before enrolling at the Institute of Cinematography. His interest in the cinema has remained with him and he has written a number of film scripts. Having begun to write under the influence of his stepfather, he published his first story, *Double Mistake*, in 1940. During World War II he worked as a war correspondent; later he wrote for an agricultural journal. He became famous with his short stories *Winter Oak* (1953) and *Komarov* (1953), consolidating his reputation with his collection of stories *Painful Happiness* (1958).

The short story has remained his most successful medium, notable examples being 'The Echo' (1960) and 'The Chase' (1962). The latter is one of a cycle of 13 stories written between 1954 and 1964 that describe country life in the Meschera region, south-east of Moscow. Children are a major theme of Nagibin's stories. A good example is *Clear Ponds* (1961), set in the district of Moscow where the author lived as a child; like much of his work it is strongly autobiographical. The collection *Kingdom of Childhood* (1971) is in similar vein, as is *The Spring that Fell Silent* (1979), in which Nagibin describes his struggle against deafness. Since the mid 1970s Nagibin has increasingly turned to historical themes as, for example, in *The Runaway* (1978), in which the main character is the 18th-century poet Trediakovsky.

Between 1960 and 1967 Nagibin was married to the poet Bella AKHMADULINA (he has been married five times in all). Like Akhmadulina, Nagibin is associated with the liberal wing of the Russian literary scene.

Naipaul, Sir V(idiadhar) S(urajprasad) (1932–) British novelist and journalist, born in Trinidad into a Brahmin family of Indian origin. Naipaul was educated in Port of Spain and then at University College, Oxford, after which he remained in Britain. His earliest works, such as *The Mystic Masseur* (1957), are chiefly comedies of manners, satirizing the middle- and merchant-classes in his native Trinidad. Perhaps the most successful of these was *A*

House For Mr Biswas (1961), which explored the cultural and political absorption of ethnic minorities through the comic story of the rootless Mr Biswas (partly based on Naipaul's own father) and his attempts to avoid being engulfed by his wife's family. It was followed by *Mr Stone and the Knights Companion* (1963), set in London, and *The Mimic Men* (1967), narrated by the failed politician Ralph Singh. His work became gradually darker and more political throughout the 1960s. In 1971 Naipaul won the BOOKER PRIZE with *In a Free State*, which deals with the theme of cultural displacement through the stories of a servant suddenly uprooted to Washington, a West Indian youth in London, and two Europeans in a Black African state. *Guerrillas* (1975) traces the link between political and sexual violence in the Caribbean. His 1979 novel, *A Bend in the River*, provoked comparisons with Conrad with its linking of personal and political violence and its underlying sense of the futility of most human enterprises. The novel places events in the life of Salim, a Muslim trader on the East African coast, against the background of the evolution of a new state. *The Enigma of Arrival* (1987) is a semiautobiographical work about a Trinidadian writer living in rural England. Naipaul's books of travel writing and political journalism explore similar themes to his fiction. Examples include *The Middle Passage* (1962), *An Area of Darkness* (1964), *The Return of Eva Peron* (1980), *Among the Believers: an Islamic Journey* (1981), *A Turn in the South* (1989), and *India: a Million Mutinees Now* (1990).

Natalini, Adolfo (1941–) *See* SUPERSTUDIO.

National Film Theatre A cinema complex on the South Bank in London, which is one of the most important venues for new films in Britain. It was founded in 1951 by the British Film Institute as part of the FESTIVAL OF BRITAIN and was originally known as the Telekinema. In 1958 the present cinema was built nearby, a second screen being added in 1970. The annual LONDON FILM FESTIVAL is held here.

National Philharmonic Orchestra Poland's principal national orchestra, based in Warsaw. The orchestra, which replaced the old Warsaw Philharmonic Orchestra (1930–39), was founded in 1946 as the Polish Symphony Orchestra. It was renamed the City of Warsaw Philharmonic Orchestra in 1947 and took its present name in 1955, when the new National Philharmonic Hall became its base. The orchestra gives subscription concerts and organizes concerts for young people; it has also toured throughout Europe, the US, South America, and Asia. Its conductors have included Witold Rowicki and Stanisław Skrowaczewski, while foreign guest conductors have included BARBIROLLI, Ormandy, Kondrashin, Ansermet, and Bernstein.

National Theatre *See* ROYAL NATIONAL THEATRE.

Němec, Jan (1936–) Czech film director and screenwriter, born in Prague. A graduate of the Prague film school, he won a prize at the film students' festival in Amsterdam for his 1960 short *A Loaf of Bread* and directed a short documentary, *The Memory of Our Day* (1963), while serving in the military. Němec's first feature, which he coscripted, was *Diamonds of the Night* (1964), a psychological study of the anxieties and memories of two men who escape the Nazis. His concern with the psychological effects of oppression continued in *A Report on the Party and the Guests* (1966), a story of dehumanizing tyranny within a family. He coscripted this film and *Martyrs of Love* (1966) with Ester Krumbachova, his first wife. His second marriage was to the singer Marta Kubisova; both their careers were ruined by the 1968 Soviet invasion, which Němec recorded in the striking documentary *Oratorio for Prague* (1968). The couple went into self-imposed exile in France in 1974 and did not return to Czechoslovakia until 1991, when Němec's film, *In the Light of the King's Love*, caused controversy of a different kind. Its faithful rendition of erotic and sadomasochistic episodes from Ladislav Klima's 1928 novel *The Suffering of Count Sternenhoch* made it the most talked about film of the season in Czechoslovakia.

neoexpressionism A type of painting that achieved prominence in the late 1970s, chiefly through the work of Anselm KIEFER and Georg BASELITZ in Germany; Francesco CLEMENTE, Enzo Cucci, and Sandro CHIA in Italy; and Julian Schnabel (1951–) in the US. Their works, which tend to be monumental in size and dominated by violent and doom-laden imagery, contributed to the general revival of figurative painting in the late 1970s and early 1980s. The term implies a kinship between these works, with their lurid colours, distorted forms, and air of emotional turmoil, and those produced by expressionist artists in the early decades of the century. Although neoexpressionist painting commanded high prices in the 1980s, critical opinion was violently polarized, with Baselitz and Schnabel, in particular, being denounced for crudeness and sensationalism. Neoexpressionism is sometimes known as **figuration libre** in France, the **transavantgarde** in Italy, and **Bad Art** in the US.

neorealism A movement in the Italian cinema and literature of the 1940s and 1950s, characterized by an emphasis on naturalism and a concern for the social condition of the poor. Neorealism began to emerge as a distinct style during the early 1940s, when the harsh reality of the war demanded that the cinema should reflect the suffering of the people. To these ends such directors as DE SICA and ROSSELLINI, employed nonprofessional casts and undertook much filming on location in order to make their work as real and immediate as possible. In general, directors tried not to draw attention to the presence of the camera. True neorealistic cinema faded during the 1950s but a whole generation of European directors were influenced by its techniques, among them PASOLINI and FELLINI. Perhaps the most striking example of a neorealist film remains De Sica's *Bicycle Thieves* (1948). The neorealist movement in literature is represented by such writers as PAVESE, MORAVIA, and VITTORINI.

Nervi, Pier-Luigi (1891–1979) Italian architect and engineer. After training at the University of Bologna and in the Italian army, Nervi worked in private practice in Rome from 1920; three of his four sons joined the firm in the 1950s. Nervi combined brilliant innovatory skills in the use of reinforced concrete with a refined aesthetic sensibility. His first major work was the Municipal Stadium in Florence (1929–32), which featured a 24-foot cantilevered roof and daring helicoidal stairs. His investigation of arched and curved forms in concrete developed in aeroplane hangers built at Orvieto and Orbetello on frames of intersecting arches (1935–42).

After the war, Nervi devised his technique of *ferrocemento*, whereby cement is poured over carefully calculated sections of steel mesh, so that it has some of the tensile properties of the steel. His celebrated Exhibition Halls B and C at Turin (1950) were built within seven months using this technique. The famous circular Palazzo dello Sport and Palazetto dello Sport in Rome (1956–59), whose prefabricated domes are respectively 164 ft and 328 ft in diameter, are landmarks in modern engineering. Later masterpieces include the Pirelli Tower in Milan (1955–59), the UNESCO conference hall in Paris (1953–57), and St Mary's Cathedral in San Francisco (1966–71). Nervi's particular skill was in enclosing very large spaces with efficient and economical structures, without using inner columns. Primarily an engineer, he achieved something that has eluded most architects of his era, in that his works are not only efficient but also of great beauty.

Netherlands Dance Theatre Dutch ballet company, founded in The Hague in 1959, which has become one of the most important companies specializing in work by contemporary choreographers. The troupe was formed as a reaction to the classicism of Sonia GASKELL's Netherlands Ballet (later renamed the DUTCH NATIONAL BALLET) by such leading choreographers as Benjamin Harkavy (the company's first artistic director), Hans van MANEN, and Rudi van DANTZIG. The company began by presenting ten modern ballets each year, including works by such US choreographers as Glen Tetley and Anna Sokolow; Tetley himself joined the company as resident choreographer and briefly served as codirector. Work done by the company in the 1960s had a profound influence upon the contemporary dance movement in Europe, in particular upon the Ballet Rambert (*see* RAMBERT DANCE COMPANY) in Britain. As well as works by Tetley, other notable early successes included *Carmina Burana* (1963), *Screen Play* (1968), and *Mutations* (1970), which was jointly choreographed by Tetley and van Manen.

Tetley and van Manen left the company in the 1970s (Dantzig having already gone elsewhere) and the troupe found a new leader in Jirí KYLIÁN, who took up the post of resident choreographer in 1975. Subsequently the company worked exclusively on his ballets, which combine classical and modern dance techniques. Van Manen returned in 1988 and the company now presents works by a range of modern choreographers as well as running a smaller junior troupe. The Netherlands Dance Theatre moved to a new theatre in The Hague in 1987.

Neumeier, John (1942–) US dancer, choreographer, and ballet director, who has established a reputation as one of the most significant figures in contemporary European dance. As artistic director and chief choreographer of the Hamburg Ballet (since 1973), he has become one of the dominant forces in modern German ballet, attracting a devoted following for his highly dramatic (and often very lengthy) works.

Neumeier was born in Milwaukee, Wisconsin but subsequently trained at the Royal Ballet School and danced under John CRANKO at the Stuttgart Ballet (1963–69). During this period he executed his first works as a choreographer, his most notable early successes including *Separate Journeys* (1968) and *Frontiers* (1969). In 1969 he became ballet director of the Frankfurt Ballet, where he won praise for his productions of *Romeo and Juliet* and *The Nutcracker* (both 1971) before moving to Hamburg four years later.

Under Neumeier the Hamburg Ballet emerged as one of the most popular dance theatre companies in Germany. Among the troupe's most successful productions of Neumeier's ballets have been *The Legend of Joseph* (1977), based on Balanchine's *The Prodigal Son*, the widely toured *A Midsummer Night's Dream* (1977), the epic *St Matthew Passion* (1981), which lasted more than four hours, five ballets inspired by the symphonies of Mahler, *Othello* (1985), and updated versions of such classics as *Swan Lake* (1976). Some critics find Neumeier's epic style pretentious and heavyhanded, but audiences flock to see his productions. He has also worked as a guest choreographer with the Harkness Ballet, the American Ballet Theater, and the Royal Danish Ballet, among other companies. He received a German Dance Award from the Society for Dance Teachers in 1988 to mark his 25-year involvement with German ballet.

new brutalism A style of architecture that was widely adopted in Britain in the later 1950s and 1960s, when an enormous amount of rebuilding took place after World War II. It is characterized by austere rectangular forms and an emphasis on such materials as undressed concrete and exposed steel. The deliberately provocative phrase originated in the circle of the British architects Peter and Alison SMITHSON in the early 1950s, probably in allusion to Peter Smithson's nickname 'Brutus'. It reflects the kind of uncompromising architecture, based firmly in the tradition of LE CORBUSIER and Mies van der Rohe, that the Smithsons and other young architects proposed for post-war Britain. From Le Corbusier's Unité d'Habitation at Marseilles with its 'rue intérieure' came the idea of high-level street decks, envisaged by the Smithsons for their unbuilt Golden Lane scheme (1952) and incorporated by Jack Lynn and Ivor Smith at Park Hill, Sheffield (1961). As influential was Le Corbusier's Maisons Jaoul (1956), with its use of concrete vaulting and rough brickwork; STIRLING and Gowan at Ham Common (1958) and Basil SPENCE at Sussex University (1962) closely followed the idiom. Other early British followers included HOWELL, KILLICK, PARTRIDGE, AND AMIS.

In the following decades the label 'new brutalism' was widely taken up by architectural writers, who applied it to analogous developments in the US and Continental Europe. Since the 1980s 'brutalism' has become a somewhat general term of abuse for everything most disliked about modern architecture.

New Cinema A German cinema movement that gathered pace in the 1960s and 1970s, influencing international film-makers through its intellectual rigour and political commitment. The movement was launched in 1962 by a manifesto signed in Oberhausen by a group of young directors, including Alexander KLUGE, who pledged to break away from West Germany's moribund commercial cinema. With financial help from the Kuratorium Junger Deutscher Film organization, founded in 1964 to help young film-makers, such directors as SYBERBERG, SCHLÖNDORFF, STRAUB, and HERZOG began to forge a new cinema of intellectual seriousness and high artistic standards. With films such as *Yesterday Girl* (1966), *Young Törless* (1966), and *The*

Chronicle of Anna Magdalena Bach (1967) the New Cinema gradually came to be recognized as an important new departure for European film. In the 1970s and 1980s budgets were increased and directors like FASSBINDER and WENDERS were able to tackle more ambitious subjects while remaining faithful to the ideals of the 1962 manifesto. Several of the movement's later films have enjoyed considerable commercial success, among them Herzog's *Nosferatu the Vampyre* (1979) and *Fitzcarraldo* (1982) and Schlöndorff's *The Tin Drum* (1979; from the novel by GRASS), which became the first post-war German film to win an Oscar as best foreign film.

New International Stage Belgian theatre company, based in Antwerp, which has played a major role in revitalizing Belgian drama since its foundation in 1973. The group was formed in reaction to the established theatre of the time, which allowed little opportunity for political or experimental work; it soon acquired an international reputation with its productions based on the theories of BRECHT. Since its first production, an adaptation of Dario FO's *Mistero Buffo*, the company has consistently attracted praise for its high standards of performance. Its most notable success to date came with its production of *Hercules*, a depiction of life in dockland with a strong socialist message, in 1980.

New Philharmonia Orchestra *See* PHILHARMONIA ORCHESTRA.

New Wave (*Nouvelle Vague*) A loose association of French film directors whose innovative approach transfigured European cinema in the late 1950s and 1960s. Several of the directors developed their ideas about film while working as critics for the influential journal *Cahiers du Cinéma*, the most prominent among them being Jean-Luc GODARD. The group, which included major names like CHABROL, TRUFFAUT, and RESNAIS, rejected many of the established conventions of mainstream cinema in order to develop the more challenging narrative and editing techniques pioneered a generation earlier by such figures as Hitchcock, Jean Renoir, and Jean Vigo. The first masterpiece of the New Wave was Godard's *Breathless* (*A Bout de Souffle*; 1960); like many of the films that followed, it was fast-moving, unpredictable, technically adventurous, and self-consciously intellectual. The directors associated with the movement soon developed their own distinctive styles and it is arguable whether the New Wave ever really existed as a coherent group; nevertheless its innovative attitude to film-making has proved a permanent and liberating influence upon European cinema.

Nichols, Peter (Richard) (1927–) British playwright, noted for his bitter comedies on painful subjects. His first play, *A Day in the Death of Joe Egg* (1967), was a sensitive and funny portrayal of the strains of living with a disabled relative, based on his own experiences of caring for a handicapped daughter. *The National Health* (1969) similarly challenges the taboos surrounding terminal illness, contrasting the anguished lives of the patients with those of the glamorous characters of a fictional hospital soap. A strong autobiographical element was evident in *Forget-me-not Lane* (1971), while Nichols' taste for the unpredictable enlivened such subsequent works as *Privates on Parade* (1977), in which army life is analysed through a revue format, *Born in the Gardens* (1979), *Passion Play* (1981), a marital tragicomedy, and *Poppy* (1982), a scathing comment on Britain's role in the Opium Wars with China, which makes use of pantomime and music-hall conventions. His more recent plays include *A Piece of My Mind* (1986). He has also written extensively for television and adapted several of his own plays for the cinema.

Nicholson, Ben (1894–1982) British painter. The son of the painter Sir William Nicholson, he studied for one term at the Slade School of Fine Arts (1911) but otherwise had no formal training. His first works of note, a series of still lifes and landscapes dating from the early 1920s, show an intelligent awareness of cubism. The freshness and immediacy of this early work also reflects the influence of his first wife, the painter **Winifred Nicholson** (1893–1981), and of the Cornish primitive Alfred Wallis (1855–1942), whom Nicholson 'discovered' in 1928.

From 1930 onwards Nicholson worked in close collaboration with Barbara HEPWORTH, who became his second wife, and adopted a completely abstract style. In 1932 the couple visited Paris and met leading members of the European avant-garde including Mondrian. The carved reliefs that Nicholson produced in the mid

1930s, many of them all-white (*White Relief*, 1935, Tate Gallery, London), established him as the chief exponent of geometrical abstraction in Britain and remain his best-known works. He remained at the forefront of avant-garde artistic activity in this country for the rest of the decade, becoming a founder member of the group Unit One in 1933, organizing Britain's first exhibition of entirely abstract art in 1935, and contributing to the constructivist publication *Circle* in 1937.

In 1939 Nicholson and Hepworth moved to the west of Cornwall, where they became the nucleus of the developing ST IVES SCHOOL of artists. During the 1940s figurative elements began to reemerge in Nicholson's paintings, which sometimes carry suggestions of landscape or still-life forms. His international reputation grew quickly in the later 1940s and 1950s, with a showing at the Venice Biennale in 1954 and a major retrospective at the Tate Gallery, London, in 1955. Following the collapse of his marriage to Hepworth, he moved to Switzerland in 1958. Here he embarked on a final artistic period characterized by large-scale abstract reliefs (*Tuscan Relief*, 1967). He was appointed OM in 1968.

Nielsen, Riccardo (1908–82) Italian composer, teacher, and musicologist. He studied composition in Bologna, his birthplace, later becoming superintendent of the Teatro Comunale there (1946–50). Subsequent posts included director of the Ferrara Conservatory (formerly the Liceo Musicale). He published valuable editions of Renaissance and baroque music.

His earliest works, for example the *Sinfonia concertante* (1931) and the violin concerto (1932), show the influence of Alfredo Casella, the grandfather figure of contemporary Italian music. Subsequent works, like the choral setting *Psalmus in confessione xcix* (1941), are clearly influenced by Stravinsky's neoclassicism. In the early 1940s he adopted serialist techniques in such works as the monodrama *L'incubo* (1948). His radio opera *La via di Colombo* won an Italia prize in 1953, establishing his international reputation as a composer. Important among his later post-serialist works are *Invenzioni e sinfonie* (1961) for voices and orchestra and *Varianti* (1965) for orchestra. He has also written two symphonies (1933; 1935).

Nilsen, Hans Jacob (1897–1957) Norwegian theatre director and actor, who played a major role in the revitalization of Norwegian theatre both before and after World War II. As director of the Norske Teatret (1933–34, 1946–50), the Nationale Scene (1934–39), and the Folketeatret (1952–55), he promoted a new realism in productions of such authors as Grieg, Holberg, and Ibsen, arguing that the theatre should strive for a greater social relevance. Amongst his most influential productions were the Čapek brothers' *Insect Play* (1939) and Ibsen's *Peer Gynt* (1948). He also won acclaim as an actor in plays by Scandinavian authors and in classics by Shakespeare and others.

Nilsson, Bo (1937–) Swedish composer. A pianist and sometime jazz musician, he is essentially self-taught as a composer, having learned his avant-garde style from radio concerts in the 1950s: he is, therefore, very much a product of Swedish radio's progressive programming of new music.

His precocious early works, clearly influenced by STOCKHAUSEN in their use of serialism and electronics but also showing the influence of BOULEZ in their instrumentation, initially attracted attention from the avant-garde DARMSTADT group in Germany rather than in Sweden. Particularly noted were *Zwei Stücke* (1956) for instrumental ensemble, *Frequenzen* (1957) for orchestra, his first major international success, and the cantata *Briefe an Gösta Oswald* (1959). Among the orchestral works from the early 1960s, *Szene I, II & III* and *Séance* belong to the same bright percussive sound-world, while *Entrée* reveals a return to late romanticism. A simpler and more lyrical idiom is employed in the film scores written in the later 1960s. Other important works from his prolific output include the large-scale piece *Nazm* (1973), for solo voices, chorus, jazz group, and orchestra, which combines notated with improvised music, *Szene IV* for jazz saxophone and chorus (1975), and *Madonna* (1977) for mezzo and instrumental ensemble.

Nitsch, Hermann (1938–) Austrian performance artist, one of the so-called **Vienna Actionists**. Outdoing even his compatriots Günter BRÜS and Otto MUEHL, he is regarded as the most extreme exponent of sadomasochistic themes in contemporary PERFORMANCE ART. He began public performances in 1961 and typical actions have involved disembowelling recently slaughtered animals and pouring their blood over naked assistants. Such displays have led to his arrest in Austria and Britain. Nitsch has written a good deal and is regarded as one of the most articulate spokesmen for performance art. Through his actions he "aims at catharsis: All torment and lust, combined in a single state of unburdened intoxication, will pervade me and therefore YOU. The playacting will be a means of gaining access to the most 'profound' and 'holy' symbols through blasphemy and desecration." *See* ACTION AND BODY ART.

Nolte, Ernst (1923–) German historian. After obtaining his doctorate in 1952, Nolte worked as a schoolteacher. In 1965 he was appointed professor of history at the University of Marburg and in 1973 he moved to Berlin.

In 1963 Nolte published *Three Faces of Fascism*, a comparative study of the ideologies of the Nazis, the Italian Fascists, and the Action Française. The common factor in these ideologies, he argued, was their 'resistance to transcendence' – that is, a revolt against the general tendency of modern societies to become more abstract and complicated.

In subsequent books Nolte considerably enlarged the scope of his work. In *Germany and the Cold War* (1974), *Marxism and the Industrial Revolution* (1983), and *The European Civil War* (1987) he described the rise of Marxism in response to the Industrial Revolution and interpreted fascism as primarily a response to Marxism. Nolte now argued that the crimes of the Nazis should be seen as a reaction to and imitation of earlier Bolshevist crimes, differing mainly in the degree of technical expertise available. This view triggered a furious debate among German historians, some of whom – including Nolte's main opponent, Jürgen HABERMAS – saw it as an attempt to partially excuse Nazi atrocities.

Notwithstanding some ambiguities and problems with details, Nolte's work constitutes one of the most stimulating and perceptive attempts to construct a philosophical history of the tumultous 20th century.

Nono, Luigi (1924–90) Italian composer. He studied at the Venice Conservatory (1941–45) under Malipiero and others, graduated in law from Padua University, and took further lessons from MADERNA and the conductor Hermann Scherchen. He attended the DARMSTADT summer schools from 1950, when he gained attention with his first acknowledged work, the *Variazione canoniche.* Despite his association with Darmstadt, works such as *Epitaffio per Federico Garcia Lorca* (1953), with its use of folksong and castanets, indicate that his adherence to Webernian serialism (seen at its most consistent in *Varianti*, 1958) was never entirely wholehearted. A crucial work from this period is the cantata *Il canto sospeso* (1956), which uses serial and motivic techniques to set a text taken from prisoners' writings. Nono taught at Darmstadt from 1954 to 1960, marrying Schoenberg's daughter Nuria in 1955. In 1959 he gave the now-famous lecture 'The Presence of History in Music Today', in which he rejected the ideas of John Cage, who had visited Darmstadt the previous year. The controversy aroused by his left-wing theatre piece *Intolleranza 1960* (1961) – setting texts by BRECHT, SARTRE, and others – and his political activism in the 1960s has continued to haunt discussions of his work. Nono took advantage of the collage effects and layering techniques made available by electronics in works such as *La fabbrica illuminata* (1964), memorable for its inclusion of factory noises. This phase culminated in the *musica realta* discussions organized by Nono in factories and universities in the early 1970s and the opera *Al gran sole carico d'amore* (1975).

From 1959 onwards he taught widely in Europe and (from 1967) in Latin America. Since the mid 1970s he has tended to write works for particular performers, such as the pianist Maurizio Pollini (*Sofferte onde serene*; 1975) and the La Salle String Quartet (*An Diotima*; 1980). Acoustic and electronic experiments at the Heinrich Strobel Foundation Experimental Studio at Freiberg resulted in such works as *Das Atmende Klarsein.* In the 1980s the means of sound production became all-important to Nono, with works such as the opera *Prometeo* (1985) existing more as works in progress than as finished pieces. Recent works include *Carlo Scarpa e infiniti possibili* (1984) and *No hay caminos, hay que caminar* (1987).

Nordbrandt, Henrik (1945–) Danish poet. Nordbrandt is the most classical and sensual of contemporary Danish poets; his unique blend of the concrete and the mystical has ensured that he is also one of the most popular. Much of his work deals with the individual's search for his place and identity in an ever-changing world.

His debut came in 1966 with *Poems*, which explores the poet's feelings of alienation. After *Surroundings* (1972) his poetry became simpler and more direct. Nordbrandt has written some of the most original and startling love poetry of the 20th century; the object of love is consistently presented as less important than the emotions it arouses in us. *Departures and Arrivals* (1974), *Ode to the Octopus and Other Poems* (1975) and *Glass* (1976) are all imbued with Nordbrandt's distinctive sensuality and freshness of language and imagery.

God's House (1977), a collection of poems about a house on a Greek island and its various inhabitants, contains an element of narrative. The eastern Mediterranean has provided Nordbrandt with a rich source of inspiration. *Icetime* (1977) contains a mixture of satirical, documentary, and political poems and shows Nordbrandt's growing interest in ecological affairs.

Nordbrandt's ability to capture complex moods and emotions with precision makes him one of Denmark's great poets. He has been widely translated.

Nordic Arts Festival *See* - MEA FESTIVAL OF CHAMBER MUSIC

Norén, Lars (1944–) Swedish playwright and poet. In the 1980s Norén emerged as one of the leading Swedish dramatists of the post-war era. Such plays as *Demons* (1982) and *Communion* (1985), which tackle themes including emotional breakdown and family conflict, earned Norén a strong reputation, though some found his plays too sexually explicit for comfort. His other works include two powerful trilogies for the theatre. The first, which consists of *A Terrifying Joy*, *When They Burned Butterflies on the Small Stage*, and *The Smile of the Underworld* (1981–83), explores the paradoxes of life in contemporary Sweden, while the second, consisting of, *The Courage to Kill*, *Night is the Mother of Day*, and *Chaos is a Neighbour of God* (1978–84), is strongly autobiographical.

Nørgård, Per (1932–) Danish composer and teacher. Nørgård is a central figure in modern Danish music with a reputation that has burgeoned internationally since the 1970s. From 1949 he studied composition privately with Vagn Holmboe, continuing as his student at the Copenhagen Conservatory (1952–55). Subsequently he studied with Nadia Boulanger in Paris (1956–57), winning the Lili Boulanger Prize in 1957. He taught piano and composition at the Odense Conservatory (1958–61) and composition at the Copenhagen Conservatory (1960–65). After resigning the latter post in a dispute over educational policy, he moved (1965) to the Århus Conservatory, which in consequence became the new focus for avant-garde music in Denmark.

Early works, of which *Triptychon* (1957) for chorus and orchestra is typical, show the influence of Sibelius and Holmboe. Crucial to his development was the performance of his *Konstellationer* at the 1959 ISCM festival in Rome, since the festival also acquainted Nørgård with the music of such figures as Webern, BOULEZ, and NONO. The first fruits of this new influence were the *Fragmenter* works, in which Nørgård introduced his concept of the 'infinite series' (a self-generating pitch set), which preoccupied him in the 1960s. Later developments include the use of collage techniques in the ballet *The Young Man Shall Marry* (1965). His works of the 1970s, such as his opera *Gilgamesh* (1972) and the second and third symphonies (1971, 1975), synthesize such apparently diverse elements as pentatonicism, 7- and 12-note series, microtones, the 'infinite series', and rhythmic patterns based on the golden section. His prolific output also includes four symphonies, the orchestral works *Voyage into the Golden Screen* (1968), *Illumination* (1984) and *Spaces of Time* (1991), pieces for chamber ensemble, ballets, the oratorio *Dommen* (1962), the operas *The Labyrinth* (1963) and *The Divine Circus* (1983), songs, and works using tape.

Norrington, Roger (Arthur Carver) (1934–) British conductor. Born in Oxford, Norrington was educated at Cambridge University and trained as a singer at the Royal College of Music, London. His first appointment as a conductor was with the Kent Opera (1966–84). In the 1960s and 1970s he founded several choirs to promote the work of Monteverdi and Shütz and became well known for his encouragement of period performances (*see* EARLY-MUSIC MOVEMENT). He was appointed musical director of the London Baroque Players in 1975 and of the London Classical Players in 1978. Norrington became principal conductor of the Bournemouth Sinfonietta in 1985 and has also worked as a guest conductor with many leading British and European orchestras.

North Sea Jazz Festival An annual jazz festival held in The Hague, Holland, each July. It was founded in 1975. Although the festival lasts only three days, there is continuous entertainment on about 14 different stages. It is possibly the largest jazz festival in Europe and features exponents of styles ranging from blues to acid jazz and fusion. It maintains an informal atmosphere, with the artists often joining each other on stage for impromptu improvisations.

Norwegian Opera (Den Norsk Opera) Norway's principal opera company, based in Oslo. It was established under its present name in 1957; previously, as Norsk Operaselskap (founded by the soprano Kirsten Flagstad in 1950), it had been Norway's first full-time opera company. Flagstad was also involved in its reorganization. The company's first musical director was Øivin Fjelstad, while Martin Turnovský was its musical director from 1975 until 1980. Its annual season runs from August to June.

Nossack, Hans Erich (1901–77) German writer. Nossack studied law and philosophy but then worked in a factory and as a bank clerk; from 1933 to 1956 he worked in his father's trading firm in Hamburg. Because of his ties to the Communist Party he was unable to publish between 1933 and 1945.

The central event of Nossack's life was the virtual obliteration of the city of Hamburg in a series of Allied bombing raids in July 1943. All of his personal belongings, including his complete writings and diaries to that date, were destroyed in the firestorms. Within months Nossack produced a chronicle, *The Destruction* (*Der Untergang*; 1948), which remains one of his most important writings. In it the destruction of Hamburg becomes a metaphor for the terrible uncertainty of life and the fragility of all we consider most solid and assured. The need or desire to abandon one's own past and everything to which one has become accustomed is a recurrent theme in Nossack's writings, as is his related distrust of all social conventions. In *Nekyia* (1947) a single isolated man wanders through an abandoned city, while in his most popular novel, *Wait Until November* (1955), a wealthy housewife leaves her husband, child, and home to live with a man she has known for only a few hours. *Impossible Proof* (1956) depicts the inability of a court to understand the kind of existential insecurity that motivates Nossack's protagonists. In *The Testament of Lucius Eurinius* (1965) a rational-thinking official of 1st-century Rome is bewildered by his wife's conversion to Christianity, which he sees as a rising tide of irrationalism.

Nossack's shorter prose is collected in *Interview With Death* (1948) and *The Meeting in the Hallway* (1963).

Nouveau Réalisme A phrase coined by the French critic Pierre Restany in 1960 in reference to certain contemporary painters and sculptors who incorporated real objects (often junk or other commonplace items) into their work. The movement had affinities with both POP ART and with Junk art. Restany also regarded Dada as a forerunner; in 1961 he organized an exhibition called '40 Degrees Above Dada' at his Galerie J in Paris. In the following year an exhibition called 'New Realists' was held at the Sidney Janis Gallery in New York. Among the artists whose work was shown in both exhibitions were ARMAN, CÉSAR, and TINGUELY.

In the 1960s exponents of Nouveau Réalisme were loosely referred to by several other names, notably Neo-Dadaists, Factualists, and Popular Realists. To add to the confusion, the term 'New Realism' has also been used in a completely different sense, to refer to a revival of naturalistic figurative painting that came in the wake of Abstract Expressionism.

nouveau roman (French: new novel) A type of experimental novel that developed in France in the 1950s and 1960s. Although differing considerably in their aims and methods, such writers as Alain ROBBE-GRILLET, Michel BUTOR, Nathalie SARRAUTE, and Claude SIMON shared a distrust of most of the standard novelistic conventions. In their works sequential plot, stable and consistent characters, and the use of an omniscient narrator are all dispensed with, chiefly on the grounds that such conventions create an effect of coherence – both in the external world and in the individual psyche – that is belied by our experience. Instead, *nouveaux romans* tend to dwell on minute physical and mental impressions, which the reader is generally left to interpret for him or herself.

The term *nouveau roman* began to be used in the mid 1950s but was given a much wider currency by Robbe-Grillet's critical manifesto *Pour un nouveau roman* (1963). Sarraute's collection of critical essays *The Age of Suspicion* (1956) is another important statement of the thinking behind these developments. *See also* ANTI-NOVEL.

Nouvelle Tendance (French: New Tendency) A broad movement in the visual arts in the early 1960s, characterized by the revival of constructivist values, the use of new materials and technologies, and a conscious rejection of traditional aesthetic norms. The first of several exhibitions under the 'Nove Tendencje' banner was held in Zagreb in 1961 and the name was quickly adopted by groups of artists working in France and Germany. The movement was in many respects a reaction against the subjective excesses of abstract expressionism and ART INFORMEL. Exponents of the Nouvelle Tendance cultivated a deliberately depersonalized style and often chose to work in groups (*see* GROUPE DE RECHERCHE D'ART VISUEL; GROUP ZERO). The artists associated with the movement, such as Viktor VASARELY and Gerhard von GRAEVENITZ, often had a strong interest in KINETIC ART and the aesthetic use of light and sound. Otherwise the Nouvelle Tendance shared many aims with MINIMAL ART.

Noventa, Giacomo (Giacomo Ca'Zorzi; 1898–1960) Italian poet. After taking a philosophy degree from Turin University, Noventa travelled in Germany, France, and Spain, where he made contact with anti-Fascists such as the Rosselli brothers and Carlo LEVI. Back in Italy, he was among the founders of *La riforma letteraia* (1936–39), a journal that aroused much controversy within the official culture of the time. Here he developed his ideological position, a personal blend of Catholicism and Marxism. A brilliant conversationalist, he wrote his poetry for reading aloud rather than the printed page. His pieces were collected in *Verses and Poems* (1956, 1966), edited by his close friends Pampaloni and FORTINI. The poems are in the Romantic tradition and make use of the Venetian dialect to express values considered outmoded by modern culture. Noventa also wrote a substantial number of essays, most of which were published posthumously in such collections as *Nothing New* (1960), *Beethoven's Breeches* (1965), *Café Greco* (1969), and *History of a Heresy* (1973).

Novomeský, Ladislav (1904–76) Slovak poet. Educated in Budapest and at the Teachers' Institute in Modra (Slovakia), Novomeský began teaching at an elementary school in Bratislava in 1923. After joining the Communist Party (1925) he worked for the party press. Following the German occupation of the Bohemian lands (1939) he moved back to Bratislava; he spent some months in the Ilava concentration camp (1940) and, as a member of the underground central committee, helped organize the Slovak national uprising (1944). From 1945 to 1950 he held senior party and government posts but in 1951 was expelled from the party as a 'bourgeois nationalist', in 1954 sent to prison, conditionally discharged in 1955, and rehabilitated in 1963. In 1968 he became a member of the praesidium of the Slovak, and in 1969 of the Czechoslovak, Communist Party.

Novomeský's first collection, *Sunday* (1927), was intended as Proletarian Poetry but was in fact, for all its melancholy, a close relation of Czech vitalist avant-garde verse, as represented by Vítěslav Nezval (1900–58). In contrast to the Proletarian Poets, he did not believe that poetry could change society, although *Sunday* includes stark but melodious poems of social protest. *Rhomboid* (1932), the imagery of which is based on various geometrical shapes, combines playfulness with intimate melancholy in a series of picture poems that approach surrealism. *Opened Windows* (1935) is an attempt at assessing what it means to be Slovak. The first collection he published after release from prison, *Vila Tereza* (1963), named after the Soviet legation's residence in Prague, is a cycle in praise of the Russian Revolution,

Lenin, and Czech avant-garde poets of the 1920s and 1930s (though he doubts the purity of their ideology). The most powerful of Novomeský's collections is *From There and Other Poems* (1964), a sometimes bitter but generally life-affirming reckoning with the 1950s, in particular his own trial and imprisonment.

Nureyev, Rudolf (Hametovich) (1938–93) Russian-born ballet dancer and choreographer, an Austrian citizen since 1982, who became the best-known dancer of the latter half of the 20th century. Born on a train near Irkutsk, he began as an amateur (due to parental objections) and subsequently joined the Kirov Ballet, where he quickly acquired a reputation as a prodigiously talented (and untameable) performer. While appearing in *Sleeping Beauty* in Paris in 1961, he applied for political asylum and within days was dancing with some of the best companies in the West. In the years after his defection he continued to wander from company to company, dancing the most demanding roles in the repertory with unrivalled panache. He won particular praise for his partnership with Margot Fonteyn at the ROYAL BALLET in the 1960s, as well as for his creation of leading roles in ballets by such major choreographers as ASHTON, PETIT, van DANTZIG, BÉJART, Tetley, Graham, and Balanchine.

Nureyev made his debut as a choreographer in the early 1960s, when he staged several works by Marius Petipa; in 1966 he devised his first original ballet, *Tancredi* (which met with a mixed response). His ballets since then have included *Manfred* (1979), *The Tempest* (1982), *Washington Square* (1985), and *Cinderella* (1986). As artistic director of the Paris Opéra Ballet (1983–89) he restored its reputation as one of the world's most prestigious companies with a varied programme of classical works and pieces by such contemporary choreographers as Michael CLARK. Nureyev's films include *Valentino* (1977; directed by Ken RUSSELL) and *Exposed* (1982). His decision to continue to tour as a dancer in his fifties was generally regarded as a mistake.

Nykvist, Sven (1922–) Swedish cinematographer, who won two Oscars for his work with Ingmar BERGMAN. He began his career as a 19-year-old assistant cameraman and four years later was promoted to cinematographer for *13 Chairs* (1945). *Under the Southern Cross* (1952) was a documentary about Albert Schweitzer that he also codirected and coscripted. Nykvist made his name through his long association with Bergman, which began with *The Virgin Spring* (1960). His photography, with its stark contrasts of light and dark, helped to establish the sombre mood of films such as *Through a Glass Darkly* (1961), *Winter Light* (1963), and *The Silence* (1963). Nykvist won a 1972 Academy Award for best cinematography for his work on Bergman's *Cries and Whispers*. His other Bergman films were *Autumn Sonata* (1978) and *Fanny and Alexander* (1982), for which Nykvist won his second Academy Award.

As his reputation grew, Nykvist was brought to Hollywood to make a series of films, beginning with *The Last Run* (1971), a gangster story set in a Portuguese fishing village. This was followed by *The Dove* (1974), a beautifully filmed sea adventure, Louis MALLE's *Pretty Baby* (1978), and the Dino DE LAURENTIIS films *King of the Gypsies* (1978) and *The Hurricane* (1979). His more recent US work has included *Starting Over* (1979), *Willie and Phil* (1980), an update of TRUFFAUT's *Jules et Jim*, and two sex-and-murder plots, *The Postman Always Rings Twice* (1981) and *Star 80* (1983). He returned to the Swedish cinema in 1991 when he directed *The Ox*, starring Bergman's old company players Liv Ullmann and Max von Sydow.

O

Oakeshott, Michael (1901–90) British historian, historiographer, and philosopher. A history lecturer at Cambridge University from 1929 until 1949, Oakeshott subsequently (1960) accepted a chair in political science at the London School of Economics, holding it until his retirement in 1969.

Oakeshott is best known for his political writings, which are the product of a fundamentally sceptical and conservative outlook. An ideological heir of Burke, he saw society not as a productive unit, but as a heterogeneous assemblage, held together by law, habit, and loyalty. In his view political activity should be directed primarily towards the carrying on of the governance of the nation, rather than towards any grand schemes of social reform. The state should not seek actively to promote the welfare of the governed but rather to ensure the maximum possible liberty of each individual to pursue his or her own particular interests. Oakeshott was especially concerned for the British tradition of individual liberty and wary of any accretion of power in any organization, as *ipso facto* subject to corruption. These ideas made him an important influence on the 'New Conservatism' of the late 1970s and 1980s.

His published works included *Rationalism in Politics* (1962), *Of Human Conduct* (1975), *On History* (1983), and *The Voice of Liberal Learning* (1989).

O'Connor, Frank (Michael Francis O'Donovan; 1903–66) Irish writer, best known for his short stories. Born to a poor family in Cork, he was largely self-educated. He began his career as a librarian and subsequently became director of the Abbey Theatre, Dublin. His first collection of short stories, *Guests of the Nation* (1931), was followed by *Bones of Contention* (1936) and *The Big Fellow* (1937), a biography of Michael Collins, the Irish political and military leader. His subsequent collections of short stories include *Crab Apple Jelly* (1944), *Traveller's Samples* (1951), and *Domestic Relations* (1957). Most of his stories describe the frustrations of middle- and lower-class life in the claustrophobic atmosphere of provincial Ireland.

After a spell teaching in the US, he produced two volumes of autobiography, *An Only Child* (1961) and *My Father's Son* (1969). He is also known for his verse translations from Gaelic and his anthologies of Irish poetry and prose. His criticism includes *The Lonely Voice* (1963), a volume on the art of the short story.

Odin Teatret *See* BARBA, EUGENIO.

Oelze, Richard (1900–80) German painter. Oelze was a maverick figure who led an unsettled and unstable life and to whom recognition came late. Born in Magdeburg, he studied at the Bauhaus in Weimar (1921–25) and worked in Dresden and Berlin before moving in 1933 to Paris. There he came into contact with the Surrealists; although his work was shown at the famous International Surrealist Exhibition in London in 1936 he generally remained aloof from their group activities. After short periods in Switzerland and Italy he returned to Germany in 1938 and was drafted into the army as a cartographer. After World War II he settled at Worpswede, a north German village formerly renowned for its artistic colony (one of the springboards of German expressionism), and in 1962 he moved finally to Postenholz near Hameln. Notoriously taciturn and a lover of solitude, he led a fringe existence and often suffered poverty. From about 1960 his work gained increasing recognition and he was awarded several distinctions, including the Max Beckmann Prize of the City of Frankfurt (1978), which characteristically was conferred in his absence.

Oelze was trained in a precise naturalistic style (*see* MAGIC REALISM) and he used it to create images that often have a strong feeling of science-fiction eeriness. His most reproduced work is *Expectation* (1936, Museum of Modern Art, New York), showing a group of apprehensive figures – most of them with their backs to the spectator – looking at or for something unseen in the sky.

Office for Metropolitan Architecture *See* KOOLHAAS, REM.

Okudzhava, Bulat Shalvovich (1924–) Russian poet and novelist. Although of mixed Caucasian origin, he was brought up in Moscow and writes only in Russian. After World War II, for which he volunteered before completing his schooling, he studied at Tiflis University and then taught in a village school. In 1956 a first book, *Lyrics*, appeared in the provincial town of Kaluga. From 1957 Okudzhava began to perform his poems to guitar accompaniment, at first unofficially and then, from 1960, publicly, quickly winning widespread affection and respect as a brave antimilitarist and unromantic but affecting poet of everyday Moscow life. After a second book of poems, *October* (1959), there appeared a harshly criticized short novel, *Good Luck, Schoolboy* (1961), which presented an autobiographical and completely unheroic, yet very memorable, picture of a young soldier's life at the front. Since then Okudzhava has also shown great courage by stating publicly that the last war was neither great nor patriotic but cruel and terrible.

Okudzhava has also written a series of historical novels: *Poor Avrosimov* (1969), *Merci, or the Adventures of Shipov* (1971), and, particularly entertainingly, *Journey of the Dilettantes* (1976–78), which describes St Petersburg high society in the middle of the last century. He has continued to write and publish poetry but it is for his early guitar-accompanied verses that he is likely to be best remembered.

Olivier, Laurence (Kerr), Baron (1907–89) British stage and screen actor, director, and producer, who became the first director (1963–73) of the National Theatre (*see* ROYAL NATIONAL THEATRE). Olivier's reputation as Britain's leading classical actor was established before World War II. He directed as well as taking the leading roles in the Shakespearean films *Henry V* (1944), *Hamlet* (1948), and *Richard III* (1956). After the war he became a codirector of the Old Vic company and pressed for the long-overdue foundation of a recognized national theatre company. He continued to win the approbation of the critics as actor-manager of the Old Vic company in the 1950s, scoring a particular triumph with a season at Stratford-upon-Avon in 1955. Two years later he showed his sympathy with the new British drama by taking the leading role of Archie Rice in John OSBORNE's *The Entertainer* (1957). From 1961 to 1963 he was director of the Chichester Festival Theatre; he then accepted the post of director of the newly established National Theatre, where he appeared in plays by Congreve, Chekhov, Shakespeare, and many others. He also continued to pursue the film career he had begun before the war, often producing and directing the films in which he appeared. The Society of West End Theatre presents the Laurence Olivier awards annually in his honour, and one of the theatres in the Royal National Theatre bears his name. He was the first actor to be honoured with a peerage (1970).

Olmi, Ermanno (1931–) Italian film director and screenwriter. Olmi was born into a peasant family and began work as a clerk in the Edison-Volta electric plant, where he took part in stage and film projects sponsored by the company. He advanced to become the producer and director of the electrical industry's documentary films and between 1952 and 1959 made some 40 short documentaries. He moved into features with the semidocumentary *Time Stood Still* (1959), following this with a series of films notable for the gentle realism and understated dignity with which they depict the lives of their mainly working-class characters. Olmi's almost neorealistic style (*see* NEOREALISM) is characterized by straightforward camerawork and the use of nonprofessional actors. By the late 1960s Olmi had moved into Italian television drama, although films such as *The Scavengers* (1969), *During the Summer* (1971), which he coscripted, photographed, and edited, and *The Circumstance* (1974) were subsequently released to cinemas. He was awarded the Gold Palm at the 1978 CANNES FILM FES-

TIVAL for *The Tree of Wooden Clogs*, a three-hour epic about a peasant family in 19th-century Lombardy that has come to be regarded as a classic of modern Italian cinema.

In 1980 he founded an innovative film school, Ipotesi Cinema, and has supervised the making of many shorts there by young film-makers. In 1987 he directed *Long Live the Lady*, an allegory about capitalism and freedom. A year later, Olmi was awarded the Golden Lion at the Venice Festival for *The Legend of the Holy Drinker*, adapted from Joseph Roth's novel. In 1991 he made *Down the River*, a documentary about the pollution of the river Po.

Oort, Jan Hendrik (1931–92) Dutch astrophysicist. Oort studied at Groningen University and was appointed astronomer at Leiden Observatory in 1924, later becoming director (1947–70).

Oort's initial work was largely concerned with the study of the Galaxy. He expanded on the work by the Swedish astronomer Bertil Linblad, confirming the position of the sun relative to the galactic centre in Sagittarius and determining a reasonably accurate mass for the Galaxy. After the discovery of the 21-cm radio emission from neutral hydrogen (by van de Hulst) in 1951, Oort was able to map the spiral arms, and thus the large-scale structure of the Galaxy. In 1950 he suggested that comets have their origin in a distant spherical shell, about one light-year in radius. This is now known as the Oort Cloud. In 1956 Oort and Theodore Walraven determined that light from the Crab nebula, the remnant of a supernova explosion in 1054 AD, is polarized and thus arose by 'synchrotron radiation', emitted by electrons moving in extremely strong magnetic fields.

Op art A type of abstract art in which the artist exploits certain optical phenomena to create patterns that seem to flicker or vibrate. Op art flourished chiefly in the 1960s; the term – an abbreviation of 'optical art' (on the analogy of POP ART) – was first used in print in *Time* magazine in 1964 and achieved wide currency in 1965 with the exhibition 'The Responsive Eye' at the Museum of Modern Art in New York. Most of the works shown were characterized by repeated small-scale patterns (often alternating 'positive' and 'negative' forms) arranged in such a way as to suggest underlying secondary shapes. This type of picture, essentially a development of the kind of optical illusion to be found in psychology textbooks, remains the most familiar form of Op art (partly because it retains much of its effect in reproduction). The genre also embraces constructions that depend on light and/or movement for their effect; thus the fields of Op and KINETIC ART sometimes overlap. The two best-known exponents of Op art are Victor VASARELY and Bridget RILEY. Their work illustrates not only the vigour and sophistication of the best Op art but also the considerable impact it made on popular design in the 1960s; a Vasarely has been used on the plastic carrier bag given away by a chain of French stores and in 1965 Riley unsuccessfully tried to sue a fashion company for using one of her designs on a dress.

Opéra Bastille An opera house (capacity 2700) in the Place de la Bastille, Paris, designed by the Canadian architect Carlos Ott and opened in July 1989 to celebrate the bicentennial of the French Revolution. The project was instigated by François Mitterand with the aim of providing a world-class venue capable of staging innovative productions for a mass audience. The building represents a considerable architectural and technical achievement and provides staging facilities that are the envy of opera companies worldwide. In January 1989, however, only months before the grand opening, the euphoria surrounding the project was marred by a bitter controversy provoked by the sacking of the musical director Daniel Barenboim. He was replaced by the South Korean pianist and conductor Myung-Whun Chung.

Orchestre de Paris French symphony orchestra founded in 1967 by the conductor Charles MÜNCH as successor to the disbanded Paris Conservatoire Orchestra. It was the first fully state-subsidized concert orchestra in Paris and made its debut under Münch on 15 November 1967. Other conductors have included Herbert von KARAJAN, Sir Georg SOLTI, and (1975–89) Daniel Barenboim.

Orff, Carl (1895–1982) German composer and music teacher. Born in Munich, Orff studied at the Munich Academy and with the composer Heinrich Kaminski. In 1924 he cofounded the Günther School, Munich, the beginning of a lifelong interest in music education for children. He also worked as an editor of the works of Monteverdi. His own compositions, almost all of which were originally written for the stage, reflect his interest in primitive musical styles in their driving ostinato rhythms, basic harmony, and heavy use of percussion; important influences were Stravinsky and medieval music, especially plainsong. The remarkably successful *Carmina Burana* (1937), inspired by a group of secular medieval Latin songs, exemplifies the physicality and excitement of Orff's mature work. Other major works include *Orpheus* (1925), *Catulli carmina* (1943), *Der Mond* (1939), *Antigonae* (1949) *Astutuli* (1952), *Oedipus der Tyrann* (1959) and *Ein Sommernachtstraum* (1964; incidental music for Shakespeare's *A Midsummer Night's Dream*). Orff also gave his name to the system of music education Orff-Schulwerk, which aims to develop children's musical sensibility through dance, songs, and the use of simple tuned percussion instruments.

Orkeny, Istvan (1912–79) Hungarian playwright, who built up a strong reputation with plays exploring the absurdities of life in communist Hungary. His experiences as a soldier and a prisoner of war in World War II had a profound effect upon his early works, which are written in a highly naturalistic style. In the 1960s he developed the 'grotesque' manner for which he became famous in a series of satires on everyday life in Hungary, winning great acclaim for such absurdist pieces as *The Toth Family* (1967), *Stevie in the Bloodstorm* (1969), *Blood Relations* (1974), *Keysearchers* (1975), and *Screenplay* (1979). His most successful play was, however, *Catsplay* (1966) – a nostalgic recreation of life in Hungary prior to World War I that has been toured widely throughout Europe.

Orlikowsky, Vaslav (1921–) Soviet-born Swiss dancer, choreographer, and ballet director, who led a revival in Swiss ballet in the 1950s and 1960s. Born in Kharkov, Orlikowsky began his career as a dancer with companies in Kharkov, Tiflis, Prague, and Lvov and also toured widely with the company of Antonina Tumkovskaya. In 1950 he became ballet master of the Classic Russian Ballet in Munich, moving two years later to take over the company at Oberhausen – where he produced the first post-war German version of *Swan Lake* (1955). In 1955 he became ballet master of the Basel Ballet.

During his period (1955–67) as head of the Basel Ballet the company led a resurgence in Swiss dance with a series of classical productions under his direction; the most successful included *Sleeping Beauty*, *The Nutcracker*, and *Romeo and Juliet*. Among other works were *Fountain of Bakhchisarai*, *Peer Gynt*, and *The Prince of the Pagodas*. Eventually Orlikowsky handed control of the Basel Ballet to his protégé Heinz SPOERLI and accepted the directorship of the Vienna State Opera (1966–71); subsequently he took over as director of the Graz Opera.

Ortese, Anna Maria (1914–) Italian novelist and short-story writer. Born and brought up in Rome, she lived in Naples in the 1930s and subsequently in Milan, Rome, and Rapallo. She has been a regular contributor to Italian journals and newspapers. The combination of fiction and nonfiction, the fabulous and the autobiographical, in her work has led some critics to see her as an early exponent of MAGIC REALISM. Her first publication, the collection of stories *Angelic Sorrows* (1937), was followed by the novel that established her early reputation, *The Bay is not Naples* (1953). First published in VITTORINI's journal *Gettoni*, the novel depicts poverty and loneliness in the Neapolitan slums in a style that mixes realism with reverie. Other works include *Silence in Milan* (1958), the fantasy novel *Iguana* (1965), the Strega-Prize-winning *Poor and Simple People* (1967), which portrays the life of her neighbourhood, *The Moon on the Wall* (1968), *The Harbour of Toledo* (1975), and *The Plumed Hat* (1979). Recent publications include *The Russian Train* (1983), a collection of stories written 20 years earlier, and a new series of stories *Between Sleeping and Waking* (1987).

Orton, Joe (1933–67) British playwright, who enjoyed considerable success with a series of outrageous black comedies before his murder at the hands of his homosexual lover. Orton's plays are chiefly parodies of popular theatre, lampooning the conventions of farce and satirizing public morality. Sexual deviation and official corruption are themes that run through his best-known plays, which are *Entertaining Mr Sloane* (1964), in which a murderer finds himself at the mercy of two people he hoped to exploit, *Loot* (1965), in which much of the comedy revolves around attempts to dispose of a dead body, and *What the Butler Saw* (1969), an hilarious farce set in a psychiatrist's consulting room. Several of the plays were given West End productions and have been regularly revived since Orton's death. The circumstances of his murder and his well-documented homosexuality at a time when pressure was mounting for increased sexual tolerance in Britain provided the material for a provocative biography, *Prick Up Your Ears* by John Larr, which was subsequently filmed (1987).

Osborne, John (James) (1929–) British playwright and actor, who established his reputation as the leading representative of the so-called ANGRY YOUNG MEN of the 1950s. Osborne's *Look Back in Anger* (1956), the first of the author's plays to be accepted for production, ushered in a new era in British theatre with its attacks on conventional middle-class values and its introduction of the vituperative antihero, Jimmy Porter. The forerunner of many so-called kitchen-sink dramas, it provided the ENGLISH STAGE COMPANY at the Royal Court Theatre with one of its greatest triumphs. Subsequently Osborne consolidated his success with *The Entertainer* (1960), about a seedy music-hall comedian, which appeared at the Royal Court with OLIVIER in the main role. Among the plays that followed, the best received have been *Luther* (1961), *Inadmissible Evidence* (1964), *The Hotel in Amsterdam* (1968), and *A Patriot for Me* (1969). In the 1970s, however, such plays as *West of Suez* (1971) and *A Sense of Detachment* (1973) failed to please either audiences or critics. Osborne had no new play produced on the British stage between the failure of *Watch It Come Down* (1975) and the premiere of *Déjà Vu* (1992), a sequel to *Look Back in Anger* that looks at Jimmy Porter 35 years after his first appearance.

Osborne has also written for television and the cinema and was a director of the influential Woodfall film company, which filmed several classic plays of the 1950s and 1960s. His screenplay for *Tom Jones* (1964) won him an Oscar. He has written two volumes of autobiography; *A Better Class of Person* (1981) deals with his early life and gives a deeply hostile picture of his mother, while *Almost a Gentleman* (1991) has been described as by a critic as 'dancing on the graves' of two of his deceased wives, the actresses Mary Ure and Jill Bennett.

Osborne, Nigel (1948–) British composer. Born in Manchester, he studied under Egon Wellesz at Oxford University and then with Witold Rudziński in Warsaw (1970–71), where he also began to work with a live electronic music group. In 1971 his cantata *7 Words* won the Swiss Radio prize. His opera *The Electrification of the Soviet Union*, with a text by Craig Raine after PASTERNAK, was performed at Glyndebourne in 1987. His fascination with modern Russian literature is also apparent from *Remembering Esenin* (1974) for voice and piano, and the poetry settings in *The Sickle* (1975) for soprano and orchestra. His prolific output also includes *Heaven-tree* (1973), a setting from Joyce's *Ulysses* for unaccompanied chorus, *I am Goya* (1977) for baritone and four instruments, *In Camera*, (1979) for 13 instruments, a flute concerto (1980), and two sinfonias for orchestra (1982, 1983). His most recent work includes *Terrible Mouth* (1992), an opera about Goya with a libretto by Howard BARKER.

Otero, Blas de (1916–79) Spanish poet. Born in Bilbao, Otero is usually considered the most significant Spanish poet to have emerged since the Civil War. His early work is introspective and much taken up with religious and metaphysical broodings; the influence of the thinker and poet Miguel de Unamuno (1864–1936) is predominant. At this stage his style was intricate and rich in imagery. After World War II Otero became convinced of the need for radical change in Spanish society and began to preach a gospel of social and political liberation. As the content of his work shifted, his style became increasingly direct in order to appeal to the 'immense majority' of working men and women for whom he now claimed to speak. Many of his post-war works were banned or censored in Spain. The poems in *Fiercely Human Angel* (1950) and *Drumroll of Conscience* (1951), his most powerful collections, reflect the tensions between his political anarchism and his religious yearnings, and between both of these and his personal desires and passions. The style is intense and anguished. Less fine are *I ask* *for Peace and the Right to Speak* (1955), where Otero's anger becomes repetitive, and *In Castilian* (1959). *Ancia* (1958), an excellent anthology of earlier work, was censored. Later volumes include *About Spain* (1964), *Expression and Reunion, 1941–69* (1969), and *Meanwhile* and *Written for* (both 1974).

Otto, Frei (1925–) German architect specializing in tensile structures, an interest he developed from his early fascination with aircraft. After military service he studied at the Technical University, Berlin (1947–52) and in 1953 published his doctoral thesis on suspended roofs. In 1967 and 1969 followed the two-volume *Tensile Structures*, the first part dealing with *Pneumatics* and the second with *Cable Nets and Membranes*.

Apart from a housing estate built in 1955, all Otto's work is with lightweight structures. He is said to have 'reinvented the tent' to produce a novel architecture at once practical and romantic. His elaborately sculptural fabric roofs on steel cables were initially successful in Germany's many garden exhibitions. In 1957 Otto founded the Development Centre for Lightweight Construction in Berlin with the tentmaker Peter Stromeyer. From their research evolved a series of retractable roofs for open-air pools and theatres, for instance at Bad Hersfeld (1968), and larger cable-net tents for exhibitions at Lausanne (1964), and Montreal (Expo '67). From these evolved the vast and beautiful roofs of the Olympic stadium at Munich (1970–74). Otto has since explored lattice shell construction to build permanent tents of huge size, chief among which have been a hotel, conference centre, and mosque in Riyadh (1967–76) and a sports hall in Jeddah (1979–81), both with Rolf Gutbrod and Tom Happold of Ove ARUP and Partners.

Otto, Teo (1904–68) German stage designer, who was involved with the first performances of several of BRECHT's most celebrated plays. A graduate of the Bauhaus, Otto began his career in stage design with sets for several radical political plays in the 1920s. He subsequently executed designs for the Kroll Opera in Berlin before emigrating to Switzerland in 1933. He met Brecht in Zürich and went on to produce striking designs for the premieres of *Mother Courage* (1941), *Galileo* (1943), and *The Good Person of Setzuan* (1943). After World War II he worked on the first performances of major works by DÜRRENMATT and FRISCH and consolidated his reputation as a designer for the opera; his atmospheric but often severe designs were seen at leading venues throughout Europe in the 1950s. Of particular note were his designs for Gustav Gründgens's revival of Goethe's *Faust* in 1957. He was also the author of two books on theatrical design, *Never Again* and *My Scene*.

P

Pablo, Luis de (1930–) Spanish composer and teacher. One of the most influential figures in contemporary Spanish music, Pablo is self-taught as a composer, having studied law at Madrid University, where he later became a music professor. In 1957 he was one of the founding members of the Grupo Nueva Música in Madrid, which in 1958 established its concert series Tiempo y Música for the promotion of new music. 1958 was also the year in which Pablo first attended the summer course at DARMSTADT. In 1965 the Grupo Nueva Música was superseded by the group Alea, which in 1968 became a live electronic ensemble.

Despite its intellectual cast, Pablo's music shows an obvious delight in rhythm. His musical language developed from a style dominated by MOMPOU and Falla, through a period when Stravinsky and Bartók were the main influences, to atonality and then SERIALISM in the mid 1950s. His first serial work was *Cinco invenciones* (1957) for flute or violin and piano, which he numbered 'op. 1', suppressing all previous works; the last orthodox serial piece was *Cuatro invenciones* for orchestra (1959; revised 1962). This phase was followed by freer post-serialist works, which display a fondness for abstract structures. The aleatoric works of the 1960s explore new forms built up from 'modules' – Pablo's term for the smallest possible musically coherent unit. Works of this period include *Radial* (1960) and *Libro para el pianista* (1961). His fascination with electronics in the late 1960s and 1970s coincided with a newfound interest in theatre works. His output is extensive, consisting mostly of instrumental and electronic pieces.

Pagnol, Marcel (1895–1974) French writer and film-maker. Pagnol grew up in Marseille and after service in World War I worked as a schoolteacher, writing novels and plays on the side.

His breakthrough came with *Topaze* (1928), a comedy play about a shy schoolteacher who is initially used as a front by a ruthless businessman but later outwits him. Pagnol then enjoyed further success with the trilogy of plays *Marius* (1929), *Fanny* (1931), and *César* (1936), about a fishing family in Marseille. In the 1930s Pagnol became involved in the film business, starting the magazine *Cahiers du Film* in 1931 and opening his own studios near Marseille in 1934. He had already turned the first two parts of his Marseille trilogy into screenplays for other directors, and in 1936 he filmed the third part himself. In collaboration with the Provençal novelist Jean Giono, Pagnol went on to create a series of classic films set in the South of France: *Harvest* (*Regain*; 1937), *The Baker's Wife* (1938), and *The Well-Digger's Daughter* (1940). His most successful post-war film was his adaptation of Daudet's *Lettres de mon moulin* (1954).

In 1946 Pagnol became the first movie maker to be elected to the Académie Française. In 1957 he published a memoir evoking his idyllic childhood in Provence, *La Gloire de mon père*, following this with a similar volume, *Le Château de ma mere*, a year later. The autobiographical sequence continued with *The Time of Secrets* (1960) and *The Time of Love*, published posthumously in 1977.

Recent years have seen a remarkable upsurge of interest in Pagnol's work. In the late 1980s BERRI's two-part film *Jean de Florette* (1986) and *Manon des Sources* (1987), adapted from two novels that Pagnol had based on his own earlier film *Manon des Sources* (1953), played to packed houses in France and abroad. This was followed by the Yves ROBERTS films *La Gloire de mon père* and *Le Château de ma mère* (both 1991), which dramatized incidents from Pagnol's memoirs.

Palitzsch, Peter (1918–) German theatre director, who did much to promote the EPIC THEATRE of Bertolt BRECHT in West Germany in the early 1960s. Palitzsch emerged as an important director with the BERLINER ENSEMBLE, directing the first performance of Brecht's *The Resistible Rise of Arturo Ui* in 1959. His influential productions have included his adaptation of the ROYAL SHAKESPEARE COMPANY's *The Wars of the Roses* cycle (1967) and new plays by DORST and WALSER. In 1992 he was one of five leading directors brought in to save the ailing Berliner Ensemble from collapse.

Panduro, Leif (1923–77) Danish novelist and writer. After a tragic youth in occupied Denmark, Panduro began to write as a form of therapy. He published his first novel, the satirical *Out, My Gold Tooth*, in 1951; the main character is, like Panduro himself, a dentist.

Panduro's next novel, *Stuff Tradition!* (1958), concerns the attempts of David, a troubled adolescent, to avoid adult 'normality' and find his own way in the world. *The Indecent Ones* (1960) and *Lizard Days* (1961), perhaps his most ambitious book, explore similar themes of rebellion and conformity. Panduro's next three books, *Far from Denmark* (1963), *The Mistake* (1964), and *The Mad Man* (1965), portray older men and explore the problems of split identity.

The Way to Jutland (1966) is the humorous tale of a rich Danish-American coming home to Denmark. In *Daniel's Other World* (1970), a more sombre work, the protagonist lives in fear of becoming mad like his parents. His last novel, *Hayfever*, appeared in 1975.

Panduro reached a wider audience through his television plays, which include *In Pieces* (1966), *Goodbye Thomas* (1968), *Bella* (1970), *Home With William* (1971), and *Louise's House* (1977), in which a woman rebels against her husband's manipulative world. Panduro's deep sympathy for human weakness and his understanding portrayal of his characters endeared him greatly to his audience. He won many prizes including the Critic's Prize for 1963, the Danish Academy Literature Prize in 1971 and the Holberg Medal, also in 1971.

Pane, Gina (1939–) Franco-Italian body artist (*see* ACTION AND BODY ART). She was born in Biarritz, France, and has lived in Paris for most of her life (settling there in 1961) but acquired Italian nationality in 1960. She studied at the Liceo Artistico in Turin (1954–58) and the Ecole des Beaux-Arts in Paris (1961–66) and concentrated on painting, sculpture and lithography until 1968 when she turned to body art. Her performances, which are often recorded on video, generally involve self-inflicted pain, which she believes has a purifying effect necessary 'to reach an anaesthetized society'. In *Action Sentimentale* (1973) she pushed a row of tacks into her forearm and in other performances she has forced herself to regurgitate meat and has lain on an iron bed made painfully hot by candles burning underneath it. She writes that "My corporal experiments show that the body is invested and fashioned by Society; they have the aim of demystifying the common image of the body experienced as a bastion of our individuality". *See also* PERFORMANCE ART.

Pannenberg, Wolfhart (1928–) German Protestant theologian. Pannenberg has taught systematic theology in Heidelberg, Wuppertal, Mainz, and Munich (since 1967).

He is a leading proponent of the view that religious knowledge and human reason are complementary rather than incompatible. According to Pannenburg, theology must subject the various conceptions of God presented throughout the history of philosophy and theology to rational examination, avoiding any emotionalist approach. In his book *Revelation as History* (1961) he denies that there has been any final revelation of God in Biblical history, arguing rather that the whole of history must be considered the gradual self-revelation of God and that this process will remain incomplete until the end of time. The death and resurrection of Jesus Christ is seen as pointing to the end of history and the completion of God's revelation. In his book *Theology and the Philosophy of Science* (1976) he argues that all branches of human knowledge can contribute something to the understanding of God, who constitutes the hidden centre of everything. Other publications include *Jesus: God and Man* (1968), *Revelation as History* (1969), *The Apostle's Creed* (1972), *Christianity in a*

Secularized World (1989), and *Metaphysics and the Idea of God* (1990).

Panufnik, Sir Andrzej (1914–1991) Polish composer. Panufnik studied composition with Sikorski at the Warsaw Conservatory (1932–36) and conducting in Vienna (with Weingartner), Paris, and London. His early works were destroyed in the Warsaw uprising of 1944. He pursued a conducting career in Poland until 1954, when he moved to England, taking British nationality in 1961. From the 1960s onwards Panufnik gave up regular conducting, devoting himself to composition. In 1990 he returned for the first time to Poland, where his music had been banned for nearly 30 years. Knighted shortly before his death, he was posthumously awarded the Polish equivalent (the Knight's Cross of the Order of Polonia) on the orders of President Wałesa.

With LUTOSŁAWSKI, Panufnik was the major post-war figure in Polish music. However, the new political order in Poland, and the restrictions it placed upon artistic experimentation, caused a stylistic narrowing in Panufnik's music after 1948. With notable exceptions (*Sinfonia rustica*; 1948) the music of this period is remarkably conservative. The works of the early 1960s mark a return to the brilliance of earlier years. The *Sinfonia sacra* (1963) is generated from small fragments of ideas, which are developed in a mood of deep solemnity, a hallmark of Panufnik's later style. The *Universal Prayer* (1969), a choral setting of Pope's poem, evolves from a single group of three notes. His later scores combined this preoccupation with motivic economy with the use of geometric patterns to fashion the overall structure of a piece. The tenth symphony (1988), for example, uses elliptical shapes as the basis for its single-movement structure. Apart from his ten symphonies Panufnik's works include concertos for piano (1961) and violin (1971), three string quartets, and much ballet music. His last work, a concerto for cello, was given a posthumous first performance by Rostropovitch in 1992.

Paolozzi, Sir Eduardo (1924–) British sculptor and printmaker, born in Edinburgh of Italian parents. He studied at Edinburgh School of Art (1943) and at the Slade School of Fine Arts, London (1944–47). In 1947 he gave his first one-man exhibition as a sculptor at the Mayor Gallery, London, and in the same year he created his well-known collage *I Was a Rich Man's Plaything* (Tate Gallery, London), which is regarded as prefiguring POP ART. From 1947 until 1950 he lived in Paris, where he was influenced by the legacy of Dada and surrealism. In the early 1950s he was a member of the INDEPENDENT GROUP, whose meetings at the Institute of Contemporary Arts, London, were the nursery of British Pop art. His most characteristic works of the 1950s were bulky sculptures (often incorporating industrial components), showing his interest in modern technology and popular culture. In the 1960s his work became lighter and more colourful. Paolozzi enjoys working on a large scale and in the 1970s and 1980s he carried out several major public commissions in Britain and Germany, notably mosaics for Tottenham Court Road underground station in London (commissioned 1979, installed 1983–85). He was knighted in 1989.

Paradjanov, Sergo (1924-90) Russian film director. Born in Georgia of Armenian parents, Paradjanov studied both music and cinema prior to joining the Douzhenko Studios in Kiev as an assistant director. He made several shorts and features before directing the poetic *Shadows of Our Forgotten Ancestors* (1964), in which young love overcomes a quarrel between families. Paradjanov's rejection of socialist realism resulted in the Soviet authorities turning down ten of his suggested scripts in five years. Although he finally received permission to make *The Colour of Pomegranates* (1969), the first of a trilogy of tableaux films, this surrealistic treatment of the life of the 18th-century poet Sayat Nova was subsequently banned.

In 1973 Paradjanov was sentenced to six years hard labour for allegedly speculating in art and being a homosexual, amongst other offences. He served five years before worldwide protests secured his release and returned to the cinema in 1984 with *The Legend of the Suram Fortress*, the second part of his trilogy. The story of a young man who is buried alive when the walls of a crumbling fortress collapse on him, the film carried an obvious political symbolism. Nevertheless, the gathering cultural thaw in the Soviet Union permitted its release in the West. In 1986 Paradjanov completed his trilogy with *Ashik Kerib* and made the short *Arabesques on the Pirosmanashvili Theme*, a warm tribute to the Georgian folk painter Niko Pirosmanashvili (1863–1918).

Páral, Vladimír (1932–) Czech novelist. After taking a degree in chemical engineering, he worked in various factories until 1967, when he became a freelance writer, which he has remained, except for the period 1972–79, when he was a publisher's editor. His three experimental comic novels, *Tradefair of Fulfilled Desires* (1964), *Private Gale* (1966), and *Catapult* (1967), satirize socialist consumerism, food and sex fetishism, and the emotional desert of modern society; their characters, nearly all automata, try to escape boredom through sex, which leads to further boredom and in one case eventual death. Páral's masterpiece, *Lovers and Killers* (1969), depicts life as a permanent struggle between barbarian workers and *embourgeoisé* socialist management, while a helpless God looks on at man's destructive sexual and material greed. After *Joy Until Morn* (1975), a sarcastic satire on the petty-bourgeois ideals of post-Dubček socialist society, embellished by bouts of synchronized sex in prefabricated tower-blocks, Páral's novels begin to lose some of their vitality. At the same time they become ever more mockingly political; *Decameron 2000 or Love in Prague* (1990) represents this period of his work.

Parise, Goffredo (1929–86) Italian novelist and writer. Parise was born in Vicenza, where he spent most of his childhood and adolescence. In 1960 he moved to Rome, becoming a film scriptwriter and a journalist. *The Dead Boy and the Comets* (1951) marked his debut as a novelist. Like much of his later work, this is notable for the author's close and ironic observation of the bigotted and provincial lower middle classes in a small northern Italian town. Events and characters alike develop a surreal quality owing to Parise's skilful use of the macabre and the grotesque. In his masterpiece *Don Gastone and the Ladies* (*Il prete bello*; 1954) Parise employs the same techniques to intensely satirical effect. The novel revolves around the figure of the vain Don Gastone, a failed social climber who becomes a priest, and the life of his parish during the years of Fascism.

Other works include *The Boss* (1965), a grotesque allegory of capitalism, *The Vienna Crematorium* (1969), and the collections of prose poetry *Spelling Book I* (1972) and *Spelling Book II* (1982). He also produced a number of travel books including *Dear China* (1966), *Two or Three Things about Vietnam* (1967), *Biafra* (1968), and *New York* (1977).

Parker, Alan (William) (1944–) British film director, screenwriter, and novelist. Parker began his career in television. His first successful cinema feature was the popular gangster-film parody *Bugsy Malone* (1975), made with a cast of children. He enjoyed further commercial success with *Midnight Express* (1978), about the experiences of a drug smuggler in a Turkish prison, *Fame* (1979), about a school for the performing arts in New York, and *The Wall* (1982), based on the album by the rock group Pink Floyd. Although he has been admired for his technical virtuosity, his films have sometimes been criticized for their alleged lack of content. *Mississippi Burning* (1988) was a controversial and emotionally charged thriller about an investigation into the murder of three civil rights workers in Mississippi in 1964. Parker's most recent film was *The Commitments* (1991), an exhilarating depiction of an aspiring soul combo in working-class Dublin.

Pärt, Arvo (1935–) Estonian composer. Pärt studied composition with Heino Eller at the Tallin Conservatory until 1963 and worked with Estonian state radio (1958–67). He soon advanced beyond the officially approved style of his early works to explore the possibilities of serialism, *klangfarbenmelodien*, collage techniques, aleatory procedures, minimalism, and avant-garde methods. At the same time he has retained an essentially conservative approach to melody, harmony, and structure that makes his work more accessible than much contemporary music. His output includes *Nekroloog* (1960) for orchestra; three symphonies (1964, 1966, 1971); *Credo* (1968) for piano, chorus, and orchestra; *Tabula Rasa* (1977), for strings and piano; *Cantus in Memory of Benjamin Britten* (1977) for string orchestra and glockenspiel; and *If Bach had Kept Bees* (1978), a concertino for harpsichord, electric bass guitar, electronic tape, and ensemble. His work of the 1970s and 1980s has been profoundly influenced by the music and teaching of the Orthodox church. Pärt emigrated from the Soviet Union in 1980, settling in West Berlin in 1982. *See also* MINIMAL MUSIC.

Partridge, John A(lbert) *See* HOWELL, KILLICK, PARTRIDGE, AND AMIS.

Paskandi, Geza (1933–) Hungarian playwright, who made his reputation with a series of plays written in the absurdist tradition (*see* ABSURD, THEATRE OF THE). He spent his childhood in Romania, where he was imprisoned (1957–63), and subsequently (1974) moved to Budapest, where he continued to develop his so-called 'absurdoid' style. This differs from the classical absurdism of BECKETT or IONESCO, in that the absurdity is always presented as a result of human folly (often by the representatives of the state) rather than as a condition of existence itself. His best-known theatrical works include the history plays *Sojourn* (1970) and *Residents of the Windmill* (1981); his other writing includes poetry, essays, and short stories.

Pasmore, Victor (1908–) British painter, who has gained equal renown for his abstract and figurative work. Born at Chelsham, Surrey, he showed early artistic talent but the death of his father in 1926 prevented his going to art school; from 1927 to 1937 he worked as a clerk for the London County Council, attending evening classes at the Central School of Arts and Crafts. In 1934 he became a member of the London Group (a progressive exhibiting society founded in 1913). By this time he was experimenting with abstraction but he soon returned to naturalism; in 1937 he was one of the founders (with William COLDSTREAM) of the Euston Road School, which became the focal point for a distinctive type of sober direct figurative art.

In 1948, however, Pasmore suddenly turned to geometric abstract art, first in paintings and then (from 1951) in reliefs influenced by those of Ben NICHOLSON. In 1951–53, with Nicholson and Barbara HEPWORTH, he was a member of the Penwith Society, St Ives, which organized Britain's first post-war exhibitions devoted entirely to abstract art. From 1954 until 1961 Pasmore was head of the painting department at King's College, Newcastle upon Tyne (Durham University), where he proved an influential teacher, his 'basic design' course (based on Bauhaus ideas) spreading to many British art schools. He has been concerned to bring abstract art to the general public, notably as consulting architectural designer to Peterlee New Town, County Durham, a post to which he was appointed in 1955. Pasmore now lives in London and Malta.

Pasolini, Pier Paolo (1922–75) Italian film director, poet, novelist, and artist, whose films criticizing contemporary Italian society and morality aroused considerable controversy. A native of Bologna, he first established a reputation for his poems, novels, and other writings, drawing on his experiences of life in the slums of Rome, where he lived during the 1940s. His sympathy for the poor and his communist leanings were apparent from his first screenplays, which include those for FELLINI's *Nights of Cabiria* (1957) and BERTOLUCCI's *The Grim Reaper* (1962). Pasolini made his debut as a director with *Accattone* in 1961. This neorealist story of Rome's underworld and its inhabitants, in which Pasolini made effective use of non-professional actors, was widely praised; it also provided the director with an opportunity to expose the conflicts in a society that embraces both Catholicism and Marxism.

His second film, *Mamma Roma* (1962), treating similar themes and starring Anna Magnani, failed to match the confident style of its predecessor. Far more successful was his third film, *The Gospel According to St Matthew* (1964), in which Pasolini again examined the relationship between Christian and Marxist values, this time by filming the story of Christ with a peasant cast in poverty-stricken southern Italy.

After *Hawks and Sparrows* (1966), a strange fantasy in which a talking crow discusses Marxist theory with two peasants (and the credits are sung), Pasolini embarked on a series of films based on mythological subjects. *Oedipus Rex* (1967) was a virtually silent version of the legend, in which the Freudian aspects of the tragedy are brought to the fore.

Theorem (1968) was a provocative depiction of the shallowness of bourgeois values, while in *Pigsty* (1969) Pasolini ran together the stories of a medieval cannibal and a decadent rebel in contemporary Italy to demonstrate that modern morality is even less appealing than that of previous ages. Subsequent films included a trilogy based on the tales of sexual intrigue in Chaucer, *The Decameron*, and *The Arabian Nights*. His film career concluded with *Salò, or the 120 Days of Sodom* (1975), an odyssey into the extreme limits of sexual perversion, in which a notorious work by the Marquis de Sade is updated to Mussolini's Salò Republic.

Pasolini's murder – he was found, brutally beaten to death in the slums of Rome – was probably an outcome of his homosexual private life (although others have suggested that his allegations of corruption in the Italian Establishment may have had some bearing on the matter).

Pasternak, Boris (Leonidovich) (1890–1960) Russian poet, translator, and prose writer. His parents, Leonid, a celebrated painter and Roza (neé Kaufman), a talented pianist, were Jewish, but Pasternak claimed to have been baptised into the Orthodox Church as a child. Under the influence of his mother and the composer Scriabin, Pasternak seemed destined for a musical career. In 1909, however, he abandoned music for poetry. Strongly influenced by such figures as Aleksandr Blok, Andrei Belyi, Vladimir Maiakovsky, and Rainer Maria Rilke, he tended to avoid literary groupings. His desire to understand the revolutionary upheavals through which he lived can be seen in his narrative poems *1905* and *Lieutenant Schmidt*, both dating from 1927. He is better known, however, for the short lyrics in such collections as *Twin in the Stormclouds* (1914), *Over the Barriers* (1917), *My Sister Life* (1922), *Themes and Variations* (1923), *The Second Birth* (1932), *On Early Trains* (1943), and *When the Weather Clears* (1956–59). During the 1930s Pasternak was forced to turn to translating and produced classic versions of eight Shakespeare plays, including *Hamlet*.

In Russia Pasternak is known mainly as a poet; in the West, however, his fame rests largely on his novel of the Russian Revolution and Civil War *Dr Zhivago*, for which he was awarded the Nobel Prize for literature in 1958. The book was banned in Russia and published in Milan in 1957. After a vitriolic press campaign against him, Pasternak was forced to decline the prize. Sometimes described as a 'poet's novel', *Dr Zhivago* may be viewed as a prose commentary to the 25 poems that end the book. Only in 1988 was the novel published in Russia. Other prose works include *Childhood of Lyuvers* (1918), *The Tale* (1929), and two autobiographical pieces, *Safe Conduct* (1930) and *Autobiographical Essay* (1956).

Pasternak's influence on such modern Russian poets as VOZNESENSKY has been immense and his grave at Peredelkino, near Moscow, is a place of pilgrimage.

Paustovsky, Konstantin Georgievich (1892–1968) Russian prose writer. Born in Moscow, he spent his childhood in Kiev; his first story was published in 1911. From 1914 until 1923 he held a series of jobs, including tram conductor, medical orderly, factory worker, and journalist. While working as a journalist in Odessa in 1920 he met a number of writers of the Odessa School, who liked to contrast the colour and exoticism of the south with the northern greyness of St Petersburg. Chief among these was Izaak Babel' (1894–?1941), about whom Paustovsky left an important memoir and whose style influenced his early stories. After leaving Odessa, Paustovsky worked in the Caucasus before returning to Moscow in 1923. His first collection, *Sea Sketches*, appeared in 1925 and was followed by further collections in 1927 and 1928 and two five-year-plan novels, *Kara-Bugaz* (1932) and *Colchis* (1934). His later work is often set in the countryside around Riazan', where the author lived for 20 years. His fiction is, however, largely forgotten, with the exception of a few short stories. Best known among these is *The Telegram* (1946), based on a real-life incident and appropriated by KAZAKOV for the basic plot of his *Smell of Bread*. In 1955 he published *The Golden Rose*, a volume devoted to the writer's craft. Far more important are his memoirs, *Story of a Life* (1946–64), which established his position as the senior liberal figure in Russian literature. This position was consolidated by his speech in defence of DUDINTSEV's novel *Not by Bread Alone* in October 1956 and by his editing of two key documents of the THAW - the second volume of *Literary Moscow* and the almanac *Pages from Tarusa* (1961).

Pavese, Cesare (1908–50) Italian novelist, poet, critic, and translator. Pavese was born into a lower middle-class family of peasant origin in the Langhe district of Piedmont; the simplicity of his native region remained with him as an ideal for the rest of his life. After taking a degree in literature at Turin University, he worked as a translator of English and American literature, introducing the Italian public to works by Melville, Dos Passos, Defoe, and Joyce, amongst others. In the 1930s he was a founder of the Einaudi publishing house and worked for the anti-Fascist journal *La Cultura* until his imprisonment in 1935. After World War II he returned to Turin and worked for Einaudi until his suicide at the age of 42.

Pavese's experience of imprisonment is reflected in *Hard Labour* (1936), a collection of Whitmanesque poems written in gaol, and the story 'The Political Prisoner' (1949; written 1938–39). His first published novella *The Harvester* (1941) uses innovative and symbolically charged language to evoke his childhood landscapes. Like much of his later work it is strongly autobiographical and concerned with such themes as memory and the pain of solitude. His ideas about childhood, myth, and symbol are most clearly set out in his *Dialogues with Leukothea* (1947). Pavese's post-war novels, which made an important contribution to Italian NEOREALISM, include *August Holiday* (1946), *The Comrade* (1947), *Before the Cock Crows* (1949), *The House on the Hill* (1948), and *The Beautiful Summer* (1949), which won the Strega Prize. In *The Moon and the Bonfires* (1950), regarded by many as his best work, he again evokes the 'mythical reality' of Piedmontese country life and the mystery of childhood, while also addressing such historical realities as the wartime Resistance and the continuing class struggle.

Pavese's posthumously published works include the poignant love poems in *Death will come and its eyes will be yours* (1951), *American Literature: Essays and Opinion* (1951), a collection of critical writings dealing especially with the role of myth and symbol, and an important diary, *The Job of Living* (1952), which is highly revealing of both his personal uncertainties and his deliberations as an artist. *Festival Night* (1953) and *Hi, Masino* (1969) are collections of short stories written in the 1930s.

Pavić, Milorad (1929–) Yugoslav (Serbian) novelist. Pavić was born and educated in Belgrade. Finding himself unable to publish or follow an academic career in Tito's Yugoslavia, he left for the West as a young man. Subsequently he spent many years teaching literature at the Sorbonne and at various institutions in Germany. He is now professor of the history of literature at the University of Belgrade, where he specializes in the writing of the Serbian baroque era.

With his first novel, *The Dictionary of the Khazars*, published in 1984 but conceived some 30 years earlier, Pavić became one of the very few Serbo-Croat writers to find an international audience. The book became a bestseller in several Western countries and has been translated into over 25 languages. An erudite historical fantasy in the tradition of CALVINO and Borges, it is remarkable for its virtuoso style and structural ingenuity. Notoriously, the book appeared in two slightly but crucially different editions – one 'male', the other 'female'. This formal experimentation was taken even further in Pavić's second novel, *Landscape Painted With Tea* (1988), much of which appears in the form of a crossword; the chapters can be read either 'across' or 'down' to provide two different narratives.

For most Western readers, the playful and fantastic elements in Pavil's works wholly obscured their political content until the violent disintegration of Yugoslavia in the early 1990s brought such issues to world attention. It is now apparent that the 'Khazars' of his first novel – a Turkic people who disappeared from history in the Middle Ages through a failure to maintain their cultural identity – are in part meant to stand for the Serbs and their 'submergence' within a multiethnic Yugoslavia. Contemporary parallels are also evident in his third novel, *The Inner Side of the Wind* (1991), about a church architect who continues stubbornly to build in the midst of a destructive civil war. Pavić has recently identified his central theme as "the tragic position of East European Christianity...my books are a kind of SOS for this civilization". He has also published several volumes of poetry.

Peeters, Flor (1903–86) Belgian organist, composer, and teacher. Peeters was a pupil of the French organist-composers Marcel Dupré and Charles Tournemire and his own work shows a clear debt to the music of both men. After studying at the Lemens Institute, Mechelen, he became a professor there in 1923 while also serving as organist at the Cathedral of St Rambout in that city. Subsequent appointments included organ teacher at Ghent Conservatory (1931–35) and Tilburg Conservatory (1935–48) and director of Antwerp Conservatory (1952–68). He also toured widely as a concert organist. In his compositions, which include nearly 500 works for the organ as well as sacred, choral, and piano music, Peeters combined a classical attitude to form with a gift for melody; influences include Gregorian chant and Flemish folk music. He also wrote an important organ treatise, *Ars Organi* (3 vols: 1952–54).

Peichl, Gustav (1928–) Austrian architect, born and based in Vienna. His works are remarkable for their purity of form – a recent Austrian preoccupation – and develop the ideas of the 1930s International Style whilst also owing something to Adolf Loos.

Early works, like the Krim Elementary School (1961) and the Dominican convent (1963–65), both in Vienna, were followed by a series of stations for Austrian Radio (ORF): Dornbirn, Innsbruck, Linz, and Salzburg (all 1968–72), and Graz and Eisenstadt (1979–81). Each station comprises a circular series of stepped studios bisected by a projecting square office block. Also for ORF he built a satellite station at Aflenz (1976–79), set largely underground in a circular hollow, and an archive building in Vienna (1982–83) – a simple block with a range of Diocletian windows set into a largely blank façade that complements the adjacent 1930s building. Most remarkable of all his buildings, however, must be his hospital in Vienna (1966–68; completely symmetrical, with a dramatic series of stepped horizontals and angles) and his PEA phosphate elimination plant in Berlin-Tegel (1979–83; another white building designed inside out and relieved by a few portholes).

Peichl's recent work has been even more geometric and pure in its form. His extension to the Städel Museum, Frankfurt (1987–90) is a curved white building with stark Loosian openings that include some triangular windows, whilst his Art and Exhibition Centre in Bonn, designed in 1986 and begun in 1989, is a vast flexible square space topped with three mighty memorial cones and a sculpture garden.

Peixinho, Jorge (Manuel Rosado Marques) (1940–) Portuguese composer and pianist. After studying piano and composition at the Lisbon Conservatory (1951–58), he took up a series of travelling scholarships, training with, amongst others, PETRASSI in Rome (1960–61), BOULEZ, STOCKHAUSEN, and Gottfried Michael Koenig in Basel (1962–63), and NONO in Venice (1962–63). From 1960 onwards he also attended the DARMSTADT summer courses. In 1970 he was a founder member of the avant-garde music group Grupo de Música Contemporânea de Lisboa. He teaches composition at the Oporto Conservatory and has also taught in Brazil.

Peixinho quickly established his leading position within avant-garde Portuguese music circles with such early works as *Successões simétricas I* for piano (1961). These early works were particularly indebted to Boulez and Nono; later (post 1970) works, which make increasing use of improvisation, owe more to Stockhausen. He has written mostly instrumental and orchestral pieces, significant among which are the *Aleatoric Kinetofonias* (1965–69) for 25 strings and 3 tapes, and the group improvisation *Con-sequência* (1974); there are also vocal, piano, and electronic works.

Penderecki, Krzysztof (1933–) Polish composer. He studied (1955–58) at the Krakow Conservatory with Malawski and Wiechowicz and has taught composition there since graduating. In the early 1960s Penderecki's music won international acclaim, both for its originality and for its powerfully dramatic and emotional qualities, which make an immediate appeal to audiences. Although he has experimented with electronic sounds, Penderecki prefers to use conventional orchestral instruments to produce the abstract sonorities favoured by XENAKIS and STOCKHAUSEN; note clusters, new string effects, and sophisticated percussion sounds are all utilized.

His first international success was *Threnody to the Victims of Hiroshima* (1960) for 52 string instruments, a piece that has greatly enhanced the vocabulary of modern music and its notation. Like his first opera, *The Devils of Loudou* (1969), and the large-scale religious choral works (*St Luke Passion*, 1965; *Dies Irae*, 1967), the *Threnody* combines experimental techniques (microtones and indeterminacy) with an emotional drive that verges on the expressionist. Since the 1970s his music has become more thematic, relying less heavily on fragmentary techniques, and has explored more traditional avenues (first and second symphonies, 1973 and 1980; viola concerto, 1983). More recent works include the *Polish Requiem* (1984) and the opera *The Black Mask* (1986).

Penna, Sandro (1906–83) Italian poet. Born in Perugia, he lived most of his life in Rome, where he worked as a bookshop assistant, antiquarian, and translator. Penna's homosexuality made him a loner, very jealous of his privacy, though he never denied his erotic tendencies either in his life or in his poetry. His first collection of verse came out in 1939 and was followed by *Notes* (1950). His major work was collected in *All the Poems* (1970), while *The Sleepless Traveller* (1977) was published posthumously.

The subject matter of Penna's verse is drawn mainly from his own life; he is especially concerned with those moments of illumination that may arise from an impression, a gesture, a transient image, or memory. In the poem 'Life is Remembering an Awakening', for example, the essence of life is concentrated into a few moments of awakening from sleep on a train journey. Penna's poetry is lyrical and epigrammatic with a strong vein of melancholy. His language blends the literary and the demotic in a simple musical style.

Penrose, Roger (1931–) British mathematician and theoretical physicist. Penrose, the son of the geneticist Lionel Penrose, graduated from University College, London, and obtained his PhD in 1957 from Cambridge University. After holding various lecturing and research posts in London, Cambridge, and the US at Princeton, Syracuse, and Texas, Penrose was appointed professor of applied mathematics at Birkbeck College, London, in 1966. In 1973 he was elected Rouse Ball Professor of Mathematics at Oxford.

Penrose has done much to elucidate the fundamental properties of black holes. These result from the total gravitational collapse of large stars that shrink to such a small volume that not even a light signal can escape from them. There is thus a boundary around a black hole inside which all information about the black hole is trapped; this is known as its 'event horizon'. With Stephen HAWKING, Penrose proved that at the centre of a black hole there must be a 'space–time singularity' of zero volume and infinite density where the present laws of physics break down. He went on to propose his hypothesis of 'cosmic censorship': such singularities cannot be 'naked' – they must possess an event horizon. The effect of this would be to conceal and isolate the singularity with its indifference to the laws of physics.

Penrose went on to describe (1969) a mechanism for the extraction of energy from black holes. He has also done much to develop the mathematics needed to unite general relativity (which deals with the gravitational interactions of matter) and quantum mechanics (which describes all other interactions). Recent publications include *The Emperor's New Mind* (1989).

performance art A type of art in which the exponent performs in (or directs) a live event, usually combining elements of theatre, music, dance, and the visual arts. The artist invariably appears as him- or herself, rather than assuming a dramatic character. Performance events may be carefully structured but more often involve a considerable amount of improvisation. The content is often either deliberately shocking (*see* ACTION AND BODY ART) or wilfully tedious and obscure. Although avant-garde groups such as the futurists, the Dadaists, and the surrealists had sometimes staged provocative events to draw attention to their ideas earlier in the century, it was only in the late 1950s that performance art began to emerge as a distinct genre. Its growth in the 1960s had much to do with the vogue for CONCEPTUAL ART, with its emphasis on ideas rather than the creation of artefacts. Performance art has often been used as a vehicle for the expression of political dissent. In the 1960s HAPPENINGs, performance events involving a large element of audience participation, became fashionable. Noted European exponents of performance art include Yves KLEIN, Josef BEUYS, and GILBERT & GEORGE.

Perutz, Max Ferdinand (1914–) British biochemist, born in Austria. While studying chemistry at Vienna University, Perutz became interested in X-ray diffraction techniques and moved to Britain to work on the X-ray diffraction of proteins with William L. Bragg at the Cavendish Laboratory, Cambridge.

During the war Perutz worked in a team under Lord Mountbatten examining various applications of science for the war effort. Following the war he organized the setting up, in 1946, of the molecular biology laboratory in Cambridge, where he was soon joined by John Kendrew. His chief objective was to establish the three-dimensional structure of haemoglobin, a molecule containing some 12 000 atoms. In 1953 he applied the heavy atom or isomorphous replacement technique to his work, incorporating heavy metal atoms into the molecule under study. This alters the diffraction patterns, making it easier to compute the positions of atoms in the molecule. By 1959 he had shown haemoglobin to be composed of four chains, together making a tetrahedral structure, with four haeme groups near the molecule's surface.

For this achievement Perutz received the 1962 Nobel Prize for chemistry sharing it with Kendrew, who had worked out the structure of the muscle protein, myoglobin, using similar methods. In later work Perutz demonstrated that in oxygenated haemoglobin the four subunits are rearranged. Perutz has also investigated the various mutated forms of haemoglobin characteristic of inherited blood diseases. He was chairman of the MRC Laboratory of Molecular Biology (1962–79), where he remains a member of staff.

Petit, Roland (1924–) French dancer, choreographer, and ballet director, usually considered the most prominent figure in French dance since World War II.

Petit studied dance at the Paris Opéra Ballet School, where he was coached by Serge Lifar, and subsequently joined the Paris Opéra Ballet in 1940. Lifar's domination of the company prevented Petit from developing his own talents to the full, however, and in 1944 he left to form Les Ballets des Champs-Elysées with Jean Cocteau and others, taking the roles of principal dancer and choreographer himself.

In 1948 Petit formed another company, the Ballets de Paris with which he toured widely in France and abroad. Among his most successful ballets of this period were *Le Jeune Homme et la mort* (1946), an existential study of despair in which a lover contemplates suicide, and *Carmen* (1949), an exotic version of Bizet's opera. *Carmen* enjoyed great popular success with its chic images and highly sensual choreography; Petit himself played the role of Don José while Renée 'Zizi' Jeanmaire (later Petit's wife) danced the part of Carmen.

Petit's career continued to flourish in the 1950s and 1960s with a series of works created for various companies, among them *Ballabile* (1950), *Le Loup* (1953), *Cyrano de Bergerac* (1959), *Notre-Dame-de-Paris* (1965), *Pelléas et Mélisande* (1969), and *Kraanerg* (1969). Other successes included a number of dance revues starring Petit and Jeanmaire and work as a director and choreographer for cinema and television; among the films to which he contributed were *Hans Christian Andersen* (1952), *The Glass Slipper* (1954), *Daddy Longlegs* (1955), and *Anything Goes* (1956).

In 1972 Petit became head of the Ballet de Marseille, where he was highly praised for his revivals of *Coppélia* (1975) and other classical ballets as well as for such original pieces as *La Rose malade* (1973), *The Phantom of the Opera* (1980), and *The Blue Angel* (1985).

Petrassi, Goffredo (1904–) Italian composer and teacher. In 1913 he entered the Roman choir school (the Schola Cantorum), where he studied plainchant and Renaissance and baroque music. After further private studies, he attended the Conservatorio di S Cecilia (1928–33), where his composition teachers were Vincenzo di Donato and Alessandro Bustini. In 1932 he became a protégé of the composer Alfredo Casella (1883–1947), after Casella heard his *Tre cori*. A year later he won international recognition when his prize-winning *Partita* for orchestra was performed at the 1933 ISCM festival in Amsterdam. From 1934 until 1936 he taught at the Accademia di S Cecilia. Subsequent posts include general director of the Teatro La Fenice in Venice (1937–40) and head of composition at the Conservatorio di S Cecilia (1939–59). In 1959 he succeeded Ildebrando Pizzetti as professor of composition at the Accademia di S Cecilia, remaining there until his retirement in 1974. In the post-war years Petrassi taught widely in Europe and the US until eyesight problems put an end to these trips in 1965.

Petrassi's music was marked from the outset by its technical mastery. The neo-classical influences evident in his music of the 1930s gave way in the 1940s to a more lyrical and introverted idiom. Central to his output are the eight concertos for orchestra, *Estri* (1967), the operas *Il cordovano* (1944–48) and *Morte dell'aria* (1950), and his large-scale choral works. His pupils have included the British composers Peter Maxwell DAVIES and Cornelius CARDEW and the Italian Aldo CLEMENTI.

Petri, Elio (1929–) Italian film director, screenwriter, and political satirist. Pietri studied literature at Rome University before joining the communist newspaper *L'Unita* as a film critic. He began his cinematic career by directing documentaries and coscripting films for DE SANTIS and other directors. His own directorial debut came in 1961 with *The Lady Killer of Rome* (1961), followed by *The Tenth Victim* (1965), *We Still Kill the Old Way* (1967), and *A Quiet Place in the Country* (1968), all of which express concern for contemporary Italian society. He came to international attention with *Investigation of a Citizen Above Suspicion*, a political thriller that won the Academy Award for best foreign film of 1970. Its plot centres on a Fascist police chief who murders his mistress and, believing himself above the law, leaves evidence of his guilt. After making *The Working Class Goes to Heaven* (1971), Petri enjoyed further success with *Lulu the Tool*, which took the Grand Prize at the 1972 CANNES FILM FESTIVAL. Later notable films include *Property is No Longer Theft* (1973) and *Todò Modo* (1976).

Petrushevskaia, Liudmila Stefanovna (1938–) Russian writer and dramatist. Having studied at Moscow University, she worked from 1972 as a television editor. Petrushevskaia began writing stories in the mid 1960s, but a decade later found her voice as a playwright; since then she has written more than 20 works for the stage. It is only recently, however, that they have been accepted for performance by the leading Moscow theatres, being at first staged mainly by amateur groups in studio theatres. For many years, in fact, her high reputation was offset by a persistent lack of official recognition; her work remained unpublished until the late 1980s. Amongst Petrushevskaia's best plays are *The Violin* (1973), *Love* (1979), *Come into the Kitchen* (1979), and *Three Women in Blue* (1983). They show Muscovites contending with typically Soviet problems, such as rivalry over property, the housing shortage, and social differences in a supposedly classless society, as well as reflecting more universal concerns, such as family relationships. Remote from any ideology, they are, typically, small-scale and undramatic with little plot, though at the end of the plays the spectators are left with a very changed perception of the characters on stage. Petrushevskaia's particular strength lies in her grasp of psychology, mastery of (Muscovite) local colour, and acute ear for dialogue. She is one of the most respected contemporary Russian playwrights.

Pettersson, (Gustaf) Allan (1911–80) Swedish composer and violinist. Pettersson was essentially self-taught as a composer, attending the Stockholm Conservatory as a violinist and violist (1930–39); his teachers there included BLOMDAHL. Further studies in Paris were cut short by the German occupation in 1940 and he returned to Sweden becoming a professional violist with the Stockholm Philharmonic Orchestra (1940–51). His playing career was brought to an end by rheumatoid arthritis in 1964.

Pettersson made his public debut as a composer in 1949, when his concerto for violin and string quartet was premiered. The hostile criticism it received induced him to return to Paris for further training under Honegger and LEIBOWITZ. Despite studying serialism with Leibowitz, Pettersson's musical roots remained in Bach and Beethoven rather than in the avant-garde. The premiere of his seventh symphony in 1968 gave Pettersson his first important public success. His 15 symphonies (written between 1953 and 1978) make up a significant part of his output; other works include concertos, including a much-acclaimed viola concerto (first performed in 1988), songs, and chamber works. Typically his music features triadic harmonies, complex percussion parts, and extreme contrasts between violent dissonances and more relaxed writing.

Pevsner, Sir Nikolaus (1902–83) British historian of art and architecture, born in Germany. One of the most influential architectural writers of the 20th century, he was educated at the universities of Leipzig, Munich, Berlin, and Frankfurt. A Jew, his distinguished academic career in Germany as an art historian was cut short by the rise of the Nazis; he moved to London in 1934. He worked first as a lecturer, establishing his name in Britain with his *Pioneers of the Modern Movement* (1936) and later becoming editor of the *Architectural Review* (1942–45). However, his greatest achievements came as a result of his collaboration with Penguin Books on *The Buildings of England* (1951–74), a series of volumes that aimed to describe every building of architectural importance in England. Most of the original 47 volumes were written by Pevsner himself, and he personally visited almost every building described. Organized by county, the series is unmatched in any other country in the world.

Another series, *The Pelican History of Art* (1953–), under Pevsner's general editorship, established itself as one of the most authoritative works on the visual arts in the English language. He produced numerous other books and carried on a full career as a teacher and lecturer. Although some of his modernist views have ceased to be fashionable, his work has undoubtedly raised the profile of architecture and the visual arts in Britain.

Peyrefitte, Roger (1907–) French writer. After studying philosophy and political science, Peyrefitte began a career in the French foreign ministry. From 1933 to 1938 he was legation secretary in Athens. After World War II he devoted himself entirely to literature.

The work of Peyrefitte is dominated by two main preoccupations: homosexual love and nostalgia for the past. With his first novel *Special Friendships* (1944), which described the mutual attraction of two sensitive boys in a boarding school, Peyrefitte incurred severe criticism from the Church. In return, he attacked the religious establishment in such novels as *The Keys of Saint Peter* (1955) and *The Prince's Person* (1963), where his irony is often reminiscent of Voltaire's. The diplomatic service is satirized in *Diplomatic Conclusions* (1953). He has also shown an ability to evoke the atmosphere of past times with great precision, as in *The Prince of the Snowland* (1948). More recent works include biographies of Alexander the Great (1977–81) and Voltaire (1985). Peyrefitte's work combines personal confession, an intense love of beauty, and precise descriptions of places and peoples.

Philharmonia Orchestra An orchestra founded in London in 1945 by the record producer Walter Legge both to give concerts and to make recordings. From 1964 (when the players took over responsibility for the orchestra) until 1977 the orchestra was known as the **New Philharmonia Orchestra**; it then reverted to its original name. Its principal conductors have included Otto Klemperer and, currently, Giuseppe SINOPOLI. The **Philharmonia Chorus** has been independent from the orchestra since 1964.

Piaget, Jean (1896–1980) Swiss psychologist. Piaget showed an early interest in natural history, publishing some respected papers on molluscs while still in his teens. After taking a degree in zoology at the University of Nêuchatel he studied psychology in Zürich and Paris. He worked at the Institute J-J Rousseau from 1921 and became a professor at the University of Geneva in 1929. He was professor of developmental psychology at the Sorbonne from 1952 to 1963. In 1955 he founded the International Centre for Genetic Epistemology in Geneva, which he directed for the rest of his working life.

In his work as a psychologist Piaget concentrated almost exclusively on the development of children's logical faculties. He argued that a child comes into the world with a few innate reflexes but without the mental structures that would allow it to be logical; even such basic concepts as time and space have to be acquired from experience. At the same time he opposed behaviourism and stressed the interaction of subject and object in the process of knowledge formation. His many books include *The Language and Thought of the Child* (1923), *Introduction to Genetic Epistemology* (1950), and *The Early Growth of Logic in the Child* (1964). Piaget's work has had a considerable influence on education, moral philosophy, and sociology.

Pialat, Maurice (1925–) French film director, actor, and artist, who confirmed his position as a leading director in the 1980s. Previously a painter, Pialat entered the cinema in the late 1950s, making several admired shorts and films for television before embarking on his first full-length feature film, *Naked Childhood* (1968), about a young delinquent. In this and subsequent films he depicted everyday emotional traumas in a supremely naturalistic style, often employing amateur actors. In *We Won't Grow Old Together* (1972) he traced the break-up of two lovers, while *A Mouth Agape* (1973) was a sensitive portrayal of a woman's slow death from cancer. The uncharacteristically cheerful *Passe Ton Bac D'Abord* (1976) was a study of teenage preoccupations.

Pialat came to international attention with *Loulou* (1980), starring Gérard Depardieu and Isabelle Huppert as two lovers in the run-down suburbs of Paris. A similarly bleak view of the world characterized *To Our Loves* (1984), in which a promiscuous 15-year-old falls out with her family; Pialat played her sympathetic father. *Police* (1985), again starring Depardieu, was another drama of emotional conflict. The acclaimed *Under Satan's Sun* (1987), based on the novel by Bernanos, is an intense analysis of the nature of evil and religious faith, with Depardieu as a self-doubting priest and Pialat as his superior. In 1992 he released *Van Gogh*, a highly praised biopic of the artist.

Piano, Renzo (1937–) Italian architect. Born in Genoa and trained in Milan, Piano has built in most parts of the world. In 1970 he formed a partnership with Richard ROGERS and a year later (with Ove ARUP and Partners) they won the prestigious competition for the Beaubourg or POMPIDOU CENTRE, completed in 1977. If its external appearance is characteristically Rogers's, the structure and logic is Piano's. Subsequently Piano has moved away from the ARCHIGRAM-like openness of the Pompidou and even from 'high-tech' steelwork: he has devoted much time to urban regeneration, natural materials, and self-help schemes, both in Italy and in the Third World. He has specialized in adapting existing buildings to modern uses, such as the Schlumberger Factory in Paris (1981–84) and the Fiat Lingotto plant at Turin (1983–87).

Piano's new buildings are few but striking. The De Menil Collection Museum in Houston, US (1981–86), has been called the world's most beautiful museum for its ferrocement solar-panelled roof, which gives a diffuse natural light. This was followed by a town centre at Berey-Charenton, France (1987) and by two dramatic sports stadia in Italy: a hall in Ravenna (1986) and the Bari Football Stadium (1987–90), which provided a spectacular setting for matches in the 1990 World Cup. He has also built exciting metro stations in Genoa.

In 1989 Piano won a competition for a new international airport at Kansai, Japan. His scheme, an extraordinary wing-shaped design, was the only one to consider the sensitive ecology of the area. In 1992 he was hired to rebuild the Potsdameraplatz, Berlin, a desolate area formerly occupied by sections of the Wall.

Piccolo Teatro della Città di Milano *See* GRASSI, PAOLO; STREHLER, GIORGIO; TEATRO STABILE.

Piene, Otto (1928–) German experimental artist. Born in Laasphe in Westphalia, Piene studied art at the Hochschule der Bildenden Künste in Munich (1948–50) and at the Staatliche Kunstakademie in Düsseldorf (1950–52), and philosophy at the University of Cologne (1953–57).

After specializing in screen-processed monochromes in the mid 1950s Piene became fascinated by the artistic possibilities of light and fire. In 1957 he cofounded the ZERO GROUP, which advocated KINETIC ART. In the early 1960s Piene produced shadow drawings and pictures and also a series of 'light ballets', in which changing light effects were created by using motorized constructions and balloons filled with coloured gases. From 1967 onwards he produced large freestanding 'light spheres' and objects made of plexiglass. In the 1970s he designed several gigantic light sculptures that encompassed entire buildings.

In 1964 Piene was appointed guest professor at an American university and thereafter divided his time between the US and Germany. His work has been exhibited widely in Germany, the US, and Britain.

Pierrot Players *See* FIRES OF LONDON.

Pietilä, (Frans) Reima (1923–) Finnish architect. His work resembles that of Alvar AALTO in its response to a site and to materials but is infinitely more mannered. Until the 1980s he had built little, though he had held a professorship in design at the University of Oulu until 1979.

Pietilä's initial breakthrough was with the Kaleva church (1959–66), by contrast to Aalto's cool spaces a high multifaceted nave with strong narrow vertical lights and an expressionistic concrete pulpit. This love of complex plastic space was taken further in the 'Dipoli' student centre at Otaniemi (1961–66): with three great wedges of hall, bars, and restaurants bursting from under a great concave roof its effect is overwhelming. His Finnish Embassy in New Delhi, designed in 1963, was not built until 1980–85. Its roof is a convex curve, said to have been inspired by a snowdrift.

In 1973 came Pietilä's next commission, an extension to the Sief Palace in Kuwait that included many ministerial buildings, all decorated with brilliant tilework. Bright tiles were used again, with brick, in his first large scheme in Finland – a congregational centre, leisure complex, and shopping mall for the new Hervanta area of Tampere. After their completion in 1979, Pietilä added libraries and cinemas, which opened in 1984. He has also designed a library for Tampere itself (1978–86). By contrast to these loosely linked projects his rebuilding of Lieska church (1978–82) was a formal composition in the manner of a Greek cross.

Most of Pietilä's later works are jointly credited to his wife, **Raili Pietilä**, whom he married in 1961.

Pignon, Edouard (1905–) French painter. Pignon was born in Bully in north-east France and brought up at Marles-les-Mines. During his early years he worked in the local mines (1921–27). He then moved to Paris, where he held a variety of jobs while studying sculpture at evening classes and painting in his spare time. He met and was encouraged by Picasso.

During the 1930s Pignon began to produce large paintings showing the life of working people. From the mid 1940s he often painted series of pictures on particular themes, such as his *Catalans* (1945–46). In the 1950s his work became more expressive and powerful (as in *Le Mineur Mort*, 1952). From 1958 to 1962 he spent his summers in Italy, resulting in such paintings of agricultural life as *Corn-gatherers* and *Threshing*. He also designed ceramics and sets for the Théâtre National Populaire in Paris and for a production of BRECHT's *Mother Courage*.

Pilinszky, János (1921–81) Hungarian poet and essayist. Pilinszky, who studied literature and art history at the University of Budapest, published his first poems in 1940 and his first volume of poetry in 1946. He was called up for military service in 1944 and witnessed considerable hardship as a prisoner of war in Germany and Austria, an experience which provides a recurring theme in his poetry. He was a devout Roman Catholic and the profoundly – if unconventionally – religious character of his poetry met with the disapproval of the post-war Stalinist regime in Hungary. He was prohibited from publishing in 1949 and his second volume of poetry did not appear until 1959. He is now widely recognized as the most accomplished and internationally accessible Hungarian poet of the post-war period. His poetry recreates a timeless world of unremitting spiritual suffering and existential anguish, only partly mitigated by religious faith. Through his stark, undecorative, yet highly inventive, imagery, however, he sustains an intensity of self-awareness that itself produces a sense of epiphany. This is particularly evident in the later volumes, *Crater* (1976) and *Apocrypha* (1981), the title poem of the latter volume being one of the most powerful lyric poems in the Hungarian language. From 1957 until his death, Pilinszky contributed memorable short prose meditations to the Catholic weekly *New Man*, the best of which were collected in the posthumous volume *Nail and Oil* (1982).

Pimenov, Yury Ivanovich (1903–77) Soviet painter. Born in Moscow, Pimenov studied (1920–25) at the Vkhutemas art school. In 1925 he joined Ost, the Society of Easel Artists, of which he became a leading member. The Society championed easel painting and figurative art at a time when modernist movements were in the ascendant in the new Soviet Union. In the 1920s Pimenov came under the influence of German expressionism and his style became more emotional. Works of this period include landscapes, portraits, still lifes, and nudes.

When the Soviet state-sponsored style of socialist realism emerged in the 1930s Pimenov felt unable to give it his unqualified support. Instead, he devoted considerable energy to the design of theatre sets and posters, a field in which there was more freedom than in painting. When he did paint scenes of Soviet life, as in *New Moscow* (1937, Tretyakov Gallery, Moscow), the works are notable for their human interest and evocation of atmosphere.

After World War II he taught at VGIK, the All-Union State Institute of Cinematography in Moscow. His later paintings include sensitive depictions of young people; for example, *The Beginning of Love* (1960, Kiev Museum of Russian Art), in which a boy on a bus looks fondly at the girl in front of him.

Pinter, Harold (Harold Da Pinta; 1930–) British playwright, regarded as one of the most important writers for the contemporary stage. His use of oblique or evasive dialogue to evoke a sense of menace, his penchant for long pauses, and his ear for the bizarre idiosyncracies of ordinary speech combine to provide the characteristic 'Pinteresque' style. His early plays, *The Room* (1957) and *The Birthday Party* (1958), were greeted with incomprehension; it was only gradually that the originality and complexity of his writing came to be appreciated. *The Caretaker* (1960), another play full of brooding menace, marked the transition to acceptance with the critics; it was also the first of Pinter's plays to be filmed. Subsequent plays include *The Dumb Waiter* (1960), a tense one-act drama about two gangsters preparing to kill an as yet unknown victim, *The Homecoming* (1965), *Old Times* (1971), which explores a stable marriage that is suddenly threatened by a third party, and *No Man's Land* (1975). *Betrayal* (1978) uses a reversed time sequence to explore the mutual deceptions involved in a three-way relationship.

Since *Betrayal* Pinter has produced no full-length dramas, concentrating instead upon writing for the screen and adopting a prominent role as a campaigner for left-wing causes. The collection of three short plays *Other Places* (1982) included *A Kind of Alaska*, in which a woman wakes from a long period of sleeping sickness to find that she has missed most of her life. Among Pinter's most recent work is *One for the Road* (1984) and *Mountain Language* (1988), concerning the plight of people who are forbidden by the state to speak their native language. *Party Time* (1992), his most substantial piece for a decade, is set in a quasi-fascist Britain of the near future.

Pinter's writing for the cinema includes screenplays for *The Servant* (1963), *Accident* (1967), *The Go Between* (1971), *The French Lieutenant's Woman* (1981), *Turtle Diary* (1985), and *The Handmaid's Tale* (1990).

Piper, John (1903–92) British painter, graphic artist, designer and writer, born at Epsom, Surrey. The son of a solicitor, he reluctantly became an articled clerk in his father's firm (1921–26): after his father's death in 1926 he studied at Richmond and Kingston Schools of Art and at the Royal College of Art in London. From 1928 to 1940 he worked as an art critic for various periodicals and was among the first to recognize the talents of such contemporaries as Ivon HITCHENS and Victor PASMORE. At this time his own work was abstract: from 1935 to 1937 he and his wife, Myfanwy Evans, published *Axix*, a quarterly journal of abstract art. By the end of the 1930s, however, he had turned to figurative work, concentrating on architectural and landscape subjects and becoming one of the outstanding representatives of British Neoromanticism, a movement that sought to revive and reinterpret the visionary tradition of William Blake and Samuel Palmer. During World War II he was an Official War Artist and some of his most famous paintings are of bomb-damaged buildings. After the war his work diversified. In particular he won renown as a designer of stained glass – notably at the new Coventry Cathedral (1962) – and for the stage; he also made prints and book illustrations and designed pottery and textiles. He wrote *British Romantic Artists* (1942) and various architectural guidebooks, sometimes in collaboration with his friend Sir John BETJEMAN (who wrote a book on Piper in the Penguin Modern Painters series, 1944). Piper also wrote poetry.

Pires, José Cardoso (1925–) Portuguese playwright and novelist, who established his reputation in the theatre on the strength of just two plays. *Relieving the Heroes* (1965), about a peasant uprising in the 1840s, attracted enormous attention in Portugal for its combination of Brechtian techniques with stock characters and devices from the Portuguese theatrical tradition. His second play, *Body of Evidence in the Hall of Mirrors* (1979) shows the influence of GENET and employs absurdist techniques to lampoon the regime of the dictator Salazar (*see* ABSURD, THEATRE OF THE).

Piriev, Ivan *See* PYRIEV, IVAN.

Piscator, Erwin (Friedrich Max) (1893–1966) German theatre director, whose development of a new kind of political drama incorporating multimedia techniques had a profound influence upon European theatre both before and after World War II. Piscator established himself as a theatrical force to be reckoned with in the 1920s, when he worked closely with BRECHT and experimented with the use of photographs, film clips, etc. to emphasize the political relevance of his productions. The success of such works as the revue-style entertainment *Despite All!* (1925), which covered major events in German history since 1914, won Piscator a post at the Berlin Volksbühne, but his radical left-wing politics and unconventional directorial style led to his dismissal in 1927. Piscator then set up his own company and continued to explore the possibilities of multimedia theatre and innovative stage design. His experiments were later to have a major impact upon the development of EPIC THEATRE and DOCUMENTARY THEATRE, most directly through hs book *The Political Theatre* (1929).

During World War II Piscator taught drama in New York. He returned to Germany in 1951, becoming director of the West Berlin Volksbühne in 1962. Piscator remained one of the most significant figures in contemporary German drama until his death, championing in particular the documentary theatre of such younger playwrights as HOCHHUTH, KIPPHARDT, and WEISS. His ideas had a profound effect upon Joan LITTLEWOOD's Theatre Workshop in Britain and the Federal Theater Project in the US.

Pistoletto, Michelangelo (1933–) Italian painter and sculptor. Pistoletto was born in Biella in north-west Italy. He later worked in Turin with his father, a picture restorer, and taught himself to paint. His earliest works, which date from the mid 1950s, included a series of large self-portraits painted in acrylic on varnished bases. The reflective quality of these bases stimulated Pistoletto to develop a way of incorporating reflected images in his works. The outcome was a series of 'mirror pictures' beginning in the early 1960s. He generally worked by taking a life-sized photograph, usually of a figure (or figures) in arrested motion, tracing its outline on paper, and attaching the figure so produced to a sheet of polished steel before painting it. The idea was that the viewer's own image should become part of the composition as he or she appeared reflected on the steel. Pistoletto's mirror pictures attracted considerable interest and made him famous.

Pistoletto's interest in reflection led to other works employing mirrors, such as the sculpture *Cubic Metre of Infinity*, which consists of mirrors facing each other across a cube format. In the late 1960s he also participated in HAPPENINGs, as with the group 'Zoo', a street theatre troupe that performed in the US from 1968 to 1970. In the 1970s he produced silkscreen prints on polished steel and in the 1980s much abstract sculpture, including a number of works consisting of heaps of coloured rags.

Planchon, Roger (1931–) French theatre director, actor, and playwright, who emerged as one of the leading directors associated with the policy of DÉCENTRALISATION DRAMATIQUE in the 1970s. Planchon's work with the theatre company he founded in Lyon in 1950 did much to draw critical attention from Paris to the provinces, and he soon won praise with his productions of new plays by such writers as ADAMOV, BRECHT, and IONESCO. In 1957 he moved to the nearby town of Villeurbanne, where he has since remained, concentrating on drama with a Marxist message.

Early successes included Adamov's *Paolo-Paoli* (1957), radical political versions of *Richard III* (1966) and other works by Shakespeare, and Molière's *Tartuffe* (1962 and 1973). He has also produced plays by Racine, Marivaux, and many of his own dramas, in several of which he also appeared as an actor. Among the most successful of his own plays have been *Infamy* (1969) and *Gilles de Rais* (1976).

The importance of Planchon's role as a champion of new writing aimed at predominantly working-class audiences was formally recognized in 1972, when his theatre at Villeurbanne was renamed the Théâtre National Populaire (previously the title of VILAR's theatre at Chaillot).

Plastov, Arkady (1893–1972) Soviet painter. Plastov was born of peasant stock in Prislonikha, a village east of Moscow in the region of the Volga River. His father, grandfather, and great-grandfather had all been church painters. Plastov studied sculpture at the Stroganov Central Artistic-Industrial College in Moscow (1912–14) and sculpture and painting at the Moscow College of Painting, Sculpture, and Architecture (1914–17). In 1917 he returned to Prislonikha where he worked as a peasant and painted in his spare time. In 1931 he joined a collective farm.

In 1931 a fire destroyed many of Plastov's works. Thereafter he devoted himself to painting, depicting scenes of agricultural life in and around Prislonikha. His paintings were exhibited in Moscow in 1935 and attracted considerable attention, being seen as examples of the new officially sponsored style of socialist realism. During World War II Plastov painted war scenes, but was unable to achieve any depth in this work. After the war, back in Prislonikha, he returned to scenes of rural life. In the 1950s he began to paint portraits, starting with members of his family, old friends, and villagers. In 1962 he was awarded the title 'People's Artist of the USSR' and in 1966 received a Lenin Prize. Plastov achieved high standards of composition and depicted his subjects with real subtlety. His paintings are among the most aesthetically successful products of socialist realism.

Pluchek, Valentin (1909–) Russian theatre director, who became famous for his consummate skill in presenting the great satirical classics of modern Russian theatre. Pluchek trained under Meyerhold in the 1920s and began a career as an actor before founding the shortlived Theatre of Young Workers and then (1939) a new experimental studio in Moscow (with Aleksei ARBUZOV). The studio quickly gained respect and in 1942 Pluchek was appointed director of the Theatre of the Northern Fleet, subsequently becoming director of the Moscow Touring Theatre (1945–50) and ultimately (1957) artistic director of the Moscow Theatre of Satire, where he remained until his retirement. In Pluchek's hands the Theatre of Satire became internationally known for its inventive constructivist versions of works by Maiakovsky, including *Mystery-Bouffe* (1957), Shaw, BRECHT, Ostrovsky, ROZOV, and many others.

Polanski, Roman (1933–) French film director of Polish descent, who emerged as one of the most controversial figures in the commercial cinema in the 1960s. Born in Paris, Polanski accompanied his family to Poland before World War II; his parents were subsequently imprisoned in Nazi concentration camps, his mother dying in Auschwitz. After the war, he worked as an actor and directed a number of surreal shorts in which his black sense of humour and macabre imagination found full expression. Polanski's first feature film was the imaginative thriller *Knife in the Water* (1962), in which a couple play out a series of dangerous emotional games with a complete stranger; the film won a prize at the Venice Film Festival. He then made two films in Britain that won major prizes at the BERLIN FILM FESTIVAL: *Repulsion* (1965), with Catherine Deneuve, was acclaimed as a horror film of rare intelligence, while the similarly violent *Cul-de-Sac* (1966) portrayed the destruction of the ordered life of a couple on a remote island.

Polanski moved to the US to make *Rosemary's Baby* (1968), a supernatural chiller, but a year later his private life was shattered when his pregnant second wife, the US actress Sharon Tate (1943–69), was murdered by members of the notorious Manson gang. Some critics interpreted the violence of Polanski's next film, *Macbeth* (1971), as a reflection of this tragedy. After making the acclaimed thriller *Chinatown* (1974) in the US, Polanski became headline news once more when he was convicted of having unlawful sex with a 13-year-old girl; he fled to France for his next major project, *Tess* (1979), an accomplished adaptation of Hardy's *Tess of the D'Ubervilles*. Recently he has worked in the theatre and directed the films *Pirates* (1986), a parody of the swashbuckling genre, *Frantic* (1988), a thriller, and *Bitter Moon* (1992). Polanski's autobiography, *Roman*, was published in 1984.

Poliakoff, Serge (1900–69) French painter. Born in Moscow, Poliakoff showed early talent as a musician. He left Russia after the Bolshevik Revolution, travelling to Istanbul with an aunt who was a singer. They toured Europe and then, in 1923, settled in Paris. For the next 20 years Poliakoff earned a living as a cabaret guitarist. He began to paint in 1929 and studied in Paris with Othon Friesz and in London at the Chelsea School of Art and the Slade School of Fine Art (1935–37).

After his return to Paris in 1937 Poliakoff met the pioneering abstract painter Wassily Kandinsky – another Russian emigré – and also became a friend of the painters Robert and Sonia Delaunay. With their encouragement, Poliakoff began to paint in an abstract style. His primary interest was in colour, rather than line or form. His early abstract work was complex but from the late 1940s onwards he began to simplify his compositions. Poliakoff became recognized as one of the leading French exponents of abstract painting during the 1950s, when his works were widely exhibited. He was given a retrospective exhibition in the Kunsthalle in Berne in 1960 and exhibitions at the Whitechapel Gallery in London in 1963 and 1969.

Poliakoff, Stephen (1952–) British playwright and film director, who emerged as one of the most original newcomers to the British theatre in the 1970s. *Hitting Town* (1975) and *City Sugar* (1975) established his reputation for challenging drama; both address the alienating superficiality of modern society and are noted for their contemporary urban settings. Of his subsequent plays, the most effective have included *Strawberry Fields* (1977), depicting neo-Nazi violence, and *Breaking the Silence* (1984), a portrayal of the flight of the author's grandfather from revolutionary Russia, which was first staged by the ROYAL SHAKESPEARE COMPANY. More recently *Coming in to Land* (1987), concerning the difficulties faced by a Polish refugee in Britain, *Playing with Trains* (1989), another RSC success, and *Sienna Red* (1991) have been well received. His writing for the screen has included the television play *Caught on a Train*, with Peggy Ashcroft, and the film *Close My Eyes* (1991), which he also directed.

Pollini, Gino *See* FIGINI, LUIGI.

Pomodoro, Arnaldo (1926–) Italian sculptor and theatrical designer. Pomodoro was born in Morciano di Romagna and later moved to Orciano, near Pesaro. He studied architecture and jewellery design. From 1950 to 1954 he worked in Pesaro as a designer of jewellery and stage sets and also took up sculpture. In 1954 he moved to Milan, where he gave his first exhibition the following year. His work was influenced by that of Paul Klee and Pablo Picasso, amongst others, and by his travels in Europe (1958–59) and the US (1959–60).

In the 1960s Pomodoro emerged as one of the leading abstract sculptors in Europe. His sculptures typically take the form of a very large simple shape – such as a column, wheel, cube, sphere, or block – and are usually cast in bronze. Although most of these works are given a polished exterior many also have a section cut away to reveal an intricate inner structure. In 1963 Pomodoro was awarded the international prize for sculpture at the São Paulo Bienale, and in 1964 the prize for Italian sculpture at the Venice Biennale. From the late 1960s onwards he received numerous commissions, including one from Modena for a memorial to Italian Resistance fighters of World War II. In 1988 he exhibited at the Venice Biennale and at the World Expo in Brisbane. He continues to design for the theatre and opera.

Pompidou Centre (in full, Centre National d'Art et de Culture Georges Pompidou) A cultural centre in Paris named after Georges Pompidou (1911–74), president of France (1967–74), who soon after his election declared: "I passionately wish that Paris could have a cultural centre that would be both a museum and a centre for creativity – a place where the plastic arts, music, cinema, literature, audiovisual research, etc. would find a common ground." The site chosen for the centre was the Plateau Beaubourg, a once thriving area near the heart of the city that had become derelict. A competition for the design drew almost 700 entries (including bizarre ideas such as a giant egg); the winner – chosen by an international jury – was submitted by Sir Richard ROGERS and Renzo PIANO. Constructed in 1971–77, their huge building is the world's most celebrated example of 'high-tech' architecture and quickly became one of the most famous sights of Paris. The brightly coloured service ducts of the building – green for water, blue for air-conditioning, and so on – are fully exposed in a provocative display. As architecture the Centre has aroused great controversy; to some it is an ebullient masterpiece, to others a bad joke. The plaza in front of the building is an integral part of the Centre and is the main platform for Paris's street performers.

The Centre was inaugurated in 1977 with a retrospective exhibition of the work of Marcel Duchamp. It houses the national collection of modern art (one of the most important in the world) and stages numerous exhibitions of contemporary art. Also part of the Pompidou Centre are a public library, an industrial design centre, a children's workshop, a cinema archive, and the experimental music laboratory of IRCAM.

Ponge, Francis (1899–1988) French poet. Ponge studied philosophy and law in Paris before seeing action in the closing months of World War I. He subsequently worked in publishing, journalism, and academic life.

In the 1920s Ponge associated with the surrealists and began to write the short prose poems for which he has become celebrated. Typically, these pieces describe ordinary everyday objects in precise physical detail without recourse to symbolism or conventional rhetoric. Ponge aims to show the unknown and the exotic near at hand and to translate something of the mystery of the silent world of objects into language. Regarded with curiosity and love, the objects Ponge writes about confront man with their otherness and his own finiteness (*Twelve Little Writings*, 1926; *The Voice of Things*, 1942). As the texts of Francis Ponge are original and unexpected he did not have much success until the 1960s. He is now regarded as belonging to the first rank of modern French poets.

Pontecorvo, Gillo (Gilberto Pontecorvo; 1919–) Italian film director, born in Pisa. The younger brother of the scientist Bruno Pontecorvo, he took a degree in chemistry but thereafter worked in journalism, becoming a Paris correspondent for several Italian publications. During World War II he led a group of partisans; he was a member of the Communist Party until 1956. His career in films began after the war, when he worked as an assistant to such directors as Yves Allégret and Mario MONICELLI; in 1953 he directed the first of several documentary shorts. He also contributed an episode to *Die Windrose*, a feminist film made in 1956 in East Germany. A year later he made his debut as a director of features with *La Grande Strada Azzurra*, followed in 1960 by *Kapo*, about the experiences of a young girl in a Nazi concentration camp.

Pontecorvo's reputation depends largely on the historical epic *The Battle of Algiers* (1966). Subsidized by the Algerian government, it told the story of that country's rebellion against the French. Critics applauded the use of grainy images and amateur actors to achieve the realistic look of newsreel footage and the film won the Golden Lion at the Venice Film Festival. The film's quasi-documentary style was a major influence on such political film makers as ROSSI and COSTA-GAVRAS. His next film, the Italian-French *Burn!* (1969), starred Marlon Brando as a diplomat who becomes involved with revolutionaries after being sent to a Caribbean island to end a sugar monopoly. After the failure of this film, Pontecorvo was little heard of until the late 1980s, when there was a revival of interest in his work. His later features have included *Operation Ogro* (1979), about the struggle of Basque terrorists against the Franco regime, and *The Devil's Bishop* (1988). Despite his meagre output he is now regarded as one of the masters of post-war film making.

Ponti, Carlo (1910–) French film producer, born in Italy. Ponti attended the Universita degli Studi in Milan and practised law (1935–38) before moving into film production in the early 1940s, when he worked with such directors as ZAMPA, COMENCINI, and LATTUADA. In 1950 he established with DE LAURENTIIS the Ponti-De Laurentiis production company, which during its seven-year existence was responsible for such films as FELLINI's *La Strada* (1954) and *The Nights of Cabiria* (1956), *Attila the Hun* (1952), *Ulysses* (1954), and the US-Italian coproduction *War and Peace* (1956). After the partnership dissolved Ponti produced films in Britain, France, and Hollywood.

His personal life has often loomed larger than his films. In 1957 he married the actress Sophia Loren in Mexico; the union was not recognized in his native country and in 1964 Ponti became a French citizen, although he continued to produce in Italy, Britain, and the US. In 1979 an Italian court convicted him in absentia of smuggling art and currency abroad and, although he could not be extradited from France, sentenced him to four years imprisonment and a fine of $25 million.

Other films produced by Ponti include *Roma Città Aperta*, which won the New York Critics' Prize in 1947, the romantic melodrama *The Black Orchid* (1958), the Western spoof *Heller in Pink Tights* (1960),

ZAVATTINI's *Two Women* (1960), a World War II tale that won Sophia Loren an Oscar for best foreign actress, *Yesterday,Today, Tomorrow* (1963), named best foreign film at the Academy Awards, LEAN's *Doctor Zhivago* (1965), which took three Oscars, the ANTONIONI films *Blow-Up* (1966), *Zabriskie Point* (1970), and *The Passenger* (1975), *Andy Warhol's Frankenstein* (1975), and the rail-disaster film *The Cassandra Crossing* (1977).

Pop art An artistic movement of the 1950s and 1960s, characterized by the use of images from popular commercial culture. The style developed independently in Britain and the US. In Britain the movement grew out of the concerns of the INDEPENDENT GROUP, a group of critics and artists who met in London in the early 1950s and found they shared a fascination with the new US culture of cinema, advertising, and popular music. The term 'Pop' was coined by a member of the group, the critic Lawrence Alloway. Another member, Richard HAMILTON, began to reflect this interest by incorporating advertisements and items from magazines in collage paintings, such as the famous *Just What is it that Makes Today's Homes so Different, so Appealing?* (1956; private collection). This work was shown in the important 1956 exhibition organized by the Independent Group 'This Is Tomorrow', which greatly influenced younger artists such as Peter BLAKE. At the end of the 1950s a new group of artists emerged, mainly from the Royal College of Art, who had been influenced by the early Pop art of Hamilton and Blake. They included R.B. Kitaj, David HOCKNEY, Allen JONES, and Peter Phillips. These artists made a strong impact on the general public in the 'Young Contemporaries' exhibition of 1961 and the exhibition 'The New Generation' at the Whitechapel Art Gallery in 1964.

In the US Pop art developed in the mid 1950s as part of the reaction again abstract expressionism. Artists such as Jasper Johns and Robert Rauschenberg began to depict ordinary mass-produced objects and to incorporate them physically in their works. Other artists either looked to commercial culture for their subject matter (for example, Andy Warhol) or produced works in the style of popular commercial art (for example, Roy Lichtenstein). Pop art influenced several artists in continental Europe (for example, Valerio ADAMI) but there were no coherent movements comparable to those in Britain and the US (although French NOUVEAU RÉALISME has sometimes been seen in this light). Within Pop art there was some tension between two aims: that of breaking down the distinction between high art and popular culture and that of using elements of popular culture in order to comment critically on modern society.

Popov, Evgenii Anatol'evich (1946–) Russian writer and dramatist. Born in Krasnoiarsk, Popov studied and then worked in geology but showed an early inclination to become a writer. His first publication was in a provincial paper in 1962, but attempts to enter the official literary world met constant obstacles, including refusal of admission to the Gorkii Literary Institute in 1972. Four years later, however, some of his work appeared after great delay in the prestigious journal *Novyi Mir* and two years after that he was admitted to the Writers' Union. Like other young writers at this time, Popov was under constant pressure to conform ideologically and in 1979 he rebelled by participating actively in the unofficial almanac *Metropole* organized by AKSENOV. There followed a total ban on his publications and expulsion from the Union. Popov joined the so-called Belle Lettrists' Club whose publication *Catalogue* (1982), like *Metropole*, was published in the US. In 1986, however, one of his stories appeared in a Soviet journal, and Popov is now, at last, being recognized as a major literary voice.

Like Zoshchenko in the 1920s and SHUKSHIN in the 1960s, Popov portrays the lower echelons of society, seemingly taking violence, fear, and crude sex for granted, but bringing an element of uncertainty into his ostensibly realistic stories that disquiets and intrigues the reader. His use of unliterary narrators and their grotesquely distorted language helps to create a world of confusion and disorientation. Popov is a prolific writer; up to 1980 he had produced over 200 short stories and ten short and two full-length plays. Apart from the contributions to *Metropole* and *Catalogue*, his published works are mainly to be found in *The Merriment of Russia* (1981), which appeared in the US. The first translations of his stories appearing in the 1990s should bring him a much wider audience.

Popper, Sir Karl (Raimund) (1902–) British philosopher, born in Austria. Popper's father was a lawyer with an interest in literature and philosophy. After obtaining his PhD from the University of Vienna in 1928, he worked as a schoolteacher and then lectured at various universities in Britain in 1935 and 1936. In 1937 he was appointed to a lectureship in philosophy at the University of New Zealand, Christchurch. After World War II Popper joined the London School of Economics, where he served as professor of logic and scientific method from 1949 until his retirement in 1969.

Popper is noted for his philosophy of science, first fully formulated in his *The Logic of Scientific Discovery* (1934). To Popper, science is not inductive. Laws and theories are not arrived at by carefully collected observations. Science begins not with observations but with problems, which are dealt with by constructing theories, laws, or hypotheses. No matter how many observations confirm a theory, it is not possible to say that it is correct. We can, however, frequently show that theories are undoubtedly false.

Popper insists that the basic procedure of science consists of strenuously attempting to falsify such conjectures and accepting those that have survived the most severe attempts at falsification. This acceptance does not confer truth on the conjecture. That a hypothesis has so far resisted attempts to falsify it is no guarantee that it will continue to pass future tests.

With such an intellectual framework Popper could easily solve the demarcation problem. Scientific theories can conceive of and describe facts that could falsify them, while what he terms the 'pseudo sciences', such as Marxism and psychoanalysis, are able to interpret any event within their theory. This, for Popper, was a point of more than academic significance. In his *The Open Society and its Enemies* (1945) he attacked totalitarianism, while in *The Poverty of Historicism* (1957) he argued strongly against inexorable laws of historical destiny.

In *Objective Knowledge* (1972) Popper argued that the development of human knowledge by the constant falsification of untenable hypotheses was a case of evolution by natural selection. He also introduced the idea of a 'third world' of theories and arguments distinct from both the objective world of things and the subjective world of experience. Recent publications include *A World of Propensities* (1990).

Porter, George, Baron (1920–) British chemist. Porter was educated at the universities of Leeds and Cambridge. After working on radar during World War II, he returned to Cambridge until he was appointed professor of chemistry at Sheffield University (1955–66). He was the director of the Royal Institution (1966–85) and became a professor at the Imperial College in 1990.

In collaboration with his Cambridge teacher, Ronald Norrish, Porter developed from 1949 onward the new technique of flash photolysis. There were good reasons for thinking that the course of a chemical reaction was partly determined by a number of intermediate species too short-lived to be detected. Porter therefore set out to study what he called the spectroscopy of transient substances.

A long glass tube containing the gas to be investigated was subjected to a brief pulse of intense light causing photochemical reactions to occur in the gas. The free radicals and excited molecules produced have only a transient existence, but could be detected by a second flash of light, directed along the axis of the tube, used to record photographically an absorption spectrum of the reaction mixture. In this way the spectra of many free radicals could be detected.

In addition, it was possible to direct a continuous beam of light down the reaction tube and focus on one particular absorption line of a species known to be present. The change of this line with time allowed kinetic measurements of the rates of very fast gas reactions to be made. Porter shared the Nobel Prize for chemistry in 1967 with Norrish and with Manfred Eigen for these studies.

Portoghesi, Paolo (1931–) Italian architect and writer, since 1964 professor of architecture at Milan Polytechnic. His historical understanding of baroque – his *Guarino Guarini* (1964) is a major piece of research – pervades all his work. He is one of the leading European exponents of POSTMODERNISM.

Early works such as the Andreis House, Scandriglia (1963), and Papanice House, Rome (1967) played with baroque angles and massing in shuttered concrete. His Industrial and Technical Institutes at L'Aquila (1968) comprise a series of stepped boxes, while his Church of the Holy Family at Salerno (1968) has a stepped conical roof over curved concave screens. Subsequent works, such as his round Bevilacqua House at Gaeta (1975), were characterized by geometrical shapes and traditional materials. Much of his 1970s work was for traditionally minded Arab clients, including Khartoum Airport (1973), the Royal Court of Amman (on a square grid, 1974), and a mosque and Islamic Cultural Centre in Rome (1975–78, with skeletal columns interwoven with concrete arches and a dome). His Academy of Fine Arts at L'Aquila (1978–82) is a five-sided atrium, whilst his Agenzia del Monte dei Paschi at Siena is Art Deco. Subsequently his work has become more classical: first apparent in his centre for Musignano Canino (1978–81) with its circular forms and Diocletian windows, this tendency continued with his cupola-topped housing of the 1980s in Salerno and dominates his competition-winning design for a law centre at St Peter's College, Oxford (1991).

Portoghesi was the director of the architectural section of the 1980 Venice Biennale – an occasion that marked the international coming-of-age of postmodernism and confirmed Portoghesi as one of its leaders. Since 1984 he has been the Biennale's overall director. In addition to writing books, he has been editor of the journals *Controspazio* (1969–83) and *Eupalino*.

postmodernism Those tendencies in the culture of late 20th-century Western societies that represent a departure from the ideas and practices of classical modernism. Although the term became ubiquitous in cultural debate in the 1980s, its meaning and usefulness are both disputed.

The concept of postmodernism is clearest in the field of architecture, where a conscious reaction against the austerities of the International Style began in the US in the 1960s. Architects such as Robert Venturi and Charles Moore began to favour an eclectic use of materials and forms, often involving elements of art deco. In Europe the same era saw a concentration on pure geometric forms, as in the work of Aldo ROSSI and O. M. Ungers; nevertheless, there is the same preoccupation with fantasy, or what Paolo PORTOGHESI has called an 'architecture of fiction'. The term 'postmodernism' was first applied to architecture by Charles Jencks in his *The Language of Post-Modern Architecture* (1975). The style gained wide recognition at the 1980 Venice Biennale, which saw the emergence of a distinctive European formalism, based on an understanding of traditional styles, techniques, and planning. While architects like Rossi, Ungers, Portoghesi, Mario Botta, and REICHLIN AND REINHART, have expressed a deeply felt classicism through modern materials, in Britain the reaction to modernism has been more superficial. Here postmodernist architecture has usually taken one of two related forms. The first is a return to 18th-century classicism, often as a façade, championed by Quinlan Terry and Robert Adam. The second is the more American approach adopted by Piers Gough, Terry Farrell, and the developer Ian Pollard, combining overscaled Hollywood pastiche with little jokes and a concern for townscape.

In fields other than architecture, the label 'postmodernist' has been attached to a wide variety of cultural phenomena – from Madonna videos to the novels of Salman RUSHDIE – that appear to have very little in common. To qualify as postmodernist an artefact usually has to blend disparate styles and genres, make knowing use of earlier cultural references, or playfully emphasize style and surface at the expense of depth and 'authenticity'. Since the 1980s the term has often been used in a still vaguer sense to denote a general cultural condition affecting all aspects of life in the West. It is argued that in a society dominated by technology and the mass media culture will inevitably be eclectic, hybrid, fragmentary, and superficial. The boundaries between styles and genres will be dissolved, as will the traditional distinction between high and low culture. In such a milieu, it is argued, the qualities of depth, seriousness, and originality – prized equally by traditionalists and the earnest exponents of the avant-garde – lose all force as aesthetic criteria. Leading theorists of the postmodern condition have included Jean-François LYOTARD and Jean BAUDRILLARD.

poststructuralism An umbrella term for a number of intellectual tendencies that developed from French STRUCTURALISM in the later 1960s. The concept embraces the deconstruction of Jacques DERRIDA, the psychoanalysis of Jacques LACAN, the later work of Roland BARTHES, and the theoretical writings of Julia KRISTEVA and Michel FOUCAULT amongst others. All these thinkers were reacting to some degree against the scientific and totalizing claims of classical structuralism. They have in common a subversive attitude to the idea of determinate meaning and to all fixed categories, including those of personal and sexual identity.

Potter, Dennis (Christopher George) (1935–) British playwright and novelist, best known for his screenplays for television and the cinema. After several years as a television critic and journalist, Potter wrote his first play for television in 1965 and subsequently became established as a prolific writer of offbeat plays and adaptations. Several of his works have provoked controversy, notably *Brimstone and Treacle*, which was filmed in 1976 but not shown until 1987 because of objections to a scene in which a Satanic young man apparently cures a severely disabled girl by raping her. The television serial *Pennies from Heaven* (1978), which used popular songs from the 1930s to tell the story of a doomed love affair between a travelling salesman and a married woman, confirmed Potter as one of the most original writers for the small screen. Subsequent works have included *Blue Remembered Hills* (1979) and the extraordinarily successful serial *The Singing Detective* (1986), in which Potter took his experiments with narrative structure to new limits. Much less successful was *Blackeyes* (1989), an impenetrable series about the exploitation of women in the fashion business, which Potter directed himself. In 1993 he wrote and produced *Lipstick on Your Collar*, another serial with songs, this time set in the War Office during the Suez Crisis. Potter's novels include *Hide and Seek* (1973) and *Ticket to Ride* (1986).

Poulenc, Francis (1899–1963) French composer and pianist. He studied composition with Charles Koechlin and was influenced by the music of Satie, AURIC, Ravel, and especially Stravinsky. In his twenties he was a member (with Auric, Durey, Honegger, Milhaud, and Tailleferre) of Les Six, a group of French composers whose work represents a reaction against both romanticism and impressionism. In 1935 he rediscovered his Catholic faith and there followed a series of remarkable sacred works, including his mass in G (1937). After World War II he pursued an international career as a pianist, performing his own music and accompanying the tenor Pierre Bernac.

Poulenc's music is remarkable for its restraint and Gallic wit. The apparent simplicity of his scores belies their sophisticated technique and subtlety of harmonic and melodic effect. He excelled in setting poetry (Apollinaire, Cocteau, Eluard, and Lorca) and completed three operas, *Les Mamelles de Tirésias* (1947), *Dialogue de carmélites* (1957; libretto after Georges Bernanos), and *La Voix humaine* (1959), as well as the melodrama *Babar the Elephant* (1945). His instrumental music is neoclassical in inspiration and ranges from concertos (harpsichord, 1928; two pianos, 1932; organ, 1938; piano, 1949) to the popular sonatas for wind instruments and piano (flute, 1956; clarinet, 1962; oboe, 1962).

Pousseur, Henri (1929–) Belgian composer. Pousseur attended the conservatories at Liège (1947–52) and Brussels (1952–53) but far more important for his future development as a composer were his studies with Pierre BOULEZ, whom he first met in 1951. In the 1950s and 1960s he emerged as a major figure in the musical avant-garde, helping to found the pioneering electronic music studies in Cologne (1954) and Milan (1956) and the Apelac studios in Brussels (1958). During this period he associated with STOCKHAUSEN and BERIO, both of whom influenced his work, and taught at the DARMSTADT Institute (1957–67). He has also taught in Basel, Cologne, New York, and Paris.

Since moving away from strict SERIALISM in the 1960s, Pousseur's works have become extremely diverse in style and method, often employing widely different, apparently incompatible, elements in the same piece. He has made far-reaching use of aleatory procedures in such works as *Répons pour sept musiciens* (1960), where the course of the piece is decided partly by the movements of counters on a draughtboard (*see* ALEATORY MUSIC). The opera *Votre Faust* (1960–69) has a number of different endings, one of which must be selected by the audience on the night. Other works include *Couleurs croisées* (1968), an eccentric series of variations on the song 'We Shall Overcome', *Invitation à l'Utopie* (1971), one of several works to reflect Pousseur's Utopian political ideas, 19√8/4 for solo cello with unconventional tuning, and *Songs and Tales from the Bible of Death* (1979). He has also written widely on contemporary music.

Powell, Anthony (Dymoke) (1905–) British novelist and writer. Powell was educated at Eton and Balliol College, Oxford. In the 1930s he worked in publishing and wrote a series of novels satirizing the Bohemian society in which he moved. In the first of these, *Afternoon Men* (1931), a pleasure-seeking group of young people attempt to find a purpose to their lives. His other pre-war novels include *From a View to a Death* (1933) and *What's Become of Waring?* (1939). After the war, in which he served in the army, Powell embarked on a 12-novel sequence under the title *A Dance to the Music of Time*. Written from the viewpoint of one Nick Jenkins, the books follow a gallery of characters from their school days in the 1920s to the onset of old age in the 1960s and 1970s. In doing so they explore the often subtle changes that have taken place in British upper-class society during half a century; although the main emphasis is on the Bohemian fringes, the military, the business world, and politics are also scrutinized. Beginning with *A Question of Upbringing* (1951) and ending with *Hearing Secret Harmonies* (1975), the novels display a remarkable range of tone, from high comedy to tragedy. Since completing the sequence Powell has written two further novels *O, How the Wheel Becomes It!* (1983) and *The Fisher King* (1986). He has also published his memoirs in four volumes under the general title *To Keep the Ball Rolling* (1976–82) as well as two volumes of criticism *Miscellaneous Verdicts* (1990) and *Under Review* (1992).

Powell, Cecil Frank (1903–69) British physicist. Powell, the son of a gunsmith, was educated at Cambridge University, and obtained his PhD there in 1927. He spent virtually his entire career at Bristol University where he became Wills Professor of Physics in 1948 and director of the Wills Physics Laboratory in 1964.

Under Powell Bristol became a leading centre for the study of nuclear particles by means of photographic emulsions. In this technique an ionizing particle crossing a sensitive plate coated with grains of silver bromide leaves clear tracks of its passage. From the size and path of the track much information about the nature of the particle can be inferred. It was this technique that allowed Powell to discover the pi-meson (or pion) in 1947 in the plates of cosmic rays. The existence of such a particle had been predicted in 1935 by Hideki Yukawa, and Powell's discovery thus went some way to establish a coherent picture of nuclear phenomena.

For his discovery Powell was awarded the 1950 Nobel Prize for physics.

Powell, Michael (1905–90) British film director and screenwriter, who in collaboration with Emeric PRESSBURGER created some of the most inventive and influential films to issue from the British cinema in the 1940s and 1950s. Powell's career began in the 1920s, when he worked as an actor and assistant director; he directed his first film, *Two Crowded Hours*, in 1931. After a number of unambitious comedy thrillers his mature directorial style emerged in 1937 with *The Edge of the World*, which led to work with Alexander Korda and his meeting with Pressburger.

In his first film with Pressburger, the thriller *The Spy in Black* (1938), Powell experimented with the mystical, fantastical, and witty style that became a hallmark of his later films. The war years witnessed the making of several of the pair's most memorable works (usually under the auspices of Archer Films, the company they founded in 1942). These included *49th Parallel* (1941), a propaganda film calling for US intervention in the war, *One of Our Aircraft is Missing* (1942), *The Life and Death of Colonel Blimp* (1943), which traced the changing nature of warfare in the 20th century, and *A Canterbury Tale* (1944). *I Know Where I'm Going* (1945) and *A Matter of Life and Death* (1946) were both highly unusual dramas making clever use of the supernatural.

Outstanding among the films that followed were *Black Narcissus* (1946), set in the Himalayas, *The Red Shoes* (1948), a tragedy set against the background of the ballet, featuring many leading dance figures, and *The Small Back Room* (1948). Later films, among them *The Tales of Hoffman* (1951) and *The Battle of the River Plate* (1946), lacked the brilliance of their earlier work.

Of Powell's last films, the most interesting was *Peeping Tom* (1960), about a sadistic voyeur, in which the director played the killer's father. He travelled to Australia in 1966 and there made such films as *They're a Weird Mob* (1966) and *Age of Consent* (1969), before returning to Britain for one last collaboration with Pressburger, the children's fantasy *The Boy Who Turned Yellow* (1972). *See also* HECKROTH, HEIN.

Powell and Moya British architectural partnership of **Sir Philip Powell** (1921–) and **Hidalgo Moya** (1920–), founded in 1946 when they won a competition for the Churchill Gardens estate, London. The first important post-war housing scheme in Britain, it was completed in 1962. Their Skylon, the landmark of the FESTIVAL OF BRITAIN, won them still greater prominence. Since then their small office has continued to design for the public sector; their buildings are usually very rational and expressive of their concrete structure but exhibit a grace and humanity that has set them above those of their peers. Apart from Yorke, Rosenberg, and Mardall, they have been the only major practice to build extensively for the National Health Service, with hospitals at Swindon (1961–72), Slough (1966), High Wycombe (1966–75) and admissions units at Fairmile (1957) and Borocourt (1959–64). The reduction of hospitals to less intimidating single-storey units became a speciality.

The much-acclaimed Mayfield school for girls in Putney (1955) was followed by swimming baths nearby and by a series of college residences, firstly at Oxford for Brasenose (1962) and Christ Church (1968) Colleges, and then at Cambridge, where the Cripps Building at St John's College is a most successful addition to the historic riverscape. These were followed in 1974 by the new Wolfson College, Oxford, for mature students. The Festival Theatre in Chichester (1961) showed that Powell and Moya could produce an exciting thrust-stage theatre on a tight budget, and the Museum of London (1974–76) that they could handle an awkward site successfully. This was demonstrated once more when their Queen Elizabeth Conference Centre (1981–86) was built directly opposite Westminster Abbey. Despite its more sophisticated steel trim, this has something of the assertive yet unaggressive formal beauty of their best work.

Prades Festival An annual music festival held in Prades, France, during July and August. It was founded in 1950 by Pablo Casals (1876–1973), the Spanish cellist and composer, to mark the bicentenary of Bach's death. Casals had exiled himself to Prades, a village on the French side of the Pyrenees, following the Spanish Civil War; he continued to direct the festival until 1968. The programme concentrates on music of the baroque and classical eras.

Prague Spring Festival An annual music festival held in Prague. Founded in 1946 to attract artists and performers to Czechoslovakia after World War II, the festival takes place over three weeks each May. The operas, ballets, concerts, and recitals are staged in Prague's restored churches, theatres, and palaces.

Prague String Quartet Czech string quartet. The current members are Bretislav Novotný (first violin), Karel Přibyl (second violin), Lubomír Malý (viola), and Jan Širc (cello). The original members of the quartet, which made its debut in Prague in 1956, were Novotný (first violin), Miroslav Richter (second violin), Hubert Šimácek (viola), and Zdeněk Koníček (cello). In 1957 Richter was succeeded as second violinist by Karel Přibyl (until then leader of the National Theatre Orchestra) and the violist Šimácek by Jaroslav Karlovský. A further change of personnel occurred in 1968 when Karlovský was replaced by Lubomír Malý and the cellist Koníček by Jan Širc (until then with the Prague Radio Symphony Orchestra). The enduring member of the group, Novotný, teaches at the Prague Conservatory, where he was formerly a student; Přibyl and Malý teach at the Prague Academy.

In 1958 the Prague string quartet won the Liège International Quartet Competition, thus inaugurating their international career. In 1961 they became an official ensemble of the Prague Symphony Orchestra, which released them from orchestral duties. They have toured extensively. Their wide repertory includes, besides the standard works, quartets by Czech composers such as Dvořák, Smetana, Janáček, and Martinů.

Prassinos, Mario (1916–85) French painter and designer. Prassinos was born in Istanbul, to Greek parents. In 1922 he moved to France with his family and from 1932 to 1936 studied languages at the Sorbonne. During this time he took up painting and made contact with the Paris Surrealist group. During the 1930s and 1940s he produced grotesque works that show the influence of surrealism as well as several delightful pictures of cats. His painting was briefly interrupted by service as a volunteer soldier in 1939–40. He became a French citizen in 1940.

In the 1950s his work was much influenced by ART INFORMEL, the European equivalent of US abstract expressionism. His works (many of them paintings of trees and the countryside) became increasingly abstract and made considerable use of black brushstrokes. In the 1960s and 1970s he painted several 'hidden portraits' of the US singer Bessie Smith and of his own grandfather – paintings in which the apparently abstract composition has suggestions of a figure hidden within it. His abstract work of the late 1970s was very dense but in the 1980s he returned to painting trees. Prassinos also produced etchings and engravings, designed stage sets, and produced book illustrations, including those for SARTRE's *Le Mur*. From 1951 onwards he also designed tapestries, such as *Homage to Shakespeare* (1966). His paintings have been widely exhibited in Europe.

Pratolini, Vasco (1913–91) Italian novelist. Born in Florence to working-class parents, Pratolini was mainly self-educated. In the late 1930s he began to move in Florentine literary and artistic circles and to publish short stories. He was a founder (1939) of the journal *Campo di Marte*, later closed by the Fascists. In 1951 he moved to Rome where he lived until his death.

His first major novel *A Tale of Santa Croce* (*Il quartiere*; 1945) gives a realistic picture of the rise of class consciousness among a group of young working-class people in a poor quarter of Florence. Similar themes are explored in the novels from *The Two Brothers* (*Cronaca familiare*; 1945) and *A Tale of Poor Lovers* (1947) to *The Girls of San Frediano* (1949). In 1955 he published *Metello*, the first part of the historical trilogy *An Italian Story*, which also includes *The Waste* (1960) and *Allegory and Derision* (1966). Here Pratolini draws a complex portrait of Florentine society over a period of 70 years (1875–1945). Major historical events – class struggle in *Metello*, life under Fascism in *The Waste*, and the post-war crisis in *Allegory and Derision* – are explored through their impact on the private lives of his protagonists. Pratolini's own brand of Marxism was much influenced by the writings of the political thinker Antonio Gramsci (1891–1937).

His other works include the novel *The Constancy of Reason* (1963), the collection of poetry *My Town is Thirty Years Old* (1967), and, more recently, *Natascia's Sheaf* (1985), a volume including both verse and prose. He has also been active as a critic of art and cinema, a screenwriter, and a journalist.

Pressburger, Emeric (1902–88) Hungarian-born British film director, producer, and screenwriter, best known for his collaborations with Michael POWELL. Pressburger attended the universities of Prague and Stuttgart and worked as a journalist before beginning to write scripts for Austrian and German films. Following Hitler's rise to power, Pressburger worked in France before moving to Britain in 1935. He met POWELL in 1937 while working on Alexander Korda's film *The Challenge* (1938) and the two collaborated for the first time on Korda's *The Spy in Black* (1939). Having formed a production partnership in 1941 as 'The Archers', Powell and Pressburger worked together on the writing and direction of their films until 1956. Although none of their films was a great commercial success all were marked by high artistic and technical qualities. The first of their films to appear was *The Life and Death of Colonel Blimp* (1943), based on the famous cartoon creation of David Low. Other remarkable features included *A Matter of Life and Death* (1946), an ambitious film about the trial of a British airmen in heaven that was chosen for the first Royal Film Performance, *Black Narcissus* (1947), in which Anglo-Catholic nuns in the Himalayas succumb to local superstitions, the ballet story *The Red Shoes* (1948), which received an Academy Award nomination for best film, and *The*

Battle of the River Plate (1956), about the sinking of the German pocket battleship *Graf Spee*.

After the break-up of the partnership Pressburger wrote, produced, and directed *Miracle in Soho* (1957), about a romance between a roadworker and a barmaid, and scripted and produced the US film *Behold a Pale Horse* (1964), an adaptation of his own novel *Killing a Mouse on Sunday*. He also wrote the Carlo PONTI release *Operation Crossbow* (1965), about a World War II mission to destroy a Nazi rocket plant. In 1983 the British Film Institute awarded BFI Fellowships to Pressburger and Powell.

Prévert, Jacques (1900–77) French poet and screenwriter. Born in Neuilly-sur-Seine, Prévert was associated with the surrealist movement in the late 1920s but later developed a more accessible style of poetry influenced by popular balladry. He became famous with his long story-poem *Attempt to Describe a Dinner of Important People in Paris* (1931), a satirical attack on the powerful, the rich, the learned, and the conceited, on behalf of poor, simple, and honest people. This antiestablishment attitude remained constant throughout his work, as Prévert attacked war, capitalism, and organized religion while praising the power of romantic love to redeem even the hardest life. His polemic often depends on a simplistic distinction between 'us' and 'them' but is generally enlivened by his anarchic sense of humour. Many of his poems have become popular songs, notably those set to music by Josef Korma. *Paroles* (1946), his first volume, was followed by such collections as *Spectacle* (1951), *Stories and Other Stories* (1963), and *Things and Other Things* (1972).

Prévert also wrote a number of successful screenplays for the director Marcel Carné: *Port of Shadows* (1938), *Daybreak* (1939), and most famously *Les Enfants du paradis* (1945), a magnificent celebration of the theatre and romantic love.

Pritchett, Sir V(ictor) S(awdon) (1900–) British writer of novels and short stories. Born and educated in London, he entered the leather business before working as a journalist in Ireland, France, and Spain. His first novel, *Clare Drummer*, was published in 1929; although it was followed by several others, including *Mr Beluncle* (1951), it is for his short stories that he is now best known. These began to appear in the *New Statesman* and other journals in the 1920s; his first published collection was *The Spanish Virgin* (1930). His stories are characterized by their wide range, their gentle irony, and their keen insight into human nature. Other volumes include *You Make Your Own Life* (1938), *When my Girl Comes Home* (1961), *The Camberwell Beauty* (1974), *On the Edge of the Cliff* (1980), and *A Careless Widow* (1991). His collected stories were published in two volumes in 1982 and 1983 and his *Complete Short Stories* in 1990. His two volumes of autobiography *The Cab at the Door: Early Years* (1968) and *Midnight Oil* (1971) have also won much praise. Pritchett's criticism appeared regularly in the *New Statesman* (of which he became a director in 1946) and has been collected in such volumes as *The Living Novel* (1946); his *Complete Essays* were published in 1991. Other writings include biographies of Chekhov and Turgenev – both of whom have noticeably influenced his own work – and travel books about Spain, New York, and Dublin.

Prix Italia Festival An international competition held each September by Radiotelevisione Italiana (RAI) for TV and radio productions up to 90 minutes in length. The six Italia prizes of 15,000 Swiss francs each are awarded to the best TV and the best radio production in the three categories of drama, music, and documentary. Two entries are accepted from the national broadcasting organizations of each country. Six RAI prizes of 1,250,000 lire each are also awarded at the festival. The competition was established in 1948.

promenade performance In the theatre, a production in which the audience moves from one location in the auditorium to another as the play progresses. A feature of post-war theatre in Europe, the promenade performance allowed directors new possibilities in terms of audience participation and visual spectacle. In some productions the audience is seated at each location; more usually, however, the audience remains on its feet while the action takes place all around them – and even amongst them. The technique attracted considerable attention in the 1970s, being employed with particular success in MNOUCHKINE's acclaimed *1789* (1970) with the Théâtre de Soleil, by the ROYAL

SHAKESPEARE COMPANY in a production of Arthur Miller's *The Crucible*, and by Peter STEIN in a version of Shakespeare's *As You Like It* in Berlin. Other admired promenade performances have included revivals throughout Europe of medieval works, notably the various mystery plays presented on a regular basis at certain sites in Britain.

Prouvé, Jean (1901–84). French blacksmith turned architectural engineer. Prouvé was born and trained in Nancy, where he opened his first workshop in 1923. He pioneered lightweight metal structures, recognizing from first principles that sheet-metal, if crimped and folded, had the strength of large girders. He first demonstrated his ideas in an unbuilt housing project for Citroën. His Rolan Garros Flying Club (1937, with Eugène Beaudouin and Marcel Lods) has been called the first totally industrialized building; it was followed by the Maison du Peuple, Clichy (1938–40), a supremely adaptable market hall, function room, and cinema built in sheet metal.

After serving in the Resistance, Prouvé opened a new factory at Maxéville (1944) to build prefabricated houses, based on a design conceived in 1939 with Pierre JEANNERET and Charlotte Perriand. Cheap and supremely rational, some 800 houses were built before his factory was nationalized in 1954 and Prouvé found himself 'kicked upstairs' to a Paris consultancy. He built himself a house in Nancy with left-over prefab panels. Prouvé worked with most of France's leading post-war architects, including LE CORBUSIER and Bernard ZEHRFUSS, dominating the fields of curtain walling and light roofs. His huge output included schools, sports halls, workshops, and housing, and he also designed metal furniture. Although under French law he was never cited as designing his own buildings, the Palais de la Foire in Grenoble (1968), the La Defense Conference Centre in Paris (1958), and the Berlin Free University (1968) have since been credited to him, and in many others he took the creative lead. His influence can be seen in the work of Norman FOSTER and Richard ROGERS, whose career he advanced as the chief assessor of the Beaubourg competition in 1971 (*see* POMPIDOU CENTRE).

Puttnam, David (Terence) (1941–) British film producer, who became one of the most commercially successful producers of the 1980s. Having entered films in 1968, Puttnam attracted attention with such major features as Alan PARKER's *Bugsy Malone* (1976) and *Midnight Express* (1978), which won two Oscars, and Ridley SCOTT's *The Duellists* (1977). Puttnam has enjoyed an almost unbroken run of successes since 1978, when he became chairman of Enigma Productions. Hugh Hudson's *Chariots of Fire* (1981), a story about the rivalry of two British runners, won four Oscars and became a classic of the British cinema, while Bill FORSYTH's *Local Hero* (1982) and Roland JOFFE's *The Killing Fields* (1985), winner of three Oscars, and *The Mission* (1986), one Oscar, were all awarded major European prizes. In 1986 Puttnam became the first Briton to head a major US studio, when he was given control of Columbia. His attempts to raise artistic standards in Hollywood were not well received, however, and he resigned in 1987 to return to Britain, where he relaunched Enigma. Among his productions since then have been *Memphis Belle* (1990), about a US bomber crew in World War II, and Istvan SZABÓ's *Meeting Venus* (1991).

Pyriev, Ivan (1901–68) Soviet film director and screenwriter, noted for his adaptations of Dostoevskii. Pyriev began as an actor, appearing in a stage production by Eisenstein in 1923. Having chosen the cinema, he progresed in six years from assistant director to screenwriter to director. He subsequently won international recognition for his work in several genres, including comedies, musicals, and drama. His films were intensely Soviet, with titles such as *Tractor Driver* (1939), *Secretary of the District Committee* (1942), *Tales of the Siberian Land* (1947), and *Kuban Cossacks* (1949). Other films include *Our Mutual Friend* (1961), *Light of a Distant Star* (1965), and the Dostoevskii adaptations *The Idiot* (1958) and *The Brothers Karamazov* (1968), which he also scripted.

Q

Queneau, Raymond (1903–76), French writer. Having come to Paris in order to study philosophy, Queneau associated with the Surrealists in the 1920s and began to write while working as a bank clerk. His first novel *Barktree* appeared in 1933. He made a career at the Gallimard publishing house and after World War II became known to a broader public with his popular songs, his play *Exercises in Style* (1949), and above all with the novel *Zazie* (1959), the story of a twelve-year-old girl's picaresque adventures in Paris. This novel was adapted as a movie by Louis MALLE. His novels and plays are characterized by a prolific verbal inventiveness, in which puns, slang, and linguistic games feature prominently. Similar qualities are to be found in his poetry, most of which was collected in *If You Think* (1951). Later novels include *The Blue Flowers* (1967) and *The Flight of Icarus* (1973). Queneau was a lifelong contributor to newspapers and journals and from 1951 a member of the Académie de Goncourt.

Quotidien, Théâtre du A European theatre movement that developed in the 1970s and has since had a particularly strong influence upon drama in Germany and France. Plays belonging to the genre present mainly working-class characters, who are prevented both by social pressures and by their own inarticulacy from expressing their alienation from society. The action tends to be naturalistic and often includes scenes of great brutality. Georges Michel was probably the first playwright to produce work of this kind; his plays *The Sunday Walk* (1966) and *A Little Love Nest* (1970) were influenced by the absurdists and by the writing of SARTRE. Subsequent writers associated with the genre have included the German playwrights Michel Deutsch, HANDKE, KROETZ, SPERR, and Jean-Paul Wenzel. Many of the most important works of the Théâtre du Quotidien were written for the Comédie de Caen and the Théâtre National de Strasbourg, where Jean-Pierre VINCENT has done much to promote them.

R

Rad, Gerhard von (1901–1971) German Protestant theologian. After completing his studies in 1930, Rad worked as a pastor for some years before returning to academic life; he subsequently taught theology of the Old Testament in Leipzig, Jena, Göttingen, and Heidelberg. One of this century's most important Old Testament scholars, Rad did much to restore the Jewish scriptures to their proper prominence in Christian thought. During the Nazi period Rad suffered much abuse for this emphasis on the Jewish roots of Christianity.

Rad insisted that the Old Testament be read as a document of God's revelation to man in history. According to Rad, the Old Testament must not be regarded as a mere foreshadowing of the New; it contains not only promise but fulfilment and the concept of Divine Grace is as important as that of Divine Law. Early Jewish religion consisted fundamentally in the celebration and remembrance of Jahweh's grace in leading his people out of Egypt to Israel, the Promised Land. Although he abstained from any dogmatic or systematic teachings, Rad's approach was widely influential. His collected *Old Testament Studies* were published in two volumes in 1958 and 1973.

Rahner, Karl (1904–84), German Roman Catholic theologian. Rahner entered the Society of Jesus in 1922 and was ordained priest in 1932. In 1934 he began his doctoral dissertation at the University of Freiburg but then moved to Innsbruck, where he taught theology until the Nazis closed the faculty in 1938. Until 1944 Rahner taught at Vienna; after the war he resumed at Pullach near Munich, returning to Innsbruck in 1949. In 1964 he was appointed to a chair of Christian *Weltanschauung* in Munich but following doctrinal conflicts he moved to Münster in 1967, remaining there until his retirement in 1971.

Rahner's dissertation *Spirit in the World* (1939) introduced his central theme of man as a spiritual being existing in a complicated material world with which he has to come to terms. Writing as a dogmatic theologian, Rahner tried to develop and reformulate Catholic doctrine to meet the pressing conditions of this century; in doing so he frequently found himself at variance with more traditional ways of presenting the teachings of the Church. In his book on meditation *Encounters with Silence* (1938) and in *On Prayer* (1949) Rahner interpreted the human condition within the world as directed towards a transcendent Being. Rahner took a major part in the Second Vatican Council (1962–65), where he was repeatedly attacked for his alleged anthropological reductionism and idealistic EXISTENTIALISM. By the late 1960s he had established a reputation as perhaps the foremost living Catholic theologian. Rahner's essays have been collected in the numerous volumes of his *Theological Investigations* (1954–84) and his major late work *Foundations of Christian Faith* was published in 1976. In this he tried to work out a viable dogmatic foundation for the Catholic faith that could withstand the challenges of relativism and scepticism.

Rainer, Roland (1910–) Austrian architect and planner. To a professorship at the Vienna Academy of Fine Arts (from 1956) Rainer added (1958–63) the post of Vienna's chief planning officer. He championed the building of low-rise public housing, his first work being a prefabricated estate designed in 1954 with Carl Auböck. His Mauerberggasse project followed in 1963, an embodiment of the ideas set out in *Die Gegliederte und Aufgelockerte Stadt*, published in 1957.

These simple buildings may be contrasted with his larger projects, in particular a series of multifunctional municipal halls. That for Vienna (1956–58) was followed by a more dramatic design for Bremen (1961–64). Its expressionist profile is formed by the concrete structure of the grandstand, which also supports a giant hyperbolic paraboloid roof that masks the size of the auditorium and permits a great glazed end overlooking a park. It is a triumph both of expressive form and structural ingenuity that was repeated in a third hall, at Ludwigshafen, Germany, completed in 1965.

Rainer also worked extensively in Austria's new towns, building a hall, lido, and housing estate at Ternitz (1961–63), and housing for Purchenau Garden City, near Linz (1966–78), where he also designed a Catholic centre (1976) using traditional facings.

Rakovszky, Zsuzsa (1950–) Hungarian poet. After studying English and Hungarian at the University of Budapest, Rakovszky worked as a librarian (1975–81) and as an editor in a state publishing house (until 1986). Since 1987 she has been a freelance writer and translator and has published three volumes of poetry. Among the most promising poets of her generation, she won the annual Robert Graves Award for the best poem of 1980 published by a young author and was awarded a major state prize for her second volume of poetry, *One House Further Away* (1988). Much of her poetry focuses on themes of spiritual isolation and despair and is distinguished by powerfully sensuous and memorably graphic imagery.

Rambert Dance Company British dance company, founded (as the **Ballet Rambert**) by Dame Marie Rambert (1888–1982) from her Ballet Club company in 1935. With their founder's guidance, the company presented a mixed programme of classical and new works, winning particular acclaim for performances of Fokine's *Les Sylphides*. The troupe toured widely, making highly successful appearances in Australia and New Zealand in the 1940s and subsequently becoming the first British ballet company to tour China (1957). Rambert herself maintained close personal control of the company, while encouraging such important new choreographers as Norman Morrice. In 1966 the company dropped its classical repertoire and began to concentrate on contemporary dance. With Morrice taking over its day-to-day management, the Ballet Rambert became one of the most respected and popular of contemporary dance troupes, staging works by such choreographers as Glen Tetley, Christopher BRUCE, Richard ALSTON, and Robert North. Alston replaced North as director in 1986 and introduced a new programme of works influenced by the US choreographer Merce Cunningham, among them dance pieces by Michael CLARK, Ashley Page, and Siobhan DAVIES. This change in emphasis was reflected by the renaming of the troupe as the Rambert Dance Company in 1987. In 1992 Alston announced that he was leaving the company.

Rame, Franca (1930–) Italian actress, playwright, and theatre manager, who has been widely praised for her work in conjunction with her husband, the satirist Dario FO, as well as for her own theatrical projects. Born into a theatrical family, Rame played a key role in the development of the **La Comune** company (founded in 1970). She has also acquired a reputation for challenging political statements on women's issues with a series of self-performed monologues.

In *The Mother* (1977) she explored the feelings of a mother for her son, who is on trial for terrorist offences; while in *The Rape* (1983) she recounted the details of an attack made on herself, possibly at the instigation of political opponents. Her collaborations with Fo – from whom she eventually separated – have included *It's All Bed, Board and Church* (1977), a compilation of four monologues, *Female Parts* (1981), and *The Open Couple* (1987), depicting the disintegrating relationship of a married couple.

Rasputin, Valentin Grigorievich (1937–) Russian novelist associated with the tendency known as 'Village Prose'. Born and educated in the Irkutsk region, he started writing in 1961, producing mainly quasi-journalistic sketches about his native Siberia. In 1967 a short but gripping novel, *Money for Maria*, about an old storekeeper's attempts to make up missing money to avoid gaol, showed Rasputin's skill as both storyteller and psychologist. Matriarchal figures also dominate *The Final Stage* (1970), in which an old woman's alienated and cold-hearted children visit their mother shortly before her death, and *Farewell to Matera* (1976), Rasputin's most ambitious work to date, which places an old woman at the centre of resistance to the flooding of her ancient island community to make way for a hydroelectric power scheme. In all these novels the author contrasts traditional values with destructive aspects of modern life. That these are not purely urban is shown in *The Fire* (1985), perhaps his bleakest work, in which we see villagers behave with crude selfishness while their neighbours' homes burn down. Rasputin's most psychologically rich novel is *Mark You This* (*Zhivi i pomni*; 1974), the only work not given a contemporary setting. In it a Soviet soldier deserts in the last months of the war to visit his native Siberian village, where he and his saintly ill-used wife are dragged into a grim spiral of violence and death. The novel, remarkable in the context of Soviet war literature, depicts not only rigid Stalinist attitudes but also human weakness, evil, and self-sacrifice on a universal level. In recent years Rasputin appears to have abandoned literature for reactionary politics, but his novels of the 1970s are amongst the most powerful examples of modern Soviet prose.

Rattigan, Sir Terence (Mervyn) (1911–77) British playwright whose well-crafted plays were among the most commercially successful of the 1940s and 1950s. Having established his reputation before World War II with the light comedy *French Without Tears* (1936), he made his name as a serious writer with the wartime play *Flare Path* (1942), based on his own experiences in the RAF. *The Winslow Boy* (1946), the true story of a naval cadet wrongly accused of stealing a postal order, quickly entered the repertory. His next drama, *The Browning Version* (1948), depicting the crisis facing a public-school teacher who sees his life collapsing all around him, was also well received. Further successes during the 1950s included *The Deep Blue Sea* (1952), a tragedy about the breakup of a marriage, *Separate Tables* (1954), concerning the private troubles of guests in a Bournemouth hotel, and *Ross* (1960), a portrayal of the latter years of T. E. Lawrence's life. The advent of the ANGRY YOUNG MEN in the late 1950s made Rattigan's adherence to the conventions of the 'well-made play' and his concentration on upper middle-class subjects seem outdated, although several of his plays have since been filmed and his best work is regularly revived.

Rattigan's other writing included several screenplays, including those for the films *The Sound Barrier* (1952) and *The V.I.P.s* (1963). He is also remembered for creating the figure of Aunt Edna, the archetypal British theatregoer, who will not accept anything that is not respectable or easily grasped.

Rattle, Simon (Denis) (1955–) British conductor. Rattle was born in Liverpool and educated at the Royal Academy of Music, London. His career began when he won the Bournemouth John Player International Conducting Competition in 1973, leading to his appointment as conductor of both the Bournemouth Symphony Orchestra and the Bournemouth Sinfonietta a year later. Among the orchestras he has since conducted are the London Philharmonic, the Berlin Philharmonic, the Los Angeles Philharmonic, Stockholm Philharmonic, and the Toronto Symphony Orchestra. He was associate conductor of the Royal Liverpool Philharmonic Orchestra from 1977 to 1980, principal conductor of the London Choral Society from 1978 to 1984, and joint artistic director of the ALDEBURGH FESTIVAL in 1982. Since 1980 he has been principal conductor of the City of Birmingham Symphony Orchestra and has been highly successful in raising the Orchestra's public profile. He has worked with period instruments but is best known for his interpretations of difficult early 20th-century works.

Ratushinskaya, Irina (1954–) Russian poet. A precociously literary child, Ratushinskaya studied physics in her hometown of Odessa. She began to write seriously in the late 1970s, by which time she had rediscovered her ancestral Catholicism and developed a highly critical attitude to the Soviet regime. After losing her teaching post in 1978 she married the human-rights activist Igor Geraschenko and moved to Kiev. In 1981 they were both briefly jailed for attending a demonstration but continued to use the *samizdat* to disseminate over 26 000 pages of banned writings, including the poetry of Osip Mandel'shtam. In 1983 Ratushinskaya was sentenced to seven years' hard labour for anti-Soviet activities, the main evidence against her being her own poems. At a strict regime camp in Mordavia she wrote over 300 poems, some on bars of soap, smuggling them out mainly by word of mouth. Her case became a *cause célèbre* in the West following the bilingual publication of *Poems* (1984), followed by *Off Limits* (1986) and the short stories in *A Tale of Three Heads* (1986). The poetry is intimate and lyrical, affirming her love of nature and religious faith even as it details the brutality and despair of the prison camp. Released on the eve of the Rejkjavic summit in October 1986, Ratushinskaya travelled to Britain with her husband. The poems collected in *No, I'm Not Afraid* (1986) and her memoir *Grey is the Colour of Hope* (1988) highlight both the inhumanity of the prison regime and the resilience and mutual support of the women prisoners. Her poems were first published in the Soviet Union in 1989.

Reed, Sir Carol (1906–76) British film director, who is remembered for the classic films he directed during the late 1940s. Reed began his career in the theatre and entered the cinema as a director at EALING STUDIOS, where, in 1933, he made his first feature *Midshipman Easy*. His other early films included *Bank Holiday* (1938), *The Stars Look Down* (1939), about a mining community in Wales, *Night Train to Munich* (1940), *Kipps* (1941) and the war-propaganda films *The Way Ahead* (1944) and *The True Glory* (1945), for which he and codirector Garson Kanin shared an Oscar.

Reed's major post-war period began with *Odd Man Out* (1947), in which James Mason starred as a hunted IRA gunman, and *The Fallen Idol* (1948), the first of three books by Graham GREENE that Reed adapted for the cinema. Greene's *The Third Man* (1949), about the illegal market in penicillin in Vienna after World War II, became in Reed's hands one of the most memorable of cinema classics, starring Joseph Cotten and Trevor Howard with a small but ominous part played by Orson Welles. With a screenplay by Greene himself and zither music composed and played by Anton Karas, this stylish and beautifully crafted thriller consolidated Reed's reputation as one of the most prominent directors of his generation. A further success was *Outcast of the Islands* (1951), taken from the novel by Joseph Conrad. He was knighted in 1952.

Reed's later career was less remarkable, although his sensitive direction of Greene's thriller *Our Man in Havana* (1959) was also praised. *Oliver!* (1968), a musical adaptation of *Oliver Twist*, brought him an Oscar for best director. He retired from the cinema in 1972.

Rego, Paula (1935–) British painter, born in Portugal. Her parents were cultured and comfortably-off Anglophiles and in 1951 they sent her to London, where she studied at the Slade School of Fine Arts (it was here that she met her late husband, the British painter Victor Willing). In the 1980s, at a time favourable for her colourful and somewhat expressionistic style, she came to the fore as one of the leading women painters of her generation. The figures in her paintings often have a cartoon-like character and her work has a welcome note of humour. Since the late 1980s her work has made use of illusionistic space and has abounded in art-historical references as well as allusions to fairy tales and nursery rhymes. Recent paintings are dominated by images of women and girls.

In 1990 Rego was appointed the first associate artist of the National Gallery, London, and in 1992 an exhibition of her work was held there – an unprecedented honour for a living painter. She also provided the large triptych *Crivelli's Garden* for the restaurant in the Sainsbury Wing of the National Gallery, which opened in 1991. The growing interest in her work was marked by the Phaidon Press's publication of a substantial monograph on her by John McEwen in 1992.

Reichlin and Reinhart Swiss architectural partnership. **Bruno Reichlin** (1941–) and **Fabio Reinhart** (1942–) met as students at Zurich University and set up in partnership in 1970. Although they teach in Geneva, their major works are nearly all in the Italian-speaking canton of Ticino. Their architecture combines rigid geometry with Palladian planning and proportions and uses both modern and traditional materials. An early example is the Casa Tonini (1972–74), based on Rudolf Wittkover's theories of Palladianism. It was followed by a timber atrium added to the House of Justice (1972–75), Sornico, and the Casa Sortori, Riveo (1976–77), a functional box given a Diocletian window as its centrepiece. They also contributed to the project *Città Analoga* (1976), with Eraldo Consolacio and Aldo ROSSI; the latter is a strong influence on their work.

A feature of Reichlin and Reinhart's work has been their interesting collaborations with other architects. Work on an extension to the Sferax factory at Cortaillod with Consolacio and Marie-Claude Bétrix (1978–81) was followed (1986) by a factory in Coesfeld Lette, Germany, with Santiago Calatrava and featuring his collapsing frame structures. Reichlin and Reinhart can also be frivolous, as is shown in their recent (1989–91) Mövenpick Motel at Bellinzona, a witty design complete with towers and a drawbridge. They have continued their early specialization in renovating older houses, as at the Casa Pellanda, Biasca (1988).

Reimann, Aribert (1936–) German composer and pianist. After studies with BLACHER and Ernst Pepping at the Berlin Musikhochschule (1955–59) he worked as a pianist, becoming well known as an accompanist to the baritone Dietrich Fischer-Dieskau. His early compositions were influenced by Webern but he abandoned serialism in 1967 when he began to compose in a more expressionist style. Principal works include the operas *Ein Traumspiel* (1965), *Lear* (1978), usually considered his greatest work, and *Die Gespenstersonate* (1984); the ballet *The Scarecrows* (1970) has a libretto by Günter GRASS. In 1992 his opera *Das Schloss*, based on Kafka's *The Castle*, was premiered at the BERLINER FESTWOCHEN. He has also composed orchestral, vocal, and chamber music.

Reisz, Karel (1926–) British film director, born in Czechoslovakia, who trained as a biochemist. He established his reputation as a director with *Saturday Night and Sunday Morning* (1960), from the novel by Alan Sillitoe; the film starred Albert Finney, who also played the lead in Reisz's *Night Must Fall* (1964), from the play by Emlyn Williams. Reisz's association with contemporary British playwrights continued with *Morgan, a Suitable Case for Treatment* (1966), based on David MERCER's play about madness. Subsequently he widened his range with such films as *Isadora* (1968), a biopic featuring Vanessa Redgrave as the dancer Isadora Duncan, *The Gambler* (1974), in which he indulged his taste for epic cinema, and *Who'll Stop the Rain?* (1978), an intelligent thriller set in the drugs subculture of the US.

Reisz's biggest commercial success came in 1981, when he directed Jeremy Irons and Meryl Streep in *The French Lieutenant's Woman*, adapted from the novel by John FOWLES. His most recent films include *Sweet Dreams* (1985), a moving depiction of an unstable marriage, and *Everybody Wins* (1990), derived from Arthur Miller's play *Some Kind of Love Story*.

Rencontres Internationales d'Art Contemporain An annual arts festival held in La Rochelle, France, in June and July. It was founded in 1973 with the Belgian musicologist Harry Halbreich as artistic adviser. Although the festival is primarily concerned with contemporary music, the programme also includes theatre, dance, cinema, and the visual arts. *See also* ROYAN FESTIVAL.

Rencontres Internationales de Musique Contemporain An international festival of contemporary music, held in Metz, France. Founded in 1972, the festival is held each autumn. The programme features the work of established modern composers as well as showcasing new talent.

Resnais, Alain (1922–) French film director, who emerged as a leading figure of the NEW WAVE in the late 1950s. Resnais began his career directing shorts, including several biopics of artists, such as Van Gogh and Gauguin.

His first feature film, *Hiroshima mon amour* (1959), caused a sensation with its innovative fragmentary style in which memories of the past intermingle with events in the present and future, enabling parallels to be drawn between a woman's love affair with an architect in modern Japan and her wartime romance with a German soldier. These innovations were taken even further in *Last Year in Marienbad* (1961), in which the past, present, and future become confused as the central characters try to work out whether they have met before.

Resnais has since returned to these themes many times. In *Muriel* (1963) an old woman is deceived by her memories of a long-past love affair; in *The War is Over* (1966) a revolutionary soldier is troubled by his recollections of the Spanish Civil War; while in *Je t'aime, Je t'aime* (1967) a failed suicide becomes hopelessly lost during an experiment in time travel.

After *Stavisky* (1974), a meditation upon a French scandal of the 1930s, Resnais made *Providence* (1977), which starred John Gielgud as an ailing writer who draws on his cynical feelings towards his family in preparing his next book. *My American Uncle* (1980) was well received for its surreal exploration of human behaviour in stressful situations and revived Resnais's reputation for technical brilliance.

More recently Resnais has courted criticism by probing ever more esoteric themes; he tackled ideas of Utopia in *Life is a Bed of Roses* (1983), combined religious and romantic elements in *L'Amour a mort* (1984), and returned to the topic of memory and its distortions in *Mélo* (1986).

Revell, Viljo (1910–64) Finnish architect, his country's first champion of architectural Rationalism. His multipurpose and lightweight 'Glass Palace' (1935; with Niilo Kokko and Heimo Riihimäki), built while he was still a student, gave Helsinki a new commercial centre. Research at Finland's Reconstruction Office from 1942 to 1949 developed his ideas of system building and prefabrication, which led to his winning Finland's first major post-war competition, for the Teollisuuskeskus Building in Helsinki (built in 1949–52). While this used industrialized construction components like strip windows, the Mäntyviita-Sufika housing at Tapiola (1954) employed precast panels and prestressed beams and slabs. His aesthetic of repeating units was meanwhile developed in the sinuous Blue Ribbon housing (1952) and distinguishes even small projects like his Meilahti School (1953) and Kärjensivu Rowhouses (1954–55).

Revell's clear systematic plans, coupled with highly advanced technical specifications, produced a finely detailed and supremely logical architecture of deceptive simplicity. These characteristics are perhaps best seen in the huge knitwear factory for Kudeneule at Hanko (1954–55) and the barracks of the Helsinki Guards (1956–62), the latter a rebuilding in curtain-wall construction on an 1840s plan following bomb damage. More expressive was his steeply arched Vatiala cemetery chapel at Tampere (1958–61).

In 1958 Revell won the competition for Toronto City Hall with Heikki Castren, Bengt Lundsten, and Seppo Valjus. They produced a powerful symbolic composition of two concave towers and a podium flanking a circular council chamber. This massive project (completed in 1964) and the tall narrow Peugot tower in Buenos Aires (1962) seem to have hastened Revell's early death.

Richards, Ceri (1903–71) Welsh painter. Born at Dunvant in South Wales, Richards studied at the Swansea School of Art (1921–24) and at the Royal College of Art in London (1924–27), where he encountered the work of the European avant-garde. He also studied drawing at the Westminster School of Art with Bernard Meninsky. After some years working as a commercial draughtsman (1927–37) he taught part-time at the Chelsea College of Art. He was head of painting at Cardiff College of Art (1940–44) and later taught at the Royal College of Art (1956–61).

Richards absorbed numerous influences from the work of his contemporaries while retaining a forceful style of his own. From 1933 to 1938 he produced relief constructions; unlike those of many continental artists, however, Richards's reliefs were not geometrical but had a pictorial, almost theatrical, quality. During the late 1940s and 1950s he produced many remarkable drawings of his daughters and his father. In 1951 he attracted popular interest with his painting *Trafalgar Square* (Tate Gallery, London), which was commissioned in connection with the FESTIVAL OF BRITAIN. He was also inspired by the poetry of Dylan Thomas and by his love of music, painting several works in response to Debussy's piano prelude *La Cathédrale engloutie*. Richards's paintings of the 1960s were bright and full of energy, incorporating images of earth and nature. Amongst other important commissions, Richards designed scenery and costumes for Sir Lennox BERKELEY's opera *Ruth* (1954) and for BRITTEN's work *Noyes Fludde* (1958).

Richter, Hans Werner (1908–) German novelist. After serving an apprenticeship as a bookseller, Richter moved to Berlin, where his experience of unemployment led him to become a member (1930) of the Communist Party. He was expelled two years later because of his Trotskyism.

After Hitler's rise to power he emigrated to Paris, but returned to Berlin to work in the Resistance; he was arrested in 1940 but had to be released through lack of evidence. In the same year he was drafted into the army. From 1943 until 1946 he was a US prisoner of war.

After his return to Germany in 1946 Richter quickly established himself as one of the leading post-war German intellectuals. He edited the influential journal *Der Ruf* with Alfred ANDERSCH and René Hocke until 1947, when it was banned by the US authorities because of its socialist ideals. Subsequently he became the main founder of GRUPPO 47, the most important literary circle in post-war Germany.

Richter's own novels are informed by his experience of totalitarianism and war. *They Fell from God's Grace* (1951) is a novel about the wartime experiences of 12 characters, including both war criminals and victims, from all the major European countries. In *Traces in the Sand* (1953) Richter describes the stifling political and cultural climate of his youth. *Thou Shalt not Kill* (1956) is a parable of the destructive power of war. Like Heinrich BÖLL Richter belongs to a post-war German literary tradition that is simultaneously committed to realism on the aesthetic level and to Utopian humanism on the ethical. Other works include *Letters to a Young Socialist* (1974), *The Flight to Abanon* (1980), and *Hours of False Triumph* (1981).

Richter, Karl (1926–81) German conductor, organist, and harpsichordist. Born in Plauen, Richter studied at the Conservatories at Dresden and Leipzig under the organist and conductor Günther Ramin. He began his career as an organist but in 1951 became director of the Munich Bach Choir and in 1953 founded the Munich Bach Orchestra. He continued to direct both ensembles for many years, frequently taking both choir and orchestra on tour. His repertory was broad but he is best known for his accomplished, if somewhat conservative, interpretations of Bach and Handel.

Ricoeur, Paul (1913–) French philosopher. Born in the Drôme area of southern France, Ricoeur studied philosophy under the Christian existentialist Gabriel Marcel. During World War II he was held prisoner in Germany and made an intensive study of the thought of Husserl, whose work he later translated and upon which he wrote several commentaries. He subsequently taught philosophy at the University of Strasbourg (1950–56), the Sorbonne (1956–66), Nanterre University (1966–70), and the University of Chicago.

Ricouer's earlier writings are mainly concerned with the philosophy of the will and the problem of human freedom. His most important work in this field appears in the sequence of volumes *Freedom and Nature* (1950), *Fallible Man* (1960), and *The Symbolism of Evil* (1969). He is better known, however, for his writings on hermeneutics, in which he tries to reconcile the insights of psychoanalysis and phenomenology. His major works on the problem of interpretation are *The Conflict of Interpretations* (1969), *Freud and Philosophy; an Essay on Interpretation* (1970), and his remarkable study of the way in which metaphor creates its own poetic truth, *The Rule of Metaphor* (1975). Recent works include *Time and Narrative* (1983, 1985). In spite of the wide scope of his investigations, Ricoeur did not receive much acknowledgement until the 1980s, perhaps because he stood somewhat aside from the dominant intellectual trends of STRUCTURALISM and POSTSTRUCTURALISM.

Ridolfi, Mario (1904–84) Italian architect. Born in Rome, Ridolfi studied at the University there, producing a graduation thesis that was already imbued with the ideas of Rationalism. In the early 1930s he collaborated on projects with Adalberto Libera (organizer of the 1928 Rationalist exhibition in Milan) and made a trip to Germany (1933) that gave his work expressionist qualities. Early works included a post office in the Piazza Bologna, Rome (1933, with a gracefully curved facade), swimming pools, and a leisure centre. With houses in the Via Villa Massimo and Via di San Valentino, Rome (1937–38) he and his longstanding partner Wolfgang Frankl turned decisively towards more traditional construction systems.

After World War II Ridolfi developed this preoccupation in his *Manuelle dell'architetto* (1946) and in a series of INA-Casa subsidized housing schemes. Much admired at the time, his combination of US social theory and traditional, even baroque, design was not always successful, as at the Via Triburtino (1949–54). The Agip Motel of 1967–70 was also deemed a failure and even a cause of his suicide years later. This contrasts with the success and influence of more vernacular projects such as the Olivetti Nursery School at Ivrea (1960) and a series of houses at Terni that include the Casa Lina (1966), Casa De Bonis (1972), Casa Lana (1974), and the Casa Briganti (1975). All are based on a central plan and use such traditional forms as tile roofs, Roman vaults, and wood frames.

At the 1980 Venice Biennale Ridolfi was honoured as a precursor of POSTMODERNISM's rediscovery of older styles and techniques.

Rie, Dame Lucie (1902–) British studio potter, born in Austria. She studied at the Kunstgewerbeschule (School of Arts and Crafts) in Vienna, where she was influenced by the city's Modern Movement, and worked as an independent potter from 1927. Following the Anschluss (1938), she settled in Britain, where she came under the influence of Bernard LEACH. From 1946 to 1958 she shared a studio with the potter Hans Coper. Her work is characterized by clear, often rather austere, forms with minimal decoration; at the same time she has achieved colouristic effects of great subtlety through glazing and staining. It is represented in many public collections in Britain and elsewhere. Rie has won numerous awards, including gold medals at exhibitions in Brussels (1935), Milan (1936 and 1954) and Munich (1964). A major retrospective of her work was held in Japan in 1989. She became a DBE in 1990.

Rifbjerg, Klaus (1931–) Danish writer. One of the most prolific and versatile writers in contemporary Denmark, Rifbjerg has produced prose, poetry, plays, and film scripts.

He made his debut as a writer in 1956 with a collection of ironic prose poems about childhood, *Findings About Myself*. His first novel, *The Chronic Innocence*, followed in 1958; set in the 1940s, it is a many-sided tale of two schoolboy companions growing up. The technical innovations of *Confrontation* (1960), a collection of poems about the ego's relationship with the external world, had a far-reaching influence on Danish poetry of the 1960s. The major poem *Camouflage* (1961) is a complex series of reflections about human personality, again prompted by childhood memories.

The novel *Anna (I) Anna* (1969) concerns a middle-class woman whose apparently perfect life is suddenly shattered by an acute crisis of identity. The book follows her trail across Europe and explores the way in which several different personalities can apparently coexist in the same human being.

Although Rifbjerg collaborated on a number of plays from his student days onwards, his first independent production was *Developments* (1965). *The Modest Ones*, a serial for radio, was broadcast in 20 episodes from 1975 to 1976; it traces the fortunes of a middle-class family through three generations. Later works by Rifbjerg include *Mythology* (1970), a collection of poems, the novel *Letter to Gerda* (1972), *The Black Hole* (1980), the play *All Quiet on the Kitchen Front* (1984), and *Angel* (1987).

Rifbjerg has also been active as a broadcaster, journalist, and literary critic. He has edited several journals, including (1959–64) the literary periodical *The Wind Rose* with Villy SØRENSEN. He has received several important prizes.

Rihm, Wolfgang (1952–) German post-expressionist composer. Rihm studied under FORTNER at the Karlsruhe Musikhochschule, with STOCKHAUSEN in Cologne, and at the DARMSTADT Institute. He has taught at Karlsruhe since 1973. His work is severely atonal. Major compositions include the chamber operas *Faust und Yorick* (1973) and *Jakob Lenz* (1980), the ballet *Tutuguri* (1982), and symhonies. He has also composed *O Notte* (with a text by Michelangelo) for baritone and small orchestra, *Cuts and Dissolves* (1977), a concerto for 29 players, five string quartets, and settings of Nietzsche, Hölderlin, and Artaud.

Riley, Bridget (Louise) (1931–) British exponent of OP ART. Born in London, Riley studied at Goldsmiths' College of Art (1949–52), where she concentrated on drawing, and at the Royal College of Art (1952–55), where she concentrated on painting. She then worked for an advertising agency and taught at Loughborough College of Art (1959), Hornsey College of Art (1960), and part-time at the Croydon School of Art (1962).

In the early 1960s, influenced by study of the French neoimpressionist George Seurat and by Victor VASARELY, Riley settled on an approach to painting that she has pursued consistently ever since. Working at first in black and white, she began to produce paintings featuring repeated simple elements arranged in tense patterns. The paintings either create an illusion of movement or otherwise disturb the retina, leaving it with shifting, vibrating images. In the late 1960s she introduced colour and over the past 20 years has gradually increased the number of colours used in any one painting and the sophistication of the patterns and colour combinations. Since the mid 1980s her work has used diagonals as well as uprights. Rather than being based on mathematical calculation or an understanding of optics, as some have thought, her works are the outcome of intuition and experimentation. Riley was quickly recognized as one of Britain's leading abstract painters. She gave her first one-woman show in 1962 and in 1963 won a prize in the John Moores Exhibition in Liverpool. She won the International Prize for Painting at the Venice Biennale of 1969. There were major exhibitions of her work at the Hayward Gallery in London in 1971 and 1992.

Ritsos, Yannis (1909–90) Greek poet. Born in Monemvasía, Greece, Ritsos worked as a legal clerk, librarian, editor, and actor until becoming a full-time writer in 1956. A prolific author, he published more than 2000 pages of poetry, as well as plays and essays. His commitment to socialism provides a constant theme in his work; he was imprisoned twice for his views and was banned from publishing during the late 1940s and early 1950s. His work is characterized by a mixture of tragic pessimism and willed political hope. In *Epitaph* (1936), one of his most successful early poems, a demonstration for political rights provides the setting for a mother's lament for her son, a protestor shot dead by police. His most famous poem, 'Romiosini' (1954), links the unending struggle against the harsh Greek climate and land with the struggle against political oppression. Ritsos's work ranges from brief epigrammatic pieces to long poems in Whitmanesque free verse; in both kinds of poem he combines a sensitivity to visual detail with an appreciation of the universal human condition. Many of his poems have been set to music, notably by his friend Mikis THEODORAKIS, with whom he often collaborated. His later publications included *Strange Things*, *The Sponge-Divers' Chorale*, and *Teiresias* (all 1983).

Robbe-Grillet, Alain (1922–) French novelist and essayist. After studying agronomy Robbe-Grillet worked for several years as a statistician and agronomist before becoming successful as a writer in the mid 1950s. He has also taught literature courses at various universities.

Four books published in the 1950s established Robbe-Grillet as a leading exponent of the NOUVEAU ROMAN: *The Erasers* (1953), *The Voyeur* (1955), *Jealousy* (1957), and *In the Labyrinth* (1959). In his collection of essays *For a New Novel* (1963) Robbe-Grillet argued that the objects of the world neither reveal nor conceal any meaning; they just are what they are. In his texts he carefully describes only the surface appearance of objects and actions. This method of objective description does not produce final clarity, however, because the evidence is incomplete or even contradictory. With their emphasis on violence and sex his novels sometimes resemble detective stories in which the solution is never disclosed: the objective world remains stubbornly silent.

His practice of presenting several different versions of the same events is taken further in *La Maison de rendezvous* (1965) and *Project For a Revolution in New York* (1970). Later books move in a more playful direction. *The Beautiful Captive* (1976) constructs a network of scenes around descriptions of some of Magritte's paintings, while *Djinn* (1981) was written as a textbook for American students of French; consequently the more difficult grammar is introduced only in the later chapters of this dreamlike story of conjuration. *The Mirror that Returned* (1984) and *Angélique* (1987) are the first parts of a discontinuous but clearly structured autobiography. Robbe-Grillet has also written screenplays, including those for RESNAIS's *Last Year at Marienbad* (1961) and *Trans-Europe-Express* (1966), which he directed himself.

Robert, Yves (1920–) French film director and actor. Robert made his stage debut in 1942 and switched to the cinema seven years later. Before long, he was established as a popular light leading man and supporting actor in such films as *Les Dieux du Dimanche* (1949), *Folies Bergère* (1957), *The Green Mare* (1959), *Love and the Frenchwoman* (1960), *The Passion of Slow Fire* (1961), and *Cleo From 5 to 7* (1962). Robert's first directing assignment was the short *Les Bonnes Manières* (1951). In the 1960s he began to write and direct features for the production company La Gueville, which he had set up with his wife, the actress Daniele Delorme. *The Tall Blond Man With One Black Shoe* (1972), a comedy about a secret service agent who erroneously trails a clumsy violinist, in which Robert also acted, won a Special Jury Prize at the 1973 BERLIN FILM FESTIVAL. Other films have included *War of the Buttons* (1962), *Les Copains* (1964), *Very Happy Alexander* (1968), from Robert's own story, *The Return of the Tall Blond Man With One Black Shoe* (1974), and *Pardon mon Affaire* (1976). He recently enjoyed considerable success with the PAGNOL adaptations *La Gloire de mon père* (1991) and *Le Château de ma mère* (1991).

Robert Matthew Johnson Marshall and Partners British architectural firm. Established in 1956, Robert Matthew Johnson Marshall (often known as RMJM) was one of the most important British architectural partnerships of its time. **Sir Robert Matthew** (1906–75) was born in Edinburgh and began his architectural career in the Department of Health for Scotland; by 1945 he was its chief architect and planning officer. In 1946 he was appointed head of London County Council architect's department. Under his direction such major works as the Royal Festival Hall (1951) and the new housing estate at Alton, Roehampton, were undertaken. While professor of architecture at the University of Edinburgh (1953–56) Matthew established the private practice that developed into Robert Matthew Johnson Marshall.

Sir Stirrat Johnson-Marshall (1912–81) was born in India, trained in Liverpool, and subsequently worked in various local authorities. In 1944 he was involved in the design of inflatable dummy tanks, guns, and other weapons in the run-up to D-day, gaining experience in applying manufacturing skills to new products that later proved valuable in his architectural work. As deputy architect of Hertfordshire County Council (1945–48) Johnson-Marshall was a key figure in the design of Hertfordshire schools, which represented a new direction in both school design and the use of prefabricated systems in building.

Within the new firm, Johnson-Marshall used several prefabricated building systems, including the CLASP system, at the Universities of York (1963) and Bath. The firm's output included three generating stations in Scotland, the Commonwealth Institute in London (1962), the University of Ulster (1968), and the University of Stirling (1969). The award-winning Civic Centre at Hillingdon, north-west London (completed 1978), made much more successful use of asymmetrical brick structures.

Roberts, William (1895–1980) British painter. Roberts left school at 14 and was apprenticed to a design and advertising firm. He took evening classes at the St Martin's School of Art, London, and in 1910 won a scholarship to the Slade School of Fine Arts, which he attended until 1913. A year later he joined the avant-garde Vorticist group that had grown up around Wyndham Lewis. He saw active service with the Royal Field Artillery in 1916–18 and in 1918 was appointed an official war artist. He had his first one-man exhibition in 1923 at the Chenil Gallery, Chelsea, and from 1925 to 1960 taught part-time at the Central School of Arts and Crafts. From 1948 he exhibited regularly at the Royal Academy and he continued working up to the day of his death.

Roberts was remarkably precocious in his response to French modernism, which predated his visit to France in 1913; the extreme geometrical simplification of his figures at this time shows the influence of cubism. After World War I, however, his style moved away from abstraction. The distinctive 'tubular' forms of some of his later paintings (many of them showing people in everyday settings) are reminiscent of Léger. In 1956–58 Roberts wrote a series of pamphlets in response to the 1956 Tate Gallery exhibition 'Wyndham Lewis and the Vorticists'; in these he disputed Lewis's claim that Vorticism was 'what I, personally, did, and said, at a certain period'.

Robson, Geoffrey *See* SHEPPARD, ROBSON, AND PARTNERS.

Rodhe, Lennart (1916–) Swedish painter. A native of Stockholm, Rodhe began to paint in the 1930s in a cubist style influenced by Picasso. After World War II he adopted an abstract geometrical style and soon became recognized as one of the leading Swedish practitioners of concrete art. In his paintings Rodhe sought to produce a sense of 'intangible space' through such devices as arranging angular forms in spiral compositions. Much of his work was commissioned for public buildings: an example is his relief in the Post Office at Östersund (1948–52).

Rodhe later abandoned his strictly geometrical approach and sought more spontaneous forms of expression. He taught for some years at the Stockholm Academy of Art where he influenced many Swedish painters. A skilled draughtsman, he also designed stage sets and cartoons for tapestries.

Rodrigo, Joaquín (1901–) Spanish composer. Blind from the age of three, he studied composition in Valencia and subsequently (from 1927) in Paris with Paul Dukas. Encouraged by Falla, he returned to Paris to study musicology in 1934, remaining there during the Spanish Civil War (1936–39). He returned finally to Madrid in 1939.

The international acclaim that greeted his *Concierto de Aranjuez* (1940) for guitar and orchestra established Rodrigo's reputation as a composer and led to a teaching post at Madrid University (1947), several overseas tours, and a host of both Spanish and foreign awards.

Rodrigo's lyrical and colourful music makes no attempt to come to terms with avant-garde developments; rather, it belongs squarely to the tradition of French (Dukas) and Spanish (Falla) neoclassicism in which he was trained. The guitar concerto remains his most popular work, although he has also written concertos for violin, piano, cello, and harp and flute, and produced stage works, songs, and guitar pieces. Other notable works include *Música para un jardín* (1957) and the *Cántico de San Francisco* (1986) for soprano and orchestra.

Roeg, Nicolas (Jack) (1928–) British film director and cinematographer, who established a reputation for originality in the 1970s. Roeg began his career as a clapper boy and subsequently worked as cinematographer on films by TRUFFAUT, SCHLESINGER, and Roger Corman among others, being particularly praised for his contribution to *Fahrenheit 451* (1966) and *Far From the Madding Crowd* (1967). He made his debut as a director in 1970 with *Performance* (codirected with Donald Cammell), an enigmatic film about the relationship between a sadistic criminal and a decadent rock star (played by Mick Jagger), in which the borderline between reality and fantasy becomes blurred. In 1971 he consolidated his success with *Walkabout*, an atmospheric piece about the clash of cultures when an Aborigine befriends two White children stranded in the Australian outback. In 1973 he won further praise with the taut supernatural thriller *Don't Look Now*, a visually dazzling film set mostly in Venice.

Subsequent films have included *The Man Who Fell to Earth* (1976), a science-fiction extravaganza starring David Bowie, the romantic tragedy *Bad Timing* (1980), and *Eureka* (1983), a less successful story about a Klondike miner who makes a fortune. More recent films include *Insignificance* (1985), in which the characters include Einstein and Marilyn Monroe, *Castaway* (1986), *Track 29* (1987), *Sweet Bird of Youth* (1989; from Tennessee Williams), *Witches* (1990), and the thriller *Cold Heaven* (1991).

Rogers, Sir Richard (1933–) British architect of Italian extraction; his cousin the Italian architect Ernesto Rogers (1909–69) was an early influence. A scholarship to Yale in 1961–62 introduced him to American technology and precise detailing; he also met Norman FOSTER. In 1963 Rogers and Foster set up the architectural practice **Team 4** with their respective wives Su and Wendy. In 1966 came the successful Reliance Controls building in Swindon, a cheap, flexible, and lightweight factory in profiled steel decking. The experience of threading in services soon led Rogers to think of placing them externally – a practice he had encountered while working with Skidmore, Owings, and Merrill in California.

Team 4 disbanded in 1967, forcing Rogers to concentrate on writing and teaching. The partnership he set up with Renzo PIANO in 1970 promised little more until, in June 1971, they won the competition for the POMPIDOU CENTRE in Paris (with Ove ARUP and Partners). The building was completed in 1976. While the technical detailing was Piano's, the flexible space (an idea descended from ARCHIGRAM theories) and the external servicing were Rogers's. This famous conceit won Rogers considerable popularity and has become almost a trademark. It is the best-known feature of Lloyd's in London (1981–86), a flexible space stacked vertically on (unusually) a concrete frame. He has since converted the Billingsgate Fish Market, London, and designed Thames Wharf offices for himself (completed 1988). Other work includes the Inmos microprocessor factory near Newport, Wales (1978–82) and the Court of Human Rights Building in Strasbourg (begun 1989).

Sadly, most of Rogers's grander projects for London remain unrealized. Those for the National Gallery (1982 competition) and Coin Street (1980–84) were especially controversial. His ideas for the capital's regeneration were published as *A New London* (1992; with Mark Fisher). He has recently designed new headquarters for Daiwa Securities (1991).

Rohmer, Eric (Maurice Henri Joseph Schérer; 1920–) French film director, best known for his psychological conversation pieces. Having taught literature in the 1940s, Rohmer became a film critic on and then editor of *Cahiers du Cinéma*, the main organ of the French NEW WAVE. After writing and directing a series of shorts, he made his first feature film in 1959, *The Sign of Leo*, a cautionary tale about a US musician who finds himself destitute in an unsympathetic Paris. The film's realist style set it apart from the bulk of New Wave films and it was not until 1963 that Rohmer embarked on his next major project. During the course of the 1960s he made six films – among them *The Collector* (1966), *My Night with Maud* (1969), and *Claire's Knee* (1970) – that are known collectively as his 'moral tales'. They concentrate on the process by which their leading characters come to make crucial decisions in their lives, mostly concerning their relationships with women. This sequence of films confirmed Rohmer's skill in observing human foibles; he was highly praised for their literate dialogue and classical style.

Die Marquise von O... (1976) and *Perceval Le Gallois* (1978) were showpieces for Rohmer's visual inventiveness, drawing, respectively, upon German Romantic and medieval paintings; both were based on literary sources, the first on a novella by Heinrich von Kleist and the second on the 12th-century epic by Chrétien de Troyes.

Rohmer embarked on a second series of films, known as the 'comedies and proverbs', with *The Aviator's Wife* (1980); the series concentrates on the emotional interaction between small groups of characters, some of whom are involved in triangular love affairs. Particularly remarkable are *Pauline at the Beach* (1982), about a young girl's psychological development through her observation of her older cousin's love affairs, *The Green Ray* (1986), in which a timid young girl optimistically sets out to find true love, and *My Girlfriend's Boyfriend* (1987), another slightly plotted film about the developing relationships between a group of lovers. Rohmer is currently working on a third cycle of films, 'Tales of the Four Seasons', of which *A Tale of Springtime* (1991) and *A Winter's Tale* (1992) have so far appeared.

All Rohmer's films are distinguished by their highly naturalistic style, achieved partly through the use of nonprofessional actors, and by their insight into unspoken feelings.

Rolfsen, Alf (1895–1979) Norwegian painter and muralist. Born in Oslo, Rolfsen studied at the Academy of Fine Arts in Copenhagen (1913–16) and subsequently travelled widely (France, Greece, Italy, Spain), gaining a good first-hand knowledge of European art history. He is chiefly known as one of the 20th century's most committed upholders of the tradition of monumental wall painting. He was much influenced by Italian Renaissance art but also by modern developments such as cubism. The many public buildings in Norway that he decorated include the church of Stiklestad near Trondheim (1930), Oslo Town Hall (1938–50), and the Hansa brewery in Bergen (1967). Rolfsen's other work included book illustrations; he himself wrote *The Language of Pictures* (1960).

Ronconi, Luca (1933–) Italian theatre director and actor, who established his reputation as a director of classic plays in the 1960s. Having found acclaim as an actor with several leading companies in Italy, Ronconi turned to direction in 1963, when he presented Goldoni's *The Good Wife* with great success. Subsequently he developed his interest in visual spectacle and imaginative staging techniques with productions of such plays as Shakespeare's *Measure for Measure*, Tourneur's *The Revenger's Tragedy*, and Ariosto's *Orlando Furioso*, which won particular praise when first presented in 1968. Since the 1960s Ronconi has continued to concentrate on classic drama, his most interesting productions ranging from Aeschylus's *Oresteia* to Ibsen's *Ghosts*. He has also worked in opera, directing versions of Wagner's *Siegfried* and Gluck's *Orpheus and Eurydice*.

Rosenberg, Hilding (Constantin) (1892–1985) Swedish composer, conductor, and teacher; a formative influence on modern Swedish music. After studying piano and organ as a child he entered (1915) the Royal Academy of Music in Stockholm, where he received lessons in composition and conducting. He first travelled abroad – Paris, Berlin, Dresden, and Vienna – in 1920, enabling him to hear the music of Schoenberg, Hindemith, and Stravinsky at first hand. In the 1920s he established a leading position in Swedish musical life, particularly through his collaborations with the theatre director Per Lindberg. During the 1930s he studied conducting with Hermann Scherchen, becoming (in 1934) chief conductor at the Stockholm Royal Opera.

In the 1920s Rosenberg's abandonment of a musical vocabulary derived from Sibelius in favour of a contrapuntal style founded on early music and Bach on the one hand, and Stravinsky, Bartók, and Hindemith on the other, marked him out as a radical. His synthesis of these elements exerted a continuing influence on his pupils in the 'Monday Group' such as BLOMDAHL and Sven-Erik Bäck. Works from this early period include the Schoenberg-influenced first string quartet (1920). From the mid 1920s Rosenberg became increasingly involved with the theatre, writing incidental music and eventually operas, of which *Journey to America* (1932) was the first. His distinctive musical style, characterized by its use of counterpoint and pedal points, is fully established in his second symphony (1935). During the 1930s, when he wrote mainly operas, this style became more accessible, employing greater lyricism and more restrained chromaticism. The fourth symphony, *The Revelation of St John* (1940), looks forward to the large-scale choral works of the 1940s, after which he returned to purely instrumental composition.

Rosenberg was a prolific composer of stage and choral works (including nine operas and six ballets), orchestral works (including eight symphonies), concertos, chamber works (including 12 string quartets), piano music, songs, incidental music, and film scores.

Rosi, Francesco (1922–) Italian film director, a prominent figure in the political cinema of the 1960s. Born in Naples, Rosi began his career in journalism and the theatre before entering films as an assistant to ANTONIONI, VISCONTI, and others. He made his own debut in 1956, when he shared the direction of *Kean*, and subsequently demonstrated his concern for social and political issues in a series of films beginning with *La Sfida* (1957). He first attracted popular attention in 1961 with *Salvatore Giuliano*, an innovative biopic about an Italian gangster murdered in 1950; in keeping with the conventions of NEOREALISM the film made use of nonprofessional actors and imaginative narrative techniques to tell the story. *Hands Across the City* (1963) employed similar methods to explore property speculation in Naples, while *The Moment of Truth* (1964) investigated the exploitation of a matador by commercial interests.

After two relatively unsuccessful forays into comedy, Rosi returned to more serious concerns with *The Mattei Affair* (1972), a conspiracy thriller about the murder of a prominent capitalist, and *Lucky Luciano* (1974), a gangster film tracing the connections between blatant criminality and political expediency in post-war Italy. Corruption in public institutions was also the theme of *Illustrious Corpses* (1976), in which a series of murders leads to the discovery of a conspiracy involving all the major political parties. Subsequently Rosi concentrated less upon criticizing the Establishment and more on the human aspects of social issues. In *Three Brothers* (1981), for instance, he presented a nostalgic view of peasant life through the eyes of three men who return to their birthplace to bury their mother. More recent films have included *Christ Stopped at Eboli* (1982), from Carlo LEVI's book about life in the rural South of Italy, a version of Bizet's *Carmen* (1984), an adaptation of Gabriel Garciá Márquez's *Chronicle of a Death Foretold* (1987), and *To Forget Palermo* (1990), a grim film about the Mafia.

Rossby, Carl-Gustaf Arvid (1898–1957) Swedish-born meteorologist. Rossby studied at the University of Stockholm and began his scientific career at the Bergen Geophysical Institute. He emigrated to the US in 1926, being appointed professor of meteorology at the Massachusetts Institute of Technology in 1928. He became naturalized in 1938 and chairman of the department of meteorology at the University of Chicago in 1941. Rossby returned to Sweden in 1950 to found the Institute of Meteorology at the University of Stockholm.

Rossby's major contributions were to the understanding of atmospheric heat-exchange and turbulence; the interaction between the oceans and the atmosphere; and general atmospheric circulation. He also developed mathematical models of various atmospheric processes and for forecasting that were of fundamental importance in establishing a scientific basis for meteorology. He identified and derived a model for the large-scale waves in the upper atmosphere (known as Rossby waves) that occur at the boundary between cold polar air and warm tropical air; he also determined the existence of jet streams – narrow high-speed currents of air that have important effects on the origin and development of weather systems.

Rossellini, Roberto (1906–77) Italian film director, whose work had a profound influence on post-war European cinema, although he is more often remembered for his controversial marriage to the Hollywood star Ingrid Bergman. Born in Rome, Rossellini began his career as a writer and director of nature documentaries, making his debut as a director of feature-length films in 1940 with *The White Ship*, which depicted life aboard an Italian hospital ship. After two more full-length films, he made the neorealist classic *Rome – Open City* (1945), portraying the struggle of the Italian Resistance against the occupying Nazis and making brilliant use of nonprofessional actors and real locations (in spite of the war, which had not yet ended in Italy).

Rossellini's achievement in *Rome – Open City* was consolidated by his next film, *Paisà* (1946), in which the often traumatic process of liberation by the Allies provides a link between six separate stories. *Germany Year Zero* (1947) tackled the anguish suffered by victims of the war in Germany after the return of peace in 1945; it introduced the themes of spiritual crisis and redemption that were to characterize many of his later films.

Anna Magnani, who had starred in *Rome – Open City*, also took the lead in *L'Amore* (1948) and *The Machine That Kills Bad People* (1948), after which Rossellini embarked on a series of five films starring Bergman, beginning with *Stromboli* (1949). In this melodrama Bergman played a wartime refugee who marries a fisherman in order to escape internment but is ground down by the harshness of her new environment; the parallels with the real-life affair of Bergman and the director were obvious. The partnership continued fruitfully through such films as *Europa '51* (1951), *Voyage to Italy* (1953), and *Fear* (1954), a melodrama about marital breakdown that reflected the state of Rossellini's own marriage (annulled in 1958).

The liaison with Bergman led to both artists being shunned by the cinema world, especially in Hollywood. Subsequently Rossellini concentrated on documentaries, often on historical themes, several of which were intended for television. He did, however, restore his international reputation with *The General della Rovere* (1959), a wartime drama that won the Grand Prix at the Venice Film Festival, and *It was Night in Rome* (1960). In his documentary films he attempted a broad history of the world with biopics of such figures as Socrates, Garibaldi, Louis XIV, Augustine of Hippo, and Christ. He died before making his planned film about the theories of Marx.

Rossi, Aldo (1931–) Italian architect and theorist, a leading writer and teacher whose ideology transcends both Rationalism and POSTMODERNISM. In the 1960s he wrote extensively for the journal *Casabella*, but is best known for his books *The Architecture of the City* (1966) and *The Analogous City* (1977). His writings reveal an unresolved tension between idealism and historicism that contrasts with the clarity of his buildings. Since his expulsion from Milan University in 1972 he has taught extensively in the US and in 1990 founded an architectural school in Florida.

Rossi's early Ronchini Villa at Versilla (1960) is a modernistic white box. More indicative of his later work is his Segrate fountain (1965) - a triangle raised between a column and a set of steps, all in reinforced concrete. His extensions and additions to the De Amicis school in Broni (1969–70) feature the giant rectangular arcades that have since dominated his work. At San Cataldo cemetery (1971–82), Modena, these are contrasted with the Doric columns of an adjacent older cemetery, while they are at their most dramatic in his Milan housing of 1969–70. His school at Fagnano Olona (1972) reveals a similar preoccupation with the pyramid-topped cylinder and the cone. The most bizarre of Rossi's works was a floating quasi-Renaissance 'Theatre of the World' for the 1979 Venice Biennale; he also designed the gateway to the 1980 Biennale. Piers and triangles add a monumental quality to his simplest terrace houses, such as those at Goito and Pegognaga (1979). Since 1980 Rossi has built relatively little; his brick chapel at Giussano (1980), flats in Berlin (1983), a new municipal centre at Borgoricco (1983–87), and offices in Turin based round a central cylinder (1984–87) all reflect the increasing purity of his classicism.

Rota, (Rinaldo) Nino (1911–79) Italian composer. The grandson of the pianist and composer Giovanni Rinaldi, he entered the Milan Conservatory as a precocious 12-year-old in 1923; in the same year his oratorio *L'Infanza di San Giovanni Battista* was performed in Milan and Lille. He later studied with Ildebrando Pizzetti, with Alfredo Casella in Rome, and at the Curtis Institute in Philadelphia (1931–32). Back in Milan he took a degree at the University and worked for a time at the Taranto Music School before moving to the Bari Conservatory, where he worked first as a teacher and later (from 1950) as director.

Rota is chiefly known for his film scores, which include music for Cass's *The Glass Mountain* (1950), Vidor's *War and Peace* (1956), ZEFFIRELLI's *The Taming of the Shrew* (1966) and *Romeo and Juliet* (1968), VISCONTI's *The Leopard* (1963), and Coppola's *The Godfather* (1972). He worked extensively with FELLINI, for whom he produced around 80 scores. Those aspects of his style that are ideally suited to film music – emotional directness, tonal bias, and rhythmic straightforwardness – appear conservative when found in the rest of his output. His music was little affected by the atonal and serialist preoccupations of his contemporaries, despite his long friendship with Stravinsky. His other works include 10 operas (of which *The Italian Straw Hat*, 1955, is the best known), three ballets, three symphonies, concertos for harp, trombone, cello, bassoon, and piano, and various choral and chamber works.

Roth, Dieter (1930–) Swiss painter, graphic artist, and designer. Born in Hannover, Roth moved with his parents to Switzerland in 1943, where he began to draw, paint, make prints, and write poetry. From 1947 to 1951 he was a graphic apprentice in Bern. He lived in Copenhagen from 1955 until 1957 and subsequently in Reykjavik, the US, Germany, and Austria.

In 1954 Roth began to experiment with OP ART and film and also produced his first 'baked sculpture'. He is best known for his preoccupation with consumer objects; in several of his exhibitions he has removed such items from their domestic context and presented them as works of art in their own right. In the late 1960s Roth collaborated on a series of prints with Richard HAMILTON and organized Dada-like HAPPENINGS. He has also been active as a typographer and as a designer of furniture and textiles. His work has been exhibited in Germany, the US, and Britain. His paintings include *Self-portrait as Drowning Man* (1974) and *Self-portrait at a Table* (1973–76; both in the Tate Gallery, London). Roth has also produced a series of books in which his own poetry is illustrated by graphic work of great sophistication.

Roy, Jules (1907–) French novelist and journalist. Roy grew up in Algeria, joining the army in 1928; in 1935 he transferred to the air corps. He fought from 1940 to 1942 in North Africa and then joined the RAF and flew nighttime bombing missions over Germany. In 1952–53 he served in the Indochina War, before resigning on grounds of conscience. In *The Battle in the Rice Fields* (1953) he praised the courage of the French soldiers while severely criticizing official policy.

Roy's first book, the poetry collection *Songs and Prayers for Some Pilots* (1943), was written in admiration of the French writer and aviator Saint-Exupéry, whose biography he later wrote. In 1946 he published *The Happy Valley*, an account of the Allied bombing missions over the Ruhr Valley, focusing on the working conditions and the psychology of the pilots. His novel *The Navigator* (1954) again deals with duty, heroism, and cowardice amongst World War II pilots. In his books *The Profession of Arms* (1948) and *The Trial of Marshal Petain* (1964) Roy explores the conflict between loyalty to the Vichy regime and sympathy with the Allied cause experienced by many Frenchmen.

In 1960 Roy went back to Algeria as a reporter and condemned the conduct of the French military in his highly controversial book *The War in Algeria.* Roy has also written several plays; in the Paris production of *The Cyclones* (1954) he himself took the leading role. His autobiography *Stranger to my Brothers* appeared in 1982.

Royal Ballet British ballet company founded in 1956 from the Sadler's Wells Ballet (formerly the Vic-Wells Ballet) and the Sadler's Wells Theatre Ballet (formerly the Sadler's Well Opera Ballet). The original company, the Vic-Wells Ballet, had been set up in 1931 by Dame Ninette DE VALOIS acting in collaboration with Lilian Baylis at the Old Vic; it had rapidly built up a strong reputation based on its outstanding dancers, who included Anton Dolin, Alicia Markova, Robert Helpmann, and Margot Fonteyn, and on the choreography of Frederick ASHTON. The Sadler's Wells Opera Ballet had been set up in 1946 as a smaller supporting company to the main troupe and proved its worth as a training ground for such choreographers as CRANKO and MACMILLAN. After 1956 the smaller company expanded and was renamed the Royal Ballet's Touring Section; it concentrates on presenting modern British works.

In 1963 De Valois handed over control of the Royal Ballet to Ashton, who developed the classic partnership between Fonteyn and Nureyev that his predecessor had established. In 1970 he was replaced by Macmillan, who added a number of important contemporary works to the company's repertoire during his six years as director. The smaller company, renamed the New Group, concentrated on experimental works for a time before returning, as the Sadler's Wells Royal Ballet (1976), to the works of such choreographers as Ashton and Balanchine. Norman Morrice and Anthony Dowell both served terms as director, Morrice securing the services of the choreographer Richard ALSTON and Dowell reviving a series of classical ballets with great success as well as presenting new works by David BINTLEY. The Sadler's Wells Royal Ballet moved from London to a new home in Birmingham in 1990 under its new title, the Birmingham Royal Ballet.

Royal National Theatre Britain's state-supported national theatre company was finally established in 1962 after over a century of discussion. The National Theatre Board was set up in 1962, partly through the efforts of Sir Laurence OLIVIER, who became the first artistic director. The company was formed from the Old Vic company, which had been performing Shakespeare's plays since Lilian Bayliss (1874–1937) took it over in 1912. Olivier's successor, Peter HALL, took over in 1975 and oversaw the company's move into its own complex (designed by Denys LASDUN) on the South Bank a year later, ending a lengthy stay at the Old Vic Theatre. The company has the use of three auditoria, the Olivier, the Lyttelton, and the smaller Cottesloe theatre; there are also several exhibition galleries. A wide range of plays has since been presented by the company, including both classics and modern drama, although the financial risks involved have prevented the production of work that is too experimental. Hall retired as artistic director in 1988 and was succeeded by Richard Eyre; at the same time the theatre was granted the right to add the prefix 'Royal' to its title, in recognition of the company's 25th anniversary.

Royal Opera An opera company based at the Royal Opera House, Covent Garden, London. Previously known as Covent Garden Opera, it adopted its current name in 1968. Since 1945 it has been Britain's national opera company. It performs operas in their original languages, employing internationally acclaimed soloists. Its musical directors have included Karl Rankl (1945–51), Rafael KUBELIK (1955–58), Sir Georg SOLTI (1961–71), Sir Colin DAVIS (1971–86), and Bernard HAITINK (since 1987). Other conductors to work there include BARBIROLLI, Kleiber, Kempe, and Giulini. The administration is currently headed by Jeremy Isaacs.

Royal Philharmonic Orchestra (RPO) An orchestra founded in London in 1946 by Sir Thomas Beecham, who remained its principal conductor until 1960. Subsequent musical directors have been Rudolf Kempe (1961–75), Antal Dorati, Walter Weller, André Previn, Vladimir Ashkenazy (1987–92), and Yuri Temirkanov (from 1993). In 1992 Sir Peter Maxwell DAVIES was appointed composer to the orchestra; both he and Yehudi Menuhin are also associate conductors. Originally founded to give subscription concerts under the auspices of the Royal Philharmonic Society, it became the resident orchestra at the EDINBURGH FESTIVAL (1948–63) and at Glyndebourne (1950–63). In 1963 the orchestra became a self-governing institution. The orchestra tours extensively throughout Britain, Europe, the US, and Canada. In 1986 the orchestra set up its own record company, RPO Records: current recording projects include a complete cycle of Tchaikovsky's symphonies. The orchestra has also recorded the complete Shostakovich symphonies, besides numerous soundtracks for films, television, and radio.

Royal Shakespeare Company Britain's best-known theatre company, which has won acclaim in a wide range of productions throughout the world. Although the idea of a theatre company specializing in Shakespearean productions had been expressed some centuries before, the RSC was not founded until 1960, when it became the resident company at the Shakespeare Memorial Theatre in Stratford-upon-Avon. Subsequently it also acquired a London base at the Aldwych Theatre, moving to the BARBICAN CENTRE in 1982, and opened other venues in Stratford (including the Elizabethan-style Swan Theatre, opened in 1986), as well as undertaking many overseas tours. With Peter HALL as its first director, the company soon established its reputation as the world's leading interpreter of Shakespeare's plays, although it went on to present work by many other historical and modern playwrights to equal acclaim. The *Wars of the Roses* cycle (1963) of Shakespeare's history plays was regarded as a particular triumph, while subsequent outstanding successes have included Peter BROOK's productions of WEISS's *Marat/Sade* (1964) and *A Midsummer Night's Dream* (1970), and the Dickens adaptation *Nicholas Nickleby* (1981), which was just one of many admired productions by artistic director Trevor Nunn. Terry Hands was promoted from artistic director to chief executive in 1986 and with such productions as *Les Liaisons Dangereuses* (1990) brought the company further acclaim, although an attempt to win a mass audience with the horror musical *Carrie* (1987) came to grief. Hands was succeeded in 1991 by Adrian Noble, who took steps to tackle the company's long-standing financial crisis.

Royan Festival One of post-war Europe's most important festivals of modern music, held in Royan, France, from 1964 until 1973. The concerts were given in the town's casino in the week before Easter; notable first performances included works by BARRAQUÉ and XENAKIS. The festival's role was taken over by the RENCONTRES INTERNATIONALES D'ART CONTEMPORAIN in 1973.

Ró˙ewicz, Tadeusz (1921–) Polish poet and playwright. Ró˙ewicz's experiences as a member of the underground Resistance to the Nazis in World War II had a profound influence on his difficult and unsettling work. Believing that the moral cataclysm of the war and the Holocaust had made conventional poetry impossible, he wrote his first book of verse *Faces of Anxiety* in a deliberately antipoetic style. Later volumes include *The Plain*, *The Green Rose*, *The Face*, and *Poetry*. His plays, which reject the accepted procedures of both traditional and avant-garde theatre, include *Card Index* (1960), *Laocoon Group* (1962), the tragicomedy *White Wedding* (1975), his best-known work, and *The Trap* (1982). Many of his works for the stage consist of collages of fragments taken from everyday conversation and newspaper articles; their cohesion depends largely upon the creative contributions of the actors and director.

Rozov, Viktor (Sergeevich) (1913–) Russian playwright and director, many of whose plays focus on the dilemnas facing the younger generation in post-war Soviet society. His plays characteristically stress the need for compromise and the redeeming power of love. After training as an actor at the Theatre of the Revolution (1934–38) in Moscow and serving with the Red

Army in World War II he set up a children's theatre in Alma-Ata in Kazakhstan; eventually he returned to Moscow as director of the Central House of Culture for Railwaymen. His plays include *Her Friends* (1949), *Good Luck!* (1954), *In Search of Joy* (1957), and *Alive Forever* (1957), which remains his most successful work. Mikhail KALATOZOV's film version of *Alive Forever*, called *The Cranes are Flying*, was also a success. This play was the first production at Moscow's Sovremennik Theatre (*see* YEFREMOV, OLEG), which has adopted the play as a staple part of its repertory. More recent works have included *The Nest of the Woodgrouse (Meet My Model Family)* (1978), in which the generation gap threatens to destroy a family, and *The Little Cabin* (1982) – both of which ran into problems with the Soviet censor and had long-delayed first performances.

Rubbra, (Charles) Edmund (1901–86) British composer. Born to working-class parents in Northampton, Rubbra left school at 14 and worked as a railway clerk. However, his talent as a pianist won him a music scholarship to Reading University and from 1921 to 1925 he studied composition at the Royal College of Music under Holst and Vaughan Williams. He subsequently worked as a pianist, critic, and teacher, eventually becoming lecturer in music at Oxford University (1947–68) and professor of composition at the Guildhall School of Music. His first symphony was performed in 1937. During World War II he formed a trio which gave concerts to servicemen.

Rubbra composed mainly in a rhapsodic style deeply influenced by the English tradition of Holst, Vaughan Williams, Ireland, and Bax, although later works show him developing a more personal idiom. His work is notable for its sustained use of polyphony. Although he wrote prolifically and in most of the traditional forms, he is best known as a symphonist and a writer of sacred music (he converted to Roman Catholicism in 1948). His 11 symphonies include the choral *Sinfonia Sacra* (1972) and the small-scale *Sinfonia da Camera* (1979). Other compositions include concertos for piano, violin, and viola, a *Festival Overture* for orchestra, and four string quartets.

Rushdie, Salman (1947–) British novelist, born in Bombay. Rushdie's novels combine extravagant fantasy with social and political history and are considered amongst the leading English-language examples of MAGIC REALISM. He was educated in England at Rugby and King's College, Cambridge. After working as an advertising copywriter, he published his first novel, *Grimus*, in 1974. Commercial and critical success came with *Midnight's Children* (1981), a complex novel that traces the development of post-independence India through the experiences of its central character, Saleem. It won the BOOKER PRIZE as well as the English Speaking Union Literary Award. *Shame* (1983) continues in a similar vein, exploring the recent history of Pakistan through the distorting mirror of the fictional 'Peccavistan'. Sadly, however, he is now best-known for the events following the publication of his 1988 novel *The Satanic Verses*, a difficult work that uses fantasy and dream sequences to explore the mental experience of Muslims living in the West. The novel's treatment of a character identified by most Muslims as the prophet Muhammed led to accusations of blasphemy and violent street demonstrations in several countries. In 1989 the Ayatollah Khomeini issued a *fatwa* condemning Rushdie to death and he has been forced to live in hiding under protective custody ever since. The Rushdie case remains a focus for debate about the conflict between secular and religious values and the concepts of free speech and blasphemy. Since his restricted life began he has produced *Haroun and the Sea of Stories* (1990), a children's fable, and a collection of essays *Imaginary Homelands* (1991).

Russell, Ken (Henry Kenneth Alfred Russell; 1927–) British film director, who earned a controversial reputation with his flamboyant and irreverent biopics. Having started as a photographer and actor, Russell became a director for television and soon attracted attention with short films on such figures as Elgar, Debussy, and Isadora Duncan. These differed from conventional documentaries in their imaginative and sometimes lyrical style. His first major success in the cinema came with his adaptation of D H Lawrence's *Women in Love* (1969), in which Oliver Reed, Alan Bates, and Glenda Jackson were much admired.

The Music Lovers (1970), an impassioned fantasy about the life of Tchaikovsky, some scenes of which were clearly designed to shock, and *The Devils* (1971), a depiction of religious fanaticism in a 17th-century convent, brought Russell his first accusations of bad taste. They also won the director a huge popular audience. Russell himself welcomed the image of *enfant terrible* and did all he could to foster it, often to the detriment of otherwise highly original films. Somewhat more restrained were *The Boy Friend* (1971) and *Savage Messiah* (1972). However, Russell continued to develop his often grotesque vision in such films as *Mahler* (1973), the rock opera *Tommy* (1974), *Lisztomania* (1975), and *Valentino* (1977), in which Rudolf NUREYEV played the silent movie star.

More recent films have included *Altered States* (1981), *Crimes of Passion* (1985), *Gothic* (1987), a typically sensationalist treatment of the Byron and Shelley circle, *The Lair of the White Worm* (1989), based on the horror story by Bram Stoker, *The Rainbow* (1989), an adaptation of Lawrence's novel, and *Whore* (1991). He has also directed a number of operas, among them *The Rake's Progress* (1982) in Florence, *Faust* (1985) in Vienna, and Gilbert and Sullivan's *Princess Ida* (1992) in London.

Russell, Willy (William Martin Russell; 1947–) British playwright, best known for his successful play *Educating Rita* (1980), about the relationship between a world-weary university tutor and a working-class student. Several of his plays were written for the Everyman Theatre in Liverpool, his home town, and reflect regional attitudes and aspirations. He achieved his first major success with *John, Paul, George, Ringo and ...Bert* (1974), an entertaining play about the Beatles, and followed it with *Breezeblock Park* (1975), *One for the Road* (1976), and *Stags and Hens* (1978). After the success of *Educating Rita*, which was also filmed, he scored another triumph with the musical *Blood Brothers* (1981) – a loose reworking of Boucicault's *The Corsican Brothers*. His most recent work includes another musical, *Our Day Out* (1983), and *Shirley Valentine* (1986), which depicts a frustrated housewife's self-discovery when she escapes from her humdrum life by taking a free holiday on a Greek island; the film version won several major awards.

Ryle, Gilbert (1900–76) British philosopher, a leading figure in the 'ordinary language' or 'Oxford' school of philosophy. Educated at Oxford, where he gained three first-class honours degrees, Ryle later became the University's Waynflete Professor of Metaphysics (1945–68). From 1948 until 1971 he edited the philosophical journal *Mind*.

An adherent of linguistic philosophy since the early 1930s, Ryle held that the prime task of the philosopher was the clarification of concepts through the elimination of linguistic confusion. In his first book, the classic *The Concept of Mind* (1949), he applied this approach to the perennial problem of the mind's relation to the body. According to Ryle, the Cartesian notion of mind as an entity distinct from body (the 'ghost-in-the-machine') is a major source of confusion. He himself described mental states solely in terms of the ability and inclination to perform physically.

In *Dilemmas* (1954) Ryle tackled the apparent incompatibilities between the scientific account of the world and our everyday experience (for example, our sense of exercising 'free will'). He saw these as arising from a confusion between the language of logic and that used to describe events.

Ryle's work was distinguished not only by incisive thought but also by a witty and brilliant style. Among his other works are *Plato's Progress* (1966), a provocative series of speculations about Plato's works and their intended meaning, *The Thinking of Thoughts* (1968), and two volumes of *Collected Papers* (1971). *On Thinking* appeared posthumously in 1992.

Ryle, Sir Martin (1918–84) British radio astronomer. Ryle graduated in physics from Oxford University in 1939; he worked on ionospheric physics at the Cavendish Laboratory, Cambridge for a short period before moving to the wartime Telecommunications Research Establishment and playing a major part in the development of airborne radar and electronic countermeasures. After the war he returned to the Cavendish and became director of the Mullard Radio Astronomy Observatory (1957) and professor of radio astronomy (1959–71). He was appointed Astronomer Royal in 1972.

Ryle's astronomical contributions initially concerned the sun and stars. He subsequently initiated an extensive series of catalogues of astronomical radio sources, which were used in the discovery of quasars and in providing evidence against the steady-state theory of cosmology (*see* BONDI). He developed radio interferometry (the use of two separated radio telescopes) and aperture synthesis (the use of variable spacing between radio telescopes to simulate a much larger single telescope); both techniques have been invaluable in radio astronomy. In 1974 Ryle shared with Antony HEWISH the first Nobel Prize for physics to be awarded for astronomical research.

S

Sacher, Paul (1906–) Swiss conductor. Sacher was born and educated in Basel, which has remained the focus of his musical activities. As director of the Basel Chamber Orchestra, which he founded in 1926, he commissioned new works from contemporary composers including Bartók, Hindemith, and Stravinsky. He also founded (1928) the Basel Chamber Choir and in 1933 established the Schola Cantorum Basiliensis, a centre for the study of early music. He was appointed conductor of the Collegium Musicum Zürich in 1941. Sacher has conducted throughout Europe but is perhaps best known for his role in establishing and directing (1954–69) the Basel Music Academy. The Academy now houses his important collection of texts and manuscripts in the Paul Sacher Foundation, which was opened in 1973.

Sachs, Nelly (1891–1970) German poet, noted for her poems about the sufferings of the Jews under the Nazis. Sachs was born in Berlin, the daughter of a wealthy manufacturer. She began to write early but her pre-war work is mostly inconsequential. A Jew, she escaped to Sweden in 1940 with the help of the writer Selma Lagerlöf and spent the rest of her life in Stockholm. She shared the Nobel Prize for literature with the Yiddish writer Shmuel Yosef Agnon in 1966.

Sachs began to write the poems for which she is remembered in the early years of her exile. In poems such as the famous 'O the Chimneys' she laments the fate of European Jewry in language at once richly metaphorical and searingly direct. In its search for consolation her poetry draws on the mysticism of the cabbala and the ethical teaching of the Chassidic tradition, with its emphasis on love, simplicity, and forgiveness. She was the most influential German woman poet of her generation. Her major collections are *In the Dwellings of Death* (1947), *Escape and Metamorphosis* (1959), *Glowing Mysteries* (1963), and *Journey beyond Dust* (1967). She also wrote a number of plays, of which *Eli: A Mystery Play of the Sufferings of Israel* (1951) is the best known.

Sagan, Françoise (Françoise Quoirez; 1935–) French novelist. Sagan has lived by her writing since the success of her first book *Bonjour Tristesse* (1953), written at the age of 18. She has written novels, plays, song lyrics, and screenplays.

In her novels Sagan describes the brief, often cynical, liaisons of characters who are aware of the fundamental loneliness and selfishness of the human condition (*Un Certain Sourire*, 1956; *Aimez-Vous Brahms?*, 1959). Love is presented as a sweet but melancholic game that is played out in a world of luxury and ennui (*Les Merveilleux Nuages*; 1961). More recent novels include *The Painted Lady* (1982), *The Still Storm* (1984), and *Un Sang d'aquarelle* (1987). Although many critics find her work shallow and repetitious, Sagan's sensitive and lively descriptions of people and circumstances have made her one of the most popular novelists of post-war France.

St Ives School A group of artists based in the small seaside town of St Ives, Cornwall, in the years during and after World War II. Although the quality of the light had attracted artists to the area since the late 19th century, a distinctive school only began to emerge when Ben NICHOLSON and Barbara HEPWORTH, Britain's leading abstract artists of the day, took refuge there in 1939. The other original members of the group were the Russian constructivist sculptor Naum Gabo (1890–1977) and the painter Peter LANYON, a native of St Ives. The group was largely responsible for keeping the ideals of abstract art alive in Britain during the war years. In the later 1940s and 1950s they were joined by a number of younger painters including Terry FROST (from 1946), Patrick HERON (from 1956), and Roger HILTON (visited regularly from 1956; settled 1965); as the group's repute grew, many other artists took to summering in the area.

Although the St Ives painters had no common programme and few stylistic similarities, their work shares certain general characteristics. In particular, it seems to represent a typically English compromise between abstraction and the native tradition of landscape painting, with its emphasis on the 'spirit of place.' Although essentially abstract, the sculpture of Hepworth and the painting of Lanyon and Hilton show a sensitive subjective response to the landscape, light, and ambience of the west of Cornwall. Typical of this approach is a series of abstract paintings executed by Terry Frost in the early 1950s, inspired by the shapes and movements of boats bobbing in the harbour at St Ives.

St Magnus Festival A week-long arts festival held annually in June in St Magnus Cathedral, Kirkwall, and at other venues throughout the Orkney Isles. It was founded in 1977 by Sir Peter Maxwell DAVIES who composed the chamber opera, *The Martyrdom of St Magnus* for the first festival. Although primarily a festival of classical music, it includes jazz, theatre, and a variety of events for children.

Sallinen, Aulis (1935–) Finnish composer. He studied (1955–60) at the Sibelius Academy, Helsinki, where his teachers included KOKKONEN and Årre Merikanto; he returned there to teach composition from 1970 to 1981. From 1960 to 1970 he was chief administrator of the Finnish Radio Symphony Orchestra.

His early works, for example the first string quartet (1958), make use of a free and sometimes darkly lyrical serialism. A new phase began in the late 1960s, when he found new ways of reconciling tonal gestures, including triadic harmony, with avant-garde structures. This can be heard in the third string quartet (1969), which uses variations form as a vehicle for applying modern techniques to a traditional Finnish folk tune. Similarly, the first symphony (1971) reflects the influence of Sibelius despite its use of such modern effects as clusters. Another decisive change of style was announced by his first opera *The Horseman* (1976), which indicated a rare talent for dramatic music – indications conformed by his later operas *The Red Line* (1978) and the SHOSTAKOVICH-influenced *The King Goes Forth to France* (1984). Shostakovich was also an influence on the mosaic-like construction of the fifth quartet and the fifth symphony (1985). Sallinen has composed extensively for orchestra and instrumental ensembles, writing six symphonies, five string quartets, and two concertos. His internatinal reputation rests largely on his four operas, of which *Kullerva* (1988) is the most recent.

Samonà, Giuseppe (1898–1983) Italian architect and planner. Born in Palermo, Samonà was director of the University Institute for Architecture in Venice (1945–71). He also wrote extensively, his themes ranging from architectural history to low-cost housing. Influences on his work ranged from LE CORBUSIER to Erich Mendelsohn and Frank Lloyd Wright. His Banca d'Italia (1968) in Padua, has four contrasting facades to integrate it into its busy historic setting. Many of his most fascinating projects were never built; nevertheless his output was considerable and included the Villa Samemi (1950–54), Mondello; the National Institute for Assistance in Work Accidents (1950–56), Venice; the Palermo Electric Light Company Ltd (1961–63) and a theatre (1970–74) in Sciacca.

Samonà also designed large quantities of low-cost housing, including projects for INA-CASA in Sciacca (1952) and for Mestre (1951–56). He also produced town plans for Brescia (1957), Trento, Palermo, Salla, Palmi, and the Venetia region (all 1961–66). But he is best remembered for his inspired teaching, even if his extrovert manner earned him a reputation for 'vitriolic intellectualism'. In the late 1940s he gathered around him a variety of architects and artists of similar socialist persuasion to form a progressive colony that remained at the forefront of Italian architecture until his retirement.

Sanger, Frederick (1918–) British biochemist. Sanger graduated from Cambridge University in 1939 and continued his research at the university until he began working for the Medical Research Council (1951–83). In 1955, after some ten years' work, Sanger established the complete amino-acid sequence of the protein bovine insulin. This was one of the first protein structures identified, and Sanger received the Nobel Prize for chemistry in 1958 in recognition of his achievement. Sanger's work enabled chemists to synthesize insulin artificially, and also generally stimulated research into protein structure.

In 1977 Sanger's team at the MRC laboratories, published the complete sequence of the 5400 nucleotides making up the DNA of the virus Phi X 174. Moreover, they found two cases of genes located within genes. Previously it had been thought that genes could not overlap. Sanger's research required the development of new techniques for splitting the DNA into different sized fragments. These are radioactively labelled and then separated by electrophoresis. The base sequence can then be worked out because it is known which base is located at the end of each fragment due to the specificity of the enzymes (the so-called restriction enzymes) used to split the DNA. Sanger was awarded the Nobel Prize for chemistry a second time (1980) for determining the base sequences of nucleic acids.

Santareno, Bernardo (Antonio Martinho do Rosario; 1924–80) Portuguese playwright, who was a leading figure in the theatre during the repressive regime of Salazar, when many of his plays were banned. In his 20-or-so plays Santareno consistently opposed the injustices of Salazar's regime, although his criticisms were often disguised as comments on past history. His first play, *The Promise* (1957), was followed by the highly praised *Crime de aldeia velha* (1959), a realistic unforgiving depiction of witchcraft hysteria in rural Portugal that won comparisons with Miller's *The Crucible*. Of the plays that followed, the most significant included *The Jew* (1966), an account of the Inquisition's trial and burning of the celebrated playwright Antônio José da Silva, and *Father Martin's Treason* (1969), which describes the tragic events that take place after an idealistic Roman Catholic priest challenges his Church's support for a brutally repressive government.

Santomaso, Giuseppe (1907–) Italian painter. A native of Venice, Santomaso studied at the city's Academy of Fine Arts. In 1937 he went to Amsterdam, where he saw paintings by van Gogh, and then to Paris, where he encountered the cubist works of Braque and Léger. After his return to Italy he joined the Corrente group, which was attempting to promote modern art in Fascist Italy. Santomaso's works at this time included still lifes painted in bright colours with wavy brush strokes.

From 1943 onwards Santomaso's painting turned towards abstraction. After the war he helped to found the FRONTE NUOVO DELLE ARTI. When this broke up in 1952 he joined the Gruppo degli Otto Pittori Italiani, a smaller group of abstract painters. During this period he gradually developed his own style of ART INFORMEL. His work of the mid 1950s featured groups of irregular coloured shapes while that produced later in the decade is characterized by thick blocks of pigment. In the 1970s many of his paintings featured luminous backgrounds with a small number of blocks of different colours superimposed. From 1940 onwards Santomaso gave numerous one-man exhibitions. In 1954 he won the first prize for painting at the Venice Biennale.

Sargent, Sir (Harold) Malcolm (Watts) (1895–1967) British conductor, organist, and composer. Born in Ashford, Kent, Sargent was educated at the Royal College of Organists, London, and became Britain's youngest doctor of music. He made his debut at the 1921 prom concerts, conducting the Henry Wood Queen's Hall Orchestra in one of his own works. Keen on promoting music, especially to the young, he became chief conductor of the Robert Mayer children's concerts in 1924. He founded the Courtald-Sargent concerts in 1929 and worked with Sir Thomas Beecham in establishing the London Philharmonic Orchestra in 1932. Sargent conducted the Hallé Orchestra (1939–42), the Liverpool Philharmonic Orchestra (1942–49), and the BBC Symphony Orchestra (1950–57), as well as conducting the Royal Choral Society and the Huddersfield Choral Society for many years. From 1948 until 1967 he was chief conductor at the London proms. He is chiefly remembered as an ardent popularizer, with a special interest in promoting new operas, and for his skill as a choral conductor.

Sarraute, Nathalie (1902–) French writer. Born in Russia, Sarraute came to

Paris as a child. She studied English literature at the Sorbonne, history in Oxford, and sociology in Berlin before training as a lawyer. After World War II she devoted herself to her writing. In 1982 she was awarded the Grand Prix National des Lettres for her complete oeuvre.

In her writings Sarraute aimed to break down the traditional structures of the novel and to forge a new relationship between language and consciousness. Her first book *Tropisms* (1939), a collection of short prose pieces, already shows her preoccupation with the hidden psychological undercurrents that accompany most human encounters. In the 1950s Sarraute became a central figure in the development of the NOUVEAU ROMAN, influencing other writers through her critical essays as well as her novels. In her collection of essays *The Age of Suspicion* (1956) she explained her distrust of the realist tradition in fiction, arguing that its conventions conceal the truth about human beings. In novels such as *Marteraux* (1953), *The Planetarium* (1959), *The Golden Fruits* (1963) and *Between Life and Death* (1968) such conventions as plot, characterization, and an identifiable narrative voice are progressively dispensed with. The social range of her novels is narrow, most of them having a domestic middle-class setting. She also wrote a number of radio plays including *Silence* (1967), and *The Lie* (1967). Her most recent novel, *Childhood* (1983), deals with the problem of memory; more accessible than many of her earlier works, it is considered to be amongst her finest achievements.

Sartre, Jean-Paul (1905–80) French philosopher and writer, who became the most prominent French intellectual of the post-war era. Born in Paris, Sartre was brought up by his mother, a cousin of Albert Schweitzer. The atmosphere of his childhood and his precocious literary ambitions are described wryly in his autobiography *The Words* (1964). After studying philosophy, psychology, and sociology at the Sorbonne, he taught at lycées in Le Havre, Laon, and Paris. In 1929 he met Simone de BEAUVOIR who became his lifelong companion. In World War II he was held in a prison camp, in which he produced his most important philosophical work *Being and Nothingness* (1943); the basic document of post-war EXISTENTIALISM, the book is a product of Sartre's immersion in the work of Husserl and Heidegger in the 1930s. The same vision of man as an isolated being forced to create his own meanings and values in a universe without a transcendent dimension informs his plays *The Flies* (1943), *Behind Closed Doors* (1945), *The Game is Over* (1947), and *Dirty Hands* (1948). Sartre's post-war writings are chiefly concerned to reconcile individualistic existentialism with the need for political commitment, which for Sartre took an increasingly Marxist form. The strain of this attempt is apparent in such works as *Existentialism is a Humanism* (1946) and *Critique of Dialectic Reason* (1960). From 1945 he edited the left-wing journal *Les Temps modernes* and took a prominent role in public affairs, travelling on political missions to the US, the Soviet Union, China, Brazil, Japan, and Israel. In 1964 he refused the Nobel Prize. Together with Simone de Beauvoir he participated in the students' revolt of 1968. The main concern of his philosophical thinking – illustrated too in his novels *Nausea* (1943) and the trilogy *Roads To Liberty* (1945) – is the relation between the isolated but free person and society.

Sastre, Alfonso (1926–) Spanish playwright, critic, and novelist, who built up a strong reputation for socially committed plays during the 1950s and 1960s. Although several of his plays were banned under Franco's regime, while others were allowed publication but not performance, Sastre remained committed to the idea of theatre as an agent for social and political reform. Many of his plays were first performed by university groups, including his own Arte Nuevo (1945–48). Other groups led by Sastre were the Teatro de Agitación Social, founded in 1950, and the Grupo de Teatro Realista, founded in 1960, both of which gave premieres of several of his plays. Such pieces as *Squad Facing Death* (1953), banned for its antimilitarist stance, *Death in the Neighbourhood* (1955), *The Raven* (1957), *Death Thrust* (1960), set against the background of the bullfight, and *In the Web* (1961), which tackled issues raised by the Algerian war, left Sastre's sympathy for the victims of repressive governments in no doubt. He himself was imprisoned in 1956 and 1961. Subsequent plays have included *The Banquet* (1965), *Roman Chronicles* (1968), *Ex-*

ercises in Terror (1970), *Magnetic Waves* (1972), and – after a break during which he concentrated upon writing novels – *It's No Laughing Matter* (1979) and *Tragicomedy of the Gypsy Celestina* (1984). In the 1970s and 1980s Sastre's plays became increasingly experimental in form, making use of nonlinear time schemes, audience participation, and a variety of unconventional techniques. His theoretical writings about the theatre are also considered of major importance.

Saura, Antonio (1930–) Spanish painter. Born at Huesca in north-east Spain, Saura took up painting in 1947 during an illness. In 1953 he travelled to Paris, where he lived until 1955. In Paris he became involved with the Surrealist group and experimented with new techniques; he tried painting in a surrealist manner himself but quickly became dissatisfied.

In 1955 Saura moved to Madrid where, in 1957, he helped to found the group El Paso, consisting of artists, writers, and sculptors who were antagonistic towards the Franco regime. The group championed modern styles in painting, especially abstract art. Saura's own work of the 1960s was expressive, even brutal and violent; many of his works are painted on torn canvases. He concentrated on figures – nudes, crucifixions, imaginary portraits. The intensity of his work soon attracted international attention; during the 1960s he won several major prizes and his paintings were exhibited in many countries.

Saura, Carlos (1932–) Spanish film director, often considered the father of contemporary Spanish cinema (in succession to BUÑUEL). Born in Aragon, he studied cinema and made a documentary before directing his first feature film, *The Hooligans* (1962), a depiction of youthful rebelliousness in contemporary Spanish society. *The Hunt* (1966) was the first of several films to probe the legacy of the Spanish Civil War. *Peppermint Frappé* (1967) was a surrealist drama, much influenced by Buñuel, about a surgeon who transforms one of his patients into a double of his brother's wife, with whom he is obsessed. With their emphasis on violence and sexual hypocrisy many of the films of this period are bitterly, if indirectly, critical of Franco's regime and such institutions as the Church and the army. Among the most successful was *Raise Ravens* (1975), which concerned the refusal of a young girl to acknowledge her parents' deaths.

With the death of Franco in 1975 the political aspect of Saura's work became less important and his subjects became increasingly varied. *Fast, Fast* (1980) traced the lives of four delinquents (played by nonprofessionals) and, like several of his earlier films, made innovative use of flamenco music. This interest came to the fore with a trilogy of films celebrating Spanish music and dance: his version of García Lorca's *Blood Wedding* (1981) was based on a ballet choreographed by Antonio GADES, the highly successful *Carmen* (1983) combined dance and drama, and *A Love Bewitched* (1986) was a supernatural love story employing the music of Falla. More recent films include *El Dorado* (1988), an epic about the conquistadors' exploration of Peru; *Ay Carmela!* (1990), a somewhat overstated allegory about a cabaret trio who find themselves behind Nationalist lines in the Civil War; and *Sevillanas* (1992), a spectacular celebration of Spanish folk dance.

Savary, Jérôme (1942–) French theatre director, actor, and playwright, who founded the Grand Théâtre Panique in 1965 with ARRABAL. Savary's writing for the Grand Théâtre Panique, which became the Grand Magic Circus in 1968, brought him to immediate public notice; he has subsequently presented a number of popular revue-style entertainments combining cabaret and social satire. He has also applied his unconventional theatrical techniques to productions of the classics, including plays by Molière. After winning further acclaim with Molière's *Le Bourgeois Gentilhomme* in 1981, he was rewarded in 1982 with the directorship of the newly established Maison de la Culture in Béziers. He is also noted as a director of operas by Offenbach and others.

Savonlinna Opera Festival An annual opera festival lasting for a month each July; performances are staged in the courtyard of the medieval Olavinlinna Castle in Savonlinna, Finland. The Festival was originally founded by the Finnish soprano Aïno Ackté in 1907 but dates in its present form from 1967, when it was totally remodelled. The programme includes newly commissioned works.

Scarpa, Carlo (1906–79) Italian architect. Scarpa was born in Venice and remained there for most of his life after graduating from the Accademia. Decisive influences were Frank Lloyd Wright, Bruno Zevi, and the De Stijl movement. Scarpa taught widely before establishing himself as an exhibition designer in the 1940s; he became responsible for the design of Venice Biennale in 1941. His reputation was made by a series of museum renovations, beginning with the Museo Abbatellis in Palermo (1953–54). This was followed by new interiors for the Accademia and Museo Correr in Venice (1954–60) and the remodelling of the Castelvecchio, Verona (1964). His work was characterized by a virtuosity of detailing in which every construction material and joint was treated with a jeweller's intricacy, a quality exemplified also in his designs for Venetian glass. Yet he was also capable of gestures of showmanship that specially suited his exhibition work, as when he took a 14th-century statue of Congrande I della Scala from its tomb and placed it high over the entrance to the Castelvecchio, set at a dramatic angle under its deep eaves.

For many people Scarpa's finest work is the Brion Vega cemetery at San Vito, Asolo, begun in 1970 and completed posthumously. Many of his largest projects were begun late in life and left uncompleted, the Banca Popolano, Verona (begun in 1973) and housing in Vicenza (1975), both being testaments to his lasting commitment to the rational purity of modernism.

Scharoun, Hans (1893–1972) German architect, whose work links the expressionist movement of the 1920s with that of the 1960s. His oddly angled and sometimes bizarre-looking buildings were always the product of purposeful planning, being mainly conceived from the inside out.

In the 1920s Scharoun was a member of the influential Berlin architectural association The Ring. This led to his contributing the masterplan and some fine blocks to the collective Siemensstadt housing development (1930) and to an ideological association with Hugo Häring (1882–1958), whose writings articulate the ideas expressed in Scharoun's buildings. Under the Nazis Scharoun was able to build little, with the outstanding exception of his Schminke House, Löbau (1933). After World War II, however, he was active in the architectural regeneration of Berlin both as professor of architecture at the Technical University (1946–48) and as city planner (1945–46). His masterplan of 1946 remained unbuilt apart from some housing, though his private flats 'Romeo and Juliet' (1954–59) were immensely popular.

Instead, Scharoun came to specialize in cultural buildings. His first theatre projects, for Kassel (1952) and Mannheim (1953), were unsuccessful, but saw his plans evolving away from the traditional proscenium arch. This process culminated in his competition-winning design for the Berlin Philharmonie in 1956. Built in 1959–63, this is Scharoun's masterpiece, though his complex hall and writhing foyer were given only a simple facade (which has been rebuilt, as has the roof). It was followed by a state library, completed alongside the Philharmonie in 1978, and a maritime museum at his home town of Bremerhaven (1970).

Schat, Peter (1935–) Dutch composer. Schat studied composition with Kees van BAAREN and piano with Jaap Callenbach at The Hague Royal Conservatory, and also privately with Matyas Seiber in London and BOULEZ in Basel. He became associated with the Studio for Electro-Instrumental Music in Amsterdam and in 1968 established his own group, the Amsterdam Electronic Circus. Many of his works involve a radical fusion of ELECTRONIC MUSIC and COMMUNITY THEATRE, often requiring collaboration between individuals from many different disciplines, such as art, architecture, filmmaking, choreography, and writing, as well as music. His compositions include the innovative operas *Labyrinth* (1962) and *Houdini* (1976), *Signalement* (1962) for six percussion instruments and three double basses, *On Escalation* (1968) for percussion and other instruments, and *The Fifth Season* (1973), a piece of music theatre about the Vietnam War designed for outdoor performance.

Schaufuss, Peter (1949–) Danish ballet dancer and choreographer, regarded as one of the most talented male dancers to emerge since NUREYEV. Schaufuss has spent most of his career outside Scandinavia, notably in Britain and the US. The son of two dancers, he made his professional debut at the age of seven and in 1967 joined the National Ballet of Canada as a soloist; he danced a number of major roles but subsequently embarked on a nomadic career moving from one leading company to another.

In the 1970s Schaufuss concentrated on dancing with the LONDON FESTIVAL BALLET (1970–74) and with George Balanchine's New York City Ballet (1974–77), as well as earning a reputation as a producer with such works as *La Sylphide* (1979), an award-winning production for the London Festival Ballet; in 1981 he produced *Napoli* for the National Ballet of Canada. In 1984 he took up the post of artistic director with the London Festival Ballet and did much to widen its repertory. He was also responsible for the appointment of Christopher BRUCE as associate choreographer and founded both the LFB (a subsidiary touring company) and, in 1988, the LFB School to encourage new talent. In 1989 he was appointed ballet director of DEUTSCHE OPER in Berlin.

Schillebeeckx, Edward (1914–) Belgian Roman Catholic theologian. Schillebeeckx entered the Dominican Order in 1934 and was ordained in 1941. He studied philosophy and theology in Paris, obtaining his doctorate in 1951; he subsequently taught theology in Louvain and in Nijmegen in the Netherlands. In 1982 he became the first theologian to be awarded the Erasmus Prize for his contribution to European civilization.

In his writings Schillebeeckx addresses himself directly to the problems of modern secularization. He regards Christian dogma as requiring continual reinterpretation according to the historical situation, so that religious truth cannot be possessed once and for all but must be renewed in every epoch (*The Understanding of Faith*; 1964). Schillebeeckx argues that many Catholic dogmas were formulated approximately, using the concepts and terminology available at the time, and must be reformulated today using today's knowledge. He makes a distinction between this approach, which he terms 'perspectivism', and mere relativism (*God the Future of Man*; 1968). Schillebeeckx's systematic writings centre on the person of Jesus Christ, regarded as the point at which human experience and divine reality coincide (*Christ: The Experience of Jesus as Lord*, 1970; *Ministry: Leadership in the Community of Jesus Christ*, 1980).

Together with RAHNER and KÜNG, Schillebeeckx has taken a leading role in the attempt to renew the Catholic church during and after the Second Vatican Council (1962–65).

Schilling, Tom (1928–) German dancer, choreographer, and ballet director, who emerged as one of the most important figures in German dance in the 1950s. Having trained at the Dessau Opera Ballet School, he appeared as a dancer with the Dresden, Leipzig, and Weimar companies in the 1950s and was appointed director and choreographer of the Dresden State Opera in 1956; he took over the East Berlin Comic Opera in 1965.

Praised for the originality of his works, Schilling was soon acknowledged as the most influential choreographer in East Germany. Among his most significant early productions was the first German version of Asafiev's *Fountain of Bakhchisarai* (1955); his works since then have included *Snow White* (1956), *Swan Lake* (1959), *The Seven Deadly Sins* (1962), *Symphonie fantastique* (1967), *Fancy Free* (1971), *Pastorale* (1979), and *A New Midsummer Night's Dream* (1981). He has worked as a guest choreographer in France, Norway, and Austria.

Schlesinger, John (Richard) (1926–) British film director, who is also known for his work in the theatre and in television. Schlesinger made a number of television documentaries in the 1950s after gaining some experience as an actor in such films as *The Battle of the River Plate* (1956). The success of the documentary *Terminus* (1960), about the British transport system, which included winning the Golden Lion award at the Venice Film Festival, enabled him to make his feature film debut with *A Kind of Loving* (1962). This award-winning story of frustrated ambition and romantic disillusion was set in industrial northern England, a setting Schlesinger returned to in *Billy Liar* (1963), a highly successful comedy starring Tom Courtenay and Julie Christie.

Julie Christie was also the star of *Darling* (1965), an exposé of jet-set society, and *Far from the Madding Crowd* (1967), an adaptation of the novel by Thomas Hardy. In 1969 Schlesinger went to the US, where he made *Midnight Cowboy*, a study of New

York low life that won two Oscars, before returning to London to make *Sunday, Bloody Sunday* (1971), about a three-way love affair.

Subsequent films have included the US-made thriller *Marathon Man* (1976), starring Dustin Hoffman and Laurence Olivier, *Yanks* (1978), about the arrival of US troops in Britain during World War II, *Madame Sousatzka* (1988), and *Pacific Heights* (1990), a chilling story about a psychopath who terrorizes the other tenants of the house in which he lives.

Schlesinger's television films have included *An Englishman Abroad* (1983) and *A Question of Attribution* (1991), both from plays by Alan BENNETT. He has also directed plays for the National Theatre and several operatic productions.

Schlöndorff, Volker (1939–) German film director, noted for his films about rebels and outcasts. Schlöndorff studied film in Paris and worked as an assistant to MALLE, RESNAIS, and MELVILLE, making his first short film in 1960 and his feature debut in 1966 with *Young Törless*. Like many of his subsequent films, this was an adaptation of a well-known book – in this case Robert Musil's story about the failure of a schoolboy to intervene when a gang of bullies kill another pupil. It won the International Critics' Prize at the CANNES FILM FESTIVAL.

Michael Kohlhaas (1969) was an adaptation of Heinrich von Kleist's novel about rural conflict in the 16th century that drew a parallel with unrest in contemporary German society. *The Sudden Fortune of the Poor People of Kombach* (1971), another rural allegory, portrayed the downfall of a peasant community after a fortune is stolen from the local tax collector. The film starred **Margarethe von Trotta**, who also worked on the screenplay; during the course of their continuing collaboration von Trotta became Schlöndorff's wife.

Summer Lightning (1972) was another joint work, starring von Trotta as a divorcée who finds her attempts to rebuild her life blighted by male chauvinism. Von Trotta then concentrated upon her own career as a director, her films including *The German Sisters* (1981), *Friends and Husbands* (1982), and *Rosa Luxemburg* (1986). She continued to collaborate occasionally with her husband, however, most notably on *The Lost Honour of Katherina Blum* (1975). Based on the novel by Heinrich BÖLL, this film about the public scorn directed at an innocent girl, because of her unknowing association with a terrorist, was widely praised for its examination of prejudice in modern German society.

Subsequent films by Schlöndorff include *Coup de grâce* (1976), set in the period following the Russian Revolution, and an adaptation of Günter GRASS's *The Tin Drum* (1979). More recently *Circle of Deceit* (1981) analysed the conflict of loyalties in war-torn Beirut while *Swann in Love* (1983) was an adaptation of Proust. His latest films are a version of Arthur Miller's *Death of a Salesman* (1985), starring Dustin Hoffman, and *The Handmaid's Tale* (1989), taken from the novel by Margaret Atwood.

Schmidt, Arno (1914–78) German writer. In 1934 Schmidt broke off his university studies in mathematics and astronomy to work in the textile industry. After service in World War II he worked as an interpreter and in 1958 he and his wife bought a small house in the village of Bargfeld, Lower Saxony, where he spent the rest of his life writing.

In one of his earliest published stories, *Leviathan* (1949), Schmidt presents his view of history as a series of meaningless catastrophes incompatible with the existence of God. He published the short essay *Atheist – Well Yes!* in 1953. Other early stories and novels focus on the lives of unremarkable people trying to hide from the truth that they live in a world of senselessness and brutality. According to Schmidt, only a minority of enlightened intellectuals are able to recognize and live with this truth. In *The Egghead Republic* (1957) Schmidt gives a satirical sketch of a Utopian state in which men of letters and science are honoured according to their true merit.

Later novels, starting with *Dump, or Mare Crisium* (1959), show the influence of Freud's theory of the subconscious; plot and dialogue are separated out from the hidden thoughts and desires of his protagonists. He carried this procedure to the limit in *Zettel's Dream* (1970), a huge book that describes a single day in the summer of 1968, largely taken up with discussions of psychoanalysis and Edgar Allen Poe (whom Schmidt has translated).

Schmidt's writing is notorious for its immense number of literary and other allusions, its use of phonetic spelling, and for its somewhat arrogant attitude to the mass of mankind.

Schmidt, Maarten (1929–) Dutch astronomer, working in the US. Schmidt graduated from the University of Groningen in 1949 and obtained his PhD in 1956 from Leiden University. After working at the Leiden Observatory from 1953 to 1959, he moved to the US, taking up an appointment at the California Institute of Technology at the Hale Observatories. He became professor of astronomy in 1964 and director of the Hale Observatories in 1978.

Schmidt is best known for his research on quasars. In 1960 Allan Sandage and Thomas Matthews identified a compact radio source, known as 3C 48, with a 16th-magnitude star-like object that was found to have a most curious spectrum. In 1963 Schmidt realized that certain broad emission lines in the spectrum of 3C 273 were the familiar hydrogen lines but shifted towards the red end of the spectrum. Red shifts of this type are caused by the Doppler effect – an increase in wavelength as the emitting source moves away from the observer. Assuming that this motion was caused by the expansion of the universe, Schmidt calculated that 3C 273 must be a billion light-years away. In that case, how could such a small source be visible at such an enormous distance? It would need to be as luminous as a hundred galaxies and it was by no means clear what mechanism could yield so much energy from such a compact source. Schmidt's work was soon confirmed by the spectra of other quasars; they all possessed unusually large red shifts. There arose a long debate as to whether the Doppler effect did explain the quasar red shift but it is now generally accepted that this is the case.

By the end of the 1960s many quasars had been discovered and their distribution mapped in the heavens. Schmidt realized that this allowed him to test the cosmological steady-state doctrine of Thomas GOLD and others, which assumes that the universe on a large scale looks the same at all times and all places. He found, however, on examining the distribution of quasars that their numbers increase with distance and that they are indeed the most distant objects in the universe – and also the youngest objects.

The discovery of the quasars with the problems they posed produced an enormous growth in astronomical research that led to the discovery of even stranger objects, such as pulsars, and the continued search for black holes. Huge black holes are indeed thought to be the source of the prodigious energy of quasars.

Schnittke, Alfred (1934–) Russian composer and musicologist, living in Germany. Schnittke was born in the German Volga Republic, the son of a journalist. After World War II his father's work took the family to Vienna, where Schnittke began private piano lessons. From 1953 onwards he studied instrumentation, composition, and counterpoint at the Moscow Conservatory under Rakov and Golubev. Schnittke himself taught at the Conservatory from 1961 until 1972. Since 1979 he has lived and taught in Hamburg.

Schnittke's work can be divided into three main periods. His early pieces, such as the oratorios *Nagasaki* (1958) and *Songs of War and Peace* (1959) were conventional in style and addressed contemporary themes in a manner acceptable to the Soviet authorities. From about 1963 onwards, however, he was increasingly influenced by avant-garde developments in Western Europe and became one of the first Soviet composers to experiment with SERIALISM and electronic music. After several years of dedicated avant-gardism he began to reintroduce tonal elements in such pieces as *Quasi una sonata* for violin and piano (1968). The beginning of a third period in Schnittke's work is announced by the first symphony (1972), which incorporates quotations from Beethoven and passages of pastiche baroque writing. He has since continued to compose in a wilfully eclectic style that combines the most heterogeneous materials and techniques; an element of sardonic parody is often apparent.

Schnittke's works include five symphonies (1972, 1980, 1981, 1984, 1988) and concertos for violin (1957, 1966, 1979, 1982) and viola (1985). His numerous chamber works include three string quartets and an affecting version of the carol *Stille Nacht* for solo violin. In 1992 *Life with an Idiot*, an absurdist opera with a libretto by Viktor Erofeev, was premiered in Amsterdam. He has also composed for tape and electronically amplified instruments and provided music for films and the theatre. His prolific musicological writings are mainly concerned with modern Russian composers.

Schöffer, Nicolas (1912–) French experimental sculptor, born in Hungary. Schöffer studied at the Academy of Art in Budapest (1932–35) and at the Ecole des Beaux-Arts in Paris (1936–39). He subsequently remained in Paris and took French nationality. At this time he was a painter, but after the war he turned to sculpture.

As a sculptor, Schöffer was much influenced by the constructivism of Naum Gabo and the abstract work of Moholy-Nagy. Most of his works are slender open towers, generally consisting of a light metal skeleton covered with plexiglass to reflect light. He called these 'spatiodynamic' constructions. In the following years he developed this basic idea by adding electric motors to produce movement (from 1950) and devices to emit sound (from 1954). Schöffer also began to build on a larger scale: in 1955 he constructed a tower 50 m high at St Cloud near Paris and in 1961 a tower 52 m high in Liège. He also developed complex 'cybernetic' sculptures which moved in response to colours and sounds (such as *CYSP 1*, produced with sponsorship from the Philips company). In 1968 he was awarded the Grand Prix at the Venice Biennale.

Schwartz, Rudolf (1905–) British conductor, born in Austria. Schwartz was born and educated in Vienna, making his debut as a conductor in 1923 at the Opera House in Düsseldorf, Germany. He went on to conduct at the Opera House, Karlsruhe from 1927 to 1933 and worked for the Jewish Cultural Organization in Berlin before World War II. A survivor of the Nazi concentration camps, he emigrated to Britain after the war. Since then he has worked with the Bournemouth Municipal Orchestra (1947–51), the City of Birmingham Symphony Orchestra (1951–57), the BBC Symphony Orchestra (1957–62), and the Northern Sinfonia Orchestra (1964–73).

Schwarz, Rudolf (1897–1961) German architect born in Strasbourg. Schwarz specialized in the building of churches, investing them with dramatic new forms. His elemental structures can be very simple in their external shapes and materials, yet find powerful expression internally by the use of concrete frames.

In 1925 Schwarz taught in Offenbach with Dominikus Böhm (1880–1955), a similarly expressive church specialist. They and Otto Bartning (1883–1959) gave German church architecture its exceptional vitality, thanks not only to their use of emotive form but also to their interest in liturgical planning. Most innovatory was Schwarz's Corpus Christi Church, Aachen (1928–30), a white box of sensational purity, whose unencumbered space sought to unite priest and congregation.

But Schwarz's most telling series of churches belongs to the period of post-war rebuilding and expansion, when the Catholic diocese of Cologne alone built 300 churches. Schwarz's masterpieces are sometimes brutally romantic. Outstanding amongst his prodigious output are St Anna, Düren (1951–56), with its altar in the bend of an L-shaped block that contrasts red sandstone and modern glass; Holy Cross, Bottrop (1951–57), a brick parabola with a glazed end; St Michael, Frankfurt (1953–54), an elongated brick ellipse; and the square Holy Family, Oberhausen (1956–58), where columns give the impression that the whole building is a baldachino.

Schwarz's sudden death left many churches to be completed by his widow, Maria Lang Schwarz, and their pupils. He also built several secular buildings, including the College of Sociology, Aachen (1931) and the Wallraf-Richartz Museum (1951–57) in Cologne, where he was the city planner from 1946 to 1952.

Sciascia, Leonardo (1921–89) Italian novelist and writer. Born in Sicily, he spent most of his life in his native town of Racalmuto, where he worked as a civil servant and teacher. After taking early retirement in 1970 he became an MEP for the Radical Party. His work uses material drawn from the darker side of Sicilian life and culture to illustrate universal moral problems and fundamental themes such as reason, truth, and justice.

Sciascia explored a variety of genres (novels, plays, essays, poetry, and short stories) while constantly searching for new forms of linguistic expression. His best work combines the skills of the historian, the investigative journalist, and the detective novelist. Irony and caustic wit are deployed against such quintessentially Sicilian ills as political intrigue and corruption, the Mafia, and the role of the clergy; Sciascia's ultimate target, however, is the ingrained conservatism that stands in the way of any attempt at reform. The crime novels *The Day of the Owl* (1961) and *A Man's Blessing* (1966) deal with the Mafia and the web of corruption and deceit surrounding its activities, while the historical novels *The Council of Egypt* (1963) and *The Death of the Inquisitor* (1964) deal respectively with 18th-century attempts at reform and the Inquisition in 17th-century Sicily.

Other works include *Pirandello and Sicily* (1961), *Equal Danger* (1971), *In Every Way* (1974), *The Moro Affair* (1978) *Candido, or A Dream Dreamed in Sicily* (1977), *From the World of the Infidels* (1979), *The Theatre of Memory* (1981), and *A Straightforward Tale* (1989).

Scola, Ettore (1931–) Italian film director and screenwriter. Born in Avellino, Scola studied law before working in journalism and radio. He began his cinematic career as a screenwriter in the early 1950s, collaborating on the scripts for such films as *Two Nights With Cleopatra* (1954), *Ghosts of Rome* (1960), *Love à la Carte* (1960), and *The Magnificent Cuckold* (1964). His debut as a director came in 1964 with *Let's Talk About Women* and he often returned to its themes of seduction and infidelity in such offerings as *The Devil in Love* (1966), *The Pizza Triangle* (1970), *We All Loved Each Other So Much* (1975), *Down and Dirty* (1976), *Passione d'Amore* (1981), and *The Family* (1987). Two of his films have taken awards at the Cannes Film Festival: he was named best director in 1976 for *Brutti, Sporchi e Cattivi* (1976) and a year later his *A Special Day* won the Special Jury Prize. His recent films include *Che Orà E?* (1989) and *The Voyage of Captain Fracassa* (1990).

Scott, Michael (1905–89) Irish architect. Scott trained simultaneously as an actor and an architect before founding his own practice in 1928. His first work was appropriately at the Gate Theatre, Dublin (1930–32). This was followed by some well-planned hospitals, notably at Portlaoise (1936, in white concrete) and Tullamore (1937). His first truly modern buildings were a house for himself (1938) and the Irish Pavilion at the 1939 New York World's Fair, whose shamrock shape was given a sophisticated curtain-wall façade.

Shortages delayed Scott's next building, the bus station in Store Street, Dublin (1948–53; also including offices for the Department of Social Welfare). Ireland's first and most famous Modern Movement building, it derived in equal measure from mid-1930s LE CORBUSIER and Mies van der Rohe, with just the right combination of clear detailing and whimsy. It established Scott as Ireland's leading architect, a status he confirmed with a series of functional factories around Dublin.

In 1959 Scott took into partnership Ronald Tallon and Robin Walker, whose design involvement was acknowledged in 1975 when the practice was renamed Scott, Tallon, Walker. Buildings like their Bank of Ireland headquarters (1968–72) and Carroll's Cigarette Factory (1967–70) show a great refinement, an unusual rapport with clients, and a commitment to incorporating paintings and sculpture. Scott's involvement with the arts led to his founding of a triennial art show in 1967 and his purchase of James Joyce's tower at Sandycove, now a museum. Most appropriate, however, was his commission (1959) to rebuild the Abbey Theatre, where he had trained, after its destruction by fire in 1951; this was completed in 1966.

Scott, Paul (1920–78) British novelist. Born and educated in London, Scott served in the Indian army during World War II, an experience that provided him with material for his later writing. Starting with *Johnnie Sahib* (1952) he wrote 13 novels, the most famous of which are the four known as the *Raj Quartet*, namely *The Jewel in the Crown* (1966), *The Day of the Scorpion* (1968), *The Towers of Silence* (1971), and *A Division of the Spoils* (1975). Through a series of intricately interrelated stories the *Quartet* dramatizes the racial, religious, and political crises besetting India at the close of the Imperial era. The atmosphere of the period is skilfully evoked. Scott's work achieved its greatest popularity with the television adaptation of the *Raj Quartet* in 1984. His last novel *Staying On* (1977), describing the lives of an English couple who decide to remain in post-Independence India, was awarded the BOOKER PRIZE.

Scott, Ridley (1937–) British film director, who began as a director of television commercials and subsequently translated the glossy imagery of these productions to his films. *The Duellists* (1978), an adaptation of a story by Joseph Conrad, was typically well shot though some critics found it superficial. The science-fiction horror story *Alien* (1979) established Scott as one of the most successful directors in the commercial cinema and was followed by the equally popular *Blade Runner* (1982), another futuristic thriller. More recent films, among them *Legend* (1985) and *Someone to Watch Over Me* (1987), have been praised for their visual qualities but again criticized for lacking content. Rather more successful was *Black Rain* (1989), which starred Michael Douglas as a US policeman working with his counterparts in Japan; the film was praised for its sensitive handling of the culture clash. *Thelma and Louise* (1991), a thriller about two women on the run in the southern US, was also admired for its intelligent characterization and provocative feminist message.

Scottish Opera An opera company founded in 1962 by Alexander Gibson, the musical director of the Scottish National Orchestra. Based in Glasgow, the company moved from its first home, the King's Theatre, to the Theatre Royal in 1975; it also gives seasons in Edinburgh and tours regularly in Scotland and the English provinces. Under the direction of Peter Hemmings (1963–87) the company developed a reputation for innovative productions making imaginative use of sets and lighting. The works of contemporary composers such as BRITTEN were performed and since 1972 there has been a policy of commissioning operas from Scottish composers. In 1971 Scottish Opera gave the first British performance of Wagner's *Ring* cycle outside London for 40 years. It formed its own permanent orchestra in 1980. The current administrator is John Mauceri.

Searle, Humphrey (1915–82) British composer, teacher, and writer. Born in Oxford, Searle studied with Vaughan Williams at the Royal College of Music and subsequently (1937–38) with Webern in Vienna. During World War II he worked for the BBC music department and in the 1950s with the Sadler's Wells Ballet; he was a professor at the Royal College of Music from 1965. His works, which are generally expressionist in style with a strong element of romanticism, show the influence of Berg and Schoenberg as well as Webern. He began to make systematic use of serial procedures after World War II. His compositions include the operas *Diary of a Madman* (1958), *Photo of the Colonel* (1963), and *Hamlet* (1968), the cantatas *Gold Coast Customs* (1949), and *The Shadow of Cain* (1951) after Edith Sitwell and *The Riverrun* (1951) after James Joyce, and five symphonies.

Seferis, George (George Seferiadis; 1900–71) Greek poet and diplomat. Seferis was born in Smyrna, now Izmir, which was taken over by the Turks in 1922, rendering him an exile from his birthplace. After studying law at Athens University and the Sorbonne he joined the Greek diplomatic service; his career involved postings in Europe, Africa, and the Middle East.

Seferis's work shows a commitment to revitalizing Greek poetry by breaking away from parochial subjects and traditional forms. While studying in France he was greatly influenced by the symbolist poets, particularly Valéry, Rimbaud, and Laforgue. Another major influence was the work of T. S. Eliot, which he encountered on his first posting to London (1931–34). The bleak and powerful symbolism of *Turning Point* (1931) and the dense complexity of *The Cistern* (1932) marked his total break from conventional styles. *Myth-history* (1935), a free-verse work written in self-consciously contemporary language, revolves around a symbolic journey – a theme reminiscent of Homer but also appropriate to Seferis's own peripatetic life.

Although Seferis's work is deeply spiritual, with a powerful sense of myth and history, the mood is often one of futility and despair. His disillusionment with politics deepened during the 1960s. His criticism of the Greek military coup (1967) brought him into official disfavour and he made no further public political comments. Seferis published volumes of his collected poems in 1940, 1950, 1960, and (posthumously) 1972, as well as the essay collection *On Greek Style* (1967) and many translations of modern English and

French poetry. He was awarded the Nobel Prize for literature in 1963.

Segal, Walter (1907–85) Swiss-born architect and teacher, who trained in Germany and practised in London from 1936. Segal was an innovator who brought Modern Movement idealism to the possibilities of timber prefabrication to produce a housing system simple enough for its occupants to erect themselves. The result is arguably more truly 'community architecture' than any traditional style championed by the Prince of Wales.

Segal showed an early hostility to the relative complexities of concrete; this may be a reason why all his works are Schumacher-like in scale and humanity. Early buildings include simple brick houses, such as St Anne's Close, Highgate (1950–52), a number of schools, and a pickle factory. He also experimented with low-rise high-density projects. Then, in 1963, he built himself temporary accommodation using a version of George Washington Snow's 'balloon framing', a nailed system resembling trellis with which Segal had first experimented in Switzerland in 1932. A series of one-off timber bungalows followed in 1968–70, culminating in 1971 with one largely built by the clients themselves at Bromeswell, Suffolk. Segal refined his system throughout the 1970s, building his first two-storey version in 1977.

In the late 1970s the London Borough of Lewisham offered Segal two steeply sloping sites unsuitable for ordinary housing if he would work with people on the council's waiting list. Segal Close (1977–82), was followed by Walter's Way (1985–87), largely supervised by his assistant Jon Broome. Their success is a tribute to Segal's lifelong idealism. His system is still used by the Walter Segal Trust and in Broome's experiments with environmentally friendly building.

Seghers, Anna (1900–83) German novelist. Seghers was born in Mainz, the daughter of the Jewish antique dealer Isiodor Reiling. She studied history, history of art, and sinology in Cologne and Heidelberg before embarking on a career as a writer. She first attracted widespread notice with the novel *Revolt of the Fishermen from Santa Barbara* in 1928. In the same year she became a member of the Communist Party and travelled to the international writers' congress in Charkow, where she became friends with the Hungarian Marxist critic Georg Lukàcs. After Hitler's rise to power Seghers fled to France, where she contributed to German journals published in exile.

At the heart of her novels is the analysis of international fascism. *Transit*, which appeared first in English in 1944, depicts the life of political refugees in Marseille under the Vichy government. The novel is a parable in the tradition of Kafka, showing the helplessness of the individual in the face of bureaucracy and totalitarianism. But it was *The Seventh Cross*, published in exile in 1942, that made her international reputation. The novel deals with the plight of Georg Heisler, an escapee from the Westhofen concentration camp, who has to rely on the help of ordinary Germans to reach the Dutch border. The novel provides a subtle and highly authentic cross-section of German society under Hitler. Seghers's assessment of the strength of German opposition to Hitler is neither over-sanguine nor wholly negative; there are no acts of spectacular heroism but many modest individual attempts to help Heisler. In 1947 Seghers returned to East Germany where she was fêted as a literary celebrity. Other important works include *The Dead Remain Young* (1949), *The Decision* (1959), *Caribic Tales* (1976), and *Strange Encounters* (1973).

Seifert, Jaroslav (1901–86) Czech poet. He left grammar school without matriculating and immediately became a member of the vanguard of Proletarian Poets. After his expulsion from the Communist Party (1929) he ceased writing for communist periodicals and, until 1949, edited various journals. After the Warsaw Pact intervention (1968), he was briefly president of the Writers' Union and is said to have wandered about Prague muttering 'After all, things were better under Hitler'. It was mainly as a symbol of resistance to neo-Stalinism that he was awarded the Nobel Prize for literature in 1984.

His first collection, *City in Tears* (1921), is a tendentious collection of revolutionary songs, in which he sees himself fighting on the barricades in the coming 'cruel, just revolution'; as proletarian and poet, he will emerge from the turmoil as a member of the new ruling class. In *On the Wireless Waves* (1925), he extols the glories of modern technology, travel, and a world united by sex and steamboats. The typographical tricks here look forward to concrete poetry. His gift for satire is evident in *Sung for the Rotary Press* (1936), though one has to be an historian to understand many of these occasional poems. After World War II, Seifert's verse tends to sentimentality (*Helmet of Soil*, 1945; *Mummy*, 1954), though sometimes it achieves simple impressionistic sensitivity (*Halley's Comet*; 1967). His last collections express a wry nostalgia and a somewhat mawkish gratitude to life (*The Plague Column*; 1977) and praise of love (*Being a Poet*; 1983).

Sereni, Vittorio (1913–83) Italian poet and writer, born in Lombardy. After graduating from Milan University, he began to teach and to contribute to avant-garde literary magazines. His experience as a prisoner of war in Africa is described in the collection of verse *Algerian Diary* (1947), in which he achieved a directness and simplicity that had eluded him in the earlier *The Border* (1941). At his best Sereni explores the universal problems of human existence in a style that is lyrical and elegiac while avoiding sentimentality. His work is much influenced by the 'crepuscular' poets of the turn of the century, especially Guido Gozzano (1883–1916). Later collections include *The Human Instrument* (1965) and *The Changeable Star* (1981).

Sereni was an accomplished translator of René CHAR, William Carlos Williams, and Apollinaire, amongst others. He also produced the novel *The Option* (1964), a volume of literary essays, *Preliminary Readings* (1973), and the collection of prose fragments *Immediate Surroundings* (1962).

serialism A method of composing music in which certain elements, usually pitch and occasionally duration, are used strictly according to a fixed order (series) that has been previously decided upon by the composer. Historically, the principle was first applied to the twelve chromatic pitches (hence the names twelve-tone music or dodecaphonic music). Invented in the 1920s by Schoenberg as a means of subverting the inevitable predominance of certain successions of notes in tonal music, twelve-tone music was developed further by his pupils Berg and Webern. It was not taken up extensively until after World War II, when it was seized upon and further developed by a diverse new generation of composers, including NONO, BOULEZ, STOCKHAUSEN and Milton Babbitt, as well as being taken up by older composers, notably Stravinsky. The term 'serialism' was first introduced at this time.

In **total serialism** all of the musical elements involved, including pitch, duration, dynamics, tempo, timbre, and articulation, adhere strictly to a fixed order. As a compositional device it arose in the 1950s as a logical extension of the methods used by Schoenberg and Webern, with MESSIAEN's *Mode de valeurs et d'intensités* (1949) serving as a crucial immediate influence on the works of POUSSEUR, Boulez, Stockhausen, and Nono. Boulez's *Structures I* (1952) is one of the most thoroughgoing examples of total serialism.

Serrau, Jean-Marie (1915–73) French theatre director, who played a major role in introducing the Theatre of the Absurd to French audiences (*see* ABSURD, THEATRE OF THE). In 1947 Serrau mounted one of the first French productions of a play by BRECHT, when he presented *The Exception and the Rule*. He continued to break new ground with plays by such absurdist authors as ADAMOV, BECKETT, GENET, and IONESCO, some of which aroused much controversy when first seen at his own Théâtre de Babylone and Théâtre de la Tempête. In the 1960s he confirmed his reputation for originality with a number of mixed-media presentations that attempted to fuse poetry with technology.

7:84 Theatre Company *See* MCGRATH, JOHN.

Shaffer, Peter (Levin) (1926–) British playwright now living in New York. *Five Finger Exercise* (1958), his first play, brought him immediate success and was followed in 1962 by the much-revived comedy double bill *The Private Ear* and *The Public Eye*, written specifically for the actress Maggie Smith. In *The Royal Hunt of the Sun* (1964), concerning the clash of cultures when the conquistadors invaded Peru, Shaffer began to explore his characteristic themes of reason versus faith and greatness versus mediocrity. The farce *Black Comedy* followed in 1965, then the one-act play *White Lies* (1967). *Equus* (1973) depicted the complex relationship between a self-doubting psychiatrist and his patient, a youth convicted of blinding six horses. Although Shaffer's implied message – that a life of demented passion may be preferable to one of dry intellect – aroused some disquiet, the play's theatrical power was indisputable. In *Amadeus* (1979) Shaffer similarly set the erratic genius Mozart against the conscientious but uninspired court composer Salieri; although critical opinion was once more divided, the play proved an enormous success, winning a series of awards. Shaffer's screenplay for Milos FORMAN's filmed version also won an Oscar.

Shaffer's more recent work has included the plays *Yonadab* (1985), *Lettice and Lovage* (1987), and *The Gift of the Gorgon* (1992), as well as plays for television and radio.

Shchedrin, Rodion (Konstantinovich) (1932–) Russian composer. Although he is a prominent musical figure in his own country, Shchedrin's works are little heard in the West. He studied composition with Yuri Shaporin and piano with Jacob Fliez at the Moscow Conservatory (1950–55) and later taught composition there (1964–69). Shchedrin's works contrived to be vibrant and diverse, incorporating modernist elements with traditional techniques and urban folk idioms, whilst remaining politically noncontroversial. His output includes the ballets *The Little Hump-Backed Horse* (1960), *Anna Karenina* (1972), and an adaptation of Bizet's *Carmen* (1968) written for his wife, the ballerina Maya Plisetskaya, as well as the opera *Not Love Alone* (1961) and symphonies, chamber music, piano music, film scores, and songs.

Shepitko, Larisa *See* KLIMOV, ELIM (GERMANOVICH).

Sheppard, Robson, and Partners British architectural firm specializing in schools and university buildings, established in 1947 by **Richard Sheppard** (1910–82), **Geoffrey Robson** (1918–), and Jean Shufflebotham. The partners met at the Architectural Association. They designed large numbers of schools, especially in Hertfordshire, Harlow, and the West Midlands, but their breakthrough came in 1959 when they won a competition for the prestigious new Churchill College, Cambridge. The complex (completed 1973), combines a traditional courtyard with monumental buildings worthy of its namesake. On more restricted budgets they also produced the early phases of Loughborough University (1961–66) and Brunel University (1965–71). They have also made major additions to existing universities and colleges, for example at Imperial College (1964–68), the City University (1969–71), Durham University (Collingwood College, 1974), and Manchester Polytechnic (1977–78). Many other firms contributed to Britain's post-war boom in educational buildings, but Sheppard, Robson were the specialists who gave the movement its backbone.

Only in the 1970s did Sheppard, Robson turn to designing noneducational buildings in any quantity, producing various offices, the huge Wood Green Shopping City (1972–80), and Lewisham Hospital (1983).

Shostakovich, Dmitri (1906–75) Russian composer. Shostakovich studied at the Petrograd Conservatory (1919–25), where his graduation piece (the first symphony) established his position in the front rank of Soviet composers when he was only 18 years old. Although his subsequent works won public acclaim, official reaction was seldom favourable and culminated in the condemnation of his opera *Lady Macbeth of Mtsensk* in *Pravda* in 1936. He subtitled his next work, the fifth symphony (1937), 'a Soviet artist's reply to just criticism' and the authorities held the work up as the epitome of approved Soviet art. During World War II Shostakovich was besieged in Leningrad, where he began his seventh symphony, a massive patriotic statement that came to be seen as a symbol of the resistance to the German invasion. In 1948 he was again condemned, along with Prokofiev and KHACHATURIAN, and only with Stalin's death in 1953 did Shostakovich return to symphonic composition. The scherzo of the tenth symphony (1953), is a brutal caricature of Stalin. His music of the 1960s and early 1970s is increasingly introspective and is mainly written for smaller ensembles. This trend is also evident in his late symphonies with their light orchestration and economy of material. His last work, the sonata for viola and piano (1975), and the last three string quartets (nos. 13–15), encapsulate the spirit of struggle and irony that lies at the heart of all Shostakovich's music.

Shostakovich's musical technique was based upon tonal harmony and the symphonic example of Mahler. His music invites interpretation both on a personal and a political level, encouraging the listener to probe beneath its often bleak or sentimental surface. He is the outstanding symphonist of the 20th century – he wrote 15 symphonies in all – and despite working within the constraints of the Soviet regime one of its most original composers.

Shukshin, Vasilii Makarovich (1929–74) Russian writer, actor, and film-maker. Born into a peasant family in the Altai region, Shukshin worked in various jobs before studying film-making in Moscow from 1954 to 1961. His first story was published in 1958 and a collection, *Rural People* (1963), was followed a year later by his first full-length film, *There Lives a Lad* (1964), which won a prize at the 16th Venice Film Festival. Other important films written and directed by Shukshin include *Your Son and Brother* (1965), *Strange People* (1969), *A Bench by the Stove* (1972) and, most famous of all, *Snowball Berry Red* (1974). Shukshin's play *Energetic People* (1974) enjoyed great success, as did two historical novels, *The Liubavins* (1965) and *I've Come to Give You Freedom* (1971), but it is for his many short stories that he is best remembered. Five collections had been published when he died of a heart attack at the age of 45 and many more have appeared since.

Shukshin's typical hero is an uprooted peasant seeking happiness and personal freedom in a confusing world in which his ambitions are foiled by the harsh Soviet authorities and victimized women alike. Many stories end with an unexpected tragicomic twist but their distinctive vitality depends on Shukshin's mastery of popular speech and its idiosyncrasies. He possessed the ability to engage readers as diverse as Brezhnev and SOLZHENITSYN and in terms of national popularity he almost equalled Vladimir VYSOTSKII. As a chronicler of the painful transition from country to city in Soviet society, Shukshin may be compared to Chekhov, who described a similar process at the turn of the century.

Šikula, Vincent (1936–) Slovak prose writer. Following studies at the State Conservatory in Bratislava and three years' teaching in Modra, he has worked for many years as a publisher's editor. The main preoccupation of his writing is the capacity of human nature to overcome suffering. *With Rozarka* (1966), about a man failing to cope with his delightful 18-year-old mentally retarded sister, reads like a modern folk story; the same may be said of many of Šikula's works from the 1960s to the 1980s. His chief work is the trilogy *The Master Carpenters* (1976–79), set during the Slovak national uprising (1944) and the beginnings of the socialist state. Using colourful language and imbued with wry humour, the trilogy shows how heroism, embodied in the figure of Imro, is rendered superfluous and impotent after the war. The one true communist is a jolly eccentric, killed at the beginning of the uprising, and the local party boss after the war is a former collaborator. Šikula's attraction to the fairy-tale tradition, particularly to the way it allows him to depict idealism and construct surreal situations, is exemplified by the short-story collection, *Études héroiques for Horses* (1987).

Simon, Claude (1913–) French writer. Born in Madagascar, Claude Simon grew up in Perpignan and went to school in Paris. He originally wanted to be a painter and did not start writing until World War II. In his novels, which are amongst the most audacious examples of the NOUVEAU ROMAN, life appears as a perpetual flux. There is little action in a conventional sense but situations, descriptions, and reflections are woven into a complex web. After writing a number of novels that are not too well known today (*The Trickster*, 1945; *The Rope*, 1947; *Wind*, 1957), he enjoyed a great success with *The Flanders Road* (1961), a novel dealing with his wartime experiences fighting in Belgium. He received the Prix de L'Expresse for this work and the 1967 Prix Médicis for *Histoire*. The novel *Triptych* (1973) epitomizes the more hermetic structures of his later work. More recent novels include *The World about Us* (1975) and *The Georgics* (1981). Simon has lectured widely in the US, South America, Japan, and elsewhere. He was awarded the 1985 Nobel Prize for literature.

Simonov, Konstantin Mikhailovich (Kirill Simonov; 1915–79) Russian prose writer, poet, and dramatist. Born in Petrograd, Simonov was educated at Saratov and at the Gorkii Literary Institute, Moscow; he published his first poems in 1935. During World War II he worked as a war correspondent for the journal *Krasnaia* *zvezda*. He is chiefly remembered now for his wartime poems, particularly 'Wait for Me', 17 million copies of which were circulated to soldiers at the Front, and 'Do you Remember the Roads of Smolensk?' His collections include *Road Poems* (1939), *With You and Without You* (1942), *Lyrical Diary* (1942), *Verses from the Front* (1942), and *Vietnam, the Winter of '70* (1971). His poems are mostly short lyrics but before the war he published six long poems, including *The Victor* (1937) and *Suvorov* (1939). His most famous prose work is the novella *Days and Nights* (1944), about the Battle of Stalingrad, together with its sequels *The Living and the Dead* (1962) and *We Are Not Born Soldiers* (1964). *Through the Eyes of a Man of My Generation*, a series of reflections on Stalin, was published posthumously in 1990. His plays are the weakest part of his output, the most famous of them being *The Russians* (1942).

Simonov was twice secretary of the Writers' Union (1954–59, 1967–79) and twice editor of its newspaper *Literaturnaia gazeta* (1938, 1950–54). He was also a conservative editor of the journal *Novyi Mir* (1946–1950). During the THAW his position was ambiguous. He attacked the portrait of the hack Soviet artist in Erenburg's novel *The Thaw* but in 1954, at the Second Congress of Soviet Writers, he called for a 'broadening' of socialist realism and the republication of 1920s satirists such as Il'f and Petrov. A writer of limited talent, Simonov nevertheless won six Stalin Prizes and a Lenin Prize. He was allegedly the model for the careerist novelist Galakhov in SOLZHENITSYN's *The First Circle*.

Simpson, Robert (Wilfred Levick) (1921–) British composer and musicologist, living in Ireland. He studied (1942–46) under Herbert Howells and subsequently worked as a music producer for the BBC from 1951 until 1980. His compositions, most of which are in traditional genres, include 11 symphonies and 15 string quartets; these works are inspired principally by the example of his great musical heroes Beethoven, Bruckner, Sibelius, and Nielsen, on all of whom he has published studies. In addition to writing such chamber pieces as the clarinet quintet (1968) and the horn quartet (1977) he has produced numerous works for brass band, including *The Four Temperaments* (1982) and *Vortex* (1989). He was composer in residence at the 1992 Malvern Festival, for which he produced four new works – a cello concerto, a flute concerto, a 15th string quartet, and an 11th symphony.

Singier, Gustave (1909–) French painter. Born in Warneton in Belgium, Singier moved to Paris in 1919. He began to paint when he was 14. Between 1933 and 1936 he served an apprenticeship with a decorative painter and then worked as a commercial artist while attending further evening classes. At this time he painted from nature and also copied old masters. He took up painting full-time in 1936.

Singier's early works were influenced by the cubists, the Fauves, and the expressionists. He later developed a more personal style of lyrical abstraction (*see* ART INFORMEL) characterized by geometric shapes and bright colours. From 1949 onwards he gave numerous one-man shows. He was commissioned to design stained glass for several Dominican houses and also designed tapestries and theatre sets.

Sinopoli, Giuseppe (1946–) Italian conductor and composer. Although he took a degree in medicine at Padua University, he also studied at the Venice Conservatory and, from 1968, at DARMSTADT where his teachers included STOCKHAUSEN and MADERNA. In 1972 he became a teacher at the Venice Conservatory and began to take lessons in conducting from Hans Swarowsky in Vienna. In 1975 he founded the Bruno Maderna Ensemble in Venice as a vehicle for the performance of contemporary music. He has since established himself as a conductor of opera, working at Covent Garden, the Metropolitan Opera House in New York, and Bayreuth. He has also become well known in Britain through his association with the Philharmonic Orchestra (since 1984). He became musical director of the Dresden Staatskapelle in 1991.

Although primarily a conductor, Sinopoli has also composed a considerable body of music. His output includes orchestral and instrumental pieces, choral music – notably the massive *Symphonie imaginaire* (1973) for soloists, children's voices, three choruses, and three orchestras – and electronic music. Stylistically, these works reflect both the impact of his Darmstadt training and the influence of his friend Franco DONATONI. Since the late 1970s he has shown a renewed interest in tonal gestures. His opera *Lou Salome* was performed in 1981.

Sinyavsky, Andrei Donatevich (1925–) Russian writer living in France. A former ardent member of Komsomol, the League of Young Communists, Sinyavsky wrote and taught at the Gorkii Institute of World Literature from 1952 until 1966 in conformity with communist doctrine. But from 1956, under the pseudonym **Abram Tertz**, he wrote novels, short stories, and critiques that circulated in the Soviet underground and were published in the West. His novels *The Trial Begins* (*Sud idyot*; 1960) and *The Makepiece Experiment* (*Lyubivom*; 1964) and his collection *Fantastic Stories* (1961) evoke the bizarre and menacing atmosphere of the last years of Stalin's rule, during which Sinyavsky's own father was arrested. At the same time they express the author's faith in the power of the imagination and his love of the fantastic. The energy and passion of his style have provoked comparisons with Dostoyevskii. Sinyavsky's prolific commentaries, such as *On Socialist Realism* (1959), attacked the view that art should glorify socialism. In 1966 he and the writer Yuli Daniel were convicted of producing anti-Soviet propaganda after a trial that drew international criticism. Sinyavsky's five years in a labour camp produced the reflections *A Voice from the Chorus* (1973), in which he juxtaposed his deeper meditations with the coarser backcloth of prison life, comically transmuting the camp into a microcosm of the world outside. On his release, Sinyavsky emigrated to Paris and taught Russian literature at the Sorbonne. His critical works, published under his own name, include important studies of Pasternak (1965) and of the poetry of the Russian Revolution (1964).

Siren, Kaija (1920–) and **Heikki** (1918–) Finnish architects. The son of the neoclassical architect Johan Sigfrid Sirén (1889–1961), Heikki Siren formed a practice with his wife, Kaija (née Tuominen), a former student of his father's, in 1948. Although they have built many offices and banks – the most spectacular of which is the Kallio Municipal Offices, Helsinki (1965), a circular complex of shops and offices with a bank tucked inside – their best work is mostly small scale and shows a sympathetic response to nature.

Their many private houses include those built for themselves at Lauttasaari (1951–60) and on Lingonso; the latter is a holiday home of logs with a summerhouse consisting of four posts completely glazed between. This has the same simplicity as their first acclaimed work, the chapel of the Technical University at Otaniemi (1957), a building of Miesian delicacy with a glazed end that looks out over a cross placed before trees. The Sirens were also involved inthe completion of Aalto's Tech Town residential campus, contributing two towers and the Retuperä blocks for graduates (1956, 1962).

The Sirens are masters of the staggered terrace house, arranged to preserve the natural landscape. This concept was exported to La Pierefitte, Val d'Yerres, France (1967–70). They have also experimented with high-quality timber prefabrication, as at Tapionsolu, Tapiola (1965) and Polar-Village (1968). But their undoubted masterpiece is the Brucknerhaus concert hall in Linz, a project won in competition in 1962 and completed in 1974. This is a deliberately neutral hall, lined in oak and fitting harmoniously into the landscape; its undramatic qualities contrast, for example, with Hans SCHAROUN's Philharmonie in Berlin.

Most recently Heikki Siren has completed (1988) the Finnish embassy at Riyadh with Jukka Siren.

Sjöberg, Alf (1903–80) Swedish theatre and film director and actor. Born in Stockholm, he trained with the Royal Dramatic Theatre and first acted professionally in 1925; he began to direct for the stage two years later. In 1930 he was appointed director of the Royal Dramatic Theatre. With his many productions of plays by Shakespeare, Strindberg, and such modern playwrights as IONESCO, BRECHT, and Stanisław Witkiewicz, he demonstrated how the modern theatre could remain faithful to the historical context of a play while emphasizing its relevance to 20th-century society. He was also much admired for his creative use of the possibilities offered by modern theatre technology.

Sjöberg was Sweden's most important film director before the emergence of Ingmar BERGMAN, whose career he helped to start. He wrote and directed a silent work, *The Strongest*, in 1929, but did not return to the cinema until the mid 1940s, when the early technical problems with sound had been overcome. He enjoyed an international success with *Frenzy* (1944), which featured Bergman's first film scenario, and later found critical acclaim with adaptations of Strindberg's *Miss Julie* (1959) and *The Father* (1969). Among other lesser films were *The Road to Heaven* (1942), *Barabbas* (1953), *Wild Birds* (1955), and *The Island* (1966).

Sjöman, (David Harald) Vilgot (1924–) Swedish film director and writer, whose reputation as a serious cinema critic has been overshadowed by the controversy surrounding his films on sexual themes. Born in Stockholm, the son of a construction worker, Sjöman worked as a clerk and prison orderly while writing several unproduced plays. He later turned one of these into a novel and a screenplay for Gustaf Molander's film *Defiance* (1952). In 1956 he was awarded a six-month scholarship to study film-making at the University of California; while in the US he also worked as an apprentice on the Hollywood melodrama *The Proud and the Profane* (1956). These experiences provided the basis for *In Hollywood* (1961), Sjöman's revealing report on the US film industry. Two years later he published *Diary with Ingmar Bergman* after assisting the director with *Winter Light* (1963; *see* BERGMAN, INGMAR). He later took a secondary acting role in Bergman's *Shame* (1968).

Sjöman made his debut as a solo director with *The Swedish Mistress* (1962), which he also scripted. His *491* (1964) incurred notoriety for its sexual content and was censored in Sweden and elsewhere while *My Sister My Love* (1966) dealt with the taboo subject of incest. *I am Curious: Yellow* (1967) also ran into international censorship, being seized by US customs. The film was eventually released in the US following a famous court battle and became an immense box-office hit. The episode played an important part in the relaxation of the hitherto rather strict US film codes. In 1968 Sjöman released a follow-up, *I Am Curious: Blue*. His more recent films have included *Blushing Charlie* (1970), *A Handful of Love* (1974), *The Garage* (1975), *Taboo* (1977), and *I Am Blushing* (1982).

Skolimowski, Jerzy (1938–) Polish film director, poet, and actor, praised for his imaginative black comedies satirizing contemporary society. A former boxer, Skolimowski scripted films by WAJDA and POLANSKI before starring in and directing *Rysopsis* (1964) while studying at the film school in Łódź. The antihero of this film was revived for *Walkover* (1965), about a boxer contemplating his next fight. Both films emphasized the individual's search for personal identity and the conflict with society that this entails.

Sexual conflict came to the fore in Skolimowski's next two films, *Barrier* (1966) and *Le Départ* (1967). The latter was made outside Poland and, when his anti-Stalinist *Hands Up!* (1967) was banned by the Polish authorities, he returned to the West to develop his career. *Deep End* (1970), filmed in London, was an atmospheric tragedy about sexual longing and alienation. The eternal triangle was the subject of both *King, Queen, Knave* (1972), taken from the story by Nabokov, and *The Shout* (1978), based on a tale by Robert GRAVES. Many critics found these films relatively shallow compared with Skolimowski's earlier work. *Moonlighting* (1982), starring Jeremy Irons, was better received for its portrayal of four Polish builders working in London while martial law is being imposed in their country. More recent films have included the disappointing *Success is the Best Revenge* (1984) and the effective thriller *The Lightship* (1985).

Skuszanka, Krystyna *See* SZAJNA, JÓZEF.

Škvorecký, Josef (1924–) Czech novelist and publisher. He read English and philosophy at Prague and then became a schoolmaster; after working in publishing from 1956 until 1963, he became a freelance writer. He left Czechoslovakia after the Warsaw Pact intervention (1968) and taught Anglo-American literature at Toronto. In Canada he and his wife founded 68 Publishers in order to publish the works of Czech writers banned in their own country. He now lives in retirement. His first novel, *The Cowards* (1958), marked the beginning of the thaw in Czech literature; it demythologizes the Czech 'revolution' against the Germans in 1945 and introduces an egocentric post-pubertal narrator, thus contravening the collectivist 'norms' of socialist realism. *The Miracle* (1972) evokes with felicitous irony the atmosphere of the Stalinist terror and presents the first balanced view of the

1968 'Prague Spring' in Czech literature. Because of the latter it horrified ex-communist dissidents and those who still believed one could have 'socialism with a human face'. *The Story of An Engineer of Human Souls* (1977) consists of a comic depiction of Czech émigré society with flashbacks to the Czechoslovakia of the narrator's youth during World War II and to life under socialism. Škvorecký has a fine sense for comic detail, is an accomplished creator of slapstick, and makes intelligent political points, but some have questioned his ultimate seriousness.

Slaatto, Nils *See* LUND, KJELL.

Slutsky, Boris (1919–86) Soviet poet. Born in Slavyansk, he graduated from the Gorkii Institute of World Literature in 1941 and fought in the army until 1945. Slutsky's war poetry eloquently records the decimation of helpless villagers by Nazi troops and the deaths of unsung Russian soldiers, often in the tone of a self-appointed public poet. A committed communist, Slutsky became a political instructor in 1945 but his verse lamented the lack of honour for ordinary men – 'the Ivans' – and criticized Stalin's economic priorities during reconstruction. Concise and earthy, his poetry achieves its power through acute observation and reiteration of theme. His writing also explores the poet's duty to speak for the inarticulate. Slutsky was unfavoured and unpublished until 1953 but his quality was gradually recognized as Stalinism was discredited. *Memory* (1957), the first of over a dozen collections to appear before his death, established him as a major figure of the THAW. *Work* (1964) extolled the value of hard work and civic responsibility, while works such as *Good Day* (1973) and *The Era of my Peers* (1977) wryly examined middle age and the individual's place in a collectivist society.

Smetana Quartet Czech string quartet, which made its debut in 1945. The current line-up, unchanged since 1955, is Jiří Novák (first violin), Lubomír Kostecký (second violin), Milan Škampa (viola), and Antonín Kohout (cello). The original members – Kostecký, Kohout, Jaroslav Rybenský (first violin), and Václav Neumann (viola) – were classmates at the Prague Conservatory. Following Neumann's decision (1947) to leave the quartet in order to pursue his conducting career, Rybenský took the rather unusual step of moving from first violin to the viola. His position as leader of the quartet was filled by Jiří Novák, who was still a conservatory student at the time.

In 1951 the members of the quartet were released from their playing commitments with the Czech Philharmonic Orchestra. Rybenský left the quartet on health grounds in 1955 and was replaced by Milan Škampa. In 1967 they were appointed to the staff of the Prague Academy. Although they have recorded the quartets of Haydn, Mozart, and Beethoven, they are best known for their commitment to Czech music and above all for establishing Smetana's and Janáček's quartets within the chamber repertory.

Smith, Stevie (Florence Margaret Smith; 1902–71) British poet and novelist. Although she was born in Hull, Stevie Smith was educated and spent most of her life in London. From the 1920s she worked as a magazine publisher's secretary and personal assistant, retiring in 1953 to look after a bedridden aunt. Her first novel, *Novel on Yellow Paper*, was published in 1936 and was followed by *Over the Frontier* (1938) and *The Holiday* (1949). However, it was as a poet that she achieved most success, her first volume *A Good Time was Had By All* (1937) being followed by seven others including *Mother, What Is Man?* (1942), *Harold's Leap* (1950), and *Not Waving But Drowning* (1957), the title poem of which remains her best-known piece. In the 1960s Smith became known to a wider public through her readings of her own work, both on the radio and in live performance. Her poetry is perhaps an acquired taste; while some are repelled by the element of whimsy in her work, others find its combination of idiosyncratic humour with a darker undercurrent beguiling. Admirers draw attention to her ear for the voices of her characters, her sophisticated use of allusion, and her sly critique of accepted religious beliefs. She was awarded the Queen's Gold Medal for poetry in 1969.

Smithson, Alison (1928–) and **Peter** (1923–) British architects and theorists whose writings and projects in the 1950s established the tenets of the NEW BRUTALISM. They met at Durham University and married in 1949. Their independent practice dates from 1950, when they won a competition for a school in Hunstanton, Norfolk. Completed in 1954, it is unique for its date in Britain, owing much to Mies van der Rohe in its bold forms and use of steel. Their Economist Building in London (1961–64) also owes much to Mies, consisting of three elegant towers of offices and flats stepped around their own courtyard. They have also designed houses, a clinic (1963), and an extension to St Hilda's College, Oxford (1968–70).

The Smithsons are equally well known for their housing projects, despite the fact that of these only the much reviled Robin Hood Gardens, London, was built (1968–72). This is a development of ideas first explored in a 1952 project for Golden Lane, London, in which LE CORBUSIER's *rue interieure* was pushed to the edge of the block to create street decks. Corbusian, too, was their unbuilt scheme for extending Sheffield University in a single organic block (1953), whilst that for Coventry Cathedral (1951) was innovatory in resembling a giant sloping tent. Denied opportunity to build for most of the 1950s, they turned instead to writing, teaching, and mounting exhibitions. As leaders of the international group Team X, they sounded the death-knell of the old guard of modernism by organizing the 1956 Congrès Internationaux de l'Architecture Moderne (CIAM) to their own ends.

Where the Smithsons' theories did achieve international recognition was in the field of town planning. Their 'cluster city' project of 1952–57 was one of the finest studies of the impact of cars on cities, and culminated in 1958 in their competition-winning project for Haupstadt, Berlin.

Sokolov, Sasha (1943–) Russian novelist living in the US. Born into a diplomat's family in Ottawa, he was brought up in Moscow but in 1975 used the accident of his place of birth to emigrate to Canada and then the US. Sokolov's reputation rests mainly on three very different novels. The first, *A School for Fools* (1976, revised 1983) is a highly lyrical postmodernist work depicting the world of a special school through the eyes and conflicting voices of a schizophrenic adolescent. Amongst events hinted at are the suicide of a favourite teacher and the first stirrings of love, but the mood and atmosphere of the book are more important than its plot. Rich in poignant and sometimes comic digressions, it may be seen as an allegory of Soviet life; in any case it is one of the most original and subtly poetic novels in Russian literature. *Between the Dog and the Wolf* (1980) also features an unreliable narrator but is so obscure as to defy close interpretation or translation. Set in the upper Volga region, it depicts, by means of hints, word play, and interpolated stories and poems, a place where night and day, the dead and the living, and even the two banks of the river, cannot be distinguished: against this scene of confusion and squalor the Oedipus tragedy is enacted. In *Astrophobia* (*Palisandriia*; 1985) Sokolov aims at a wider audience, with an extended picaresque fantasy on Soviet history, which at the same time parodies the genre of bestselling politico-sexual memoir. Palisandr, the narrator-hero, who is descended from Rasputin and Beria, describes in a language combining Soviet cliché and lofty lyricism a series of wildly scurrilous escapades for full appreciation of which a good knowledge of Russian history and literature is necessary. Though not very exportable, Sokolov is without doubt a major figure in modern Russian prose.

Soldati, Atanasio (1896–1953) Italian painter. Born in Parma, Soldati trained as an architect, receiving his diploma in 1920. In 1922 he began painting and in 1925 he moved to Milan to take up a teaching post. At this stage he mainly painted still lifes, some of which show the influence of cubism. In the 1930s he came under the influence of the De Stijl movement, which advocated an abstract art based on straight lines, right angles, and primary colours. Soldati thus became a pioneer of geometrical abstraction in Italy, though he experimented with a variety of abstract styles. During the war his studio was badly damaged and numerous paintings were destroyed.

In 1948 Soldati was a cofounder of the Movimento per l'Arte Concreta, which advocated the cause of geometrical abstraction in Italy. In the post-war years Soldati achieved a personal synthesis of the various abstract styles that had influenced him. Its distinctive features were its luminous colours and lyrical atmosphere. Often there were hints of figuration, as in

La Grande Gioia of 1948, which appears to feature a section of the sun shining brightly.

Soleri, Paolo (1919–) Italian architect and philosopher, who settled in Arizona after working with the US architect Frank Lloyd Wright in 1947–49. A brief return to Italy (1950–55) stimulated an alternative career in ceramics that has also influenced his architecture. During this period he built a ceramic factory for the Solimene family at Vietri, a bizarre green and orange-tiled building cut into a cliff and supported on Gaudí-like columns. Back in Arizona, he established (1956) the Cosanti (Before Things) Foundation to develop his ideas on the relationship between architecture and ecology – a field he terms 'arcology'. Scottsdale became home to his experimental Earth Houses (1956–74), built of concrete mixed and cast on the ground like ceramics, and a study centre for arcology. Projects included Mesa City (1967) and a book, *The City in the Image of Man* (1970).

In 1970 Soleri began to build his model city, Arcosanti, a dense ten-acre development set in 860 acres of open land on a mesa. His theory is that a city is both more environmentally sound and socially interactive if it is intensely compact. A foundry and ceramic studios were completed in 1974, having been largely built by voluntary labour in earth-coloured concrete. Since then the project has developed as a study centre rather than as a real city, although it is beginning to achieve the intended density in its later housing, workshops, and cloisters. It has also evolved more advanced ecological features, such as solar heating in Soleri's 'Greenhouse Housing'. An annual Arcosanti Art and Music Festival has prompted the development of a separate Valetta Theatre complex below the mesa.

Soloukhin, Vladimir Alekseevich (1924–) Russian poet and prose writer. Born of peasant stock at Olepino, near Vladimir, he decribes both places in his work: the first in the short story *The Law of the Alarm Bell* (1963) and the series *Olepino Ponds* (1973) and the second in the book of sketches *A Walk in Rural Russia* (*Vladimirskie proselki*; 1957). After war service, he entered the Gorkii Literary Institute in 1951. Soloukhin is one of the best of the 'Village Prose' writers and works in the tradition of the 19th-century Slavophiles, i.e. with a conviction that Russia stands apart from the main currents of European culture and must look to its own institutions, art, religion, and history in order to progress. Inevitably this has led to his being courted by the extreme nationalist right but he has so far rejected these overtures. He sided with the establishment during the PASTERNAK affair and in 1958 attacked EVTUSHENKO in an article in *Literaturnaia gazeta*; however, his novel *Coltsfoot* (*Mat'-machekha*; 1964) is explicitly anti-Stalinist. His other main prose works are *A Drop of Dew* (1960), set in his native village, *Letters from the Russian Museum* (1966), *The Third Hunt* (1967), *Searching for Icons in Russia* (*Chernye doski*; 1969), *Bread on Honey* (1978), and *Disaster with Doves* (1984).

Soloukhin began as a poet, publishing his first poems in 1946. His first collection *Rain in the Steppe* was published in 1953 and he has followed this with *She-crane* (1959), *He with Flowers in His Hand* (1962), *To Live on Earth* (1965), *Argument* (1972), and *Grey Hair* (1977). Increasingly experimental in form, his poems, short lyrics for the most part, draw much of their inspiration from the natural world. Soloukhin has also translated the poetry of Jacques PRÉVERT and the work of Bulgarian and Georgian poets.

Solstad, Dag (1941–) Norwegian novelist and short-story writer. Solstad made his literary debut in 1965 with the short-story collection *Spirals*. In the 1960s he was a leading member of the influential student group Profile, which was Marxist-Leninist in its sympathies. The writers of the Profile group played an important part in the politicization of Norwegian writing in the later 1960s and 1970s.

Solstad's early work is preoccupied with the way in which bourgeois language affects our ability to think critically about society. *Verdigris* (1969) shows how men and women are unconsciously led to accept the superficial stereotypical roles that society demands of them. *Arild Asnes 1970* (1971) is the story of an author who comes to realize the meaninglessness of his role and the powerlessness that accompanies his independence as he moves towards a Marxist-Leninist position. The novel caused much debate on its publication.

The Square of 25th September (1975) is a collective novel depicting the fortunes of a working-class family from 1945 to the referendum on European Community membership in 1972; its theme is the betrayal of the workers by post-war social democracy. The trilogy *Betrayal: Pre-war Years* (1977), *War 1940* (1978), and *Bread and Weapons* (1980) is about the betrayal of the working class during the war itself. The events are historically accurate but interpreted in Marxist-Leninist terms.

Solstad's later works are more personal and reflective, concentrating on why and how the youth rebellion of the 1960s failed to halt the development of a bourgeois materialistic society in Norway.

Solti, Sir Georg (1912–) British conductor and pianist, born in Hungary. Solti was born in Budapest and studied at the Liszt Academy there under Bartók, Kodály, and Dohnányi. He worked as a conductor and pianist for the State Opera, Budapest, from 1930 until 1939, when he left Hungary to escape the persecution of the Jews. He spent World War II in Zürich, where he was unable to conduct professionally (not being a Swiss national) and concentrated on his playing; he won the Geneva International Piano Competition in 1942. After World War II he was appointed musical director of the Bavarian State Opera in Munich (1946–52) and of the Frankfurt Opera (1952–61). In 1961 he emigrated to Britain, becoming musical director at the Royal Opera House, Covent Garden (1961–71) and conductor and director of the London Philharmonic Orchestra (1979–83). He has also been musical director of L'Orchestre de Paris (1971–75) and, most notably, of the Chicago Symphony Orchestra (1969–91), which under his leadership acquired a reputation as perhaps the finest symphony orchestra in the world. He is particularly well known for his interpretations of Wagner and Richard Strauss.

Solzhenitsyn, Alexandr Isaevich (1918–) Russian writer and historian, currently living in the US. He was born into a middle-class family six months after his father's death, trained as an engineer, and began schoolteaching just before World War II, in which he served until arrested for a political indiscretion in February 1945. The eight years spent in prison and his ensuing treatment for cancer provided the material for his major fictional writings. Rehabilitated in 1957, he worked as a teacher in Riazan'. Having written secretly since 1952, he was able to publish in 1962, thanks to Khrushchev's assistance, a sensational tale of a prison camp, *One Day in the Life of Ivan Denisovich* (1962). After only two years, however, he began to be hounded by the authorities – the process is described in his memoir *The Oak and the Calf* (1975) – and he was finally expelled from the Soviet Union in 1974, following the illegal publication abroad of his major novels and the first part of the documentary *Gulag Archipelago* (1973–75). After living in Switzerland for two years, he moved (1976) to Vermont where he has devoted himself to writing his magnum opus, an as yet incomplete multi-volume history of the Russian Revolution, *The Red Wheel*, beginning with *August 1914* (1971). Having always regarded a Russian writer as 'a kind of second government', Solzhenitsyn has in his lifetime been praised, persecuted, feared and, most recently, almost deified in the country of his birth.

Solzhenitsyn's best early stories, in addition to *One Day*, are *Matrena's Home* (1963) and *For the Good of the Cause* (1963), both showing Soviet morality in a gloomy light. Of his longer works, *The First Circle* (1968) recalls the great Russian novels of the 19th century in its lengthy and impassioned politico-philosophical conversations. Set in a special prison near Moscow, it introduces representatives of many strata of the Soviet hierarchy, including Stalin himself. *Cancer Ward* (1968) has a tauter construction and again shows a cross-section of people seeking a validity for their lives in a desperate situation. As a creative writer Solzhenitsyn's principal distinction lies in his rich use of language and in his ability to combine personal and historical elements in large-scale structures with a strong moral centre. Solzhenitsyn's principal characteristic, however, which no doubt helped to bring him the Nobel Prize for literature in 1970, is his unswerving conviction and Olympian authority. He is by any standards a major figure of our times.

son et lumière A form of theatrical entertainment that relies upon the use of lighting and sound effects, rather than the presence of live actors. Such productions usually take place in the open air at castles, country houses, or other sites of historical interest and often relate the events that have occurred at that particular location over the years. Actors are sometimes employed, chiefly for visual effect, but otherwise a recorded soundtrack and other technical effects are used to convey both atmosphere and information. Now a highly popular tourist attraction in many countries, the genre originated in performances given in France in the 1950s.

Sørensen, Villy (1929–) Danish writer. Sørensen made his literary debut in 1953 with *Strange Tales*, a collection of short stories with an absurdist flavour that already shows the humour and word-play for which he has since become famous. *Harmless Tales* followed in 1955. A major theme in Sørensen's work is the division of the self, whether in a moral, psychological, or social sense.

Poets and Demons (1959) is an essay collection dealing with subjects including artistic creation, philosophy, and the Danish welfare state. In *Tutelary Tales* (1964) Sørensen returned to the short-story form to explore themes of rebellion and authority in contemporary Europe. In the 1970s he became increasingly interested in social issues, especially those relating to the freedom of the individual. *Rebellion from the Centre* (1978, with K. Helveg Petersen and Niels I. Meyer) provoked much debate about democracy and authority. In *Seneca – the Humanist at the Court of Nero* (1976) Sørensen produced an interpretive biography of the 1st-century philosopher and politician, drawing clear parallels between his age and our own. *Weather Days* (1980), a novel in the form of a diary, shows a preoccupation with language and especially with the way words change or lose their meaning. In the late 1980s Sørensen published the first two volumes of a planned trilogy on Norse, Greek, and Judeo-Christian mythology, *Ragnarok* (1989) and *The Revolt of Apollo* (1989).

From 1959 until 1963 Sørensen was coeditor of the literary magazine *The Wind Rose* with Klaus RIFBJERG. He has published commentaries on Nietzsche, Schopenhauer, and Kierkegaard, as well as translating stories by Kafka, one of the main influences on his own work. He has been a major figure in Danish cultural and social debate since the 1950s, winning many prizes for his work.

Sostres, Josep Maria (1915–84) Spanish (Catalan) architect, writer, and theoretician. He was professor of architectural history at the Escuela Tecnica Superior in Barcelona. Inspired by the work of the rationalist architect Giuseppe Terragni (1904–41), he founded (1952) the Grupo R to recover the ideas of the modern movement lost under Franco's fascism; he was also one of the first champions of the Art Nouveau architect Antonio Gaudí. Sostres himself built little but was influential in the development of both the rational modernism and the historical awareness that are twin themes of recent Catalan architecture. The first trait is most apparent in his MMI House (1955–58), Barcelona, while his Agustí House (1953–55), Sitges, owes much to Alvar AALTO and Mies van der Rohe. The sense of history is more noticeable in his Hotel Maria Victoria Puigcerda (1956–57) and El Noticiero Universal Newspaper Building (1963–65), both undramatic but original responses to their respective settings in central Barcelona.

Soulages, Pierre (1919–) French abstract painter. Soulages was born at Rodez in Aveyron in southern France. As a schoolboy he became interested in the prehistoric remains and Romanesque art of the surrounding area and took up painting. In 1938 he went to Paris where he visited the Louvre and saw exhibitions by Cézanne and Picasso. As a result he decided not to study at the conservative Ecole des Beaux-Arts in Paris and returned to Rodez. During World War II Soulages served in the French army until 1940 and then worked as a vineyard labourer near Montpellier.

In 1946 Soulages settled in Paris, where he met the painter and designer Sonia Delaunay, who encouraged an interest in abstract art. He produced his first nonfigurative paintings in 1947 and quickly developed a distinctive style, characterized by thick dark brush strokes on a light ground. Prizes soon followed: in 1953 a prize at the São Paulo Bienale; in 1957 a prize from the Japanese Ministry of Education; in 1959 a Grand Prix for Graphic Art at the Ljubljana Biennale. During the 1950s he began to experiment with additional colours, usually dark browns, reds, or blues. In the 1970s he began to cover large areas of canvas with blocks of dark colour and to create linear textures within the blocks; in the 1980s he sometimes treated entire canvases in this way. In 1987 he was awarded France's Grand Prix National des Arts.

Sovremennik Theatre *See* YEFREMOV, OLEG (NIKOLAYEVICH).

spaghetti western A film genre of the 1960s and 1970s that established European film-makers as the leading interpreters of the western, previously very much the province of Hollywood. The rise of the European western was largely a result of the work of the Italian director Sergio LEONE, who set the pattern with location filming in Spain, US lead actors, and Italian film crews; the voices of Italian members of the cast were subsequently dubbed into English. Violent and, unlike the US originals, often wryly humorous, the spaghetti westerns breathed new life into what had become an exhausted genre. *A Fistful of Dollars* (1964), starring Clint Eastwood, is recognized as the first of the spaghetti westerns; among the best of those that followed were *For a Few Dollars More* (1965) and *The Good, the Bad and the Ugly* (1967), both also starring Eastwood. Although few further European westerns have been made since Leone's classics, the influence of the spaghetti westerns on those still being made in the US has been profound.

Spark, Muriel (1918–) British novelist of Scottish-Jewish parentage. Born Muriel Camberg in Edinburgh, she attended Heriot Watt College before marrying young and travelling to Southern Africa with her husband. She worked in British Intelligence during World War II and became editor of *Poetry Review* (1947–49). Since the late 1960s she has lived mainly in Italy.

Spark turned to fiction after winning an *Observer* short-story competition and in 1957 published her first novel *The Comforters*, which reflects her conversion to Roman Catholicism in 1954. *Memento Mori* (1959), a macabre tale in which old people receive mysterious intimations that they are about to die, is typical in its combination of social satire and the sinister – as is *The Ballad of Peckham Rye* (1960), a tale of underworld goings on with a strong hint of the supernatural. Her best-known novel, *The Prime of Miss Jean Brodie*, appeared in 1961 and was subsequently made into both a play and a film. It is a morally ambiguous tale about an Edinburgh schoolmistress's attempts to impose her ideals on her favoured pupils (her 'crème de la crème'). *The Girls of Slender Means* (1963) was an allegory about the nuclear threat, set in a girls' hostel in London, while *The Abbess of Crewe* (1974) provided an oblique commentary on the unfolding Watergate scandal in the US through its description of ecclesiastical corruption in a convent. Her later novels include *Territorial Rights* (1979), *The Only Problem* (1984), *A Far Cry from Kensington* (1988), and *Symposium* (1990). Many of her works have been adapted for the cinema and television. She has written several radio plays and *Doctors of Philosophy* (1962) for the stage. *Curriculum Vitae*, an account of her earlier life, appeared in 1992.

spatial music Music in which the location of the sound sources (whether live instruments or loudspeakers) is an integral part of the work's structure and the listener's experience. The spatial dimension can be utilized in both electronic and non-electronic works. Primarily a post-war phenomenon, the emphasis on location as a factor in musical composition belongs conceptually with other contemporary musical developments, such as SERIALISM, which seek to displace the traditional ascendancy of pitch and rhythm. Varèse's *Poème électronique* (1958), a MUSIQUE CONCRÈTE work expressly designed for its performance on 350 loudspeakers in the Philips Pavilion at the 1958 World Fair, was an influential example. Other 20th-century works with a significant spatial component include Charles Ives's *The Unanswered Question* (1906), STOCKHAUSEN's *Gruppen* (1957), and XENAKIS's *Stratégie* (1962).

Spazialismo *See* FONTANA, LUCIO.

Spence, Sir Basil (1907–76) British architect, celebrated for his rebuilding of Coventry Cathedral after wartime bombing. Spence designed a few buildings in the 1930s in his ancestral Scotland but recognition came with his contributions to the *Britain Can Make It* exhibition (1946) and the Sea and Ships Pavilion at the FESTIVAL OF BRITAIN in 1951. In that year he won the Coventry competition. A symbol of Britain's post-war regeneration, the cathedral was completed to a reduced design in 1962. Although mainly regarded today as a 'period' shell for the many fine works of art inside (by Graham SUTHERLAND, John PIPER, and others), the building confirms Spence's ability to fuse traditional and modern elements in a popular manner. Also in Coventry he built three tiny suburban churches on minute budgets (1953–57).

Subsequently Spence received an immense number of public commissions. His Sussex University (1959–75) owes a great debt to LE CORBUSIER's Maisons Jaoul and includes the outstanding Falmer House of 1962. He was also the principal architect at Southampton University and contributed to many other campuses, notably the science areas at Nottingham and Exeter. His Glasgow airport (1966) was also praised. But in the 1960s some of his work was thought too traditional, like the British Embassy at Rome (1960–71), whilst his larger London projects upset conservationists. Most controversial were the Household Cavalry Barracks at Knightsbridge (1960–70), a monumental work in brick and concrete, and the Home Office development completed in 1976 (with Fitzroy Robinson).

No other British architect of the period achieved Spence's household recognition and none was more prolific. His smaller projects, like the house at Beaulieu for himself (1961) and Swiss Cottage Library and Baths (1964), serve to remind how exciting an architect he could be.

Sperr, Martin (1944–) German playwright and theatre director, who is best known for his use of violent and brutal imagery to produce a strong reaction from audiences. Sperr first attracted attention with *Hunting Scenes from Lower Bavaria* (1966), depicting the persecution of a homosexual in a small village community; the play has since been recognized as the first expression of the revival in German folk theatre that took place in the late 1960s. After translating Edward BOND's notorious *Saved* for the German stage, Sperr adopted similar shock tactics in a number of his own plays, employing them to particularly powerful effect in the much-revived *Magic Afternoon* (1968). More recent plays, some of which bear the influence of the German dramatist Ödön Joseph von Horváth (1901–38), include *Koralle Meier* (1970), which concerns the relationship between the inhabitants of a small town and a concentration camp nearby, and *Munich Freedom* (1971), a critique of capitalism.

Spoerli, Heinz (1941–) Swiss dancer, choreographer, and ballet master, who is particularly noted for his work with the Basel Ballet Company. Born in Basel, Spoerli studied with the School of American Ballet, the American Ballet Center, and the London Dramatic Dance Centre. He began his performing career with the Basel company (1960–63) at the invitation of Vaslav ORLIKOWSKY. Subsequently he appeared with the Cologne Ballet (1963–66), the Royal Winnipeg Ballet (1966–67), the Grands Ballets Canadiens (1967–69 and 1970–71), and the Geneva Ballet (1971–73) before returning to his hometown to become ballet master with the Basel company.

Since 1973 Spoerli has established the Basel Ballet (previously overshadowed by the city's opera house) as a major company with a strong international reputation. He added important new works to the troupe's repertoire, including ballets by Balanchine, William Forsythe, and Hans van MANEN, as well as many of his own creations. His lyrical neoclassical ballets have been much praised for their theatricality and their incorporation of indigenous Swiss musical motifs. They include adaptations of traditional pieces, among them *Giselle* (1976), *Romeo and Juliet* (1977), and *The Nutcracker* (1980), versions of more recent classics, such as *The Firebird* (1973), *Petrushka* (1974), *A Midsummer Night's Dream* (1976), *Ondine* (1978), and *La Fille mal gardée* (1981), and numerous works of his own, ranging from the light hearted *Cheese* (1978), which has become a signature piece for the company, to *Orpheus and Eurydice* (1983), based on Gluck's opera, and *La Belle Vie* (1987), a lavish depiction of life in Paris during the Second Empire.

Spoerri, Daniel (1930–) French sculptor, born in Romania of Swiss parentage. Spoerri moved to Switzerland in 1942 to train as a ballet dancer and performed from 1954 to 1957 with the Berne State Opera Company. From 1955 to 1961 he published a poetry magazine, *Material*, and in 1959 settled in Paris to publish the journal *MAT* (*Multiplication d'Art Transformable*), in which he advocated the construction of works of art that can be altered by the rearrangement of their parts.

Spoerri became internationally known for his work in ASSEMBLAGE, especially his so-called *tableaux pièges* (snare pictures). These are trick sculptures constructed from ordinary consumer goods glued to chairs or tables that are then hung sideways on the wall. One such work consisted of a table of leftover breakfast dishes, including an ashtray with its cigarette. His fascination with everyday articles derived partly from the example of the Dadaist Marcel Duchamp – an influence acknowledged when Spoerri placed a sign above one New York exhibition of his pieces reading 'I accuse Marcel Duchamp'. During the 1960s Spoerri brought his powerful personality to Pierre Restany's NOUVEAUX RÉALISME movement. He has also written a book on the nature of chance, agreeing with the surrealists that the random and accidental can be a valuable resource for the artist.

Spoleto Festival of the Two Worlds An annual arts festival founded in 1958 by Gian Carlo MENOTTI, the Italian-born composer, to promote young musicians and composers and to encourage cultural links between the Old and the New Worlds. The festival is held over three weeks in June and July in the picturesque hilltop town of Spoleto, Italy. The programme includes opera, concerts, jazz, country music, dance, theatre, and the visual arts. The success of the festival has permitted the upkeep and restoration of Spoleto's 14th-century churches and 17th-century theatre, which serve as the venues for many of the performances.

Squarzina, Luigi (1922–) Italian theatre director and playwright, who emerged as one of the leading figures in Italian theatre after World War II. A graduate of the Academy of Dramatic Art in Rome, Squarzina attracted much attention with his productions of classics by such authors as Shakespeare and Goldoni and in 1962 was appointed artistic director of the TEATRO STABILE in Genoa. He subsequently moved (1976) to the Teatro Stabile in Rome, where he remained until 1983. His productions of the classics were always based on a thorough understanding of the text and did much to raise standards of production throughout Italian drama. He has found equal acclaim as a director of plays by modern writers, among them his own works and those of Pirandello.

Stalinist architecture The officially approved style of architecture in the Soviet Union and its satellites from about 1933 to about 1955. In the 1920s revolutionary Russia had embraced the modernism of the Bauhaus, producing a distinctive Russian variant, constructivism. Stalin, however, shared with Hitler a strong dislike of modernism and a desire for a more classically inspired architecture. In the final competition for the Palace of the Soviets in Moscow (1933) Stalin's influence called forth a plethora of Roman-inspired designs on a giant scale. The foundation of the All Russian Academy of Architecture in October 1933 announced the establishment of the new offical style.

By the end of World War II a number of huge projects were under way in Moscow. For public buildings and mass housing alike, huge blocks like symmetrical group of towers became the favoured solution. The Moscow State University, Lenin Hills (Rudnev, Abrosimov, Khryakov, and others; 1943–53) set the tone, being an immense cluster of buildings with deliberately harsh neoclassical ornament and colossal finials of gilded glass atop the towers. The Leningrad Hotel, Moscow (1948–52) and the Ministry of Foreign Affairs, Moscow (1952) are variations on this theme, using ornament based on vernacular Russian architecture but inflated to a huge scale. The building of the Moscow Metro provided opportunities for design on a more human scale, such as the Kurshaya Station (Zakharov and Chernysheva; 1949) in Greek Doric style and, the Kaluzhskaya Station (Polyakov; 1949–50) and the Komsomolskaya Station (Shchusev and others; 1952) in a kind of Stalinist-baroque. When the huge Volga-Don canal was built (1948–52) various features were given tremendous architectural emphasis, with locks and bridges receiving immense towers, pylons, and rostral columns.

The All Union Agricultural Exhibition of 1954 became a major showcase for the architectural establishment, as the different ministries and republics competed to produce the most splendid pavilion. The Northern Caucauses built a sort of corinthian temple, while the Siberian pavilion with its violently over-scaled ornament is more like a surrealist film-set. Stalinist architecture often employed a somewhat heavy-handed symbolism; thus the Ministry of Meat Production had colossal bulls-head capitals on their buildings, while the Pavilion of Rabbit Breeding is adorned with a huge frieze showing rabbits breeding.

The 1954 Exhibition almost marked the end of the style, for in March 1953 Stalin himself had died and a year later neoclassicism was coming under heavy criticism; the abolition of the Academy of Architecture in 1955 brought it to an abrupt end. There is no doubt that much dramatic architecture was produced, successfully establishing the character of the regime and its imperial claims. Stalinist tower-building rose in most of the satellite capitals, the most notorious being perhaps the Warsaw 'Palace of Culture'. However, it will be a long time before it can be appreciated from a purely aesthetic viewpoint.

Stangerup, Henrik (1937–) Danish novelist, writer, and film-maker. Stangerup began his career as a journalist and rapidly acquired a reputation as an *enfant terrible* of the Danish cultural scene. His films and novels explore the predicament of the nonconforming individual in an impersonal technological society in which the media are used as agents of social control. Stangerup's nonconformists generally find that resistance to the system is both futile and fatal.

His breakthrough novel, *The Man who Wanted to be Guilty* (1973), proposes the idea that far from being a purely destructive emotion guilt may be necessary to authentic human existence. It describes a man struggling to come to terms with the guilt he feels at having murdered his wife in the face of psychiatrists and others telling him that he was not responsible for his actions.

The Road to Lagoa Santa (1981), his greatest success to date, describes the attempts of the naturalist, Peter Wilhelm Lund, to come to terms with the reality of his own experience. Lund has to transcend science in order to achieve self-understanding.

Stangerup has been widely translated and is one of the most hopeful portents on the Scandinavian cultural scene today.

Steffann, Emil (1899–1968) German architect, specializing in religious buildings. A pupil of Rudolf SCHWARZ, Steffann has shown a similar intensity in his work, despite operating entirely within a continuing craft tradition. He has been described as a lonely soul unperturbed by fashion; certainly, his acceptance of fundamental principles and deep response to location give his work a timeless quality. He sought an architecture of simplicity and, indeed, poverty that allowed space for life's more essential matters.

His first work (1943) was an emergency church in Lorraine built to resemble a barn. There followed a series of churches and monastic buildings: the reconstruction of the Franciscan Friars' church (1947–52) in Cologne; St Laurentius (with S Östreicher, 1952–55), Munich; St Elisabeth (1953–58), Opladen; St Augustine's parish centre (with Nikolaus Rosing, 1961–66), Düsseldorf-Eller; and a church (1963) at Dormagen with Paul Hopmann. His last works were all designed with Gisberth Hülsmann: the Carthusian monastery of Marsenau (1962–64); the St Laurentius community centre (1962–63) in Cologne-Lindenthal; a Franciscan monastery at Euskirchen (1965); and a church (1965–68) at Oeffingen.

Stein, Peter (1937–) German theatre director, who won widespread acclaim during his long association with the Berlin Schaubühne. In the later 1960s Stein established a reputation for highly political productions, often developed on a basis of COLLECTIVE CREATION, with such successes as *Saved* (1967) by Edward BOND and *Vietnam Discourse* (1969) by Peter WEISS. The care with which Stein researched the subjects of his productions and his attention to detail over long rehearsal periods earned him much admiration. In 1970 he took over at the Schaubühne, which he initially ran as an anticapitalist collective. His most important productions with the company included *Dream of the Poor Heinrich Kleist of Prince Homburg* (1972), *As You Like It* (1977), Aeschylus's *Oresteia* (1980), and Chekhov's *Three Sisters* (1984). In several Chekhov productions of the later 1980s he attempted to reconstruct the original Moscow productions from Stanislavsky's notebooks. He left the Schaubühne in 1987. In recent years he has also worked in opera, mounting highly praised productions of Verdi and Debussy. In 1992 he was appointed director of theatre at the Salzburg Festival, where he presented a version of Shakespeare's *Julius Caesar*. Although recent productions have been praised for their theatricality and beautiful craftsmanship, admirers of his earlier work have felt uneasy at their lack of political content.

Steinert, Otto (1915–78) German photographer, who originated the concept of **Subjective Photography**. Steinert practised medicine until 1947, when he became a full-time portrait photographer. In 1948 he became head of photography at the Staatliche School in his hometown of Saabrücken and a year later cofounded the FOTOFORM group. Feeling that Fotoform's original concentration on abstract imagery was too limiting, Steinert argued for a wider concept of 'Subjective Photography' that would include any photograph that showed individual creativity and a personal interpretation of the world. Both abstract and more literal work, appeared in the first Subjective Photography exhibition, held in Saarbrücken in 1951; Moholy-Nagy and Man Ray were among the artists represented. Further exhibitions under the Subjective Photography label were held in 1954 and 1958. In the 1960s Steinert held professorships at Staatliche and Essen-Werden and wrote prolifically on his ideas. His studies of landscapes, industrial settings, and Nobel Prize-winning scientists draw their power from his stark use of shadow and his skill in evoking the mood of a subject through technical means. As a teacher and theorist he influenced a whole generation of post-war West German photographers.

Steirische Herbstfestival A music festival held in October-November each year in Graz, Austria. As well as concerts of music ranging from classical to jazz, it features symposia and discussions.

Stirling, Sir James (1926–92) British architect. One of the most influential and original of post-war European architects, Stirling was born in Glasgow and educated at Liverpool University. He worked in partnership in London with James Gowan (1956–63) and later with Michael Wilford (1971–92). Stirling and Gowan's work steered British modernism towards what became known as the NEW BRUTALISM. Their flats at Ham Common (1955–58) started a trend for brick with exposed concrete beams and the engineering department of Leicester University (1959–63) used similar materials on a heroic scale. From 1964 to 1971 Stirling's work made greater use of historical allusion, as, for example, in the Cambridge History Faculty (1964–67), the Florey Building for Queens College, Oxford (1966–71), and housing at Runcorn, Cheshire (1967–76; demolished 1991). After 1971 Stirling and Wilford made a more explicit use of historical references in form, material, and decoration, most notably in the extension to the Tate Gallery in London (1980–85), the Neue Staatsgalerie in Stuttgart (1977–84), probably his most praised building, and the Wallraf-Richartz Museum, Cologne. With the Americans Robert Venturi and Philip Johnson he may be said to represent the more thoughtful face of the POSTMODERNISM prevalent in the 1980s. Stirling's controversial design for an office development at No 1, Poultry, in the City of London, replacing a group of listed Victorian buildings, won consent after a long planning battle and awaits commencement. Stirling was a visiting professor at several universities and won most major architectural prizes.

Stockhausen, Karlheinz (1928–) German composer. Stockhausen studied under Frank MARTIN at the Cologne Musikhochschule and then in 1952–53 with MESSIAEN and Milhaud in Paris, where he made his first experiments with electronic music. On his return to Cologne he cofounded (1953) the pioneering ELECTRONIC MUSIC studios of the West German state radio and continued his explorations with such works as *Gesang der Jünglinge* (1956) for children's voices and synthesized sounds. He also explored serial techniques in such instrumental works as the *Klavierstücke* I-IV (1953) for piano. *Gruppen* (1957) for three orchestras shows Stockhausen's preoccupation with acoustics, a subject he studied at university, and with the spatial location of different musical forces (*see* SPATIAL MUSIC).

In 1958 he travelled to the US and met the composer John Cage, whose emphasis on the role of chance in musical performance greatly influenced Stockhausen's works of the 1960s (*see* ALEATORY MUSIC). In such pieces as *Carre* (1960), *Mikrophonie I* (1964), and *Kurzwellen* (1968) exact notation was dispensed with but such matters as the use and placing of microphones were specified. In *Aus den sieben Tagen* (1968) the 'score' consists of an instruction to the players to fast in silence for four days and then to improvise without conscious thought. The strain of Utopian mysticism in Stockhausen's later work is well represented by, for example, *Hymnen* (1967) for tape and orchestra, a work intended to celebrate the unity of mankind. Other principal works include *Zeitmasse* (1956) for woodwind, *Kontakte* (1960) for instruments and electronic sounds, *Momente* (1962) for soprano, choruses, and instrumentalists, and the vocal works *Stimmung* (1968), and *Sirius* (1977). Since 1977 Stockhausen has been engaged on the massive opera sequence *Licht*, which will comprise seven large-scale works named after the days of the week; so far *Donnerstag* (1980), *Samstag* (1984), and *Montag* (1988) have been completed.

Stoppard, Tom (Tom Straussler; 1937–) British playwright and novelist, born in Czechoslovakia. Writing loosely in the tradition of Continental absurdism, he established his reputation with *Rosencrantz and Guildenstern are Dead* (1966), a reworking of Shakespeare's *Hamlet* as seen through the eyes of two of the play's minor characters (*see* ABSURD, THEATRE OF THE). First seen at the EDINBURGH FESTIVAL, it subsequently enjoyed a lengthy West End run and has had many revivals. *The Real Inspector Hound* (1968), a surreal skit on detective thrillers, features two theatre critics in the audience who are gradually drawn into the action on stage; this ingenious one-acter was followed by such commercial and critical sucesses as *If You're Glad I'll be Frank* (1969), *After Magritte* (1970), and *Artist Descending a Staircase* (1973), which was written for radio. Perhaps his masterpiece of this period was the comedy *Jumpers* (1972), a skilful and eloquent parody of academic philosophy, in which long passages of moral argument are interspersed with displays by a team of acrobats (jumpers).

Travesties (1974), a comedy featuring characters including James Joyce and Lenin, was similarly rich in literary allusions and linguistic inventiveness; it also offered insights into the way in which recollections of past events can be coloured by the character of the person who remembers them. More recent works have included the political *Dirty Linen* (1976), the musical play *Every Good Boy Deserves Favour* (1977), the marital tragicomedy *The Real Thing* (1982), and *Hapgood* (1988), an intellectual spy thriller.

Stoppard has also produced adaptations and translations of foreign works, among them García Lorca's *The House of Bernarda Alba* (1973), Nestroy's *On the Razzle* (1981), and HAVEL's *Largo Desolato* (1987), as well as plays for television, including his first play, *A Walk on the Water* (1963), *Boundaries* (1975), *Professional Foul* (1977), and *Squaring the Circle* (1984). His screenplays include those for *The Human Factor* (1979), *Brazil* (1985), and *Empire of the Sun* (1987).

Storey, David (Malcolm) (1933–) British playwright and novelist. The son of a Yorkshire mining family, Storey left school at 17 and became a professional rugby league player; at the same time he studied painting at the Slade School of Fine Arts in London. *The Restoration of Arnold Middleton* (1967), his first play, was performed at the Royal Court Theatre and immediately established his reputation. His best-known work is probably *Home* (1970), an intimate drama set in a lunatic asylum; the original production featured John Gielgud and Ralph Richardson and was directed – like several other of Storey's plays – by Lindsay ANDERSON for the Royal Court. Other works for the stage have included *The Contractor* (1969), which concerns the events that take place as a marquee is erected for a wedding reception, *The Changing Room* (1971), which draws on the author's experiences as a professional rugby player, *Life Class* (1974), *Sisters* (1978), *Early Days* (1980), and *The March on Russia* (1989).

Like his plays, Storey's novels are preoccupied with the theme of social mobility and, in particular, the psychological difficulties experienced by characters who move away from their working-class origins. *This Sporting Life* (1960), his best-known novel, concerns the ambitions of a professional rugby player and his love for his landlady; it was subsequently filmed by Lindsay Anderson. His later novels include *Flight into Camden* (1960), *Pasmore* (1972), the ambitious and largely autobiographical *Saville* (1976), which won the BOOKER PRIZE, and *Present Times* (1984).

In 1992 he published *Storey's Lives*, a volume of confessional poetry.

Straub, Jean-Marie (1933–) German film director, born in France and living since 1969 in Rome. A series of collaborations with his French-born wife, **Daniele Huillet** (1936–) established Straub as a leading figure in the NEW CINEMA movement of the 1960s. Noted for their left-wing views, the Straubs made their first shorts in the early 1960s with Huillet acting as her husband's cowriter and coeditor; from 1974 she was also his codirector. Their first feature film was *Chronicle of Anna Magdalena Bach* (1967), an austere portrayal of the life of Bach. The visual and polemical clarity of this and later films quickly won the Straubs a reputation as the 'film-maker's film-makers' and most West German alternative cinema of the late 1960s and early 1970s bore their stamp.

Othon (1969) used a play by Corneille to debate the relationship between culture and communication, while *History Lessons* (1972) was a provocative political meditation based on an unfinished novel by BRECHT. *Moses and Aaron* (1974) was a screen version of Schoenberg's opera and *The Dogs of Sinai* (1976) drew on a political novel by Franco FORTINI. Subsequent films have included *From the Cloud to the Resistance* (1979), an imaginative evocation of the history of an Italian village, and *Class Relations* (1983) based on a novel by Kafka. Despite their wide influence, their uncompromising style has precluded success in the commercial cinema.

Strauss, Botho (1945–) German playwright, poet, novelist, and theatre critic, whose abstruse and elliptical plays have made him the most talked about contemporary dramatist in his own country. As resident playwright at the Schaubühne in Berlin (1970–75), he won several awards with his first play, *The Hypochondriacs* (1972), a disturbing farce in which a woman discovers that all her actions and emotions during the past five years have been controlled by a secret admirer. Subsequent plays have included *Three Acts of Recognition* (1976), *Great and Small* (1978), in which the central female character Lotte makes a depressing tour of an urban wasteland, *The Park* (1983), one of several adaptations of Shakespeare, and *Tourist Guide* (1986). *Seven Doors* (1989) is a series of weird disconnected sketches on the theme of contemporary angst, while *Schlüsschor* (1991) is a surreal comedy inspired by German reunification. In *Time and the Bedroom* (1992) a woman constantly changes her appearance and identity to conform to masculine stereotypes. His novels include *Rumour* (1980) and *The Young Man* (1984).

Strehler, Giorgio (1921–) Italian theatre director, who cofounded the celebrated **Piccolo Teatro della Città di Milano** with Paolo GRASSI in 1947. Having begun as an actor, Strehler soon distinguished himself as a director and in time was recognized as one of the driving forces behind post-war Italian theatre. The establishment of the Piccolo Teatro della Città di Milano marked the start of the influential TEATRO STABILE movement and constituted the first concerted effort to reach a new audience rarely catered for by traditional companies.

Strehler encouraged the company to explore a wide repertoire including both classic and modern plays and won particular acclaim for his championship of the works of BRECHT in the 1950s. He has presented plays by Shakespeare on a regular basis, his most successful interpretations including *Coriolanus* (1957), *King Lear* (1972), and *The Tempest* (1948 and 1978). Among other notable productions have been works by Italian playwrights ranging from Goldoni to Pirandello and several of Mozart's operas.

From 1968 to 1972 Strehler experimented with more politically committed work with a new company, the Gruppo Teatro e Azione. In the 1980s he combined his work with the Piccolo company with visits to Paris, where he directed the Théâtre de l'Europe in plays by Brecht and other leading European writers. He resigned from the Piccolo Teatro in 1992, following an investigation into his alleged mismanagement of an EC grant.

structuralism An approach to cultural studies that analyses individual phenomena in terms of their structural role within larger systems of meaning.

The principles of structuralism were first clearly stated in the structural linguistics of the Swiss theorist Ferdinand de Saussure (1857–1913). Saussure proposed that languages were self-contained systems that should be explored through the details of their internal structure rather than through comparative or historical studies. Linguistic signs he regarded as in themselves completely arbitrary, deriving their meaning from their structural relationships with other signs rather than from any inherent connection with the things or concepts signified.

The growth of a wider structuralist movement was largely the result of LÉVI-STRAUSS's application of these principles to the analysis of human cultures. In his anthropological studies Lévi-Strauss interpreted his data in terms of certain underlying structural ideas – such as oppositions and hierarchies – that he considered transcultural and ahistorical.

In the 1960s more subversive thinkers seized eagerly on the idea that cultural signs might be as arbitrary as linguistic signs, deriving their value not from any connection with 'nature' or 'reality' but from their function within a closed structure of socially determined meanings. This is the assumption behind the earlier work of Roland BARTHES, who analysed the products of both high and low culture (Racine and striptease) in terms of the larger codes and conventions that supposedly determine their meaning. The structuralist literary critic likewise approaches a written text as a self-contained verbal structure that generates meanings through the operation of certain implicit codes. The traditional assumptions that a text represents the intention of an individual author and reflects a nonverbal reality are discarded.

The term structuralism was introduced into architecture in the early 1960s to describe the approach of certain Dutch architects, notably Aldo van EYCK and Jacob Bakema (*see* VAN DEN BROEK AND BAKEMA. Taking their cue from Lévi-Strauss's attempt to relate complex cultural phenomena to a few basic structural models, they proposed that answers to a wide range of design problems could be found in a small number of formal archetypes. Other architects associated with these ideas included Hermann HERTZBERGER and Piet BLOM.

See also POSTSTRUCTURALISM.

Studio PER A loose allegiance of four Spanish architects, **Pep Bonet, Christián Cirici, Lluís Clotet** and **Oscar Tusquets Blanca** (all born 1941), who shared a Barcelona office from 1965 until the mid 1980s. In 1972 Studio PER expanded to form B D Ediciones dei Diseño to produce their ranges of furniture and construction components. Until 1983 Bonet and Cirici practised together, as did Clotet and Tusquets; in 1987 Tusquets founded the new firm of Tusquets, Diaz, and Associates. All teach extensively.

Bonet and Cirici are best known for their clean Miesian houses, such as those in Argentona, Barcelona (1982–83), and Bonet's own house at Vilamajor (1976). Bonet was the principal architect for the rebuilding of the Plaza del Universo, Barcelona (1983–85), whilst Cirici has concentrated on teaching.

Clotet's work is more historically based, veering from neoclassicism to a style influenced by POP ART. His best-known work is the Casa Vittoria, Pantelleria (1974, with Tusquets), with its lines of quasi-antique piers; their Casa Regás at Llofriu features a porticoed garage, trompe-l'oeil walls, and disconnected rhythms of windows and shutters. His quirky sense of historical correctness has led to many commissions to restore the old centre of Barcelona. His recent works include the simple but distinguished Simón warehouse, Barcelona (1986–88). For his part Tusquets has become wholly disenchanted with the modern movement and the most eclectic of the four. With Charles Diaz he has restored the Convent dels Angels (1983) and remodelled the Palau de la Música Catalana (1982–87). Truly postmodern classical (*see* POSTMODERNISM) is his Mas Abelló housing at Reus, Tarragona (1983–88).

Subjective Photography *See* STEINERT, OTTO; FOTOFORM.

Sudek, Josef (1896–1976) Czech photographer. Sudek was born at Kolín, near Prague. He trained as a bookbinder at the Royal Bohemian School of Crafts at Kutná Hora (1908–10) and then served an apprenticeship in Prague (1910–13). When his sister became a professional photographic assistant Sudek began to experiment with photography and in 1915 took his first pictures of Prague. In 1915–16 he served on the Italian front, where he lost his right arm. After the war Sudek studied photography at the new State School of Graphic Arts in Prague (1921–24). Here he encountered the work of the American Edward Weston, which influenced his early studies, such as a series of hazy photographs taken in a war veterans' home (1922–27). From 1927 onwards he worked as a professional photographer.

During the 1920s Sudek repeatedly photographed the interior of Prague's St Vitus Cathedral as stonemasons completed the medieval building, capturing both the monumental scale of the masons' work and the building's beauty and holiness. Publication of the photographs in 1928 was a great success and Sudek's business flourished until World War II, during which he retreated into his studio and experimented with still-life pictures. During the 1950s several books of his photographs were published in Czechoslovakia, even though he declined to embrace the ideals of the socialist government. In 1963 an exhibition of his work was held in Prague and proved a failure. Sudek turned back to studio work and began to produce his celebrated 'labyrinths' – series of photographs of particular items (such as stamps or record covers) or on particular themes (such as paper or glass). They are masterpieces of composition, revealing a remarkable sensitivity towards texture and light.

Sundman, Per Olof (1922–) Swedish novelist and writer, who made his literary debut in 1957 with *The Hunters*, a collection of short stories set in the Far North of Sweden. Using a remote rural community as a microcosm, Sundman explores questions of the individual's relations to others and to society. Searches and hunts – either literal or metaphorical – are a recurring motif. Sundman appears to deny the possibility of ever fully understanding another human being.

Similar preoccupations characterize Sundman's other writings. *The Investigation* (1958) and *The Marksman* (1960) both focus on the difficulties of establishing the truth, especially in questions of human motivation and character. *The Expedition* (1962) is a retelling of Stanley's expedition to the Congo, in which Sundman emphasizes the decline of Western imperialism.

The Flight of The Eagle (1967), Sundman's acknowledged masterpiece, describes an ill-fated Swedish balloon expedition to the North Pole at the end of the 19th century. Based on documents and diaries, it explores the motivation behind such expeditions and the personal relationships between the adventurers. *Without Fear, Without Hope* (1968) is a companion volume to the novel, providing background material in the form of annotated documents.

The Story of Såm (1977) is a reworking of the 13th-century *Hrafnkels's Saga* in a contemporary setting. A violent story about a dispute over land, it reveals more clearly than Sundman's other works the debt he owes to the narrative tradition of the sagas.

Superstudio Italian architectural practice founded in 1966 by **Adolfo Natalini** (1941–), a Florentine painter turned architect who from 1973 has also been Professor of Architecture at the University of Florence. His partners were the designers Cristiano Toraldo di Francia (1941–) and Piero Frassinelli (1939–), and the Magris brothers Roberto (1935–) and Alessandro (1941–). Theoretical projects included *Il Monumento Continuo* (1969) and *Twelve Ideal Cities* (1971), as well as such exhibitions as *Italy the New Domestic Landscape* (1972) and *Mindscapes* (1973–75). They became regular contributors to the Venice Biennale and Milan Triennale. Since 1979 Natalini has worked on many projects for historic cities, including Mannheim, Jerusalem, Strasbourg, Pistoia, and Parma.

However, Superstudio differed from other theorists in building extensively, particularly shop interiors. Most important were a series for the Banca Tuscana, for whom they also worked on prefabricated structures. Natalini's preoccupation with the grid, both in his interiors and in later buildings, developed from this work. A system for airports led to the building of two terminal concourses (with Archizoom, 1970), a bank at Alzate Brianza (1978–83), an electrical factory in Bologna (1979–81), and a market centre in Pistoia (1982–88), all underlaid by a rigid grid and using prefabricated parts but relieved by bright colour, curves, or porthole windows. Much use is made of laminated timber trusses. The Compagnia Theatre, Florence (1984–87) is externally of stone but has a high-tech roof. Superstudio finally broke up in 1986.

Susskind, (Ian) Walter (1913–80) British conductor, pianist, and composer, born in Czechoslovakia. Susskind was born in Prague and studied at the State Academy of Music with the composers Suk and

Hāba and the conductor Szell. After several years with the German Opera in Prague (1933–38) he emigrated to Britain, where he played with the London Czech Trio (1938–42). He was subsequently conductor of the Royal Carl Rosa Opera Company (1943–45), principal conductor of the Scottish National Orchestra (1946–52), and a guest conductor with the Sadler's Wells Opera Company and the Glyndebourne Opera. In the 1950s and 1960s he spent long periods in Canada and Australia, becoming principal conductor of the Victoria Symphony Orchestra, Melbourne (1953–55), the Mendelssohn Choir, Toronto (1956–64), and the Toronto Symphony Orchestra (1956–65). An enthusiastic promoter of music for the young, he founded the National Youth Orchestra of Canada in 1958. He later founded and directed the St Louis Symphony Orchestra (1968–75) and appeared as a guest conductor of numerous festivals in Europe and the US. His own compositions include works for piano, violin, and orchestra, and music for the theatre and cinema; he is also known for his orchestral arrangements of pieces originally written for piano.

Sutherland, Graham (1903–80) British painter and graphic artist. Born in London, Sutherland attended Goldsmith's School of Art (1921–26) after abandoning an apprenticeship to the engineering department of a railway company. At Goldsmith's he specialized in engraving and began to produce a series of etchings of idyllic landscapes inspired by the work of the 19th-century English painter Samuel Palmer. When the market for fine printing collapsed in the 1930s he worked as a commercial designer, producing posters, crockery, and glassware; he also taught at the Chelsea School of Art (1927–39).

In 1934 Sutherland made the first of many visits to Pembrokeshire, Wales. Inspired by the distinctive character of the area, he began to produce a series of semi-abstract landscapes in oils and watercolour in which natural features such as roots, rocks, and vegetation assume a fantastic anthropomorphic character. The writhing forms and harsh colours create a mood of disquiet. Sutherland continued to work in this vein during World War II, while also producing images of bomb damage and work in mines and quarries in his capacity as an official war artist.

After the war, Sutherland, a Catholic convert since 1926, acquired a reputation as Britain's foremost living religious artist. His first major religious work was a crucifixion for St Matthew's Church, Northampton (1944–46); its anguished depiction of Christ owes something to photographs of the Nazi death camps and to the work of Sutherland's friend Francis BACON. In 1962 he completed the enormous tapestry of Christ in Majesty for the rebuilt Coventry Cathedral.

From 1947 onwards Sutherland worked mainly in the South of France, where he largely abandoned landscape painting in favour of still lifes and studies of animals (especially reptiles and insects). He finally settled on the Côte d'Azur in 1955. He also produced a number of controversial portraits of famous sitters, including Somerset Maugham (1949) and Sir Winston Churchill (1954); notoriously, the latter so disliked the painting that Lady Churchill eventually destroyed it. By the mid 1950s Sutherland had emerged as Britain's best internationally known artist, with a particularly strong reputation on the Continent. He was appointed OM in 1960. However, his later work is now generally considered inferior to the landscapes of the 1930s and 1940s.

Süto, András (1927–) Romanian playwright and novelist of Hungarian ethnic background. Born in Transylvania, Süto began his career in journalism, becoming chief editor of the pictorial *Uj Elet* in 1957. Although he has published novels, short stories, essays, and travelogues since the 1950s, it is for his dramatic works that he is now best known. Seen as a spokesman for the Hungarian minority in Romania, Süto is admired for his poetic language and the sympathy for the individual shown in such dramas as the historical plays *The Palm Sunday of a Horse Dealer* (1974), *Star at the Stake* (1975), and *The Wedding Feast at Susa* (1981). Other plays on traditional themes include the widely performed *Cain and Abel* (1977), which has been translated into several languages, and *Advent a Hargitán* (1985). Despite their historical settings his plays generally address issues in contemporary society.

Svankmajer, Jan (1943–) Czech animator, noted for his fantastic and macabre style. Svankmajer was born in Prague, where he still lives, and became a member of the Czechoslovakian Surrealist Group in 1970. In early shorts such as *The Flat* (1968) he created a nightmarish world in which inanimate objects take on a malevolent life of their own and persecute human beings. The vein of black humour in his work owes something to both BUÑUEL and FELLINI. He was proscribed from film making for most of the 1970s but continued to work underground. In *Dimensions of Dialogue* (1982), perhaps his most gruesome piece, a series of clay figures eat each other and then vomit to create new figures, who continue the cycle. A preoccupation with cannibalistic imagery marks much of his work.

Svankmajer first became generally known in the West with *Alice* (1988), a typically dark interpretation of *Alice's Adventures in Wonderland.* His first full-length feature, it was made in the face of considerable difficulties and with foreign funding. Following the critical success of this work he has received several commissions from Western broadcasting organizations and become a highly fashionable figure. The BBC screened two films about his work in 1992. Recently, his style has had a noticeable influence in such fields as advertising and rock videos.

In 1992 Svankmajer opened his Surrealist Gallery in Prague. He continues to draw, paint, sculpt, and design puppets as well as to make films. At present he is working on a full-length treatment of the Faust story. His wife, the artist Eva Svankmajerova, has collaborated on a number of his projects.

Svoboda, Josef (1920–) Czech stage designer and architect, who was head designer of the National Theatre in Prague for nearly 30 years (from 1951). Svoboda has produced over 500 designs for theatres all over Europe, including major venues in Belgium, France, Italy, Germany, and Britain, and has had a profound influence over other designers. His many innovative sets have included those for Gogol's *The Government Inspector* (1948), Shakespeare's *Hamlet* (1959), Ostrovsky's *The Storm* (1966), Chekhov's *Three Sisters* (1967), Dostoevskii's *The Idiot* (1970), and Claudel's *Partage de Midi* (1984). He was a founder of the Laterna Magika, a company that presents productions combining cinematic and live performances; he became its artistic director in 1973. Since the early 1980s the Laterna Magika has been part of the National Theatre in Prague. In 1971 he was appointed General Secretary of the International Organization of Scenographers and Theatre Technicians.

Syberberg, Hans-Jürgen (1935–) German film director, who established his reputation during the 1970s with his highly original, often bizarre, films on themes drawn from German history and culture. Syberberg's unique cinematic style, in which he rejects any pretence of realism or conventional narrative, owes much to his early association with Bertolt BRECHT and the productions of the BERLINER ENSEMBLE, several of which he filmed in the 1950s.

Syberberg subsequently moved to West Germany and during the 1960s gained experience working on documentaries for television. He made his feature-film debut in 1968 with *Scarabea*, based on a story by Tolstoy. However, he first attracted serious attention in 1972 with *Ludwig – Requiem for a Virgin King*, a visual extravaganza in which the Germany of Wagner and the Romantics is contrasted with the militarism of Bismarck and Hitler, both of whom appear in the film.

Syberberg continued to develop his epic vision of German identity in *Ludwig's Cook* (1973), in which Ludwig's court is seen through the eyes of his kitchen staff, and *Karl May* (1974), a film with similar themes that starred well-known actors from the Nazi cinema. He adopted a more documentary style for the five-hour film *The Confessions of Winifred Wagner* (1975), in which the composer's daughter-in-law defends the memory of Hitler as a patron of the arts. He further explored the links between German culture and Nazism in the seven-hour *Hitler, A Film from Germany* (1977), in which biographical elements are once again intermingled with extravagant fantasy. The film combines the use of living performers with tableaux featuring waxworks, puppets, and back projection. Syberberg's most recent films have included *Parsifal* (1981), an interpretation of Wagner's opera, and a series of scaled-down one-woman pieces with the actress Edith Clever.

Szabó, István (1938–) Hungarian film director, who emerged as the leading figure in Hungarian cinema in the 1970s and 1980s. Born in Budapest, he won praise for the film *Concert* while still at film school; he made his debut as a director of feature films in 1964 with *The Age of Illusions*, an allegorical love story that carried sharp comments on the political and moral state of modern Hungarian society. Similar themes dominated *Father* (1966) and *25 Fireman's Street* (1973), both of which examined the problems of post-war Hungary through the stories of individuals.

Szabó's international reputation was established in 1979 with *Confidence*, a claustrophobic depiction of two people obliged to masquerade as husband and wife during the Nazi occupation. Further acclaim came in 1981 with *Mephisto*, in which an actor (played by Klaus Maria Brandauer) attempts to justify the moral compromises he makes in order to advance his career under the Nazis. Brandauer also starred in *Colonel Redl* (1985), in which a man repudiates his family, his Jewish identity, his homosexuality, and his friends to rise within the intelligence network of the Hapsburg Empire – only to find that he is still regarded as an outsider and an ideal scapegoat. The same theme of self-betrayal figured in *Hanussen* (1988). Szabó's *Sweet Emma, Dear Böbe* (1991), about two Russian teachers struggling to make sense of a post-communist world, won the Silver Bear award at the Berlin Festival. *Meeting Venus* (1992), a comedy of manners set in the world of international opera, draws on Szabó's own experience of producing Wagner in Paris.

Szajna, Józef (1922–) Polish theatre director, designer, and artist. A survivor of Auschwitz and Buchenwald, Szajna lectured at the Academy of Arts in Cracow from 1953 and worked as a scenographer with the People's Theatre in Nowa Huta, which he cofounded in 1954. He became director of the People's Theatre in 1963 and subsequently worked at the Stary Theatre in Cracow (1966–70) and as director of the Theatre Studio in Warsaw (1971–82). Szajna became a familiar figure at international theatre festivals, where he presented works by Dante and Shakespeare as well as plays by contemporary Polish playwrights. His *Macbeth* was much admired when seen in Britain in 1970, while more recent successes have included *Cervantes* (1976), *Dante Alive* (1981), and *Dante III* (1985). He has also exhibited his paintings all over the world and published several books on the theatre. In 1982 he retired from the teaching of scenography to concentrate on directing and designing. He is married to the theatre director **Krystyna Skuszanka** (1924–), whose productions have included Gozzi's *Turandot* (1956) and Shakespeare's *The Tempest* (1959).

T

Tabucchi, Antonio (1943–) Italian novelist. Tabucchi has taught Portuguese Literature at Genoa University since 1977 and was for a period director of the Italian Institute in Lisbon. He is also an accomplished translator of the great Portuguese poet Fernando Pessoa (1888–1935), to whom he has devoted several critical essays. Portuguese and Latin American literature have strongly influenced his own work. Tabucchi employs a multiplicity of narrative voices and favours somewhat mysterious plots involving the existential strivings of eccentric protagonists. His works include the novels: *Square of Italy* (1975), *The Little Sailing Ship* (1978), *Indian Nocturne* (1984), and *Vanishing Point* (1986). His collections of short stories include: *The Reverse Game* (1981), *The Woman of Porto Pim and Other Stories* (1983), *A Little Misunderstanding of No Importance* (1985), and *The Birds of Beato Angelico* (1987). He is also the author of the one-act play *Failed Dialogues* (1988).

tachisme A style of nongeometrical abstract painting, characterized by the use of random blotches of colour to express the emotions or unconscious of the artist, that emerged in France in the years after World War II. Like US action painting (a contemporary development), it emphasized the value of spontaneous and unplanned composition. The term (from French *tache*, stain or spot) was introduced by the French critic Charles Estienne in 1954. It is now used more or less interchangeably with the slightly more general term ART INFORMEL.

Tafdrup, Pia (1952–) Danish poet. Tafdrup made her debut with a series of poems published in the journal *Chancen* in 1980. Her first collection, *When an Angel's been Grazed* (1981), includes poems about childhood and a number of frankly erotic pieces. Much of Tafdrup's imagery is drawn from the natural world, which she describes in precise sensuous language vibrant with life. *The Innermost Zone* (1983) sets out to explore unknown regions of the body and mind; Tafdrup is much preoccupied with the body as a source of sensation. *Spring Tide* (1985), one of her most popular collections, is a lyrical celebration of desire in which the birth, growth, and waning of passion are set against the larger rhythms of the natural universe.

Tafdrup has also edited two anthologies of Danish poetry and written a play. She has been translated into several languages and is considered one of the most promising contemporary Danish poets.

Taganka Theatre The familiar name of the Theatre of Drama and Comedy, which was founded in Moscow in 1946. One of the two most important theatrical venues to be founded in Russia since World War II (the other is the SOVREMENNIK THEATRE), the Taganka seats 600 people and has earned a strong reputation for its productions of contemporary drama. In its early years it was restricted to Soviet works, but in recent times plays by BRECHT, Molière, and Shakespeare have been performed there. Iurii LIUBIMOV took over from Nikolai Gubenko as head of the theatre in 1989.

Takis (Panayotis Vassilakis; 1925–) Greek exponent of KINETIC ART. Born in Athens, he began to sculpt in his early twenties, having had no formal training. His career began to develop seriously when he settled in Paris in 1954; he also lived briefly in London in the mid 1950s. Between 1954 and 1958 Takis specialized in creating his so-called 'signals', abstract moving sculptures of steel wire that were put in motion either by weights or springs. An example is *Signal Rocket* (1955, The Museum of Modern Art, New York). These works gave their name to London's Signals Gallery, with which Takis was associated at this time. He also exhibited at the Hanover Gallery, London (1955), the Galerie Iris Clert, Paris (1959), and the Iolas Gallery, New York (1960).

It was during the 1960s that Takis began to create the electromagnetic works for which he is best known. These used powerful magnets to move metal objects such as iron filings in changing patterns, often in time to music and lighting effects. In 1960 he even suspended the poet Sinclaire Beiles in a magnetic field in the Galerie Iris Clert. A major 20-year retrospective exhibition of Takis's work was held in 1972 at the Centre National d'Art Contemporain in Paris. In 1975 he introduced musical electromagnetic kinetic discs at London's ICA Galleries.

Talev, Dimitär (1898–1966) Bulgarian writer. Born in Prilep, Macedonia, Talev studied medicine in Zagreb and Vienna. In 1921 he settled in Sofia, where he became professor of Slavonic languages at the St Kliment of Ohrida University and edited the newspapers *Makedoniya* and *Zora*. Talev first gained attention for his short stories, consolidating his reputation with the tetralogy of novels *The Iron Candlestick* (1952), *The Day of St Elias* (1953), *The Bells of Prespa* (1954), and *I Hear Your Voices* (1966), which depicts the struggles of the Macedonian peoples for religious freedom and national liberation between 1820 and 1924. Talev also wrote historical novels about leading Bulgarian literary figures but his works were virtually banned after the socialist government took power in 1944. In the 1960s he was permitted to rejoin the Union of Bulgarian Writers and his books were republished. They have since been translated into English, Chinese, and many other languages. He is usually considered the leading figure to have emerged in Bulgarian literature since World War II.

Tampere International Theatre Festival An annual festival of drama held in Tampere, Finland. It lasts for a week in August and features performances from around the world, but particularly from Scandinavia, the Baltic states, and eastern Europe. Founded in 1967, it is still Finland's only festival of drama. The city's fine modern architecture provides a backdrop for street theatre and cabaret as well as for large outdoor productions. There are also seminars and workshops.

Tàpies, Antoni (1923–) Spanish (Catalan) abstract painter. Born in Barcelona, he studied law at the university there but took up art in 1945 while convalescing from an illness. In the late 1940s Tàpies passed through a surrealist period, during which he was much influenced by Paul Klee and Joan MIRÓ. In 1948 he held his first exhibition at Barcelona's Salón de Octubre and helped to form the Dau al Set (Seven on the Die) group of young Catalan painters and writers. The movement broke up in 1951.

Tàpies held his one-man exhibition in Barcelona in 1950 and spent the next few years in Paris on a French government scholarship. Following his one-man exhibition in New York in 1953 he became a frequent visitor to the US.

In the mid 1950s Tàpies began to produced mixed-media works in the style – sometimes known as 'matter painting' – for which he has become internationally celebrated. These combine painting in a lyrical expressionist style (*see* ART INFORMEL) with elements of collage. Humble or discarded materials such as cardboard, rags, or string, are embedded in a thick impasto that sometimes includes pulverized marble or latex. He sometimes scratches or cracks the surface to produce an effect resembling old walls.

Tàpies settled at St Gall in Switzerland in 1962 and executed a mural for the theatre there in 1971. He took up sculpture in 1970, the year in which he published *The Practice of Art*. He has written several other books, including his autobiography, *Memoria personal* (1978).

Tardieu, Jean (1903–) French dramatist and poet. Tardieu studied literature at the University of Paris and published his first poems in 1927. From 1944 until 1964 he worked for French Radio and Television (RTF), where he was head of the experimental drama studios for 15 years. Tardieu made his name in the 1950s with a series of short witty plays in the absurdist mode (*see* ABSURD, THEATRE OF THE). Typically, they present ordinary people who are suddenly confronted with events that undermine all their assumptions about the world.

In *Who Goes There?* (1949) and *Courtesy Doesn't Pay* (1950) malign forces destroy the protagonists' faith in normality at a single blow. In *The Enquiry Office* (1955) a man asks initially for the time of his train, but then for answers to all the questions raised by his unimportant life; eventually he obtains the information that he is about to die. In *The Keyhole* (1955) a woman strips for a voyeur, but goes on to remove her skin, flesh, and internal organs, leaving only a skeleton; the voyeur knows he has met his death. In some other plays, notably *The Sonata and the Three Gentlemen* (1966), language is used purely for its musical, rather than its semantic, qualities. His complete poems were published as *The Hidden River* (1968).

Tarkovsky, Andrei (1932–86) Soviet film director, who emerged as a leading figure in serious art cinema in the 1960s. The son of a poet, Tarkovsky made his first shorts at film school; these already display the preoccupations of his later work, notably a concern with the nature of art. His first feature film, admired especially for its atmospheric use of landscape, was *Ivan's Childhood* (1962), a sombre account of the adventures and eventual death of a young spy for the Soviet Resistance during World War II. Religious themes were central to Tarkovsky's next major success, *Andrei Rublev* (1966), in which the great 15th-century icon painter is shown as losing his faith in the face of the horrors of war. Praised for its convincing evocation of life in medieval Russia, the film was nevertheless banned in the Soviet Union until 1971, when it appeared in censored form.

Less successful was *Solaris* (1972), a somewhat self-indulgent science fiction epic that was apparently intended as a socialist answer to the US film *2001: A Space Odyssey* (1969). Like Tarkovsky's earlier films, *Stalker* (1979) attracted praise for its visual qualities but was found obscure and over cerebral by some critics. Subsequent films included *Nostalgia* (1983), a melancholy story about one man's search for personal identity, and *The Sacrifice* (1986), a doom-laden drama in which a retired actor attempts to prevent the destruction of the world by offering up his own life to God as a sacrifice. Shortly after this was completed, Tarkovsky died of cancer. The last two years of his life had been spent in exile in the West. His diaries were published in 1991.

Tati, Jacques (Jacques Tatischeff; 1908–82) French film actor and director, who is remembered chiefly for his films featuring the character Monsieur Hulot. A professional rugby player, Tati became a popular star of music hall in the 1930s with his mimed impressions of famous sporting personalities; he also appeared in films by René CLÉMENT and Claude AUTANT-LARA. He made his debut as a director in 1946 with the short *L'Ecole des facteurs*, which in 1949 he expanded into *Jour de fête*, the first of his five feature films. This highly visual comedy about the efforts of a postman to perform his job faster and more efficiently won several awards and established Tati as the cinema's only true successor to Buster Keaton and Charlie Chaplin.

Monsieur Hulot's Holiday (1953) introduced the ludicrously inept title character and is usually considered the best of all his films. In it he demonstrates both his skill as a performer and as a director sensitive to the absurdities of human behaviour. Hulot reappears in *Mon Oncle* (1958), in which he wrestles with a modern house fitted out with a battery of technological gadgets, *Playtime* (1967), which follows his chaotic progress through a surreal contemporary Paris, and *Traffic* (1970), which makes fun of society's love affair with the car. As Tati's career progressed he became increasingly preoccupied with the satirical thrust of his films – somewhat to the detriment of the comedy. He ended his career with *Parade* (1974), a film for television based on his early mime act; he was declared bankrupt the same year.

Tátrai Quartet Hungarian string quartet, which made its debut in 1946. The current members are Vilmos Tátrai (first violin), István Várkonyi (second violin), György Konrád (viola), and Ede Banda (cello). The original members, all players in the Budapest Municipal Orchestra (later the Hungarian State Orchestra) were Tátrai, whose name the quartet took, Albert Rényi (second violin), József Iványi (viola), and Vera Dénes (cello).

The Tátrai's international reputation dates from 1948, when it won the Bartók Competition for string quartets: they have since toured widely in Europe and Japan. Their recordings include complete Haydn, Beethoven, Bartók, and Kodály quartet cycles, and the complete Mozart quintets. Their extensive repertory also includes a considerable number of commissioned works, many by Hungarian composers.

Tavener, John (Kenneth) (1944–) British composer. The son of a London builder, he studied at the Royal Academy of Music under BERKELEY and David Lumsdaine and was organist at St John's Church, Kensington. His music is devotional in spirit and shows the influence of MESSIAEN and the late religious works of Stravinsky (especially the *Canticum Sacrum*). Tavener first came to notice with his biblical cantata *The Whale* (1969), which enjoyed considerable popularity and was recorded on the Beatles' Apple label. His early Catholic period produced such rich works as the *Celtic Requiem* (1969), *Ultimos Ritos* (1972), a meditation on the crucifixion, and *Thérèse* (1979), an opera about Thérèse of Lisieux. He converted to the Russian Orthodox church in 1976 and his later works, such as his *Liturgy of St John Chrysostom* for chorus, are generally more austere and contemplative. *The Protecting Veil*, a work for cello and orchestra, was hailed as a modern classic when premiered at the 1989 proms and became a bestseller on record. 1992 saw first performances of several major new works by Tavener, including *Mary of Egypt*, a one-act chamber opera presented at the ALDEBURGH FESTIVAL, the choral work *We Shall See Him as He Is*, and *The Last Sleep of the Virgin*, for string quartet and handbells.

Tavernier, Bernard (René Maurice) (1941–) French film director, who became a leading figure in mainstream cinema in the 1970s. He began his film career as a critic, writing for *Cahiers du Cinéma* among other publications, and made a successful debut as a director in 1972 with *The Watchmaker of St Paul*, a screen version of a thriller by Georges Simenon. The star of this film, Philippe Noiret, reappeared in Tavernier's *Let Joy Reign Supreme!* (1975), an historical epic, and *The Judge and the Assassin* (1976), which concerned a magistrate's attempts to test the truth of a suspect's insanity.

Subsequent films on varied subjects included *Spoiled Children* (1977), about a writer who becomes embroiled in both an affair with a neighbour and political protest, *Death Watch* (1980), a science-fiction drama set in Scotland, and *A Week's Holiday* (1980), an optimistic film about the maturing of the generation of 1968. Among more recent works have been the films *Clean Slate* (1981), with Noiret as a policeman who resorts to murder in East Africa during the 1930s, *Sunday in the Country* (1984), about a painter in the France of 1910 who reflects upon his life and acknowledges his own lack of originality (taken to be a comment by Tavernier upon his own career), and *'Round Midnight* (1986), which recreated the jazz clubs of Paris in the 1950s. His latest film is *L.627* (1992), a thriller about the French drug squad.

Taviani, Paolo (1931–) and **Taviani, Vittorio** (1929–) Italian film directors, who have collaborated on a series of highly imaginative films exploring themes of myth and memory. The two brothers were inspired by ROSSELLINI's *Paisà* to form their own film club and subsequently made their directorial debut working with Cesare ZAVATTINI on *San Miniato, July 44* (1954), a documentary about a Nazi atrocity in the home village of the Taviani family. More documentaries followed, during which the brothers perfected their system of taking turns to direct scenes in each movie; they usually worked to their own screenplays and, to begin with, used the techniques associated with NEOREALISM.

After work with Rossellini and others, the brothers made their own feature-film debut in 1962 with *A Man for the Burning*, which introduced the themes of self-sacrifice, political idealism, and subversive fantasy that were to characterize much of their subsequent work. Several of their earlier films were openly political, tackling such issues as Italian divorce law, the public image of the Communist Party, and the solitary confinement of political prisoners.

After *Allonsanfan* (1974), about a rebellion in historical Sicily, the Tavianis won international praise for *Padre Padrone* (1977), an emotional story about the experiences of a Sardinian shepherd boy in the Italian army. The brothers consolidated their success with *The Night of San Lorenzo* (1982), a tragicomedy celebrating Italian resistance to the Nazis during World War II. The diversity and confusion of life provided the central theme for *Kaos* (1984), which was based on short stories by Pirandello, while *Good Morning, Babylon* (1987) describes the impressions of two brothers who travel to Hollywood to work on the set of D W Griffiths's *Intolerance.*

Team 4 *See* FOSTER, SIR NORMAN; ROGERS, SIR RICHARD.

Teatro Popolare Italiano *See* GASSMAN, VITTORIO.

teatro stabile Any of the professional theatre companies set up in Italian cities, mainly in permanent homes, after World War II in order to lend an element of stability to the theatrical scene. Leading examples include the celebrated **Piccolo Teatro della Città di Milano**, founded in 1947 by Giorgio STREHLER and Paolo GRASSI, the Teatro de Arte in Genoa, founded in 1951, and the Teatro Stabile in Turin, founded in 1955.

Tendriakov, Vladimir Fedorovich (1923–84). Russian prose writer. Tendriakov was born in Makarovskaia in Vologda province, the setting of many of his rural stories. Wounded while on active service in August 1943, he went to Moscow in 1945 to study painting; he entered the Gorkii Literary Institute in 1946 and had his first story, *Affairs of my Platoon*, published in 1947. He became a full-time writer following the publication of *The Fall of Ivan Chuprov* (1953). This, like most of Tendriakov's prolific output, is a short novel or *povest'*. During the 1950s his writing became steadily more pessimistic, the author seeing everywhere the persistence of evil in Soviet society despite the reformist rhetoric of the post-Stalinist Party. Such pessimistic works include *Ruts* (1956), *The Miracle-Working Icon* (1959), *Three, Seven, Ace* (1960), *The Trial* (1961), *Short Circuit* (1962), the satirical *Creature of a Day* (*Podenka – vek korotkii*; 1965), *Death of the Boss* (*Konchina*; 1968), *On Apostolic Business* (1969), *Spring Somersaults* (1973), *Eclipse* (1977), and *Retribution* (1979). The last of these deals with alcoholism and domestic violence and is a good example of the urban literature that succeeded the 'Village Prose' of the 1960s and early 1970s. He also produced several full-length novels, notably *Beyond the Current Day* (1959) and *Meeting with Nefertiti* (1964). Tendriakov was a liberal who contributed to the almanac *Literary Moscow* in 1956 and in 1967 signed a letter of support for SOLZHENITSYN. A number of his posthumously published works, notably *The Witch-Hunt* (*Okhota*), are remarkable in their outspokenness.

Tertz, Abram *See* SINYAVSKY, ANDREI DONATEVICH.

Testi, Flavio (1923–) Italian composer and musicologist. Testi studied at the Turin Conservatory and subsequently took private lessons while a student of literature at Milan University. After a career in music publishing with Suvini Zerboni (1952–54) and Ricordi (1955–65), he became a lecturer at the Padua Conservatory in 1972 and at the Milan Conservatory in 1974.

His style is essentially atonal and polyphonic, with his works of the 1960s and 1970s developing a greater density of texture and a stronger sense of instrumental sound. He has produced a considerable body of work, including the operas *Il furore di Oreste* (1956), *La celestina* (1963), and *L'albergo dei poveri* (1966). Notable among his orchestral and chamber music are the double concerto for violin and piano (1959), the five works entitled *Musica da concerto* (1957–69), and the string quartet *Tempo* (1976). His vocal and choral compositions include four cantatas. He has also written two music history textbooks.

Testori, Giovanni (1923–93) Italian novelist, poet, playwright, and art critic. Born in Novate near Milan, Testori studied philosophy before devoting himself to literature and art. His studies of Piedmontese and Lombard paintings of the baroque era have made a significant contribution to art history.

His first work of fiction *The God of Roserio* (1954; subsequently included in the collection of short stories *The Bridge of the Ghisolfa*, 1958) also represents the beginning of the cycle *The Secrets of Milan*. The other volumes in the sequence are the novel *Gilda of MacMahon* (1959), the plays *Maria Brasca* (1960) and *Arialda* (1961), and the novel *The Large Factory* (1961). Testori depicts the solitary and alienated lives of manual workers, prostitutes, pimps, and homosexuals in the bleaker Milanese suburbs with vigorous realism. His language combines standard Italian with dialect.

His later works include *Crucifixion* (1966), a collection of poetry, the play *The Nun of Monza* (1967), and the Shakespearean parodies *Ambleto* (1972) and *Macbetto* (1974). The verse dialogues *Conversation with Death* (1978) and *Interviewing Mary* (1978) were followed by *The Betrothed Put to the Test* (1985), a theatrical piece on a theme from Manzoni. In 1986 he published a further collection of poems, *Diadémata*.

Thaw, the The relaxation of controls in the political, social, economic, and cultural life of the Soviet Union after the death of Stalin on March 5 1953. It took its name from an artistically undistinguished but politically important novel by Il'ia Erenburg (1891–1967), published with official backing in 1954. The movement gained impetus with Khrushchev's 'Secret Speech' to the 20th Party Congress in February 1956, in which he denounced Stalin's 'Cult of Personality'. Following Khrushchev's speech to the 22nd Party Congress in October 1961, the Thaw reached its apogee with the publication in Aleksandr Tvardovsky's liberal journal *Novyi mir* of *A Day in the Life of Ivan Denisovich* by the then unknown SOLZHENITSYN. The failure to publish the same author's *Cancer Ward*, the fall of Khrushchev, and the accession of Leonid Brezhnev in 1964 marked the effective end of the Thaw, although Solzhenitsyn's *Zakhar the Pouch* appeared in 1966 and Mikhail Bulgakov's long-suppressed novel *The Master and Margarita* was published in two censored journal instalments in 1966 and 1967. 1966 saw the trial of Andrei SINYAVSKY and the following year, the 50th anniversary of the October Revolution, brought a drive for Marxist-Leninist orthodoxy and a refreezing of the Soviet literary scene that lasted until 1985.

Even during the Khrushchev years there were significant retreats from liberalism – notably the campaign against Boris PASTERNAK after the publication in the West of *Dr Zhivago*. However, the Thaw did see the publication of a number of major works by Evgenii EVTUSHENKO (*Zima Station*, 1956; *Babii yar'* and *The Heirs of Stalin*, both 1961), Vladimir Pomerantsev (*On Sincerity in Literature*; 1953), Aleksandr Yashin (*Levers*; 1956) and Vladimir Dudintsev (*Not by Bread Alone*; 1956). Two significant almanacs were *Literary Moscow* (two vols; 1956) and *Pages from Tarusa* (1961), edited by Konstantin PAUSTOVSKY.

Theatre Behind the Gate *See* KREJČA, OTOMAR.

Théâtre des Bouffes du Nord *See* BROOK, PETER; INTERNATIONAL CENTRE OF THEATRE RESEARCH.

Théâtre des Nations An international theatre festival founded in 1954 under the auspices of the INTERNATIONAL THEATRE INSTITUTE. Using the Théâtre Sarah-Bernhardt (later renamed the Théâtre de la Ville) in Paris as its base, the festival became one of the most important cultural gatherings in the world between 1954 and 1965, attracting companies from 50 countries. Jean-Louis BARRAULT assumed control of the festival in 1965 but political disruption in 1968 led to its suspension; it has since been revived on an irregular basis in several different countries. Companies participating in the festival have included the BERLINER ENSEMBLE and the Piccolo Theatre from Milan.

Théâtre du Soleil *See* MNOUCHKINE, ARIANE.

theatre in education The use of drama for educational purposes, as promoted in recent years chiefly in Britain, although similar schemes also operate elsewhere. The movement gathered strength in the 1960s, when challenging performances aimed at younger audiences were presented at such venues as Coventry's Belgrade Theatre. Characteristics of these performances include an emphasis on audience participation and a choice of subject matter that has some social or educative value. Topics treated by leading companies specializing in such work (usually on a touring basis) have included racism, ecological disaster, drug dependency, and AIDS.

theatre-in-the-round Drama in which the audience is seated on all sides of the acting area, rather than in front of a proscenium arch stage. The abandonment of the long-established convention of the imaginary 'fourth wall', through which the audience sees the action, was a major innovation in post-war European drama. Although experiments with such an arrangement had been carried out before World War II by such directors as Okhlopkov in the Soviet Union, it was only in the 1950s that the idea was explored more fully, initially in the US. The possibilities for increased audience identification with the action and for a more intimate form of drama led to its adoption by many leading companies and a new attention to innovative stage designs in general. Theatres given over almost exclusively to such productions have included the Royal Exchange Theatre in Manchester and the Théâtre en Rond de Paris.

Théâtre National Populaire *See* VILAR, JEAN; PLANCHON, ROGER.

Theatre of Cruelty *See* CRUELTY, THEATRE OF.

Theatre of Fact *See* DOCUMENTARY THEATRE.

Theatre of the Absurd *See* ABSURD, THEATRE OF THE.

Théâtres Nationaux *See* DÉCENTRALISATION DRAMATIQUE.

théâtre total A theory of theatrical technique that gained widespread currency in Europe after World War II. According to this theory, responsibility for all matters of interpretation and artistic control lies solely with the director (compare COLLECTIVE CREATION). Sometimes the director's influence has even been extended to the text itself; Jean-Louis BARRAULT, one of the best-known directors to advocate *théâtre total*, has often had a hand in creating the scripts of his productions.

Theatre Workshop *See* LITTLEWOOD, JOAN.

Theodorakis, Mikis (1925–) Greek composer and politician. Theodorakis served with the Resistance during World War II and was subsequently deported for his leftist views during the Greek Civil War of 1947–52. Influenced mainly by his childhood experiences of Byzantine chant and Cretan folk music, he was essentially self-taught as a composer until he enrolled at the Paris Conservatoire at the age of 29, where he studied with MESSIAEN. In Paris he began to write the modern folk songs for the bouzouki with which his name is mainly associated. His first significant success came with the Covent Garden production of his ballet *Antigone* in 1959: emboldened by this triumph he felt able to issue a statement condemning the Greek musical establishment on his subsequent return to Greece (1961).

In the 1960s Theodorakis had considerable influence in left-wing Greek cultural circles, extending his ideas about the social function of music to poetry, film, and theatre as well. He was elected as a communist MP in 1964. When the colonels came to power in Greece in 1967, Theodorakis was imprisoned (remaining so until 1970) and his music banned. In the 1980s and early 1990s he spent several further periods as an MP; in 1992 he resigned his position as minister without portfolio in order to concentrate on his musical career.

His many works include song cycles, oratorios, ballets, and film scores – most famously for CACOYANNIS's *Zorba the Greek* (1965), the theme tune of which became an international hit. More recent works include the opera *Kostas Kariotakis* (1985).

Thomas, R(onald) S(tuart) (1913–) Welsh poet and clergyman. Thomas was educated at University College, Bangor and ordained (1936) in the Church of Wales. He subsequently served as rector to several parishes in rural Wales before retiring in 1978. His first volume of poetry *The Stones of the Field* was published in 1947; further collections included *Song at the Year's Turning* (1955), *Tares* (1961), *Pieta* (1966), *Not that He Bought Flowers* (1968) and *Laboratories of the Spirit* (1975). In 1974 his *Selected Poems 1946–68* was published and *Later Poems 1972–1982* appeared in 1983. Subsequent collections include *Welsh Airs* (1987) and *Counterpoint* (1990). As a poet Thomas draws most of his subject matter from the harsh lives of the hill farming communities to which he ministered for over 40 years. Style and diction are kept severely plain and the tone of both his religious and his pastoral poetry is determinedly unsentimental. Some of his later work shows an interest in the physical sciences. He edited *The Penguin Book of Religious Verse* (1963). In the 1980s he became increasingly militant and outspoken in his support for Welsh nationalist causes. His *Collected Poems* were published in 1993.

Tinbergen, Nikolaas (1907–88) Dutch zoologist and ethologist. After gaining a PhD in zoology (1932) at Leiden University, Tinbergen taught there until 1949, becoming professor of experimental biology. He then moved to Oxford University, where he helped to originate the Animal Behaviour Research Group, within the department of zoology, becoming first reader (1962) and then professor of animal behaviour (1966–74).

Like Konrad LORENZ, Tinbergen considerably influenced the comparatively new science of ethology. His work (like Lorenz's) emphasizes the importance of field observations of animals under natural conditions, though amplified by laboratory experiment designed to trigger responses under controlled conditions. His studies embrace both vertebrate and invertebrate animals, from arctic foxes to snails, investigating such topics as animal camouflage, social, courtship, and mating behaviour. One of Tinbergen's most important theses is that a study of aggression in animals could lead to a greater understanding of such behaviour in man and perhaps provide some means of modifying it. His work in relating ethology to the human condition led to his being awarded, jointly with Lorenz and Karl von Frisch, the Nobel Prize for physiology or medicine in 1973. His most influential publication, *The Study of Instinct* (1951), presents a summary of the work of ethologists in the first half of the 20th century. His brother is the Nobel-Prize-winning economist Jan Tinbergen (1903–).

Tinguely, Jean (1925–91) Swiss mechanical sculptor and pioneer of KINETIC ART. Born in Freibourg, he attended the Basel School of Fine Arts on an irregular basis between 1941 and 1945. He settled permanently in Paris in 1952 and began to create the moving metal and wire sculptures he called *Métamécaniques*. Tinguely held his first exhibition of 'metamechanic reliefs', some of which were powered by small electric motors, in Paris's Arnaud Gallery in 1953. His surreal sculptures were usually assembled from such discarded items as bent wheels, saws, barrel hoops, and bicycle parts. Some produced clattering or ringing sounds by rapping on metal pans or bottles; some even gave off odours. At the 1957 Paris Biennale he exhibited his 'metamatic-self-moving-odorous-and-sonorous' machine, which emitted noises and fumes while producing some 40 000 'gesture' paintings.

Tinguely was one of nine artists influenced by Yves KLEIN's anti-art attitude who formed the NOUVEAU RÉALISME group in 1960. His experiments were now moving away from KINETIC ART in the direction of PERFORMANCE ART or HAPPENINGS. In 1960 he exhibited his 20-minute autodestructive machine in the garden of New York's Museum of Modern Art; as well as destroying itself, as planned, the sculpture (titled *Homage to New York*) malfunctioned and started a fire. More suicidal machines followed, including the complex work 'monster-sculpture-autodestructive-dynamic-and-aggressive' for the Louisiana Museum in Copenhagen (1961). In 1965 the Museum of Fine Arts in Houston, Texas, acquired the entire contents of a Tinguely exhibition held at the Alexander Iolas Gallery in Paris. Asked about the success of his unusual art, Tinguely commented simply: 'Life is a game.'

Tippett, Sir Michael (1905–) British composer. After studying composition at the Royal College of Music (1923–28) and counterpoint with R. O. Morris (1930–32), Tippett spent the 1930s developing his own musical style from a variety of influences including jazz and blues, the English madrigalists, modal harmony, strict counterpoint, and the music of Stravinsky, Bartók, and Hindemith. At the same time he worked as a conductor, particularly for socialist organizations. He was imprisoned during World War II as a conscientious objector.

Tippett's personal style emerged slowly; his first mature pieces, the concerto for double string orchestra (1939) and the oratorio *A Child of our Time* (1941), were written just before the war. His operas span the next five decades and chronicle the way his musical language has changed. *The Midsummer Marriage* (1955) is both lyrical and richly scored, while *King Priam* (1961) is more austere, using clearly distinguished blocks of sound. In *The Knot Garden* (1970) contrasted ideas are integrated into a continuous structure while *The Ice Break* (1977) and *New Year* (1989) mark a return to the opulent scoring and lyricism of earlier works. In addition Tippett has written two major choral works, *The Vision of St Augustine* (1965) and the extrovert *The Mask of Time* (1983). For all these works Tippett has supplied his own idiosyncratic texts, drawing freely on myth, symbolism, and Jungian psychology to interpret contemporary spiritual anxieties. He has been prolific in the field of instrumental music, completing four symphonies (1945, 1957, 1972, 1977), the triple concerto for violin, viola, and cello (1979) five string quartets, four piano sonatas, and many works for solo voice.

Tobino, Mario (1910–) Italian novelist, poet, and physician. Born in Viareggio, he worked for many years as a consultant in the psychiatric hospital at Lucca. His early poetry, written between 1934 and 1942, is characterized by an intense lyricism and a passionate subjectivity that is also to be found in his fiction. His first novel was *The*

Pharmacist's Son (1942). *The Desert of Lybia* (1951), a war diary, was followed by a brief satirical novel about university life under Fascism, *Black Flag* (1950). His most perceptive work, *The Women of Magliano*, was inspired by his experience in the psychiatric hospital. Other novels include *The Underground* (1962), about the wartime Resistance to the Fascists, *Down the Ancient Staircase* (1972), another novel set in a mental institution, and *Lost Love* (1979), which deals with the renewed stirrings of a past relationship. Among recent titles is *The Thief* (1984). He has also written short stories.

Todorov, Tzvetan (1939–) French philosopher, historian, and literary theorist, born in Bulgaria. Todorov settled in France in 1963, having secured a post as a research assistant at the Paris National Centre for Scientific Research. One of the major exponents of the structuralist approach to literature, he made his reputation with *Grammar of the Decameron* (1969), a study of Boccaccio, and *Introduction to Fantastic Literature* (1970), a structuralist analysis of the genre. He has specialized in the study of prose, publishing *The Poetics of Prose* in 1971. In his works of the later 1970s and 1980s he has adopted a more eclectic approach and shown a particular interest in the philosophical and cultural role of symbols; works of this phase include *Theories of the Symbol* (1977), *Symbolism and Interpretation* (1978), and *The Conquest of America: the Question of the Other* (1982). He has also written on Russian literary theorists, including Mikhail BAKHTIN. In 1972 he published (with O. Ducrot) the *Encyclopaedic Dictionary of the Sciences of Language*. He has written numerous essays.

Tolkien, J(ohn) R(onald) R(euel) (1892–1973) British writer, philologist, and academic, born in South Africa. A career academic, he was Merton professor of English language and literature at Oxford University from 1945–59 and published works of philology and criticism of Anglo-Saxon literature, notably *Beowulf: the Monsters and the Critics* (1936). In later life Tolkien found international fame with his fantasy novels, which draw heavily on his knowledge of early literature and his linguistic scholarship. In *The Hobbit* (1937), ostensibly a children's book, and its sequel, the massive three-volume *The Lord of the Rings* (1954–55) Tolkien created an extensively detailed mythological world, Middle Earth, complete with its own history and languages. These works have spawned many imitations, almost single-handedly creating a new genre. *The Silmarillion*, a sequence of writings describing the earlier history of Middle Earth, was published posthumously in 1977. Other works by Tolkien include *The Adventures of Tom Bombadil* and *Farmer Giles of Ham*. *Tree and Leaf* (1964) contains his earlier lecture 'On Fairy Stories', an important defence of fantasy literature. With his friend and fellow don C. S. LEWIS he was a founder member of the Inklings, a group of like-minded writers.

Tolstaia, Tat'iana (1951–) Russian short-story writer. Born in Leningrad, the granddaughter of the Soviet novelist Aleksei Tolstoi, she graduated in philology from Leningrad University in 1974 and made her literary debut with an excellent story, 'On Golden Porch', in 1983. This work gave its title to a highly acclaimed collection of 13 pieces published in 1987 and translated into English two years later. Tolstaia now lives in Moscow, although she has recently spent much time as a guest of various US universities. A second much praised collection, *Sleepwalker in a Fog*, appeared in 1991.

Tolstaia's stories are remarkable for their exuberant and richly metaphorical prose style. She stands out from her contemporaries for having developed an individual style that, as with Nabokov, is more important to her than theme or ideas. Many of her best stories are character studies or describe small episodes in the lives of lonely unremarkable people struggling in difficult circumstances. Remote from social, political, or ideological questions, she is concerned with the pathos of unfulfilled dreams and illusions, often interweaving melancholy lyricism with flashes of grotesque humour reminiscent of Bulgakov or her acknowledged master Andrei BITOV. She is widely regarded as the outstanding Russian writer of her generation.

Tomasi di Lampedusa, Giuseppe *See* LAMPEDUSA, GIUSEPPE TOMASI DI.

Torga, Miguel (Adolfo Correia da Rocha; 1907–) Portuguese writer. Born into a poor Catholic family in São Martinho de Anta, Torga fled to Brazil when only 12 years old in order to escape being sent to a seminary. After several years working on a coffee estate he returned to Portugal and studied medicine at the University of Coimbra, graduating in 1933. He subsequently practised as a doctor. From 1927 he was associated with the Presença group of poets but broke away in 1931. An opponent of the Salazar regime, he spent time in prison and some of his work was banned. Following the 1974 revolution he was fêted by the socialist government and proposed as a candidate for the Nobel Prize. He is married to the eminent literary critic Andrée Crabbé Rocha.

Torga's work combines a loyalty to the language and people of his native Trás-os-Montes region with an interest in the largest philosophical and relgious themes; a characteristic note is one of protest against the futility of life and its constant hardships. The stories in *Tales of the Highlands* (1941), *New Tales of the Highlands* (1944), and *Portugal* (1950) deal with rural Portuguese life, as does the acclaimed novel *Vindima* (1945), which deals with a catastrophic failure of the grape harvest in Douro. Despite having rejected his Catholic upbringing, he maintained a keen sense of the religious, making frequent use of transcendental language; in his novels *Liberation* (1944) and *O Senhor Ventura* (1943) he explicitly links the missions of the doctor, the priest, and the poet. His most popular work is *Bichos* (1940), in which the characters are partially anthropomorphized animals living out the inevitable cycle of birth and death. A prolific author, he has published numerous collections of poetry, four plays including *The Sea* (1941; revised 1970), 12 novels, and several volumes of essays, including the collection of political writings *Fogo Preso* (1976). His *Diaries*, published sporadically since 1941, are considered to be amongst his most important writings.

total serialism *See* SERIALISM.

Tournier, Michel (1924–) French writer. Tournier studied law, literature, and philosophy at the Sorbonne and the University of Tübingen. After failing to become an academic philosopher he worked in radio and television and for a large publishing house in Paris.

In his novels Tournier often retells existing stories or legends, giving them his own twist of philosophical speculation. His first novel *Friday and Robinson* (1967) reworks the story of Robinson Crusoe; in Tournier's version it is Friday who educates Crusoe by explaining the defects of civilization. When a ship finally arrives Friday leaves for Europe, while Crusoe chooses to remain on the island. Tournier has also published a children's version of the story, *Friday, or The Wild Life* (1977).

Erlking (1970), Tournier's second novel, takes its title from the poem by Goethe. It tells how a young Frenchman, at once fascinated and repelled, becomes involved in bizarre Nazi experiments designed to create a new race as a basis for a new civilization. The novel was awarded the Prix Goncourt. Tournier's other novels include *The Fetishist* (1974), which explores questions of 'natural' and 'unnatural' sexuality, *Gaspard, Melchior and Balthazar* (1980), which retells the legend of the three wise men and enquires into their motives, and *The Golden Droplet* (1985), the story of a young African at large in France. *The Midnight Love Feast* (1990) is a collection of stories and journalistic pieces. Tournier's novels combine a genuine gift for storytelling with philosophical reflection.

Tovstonogov, Georgiy (Aleksandrovich) (1915–89) Georgian theatre director, noted for his innovative productions of the classics. He began his career as an assistant director at the Junior Theatre in Tbilisi in 1931 and rose to the post of director of the Griboyedov Russian Drama Theatre in the same city in 1938. Subsequently he served as director of Moscow's Central Children's Theatre (1946–49), Leningrad's Komsomol Theatre (1950–56), and (from 1956) as chief director of Leningrad's Gorkii Theatre (also called the Bolshoi Dramatic Theatre). Under his guidance the Gorkii quickly became one of the most respected venues in the country, presenting a mixture of approved Soviet plays, Russian classics, and Western drama. His productions, several of which have also been seen abroad, have included Dostoevskii's *The Idiot* (1957), ARBUZOV's *It Happened in Irkutz* (1960), Sholokhov's *Virgin Soil Upturned* (1964), Chekhov's *Three Sisters* (1964), Gogol's *The Petty Bourgeoisie* (1967) and *The Government Inspector* (1972), *The Story of a Horse* (1975), derived from Tolstoi and rapturously received on Broadway, and Sukhovo-Kobylin's *Tarelkin's Death* (1984). His publications on the theatre include *On Being a Director* (1965).

transavantgarde, the *See* NEOEXPRESSIONISM.

Trauner, Alexander (Alexandre) (1916–) French cinematic art director born in Hungary, noted especially for his association with the US director Billy Wilder. Trauner began as a painter but was hired as an assistant by the art director Lazare Meerson while in Paris for an exhibition. He made his name in the industry with his work for Marcel Carné, including sets for *Hotel du Nord* (1938). Being Jewish, Trauner was obliged to lie low during the Nazi occupation but continued to work anonymously while in hiding.

After the war he began his international career by creating the bleak sets for Orson Welles's *Othello* (1952). This was followed by work on the Hollywood spectacular *Land of the Pharaohs* (1955) and with Billy Wilder on *Love in the Afternoon* (1957), *Witness for the Prosecution* (1958), and *The Apartment* (1960). Trauner's knowledge of European settings was well employed in such US productions as *Paris Blues* (1961), Wilder's *One Two Three* (1961), set in West Berlin, and *Irma La Douce* (1963), set in Paris, and *Behold a Pale Horse* (1966), a Spanish story Trauner coproduced with Fred Zinnemann. He also devised Indian sets for John Huston's *The Man Who Would Be King* (1975).

His European films have included the French version of *Lady Chatterley's Lover* (1955), *Aimez-Vous Brahms?* (1961), the British-French Nazi thriller *The Night of the Generals* (1967), *La Truite* (1979), and the French-Italian-German *Don Giovanni* (1979).

Trevor, William (William Trevor Cox; 1928–) Irish novelist, short-story writer, and playwright. Born to a Protestant family in County Cork, Trevor studied history at Trinity College, Dublin and enjoyed some success as a sculptor before turning to writing. Since the late 1950s he has lived and worked in England, initially as an advertising copywriter and subsequently as a full-time author in Devon. Although he has written about English life in such stories as 'Lovers of their Time' (1978) and 'The Children of Dynmouth' (1976), his work is mainly concerned with rural and small-town Ireland. His novels include *The Old Boys* (1964), *Mrs Eckdorf in O'Neill's Hotel* (1969), *Elizabeth Alone* (1973), and the novella *Reading Turgenev* (1991), which was shortlisted for the BOOKER PRIZE. *The Day We Got Drunk on Cake* (1969), *The Ballroom of Romance* (1972), *Angels at the Ritz* (1975), *The News from Ireland* (1986), and *Family Sins* (1991) are all collections of stories. An acute observer of manners and morals, Trevor writes about the frustrations of the lonely and unsuccessful in a sparse understated style that often yields effects of great poignancy. In writings such as the story 'Attracta' (1978) and the novel *Fools of Fortune* (1981) he has shown an increasing willingness to confront the tragedies of Irish history and the causes of the present-day troubles in Northern Ireland. His plays include *Going Home* (1972), *Marriage* (1973), and *Scenes from an Album* (1981); he has also adapted many of his own works for television. His *Collected Stories* were published in 1991.

Troell, Jan (1931–) Swedish film director, screenwriter, and editor, whose background in cinematography is reflected in his sweeping outdoor epics. Born a dentist's son in Skane, Troell worked as a schoolteacher before entering the cinema in the early 1960s. He began with shorts, assisting the director Bo WIDERBERG as a cameraman and editor before directing his own first feature, *Here's Your Life*, in 1966. After *Who Saw Him Die?* (1968), Troell directed the expensive *The Emigrants* (1971), using the BERGMAN stock players Liv Ullmann and Max von Sydow in an epic story of poor Swedish emigrants on the long voyage to America. The sequel, *The New Land* (1973), retained the same cast to portray the family's subsequent struggles in Minnesota. The following year Warner Bros employed Troell to make another frontier saga, *Zandy's Bride*, again using Ullmann, and in 1979 he directed the DE LAURENTIIS film *Hurricane* in the US. His most recent films have been made in Sweden and include *Il Capitano, A Swedish Requiem* (1991), about a notorious double-murder.

Troyat, Henri (Lew Trassoff; 1911–) French novelist of Russian origin. Born in Moscow, Troyat fled with his family to Paris during the Bolshevik Revolution. After legal studies at the University of Paris he practised as a lawyer and wrote novels in his spare time. He became a full-time writer in 1941. His work has won several national prizes and he was elected to the Académie Française in 1959.

The main influence on Troyat's work has been the 19th-century Russian novel, especially the work of Tolstoi. In his large-scale novels he recreates the important events of Russian history and provides a detailed and meticulously researched picture of a lost world. In *While the Earth Endures* (1947–50), a trilogy, he describes the adventures of a single family before, during, and after the Revolution. Another major work, the five-volume *The Light of the Just* (1959–63) deals with the failed Decembrist Revolution in St Petersburg in 1825. Other multivolume sequences include *Seedtime and Harvest* (1953–58) and *Les Eygletière* (1965–67). He has also written biographies of such important Russian figures as Pushkin (1950), Tolstoi (1967), Gogol (1973), Catherine the Great (1984), Ivan the Terrible (1986), and Alexander II (1986). Other recent publications include *Derision* (1983) and *The Solitary Sound of the Heart* (1985).

Truffaut, Francois (1932–84) French film director, actor, and screenwriter. Truffaut was the most prominent of the directors associated with the NEW WAVE of the late 1950s and the originator of the AUTEUR theory of film-making.

After a troubled childhood, desertion from the army, and a spell in gaol after his Paris film club failed, Truffaut's fortunes improved when he found work as a film critic for *Cahiers du Cinéma*. He soon established a reputation for hostility to the conventional cinema, calling for a new relevance in French filmmaking, and freedom from the constraints of detailed scripts.

After working as an assistant to ROSSELLINI and making three shorts himself, he set up his own company, Films du Carrosse. He made his debut as a director of full-length features with *400 Blows* (1959). This tale of teenage angst in which a delinquent boy turns to petty crime drew on Truffaut's own childhood and introduced the ideals of the New Wave to a wider audience.

Truffaut's second full-length film, *Shoot the Pianist* (1960), translated the conventions of the Hollywood gangster movie to Europe; like many other Truffaut films it features frequent unexpected changes in mood. *Jules and Jim* (1961), about a triangular love affair, and *Silken Skin* (1964), in which an illicit affair culminates in murder, consolidated Truffaut's position as a leading director, while in *Love at Twenty* (1962), the central character (Antoine Doinel) of his first film reappeared in a tale of unrequited love.

After *Fahrenheit 451* (1966), from the science-fiction novel by Ray Bradbury, and the Hitchcock-inspired thriller *The Bride Wore Black* (1967), Truffaut continued the saga of Doinel (played as before by Jean-Pierre Léaud) in *Stolen Kisses* (1968), in which the character becomes embroiled in an affair with an older woman. The Doinel series concluded with *Domicile conjugale* (1970), in which the central character settles into marriage, and *Love on the Run* (1979), in which he gets divorced.

The Wild Child (1969) was a widely praised story about an 18th-century scientist (played by Truffaut himself) who attempts to civilize a wild boy found in the depths of a French forest. *Anne and Muriel* (1971), a reworking of the *Jules and Jim* theme set in Wales, and *A Gorgeous Bird Like Me* (1972) were also well received. In 1973 *Day for Night*, about the trials of a film crew, won Truffaut an Oscar for best foreign film.

Truffaut's last films included the Gothic romance *The Story of Adèle H* (1975), based on a novel by Victor Hugo, *The Green Room* (1978), which starred Truffaut as a death-obsessed widower, *The Last Metro* (1980), in which Catherine Deneuve played a theatre manager during the Nazi occupation, and the thriller *Finally Sunday!* (1983).

Tubin, Eduard (1905–82) Estonian Composer. After studying composition and conducting at the Tartu Academy (1924–30), Tubin conducted the Vanemuine Theatre Orchestra in Tartu until 1944. He pursued his keen interest in new music throughout his conducting career and was influential in introducing the latest Western European scores to Estonian audiences. He conducted Stravinsky's *Symphony of Psalms* in Tallinn in 1936 and met Kodály two years later. In 1944 he moved to Sweden.

Between 1934 and 1973 Tubin produced 10 symphonies; he also wrote two operas and many orchestral works. His vocal music is mainly for solo voice accompanied by either piano or orchestra. Tubin was much influenced by the music of Bartók, particularly in his use of complex rhythm and extended melody; his compositional style was fluent and highly expressive, his orchestration being particularly accomplished.

Tudor, Antony (William Cook; 1908–87) British choreographer and dancer, who brought an introspective quality to modern ballet. His major works concentrate on characterization and show a sympathy with the afflicted that has earned him the unofficial title 'the choreographer of human suffering'.

Tudor worked in the Smithfield meat market before joining Marie Rambert's Ballet Club company in 1930. He made his debut as a choreographer in 1931 with *Cross Garter'd*, a short piece based on Shakespeare's *Twelfth Night*. *Lilac Garden* (1934), a work depicting the anguish of a woman forced into an unwilling marriage, is considered a landmark in the history of contemporary ballet. His other major works for the Rambert company included *Dark Elegies* (1937), a subdued piece danced to music by Mahler.

In 1937 Tudor and several colleagues left Rambert to form the Dance Theatre company (later renamed the London Ballet). Tudor's work with this shortlived enterprise led to an invitation to join the Ballet Theater in the US (later renamed the American Ballet Theater). Tudor and fellow-choreographer Harold Laing remained with this company for ten years; new works of this period included *Pillars of Fire* (1942), a powerful study of sexual despair in small-town America that was hailed as a masterpiece, and a one-act ballet based on themes from *Romeo and Juliet* (1943).

In 1949 Tudor visited Sweden as guest choreographer with the Royal Swedish Ballet, returning to New York in 1951 to choreograph such pieces as *Lady of the Camellias* (1951) for the New York City Ballet. As director of the Metropolitan Opera Ballet School, he spent much of his time teaching and eventually joined the staff at the Juilliard School. He revived his career as a choreographer in the 1960s with such works as *Echoing of Trumpets* (1963) for the Royal Swedish Ballet and *Shadowplay* (1967) for the ROYAL BALLET. His last works, created for the American Ballet Theater, included *The Leaves Are Fading* (1975) and *The Tiller in the Fields* (1978), both of which employed the music of Dvorák.

Tumanov, Joseph (Mikhailovich) (Joseph Mikhailovich Tumanishvili; 1905–) Russian theatre director, who communicated the ideas of Stanislavsky to a new generation of actors after World War II. A pupil of Stanislavsky himself from 1928 to 1932, he won acclaim for his productions at the Pushkin Theatre and at other theatres in Moscow; his many triumphs included a memorable stage version of Dickens's *Little Dorrit* (1953).

Turing, Alan Mathison (1912–54) British mathematician. Turing studied at Cambridge University, where he gained a fellowship in 1935; from 1936 to 1938 he worked at Princeton. During World War II he made a major contribution to the Allied victory with his role in deciphering the German Enigma codes. He was at the National Physical Laboratory from 1945 to 1948 and subsequently became reader in mathematics at Manchester University.

His most important work consisted in giving a mathematical formalism of the intuitive concept of computability. Turing developed a precise characterization of an idealized computer – the Turing machine – and equated the formal notion of effective decidability with computability by such a machine. He was thus able to show that a number of important mathematical problems could have no effective decision procedure.

Turing was able to put his theoretical work on computability into practice during his time at the National Physical Laboratory when the ACE computer was built under his supervision, and later when he became assistant director of the Manchester automatic digital machine.

Turing was a homosexual at a time when homosexual behaviour was still a criminal offence in Britain. He committed suicide as a direct result of a prosecution for alleged public indecency. His life and death are considered in the play *Breaking the Code* (1986) by Hugh Whitemore.

Turnbull, William (1922–) Scottish abstract sculptor, painter, and printmaker. Born in Dundee, he served in the RAF during World War II and subsequently studied at London's Slade School of Fine

Art (1946–48) and worked as a commercial illustrator. He then spent two years in Paris experimenting with abstract painting and held his first one-man exhibition (1950) at the Hanover Gallery in London. Two years later he began teaching at the Central School of Arts and Crafts, a position he held for two decades (1952–72). After several years of figurative work he returned to abstraction in 1956, becoming intrigued by the spatial problems presented by large canvases. During this period he abandoned his previous heavy impasto technique in favour of a style characterized by smooth surfaces and the use of single flat colours to evoke a spatial emptiness. One of the first British painters to adopt the US colour-field technique, he participated in the important 'Situation' exhibition of British abstract artists held in London in 1960. from 1960. As a sculptor, Turnbull chose figurative forms during the 1950s but thereafter produced mainly abstract geometrical forms of human height that often have a totem-like appearance. He later created geometrical works in painted steel.

Turnbull has held one-man exhibitions in New York, San Francisco, Berlin, and Toronto, as well as numerous shows in London, including nine at the Waddington Galleries (the most recent being in 1991). A retrospective exhibition of his work was held at the Tate Gallery in London in 1973.

Turner Prize A British prize for achievement in the visual arts, established in 1984 by the Patrons of New Art, a body founded in 1982 to encourage the collection of contemporary art. The £20,000 prize is awarded annually by a jury including the director of the Tate Gallery, which hosts the presentation, and a representative of the Patrons. Since 1991 the regulations have specified that the winner shall be a British artist under the age of 50 who has held a major exhibition in the previous 12 months; previously the prize was also open to critics and administrators and there was no upper age limit. The winners have been Malcolm Morley (1984), Howard HODGKIN (1985), GILBERT & GEORGE (1986), Richard Deacon (1987), Tony Cragg (1988), Richard LONG (1989), Anish KAPOOR (1991), and Grenville Davey (1992). The prize was suspended in 1990 following the financial collapse of the original sponsors, Drexel Burnham Lambert; since 1991 it has been sponsored by Channel 4 television.

Tusquets Blanca, Oscar *See* STUDIO PER.

U

Ulrich, Jochen (1944–) German dancer, choreographer, and ballet director, who established his reputation as a choreographer with the Cologne Dance Forum in the 1970s. Having trained at the Cologne Institute for Theatre Dance, he joined the Cologne Opera Ballet in 1967, becoming one of the company's most popular solo dancers.

Ulrich cofounded the Cologne Dance Forum in 1971 and has since found recognition as one of the most original choreographers in contemporary German ballet. His work has made Cologne one of the country's leading centres for dance. Although dancers with the company are coached in both classical and modern technique, the Forum presents a programme of exclusively contemporary works. His own ballets include *Des Knaben Wunderhorn* (1974), to the music of Mahler, *Walzerträume* (1977), *The Miraculous Mandarin* (1980), to the music of Bartók, and *Canto General* (1981).

Ůmea Festival of Chamber Music A week-long music festival, held in Ůmea, Sweden, each June. It is twinned with the **Korsholm Festival**, Finland, on the other side of the Gulf of Bothnia, which continues for a further three weeks. Together they form the **Nordic Arts Festival**. The current musical director is Dmitri Sitkovetsky.

Utzon, Jørn (1918–) Danish architect, who worked with Gunnar Asplund, Alvar AALTO, and Frank Lloyd Wright before setting up his own practice in 1950. Rarely has so talented an architect built so few works. No other building of the age, however, has been at once so controversial and so revered as the Sydney Opera House, for which Utzon won a competition in 1957. Arguments over costs caused him to quit in 1966, leaving others to complete the interiors of the concert hall, opera house, theatre, and cinema; but the exterior, with its zany parabolic roofscape, was completed to his design and is one of the world's most famous buildings.

A recurrent theme in Utzon's work, demonstrated at Sydney and described in his article 'Platforms and Plateaus' (*Zodiac*, 1962), is that of a pagoda roof floating over a podium platform. Only at his Bagsůaerd church, Copenhagen (1973–76), did he have the opportunity to repeat the soaring curves of Sydney, though the same idea is there in the great canopy of his new Parliament Building in Kuwait (1972). His housing combines the podium idea with an interest in courtyards and atria. A debt to Wright's organic 'Usonian' housing of the 1930s can be seen in his schemes at Helsingør (1956–60) and Fredenborg (1962–63) but most vividly in his own house at Porto Petro, Mallorca (1971–73). Bright Mediterranean titles and impressive atria are also features of his later works, such as at the Paustian showrooms, Copenhagen (1987, with his sons Jan and Peter).

V

Vaculík, Ludvík (1926–) Czech novelist and essayist. He studied at the communist-run College of Politics and Social Studies, worked as a tutor in apprentices' hostels and then, after military service, earned his living as a journalist. He was expelled from the Communist Party in 1967, banned after the Soviet occupation, and subsequently became the organizer of the main Czech *samizdat* series. All four of his novels record stages in the conscious development of his identity. *The Busy House* (1963) is a communist idyll based on his work as a hostel tutor. The linguistically and structurally sophisticated *The Axe* (1966) concerns his rural Moravian roots and, particularly, his hardline communist father; the narrator is a journalist. *The Guinea Pigs* (1977), ostensibly an allegory of communist rule by fear and manipulation of information, is in fact a discussion of how far the individual can make his own fate. *Czech Dreambook* (1983) is a ruthlessly honest account of dissident life in diary form; the author's account of his intimate life functions as an attack on the regime's invasion of his privacy. *Views on Vaculík's Czech Dreambook* (1991) gathers the responses of people who figure as characters in the novel (other dissidents and his interrogator) and those of critics; the book serves as a postscript to the *Dreambook*, giving voice and personality to characters who had been subordinated to the narrator in the novel itself.

Vadim, Roger (Roger Vadim Plemiannikov; 1927–) French film director, who is remembered as much for his personal associations with some of cinema's most beautiful women as for his films. Vadim's reputation was established with his directorial debut, *And God Created Woman* (1956), which effectively launched its star, Brigitte Bardot, as the sex symbol of the decade. Married in 1952, Bardot and Vadim subsequently divorced; after a second marriage failed, Vadim married another of his female leads, the US actress Jane Fonda, who had starred in his remarkable science-fiction sex fantasy *Barbarella* (1967). When this marriage also collapsed he married (and divorced) the actress Catherine Deneuve. Vadim's early films were greeted as low-brow expressions of the intellectual rebelliousness that inspired the French NEW WAVE; at various points in his career he was invited to work with such contemporaries as MALLE and FELLINI. His later films have mainly been mild sex comedies and unambitious thrillers. Vadim directed a second film entitled *And God Created Woman* in 1987 but this failed to recreate the sensational impact of the original.

Vago, Pierre (1910–) French architect, born in Hungary. Vago emigrated to France in 1928 and established an architectural practice in Paris in 1934. There he studied under Auguste Perret (1874–1954), father of the architectural use of reinforced concrete, who was a most important influence on his work. Vago founded the Réunions Internationales des Architectes in 1932; subsequent conferences in 1933 and 1935 proved important meeting-points for proponents of modernism from most European countries. In 1948 this was reconstituted as the Union Internationale des Architectes, a forum for architects from both sides of the Iron Curtain. In 1947 he was appointed chief architect for the development of the historic towns of Avignon, Arles, and Beaucaire. Vago designed the library for the University of Bonn in 1968. Probably his best-known works are the Church of St Pius at Lourdes (with the engineer Eugene Freyssinet; 1958) and the museum and hostel there (1977).

Vailland, Roger (1907–65) French writer. From 1930 to 1940 Vailland was a foreign correspondent in the Balkans, the Middle East, and Ethiopia. In World War II he joined the Resistance and became a member of the Communist Party. After the war he worked as a full-time writer, quitting the party in 1956 after the Soviet-led invasion of Hungary.

Vailland's first novel, *Playing With Fire* (1945), is often considered his best. The book gives a realistic picture of a group of Resistance workers in Paris in 1944, revealing not only their heroism but also less admirable qualities such as selfishness and greed. Vailland's later novels often combine a plea for communist revolution with descriptions of romantic and physical love. He became internationally famous with his novel *The Law* (1957), which focuses on a tavern game of brute power in which the winner has the right to humiliate the loser. Set in a barren landscape near a southern Italian seaport, the novel was later filmed by Jules Dassin. His last novels *La Fête* (1960) and *A Young Trout* (1964) again take up the themes of free love and sexuality in a world largely dominated by brute force.

Valente, José Ángel (1929–) Spanish poet. Born in Orense, Galicia, Valente studied modern languages in Madrid (1947–53) and lectured at Oxford University from 1955 to 1958. He subsequently settled in Geneva. His debut volume *A Kind of Hope* (1955) and its successor, *Poems for Lazarus* (1960), both won prizes. He also published *On the Place of the Song* (1963), *Memory and Sighs* (1966), *Brief Sound* (1968), *The Innocent* (1970), and *Point Zero* (1972) amongst other collections, as well as translations of Hopkins and Cavafy and a volume of literary criticism, *The Words of the Tribe* (1971).

Typically, his poetry explores the complex emotions aroused by everyday incidents and shows a marked bias towards such sombre themes as death, exile, and the loneliness of ordinary people. Arguably the most intellectual Spanish poet of his generation, he employs a compressed and antirhetorical style that nonetheless achieves effects of great intimacy and emotional power. Although there is a strong vein of social realism in his work and he was outspoken in arguing for greater intellectual liberty in Franco's Spain, he is not primarily a political poet. He has expressed a hope that the effort of clarifying his own experience by writing about it may help others to profit from it.

Valkepää, Nils Aslak (1943–) Norwegian poet. Valkepää is the most prominent Samisk (Lapp) writer in Scandinavia and a champion of the rights of indigenous peoples worldwide. His work takes its themes from the culture and traditions of the Sami people and draws on the richness of the Samisk language in its exuberant descriptions of nature. His poetry is based on the *joik*, a rhythmical monotone chant originally employed in shamanistic rituals. Valkepää is a musician and a painter as well as a poet.

His first book *Greetings from Sami Land* (1971) introduces many of his characteristic themes, notably the relationship between Samisk life and art and the natural world. *The Ways of The Wind* (1987), a collection of poetry written between 1974 and 1981, uses new forms to convey a mystical apprehension of nature. Valkepää's most celebrated work, *The Sun, My Father* (1991), is a collection of poems and photographs assembled over a six-year period. Not only a richly imaginative work of art but also an important source of information about Samisk life and culture, this collection has been awarded a Norwegian literary prize and stands as a milestone in Samisk literature.

Valle, Gino (1923–) Italian architect, who with his father and sister founded (1952) the Studio Valle architectural practice in Udine. In 1951–52 he travelled in the US; his early Udine Savings Bank (1955) owes its tetrahedral styling to the US architect Buckminster Fuller. The Latisana Savings Bank (1956) and Treppo Carnico Town Hall (1958) are quietly understated, the latter using local stone; the Portugruaro Hospital (1955) is more aggressive. Maturity arrived with the assertive strength of his Zanussi factory at Pordenone (1959–61), 'a piece of heroic engineering' (Rayner Banham) usually considered Valle's masterpiece. His Udine Theatre (1963) maintained this textural richness, whilst his Monument to the Resistance (designed 1959, erected 1967–69) is a dramatic open box.

His industrial buildings combine great variety in style and materials with a constant predilection for prefabrication and strip windows. He has designed a number of lightweight aluminium sheet structures that he terms 'non architecture', including warehouses for Zanussi (1963), a factory for Sipre (1962–63), the Messaggero Veneto printing works (1967–68), and a factory for Zanussi at Porcia (1966–70) that features horizontal banding in vivid colours. Other buildings were precast to resemble shuttered concrete, notably Casarza Town Hall (1972–74). Concrete and aluminium are combined in his massive offices at Pordenone (1972–82). Particularly elegant are his Fantoni factory at Osoppo (1972–75), eight prefabricated schools in prestressed reinforced concrete (1974–76), and the IBM distribution centre at Basiana (1980–83). He has used colour to brighten the barest housing projects, such as those at Udine (1976–79) and Buia (1977–79), whilst those at Giudecca (1980–86) are of brick on tall piers. Brick is a feature of Valle's latest works, like his offices for Olivetti at Ivrea (1985–88). He is currently involved in regeneration projects in the Marttima docks and Valle d'Aosta.

Vampilov, Aleksandr (Valentinovich) (1937–72) Soviet playwright. Vampilov was considered the most important writer for the Soviet theatre of his generation and his brief career subsequently had a profound influence upon contemporary Eastern European drama. He began as a journalist before studying at the Gorkii Literary Institute in Moscow, during which time his short comedy *The House Overlooking a Field* (1964) was published, attracting much attention. With the encouragement of ARBUZOV and Viktor Rostov he joined the Writers' Union and went on to explore such themes as disillusion and man's relationship with nature in *Farewell in June* (1965), *The Elder Son* (1967), and other plays.

Vampilov won particular praise for *Duck Hunting* (1967) and *Last Summer in Chulimsk* (1971), in which he voiced his own bitterness and despair through the cynicism of the central characters who, driven by self-pity and hopelessness, subject each other to vicious abuse. Influenced by Gogol and Chekhov, with whom he is sometimes ranked, his plays inspired numerous other writers, the most notable being Arbuzov himself and Aleksandr Volodin. Vampilov's last plays included the unfinished farce *The Incomparable Nakonechnikov* (1971) and the double bill *Provincial Anecdotes* (1971); his career ended abruptly when he died of a heart attack following a boating accident.

van Dantzig, Rudi *See* DANTZIG, RUDI VAN.

Van Den Broek and Bakema. Dutch architectural partnership formed in 1948 by **Jacob Bakema** (1914–81) and **J. H. van den Broek** (1889–1978). Van den Broek was born in Rotterdam and trained at the Rijswerkschool, Nijmegen, working in partnership with Johannes Brinkman from 1937. Bakema, born and trained in Groningen, was the more influential, being a prolific writer as well as designer. The partnership became the largest architectural practice in the Netherlands, with over 200 staff. Both were members of Team X, the group of young architects who prepared the tenth and last Congrès Internationaux d'Architecture Moderne (CIAM), although only Bakema contributed to its publications. The partners remained loyal to modernism and the functionalism propounded by the De Stijl movement in a period when Dutch architecture saw a partial return to traditional planning. Although their output includes all building types, their most important work is in public housing, the best of which is at Leeuwarden and Kampen (1959–68). Their approach to planning is characterized by the abandonment of all traces of traditional formalism or geometry and the mixture of large and small scales. The partnership has also been responsible for notable public buildings and urban redevelopment projects, for instance the Lijnbaan in Rotterdam (1949–53), the Town Hall at Terneuzen (1961), and the Kurhaus District of Scheveningen (1973). The Lijnbaan centre was a pioneering example of the pedestrianized shopping street with tower blocks linked by lower buildings, a type that has now become familiar across Europe and North America.

van Eyck, Aldo (1918–) *See* EYCK, ALDO VAN.

Varda, Agnès *See* DEMY, JACQUES.

Vasarely, Victor de (Viktor Vasarhelyi; 1908–) French painter and sculptor, born in Hungary: the foremost pioneer of OP ART. After briefly studying medicine, Vasarely trained at a school of applied arts in Budapest (1928–29). He held his first one-man show in that city in 1930 but settled in Paris later the same year. He worked in publicity and advertising from 1936 until 1944, when he devoted himself to painting, developing his characteristic style of geometrical abstraction from about 1947 onwards. In the 1955 show 'Mouvement' at the Denise René Gallery he exhibited his first Op art works, a series of compositions in which staggered receding planes were used to create an illusion of movement. His first such works used only black and white, but he soon added other unmixed colours. Concurrently with the 1955 exhibition Vasarely expounded his radical artistic ideas in his 'yellow manifesto' *Mouvement*. Vasarely greatly influenced younger artists such as those associated with the NOUVELLE TENDANCE movement and the GROUPE DE RECHERCHE D'ART VISUEL. He has also created Op art reliefs of coloured glass and used metallic surfaces to decorate large wall spaces, as in his mural at the University of Caracas, as well as working in ceramics, tapestries, and other media.

Vasarely is represented in most major museums of modern art, including New York's Guggenheim Museum, London's Tate Gallery, and Paris's Musée St Etienne. In 1970 he opened his own Musée Didactique, which contains about 550 of his works. The Musée Vasarely was inaugurated in 1976 at his birthplace, Pécs; a Vasarely Centre opened in 1978 in New York and one in Oslo in 1982.

Vasiliov, Vladimir *See* KASATKINA, NATALIA DMITRIEVNA.

Vassalli, Sebastiano (1941–) Italian novelist and writer. Born in Genoa, he contributed to the neo-avant-garde movement of the 1960s and 1970s with such experimental narratives as *Narcissus* (1968) and *The Arrival of the Lotion* (1976). The poetry in *Shadow and Destiny* (1983) is highly critical of literary and political clichés.

In such later works as *To Inhabit the Wind* (1980) and *Blue Sea* (1982) Vassalli has adopted more traditional narrative forms without abandoning his ironic tone. More recently he has published *The Night of the Comet* (1984), a biography of the poet Dino Campana, and the novels *The Gold of the World* (1987), *The Chimera* (1990), and *Marco and Mattia* (1992).

Vauthier, Jean (1910–92) French avant-garde playwright, born in Belgium. Vauthier is best known for his plays featuring the character Captain Bada, a grotesque anti-social misogynistic figure who embodied many of the author's personal traits. Bada first appeared in *Capitaine Bada* (1952) and was revived in *Badesque* (1965), set in the afterlife. Other works include *The Fighting Character* (1956), which provided BARRAULT with one of his most famous roles, and *Blood* (1970), which was commissioned by Marcel MARÉCHAL. Vauthier also created a new version of Machiavelli's *La Mandragola* (1952) and radical adaptations of plays by Shakespeare and Euripides amongst others. His last play, *Island of Birds* (1992), was produced after his death. Vauthier's work owes much to the tradition of Artaud and the theatre of cruelty (*see* CRUELTY, THEATRE OF).

Vedova, Emilio (1919–) Italian abstract painter. Born in Venice, he began to paint at an early age but had no formal training. From the age of 17 he began to exhibit landscapes and soon developed a more contemporary style under the influence of Picasso and Georges Rouault. During World War II he opposed the Fascist regime and fought with the partisans. In 1946 he became a member of the FRONTE NUOVO DELLE ARTI, the first post-war Italian movement directed towards abstraction. When this broke up, Vedova became one of the Gruppo degli Otto Pittori Italiani (Group of Eight Italian Painters).

After early phases influenced by expressionism and cubism, Vedova developed a violent and expressive abstract style combining the dynamic-rhythmic construction of futurism and elements of post-war ART INFORMEL. Interwoven strokes, usually black, are combined with touches of intense colour. Some critics have found a political meaning in his work, seeing it as an expression of his hatred of tyranny. In 1964 Vedova began a series of experiments in spatial painting that he called *plurimi*. These consisted of panels painted on both sides and connected at various angles to form complex constructions. Vedova has held one-man shows in Germany, the US, and in South America as well as in most of Italy's major cities.

Velde, Bram van (1895–1981) Dutch abstract painter. The elder brother of Geer van Velde, he served an apprenticeship to a painter and decorator before receiving any formal training. In the early 1920s he stayed at Worpswede, the German artistic colony, where he absorbed the expressionist heritage, and then studied in Paris, where he came under the influence of first fauvism and then cubism. Apart from a few years painting on Majorca (1932–36), he spent the rest of his active years in Paris. He died in Geneva.

Bram van Velde's early paintings are mainly landscapes and still lifes rendered in vivid expressionistic colours. During the 1930s his subjects became increasingly obscured by his treatment and before the outbreak of World War II he had developed a completely abstract approach. After the war his reputation as one of the most original exponents of European expressive abstraction (*see* ART INFORMEL) grew steadily. His most characteristic works feature somewhat amorphous coloured shapes, often vaguely suggestive of figures or faces, superimposed on a monochrome background. Bram van Velde's painting found an early champion in Samuel BECKETT, who described it as "primarily a painting of the thing in a state of suspense...the thing alone...the thing immobile in the void."

Velde, Geer van (1898–1977) Dutch abstract painter. Born at Lisse, the younger brother of Bram van Velde, he received no formal training as a painter. He settled in Paris in 1925 and the following year exhibited at the Salon des Indépendants. His works were also shown at the Salon de Mai, the Salon d'Automne, and the Salon des Tuileries. He moved to Cagnes-sur-Mer during World War II, returning to Paris in 1946 for a one-man show at the Galerie Maeght. Two years later he held a joint exhibition with his brother at the Kootz Gallery in New York.

Geer van Velde made his reputation with his numerous abstracts in light delicate colours (most often blues); an example is *Composition* (1948, private collection). Although his paintings usually have a geometrical framework his forms often suggest features of the external world – often an interior as in *Les Outils Naturels* (1946, private collection).

Vesaas, Tarjei (1897–1970) Norwegian novelist, poet, and playwright. Vesaas wrote in Nynorsk, the less common form of the Norwegian language. He is recognized as one of the greatest Norwegian writers of the century.

Vesaas made his literary debut in 1923 and continued to write successfully until his death. His earlier books mostly deal in a realistic vein with life in Norway's traditional rural communities and consider the search for meaning and identity in life. His breakthrough came in 1928 with the novel *The Black Horses,* which was followed by a further seven novels and two short-story collections in ten years. His later works are highly lyrical and characterized by the use of symbolism drawn from the natural world. During World War II he wrote *The Seed* (1940), describing the spread of evil and mass violence, and *House in the Dark* (1945), an allegory about the occupation of Norway. Later works include *The Birds* (1957), a novel with a mentally subnormal hero, *The Ice-Palace* (1963), a lyrical story of the friendship of two young girls for which Vesaas won the Nordisk Råd Prize for literature, and *The Bridges* (1966), in which he experiments with style, mixing the realistic with the fantastic. Vesaas published several later collections of short stories including *The Winds* (1952) and *The Boat in the Evening* (1968), which is partly autobiographical. His poetry, published in six collections, is similar in theme to his novels. His work has been translated into many languages and filmed in Norway and abroad. He was married to the poet Halldis Moren Vesaas.

Vestdijk, Simon (1898–1971) Dutch novelist, poet, and essayist. After studying medicine Vestdijk worked for some years as a ship's doctor but in 1933 decided to live as a writer and journalist. He lived in the same small village in Utrecht from 1939 until his death. Between 1932 and 1971 Vestdijk published some 40 novels, 10 collections of short stories, 30 books of criticism and essays – many of them about music – and 20 volumes of poetry. He is usually considered the most important Dutch writer of the mid century.

As a novelist, Vestdijk advocated a clear sober style and called himself a 'psychological realist'. Among his best-known works are the eight volumes of the 'Anton Wachter' sequence based on the author's younger years. The key to the entire series is the unhappy love affair of the 14-year-old protagonist, described in minute psychological detail in the volume *Back to*

Ina Damman (1934). In other novels Vestdijk described the destruction of true love by the prejudices of provincial Dutch society (*The Garden Where the Brass Band Played*; 1950). The tone of his work is often bitter.

Vestdijk also wrote a number of historical novels set in various places and times; these are notable for their wealth of meticulously researched detail as well as their psychological portraits of well-known historical figures (Pontius Pilate and El Greco amongst others).

Viani, Alberto (1906–) Italian sculptor. Born at Quistello, Mantua, he studied at the Academy of Art in Venice, where he was a pupil of the sculptor Arturo Martini (1889–1947). He subsequently moved to Venice and began to shift from his early classicism to a semiabstract style featuring simplified forms that are often suggestive of the female body. Major influences on his later work were Constantin Brancusi and the surrealist sculptor Hans Arp. In 1946 Viani became a member of the FRONTE NUOVO DELLE ARTI, Italy's first important abstract movement. He worked mostly in marble.

Vieira da Silva, Maria Hélèna (1908–92) French abstract painter and engraver born in Lisbon, Portugal. In 1927 she settled in Paris, where she studied printmaking with Stanley HAYTER and painting with Roger Bissiére, Fernand Léger, and Othon Friesz. In 1930 she married the Hungarian abstract painter Arpad Szenés. During the 1930s Vieira de Silva moved away from her early expressionist style to become a mainly abstract painter, exhibiting regularly at the Salon de Mai. Her works – such as *Composition* (1934, private collection, Paris) – are characterized by neutral backgrounds of soft greys and whites with random lines or flecks of almost iridescent greens, blues, oranges, and violets superimposed to form diagonals or net-like patterns.

Vieira de Silva moved to Brazil for the duration of World War II, where she further developed her style by juxtaposing square, rectangle, and diamond shapes to create a sense of twisting movement across the canvas. After her return to Paris in 1947 she quickly gained recognition as a leading exponent of expressive abstraction (*see* ART INFORMEL). She exhibited frequently in New York, Paris, and London and in her later years received honours from both the French and Portuguese governments.

Vienna Actionists (Wiener Aktionismus) *See* BRÜS, GÜNTER; MUEHL, OTTO; NITSCH, HERMANN.

Vienna Festival (Wiener Festwochen) An annual music festival held for a fortnight in June in Vienna. It was founded in 1951 and concentrates on opera, although the programme also includes ballet. Every other year it links up with festivals promoted by the Gesellschaft der Musikfreunde, a Viennese music society (established 1812) whose conservatory is the city's leading music school.

Vik, Bjørg (1935–) Norwegian writer. Vik began to write short stories while working as a journalist and in 1963 published the novella collection *Sunday Afternoon*. The short story remains her favoured genre but since the publication of *Two Acts for Five Women* in 1974 she has written several dramatic pieces that have been successfully staged in Norway.

Her early work created a public outcry with its open discussion of sexual matters as seen from a female perspective. Vik was the first writer to bring the feminist issues of the 1970s to public consciousness in Norway, writing of the repressive upbringing and systematic exploitation of women both at home and in the workplace. Her most popular work to date, *An Aquarium of Women* (1972), is a cycle of nine stories dealing with the factors that inhibit women's potential, from the socialization of girls and adolescents, to the disillusionment of middle age, and the problems of women seeking to redefine the female role.

In later collections such as *Soon it Will be Autumn* (1982) and *A Forgotten Petunia* (1985) Vik adopts a less oppositional stance; her protest emerges more subtly from the content of the stories, which tend to dwell on the frustrations of everyday life. Her ability to evoke the significance of the everyday in a few simple sentences and her gift for dialogue have made her one of Norway's most accessible and widely read authors.

Vilar, Jean (1912–71) French theatre director and actor, who exerted a profound influence upon French theatre through his attempts to create a new drama of political and social relevance that was accessible to all. Having trained with Dullin, Vilar began working as a director during World War II, presenting avant-garde productions of Strindberg and other modern playwrights. In 1947 he founded the **Avignon Festival** as a showcase for contemporary drama in the provinces; the success of the festival, now France's most important such event, did much to promote the policy of DÉCENTRALISATION DRAMATIQUE and provided Vilar with the opportunity to develop the techniques that he subsequently applied to productions in Paris and elsewhere.

Vilar attracted particular attention with his austere sets, which were equally suitable for both classical and modern plays. He was also admired as an actor, especially when appearing alongside Gérard Philipe. His efforts to open up the theatre to all classes were rewarded in 1951, when he was appointed head of the revived **Théâtre National Populaire** at Chaillot, which he transformed, dispensing with all the paraphenalia of footlights, curtains, and painted scenery and presenting demanding new works by such authors as BRECHT and T. S. Eliot alongside the classics. In 1963 he left Chaillot in order to return to Avignon, where he undeservedly became a target for left-wing demonstrators during the upheaval of 1968.

Vilikovský, Pavel (1941–) Slovak prose writer. While still an undergraduate reading Slovak and English at Bratislava, he joined the editorial board of the chief Slovak literary journal, which he was obliged to leave for political reasons in 1970; he was able to join another journal, *Romboid*, in 1976, where he still works. His first book, a collection of lyrical short stories, *A Sentimental Education in March* (1965), gives very few indications of his later development. He was not allowed to publish another book until 1983, when the novel *The First Movement of Sleep* appeared; it is a wry account of a society in which almost everyone plays selfish games with everyone else. Vilikovský came into his own with a satirical novel written in the 1970s, *Ever Green is the...* (1989), whose narrator, a secret agent with a forged British passport, is being interrogated sitting over a bath of sulphuric acid on a spike of ice rammed up his rectum; the ice is slowly melting. Set mainly in Slovakia and Bucharest, the novel satirizes national, social, and political myths, jargon, sex and sexology, the military, spies and spying, the Cold War and détente, socialism and capitalism, Czech-Slovak relations, and ideas of Slovak identity. Such ideas are also satirized in the short-story collection *The Escalation of Emotion* (1989); on the whole, however, an ironic attitude towards modern man's lack of spirituality, rather than social satire, dominates this work. The starting-point of *A Slovak Casanova* (1991) is the idea of the party bureaucrat as primarily an orgiast; the novella develops into a witty satire on communist hypocrisy, moral opportunism, scientific atheism, and the rule of fear within the party.

Vinaver, Michel (Michel Grinberg; 1927–) French playwright and novelist, who emerged as a leading writer for the French stage in the 1950s. Having begun his career as a novelist, he attracted attention in the theatre with *The Koreans* (1956), which was staged by Roger PLANCHON and depicted the contrasting experiences of French soldiers and Korean peasants during the Korean War. Subsequent plays have included *Iphigénie Hotel* (1960), about De Gaulle's return to power in 1959, *Overboard* (1972), a highly comic portrayal of life in a toilet roll company, and *A Smile on the End of the Line* (1979), similarly depicting the experiences of a group of employees in a small company. These last two plays reflect Vinaver's former employment as a business executive. Generally realistic in style, Vinaver's plays have been linked with the Théâtre du Quotidien (*see* QUOTIDIEN, THÉÂTRE DU), although several of his works also call on mythology and employ non-naturalistic devices.

Vincent, Jean-Pierre (1942–) French theatre director, who came to prominence during the 1970s. A cofounder of the Théâtre de l'Espérance at the Montmartre Palace in 1972, he won acclaim for his productions of plays by BRECHT, Büchner, and modern French writers. He transferred to the Théâtre National de Strasbourg in 1975 and in 1983 crowned his career by becoming director of the Comédie-Française, resigning three years later. His most admired productions include works belonging to the tradition of the Théâtre du Quotidien (*see* QUOTIDIEN, THÉÂTRE DU), influenced by contemporary German drama, and adaptations of novels by Zola and other French and German novelists.

Vinogradov, Oleg Mikhailovich (1937–) Russian dancer, choreographer, and ballet master, who in 1972 became artistic director of the Kirov Ballet. Vinogradov began his career as a choreographer working on operatic productions with the Novosibirsk Theatre company. In 1964 he choreographed Prokofiev's *Cinderella*, following this a year later with the same composer's *Romeo and Juliet*. Both productions were praised for their innovative staging and established Vinogradov as one of the most promising choreographers of his generation. He took over the Kirov Ballet in 1972, where his productions have included *Useless Precautions* (1971), *Coppélia* (1973), and *The Battleship Potemkin* (1983).

Visconti, Luchino (Count Don Luchino Visconti di Morone; 1906–76) Italian film and theatre director, noted for his opulent productions of films, plays, operas, and ballets. Visconti was born into an aristocratic family in Milan and showed an interest in horse-breeding before entering the theatre as a set designer. He subsequently designed costumes and worked as an assistant to the film director Jean Renoir. He made his debut as a director with *Obsession* (1942), a reworking of *The Postman Always Rings Twice*, in which he demonstrated an interest in NEOREALISM, although his later films moved away from a naturalistic style. The implied homosexuality of one of the characters and the film's preoccupation with moral failure led to its being banned by the Fascist authorities.

The director's Marxist sympathies were evident in several post-war films showing the hardships suffered by the poor in rural Italy and the disappointments experienced by those hoping to better their lot. *Senso* (1954), about an adulterous romance between an Italian countess and an Austrian officer, was also broadly political although the lavish settings and historical authenticity of the film were perhaps its strongest features.

After *White Nights* (1957), an intense love story based on a tale by Dostoevskii, Visconti was widely praised for *Rocco and his Brothers* (1960), a powerful account of a family's disintegration in the face of a variety of crises. Visconti's love of the historical epic was indulged to the full in his next film, *The Leopard* (1963; from the novel by LAMPEDUSA), which won the Golden Palm award at the CANNES FILM FESTIVAL.

Subsequent work included *The Damned* (1969), an uneasy tale of decadence in Nazi Germany starring Dirk Bogarde, and the moving *Death in Venice* (1971), in which Bogarde played a composer whose infatuation with a young boy leads him to remain in the plague-ridden city, where finally he dies. Visconti ended his career with *Ludwig* (1972), an extravagant portrait of the 'mad' king of Bavaria, *Conversation Piece* (1974), a subtle study of old age and death, and *The Innocent* (1976), a period piece about marital infidelity.

As a stage director, Visconti concentrated on modern dramas that reflected his socialist principles, although he was also praised for his productions of plays by Goldoni, Shakespeare, and Chekhov. As a director of opera he was particularly admired for his Verdi productions.

Vitez, Antoine (1930–) French theatre director and actor, born in Russia, who is noted for his radical left-wing political stance. Vitez emerged as a leading director in the 1960s, working under VILAR and at various venues in the provinces under the policy of DÉCENTRALISATION DRAMATIQUE. He served (1971–80) as director of the Théâtre des Quartiers d'Ivry and subsequently (from 1981) as director of the theatre at Chaillot, consolidating his reputation for politically committed and technically experimental work. His productions have ranged from the classics to plays by such modern playwrights as BRECHT and Claudel. He is particularly admired for his creative approach to the text, encouraging performers to explore their own physical and intellectual reactions to the script.

Vittorini, Elio (1908–66) Italian novelist and literary critic. Born into a working-class family on Sicily, Vittorini left school at 17 and worked as a labourer and a proofreader for a newspaper. Having taught himself English, he began to publish the translations of English and US literature that were his main source of income until World War II. His translations of Faulkner, Hemingway, and others make him (with PAVESE) one of the pioneers of American studies in Italy.

In the 1930s Vittorini published a number of short stories and his first novel, *The Red Carnation* (1933), which sets the personal and sexual difficulties of an adolescent boy against the political turbulence of the Fascist era. This was followed by his most significant novel, *Conversation in Italy* (1941), in which the narrator makes an anguished return to the island in search of his roots; the mood is one of personal and political despair. The Fascist authorities interfered with the publication of both novels and interned their author in 1943.

After World War II Vittorini emerged as one of the leaders of left-wing thought in Italy. His journals *Il Politecnico* (1945–47) and *Il Memabò* (1959–67) became a focus for spirited and controversial debates about literature, culture, and society. Vittorini's post-war novels were *Men and Not Men* (1945), an epic account of the Resistance movement in Milan, *The Twilight of the Elephant* (1947), and *Women of Messina* (1949); in 1956 he published the unfinished *Erica* and *The Garibaldina*, a story of a girl who, during the Depression, resorts to prostitution to feed her younger brothers. After this he published no new fiction, concentrating on his work as a literary critic and theorist. An important collection of critical essays, *The Two Tensions*, was published posthumously in 1967.

Vlach Quartet Czech string quartet, founded in Prague in 1951. The current members are Josef Vlach (first violin), Václav Snítil (second violin), Josef Kodousek (viola), and Viktor Moučka (cello). The original members, all players in the Czech Chamber Orchestra under Václav Talich, were Vlach (whose name the quartet took), Snítil, Saběslav Soukup (viola), and Moučka.

The quartet was for some years associated with the Prague National Theatre, where they played both as an ensemble and as orchestral members until 1957. The quartet came to prominence in 1955, when they won the Liège International Quartet Competition. Until 1971 they were the resident chamber ensemble for Prague radio. Vlach himself remained leader of the Czech Chamber Orchestra and a guest conductor with the Czech Philharmonic Orchestra. All the quartet members teach at the Prague Conservatory and Academy of Musical Arts. They perform and have recorded the standard quartet repertory, with special emphasis on the works of Czechoslovakian composers such as Dvořák, Smetana, and Janáček.

Vladimov, Georgii Nikolaevich (Georgii Nikolaevich Volosevich; 1931–) Russian novelist living in Germany. Born into a family of teachers, he studied law before beginning work as a critic in 1954, and serving as an editor on the prestigious literary journal *Novy Mir* from 1956 to 1959. His short novel, *The Great Ore* (1961), was written in the realistic mode to which Vladimov has remained faithful but was notable for avoiding the false glorification of labour then still characteristic of Soviet prose. Similarly true to life was *Three Minutes of Silence* (1969, revised 1982), a novel about work on the North Atlantic fishing fleet, again emphasizing the strain of hard physical work and the conflicts arising between individuals and the authorities. Vladimov's masterpiece, however, is *Faithful Ruslan* (1975), the allegorical story of a guard dog who proves unable to adjust to a new way of life when the camp in which he worked closes. For many years this affecting and resonant story circulated anonymously in *samizdat*, attracting various attributions, but after his enforced exile in 1983 (the result of a consistently liberal public stance), Vladimov was able to claim authorship of this brilliant and original piece of prison-camp literature. Before his exile the writer had suffered considerable KGB harrassment, described with dignity in a chilling short documentary story, *Pay No Attention, Maestro* (1983). In the West Vladimov's high principles have also brought him into conflict with some émigré factions, but he has continued to write. His latest major work, *The General and his Army* (1990) is about World War II, the first of his novels on this theme.

Voinovich, Vladimir Nikolaevich (1932–) Russian satirist living in Germany. After various manual jobs and four years as a private in the Red Army, he began to write in 1960. Voinovich's early stories, which provided realistic pictures of Soviet rural and urban life, soon aroused controversy by depicting endemic cynicism and disillusion, as in 'I Want to Be Honest' (1963) or 'Two Comrades' (1967). In 1975, however, he committed the ultimate sacrilege by publishing in Paris a hugely comic novel set at the time of the German invasion of the Soviet Union, *The Life and Adventures of Private Ivan Chonkin*. In complete contrast to the official literature of heroic glorification, this novel (which had long circulated in *samizdat*) portrays the conflict as a farce and the eponymous hero as a voice of almost simple-minded sanity amidst the lunacy of Stalin's Russia. The sequel, *Pretender to the Throne* (1979), is more bitterly satirical but lacks its predecessor's lightness of touch. In 1974 Voinovich had been expelled from the Writers' Union for his too independent political stance and there ensued various kinds of harrassment, from an inept attempt to keep him out of a flat to which he was entitled, hilariously described in *The Ivankiad* (1976), to sinister intimidation, including poisoning, by the KGB. Forced to emigrate in 1980, he has continued to write in exile. *The Anti-Soviet Soviet Union* (1985) is a collection of short satirical essays on life, literature, and politics in the USSR. Other notable works include a play, *Tribunal* (1985), and an ambitious satire, *Moscow 2042* (1986), which mocks many features of Brezhnev's regime by taking them to their logical conclusion in an imaginary Moscow of the 21st century.

von Karajan, Herbert *See* KARAJAN, HERBERT VON.

von Rosen, Elsa-Marianne (1927–) Swedish ballet dancer and choreographer, who was a ballerina with the Royal Swedish ballet in the 1950s and subsequently led a number of distinguished dance companies. Having trained at the Royal Danish Ballet School, she won acclaim as a dancer with the Ballets Russes de Monte Carlo and in 1950 cofounded the Swedish Ballet with her husband. She danced all the major ballet parts with the company over the next decade, creating the title roles in CULLBERG's *Miss Julie* (1950) and *Medea* (1951). She established the short-lived Scandinavian Ballet in 1960 and toured Sweden, Germany, and Denmark, before disbanding the troupe a year later. Since then she has worked with the Ballet Rambert (*see* RAMBERT DANCE COMPANY), the Royal Danish Ballet, and – as ballet director (1970–76) – with the Gothenburg Ballet. She is particularly noted for her productions of the ballets of August Bournonville and has choreographed several ballets herself, including *La Sylphide* (1960), *Don Juan* (1967), *Swan Lake* (1971), and *A Girl's Story* (1975), which used rock music by Emerson, Lake and Palmer.

von Trotta, Margarethe *See* SCHLÖNDORFF, VOLKER.

Vormingstoneel (Dutch: education theatre) A theatre movement of the early 1970s that did much to promote the performance of politically aware drama in both Belgium and the Netherlands. The late 1960s and early 1970s saw the emergence of a number of companies in both countries who emphasized the theatre's role as an agent of social change. Drawing on the theatre of BRECHT and Marxist ideology, they took drama into the heart of the community, with performances in schools, factories, etc. and encouraged discussion of the issues raised with audiences afterwards. Although much of the work done by companies associated with the Vormingstoneel movement had a strong educative element, the Dutch companies lost state support in the mid 1980s and the movement as a whole failed to survive.

Vostell, Wolf (1932–) German collage artist and creator of HAPPENINGS. He was born at Leverkusen on the Rhine and studied graphic techniques, especially photolithography, in Cologne (1950–53). He continued his lengthy training with studies in painting and typography at Wuppertal (1954–55), the Ecole des Beaux-Arts in Paris (1955–56), and the Düsseldorf Academy (1956–57). In 1956 Vostell began to produce his *décollages*, a type of anti-collage created by tearing pieces off posters and other pre-existing images rather than by assembly. The results were often overpainted or scribbled on by Vostell. In the late 1950s he came to international attention with a series of 'Décollages-Happenings' held in Ulm, Wuppertal, Berlin, New York and elsewhere. These were ritual actions with an emphasis on violence and destruction.

Voznesensky, Andrei Andreevich (1933–) Russian poet, one of the most prominent of the THAW generation. Born into an intellectual Muscovite family – his father was a professor of engineering – Voznesensky was evacuated to the Urals during World War II. Originally a student of architecture, he made his name in the literary world with two collections published in 1960, *Mosaic* and *Parabola*. In the same year, together with his almost exact contemporary Evgenii EVTUSHENKO, Voznesensky visited the US. Since then he has made frequent visits abroad and his enduring fascination with the mutual influence of Russia and the US can be seen throughout his work, notably in the long poem *Perchance* (1970). Voznesensky, like Evtushenko, is famous for his public recitations of his work, particularly the heavily assonantal and onomatopoeic 'Goya' (1959); in 1962 he was among the poets who drew an audience of 14 000 to the Luzhniki Ice Hockey Stadium in Moscow. His career appeared to falter briefly after a brush with the Soviet literary bureaucracy in 1967 but revived with the publication of *The Shadow of Sound* (1970) and *Look* (1972). His *Collected Works* appeared in 1983 and in the Gorbachev era he again became a spokesman for the new freedoms, notably in his outspoken long poem *The Ditch* (1986), which deals with the desecration of the site of a wartime atrocity. In 1987 he became Chairman of the Legacy of PASTERNAK, a poet whose profound influence on him is recorded in the prose piece 'I am Fourteen' (1980).

Voznesensky's thematic range is wide and his style innovative to the point, on occasions, of obscurity. A leitmotif in his work is the isolation of the individual, particularly the artist, a theme which he develops through a series of historical parallels in such poems as *Craftsmen* (1957) and a series of poems dedicated to Michelangelo (1975). Voznesensky's work has been translated into English by, among others, W. H. Auden.

Vysotskii, Vladimir Semenovich (1938–80) Russian songwriter, poet, and actor. Brought up near Berlin, where his father served in the army, he studied at the Moscow Art Theatre Drama School and acted in various Moscow theatres before in 1964 joining Iurii LIUBIMOV's Taganka Theatre, where he soon became a major star. In addition to his acting career Vysotskii quickly established a parallel reputation as a guitar poet, whose songs about myriad aspects of Soviet life and history touched a nerve throughout Russia, circulating by means of crude amateur recordings from unofficial recitals. The texts of Vysotskii's songs were not published in his lifetime and yet many were widely known by heart, such was the vitality of his personality and the recognized truth of his work. Marriage to the French actress Marina Vlady enabled him to travel, and he made some notable recordings at concerts in Paris, New York, and Toronto, although for many admirers the old amateur tapes contain his most authentic performances. Vysotskii's early death as a result of alcohol and drug abuse was deliberately given no official recognition and yet his funeral attracted tens of thousands of mourners from all ranks of society – a unique event in the history of the Soviet Union. After his death an authorized collection of 300 partially censored poems, *Nerve* (1981), appeared and just as quickly disappeared (a train load of copies was hijacked in central Russia); subsequently a smuggled Western facsimile edition of this book circulated widely. But it is the US-published three-volume edition *Songs and Verses* (1981–83) that provides the best memorial to a man whose songs captured with both humour and pathos the poetry and squalor of Soviet life.

W

Wajda, Andrzej (1926–) Polish film director, widely considered the most important figure in contemporary Polish cinema. After World War II, during which he fought with the Resistance, Wajda studied at the film school at Łódź and made a number of shorts. His first feature film was *A Generation* (1954), the first of a trilogy depicting the horrors of the war. Both *A Generation* and *Kanal* (1957) dealt with the activities of the Resistance in Warsaw, while the third part of the trilogy, *Ashes and Diamonds* (1958; from the novel by ANDRZEJEWSKI), focused on a young antihero whose plans to kill a communist official end in his own death. The central role was played by Zbigniew Cybulski, who thereby acquired the status of a Polish James Dean. Wajda subsequently experimented with a wider range of subjects, from *Innocent Sorcerers* (1960), which voiced the frustrations of modern youth, to *The Siberian Lady Macbeth* (1961).

His next major triumph came with *Everything for Sale* (1968), about the traumas of a film crew when the leading actor goes missing; the film was partly inspired by the accidental death of Cybulski, whose career had become inseparable from that of the director. Less remarkable films followed, among them *The Birchwood* (1971), *The Wedding* (1972), and *The Shadow Line* (1976). Wajda's next significant achievement, *Man of Marble* (1977), was banned in Poland but won international acclaim for its scathing indictment of official corruption. Similar political themes were addressed in *Rough Treatment* (1978) and *Man of Iron* (1981), in which the Polish state is shown conducting a smear campaign against Solidarity activists. Subsequent films have included the historical dramas *Danton* (1982), starring Gérard Depardieu; *A Love in Germany* (1983), based on a novel by Rolf HOCHHUTH; and *Korczak* (1990), which recounts the heroic efforts of a Polish-Jewish doctor to assist the children of the Warsaw ghetto during the German occupation. Wajda was a senator of the Polish Republic from 1989 until 1991.

Wakhévitch, Georges (1907–84) Soviet art director for the stage and the international cinema, who worked with such directors as Renoir, BUÑUEL, and Peter BROOK. Born in Odessa, he studied painting and the decorative arts in Paris before working as an assistant art director to Lazare Meerson on various French films of the 1920s. Wakhévitch subsequently designed sets and costumes for Hollywood, as well as for the theatre, opera, and ballet. Films to feature his work include *Madame Bovary* (1934), Renoir's *La Grande Illusion* (1937) the British production of *The Beggar's Opera* (1953), the US production of *King of Kings* (1961), Buñuel's *Diary of a Chambermaid* (1964), the British-French *Mayerling* (1968), and the British-Danish *King Lear* (1970). His artwork was especially appropriate in two films with Georgian themes, *Pirosmani* (1973), an attentive look at a Georgian primitive artist, and the flamboyant musical *Melodies of the Veriyski Neighbourhood* (1974). Wakhévitch's brother, Eldar, was a film director.

Walser, Martin (1927–) German writer. After growing up in Wasserburg and Lindau, Walser studied literature, history, and philosophy in Regensburg and Tübingen. He received his doctorate (1951) for a thesis on Franz Kafka. In 1953 he became a member of GRUPPE 47. Today he lives on Lake Constance.

Walser is the novelist of the post-war German middle class. Typically, he portrays male protagonists in their struggles to climb the social ladder and to fulfil the other expectations of their class. This is the topic of *Marriage in Philippsburg* (1957), in which the journalist Hans Beaumann succeeds in becoming a respected member of middle-class society, yet only at the price of self-alienation. The next three novels *Half-Time* (1960), *The Unicorn* (1966), and *The Fall* (1973), depict the personal and professional frustrations of Anselm Kristlein, who drops his studies in order to become a salesman. Walser's characters, who tend to suffer from a lack of self-confidence and clear identity, generally fall back on a strategy of resignation in order to survive in the alienating environment of the business world. Other works of fiction include *The Swan House* (1980), *Letter to Lord Liszt* (1982), *Breakers* (1985), and *The Defence of Childhood* (1991). He has also written plays and numerous essays.

Walter, Erich (1927–) German dancer, choreographer, and ballet director, who emerged as one of the most influential contemporary German choreographers in the 1950s. Having begun his career with the Nuremberg Opera Ballet (1946–50), Walter subsequently joined the Göttingen Ballet (1950–51) and the Wiesbaden Ballet (1951–53) before becoming ballet master of the Wuppertal company (1953–64), which he transformed into one of the most important European troupes. Here he made his debut as a choreographer (in collaboration with the designer Heinrich Wendel).

After such early successes as *Pelleas and Melisande* (1955), *Jeux* (1958), *Romeo and Juliet* (1959), *L'Orfeo* (1961), and *Ondine* (1962), he was appointed ballet director of Düsseldorf's German Opera on the Rhine (1964), which he likewise built up into one of the country's most prestigious companies. Among his many highly praised ballets for this and other companies have been *Dance Around the Golden Calf* (1968), *Le Sacre du Printemps* (1970), *Third Symphony* (1974), and *Fantaisies* (1980).

Walton, Sir William (1902–83) British composer. Walton trained as a chorister and then studied music at Christ Church, Oxford but was largely self-taught as a composer. In 1919 he was befriended by the Sitwell family, who supported him during the first decade of his career as a composer. Most notable among his early works is the entertainment *Façade* (1923), a setting of Edith Sitwell's poetry, which shows the influence of jazz and the chic witty world of POULENC and Les Six. At about the same time, Walton became acquainted with the music of Schoenberg and wrote a string quartet which Berg admired, although it was subsequently withdrawn by the composer. The viola concerto (1929) established his mature style, which is predominantly lyrical and romantic with occasional touches of parody and humour.

His short oratorio *Belshazzar's Feast* (1931) combines the English choral tradition of Handel, Stanford, and Elgar with the exotic orchestration of Ravel and Stravinsky. His later works are mostly for large orchestra; these include two symphonies (1935, 1960), *Variations on a Theme by Hindemith* (1963), and the operas *Troilus and Cressida* (1954) and *The Bear* (1967). Other works include the ballets *The Wise Virgins* (1940) and *The Quest* (1943), songs, chamber music, and church music. He was also a skilled writer of atmospheric film music, notably for OLIVIER's productions of *Hamlet*, *Henry V*, and *Richard III*. Most of Walton's later music was written on the Italian island of Ischia, where he settled in 1949.

Ward, Edmund *See* GOLLINS, MELVIN, WARD.

Warsaw Autumn Festival An annual music festival held each autumn in Warsaw, Poland. Established in 1956, it promotes the work of Polish and East European composers and performers, with an emphasis on newly commissioned and experimental work.

Waugh, Evelyn (1903–66) British novelist. Waugh was educated at Lancing and Hertford College, Oxford, where he mixed in high society and with such aesthetes as Harold Acton. After graduating with a third-class degree in modern history he worked as a teacher, a profession which provided material for his first novel *Decline and Fall* (1928), a brilliant farce that won instant critical acclaim. It was followed by *Vile Bodies* (1930), a satire set in the London of the Bright Young Things. During the 1930s Waugh travelled extensively in Africa and South America, publishing three works of travel journalism, *Remote People* (1931), *Ninety-Two Days* (1934), and *Waugh in Abyssinia* (1936). His African experiences are reflected in *Black Mischief* (1932) and *Scoop* (1938). After a brief, bitterly unhappy, marriage he was received into the Roman Catholic Church in 1930; this experience may account for the darkening tone in *A Handful of Dust* (1934), perhaps the finest of his early works. In 1939 Waugh was commissioned into the Royal Marines, serving in the Middle East and Yugoslavia. His wartime experiences feature in the *Sword of Honour* trilogy, *Men at Arms* (1952), *Officers and Gentlemen* (1955), and *Unconditional Surrender* (1961). His most popular work is *Brideshead Revisited* (1945), a sumptuous elegy for the English aristocracy in the century of the common man. Other works include *The Loved One* (1948) and the excoriating self-caricature *The Ordeal of Gilbert Pinfold* (1957).

Weigel, Helene *See* BRECHT, (EUGEN) BERTOLT (FRIEDRICH).

Weir, Judith (1954–) Scottish composer. Born in Aberdeen, she studied with John TAVENER and later with Robin Holloway at Cambridge University. She also experimented (1973) with computer music at MIT. Weir has taught at the Universities of Glasgow and Cambridge and is currently composer in residence at the Royal Scottish Academy of Music and Drama. Although she came to the attention of the critics with such pieces as *The Art of Touching the Keyboard* (1983) for piano, it was with her opera *A Night at the Chinese Opera* (1987) that she found a wider audience. A second opera, *The Vanishing Bridegroom*, was performed in 1990. 1992 saw the premiere of *The Small Moments (in Life)*, a theatrical piece worked out with the director Martin Duncan, and *I Broke Off a Golden Branch*, a piano quintet.

Weiss, Peter (Ulrich) (1916–82) Swedish playwright, artist, novelist, and theatre director, born in Germany; he is best known for the savage work of DOCUMENTARY THEATRE usually known as the *Marat/Sade* (1964). Titled in full *The Persecution and Assassination of Jean-Paul Marat as Performed by the Inmates of the Asylum of Charenton under the Direction of the Marquis de Sade*, it provided the ROYAL SHAKESPEARE COMPANY with one of its most notable early successes (under the direction of Peter BROOK).

Subsequent plays, which became increasingly political, included *The Investigation* (1965), a dramatization of events during a recent war crimes trial that was staged simultaneously in 14 German theatres. This success was followed by *The Tower* (1967), *Vietnam Discourse* (1968), *The Insurance* (1969), *Trotsky in Exile* (1970), *Hölderlin* (1971), and *The New Investigation* (1981).

Wekworth, Manfred (1929–) German theatre director, who established his reputation working with BRECHT and the BERLINER ENSEMBLE in the early 1950s; he became chief director of the company in 1963 and manager in 1977. His collaborations with Brecht included adaptations of plays by Gorkii and Shakespeare among others. In 1971 he left the Berliner Ensemble for six years, arguing that the company had moved away from Brecht's original concept; during this period he worked with the British National Theatre and elsewhere. His many theoretical writings on the theatre have included *Brecht?* (1968) and *Theatre in Discussion* (1982).

Weldon, Fay (Franklin Birkinshaw; 1931–) British novelist, dramatist, and screenwriter. Although born in England, Weldon was brought up in a family of women in New Zealand. After studying economics and psychology at the University of St Andrews she worked for a time in advertising and began to write for television. Her first novel, *The Fat Woman's Joke*, was published in 1967. She was closely involved in the British women's movement in the late 1960s and early 1970s, and sexual politics and the role of women in society remain major themes in her work. Her novels combine acerbic social comedy with a vein of macabre fantasy. The author's tone is generally one of caustic disenchantment. Her earlier works include *Down Among the Women* (1971), *Female Friends* (1975), and *Praxis* (1978). *Puffball* (1980), one of several novels to show an interest in women's reproductive role, deals with a young couple stranded in a rural idyll that soon develops into a nightmare. With their short scenes and pointed dialogue her novels often resemble screenplays and have adapted well for television. In this way several of her later novels have reached a large audience, notably *The Life and Loves of a She-Devil* (1983), *The Heart of the Country* (1987), and *The Cloning of Joanna May* (1989). Her most recent novels are *Darcy's Utopia* (1990), *Growing Rich* (1991), and *Life Force* (1992).

Welsh National Opera (WNO) An opera company based in Cardiff, founded in

1946. Originally an amateur company that engaged professional soloists and orchestral players, it has evolved into a wholly professional body. It is noted for its chorus and for its innovative productions of both mainstream and new works, often with invited foreign producers. Productions have included Wagner's *Ring* cycle (produced by Göran Järvefeld; completed 1986), Berlioz's *The Trojans* (1987), and works commissioned from such Welsh composers as Alun HODDINOTT and William Mathias. Musical directors have included Charles GROVES (1961–63), Richard Armstrong (1973–86), and Charles Mackerras (since 1987). The WNO orchestra was formed in 1970 as the **Welsh Philharmonia**, a name it retained until 1979.

Wenders, Wim (Wilhelm Wenders; 1945–) German film director, whose films mostly concern the search for personal identity in contemporary society. Wenders emerged as an important talent in European cinema in the 1970s, having trained at the film school in Munich and begun his career making short documentaries. His first major feature, *The Goalkeeper's Fear of the Penalty* (1971; from the novel by Peter HANDKE), established the existential preoccupations that were to dominate much of his later work. As with several other films by Wenders the soundtrack included US rock music – a reflection of the director's love-hate attitude towards US popular culture.

After a screen version of Hawthorne's *The Scarlet Letter* (1972), Wenders made *Alice in the Cities* (1974), about a girl's search for her grandmother in a Germany that has surrendered itself almost completely to the materialist values of the US. Wenders then directed two films in the tradition of the US road movie, *Wrong Movement* (1975; with a screenplay by Handke), and *Kings of the Road* (1976), an epic account of the wanderings of two men along the border between the two Germanies.

In *The American Friend* (1977) Wenders recreated the atmosphere of US *films noirs* of the 1930s (*see* FILM NOIR). The film featured performances by the directors Samuel Fuller and Nicholas Ray. Wenders's next film was a documentary about Ray's death from cancer entitled *Lightning Over Water* (1981). *Hammett* (1982), another black thriller, speculated on the circumstances that led Dashiel Hammett to write *The Maltese Falcon*, while *The State of Things* (1982) depicts a cinema crew's inertia when the film they are working on is halted by lack of funds.

Wenders enjoyed considerable commercial success with *Paris, Texas* (1984), a melancholy story about the reunion of a man, his wife, and their son set largely in the Texan desert; the film was particularly admired for its evocative soundtrack and for the acting of Harry Dean Stanton and Nastassia Kinski.

Among Wenders's films since then have been *Tokyo-Ga* (1985), a documentary about modern Japanese society, and *Wings of Desire* (1987), about an angel who decides to become human in order to participate in the life of modern Berlin. Wenders's 1992 offering *Until the End of the World* – a fantasy filmed in locations all around the world – was widely attacked as overblown and pretentious.

Weöres, Sándor (1913–89) Hungarian poet and translator. Weöres, who published his first poems at the age of 14, studied at the University of Pécs where he completed a doctoral dissertation on 'The Birth of the Poem' in 1939. After the publication of his tenth volume of poetry, *The Colonnade of Teeth* (1967), he was forced by the Hungarian Stalinist regime to restrict his attention to literary translation and the writing of children's verse; this situation continued until the revolution of 1956. Between 1956 and his death, Weöres published over 25 volumes of poetry, including a three-volume *Collected Works* (1975), and a remarkable anthology of neglected early Hungarian literary texts under the title *Three Sparrows with Six Eyes* (1977).

Weöres is widely recognized as the master craftsman of post-war Hungarian poetry. His verse is characterized by its extraordinary thematic and stylistic range – from the profoundly philosophical to the comic and light-hearted – and by its unparalleled technical virtuosity. Weöres continually recreates his elaborate personal mythologies as his work shifts between the idioms of primitive ritual and folksong on the one hand and the invention of sophisticated literary personae on the other. The depth of his identification with these personae is best illustrated by the volume *Psyche* (1972), a collection of verse and prose offered as the autobiographical work of an invented Hungarian woman poet of the early 19th century.

Werkteater (Dutch: work theatre) Dutch theatre organization noted for its promotion of actor-based drama and its investigation of acting technique, in particular regarding physical movement. Founded in Amsterdam in 1970, the Werkteater has won praise for its high performance standards in such socially relevant plays as *Situations* (1972), which depicts life in a mental hospital, *Sunset Way* (1973), which tackles old age, and *In for Treatment* (1979), about the experiences of a cancer patient. The Werkteater has inspired several similar groups and has also spawned Werkteater II, which has developed the original company's innovative work.

Werner, Gosta (1908–) Swedish film director of imaginative short subjects, who has also written widely on cinema. After a career in journalism, Werner came to the cinema at the age of 37 and won immediate acclaim for such lyrical shorts as *Early Morning* (1945), *Midwinter Sacrifice* (1946), *The Train* (1948), *Land of Liberty* (1958), *A Glass of Wine* (1960), *Living Colour* (1962), *Huan Landscape* (1965), and *When People Meet* (1966). Werner's features, mostly rather sombre films that have found less approval, are *Loffe the Vagabond* (1948), *Miss Sun-Beam* (1948), *The Street* (1949), *Backyard* (1950), *Meeting Life* (1952), and *Matrimonial Announcement* (1955).

Wertmuller, Lina (Arcangela Felice Assunta Wertmuller von Elgg; 1928–) Italian film director, who became a cult figure in the 1970s for her sociological parables full of sex and violence. The daughter of a Roman lawyer, Wertmuller was expelled from more than a dozen Catholic schools before becoming a schoolteacher herself. She left to study at Rome's Theatre Academy, graduating in 1951 and touring Europe as a puppeteer. She subsequently worked as an actress, playwright, and theatre director, establishing a reputation for temperament as well as talent and writing a number of musicals and comedies for television. In 1963 she worked as an assistant to FELLINI on his celebrated film *8½* and wrote and directed her own first feature *The Liz- ards*, which won a Locarno Film Festival award.

Wertmuller's career took off after she formed the production company Liberty Films with the actor Giancarlo Giannini. In 1972 she won the best director award at Cannes for *The Seduction of Mimi* (1972), a controversial tragicomedy about a helpless individual overwhelmed by social, sexual, and political problems. Similar themes were explored in *Love and Anarchy* (1973), *All Screwed Up* (*Tutto a posto e niente in ordine*; 1974), and *Swept Away* (*Travolti da un insolito destino nell'azzuro mare d'agosto*; 1974).

Wertmuller received the highest critical acclaim of her career for *Seven Beauties* (1976), a moving and often absurd depiction of life in a Nazi concentration camp. The film led to a contract with Warner Bros to direct four pictures in English, but this was terminated when her first effort, *The End of the World in Our Usual Bed in a Night Full of Rain* (1977) proved disappointing. Although her work has been praised for its spontaneity and inventiveness, some have found its mingling of humour with scenes of human suffering distasteful. She has written all her films and her artist husband, Enrico Job, regularly designs her sets. In 1990 she was put in charge of Rome's celebrated film school, the Centro Sperimentale di Cinematografia, with a brief to reduce its administrative bureaucracy.

Wesker, Arnold (1932–) British playwright, who was hailed as a leading representative of the ANGRY YOUNG MEN of the late 1950s. *Chicken Soup with Barley* (1958), first shown at Coventry's Belgrade Theatre, was the first part of a trilogy about the experiences of the Kahn family in post-war British society, the subsequent parts being *Roots* (1959) and *I'm Talking About Jerusalem* (1960). Like many of his subsequent plays these works reflect Wesker's own upbringing in the Jewish community of London's East End; in the trilogy the socialism and idealism of the younger members of the family are often in conflict with the disillusionment of the older members. *The Kitchen* (1959) made use of Wesker's memories of his four years' working as a pastry cook, while *Chips with Everything* (1962), first presented by the ENGLISH STAGE COMPANY, was based on his National Service with the RAF.

Many of Wesker's plays deal with the struggles of the idealist in unsympathetic surroundings, a situation in which he has often found himself in real life: a natural supporter of liberal causes, he was imprisoned briefly for his commitment to the antinuclear movement. In 1961 he established the Centre 42 project with the aim of bringing the arts to working-class audiences, subsequently acquiring the Round House in Chalk Farm, London as a base (with assistance from the Labour government); the centre was wound up in 1971 for financial reasons. Although Wesker's best-known plays belong to his early period, he has continued to please audiences, if not always the critics, with such pieces as *The Merchant* (1976), a reworking of Shakespeare's *The Merchant of Venice*, *Caritas* (1981), about a medieval anchoress, the monologues *Mothers* (1982) and *Annie Wobbler* (1983), *Whatever Happened to Betty Lemon* (1986), and *Beorhtel's Hill* (1989). He has also written for television and radio.

Wexford Festival An annual music festival held in Wexford, Ireland since 1951. Taking place over three weeks in October and November, the festival focuses on opera with an emphasis on unusual and lesser known works; the programme also includes concerts and recitals. The performances take place in the town's 18th-century theatre.

Widerberg, Bo (1930–) Swedish film director and writer, noted for his lyrical style and his use of historical subjects to convey a contemporary social message. Widerberg worked in a mental hospital before entering journalism as the editor of a small-town newspaper. In the early 1950s he began writing short stories, publishing the collection *Kissing* along with a novel, *Autumn Term*, in 1952. After a year as film critic for Sweden's largest newspaper, he codirected a short, *The Boy and the Kite* (1961), with Jan TROELL. In 1962 he published *The Vision of Swedish Cinema*, a controversial attack on leading figures in the Swedish film industry, especially Ingmar BERGMAN, whom Widerberg accused of dictating taste and monopolizing talent.

Widerberg first came to international attention with *Elvira Madigan* (1967), a slow-moving but intensely lyrical account of the doomed romance between an army officer and a circus artist. With its exquisite photography (Jorgen Persson) and haunting use of the slow movement from Mozart's piano concerto No. 21 the film created an unforgettable dreamlike atmosphere. Other period pieces followed, most notably *Adalen 31* (1969), in which small-town strikers tragically confront government troops; the film took the Academy Award for best foreign film. His more recent releases have been *Stubby* (1974), the Swedish-German coproduction *Victoria* (1979), *The Man from Majorca* (1985), and *The Serpent's Way* (1987). He has continued to publish novels, short stories, and essays.

Wilkins, Maurice Hugh Frederick (1916–) British biophysicist, born in New Zealand. After graduating in physics from Cambridge University in 1938, Wilkins joined John Randall at Birmingham University to work on the improvement of radar screens. In 1944 he went to the University of California, Berkeley, as one of the British team assigned to the Manhattan project and development of the atomic bomb. The results and implications of this work caused him to turn away from nuclear physics and in 1945 he began a career in biophysics, firstly at St Andrews University and from 1946 at the Biophysics Research Unit, King's College, London, where he was professor (1970–81).

The same year that Wilkins joined King's College, scientists at the Rockefeller Institute announced that genes consist of deoxyribonucleic acid (DNA). Wilkins began studying DNA molecules by optical measurements and chanced to observe that the DNA fibres would be ideal material for x-ray diffraction studies. The diffraction patterns showed the DNA molecule to be very regular and have a double-helical structure. The contributions of Wilkins' colleague, Rosalind FRANKLIN, were especially important in showing that the phosphate groups are to the outside of the helix, so disproving Linus Pauling's theory of DNA structure.

Wilkins passed on his data to James Watson and Francis CRICK in Cambridge who used it to help construct their famous molecular model of DNA. For their work in elucidating the structure of the hereditary material, Wilkins, Watson, and Crick were awarded the 1962 Nobel Prize for physiology or medicine. Wilkins went on to apply his techniques to finding the structure of ribonucleic acid (RNA).

Williamson, Malcolm (1931–) Australian composer, working in Britain. He studied with Goossens in Sydney and Seiber and LUTYENS in London. In 1954 he settled in London and was appointed Master of the Queen's Music in 1957. A distinguished organist and pianist, he was involved in the performance of most of his early works. He was heavily influenced by the music of MESSIAEN and BOULEZ, although his own style contains a bewildering variety of idioms. His early successes were in opera (*Our Man in Havana*, 1963; *The English Eccentrics*, 1964) and instrumental music (three piano concertos; 1958, 1960, and 1962). Williamson did not follow up his early achievements in opera and, in general, his later music forfeits sophistication in its attempt to win a broad popular audience. In the late 1950s he worked as a night-club pianist and the influence of light music can be felt in his subsequent dramatic works, which take the form of entertainments for adults or children, often with audience participation. Williamson's eight symphonies have been unjustly neglected; together with his elegiac violin concerto, written for Menuhin in 1965, they embody the best of his eclectic style.

Wilson, Sir Angus (Frank Johnstone) (1913–91) British novelist and short-story writer. He was educated at Westminster and Merton College, Oxford, after which he worked in the Library of the British Museum. During the war he worked in the Ministry of Information, returning to the Museum in 1946. He began to write as therapy following a nervous breakdown and found instant recognition with two volumes of satirical short stories, *The Wrong Set* (1949) and *Such Darling Dodos* (1950). His first novel, *Hemlock and After* (1952), dealing with the attempts of a repressed homosexual novelist to establish a writers' colony, displays the broad social range, acute moral sense, and rich humour that characterize all his subsequent work. *Anglo-Saxon Attitudes* (1956; televised 1992), describes a crisis in the life of a successful middle-aged historian as he ponders the lies, both emotional and professional, on which his eminence is based. This was followed by another volume of stories, *A Bit Off The Map* (1957), and *The Middle-Age of Mrs Eliot* (1958), a compassionate study of a woman who finds herself suddenly widowed in middle age. *The Old Men at the Zoo* (1961) is a curious black comedy about zoo keepers in a quasi-fascist Britain of the near future, while *Late Call* (1964) uses a soulless New Town as a symbol of post-war Britain. *No Laughing Matter* (1967), his most ambitious and experimental work, covers 50 years in the life of the Matthews family. *As if by Magic* (1973) follows the restless globetrotting of Hamo Langmuir, a homosexual agronomist, and his goddaughter Alexandra as they search for meaning in their lives. His final novel *Setting the World on Fire* (1980), another acute examination of English mores, follows the fortunes of two brothers of very different character who jointly inherit a great house. Wilson also wrote studies of Zola, Dickens, and Kipling, and examined his own creative processes in *The Wild Garden* (1963). Wilson became a sadly neglected figure in his later years but there has been a major revival of interest in his work since his death.

Wilson, Georges (1921–) French theatre and film director and actor, who was manager of the Théâtre National Populaire (1963–72). After beginning his career with the Grenier-Hussenot company in 1947, he joined the TNP in 1952, quickly becoming the company's leading actor. He appeared in plays by Jarry and Musset among others, usually under the direction of Jean VILAR. As a director and company manager, he enjoyed success with plays by a wide range of authors, from Shakespeare to BEHAN, BOND, and BRECHT but in the 1960s found his policies increasingly out of step with the rapidly changing political climate. After the company disbanded in 1972 he worked at the AVIGNON FESTIVAL and elsewhere and added to his reputation as a director for the cinema with such films as *Asphalt* (1981) and *Tango, the Exile of Gardel* (1985).

Winter, Fritz (1905–) German abstract painter. Winter was born into a mining family in the Ruhr and worked as a miner while training to be an electrician. His artistic talents, however, brought him a scholarship to the Dessau Bauhaus (from 1927) where he studied under Paul Klee, Wassily Kandinsky, and Oskar Schlemmer. He also worked briefly with Naum Gabo in Berlin before the Nazis condemned his work as degenerate and forbade him to exhibit. During World War II he was wounded and taken prisoner, returning in 1949 to help found the Zen group of expressive abstractionists. In 1951 Winter was awarded a prize at the Venice Biennale and a year later gave his first US one-man show at New York's Hacker Gallery. In 1955 he began to teach at the College of Fine Arts in Kassel.

Winter's style developed constantly. In 1930–32 he painted in thick layers of paint mixed with sand and other material but soon developed a new style characterized by the use of imaginative semiabstract forms. He then went a decade (1934–44) without painting before returning with a series he called *Triebkräfte der Erde* (Force-Impulses of the Earth), which combined his earlier styles. His work of the 1950s tends to feature free-floating abstract shapes – often bars of black or grey – set against coloured backgrounds. In the 1960s he dispensed with these forms and divided his canvas into zones of pure colour in the manner of British and US colour-field painters. His work has become increasingly respected and some critics now regard him as the most original of Germany's post-war abstract artists.

Wohmann, Gabriele (1932–) German novelist. Wohmann grew up in Darmstadt in a strongly Protestant family. She started publishing in 1956 and is now a member of PEN and of the German Academy of Language and Poetry. She has received many literary prizes and is one of the most widely read of post-war German writers.

Wohmann's repressive upbringing has had a major influence on her work. Her many novels and short stories offer an unflinching diagnosis of the pathologies of middle-class family life, analysing, for example, the crippling emotional dependence of grown-up children on their parents and their resulting inability to cope with life. Many of her protagonists are women who are unable to develop their own personalities and consequently perpetuate the pathology in their own relationships. Wohmann is a masterly satirist of the bourgeois pseudo-idyll and a shrewd analyst of the many ways in which people fail to communicate. Among her imortant works are *Farewell for Long* (1965), *Counter-Attack* (1972), *Paulinchen Stayed at Home Alone* (1974), *An Outing with the Mother* (1976) and *Early Autumn in Badenweiler* (1978).

Wolf, Christa (1929–) German writer. Christa Wolf spent a quiet childhood in Landsberg (today Gorzów); the family had to flee to Mecklenburg in 1945. She worked as a secretary before completing her higher school education in 1949. Like others, Wolf reacted to German war guilt by identifying with the ideals of the newly founded socialist East Germany, becoming a party member in 1949. After studying German literature in Jena and Leipzig she worked as an editor on the writers' journal *New German Literature* and with the publishing house Neues Lebe. She is married to the writer Gerhard Wolf.

Wolf is probably the best-known writer to have emerged from the former East Germany. Her first international success was her novel *The Divided Heaven* (1963), which sets the story of a disintegrating relationship against the background of the historical events of 1961, when the Berlin Wall was erected. Although officially honoured by the authorities as a model writer, Christa Wolf freed herself from the dogmatism of social realism very early. Thus, for example, her second novel *The Quest for Christa T.* (1968) was denounced in East Germany for its emphasis on the value of subjective experience. The book is the fictional biography of Christa T., a romantic outsider in East German society. Most of her subsequent novels were highly acclaimed in the West but critically received in the East. *A Model Childhood* (1976) is a semi-autobiographical novel in which Wolf reconstructs her Nazi childhood, implicitly questioning the official East German claim to have come to terms completely with the fascist past. This was followed by *No Place on Earth* (1979) and *Kassandra* (1982), Wolf's most feminist novel. After the coming down of the Berlin Wall in 1989 she published *What Remains*, a novella based on her personal experience of STASI surveillance in the late 1970s. The book caused a heated controversy in Germany about the role of Wolf and other intellectuals in East German society.

Wolkers, Jan (1925–) Dutch novelist and sculptor. Born at Oegstgeest, a village near Leiden, Wolkers studied sculpture in Amsterdam, Salzburg, and Paris. He published his first book in 1961.

His early work, such as the stories in *Serpentina's Petticoat* (1961) and the novel *Crew Cut* (*Kort Amerikaans*; 1962), contains vigorous attacks on the conservatism of Dutch society. The style combines realism and fantasy, while the tone is frequently sarcastic. In *Oegstgeest Revisted* (1965) Wolkers described a visit to his native village; the book combines childhood memories with the more critical perceptions of the adult narrator. In 1969 he enjoyed a huge success with *Turkish Delight*, a straightforward story of passionate love and sex ending in tragedy. His later books include the melodramatic *The Dodo* (1974), *The Kiss* (1977), and *The Peach of Immortality* (1980), which explores the bitterly unhappy marriage of two former Resistance workers, 35 years after the war. At their best, Wolkers's books combine sharp-edged criticism of modern Dutch and Western society with a fundamental love of life in all its variety and chaotic beauty.

World Theatre Season An important international theatre festival that was founded in London in 1964 by Peter Daubeny. Based at the Aldwych Theatre, the festival attracted many of the world's leading companies, including the Comédie-Française from France, the Abbey Theatre from Ireland, the Moscow Art Theatre from the Soviet Union, and companies from Austria, Belgium, Czechoslovakia, Germany, Greece, Italy, Poland, Spain, and Sweden. The festival ended as an annual event in 1973, with one further staging in 1975.

Wotruba, Fritz (1907–75) Austrian stone sculptor, who founded the post-war Austrian school of abstract sculpture. Born in Vienna, he trained as an engraver before becoming a pupil (1925) of the sculptor Anton Hanak at the Vienna Academy. He first came to international notice in 1929 when his *Torso of a Man* was shown at an exhibition of Austrian art in Paris. Wotruba spent World War II in Switzerland, returning to Vienna in 1948 to become a professor at and then rector of the Academy. During this period he produced many striking variations on the human form, notably the series *Human Cathedrals* (1946–49). A major exhibition of his work was held in 1948 at the Venice Biennale. In 1964 he exhibited at the Marlborough-Gerson Gallery in New York and executed a large relief frieze for Marburg University in Germany.

During his career, Wotruba shifted gradually from a figurative to an abstract style of sculpture. He began this process by eliminating details from the human figure in the manner of the Romanian Constantin Brancusi but after the war began to produce monumental block-like forms that he left in a rough primitive state. He generally carved directly onto unrefined blocks of hard stone. Wotruba also produced some notable pieces in bronze. His work was largely responsible for reviving sculpture in post-war Austria and now enjoys an international reputation.

Wuppertal Dance Theatre *See* BAUSCH, PINA.

X

Xenakis, Iannis (1922–) French composer, architect, and writer, born in Romania to Greek parents. Xenakis absorbed his earliest musical influences, Romanian folk music and Byzantine chant, before the family's return to Greece in 1932. During World War II he trained as an engineer and joined the anti-Nazi Resistance; after being partially blinded in action he escaped to Paris, where he settled in 1947 (taking French nationality in 1965). He studied at the Ecole Normale de Musique with Honegger and Milhaud and at the Paris Conservatoire with MESSIAEN (1950–51). He also took lessons in Switzerland from Hermann Scherchen. More significant, however, was his involvement with the building projects of LE CORBUSIER from 1948 until 1959. The close structural links between his first composition *Metastaseis* (1954) and the Philips Pavilion at the Brussels World Fair Exhibition (1958), which Xenakis designed, exemplify his belief that there is a correlation between music and architecture. His association of music with mathematical theory led him to found the Equipe de Mathématique de d'Automatique Musicales in Paris in 1966. Subsequently, while teaching at Indiana University, Bloomington (1967–72), he founded a US counterpart, the Center for Musical Mathematics and Automation.

Xenakis has often drawn on mathematical models – such as set theory in *Herma* (1960–64), Markovian chains in *Analogiques* (1958), and game theory in *Duel* (1959) and *Stratégie* (1959–62) – to provide a structure for his works. His computer-generated 'stochastic' pieces explore the mathematics of probability; although the composer can determine the overall structure of such a piece, the large number of different elements involved makes their short-term behaviour unpredictable. In recent years he has concentrated on developing computer technology for the graphic generation of music. He has written orchestral, chamber, and choral works, as well as a number of large-scale mixed-media events designed for performance outdoors. Recent pieces include *Tuorakemsu* (1990), *Kyania* (1990), and *Dox-orkh* (1991).

Y

Yefremov, Oleg (Nikolayevich) (1927–) Russian theatre director and actor, who established his reputation while chief producer at Moscow's **Sovremennik Theatre** (1956–70), which he founded. He has won particular praise for his work with younger audiences and installed his own company of young actors (for many years considered the best in the Soviet Union) at the theatre in 1958 to present plays by leading contemporary writers. Successes from this period included *Alive Forever* (1957) by Viktor Rostov, who with Aleksandr Volodin became the company's resident playwright; he also intrigued Moscow audiences with his productions of works by foreign writers, including OSBORNE's *Look Back in Anger* (1966) and Albee's *Ballad of the Sad Café* (1967). Also active in films, Yefremov finally left the Sovremennik Theatre in 1970 and succeeded Boris Livanov as head of the Moscow Art Theatre (where he had been trained). Since taking over the theatre he has attempted to revive its flagging reputation for challenging drama by presenting plays by such writers as BUERO VALLEJO, Volodin, and others, meeting with only partial success. In 1989 his production of Chekhov's *Uncle Vanya* went on tour to London's ROYAL NATIONAL THEATRE, where it was well received.

Yehudi Menuhin Festival of Music (Alpengala) A music festival held annually in Gstaad, Switzerland. It lasts for five weeks during August and September. The programme concentrates on celebrity performances of well-established classical works. The violinist Sir Yehudi Menuhin, who has been a local resident, is the best known of the festival's musical directors.

Yevtushenko, Yevgeny (Aleksandrovich) *See* EVTUSHENKO, EVGENII (ALEKSANDROVICH).

Z

Zadek, Peter (1926–) German theatre and film director, who is considered one of the most important figures in contemporary German theatre. Zadek established his reputation in the 1960s while artistic director at Bremen (1964–67) and subsequently at Bochum (1972–75), producing politically committed and innovative versions of plays by authors ranging from Shakespeare to BEHAN. He also won acclaim for his productions of new plays by contemporary writers, notably DORST and FORTE, who shared the same antiestablishment stance. Most popular of all, however, have been his adaptations of several novels by Hans Fallada (1893–1947) as satirical revues – among them *Little Men – What Now?* (1972) and *Each Dies for Himself Alone* (1981). In 1992 he was one of five German directors called in to save the ailing BERLINER ENSEMBLE from collapse.

Zadkine, Ossip (1890–1967) French sculptor, born in Russia. Born in Smolensk, he was sent to England to learn the language (he had British ancestors) in 1905 and attended art schools in Sunderland, London, and Paris, where he settled in 1909. He became one of a group of artists – including Archipenko, Laurens, and Lipchitz – who experimented with cubism in sculpture; in his own work he often made use of hollows and pierced openings. In 1915 he joined the French army and after being severely gassed worked as an interpreter to the Russian Brigades. He spent most of World War II in New York, returning to Paris in 1944. The house in which he lived from then until his death is now a museum devoted to his work – one of the most delightful small museums in France.

Zadkine's style was emotional and expressive and his sculpture can seem rather overblown (and repetitive when seen *en masse*). However, his most famous piece is generally regarded as one of the greatest public monuments of the 20th century; it is the huge bronze *To the Destroyed City* (1953) in Rotterdam, commemorating the almost complete destruction of the city in World War II. This work brought Zadkine international fame and led to several other major public commissions.

Zagreb Festival of Contemporary Music A biennial festival of modern music held in Zagreb, Croatia, during May; it was founded in 1961. The programme covers a wide range of contemporary music, opera, concerts, and ballet.

Zampa, Luigi (1905–) Italian director and screenwriter of films in the neorealist manner (*see* NEOREALISM). Born in Rome, he abandoned his engineering studies in 1928 for the stage, working both as an actor and a playwright. He enrolled at Rome's Centro Sperimentale di Cinematografia in 1935 and three years later entered the Italian cinema as a screenwriter, a role he continued to exercise after directing his first film, *L'Attore Scomparso*, in 1941. As a director, Zampa made an important contribution to neorealism with his first major film, *To Live In Peace* (1946), which argued that most Italians had opposed World War II. Other films in a similar vein included *Angelina* (1947), a comedy starring Anna Magnani as a poor housewife who learns to speak out on social and political matters, and *Difficult Years* (1948). With the advent of the so-called New Italian Cinema of the 1950s, Zampa's later films proved less successful. These include *The Love Specialist* (1957), *The Magistrate* (1959), *A Question of Honour* (1965), *A Girl in Australia* (1971), *Il Mostro* (1977), and *Letti Selvaggi* (1979).

Zampi, Mario (1903–63) Italian-born British film director, screenwriter, and producer, who won applause for his zany black comedies. A native of Rome, Zampi was a child star in Italian films before moving to London at the age of 19 and working as a film editor for Warner Bros. He co-founded Two Cities Films in 1937 and produced such films as *Spy for a Day* (1940) and the thriller *The Fatal Night* (1948). In the 1950s he wrote, produced, and directed a string of delightful farces epitomized by *Laughter in Paradise* (1951), in which a millionaire leaves each of his relatives a fortune on condition that they perform specified acts that are either humiliating or illegal. Other offerings include *Top Secret* (1952), about a sanitary engineer mistaken for a spy, *Happy Ever After* (1954), in which Irish villagers attempt to murder their obnoxious squire, *The Naked Truth* (1957), about a group of celebrities who conspire to kill a blackmailer, *Too Many Crooks* (1958), the US musical comedy *Bottoms Up* (1960), and *Five Golden Hours* (1961), in which a con man plots to murder three widows. Zampi's comedies featured such stars as Spencer Tracy, Peter Sellers, Terry-Thomas, David Niven, and Joyce Grenfell.

Zanuso, Marco (1916–) Italian architect and designer. Zanuso studied at the Milan Polytechnic and served in the Italian Navy (1940–45) before establishing a practice (1945) in Milan. He has since held numerous academic posts and edited the architectural magazines *Domus* and *Casabella*. His reputation as a leading designer was established with work on household and industrial objects, such as the 'Lady' chair (1951), an early combination of metal and foam rubber, the enamelled sheet-metal 'Lambda' chair (1962), and the 'Mancuso' coffee table (1971). Zanuso designed a number of houses in the 1950s but by the late 1960s he was concentrating more on industrial building, claiming that the factory was the heart of modern society. He has shown great skill in housing several different activities under one roof as, for example, at the headquarters of Edgar's Stores in Johannesburg (1970–72). Zanuso believed that an architect should never 'resist' the landscape in which his buildings are sited. Accordingly, when planning his IBM Italia factory at Palomba, Rome (1979–82) he rejected the idea of a camouflaged development for this very large group of buildings in favour of a design in which the blocks followed the contours of the site.

Zanussi, Krzystof (1939–) Polish film director and screenwriter, living in Germany. While studying for a physics degree at the University of Warsaw, Zanussi took a film course that altered his career plans. In 1960 he began six years of training at the Łódź film school; his half-hour *Death of a Provincial* (1966) won several awards at film festivals. Zanussi's films are noted for their stoic intellectual characters and the director's austere camerawork. His many award-winners include the television production *Family Life* (1971), a fascinating study of a young man's uncomfortable visit to his old family home that won the Grand Prix at the San Remo International Film Festival, and *Illumination* (1973), the story of a troubled scientist who fails to find absolute scientific truth, which took the Grand Prix in Locarno. *The Balance* (1975), about a woman's escape from a doomed marriage, won the OCIC Prize at the BERLIN FILM FESTIVAL.

Zanussi subsequently won the OCIC Best Director award at Cannes for *The Constant Factor* (1980), in which a man is punished by society for resisting the corruption around him. This was one of several films in which Zanussi criticized the socialist system. *Camouflage* (1977) showed a professor battling against academic bureaucracy, while *The Contract* (1980) attacked the corruption and complacency of the socialist state in a farce about a disastrous wedding party. His most recent offerings are *Life for a Life* (1991), about Saint Maksymilian Kolbe, who offered himself in the place of a condemned man in the Nazi concentration camp at Auschwitz, and the documentary *Russia Today* (1991), which he also scripted. He has been president of the European Federation of Film Directors since 1990.

Zanzotto, Andrea (1921–) Italian poet. Zanzotto was born in the Venetian province of Treviso, where he spent most of his working life as a schoolteacher. His first collection of poems, *Behind the Landscape* (1951), was followed by *Vocative* (1957), *Nine Eclogues* (1962), and *Beauty* (1968). His poetry has achieved an international reputation. Earlier works show the influence of the hermetic poetry of MONTALE and Ungaretti, while drawing much of their imagery from the pastoral landscape of the poet's native region, made tragic by the two World Wars.

With *Beauty* (1968) Zanzotto embarked on a programme of audacious linguistic experimentation in which he set out to exploit the resources of the Italian language to the full. The poems blend the languages of literature, technology, and science with vocabulary drawn from everyday conversation, advertising and the mass media, and regional slang. The poem 'Elegy in Petél' is written in 'petél', a kind of baby talk that cannot be translated although it hovers on the edge of recognizable language.

Later volumes include *Easters* (1973), *Filò* (1976), *The Woodland Book of Manners* (1978), *Fosfeni* (1983), and *Idiom* (1986). In these collections Provençal, Latin, Petrarchan references, and Venetian dialect are all added to the linguistic mix.

Zavattini, Cesare (1902–89) Italian screenwriter, film theoretician, and novelist; a key figure in Italian NEOREALISM. After a stint as a journalist, Zavattini published a number of short stories and novels in the early 1930s before writing his first screenplay in 1935. His theoretical writings had a powerful influence on post-war neorealism, which was reinforced by the acclaimed screenplays he wrote for DE SICA and others in the movement. These include the script for De Sica's classic *Bicycle Thieves* (1948), about an unemployed worker who searches Rome for his stolen bicycle, which won Zavattini an Academy Award. His other screenplays include those for DE SANTIS's *Rome Eleven O'Clock* (1952), De Sica's *Umberto D* (1952), PONTI's impressive *Two Women* (1960), about a woman and her daughter escaping from the bombing of Rome during World War II, FELLINI's *Boccaccio '70* (1962), *Yesterday, Today and Tomorrow* (1963), a film combining three stories of sexually liberated women, the US-Italian crime farce *After the Fox* (1966), *The Garden of the Finzi-Continis* (1971), adapted from the novel by BASSANI, and the US-Mexican film *The Children of Sanchez* (1979), about the attempts of a Mexican and his daughter to rise above their poverty. Zavattini's poignant stories and telling dialogue ensured that he remained a force in the cinema long after the heyday of neorealism.

Zeffirelli, Franco (1923–) Italian opera, theatre, and film director and designer. Zeffirelli began his career as an actor in 1945 with the Morelli Stoppa company in Florence; he subsequently worked as a designer, creating sets and costumes for Shakespeare's *As You Like It* with Salvador Dali in 1948. After attracting attention with his sets for plays by Tennessee Wiliams, Chekhov, and others, he was entrusted (1952) with the production and design of several operas at La Scala, Milan; many of the productions he staged there were subsequently seen all over the world, among them *Pagliacci* (1959), *Tosca* (1964), *Don Giovanni* (1972), *Otello* (1972), *La Bohème* (1981), and *Turandot* (1983).

Zeffirelli's later stage productions include *Romeo and Juliet* (1960) at London's Old Vic Theatre, DE FILIPPO's *Saturday, Sunday, Monday* (1973) for the National Theatre in London, Arthur Miller's *After the Fall* (1964) in Rome, and Albee's *Who's Afraid of Virginia Woolf?* (1964) in Paris.

Romeo and Juliet was one of a number of Zeffirelli's stage productions to transfer to the screen under his direction (1967). Other films, characterized by their strong romantic ambience, have included *Brother Sun and Sister Moon* (1973), *Endless Love* (1981), and the operas *La Traviata* (1983), *Cavalleria Rusticana* (1983), and *Otello* (1986). The television series *Jesus of Nazareth* was screened in 1977.

Zeffirelli has also produced the ballet *Swan Lake* (1985), an autobiography, *Zeffirelli by Zeffirelli* (1986), and the biopic *The Young Toscanini* (1987).

Zehrfuss, Bernard (1911–) French architect, who after training in Paris established his career in Tunisia. From 1943 to 1948 he led a successful team charged with post-war rebuilding in the colony, designing many public buildings, as well as a hippodrome, and a cemetery. He returned to design Tunis University (1960 and 1965) and housing (1979). His achievement won him important commissions back in France, including the Renault complex at Flins (1952), two embassies, and housing projects around Paris, Nancy, and St Etienne (1958–78).

But it was his involvement in the construction of the Unesco headquarters in Paris (1958, with Marcel Breuer and Pier Luigi NERVI) that brought him greatest renown. He was later solely responsible for the numerous extensions and new buildings in the complex, all designed to his exacting standards. In the 1970s Zehrfuss's talent for providing headquarters buildings was taken up by many multinational firms, including Siemens (1972), Sandoz (1972), Jeumont Schneider (1973), and Spie Batignolles (1974); he also designed the headquarters of the French National Railways (1978). Less successful was his National Centre for Industry and Technology at La Défense in Paris (1950, with Camelot and de Mailly); here the success of the dynamic engineering has been overshadowed by controversy about the setting.

Zeman, Karel (1910–89) Czech animator and director of special-effect fantasy films. Born in Moravia, Zeman worked as a window-dresser and poster artist before making a number of advertising films and entering the cinema in the 1940s. He combined various forms of animation with puppetry and created 'Mr Prokouk', a popular cartoon character first introduced in 1947 in *Prokouk the Bureaucrat.* In the early 1950s Zeman began to mix live action with animation in several innovative feature-length films noted for their fantastic effects. His features included *The Treasure of Bird Island* (1952), the well-received *Journey to Primeval Times* (1955), *The Fabulous World of Jules Verne* (1957), the internationally known *Baron Munchhausen* (1961), and *Sinbad the Sailor* (1974).

Zero Group A group formed in Düsseldorf in 1957 by the German artists Heinz MACK and Otto PIENE to pursue their interest in KINETIC ART and the use of moving light in sculpture; they were joined in 1962 by Gunther Uecker. The group's ideas were publicized in a periodical also named *Zero* (1958–61) – the name having been chosen to suggest the idea of a space not yet explored and an entirely fresh start. The group was essentially part of the broader NOUVELLE TENDANCE movement, which also included such experimental teams as Group 'T' from Milan and Group 'N' from Padua.

Influences on the group included the radical artists Yves KLEIN, Lucio FONTANA, and Laszlo Moholy-Nagy. Their work was also a reaction against pessimistic trends in the arts, with the group's leaders looking optimistically towards a future of 'new idealism'. They largely abandoned concrete forms for colour, light, and movement, stating, "We are interested in light...the illimitable possibilities to plan a better and a clearer world." Piene used pure colour, usually red or black, in his spherical sculptures and even created 'light ballets' by filling balloons with coloured gases. Mack concentrated on reliefs using mirrors and luminescent metals. The group also experimented in collective work, exhibiting in 1961 at the Howard Wise Gallery in New York, in 1964 at the Institute of Contemporary Art, Pennsylvania University in Philadelphia, and the next year at the Kestner-Gesellschaft in Hanover. The group was disbanded in 1966.

Zimmermann, B(ernd) A(lois) (1918–70) German composer. Born near Cologne, Zimmermann studied at Bonn, Königsdorf, and Berlin universities. His early compositions, which date from after World War II, show the influence of Milhaud and Stravinsky and the serialist procedures he absorbed while studying with FORTNER and LEIBOWITZ at the DARMSTADT Institute. From 1950 until 1952 he taught the history of music theory at Cologne University and from 1957 composition at the Cologne Musikhochschule. During this period his work developed through a phase of total SERIALISM influenced by Webern towards a more miscellaneous and idiosyncratic style that Zimmermann himself termed 'pluralistic'. The works of this phase make use of a wide range of elements including electronic sounds, quotations from other works, and mixed-media techniques; principal among them are the opera *Die Soldaten* (1960) and the *Requiem for a Young Poet* (1969). The pluralistic style was in part an attempt to exemplify Zimmermann's speculative ideas about the nature of time, which he held to be 'spherical'.

Zinov'ev, Aleksandr Aleksandrovich (1922–) Russian philosopher, political commentator, and satirist living in Germany. Born the son of an artist in a village in central Russia, he attended school in Moscow, served as a fighter pilot in World War II, and subsequently studied philosophy at Moscow University. Zinov'ev's career as a professional philosopher was centred on mathematical logic, in which field he won an international reputation; in the 1970s, however, he increasingly came into conflict with the Soviet regime. A turning point was reached in 1976 when his gargantuan satire *The Yawning Heights* was published in the West, leading to its author's expulsion from the Soviet Union in the following year. Since then he has lived in Germany, publishing a huge quantity of political satires and commentaries. Major works include *The Radiant Future* (1978), *The Yellow House* (1980), *Homo Sovieticus* (1982), and *Our Youth's Flight* (1983), – the latter, it seemed to many in the West, a blatant defence of Stalinism. Very much a loner, Zinov'ev has appeared to court controversy, scorning his fellow writers and regarding himself as the only truly modern one. In *The Yawning Heights*, probably the most typical and the best of his novels, the Soviet Union is represented as a huge decrepit village whose inhabitants (some of them thinly disguised political and cultural figures) endlessly discuss various, usually parodoxical, propositions with the aid of (mainly scabrous) anecdotes, poems, and pictures. Zinov'ev's diffuse and sometimes self-indulgent but always witty satires amount to a scathing indictment of Soviet life and thought.

Zunzunegui, Juan Antonio de (1901–) Spanish (Basque) novelist. Zunzunegui, a realist in the tradition of Balzac and the Spanish historical novelist Benito Pérez Galdós (1843–1920), is very widely read in Spain. Sometimes brutal and shocking, his work has affinities with the school of *tremendísmo* and several of his books were banned under Franco. Many of his novels and stories attack corrupt political leadership. His longer narratives include *O-These Children!* (1943), *The Ship of Death* (1945), *The Failure* (1947), *The Supreme Good* (1951) – an excellent three-generation family saga – *Life As It Is* (1954), and *Life Goes On* (1969). *The Prize* (1962), a satire on literary prizes, won the National Prize.

His books, mainly set either in the Bilbao business community, of which he has first-hand experience, or in the Madrid underworld, are closely observed social satires with a strong emphasis on local colour and customs. They are direct in style, broad in their characterization, and generally pessimistic in their conclusions.

REF NX 542 E93 1993
European culture : a
contemporary companion
1993.

For Reference
Not to be taken from this room

Not to be taken from this room